Power Programming with RPC

Power Programming with RPC

John Bloomer

O'Reilly & Associates, Inc.
103 Morris Street, Suite A
Sebastopol, CA 95472

Power Programming with RPC
by John Bloomer

Copyright © 1992 O'Reilly & Associates, Inc. All rights reserved
Printed in the United States of America.

Editor: Dale Dougherty

Printing History:

February 1992:   First Edition.

September 1992:   Minor corrections.

This book is printed on acid-free paper with 50% recycled content, 10-15% post-consumer
waste. O'Reilly & Associates is committed to using paper with the highest recycled content
available consistent with high quality.

ISBN: 0-937175-77-3

Table of Contents

Preface *xxv*

Scope of This Handbook xxvi

Some Assumptions About the Reader xxx

    Software Mentioned in This Book xxx

    Examples xxxii

Additional Sources of Information xxxiii

Conventions xxxiv

Acknowledgments xxxv

Chapter 1: Introduction to Remote Procedure Calling *1*

Client/Server Computing 1

    Remote versus Local Procedure Calling 2

RPC Application Development 3

    Defining the Protocol 4

    Developing Server and Client Application Code 6

    Compiling and Running the Application 9

RPC Makes Interprocess Communications Less Painful 10

How RPC Systems Work 11

    RPC Systems and the OSI Reference Model 13

    What is "State" and Why is it Important? 15

Top Twenty Distributed Computing Terms and Acronyms 16

Chapter 2: Network Computing Today *19*

Distributed Computing Standards 19

    Features of a Distributed Computing Environment 20

    NCS 21

    ONC 22

Examining ONC and NCS 24

    Machine-independent Data Representation 24

    RPC Mechanism 26

    Protocol Compilers: The Most Important Feature 29

    Authentication Services 30

    Network Resource Naming Services 30

    Network Time Service 30

Distributed File System 31

There May be a Common Application Environment in Your Future 31

Netwise: A Second ONC Alternative 32

Machine-independent Data Representation 33

RPC Mechanism 33

Protocol Compiler 34

Authentication Services 34

Network Resource Naming Services 34

Network Time Service 35

Distributed File System 35

Summary of Distributed Computing Environments 35

Rapid Evolution 38

Which One Should You Choose? 40

Put the ONC Suite on Your Machine for Free 40

Chapter 3: Developing High-level RPC Applications 43

Development Overview 43

From Local to Remote Directory Reading 44

Define the Protocol 47

Data Types 47

Program, Procedure, and Version Numbers 47

High-level ONC RPC Library Calls 48

At the Server 49

At the Client 50

Shared XDR Routines 50

Using the XDR Library 51

Writing the Client and Server Programs 54

At the Server 54

At the Client 55

Compile, Link, and Run 56

Why High-level Calls and Not Protocol Compiling? 58

Some Limitations of the High-level Calls 58

TCP Transport Requires Lower-level Calls 59

Chapter 4: Protocol Compiling and Lower-level RPC Programming 61

Development Overview 63
  Filename Conventions and Make 63
Using RPCGEN 65
The Protocol Definition Language 68
  Definitions 68
  Symbolic Constants 69
  Enumerations 69
  Structures 70
  Unions 71
  Typedefs 71
  Programs 72
  Declarations 74
  Special Cases 76
  Booleans 76
  Strings 77
  Opaque Data 77
  Voids 78
Preprocessor Symbols and Control 78
Lower-level ONC RPC Library Calls 79
  At the Client 79
  At the Server 80
An Example: One Client Talks to One Server 81
Debugging 89
  Step 1: Debug Without the Network 90
  Step 2: Use the Raw Transport 94
  Step 3: Debug Over the Network 97
Deploying Servers During Development 100
Real RPC Power Means Using IPC 101

Chapter 5: UNIX Networking and Interprocess Communication 103

A Network Protocol Primer 104
  Internet Addressing 104
  Connectionless at the Lowest Level 105

Internet Protocols 105

Applications Protocols 107

Connections and Well-known Ports 107

Types of Servers 108

Network Transport Selection: UDP or TCP? 109

Adding a Server to the System 110

inetd and Other Lurking Network Daemons 111

Installing a Server Yourself 113

A Digression on Remote Execution Daemons 113

Configuring inetd 114

An Overview of UNIX Interprocess Communication 119

Pipes and FIFOs 119

Message Queues, Semaphores, and Shared Memory 120

Berkeley Sockets and System V TLI 121

Data Representation or Byte Ordering 121

Retrieving Host, Network, and Address Information 122

Getting ONC RPC Information 124

Berkeley Sockets 125

Yeah, But How Do I Use Sockets? 127

Socket Examples 128

Advanced Socket Programming Issues 142

Remote Execution, Security, and Authentication 144

Chapter 6: *Application Development: Networked Parallel Image Processing* 147

Developing Parallel Algorithms for a Multi-server Network 148

A Simple Model For Parallel Processing on a Network 149

System Requirements and Network Constraints 151

Server Access 151

Server and Network Performance 151

Brute-force Scheduling Using Process Control 152

Programming Asynchronous and Concurrent Processing at the Client ... 152

Making Use of Timers to Watch Child Processes 156

Development Steps 160

Remote Image Processing (RIP) 164

Specifying Filter Coefficients 164

rip Development: It's as Easy as 1 2 3 166

    Step 1: Define the Protocol 166

    Step 2: Building the Client Procedure 168

    Step 3: Developing the Server Procedure 179

Testing and Running the Program 183

Extending RIP 184

Fast SunView Frame Buffer Access Needed 185

Chapter 7: Distributing Existing Applications   *187*

A Local Image Manager 187

    The Header File 188

    Modularity 189

    Functions 192

    Compile, Link, and Run 197

Moving a Local Application to the Network 197

    Answer Fourteen Questions First 197

    The Strategy 200

Chapter 8: Managing RPC Servers   *215*

How to Start the Remote Server 216

    Shell Scripts For Starting Servers 217

    Starting a Remote Server From within Your Client Application 221

Terminating Your Services 223

    System Error: "%STF-E-OPENIN, Server Too Fat" 225

    Hit Reset 226

Report Server Information with rpcinfo 227

    Changes Under TIRPC 231

Data Sharing: NFS versus Sending it Yourself 231

Host-qualified Filenames 232

Chapter 9: Multiple Clients and Servers   *235*

Remote Asynchronous Calls, Multi-server Processing 235

    ONC RPC Support 236

    The Follow-up RPC 250

Multi-tasking at the Server 262

    Multi-tasking with Child Processes 263

    Alternatives to Avoid Run-time Process Creation 267

Combining Asynchronous and Multi-tasking at the Server 268
Lightweight Processing 270
Remote Asynchronous Calls with LWP 271
    A Minimal Set of LWP Routines 271
    Client Multi-server Example 273
    Server Multi-tasking Example 278
    Caveats 282

Chapter 10: RPC Under Windowing Systems   *283*

The X Window System 284
    X Toolkit Client Application Flow of Control 284
    Low-level RPC and X Protocol Similarities 285
Strategies for Using RPC Under X 285
    Placing and Servicing RPCs in an Event-driven Environment 286
RPC and XView 290
    Synchronous RPCs with a Timer 290
    Remote Asynchronous Calls, FRPC Polled with a Timer 292
    The Event Notifier and Associated Complications 296
    Remote Asynchronous Call Servers Using notify_enable_rpc_svc() 298
RPC and Xol/Xt 300
    Watching IPC with XtAppAddInput(3Xt) 301
    Remote Asynchronous Calls, Servers Using XtAppAddInput() 308
Comparing Network Windowing Systems and RPC 313
    A Digression: Performance of Typical versus Network Windowing
        Systems 314
    Windowing System Evolution Can Hide a Frame Buffer 314
    X11 Pixmaps versus SunView Pixrects 315
    Augment Typical Windowing Systems with RPCs 322

Chapter 11: ONC Transport-independent RPC   *323*

Maintains the ONC RPC Protocol 324
Run-time Transport Independence 325
    Network Selection 326
Uniform Addressing 326
TIRPC API 326
    Backward Compatibility 327
    Levels of the Library 327

An Example 330

Availability 332

Chapter 12: Advanced Programming Issues *333*

Authentication and How to Use It 333

    ONC RPC Credentials and Verification at the Client 334

    Adding Authentication to the dim Client 339

    Authentication at the Server 344

    Adding Access Control to the dim Server 346

Error Reporting Summarized 350

Fault Tolerance, Connection Errors, and Crash Recovery 351

    Connection Errors and Recovery 351

    Caching Replies at the Server 353

    Broken Connections and Testing 353

    Crash Recovery 356

The ONC RPC Programming Reference *359*

Section One: ONC XDR Library Routines 361

Section Two: ONC Portmap Library Routines 377

Section Three: ONC RPC Library Routines 381

Section 1: ONC XDR Library Routines *361*

Overview 361

    XDR Streams and Their Management 363

    Conversion Filters 364

Synopsis 368

    xdr_array( ) 368

    xdr_bool( ) 368

    xdr_bytes( ) 368

    xdr_char( ) 369

    xdr_destroy( ) 369

    xdr_double( ) 369

    xdr_enum( ) 369

    xdr_float( ) 369

    xdr_free( ) 369

    xdr_getpos( ) 370

    xdr_inline( ) 370

xdr_int( ) 370

xdr_long( ) 370

xdrmem_create( ) 370

xdr_opaque( ) 371

xdr_pointer( ) 371

xdrrec_create( ) 371

xdrrec_endofrecord( ) 371

xdrrec_eof( ) 372

xdrrec_readbytes( ) 372

xdrrec_skiprecord( ) 372

xdr_reference( ) 372

xdr_setpos( ) 372

xdr_short( ) 373

xdrstdio_create( ) 373

xdr_string( ) 373

xdr_u_char( ) 373

xdr_u_int( ) 373

xdr_u_long( ) 374

xdr_union( ) 374

xdr_u_short( ) 374

xdr_vector( ) 374

xdr_void( ) 374

xdr_wrapstring( ) 375

Section 2:   ONC Portmap Library Routines

Section 2:   ONC Portmap Library Routines   377

Overview 377

Synopsis 378

pmap_getmaps( ) 378

pmap_getport( ) 378

pmap_rmtcall( ) 378

pmap_set( ) 378

pmap_unset( ) 379

xdr_pmap( ) 379

xdr_pmaplist( ) 379

Section 3: ONC RPC Library Routines   *381*

  Overview 381
  Functional Summary 381
    Building Client Authentication 381
    Making the Call from the Client 382
    CLIENT Handle Management 383
    Server Registration With The Portmap 383
    SVCXPRT Service Transport Handle Management 384
    Server Side Error Handling And Reporting 384
    Server I/O and Utility 385
    Direct XDR Access 386
    Making Secure RPCs 386
  Synopsis 387
    authdes_create() 387
    authdes_getucred() 388
    auth_destroy() 388
    authnone_create() 388
    authunix_create() 388
    authunix_create_default() 388
    callrpc() 389
    clnt_broadcast() 389
    clnt_call() 389
    clnt_control() 390
    clnt_create() 391
    clnt_create_vers() 391
    clnt_destroy() 391
    clnt_freeres() 391
    clnt_geterr() 392
    clnt_pcreateerror() 392
    clnt_perrno() 392
    clnt_perror() 392
    clntraw_create() 392
    clnt_spcreateerror() 393
    clnt_sperrno() 393
    clnt_sperror() 393
    clnttcp_create() 393

clntudp_bufcreate() 393

clntudp_create() 394

get_myaddress() 394

getnetname() 394

getrpcport() 394

host2netname() 395

key_decryptsession() 395

key_encryptsession() 395

key_gendes() 396

key_setsecret() 396

netname2host() 396

netname2user() 396

registerrpc() 396

rpc_createerr 397

svc_destroy() 397

svcfd_create() 397

svc_fds 397

svc_fdset 397

svc_freeargs() 398

svc_getargs() 398

svc_getcaller() 398

svc_getreq() 398

svc_getreqset() 398

svcerr_auth() 399

svcerr_decode() 399

svcerr_noproc() 399

svcerr_noprog() 399

svcerr_progvers() 399

svcerr_systemerr() 400

svcerr_weakauth() 400

svcraw_create() 400

svc_register() 400

svc_run() 400

svc_sendreply() 401

svctcp_create() 401

svcudp_create() 401

svcudp_bufcreate() 401

svc_unregister() 402

user2netname() 402

xdr_accepted_reply() 402

xdr_authunix_parms() 402

xdr_callhdr() 402

xdr_callmsg() 402

xdr_opaque_auth() 403

xdr_rejected_reply() 403

xdr_replymsg() 403

xprt_register() 403

xprt_unregister() 403

Error Codes 404

Appendix A: Obtaining RFCs (Internet Standards, Request for Comment)   *407*

Appendix B: An RPC Case Study: Networked Ray Tracing   *409*

Introduction to Ray Tracing 409

Accelerating Ray Tracing 411

Multiple Processor Ray Tracing and Data Distribution 413

Networked Ray Tracing Using RPC 415

Dynamic Scheduling and Load Balancing 417

But Why Scan-line Parallelism and Not Frame Parallelism? 418

Performance Results 421

Conclusions 421

References 423

Documentation and Source Code 426

Comments on Augmenting the Client to Run Under X11 with the XView Toolkit 451

Appendix C: Generalized Server Initialization, Inquiry, and Removal   *453*

Appendix D: Parallel Processing In A Nutshell   *457*

Parallelism 458

Interprocess Control 459

Interprocess Communication 459

Buzzwords: A Glossary   *461*

Index   *469*

List of Figures

Figure P-1 Book organization and reading strategy xxvii
Figure 1-1 Local and remote procedure call communication 3
Figure 1-2 ONC RPC client/server setup 12
Figure 1-3 RPC communication 13
Figure 1-4 RPC systems within the OSI reference model 14
Figure 2-1 The Network Computing Architecture and System 23
Figure 2-2 The Open Network Computing architecture 25
Figure 3-1 Developing a network application with high-level RPC 44
Figure 3-2 High-level RPC 46
Figure 4-1 Developing a network application with RPC Protocol Compiler 62
Figure 4-2 Application development with RPCGEN 64
Figure 4-3 Reducing an RPC application for local debugging 91
Figure 5-1 The TCP/IP Internet Protocol suite layers 106
Figure 5-2 Network servers can be one of six different types 111
Figure 5-3 Connection-oriented (left) and connectionless (right)
            IPC protocols 126
Figure 6-1 Modeling the distributed computing environment for parallelizing
            algorithms 150
Figure 6-2 RIP application development layout 161
Figure 6-3 A model for Remote Image Processing 165
Figure 9-1 Synchronous RPC 236
Figure 9-2 Three asynchronous alternatives to avoid client blocking 237
Figure 9-3 Asynchronously collecting results within the client avoids blocking
            at the client 252
Figure 9-4 Using a second client process (a local collection daemon) FRPC to
            avoid blocking at the client 262
Figure 9-5 A multi-tasking server 263
Figure 9-6 Server multi-tasking via multiple processes 264
Figure 10-1 Distributed X Window applications using widget sets and
            toolkits 286
Figure 10-2 Remote asynchronous calls monitored with an interval timer
            in XView 293
Figure 10-3 The Notifier as placed between the XView server and client
            application 296

Figure 10-4   Asynchronous X client and server using XtAppAddInput() to listen for an FRPC 303

Figure 10-5   An RPC server using the Xt dispatch loop to replace svc_run() 308

Figure 11-1   Layers of the TIRPC interface 324

Figure 12-1   ONC RPC error reporting framework 351

Figure B-1   The ray tracing, image synthesis paradigm (adapted from [Sam89]) 410

Figure B-2   Overview of the network parallel ray tracing application 414

Figure B-3   Benchmark scene generated by the ray tracer 415

Figure B-4   Multiple ray tracing servers using process control 418

Figure B-5   Parallel network ray tracing time for 420x320 images as a function of number of servers 422

Figure B-6   Parallel network ray tracing time for 840x640 images, as a function of number of servers 423

List of Tables

Table 2-1 Apollo/HP Distributed Computing Acronyms...22
Table 2-2 Sun/AT&T Distributed Computing Acronyms 23
Table 2-3 Distributed Computing Environment Features...35
Table 2-4 The ONC Development Road Map 38
Table 2-5 DCE Development for NCS Release 2.0...39
Table 3-1 ONC RPC Program Numbers..48
Table 3-2 Primitive ONC XDR Filters for C Built-in Data Types.............................52
Table 3-3 ONC XDR Filters for Handling Complex C Data Types 53
Table 4-1 RPCGEN Command-line Options 66
Table 4-2 RPCGEN.NEW Command-line Options 67
Table 4-3 Preprocessor Symbols Built-in to RPCGEN..78
Table 8-1 Rpcinfo Options..227
Table 11-1 Net Type Values and Transport Selection..326
Table 11-2 The New Preferred Calls...327
Table 12-1 Flavors of Authentication,
            (CLIENT *clnt)->cl_auth->ah_cred.oa_flavor.......................................335
Table 12-2 Functions for Error Reporting at the Client after an RPC.....................338
Table 12-3 Possible Authentication Errors, rpc_err.re_why 339
Table 12-4 Functions for Error Reporting at the Server 345
Table B-1 Parallel Ray Tracing: Frames or Scan-lines?...419

List of Examples

Example 1-1 RPCL protocol definition: rdb.x 5

Example 1-2 Portion of header file: rdb.h 6

Example 1-3 Remote database service procedures: rdb_svc_proc.c 6

Example 1-4 The client application for rdb: rdb.c 8

Example 3-1 Directory listing with local procedure calling: lls.c 44

Example 3-2 Directory listing procedure: read_dir.c 45

Example 3-3 Common include definitions for the RPC directory lister: rls.h 48

Example 3-4 XDR conversion routine shared by the RPC remote directory read
client and server: rls_xdr.c 51

Example 3-5 RPC server for reading directory files: rls_svc.c 55

Example 3-6 RPC client for reading remote directory files: rls.c 56

Example 4-1 Rules for simple RPCGEN application development: makefile 64

Example 4-2 Remote directory listing protocol: rls.x 82

Example 4-3 Header file generated by RPCGEN: rls.h 83

Example 4-4 Remote read directory service: rls_svc_proc.c 84

Example 4-5 Remote directory listing client: rls.c 86

Example 4-6 Two forms of local debugging: makefile 92

Example 4-7 A simple shell archiving script: bundle 93

Example 4-8 Server stub edited to use Raw transport for local debugging:
rls_svc.c 95

Example 4-9 Client application using Raw transport for local debugging: rls.c 96

Example 4-10 A shell script to kill processes by name: slay 101

Example 5-1 AF_UNIXserver.c – UNIX domain socket server 129

Example 5-2 AF_UNIXclient.c – connection-oriented UNIX domain socket
client 131

Example 5-3 TCP_AF_INETserver.c – TCP Internet socket server 134

Example 5-4 TCP_AF_INETclient.c – TCP Internet socket client 135

Example 5-5 UDP_AF_INETserver.c – UDP Internet socket server 138

Example 5-6 UDP_AF_INETclient.c – UDP Internet socket client 140

Example 5-7 Reading and writing a socket requires special care:
myReadWrite.c 143

Example 5-8 Using rexec() for remote execution: remote.c 145

Example 6-1 Catching SIGCHLD from child deaths using fork(), kill(), and signal(): stest.c 153

Example 6-2 wait() watches for child processes that die: wtest.c 154

Example 6-3 Asynchronous concurrent processing using fork() and signal (): status.c 155

Example 6-4 Interval timer and signals monitor how long the kids are out: childTimer.c 157

Example 6-5 Using time-of-day to watch child processing tim: day.c 159

Example 6-6 A template for RPCGEN RPC development: makefile 161

Example 6-7 Sample input script for rip 165

Example 6-8 Protocol for client/server remote image processing exchanges: rip.x 167

Example 6-9 Definitions and macros shared between user client and server RIP code: rip_shared.h 169

Example 6-10 Client procedures for RIP: rip.c 170

Example 6-11 Server procedures for RIP: rip_svc_proc.c 180

Example 7-1 Header file for the local image manager: im.h 188

Example 7-2 Main procedure for the local image manager: im.c 190

Example 7-3 Archive access functions for the local image manager: im_proc.c 193

Example 7-4 RPCL protocol definition for the distributed image manager: dim.x 202

Example 7-5 Client main for the distributed image manager: dim.c 205

Example 7-6 The server procedures for the distributed image manager: dim_svc_proc.c 208

Example 8-1 C shell script to start remote servers: sstart.csh 218

Example 8-2 A Bourne shell script to start remote server process (better): sstart.sh 219

Example 8-3 Direct ls servers using sstart.sh: ~/.ls 221

Example 8-4 A skeleton for starting servers from the client 222

Example 8-5 A skeleton for server self-termination after lack of use 224

Example 8-6 Server termination through an RPC: die_1() 225

Example 8-7 A skeleton for setting server process priority 226

Example 8-8 Restarting the server with an RPC: restart_1() 226

Example 9-1 Combined one-way and synchronous RPC protocol for remote directory listing: one-way.x 240

Example 9-2 Server procedures including a one-way, request-only RPC service: one-way_svc_proc.c 242

Example 9-3 Client places one-way RPC requests: one-way.c 243

Example 9-4 Utility to ask the network if a service is available: broadcast.c 248

Example 9-5 Service request loop: svc_run() 250

Example 9-6 A service procedure makes an FRPC: doit_1() 252

Example 9-7 Header file included by asynchronous clients and servers:
asyncRls.h 254

Example 9-8 Client side of an asynchronous server routine: asyncRls.c 255

Example 9-9 Server responds asynchronously using FRPCs: asyncRls_svc.c 258

Example 9-10 Server multi-tasking through process creation:
HighLevelServer.c—DOES NOT WORK! 264

Example 9-11 Multi-tasking service that works: multi-Rls_svc.c 265

Example 9-12 Asynchronous, multi-tasking service: multiAsyncRls_svc.c 268

Example 9-13 Lightweight processing for asynchronous remote calls from a
client: rteleLWP.c 275

Example 9-14 Lightweight processing svc_run() server loop: svc_runLWP.c 278

Example 9-15 Lightweight processing for asynchronous remote calls from a
client: rteleLWP_svc_proc.c 280

Example 10-1 XView client with synchronous RPCs launched from callback
function: syncCallback.c 287

Example 10-2 makefile for Xt and Xv applications 289

Example 10-3 Using an interval timer in XView to place synchronous RPCs:
itimer.c 291

Example 10-4 XView interval timer looks for asynchronous FRPC requests:
asyncCallback.c 293

Example 10-5 Using notify_enable_rpc_svc() in the XView Notifier:
notifyServer.c 298

Example 10-6 Dispatcher registered for XView and Xt/Xol RPC server
applications: dispatch.c 299

Example 10-7 A simple Xt/Xol example: hello.c 300

Example 10-8 Xt socket-based client, Internet addressing, and TCP transport:
Xt_sockets_AF_INET_client.c 303

Example 10-9 TCP_AF_INETserver.c modified for repeated use:
Loop_TCP_AF_INET_server.c 306

Example 10-10 UDP transport RPC server activated by the Xt event dispatcher,
using XtAppAddInput(): udpDispatchServer.c 308

Example 10-11 TCP transport with XtAppAddInput is more complex:
tcpDispatchServer.c 311

Example 10-12 Synchronous remote directory listing client using TCP transport:
tcpRls.c 313

Example 10-13 X client loads a Sun rasterfile(5) format image into a window:
xwload.c 315

Example 10-14 Load a Sun rasterfile(5) format image into a SunView window:
wload.c 318

Example 10-15 Sun rasterfile format utilities: raster.c 320

Example 10-16 Sun rasterfile format support: raster.h 321

Example 12-1 Adding authentication to the client: dim.c 340

Example 12-2 Automating authentication changes to server dispatch stub:
          makefile 347

Example 12-3 Macros included into the server dispatch routine for
          authentication: auth.h 348

Example 12-4 Access control added to server delete procedure:
          dim_svc_proc.c 349

Example 12-5 repairDB() now restores the database 357

Example R-1 Reading and writing XDR data through simple filters: portable.c 365

Example R-2 Using fast XDR macros: macro.c 367

Example B-1 Manual page for the network ray tracer rtrace 426

Example B-2 Input file for the network ray tracer rtrace: bdata.i 427

Example B-3 Protocol definition for the network ray tracer rtrace: rtrace.x 428

Example B-4 Other shared definitions for the network ray tracer client and server
          procedures: rtrace_shared.h 429

Example B-5 Client side of the network ray tracer: rtrace.c 430

Example B-6 Server procedures for the network ray tracer rtrace:
          rtrace_svc_proc.c 442

Example B-7 makefile for the rtrace network ray tracer 450

Example C-1 Making RPCSRC 4.0 rpcinfo.c do other things: patchFile 454

Preface

Are you *compute-bound?* Within your workstation lies a tool to capture huge amounts of CPU horsepower from your network without spending another dime. This tool gives you the ability to put any number of machines at the service of your application.

My first real experience with RPC came in the middle of developing image processing algorithms for a research project. Before using RPC, I found myself drinking lots of coffee while I waited to see results. I wanted to be more productive. I needed to prototype algorithms more quickly and produce on-line demos more easily. I considered purchasing or designing special-purpose hardware and software (e.g., a subsystem or plug-in boards like Sun's TAAC or VX/MVX), but I had no extra card slots in my Sun 3/60. Besides, I had a small budget and tight time constraints.

I began thinking about the 300+ UNIX machines in our laboratory. There are lots of workstations and a number of multiprocessor compute servers and graphics engines—all available over Ethernet. How could I exploit the computing power of these machines on the network? The answer is RPC, the remote procedure call facility developed by Sun Microsystems.

Remote procedure calling is the ability to call procedures outside of an application's current address space. In other words, a local program can execute a procedure on a remote machine, passing data to it and retrieving the result. RPC allows you to write a distributed application that can make use of the computing resources of a network.

☞ **RPC Defined.** An RPC system is the collection of software necessary to support remote procedure call programming and the necessary run-time services. An RPC system is a logical subset of a distributed computing environment. RPC is used in this book to refer to an RPC system.

This book provides an understanding of how to use the RPC libraries to build distributed applications. I address the questions I had when I first looked into RPC, interprocess communication mechanisms, and the related tools on my Sun workstation. I show lots of program examples, some of which will get you started writing your own programs while others present techniques useful for tackling more complex applications. If you're anything like me, you will try the programs in this book, see what breaks, and learn from it.

This book covers the RPC facility developed by Sun Microsystems' Open Network Computing (ONC) group. As I explain at the end of Chapter 2, my rationale for choosing ONC RPC was that it was the only RPC freely available then and now. I also cover elements of the Open Software Foundation's (OSF) Distributed Computing Environment (DCE†), a competing standard that defines its own RPC. I try to make some sense of the confusion over what the ONC and DCE standards propose. RPC implementations can be abstracted at some level to look the same, independent of the machine's operating system. So, a programmer who follows the examples in this book will learn the general art of remote procedure calling under UNIX and can apply these techniques to the RPC system of choice.

Scope of This Handbook

Figure P-1, on page xxiii, illustrates the organization and interdependence of the material presented in this book. Use it as a road map to navigate through the book.

Chapter 1, *Introduction to Remote Procedure Calling*, explains how remote procedure calling works and the mechanisms on which it is built. Chapter 1 takes you through the development of a trivial RPC example.

Chapter 2, *Network Computing Today*, profiles evolving standards in distributed computing environments. A *distributed computing environment* is the name given to a suite of tools, including a remote procedure call mechanism and programming library. These tools facilitate the development and hosting of distributed, networked applications. I cover ONC and DCE, as well as some specific RPC application development tools, such as protocol compilers, including Sun's RPCGEN, the Netwise RPCTOOL, and NCS NIDL.

Chapter 3, *Developing High-level RPC Applications*, covers the basics of RPC application development and finally gets down to some real examples. It starts with a simple, hand-compiled client/server protocol example. This example introduces the high-level ONC RPC library functions that enable you to tie a client and server together over the network with only a few additional lines of code. When clients and servers converse only a few times, use the UDP transport and pass data struc-

---

† OSF uses the term DCE to denote its product offering, so we will avoid using the acronym DCE for a generic distributed computing environment.

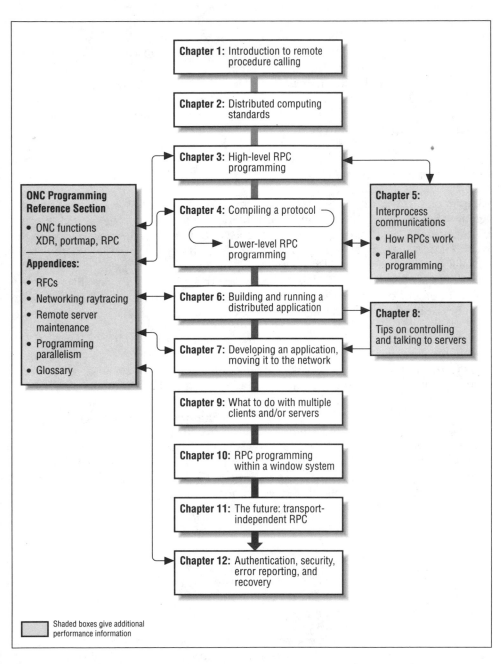

Figure P-1. Book organization and reading strategy

tures of limited complexity, the high-level interface is an easy way to put together a
distributed application.

Chapter 4, *Protocol Compiling and Lower-level RPC Programming,* addresses situations where the communication between the client and server is more complex. A protocol compiler should be used when complex data structures or several service procedures are involved. Protocol compilers take your high-level definition of the exchange and compile interface routines that your client and server programs call. The definition includes the names of the service program and its procedures, as well as the data types to be passed in and out. A protocol compiler becomes a real productivity tool when you have anything more than simple client/server exchange. Program development is similar regardless of which protocol compiler you choose: RPCGEN, Netwise RPCTOOL, or NCS NIDL. In this chapter, we deploy and debug a small, synchronous application that provides a simple, one-at-a-time client/server interaction.

Chapter 5, *UNIX Networking and Interprocess Communication,* explores the close relationship between RPC and the UNIX interprocess communication (IPC) mechanism. After all, sockets, descriptors, protocols, and transports are what make up the world of networking. If you need specialized or high-performance networked applications, you must often deal with low-level IPC. If you like to roll your own, this chapter is a must, filled with lots of examples that illustrate IPC mechanisms. We build a number of different client/server pairs, and later implement the same thing with RPC. Seasoned UNIX hackers may skip this chapter.

Chapter 6, *Application Development: Networked Parallel Image Processing,* first covers the practical limitations of networking then develops a scheduled, multiple-server image processing network application. Chapter 6 uses the interprocess communication discussed in Chapter 5 to build a large-scale distributed application. This chapter should prepare you for more complicated, multiple-server applications. If one of your goals is to achieve speed-up through parallel concurrent computation, then you want to think about the overall client/server structure before coding. *Handling multiple servers or clients concurrently is, in my estimation, the real strength of RPC.* Not only can you control remote program execution, you can manage many of them at once. As standards develop, more help for concurrency will be provided in the application development tools. I'll build a simple, asynchronous, process control-based scheduling mechanism that we'll re-use later in the book.

Chapter 7, *Distributing Existing Applications,* follows the development of another application; this one manages collections of images. We take this application and re-design it to run over the network. The purpose of this chapter is to present some general techniques for changing existing applications so that they use RPC and take advantage of network computing.

Chapter 8, *Managing RPC Servers,* defines and presents solutions for various issues, including those specific to distributing applications across a large number of servers. A remote procedure call system depends upon the utilities provided by distributed computing environments for starting, finding, registering and binding to services. By making use of existing RPC-based utilities like distributed file systems and name servers, RPC becomes more versatile, extensible and reliable for an applications developer.

Chapter 9, *Multiple Clients and Servers,* addresses many of the challenges raised in Chapter 6 as we consider developing multiple clients and servers to communicate in asynchronous and concurrent fashions. This chapter presents some of the most important information in the book. At this point in the evolution of system software, RPC system calls alone are not enough to get a multiple client or server-distributed application running concurrently. You need to add your own IPC and control techniques. Strategies for remote asynchronous calls and concurrency at both the client and server sides of an RPC are detailed. Examples use UNIX IPC and lightweight process threads along with ONC RPC functions to get a number of clients and servers working together.

Chapter 10, *RPC Under Windowing Systems,* addresses how RPC complements a windowing system like X. The event-driven nature of windowing systems requires a different RPC programming approach. The issues of integration can be complicated, especially when process control or IPC is required. In one example, RPC is slid-in underneath Sun's X11/NeWS Openwin windowing system with the XView programming library. Using X11 with low-level IPC is not to be overlooked. For simple tasks, X11 and associated toolkits have the ability to do I/O multiplexing from a number of display clients. Thus, you can use multiple RPC servers or multiple X11 clients to accelerate or distribute an application. This chapter assumes some knowledge of X programming.

Chapter 11, *ONC Transport-independent RPC,* presents the proposed future of RPC systems. By isolating the application programmer from the details of addressing and transports, code not only becomes more portable across networks and operating systems, but is easier to write. The recently released ONC TIRPC software is presented. Changes from, and compatibility with, the earlier version 4.0 release are discussed.

Chapter 12, *Advanced Programming Issues,* introduces the need for authentication (credentials and verifiers) and security schemes. The three flavors of ONC-supported credentials are discussed via examples. Chapter 10 briefly treats the large topic of RPC application fault tolerance in terms of error detection and recovery.

The ONC RPC Programming Reference offers complete details on the ONC functions used in the book. The reference guide covers the backbone of the ONC distributed computing environment. The library routines are described as they are used throughout the book. They are discussed in more detail as complete libraries in the reference guide. *The ONC RPC Programming Reference* has three sections. The first section is a reference for ONC XDR functions; the second section is a reference for Version 4.0 Portmapper binder service; and the last section is a reference for the RPC programming libraries.

Appendix A, *Obtaining RFCs (Internet Standards, Request for Comment),* discusses how to find out more about the standards discussed in this book.

Appendix B, *An RPC Case Study: Networked Ray Tracing*, presents a more elaborate application than the one in Chapter 6. This chapter is more academic in tone, as it is derived from a research report. Nonetheless, it contains a lot of good code. All the techniques are demonstrated in this finale: a distributed parallel ray tracer. Synthesizing images is compute intensive. By slaving a number of available machines to the task, near-optimal speed-ups are reached. Like Chapter 6 it uses a heavyweight processing approach to server scheduling.

Appendix C, *Generalized Server Initialization, Inquiry, and Removal*, extends the RPC utility `rpcinfo` so that it becomes a server initialization, inquiry, and removal tool.

Appendix D, *Parallel Processing In A Nutshell*, is a crash-course on parallel programming, especially as it applies to a distributed network environment. This section presents the practical side of a largely academic subject. It won't make you an expert, but I have had some successes that I can share. I'll give enough keywords, topics, and issues to start you on an in-depth literature search if you so desire.

Finally, there is the *Glossary* of terms and acronyms that frequently appear in this book.

Some Assumptions About the Reader

You need to know the C programming language and the UNIX operating system. You need not be a master of either one. Nor do you need to be a networking guru.

The chapters dedicated to explaining interprocess communication mechanisms concentrate on UNIX implementations, giving the necessary background required to understand how RPC and other networking utilities work. The IPC chapters are not mandatory reading; they are more illustrative and may be boring to the more experienced programmer.

Chapters 6, 9, and 10 deal with programming behind a windowing system. Some exposure to X or SunView is expected, but you need not be an expert in windowing systems. You should be able to pick up knowledge of how to use these windowing libraries as you go along.

Software Mentioned in This Book

Chapter 2 points out that the major RPC systems are commercially available. Let's look at what RPC system software is available and where:

RPC 4.0

Sun posted the RPC source to Usenet several years ago as RPCSRC 4.0. It includes ONC RPC system source along with network utilities. It is available at file transfer protocol (FTP) RPCSRC archive sites. Release 4.0 is available from Sun as part

`#RPC-4.0-X-X-5` for a nominal processing fee. A more recent version, including transport independence, is available in System V, Release 4 (SVR4), on Internet and as user-contributed software in Berkeley 4.3.[†] Sun has recently released a BSD 4.3 VAX port of the version 4.1 ONC/NFS source code. Licensing fees can be waived.

This book emphasizes use of the publicly available Sun Microsystems, Inc. RPC version 4.0 software (RPCSRC 4.0) with the RPCGEN protocol compiler. It is copyrighted but freely distributed, with some degree of support by Sun though the Portable ONC Group. Although I'll be using RPCSRC 4.0, no major differences between earlier or later versions are exploited.[‡]

You can buy the ONC software directly from Sun, or it may be bundled in newer UNIX releases. If you have Internet access, you can bring the source code for Sun's RPCSRC 4.0 (Release 4.0) tool suite to your machine for free.

Sun's freely licensed RPC/XDR implementation, RPCSRC 4.0, is available via anonymous ftp from `bcm.tmc.edu` and by e-mail from the `archive-server@bcm.tmc.edu`. If you use the archive server, send mail to `archive-server@bcm.tmc.edu` with a subject of "send `index nfs`" to see all the names of the files. Sending a message with the `Subject` "help" will return to you more information about the archive server itself.

To use anonymous FTP, use the `ftp` program to connect to `bcm.tmc.edu`. When prompted for a user name, enter "anonymous." When prompted for a password, enter your user ID. Then change directory (`cd`) to "nfs" where you will find the RPCSRC 4.0 files. Use `mget` or multiple `gets` to up-load the 17 Bourne shell (shar) files in the main library and 4 shar files for ONC's secure RPC.

RPCSRC 4.0 is available from the Rice University archive. Use `titan.rice.edu` for anonymous FTP and `archive-server@rice.edu` for e-mail. If you use the archive server, send mail to `archive-server@rice.edu` with a `Subject` of "send `index sun-source`" to see the names of the files in the `sun-source` directory.

RPCSRC 4.0 tools are also available from `comp.sources.unix` news archive sites.

If you don't have Internet access, the Sun-Spots mailing list distributes a digest and archives lots of valuable tools. Find out more by sending requests to the `sun-spots-request@rice.edu`.

I first received the RPCSRC 4.0 source code on the 1988 Sun User's Group tape. If you cannot FTP it, contact the mail servers or locate old SUG tapes. Contact Sun at `nfsnet@sun.com` (the Internet) or `sun!nfsnet` (Usenet).

---

† While TIRPC is available now, it won't completely show up in SunOS until SunOS5.0.

‡ Due to its recent release, I present only limited experience with the ONC Transport-independent RPC system. Nevertheless, all the examples and issues presented remain relevant and compatible with the TIRPC release.

Netwise RPCTOOL

Netwise and their RPCTOOL protocol compiler are closely allied with ONC RPC. The address of Netwise is: 2477 55th St., Boulder CO, 80301. RPCTOOL, described in Chapter 2, *may become* the preferred ONC development environment.

NCS RPC

Apollo's NCS is moving out of its proprietary, parochial stage and into the main-stream as it is bundled with HP/Apollo workstations. It is available as a separate HP/Apollo product. Pieces of it will be released in 1991 by the Open Software Foundation (OSF).

OSF DCE

OSF plans to release the NCS RPC discussed in some modified form, along with a number of other support packages within the Distributed Computing Environment (DCE) of the OSF/1 operating system. A tentative Fall 1991 release date is planned. The first snapshot was released to members of OSF in 1990. Delivery price and license fees are yet to be determined for this large-scale project. Some pilot site implementations are needed first. For more details contact OSF's Marketing Department at 617-621-8700.

Courier RPC

We talk very little in Chapter 2 about one of the original RPC systems, the Xerox Courier system. Courier over TCP is publicly available as part of the user-contributed software in Berkeley 4.3.

Examples

The examples were developed under SunOS4.0, and shown to work under SunOS 4.1, as well as DEC ULTRIX® and Convex machines running the RPCSRC 4.0 release of the XDR, RPC, and Portmapper utilities and libraries.

If you have access to UUNET, you can retrieve the source code using uucp or ftp. For uucp, find a machine with direct access to UUNET, and type the following command:

```
cp uunet\!~/nutshell/rpc/rpc.tar.Z yourhost\!~/yourname/
```

The backslashes can be omitted if you use the Bourne shell (*sh*) instead of *csh*. The file should appear some time later (up to a day or more) in the directory */usr/spool/-uucppublic/yourname*.

You don't need to have opened an account to UUNET to be able to access their archives via UUCP from within the United States of America. By calling 1-900-468-7727 and using the login "uucp" with no password, anyone may uucp any of UUNET's online source collection. (You may wish to start by copying *uunet!/usr/-spool/ftp/ls-lR.Z*, which is a compressed index of every file in the archives.) As of this writing, the cost is 40 cents per minute. The charges will appear on your next telephone bill.

You don't need to subscribe to UUNET to be able to access its archives by *ftp* either. However, you need to use a machine connected to the internet. To use *ftp*, *ftp* to *ftp.uu.net* and use *anonymous* as your user name and *guest* as your password. Then type the following:

```
cd nutshell/rpc
binary (you must specify binary transfer for compressed files)
get rpc.tar.Z
bye
```

The file is a compressed tar archive. To restore files after retrieving the archive, type:

```
uncompress rpc.tar.Z
tar xf rpc.tar
```

Additional Sources of Information

Though this book is designed to be self-contained, you may want to retrieve some related references. When addressing issues concerning windowing systems, especially X and XView, O'Reilly & Associates puts out the definitive guides. The *XView Programming Manual*, Volume Seven of the series, is also invaluable as much of the later code developed here will use the XView toolkit. The low-level X11 graphics drawing, done best right at the Xlib interface as opposed to through XView, can be referenced from the Volumes One and Two of the X series. I'll also be borrowing some make tips from the Nutshell Handbook, *Managing Projects with make*.

During the development of this book, three other RPC books have been released presenting specifics of the NCS and ONC RPC libraries:

*   NCS RPC – *Network Computing System Tutorial*, by Tom Lyons, Prentice-Hall.

*   ONC RPC – *The Art of Distributed Applications*, by John Corbin, Springer-Verlag.

*   NCS RPC and ONC RPC – *UNIX Network Programming*, by Richard Stevens, Prentice-Hall.

The following are additional sources of information:

*   *Xerox Network Systems Architecture, General Information Manual, XNSG 068504*, Xerox Corporation, April 1985.

*   *Implementing Remote Procedure Calls*, by A. D. Birrell and B. J. Nelson, XEROX CSL-83-7, October 1983.

*   *Berkeley Software Architecture Manual 4.3 BSD Edition*, by W. Joy, R. Fabry, S. J. Leffler, M. K. McKusick, and M. J. Karels, Dept. of Electrical Engineering and Comptuer Science, University of California, Berkeley, April 1986.

- *Open Systems Networking Interfaces*, System V Interface Definition, Issue 2, Volume III, 1986.

- *Remote Procedure Call Programming Guide*, Sun Microsystems, Inc., 1988.

- *Assigned Numbers*, by J. Reynolds and J. Postel, DARPA RFC 923, October 1984.

- *Remote Procedure Call Protocol Specification*, Sun Microsystems, Inc., DARPA RFC 1050, June 1988.

- *rpcgen – An RPC Protocol Compiler*, Sun Microsystems, Inc., 1988.

- *STREAMS Programmers Guide*, UNIX System V Release 3, AT & T.

- *Secure Networking in the Sun Environment*, by B. Taylor and D. Goldberg, Sun Technical Report, 1987.

- *XDR: External Data Representation Specifications*, Sun Microsystems, Inc., DARPA RFC 1014, June 1987.

Conventions

Courier   Any function calls or UNIX shell commands mentioned in the text are in Courier. Source code, computer screen I/O, or extended UNIX command lines are in a smaller font.

UNIX system functions when introduced are followed by any relevant manual page section number. For example, rshd, the remote shell daemon, is mentioned as rshd(8C). The UNIX command "man 8c rshd" will bring up more complete information if the manual pages are installed on your system. If possible, get the manual pages for the ONC RPC library functions, including RPC, XDR, Portmapper, secure RPC, and support routines.

Courier Bold

Command lines that you should type are in **Courier Bold**.

Italic   Filenames are in *Italic*.

Helvetica Condensed

Examples of syntax are in Helvetica Condensed.

Function calls are always referenced with trailing "()" to differentiate them from commands, which only have trailing parentheses when enclosing a manual page section.

Often I'll use the C preprocessor cpp style of expressing include filenames. <netinet/in.h> is actually */usr/include/netinet/in.h*.

Acknowledgments

Dale Dougherty has been very patient and helped me turn a maze of experiences into something useful to the rest of the world. I am grateful to people at Sun for their review of the book. I learned quite a bit from Vipin Samar, David Brownell, Carl Smith and Geof Lewis. HP/Apollo and Netwise provided me with assistance through review and documentation. Bruce Barnett and Walt Dixon here at GE Corporate R&D and Richard Sturges at David Taylor Naval Research provided review with an in-the-trenches application programmer's point of view. Tony Mason of Transarc also provided some useful insight. Andy Oram provided a much-appreciated final review and recommended some key changes.

Thanks goes to Richard Stevens for reviewing sections of the book to help produce a more accurate and complete revised edition.

Edie Freedman designed this book and Mike Sierra created the FrameMaker template for it. Chris Reilley drew the figures. Eileen Kramer did the copyediting and final production.

My family deserves most of the credit. The kids still cannot go to sleep at night unless they hear me at the keyboard. Somehow my wife endured as she's still here after this long ordeal.

In this chapter:

- *Client/Server Com-
  puting*
- *RPC Application
  Development*
- *RPC Makes
  Interprocess
  Communications
  Less Painful*
- *How RPC Systems
  Work*

1

Introduction to Remote Procedure Calling

Remote procedure calling allows a client to execute procedures on other networked computers or servers. ONC's RPC forms the foundation for most of the distributed system utilities used today like NFS and NIS. But RPC is also a user programming tool. It makes the client/server model more powerful and easier to program in than yesterday's low-level network socket interface. When combined with the ONC RPCGEN protocol compiler, clients transparently make remote calls through a local procedure call interface.

In this chapter, we explain the basics of remote procedure calling and provide an example of an RPC application. We give an overview of how the RPC communication model works and its relation to interprocess communication (IPC) facilities. If you get lost in the terminology, consult the list of top twenty buzzwords at the end of this chapter.

Client/Server Computing

The client/server model of computing is a popular model for distributed processing. It applies to any processing environment where one set of entities requests work to be done and another set actually performs the work. The X Window System, for instance, provides a client/server model for distributed processing. An RPC system provides the same ability to execute programs remotely as the X Window System, yet with a more direct communication model and less overhead.

The X Window System and RPC use the terms *client* and *server* differently, however. In X, remote *client* applications communicate with a local *display server*.

In RPC, a local *client* application makes procedure calls that can be executed on remote *servers*.

The term *remote* does not necessarily mean that clients and servers are communicating over a network. In both RPC and X, clients and servers may exist on the same machine. Similarly, while you might think of clients and servers as separate computers on a network, they are best understood as processes, running anywhere on the network. An application may take on the roles of both client and server.

A simple RPC application consists of a single client that communicates with a single server—the machine that actually executes the procedure. The client application talks to the procedure on the remote server by passing arguments and retrieving the results. Thus, performing a synchronous remote procedure call looks pretty familiar. Your machine waits until execution is complete before control returns to the client application.

Remote versus Local Procedure Calling

So, for the application programmer, what's the difference between local and remote procedure calling? As it turns out, there is very little difference—that's been a primary goal of RPC application programming interfaces (API).

Figure 1-1 illustrates the difference between local and remote procedure calling. On the left, a calling (client) process executes a procedure in its own address space. On the right, the client and server are running as two separate processes, and no longer have to live on the same machine. The RPC library handles the communication between these two processes.

RPC uses a request-and-reply communication model. The client procedure sends *request* messages to the server procedure which returns *reply* messages. The client and server processes communicate by means of two *stubs*, one for the client and one for the server. A stub is a communications interface that implements the RPC protocol and specifies how messages are constructed and exchanged. A protocol compiler like ONC RPCGEN is typically used to generate the stubs. The stubs are then linked with the client and server programs.

The stubs contain functions that map your simple local procedure calls into a series of network RPC function calls. The client calls procedures found in its stub that use the RPC library to find a remote process and then make requests of it. This remote process, in turn, listens to the network through the server stub. The server stub performs the low-level functions that invoke your service routines with a local procedure call interface.

Clients and servers must be able to communicate using a machine-independent data representation. The ONC RPC uses a single-canonical format for data representation known as External Data Representation (XDR). Client and server stubs are responsible for translating data in and out of this one form. If you use a protocol compiler, you can specify the service procedures and data structures to be

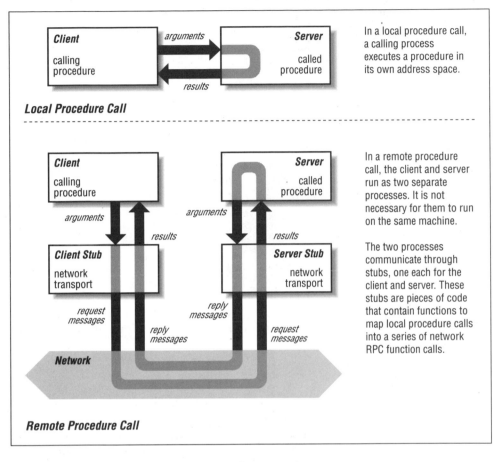

In a local procedure call, a calling process executes a procedure in its own address space.

Local Procedure Call

In a remote procedure call, the client and server run as two separate processes. It is not necessary for them to run on the same machine.

The two processes communicate through stubs, one each for the client and server. These stubs are pieces of code that contain functions to map local procedure calls into a series of network RPC function calls.

Remote Procedure Call

Figure 1-1. Local and remote procedure call communication

exchanged and leave the translation processing to the stubs. The XDR library contains filters for translating built-in C types as well as more complex types like strings and variable-length vectors.

RPC Application Development

Let's look at an example of a client/server interaction as we perform a lookup in a personnel database on a remote machine. Assume that the remote database cannot be accessed by your local machine via NFS. Before writing an RPC application, we might consider using standard UNIX shell commands. The following alias allows us

to search the database found in */usr/local/lib/personnel.dat* of the machine specified on the command line. (rodson is the name of my computer.)

```
rodson> alias rdb \
'echo name   location   extension;rsh -n \!\!·1 ' \
'egrep \!\!:2 /usr/local/lib/personnel.dat'
```

For example, if the database were on a remote machine named cortex, I could
get these kinds of results from my machine rodson:

```
rodson> rdb cortex BLOOMER
first   middle  last    phone   location
JOHN    J       BLOOMER 6964    KWC317
```

There are two major problems: the command is slow to execute and it requires an
account on the remote machine. A better alternative is to establish a server on
cortex that can respond to queries and retrieve information quicker for any user
on the network.

To develop an RPC application, we follow two steps:

1. Specify the protocol for client/server communication.

2. Develop the client and server programs.

Then we compile the programs and link the generated stubs and libraries. To test
the application, we launch the server on a remote machine and run the client application locally.

Defining the Protocol

The first step is to define the interface between the client and server, establishing
the framework for application development. If you use a protocol compiler, you
identify the names of service procedures and the data types of parameters and
return arguments in a protocol definition. The protocol compiler reads the definition and automatically generates the client and server stubs.

As we discuss in Chapter 2, there are several different protocol compilers: Netwise
RPCTOOL, ONC RPCGEN, or NIDL for OSF/NCS users. We will be using RPCGEN
and write the protocol definition in the ONC RPC Language (RPCL). The RPCL is
itself organized like the C language, using **cpp(1)** preprocessor directives and six
different types of definitions:

*   constant

*   enumeration

*   structure

*   union

*   typedef

*   program

Enumerations, structures, and typedefs are like those in C. Constants specify symbolic integer constants. RPCL unions are discriminated unions. These are somewhat analogous to Pascal variant records, quite different from C unions. Program definitions specify the service procedures to be recognized by one server.

An RPCL protocol definition file has a *.x* extension. Example 1-1 contains a sample RPCL protocol definition for a remote database server. A client can ask a server to add or delete a personnel record from a remote database. Records are stored as ASCII characters, delimited by whitespace. The fields are name (first, middle initial, last), phone number, and location.

Example 1-1. RPCL protocol definition: rdb.x

```
/* preprocessor directives */
%#define DATABASE "personnel.dat"  /* '%' passes it through */

/* constant definitions */
const MAX_STR = 256;

/* structure definitions, no enumerations needed */
struct record {
   string firstName<MAX_STR>;      /* <> defines the maximum */
   string middleInitial<MAX_STR>;       /* possible length */
   string lastName<MAX_STR>;
   int phone;
   string location<MAX_STR>;
};

/* program definition, no union or typdef definitions needed */
program RDBPROG { /* could manage multiple servers */
        version RDBVERS {
                record FIRSTNAME_KEY(string) = 1;
                record LASTNAME_KEY(string) = 2;
                record PHONE_KEY(int) = 3;
                record LOCATION_KEY(string) = 4;
                int ADD_RECORD(record) = 5;
        } = 1;   /* you set the interface version number */
} = 0x20000001; /* program number ranges established by ONC */
```

Four service procedures are defined to search through the records by first and last name, phone number, or location. Each requires a string argument and returns a struct record. In RPCL, strings are unambiguously defined as a NULL-terminated sequence of characters. The fifth procedure adds records to the database, returning a status integer. A sixth procedure, number 0 or the NULL procedure, will be inserted by RPCGEN. It is used for pinging a server to verify that it is listening for requests.

You can compile the protocol definition with the following command:

```
rodson> rpcgen rdb.x
```

RPCGEN produces a client stub, *rdb_clnt.c*, and a server stub, *rdb_svc.c*. It also produces any necessary XDR filters and a header file to be included by client and server applications and stubs. In this example, one XDR filter, *rdb_xdr.c*, is generated because struct record is the only non-trivial data structure. This bi-directional filter will be used by both the client and server.

The header file is named *rdb.h* and a portion of it is shown in Example 1-2. The DATABASE preprocessor definition is passed into the header file. MAX_STR also appears as an integer preprocessor constant. struct record will show up as a typedef structure definition in the header. The service procedures will be proto-typed as the lowercase equivalent of the specified name followed by a _version number. The client will request remote services in terms of a long integer.

Example 1-2. Portion of header file: rdb.h

```
#define FIRSTNAME_KEY((u_long)1)      /* taken from the */
#define LASTNAME_KEY((u_long)2)       /* header file */
#define PHONE_KEY((u_long)3)          /* generated by */
#define LOCATION_KEY((u_long)4)       /* RPCGEN */
#define ADD_RECORD((u_long)5)
#define RDBPOG((u_long)0x20000001)
#define RDBVERS((u_long)1)
extern record*firstname_key_1();
extern record*lastname_key_1();
extern record*phone_key_1();
extern record*location_1();
extern int*add_record_1();
```

Version numbers of a protocol are useful when multiple software generations must coexist. Some interfaces may be compatible while others may not. Your client application can decide whether a version-number mismatch constitutes an error before placing the remote procedure call.

RPCGEN also generates a server dispatch function to take care of validating requests and invoking the appropriate service procedures. The service procedures are the only server-side code you typically have to write.

Developing Server and Client Application Code

Now we can create the service procedures specified in the protocol. For sake of clarity we'll keep our example simple, doing minimal error checking, etc. We'll only return the record associated with the first key-value matched. The remote database server code is shown in Example 1-3.

With RPC, client and server parameters are passed by address. The service procedures must work with pointers for the simple reason that they are invoked by the dispatcher. The dispatcher must have an address to a static result to encode it and send the reply out over the network. Clients must pass addresses to their stubs for the same reason.

Example 1-3. Remote database service procedures: rdb_svc_proc.c

```
/*
 * Only the last name searching service is completely detailed;
 * the others are similar.
 */
#include <stdio.h>
#include <string.h>
#include <rpc/rpc.h>
#include "rdb.h"

FILE            *fp = NULL;
```

Example 1-3. Remote database service procedures: rdb_svc_proc.c (Continued)

```
static record  *pR = NULL;

int readRecord() /* a utility routine, reads one record */
{
  char buf[MAX_STR];

  if (!pR) {
    pR = (record *) malloc(sizeof(record));
    pR->firstName = (char *) malloc(MAX_STR);
    pR->middleInitial = (char *) malloc(MAX_STR);
    pR->lastName = (char *) malloc(MAX_STR);
    pR->location = (char *) malloc(MAX_STR);
  }
  if (!fgets(buf, MAX_STR - 1, fp)) return (0);
  if (sscanf(buf, "%s%s%s%d%s", pR->firstName,
    pR >middleInitial, pR->lastName,
    &(pR->phone), pR->location) != 5) return (0);
  return (1);
}

record *lastname_key_1(name)
  char **name;
{
  if (!(fp = fopen(DATABASE, "r")))
    return ((record *) NULL);
  while (readRecord())
    if (!strcmp(pR->lastName, *name)) break;
  if feof (fp) {
    fclose(fp);
    return ((record *) NULL);
  }
  fclose(fp);
  return ((record *) pR);
}

record *firstname_key_1(name)
  char **name;
{
....
  return ((record *) pR);
}

record *phone_key_1(name)
  char **name;
{
....
  return ((record *) pR);
}

record *location_key_1(name)
  char **name;
{
....
  return ((record *) pR);
}

int *add_record_1(r)
  record  *r;
{
  static int status;
....
  return ((int *) &status);
}
```

By virtue of the stub generated at the client-side, the client code written by you will make local calls with the same names as those used for your service procedures. Example 1-4 shows the client code. The main() scans for a search key and value; then attempts to place the appropriate remote calls. Before anything can be done, the client calls the server machine's portmap daemon to see if the necessary server program is registered. This itself is a well-defined RPC. If registered, the ONC RPC library function **clnt_create(3N)** returns a pointer to a CLIENT structure containing vital server communication information (e.g., the port address and an associated socket). With ONC RPC 4.0 you create a connection using either the TCP or UDP IP transports. With the latest transport-independent RPC (TIRPC), transport selection can be done at run-time to suit client, server, and user preferences and constraints.

Example 1-4. The client application for rdb: rdb.c

```
#include <stdio.h>
#include <ctype.h>
#include <rpc/rpc.h>
#include "rdb.h"

#define PRINTRECORD(pR) {\
  printf("first\tmiddle\tlast\tphone\tlocation\n"); \
  printf("%s\t%s\t%s\t%d\t%s\n", \
    pR->firstName, pR->middleInitial, \
    pR->lastName, pR->phone, pR->location); \
  }

main(argc, argv)
  int       ·           argc;
  char                  *argv[];
{
  CLIENT              *cl·     /* a client handle */
  char                *value;
  int                  key;

  if ((argc != 4) || (!isdigit(argv[2][0]))) {
    fprintf(stderr, "Usage: %s server key value\n", argv[0]);
    exit(1);
  }
  if (!(cl = clnt_create(argv[1], RDBPROG, RDBVERS, "tcp"))) {
    /*
     * CLIENT handle couldn't be created, server not there.
     */
    clnt_pcreateerror(argv[1]);
    exit(1);
  }
  value = argv[3];
  switch (key = atol(argv[2])) {
  case FIRSTNAME_KEY:
    PRINTRECORD(firstname_key_1(&value, cl));
    break;
  case LASTNAME_KEY:
    PRINTRECORD(lastname_key_1(&value, cl));
    break;
  case PHONE_KEY:{
    int       p;
    if (!(sscanf(argv[3], "%d", &p)) != 1) {
      fprintf(stderr,"\"PHONE_KEY\" requires integer value\n");
      exit(1);
    }
    PRINTRECORD(phone_key_1(&p, cl));
    break;
```

Example 1-4. The client application for rdb: rdb.c (Continued)

```
  }
  case LOCATION_KEY:
    PRINTRECORD(location_key_1(&value, cl));
    break;
  case ADD_RECORD:{
    record  *pR = (record *) malloc(sizeof(record));
    pR->firstName = (char *) malloc(MAX_STR);
    pR->middleInitial = (char *) malloc(MAX_STR);
    pR->lastName = (char *) malloc(MAX_STR);
    pR->location = (char *) malloc(MAX_STR);
    if (sscanf(argv[3], "%s%s%s%d%s", pR->firstName,
        pR->middleInitial, pR->lastName, &(pR->phone),
        pR->location) != 5) {
      fprintf(stderr,
        "\"ADD_RECORD\" requires a complete quoted record\n");

      exit(1);
    }
    if (!(*add_record_1(pR, cl))) {
      fprintf(stderr, "couldn't add record\n");
      exit(1);
    }
    break;
  }
  default:
    fprintf(stderr, "%s: unknown key\n", argv[0]);
    exit(1);
  }
}
```

Compiling and Running the Application

You are now ready to compile the client and server, linking with the stubs and XDR filters generated by RPCGEN. If you are running SunOS or ONC RPC is installed, the XDR and RPC library functions are included in *libc.a* so no extra link libraries are necessary. In later chapters, we'll present a *makefile* for automating the compilation process. For now, type the following series of commands:

Compile the client code:

        rodson> **cc -c -o rdb.o -g rdb.c**

Compile the client stub:

        rodson> **cc -c rdb_clnt.c**

Compile the XDR filters:

        rodson> **cc -c rdb_xdr.c**

Build the client executable:

        rodson> **cc -o rdb rdb.o rdb_clnt.o rdb_xdr.o**

Compile the service procedures:

        rodson> **cc -c -o rdb_svc_proc.o rdb_svc_proc.c**

Compile the server stub:

```
rodson> cc -c rdb_svc.c
```

Build the server executable:

```
rodson> cc -o rdb_svc rdb_svc_proc.o rdb_svc.o rdb_xdr.o
```

You now have client and server executables: `rdb` and `rdb_svc`, respectively.
Start the server up on a remote machine with the command:

```
rodson> rsh -n remoteHost $cwd/rdb_svc &
```

Try it and see how it really works. Here's what I get:

```
rodson> rdb cortex 2 BLOOMER
first    middle last      phone   location
JOHN     J            BLOOMER 6964    KWC317
```

You'll find `rdb` returns *much* faster than the `rdb` shell alias. The server is now
accessible to the whole network.

By the way, RPC servers don't have to be started manually, as we did here. We will
look at ways of starting RPC servers using UNIX facilities in Chapter 5 and discuss
other methods in Chapter 8.

Of course, this example gives you a simple overview of the application development process. We will be explaining this process in more detail in the chapters
ahead.

RPC Makes Interprocess Communications Less Painful

Interprocess communication (IPC) is an essential part of the client-server model.
While UNIX provides a rich set of IPC tools, IPC can be hard to use and therefore it
remains under-exploited. It can be difficult to develop, debug, and deploy multiple-
process applications, especially when the processes are distributed across a
network. With IPC, communication occurs in cumbersome and potentially machine-
dependent fashions (e.g., byte ordering and addressing problems). Error handling,
portability, and conciseness of code all suffer. While many non-UNIX operating
system development platforms include IPC support libraries, they are certainly no
easier to use.

You could use sockets to develop the network communication routines you need
for your own application. If you're out to develop a re-usable, extensible set of
communication tools, you'd have to start at a low level and define a machine-independent data representation as well as a protocol for exchanging data. Fortunately,
an RPC system allows you to avoid working at such a low level. For example, the
ONC RPC system provides the External Data Representation (XDR) library and

defines the RPC message-passing protocol. RPC systems were designed to hide all the nasty IPC details and make networked applications easier to develop.

How RPC Systems Work

In general, services make themselves known to a network of clients through an independent naming service or daemon. This service can give clients the address they need to open a communication channel with a server. The server can then accept (or deny) client requests, sending replies as necessary. The connection is closed once the remote session is completed.

How this happens is significantly different between socket-based and transport-independent flavors of RPC. Transport-independent RPC keeps addressing (e.g., server/service names, transports, client, and server addresses) at a symbolic level. In socket-based RPC systems, the default network services for a system are defined in */etc/services* and become available at boot-time. If the ONC Network Information System (NIS)[†] database server is running, services are found by calling it.

A service, identified by the port it is listening to, is a daemon waiting for a connection request. A port is a logical network communication channel. One ONC network service, the portmapper, is responsible for mapping services to ports, an essential part of client/server communication. The portmapper on every host is well-known; it is always assigned to port number 111. This allows direct access by both the client and server to a machine's portmap via **portmap(8C)**. With transport-independent RPC, port numbers are replaced by more abstract addresses and portmap is replaced by the more general rpcbind(8C) service.

Figure 1-2 outlines the steps necessary before an ONC RPC client can call a server.

1. When any ONC RPC server (daemon) is started, it establishes an address where it listens for requests. It registers the port number (address) with the portmapper. It also registers the RPC program numbers and versions that the server is prepared to service. The client and server applications have arbitrary port numbers or addresses.

2. Before a client can make a remote procedure call (using a server program number), the portmapper of the server machine is consulted to identify the port number (address) that is to receive an RPC request message.

3. The client and server can now open a communication path to perform the remote procedure execution. The client makes its request; the server sends a reply.

The sequence of events initiated by a client's remote procedure call (step 3 above) is shown in Figure 1-3. The process can only begin if the service is registered in the machine's portmap and the client has received a valid address for communication.

---

† NIS is the new name for Sun's Yellow Pages. YP is a trademark of British Telecom.

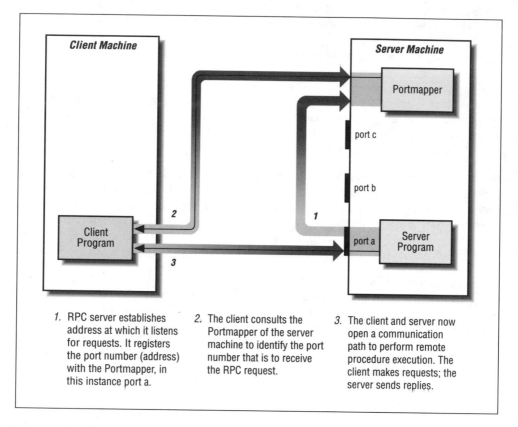

1. RPC server establishes address at which it listens for requests. It registers the port number (address) with the Portmapper, in this instance port a.

2. The client consults the Portmapper of the server machine to identify the port number that is to receive the RPC request.

3. The client and server now open a communication path to perform remote procedure execution. The client makes requests; the server sends replies.

Figure 1-2. ONC RPC client/server setup

A client procedure call sends a request message to the server and waits for a response. The server provides the requested service and sends back a reply message containing the results.[†] The client procedure call then returns the results.

To completely understand how socket-based RPC systems work, it helps to have some understanding of UNIX IPC mechanisms, especially sockets. Chapter 5 explains socket-based IPC, the communication scheme on top of which most RPC systems have been built. If at any time you find yourself thirsting for more details on IPC, jump-subroutine to Chapter 5. It's valuable information because IPCs are themselves a useful programming tool.

---

† To modularize code, a *dispatcher routine* is often used when a server provides multiple services (each a remote procedure call). The dispatcher sorts the requests, branching to the requested service procedure.

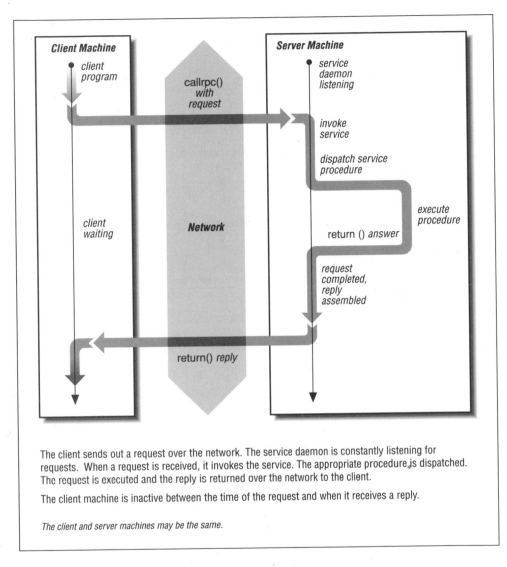

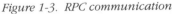

The client sends out a request over the network. The service daemon is constantly listening for requests. When a request is received, it invokes the service. The appropriate procedure is dispatched. The request is executed and the reply is returned over the network to the client.

The client machine is inactive between the time of the request and when it receives a reply.

The client and server machines may be the same.

Figure 1-3. RPC communication

RPC Systems and the OSI Reference Model

The Open Systems Interconnection (OSI) reference model defines the seven layers of network communication. Figure 1-4 shows how the components of ONC RPC 4.0 remote procedure call system can be described by this model. The user application sits at the top layer, transparently using a data representation scheme to communicate with a remote procedure call library. The ONC RPC 4.0 library, like most RPC libraries, supports the TCP(4P) and UDP(4P) transport IP(4P) protocols. These are two of the most commonly used transports under UNIX and are discussed in detail in Chapter 5 along with low-level network programming issues. Transport-independent RPC (TIRPC) libraries attempt to isolate the application from the transport used, making it easier to program for a wider variety of transports.

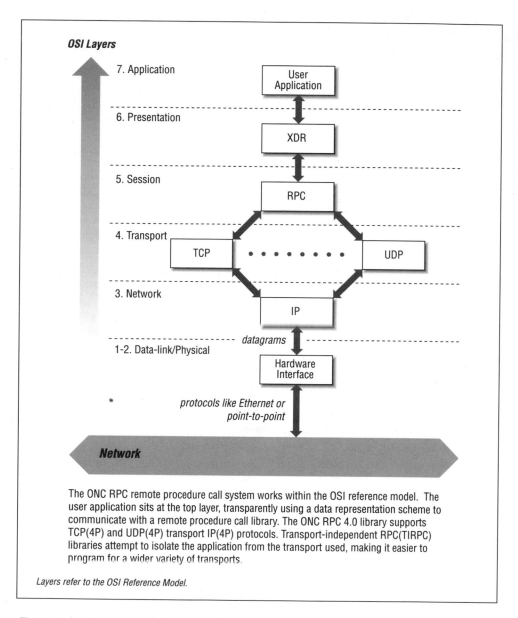

The ONC RPC remote procedure call system works within the OSI reference model. The user application sits at the top layer, transparently using a data representation scheme to communicate with a remote procedure call library. The ONC RPC 4.0 library supports TCP(4P) and UDP(4P) transport IP(4P) protocols. Transport-independent RPC(TIRPC) libraries attempt to isolate the application from the transport used, making it easier to program for a wider variety of transports.

Layers refer to the OSI Reference Model.

Figure 1-4. RPC systems within the OSI reference model

What is "State" and Why is it Important?

Because the client and server are separate processes, typically running on different machines, what happens when they cannot communicate with each other? What happens when the server crashes while executing a service procedure? What does the client do? The response depends upon whether a server is *stateless* or *stateful*. A stateless server does not maintain any information or state about interactions with clients. Stateful servers accumulate client information for remote procedure calls and require it to function properly.

Whether or not a server maintains state may not seem important yet, but it greatly affects the way clients and servers must be built. The statefulness of a server is often affected by the protocol or transport embedded within an RPC system.

Consider the `rtele_svc` database server developed earlier in this chapter. It has no concept of state. Each request can be handled independently. If the server crashes, active clients must wait until the server is available again. Once started, the new instance of the server opens the database and honors requests. At worst, client requests may time-out and require retries. Though delayed, the server still functions properly. If state is required in a client/stateless server relationship, it is maintained at the client.

Now let's say we broke the `rtele_svc` name look-up process into two steps. The first request would seek the database descriptor to the appropriate record in the file. Subsequent requests would retrieve selected information from that record. The last information request from a client would be appropriately tagged to facilitate the rewinding or closing of the file. The server is now stateful because request processing depends on earlier requests and how they left the file descriptor. Note that requests should come in groups of two or more and each client's request group must be handled separately.

If this stateful server crashed, recovery would be more complex. Unless the server somehow kept a log of processed requests to reconstruct state, it must count on the active client(s) to describe the state it was in when it crashed. The server needs to know if it was in the middle of a transaction with a client, and if so, what the active seek point(s) was.

Thus, if a stateful server crashes in the middle of an operation, the server alone has the information to know where to resume the operation. Server crash recovery can be complicated, if not impossible. If a stateless server crashes under the same circumstances, the client retains the information that's necessary for the server to resume the operation. We will cover server crash recovery in Chapter 12.

Top Twenty Distributed Computing Terms and Acronyms

As much as I hate acronyms, this book and the subject of networking is full of them. Many are similar and it can be confusing. You should make sure that you know these twenty frequently used terms and acronyms.

binding. The act of associating a server with a socket. When ONC RPC server transport handles are created they are *bound* to a certain network port (and a socket) address. A binding is a logical association between a client and server.

broker or binder service (port mapping). An intermediary between clients and servers designated to assist in network resource location.

client. An entity that requests services of a remote or local server.

daemon. A program designed to run continuously in the background, lying dormant until some condition is met. Most servers are daemons. Daemons have been around a lot longer than RPC, providing many local services within UNIX.

distributed computing environment. Generally a superset of other programming tools. Typically a coherent toolkit with remote procedure calling and data representation libraries. It includes network resource management tools and application development interfaces.

Internet Protocols. Includes TCP, IP, and UDP. Often referred to as the TCP/IP protocol family. Transmission Control Protocol (TCP) uses connection-oriented sockets. User datagram protocol (UDP) uses connectionless datagram sockets. Both are layered on top of IP.

IP. Internet protocol, an inter-network datagram delivery protocol. An IP address refers to a host.

NCA. The Network Computing Architecture (NCA), an Apollo/HP abstraction, is a collection of concepts and guidelines for distributed computing. (See also OSF.)

NCS. Baseline OSF distributed computing environment. The HP/Apollo's Network Computing System (NCS) is a particular implementation of NCA. NCS is a distributed computing environment consisting of Apollo/HP products: NCS/NCK and NCS/NIDL.

NFS. Sun's Network File System (NFS), built on ONC RPC. It uses IP with UDP.

ONC. Sun Microsystems' Open Network Computing. The ONC product suite includes RPC, XDR, NIS, NLM, rex, etc. AT&T and others support ONC tools.

OSF. Open Software Foundation (OSF). OSF is a consortium of DEC, IBM, HP/Apollo, and other major UNIX hardware vendors.

ISO/OSI. Bodies within CCITT. The Open Systems Interconnection (OSI) is a set of International Organization for Standardization (ISO)-developed standards including the seven-layer reference model for data communication systems and the ASN.1 Basic Encoding Rules.

port. A logical network communication channel.

remote procedure call system. A set of facilities including a programming library and network resource mapping and binding services to provide a mechanism for client processes to execute procedures on a remote server. A remote procedure call system is a subset of a distributed computing environment.

reply. Information assembled by a server and transmitted back to a client in response to a request.

request. Information assembled and transmitted to a server by a client to initiate some action at a server.

server. Servers are daemons that make resources available to networked clients. Servers have port and program numbers associated with them for network access by clients.

socket. An interprocess communication (IPC) channel. Once connected, processes use socket descriptor reads and writes to communicate. (See also interprocess communication.)

UI. UNIX International. Sun, AT&T, and others teamed up to develop standards in the UNIX system software. It was formed in response to OSF.

These terms and others can be found in the glossary.

In this chapter:

- *Distributed Computing Standards*
- *Examining ONC and NCS*
- *Netwise: A Second ONC Alternative*
- *Summary of Distributed Computing Environments*

2

Network Computing Today

An RPC system—an implementation of an RPC mechanism with an application programming interface (API)—is not enough to allow you to build a networked application. You need additional tools and facilities typically provided as part of a distributed computing environment.

We will examine the two most important commercial implementations of distributed computing environments: Sun's Open Network Computing (ONC) and the OSF's DECORUM DCE, based on the HP/Apollo NCS RPC. We will cover the significance of these two distributed computing environments, concentrating on the features that most affect RPC programming. Currently, the two implementations are incompatible, supporting different protocols and APIs.

This chapter is not essential to getting started writing RPC programs. You can skip ahead to Chapter 3 if you wish to do so. However, it helps to have a broader perspective on distributed computing and the various tools available to support the programmer and end user.

Distributed Computing Standards

Chances are that many people first became familiar with *distributed computing* through the trade journal debate surrounding the selection of technology by the Open Software Foundation (OSF) for its DECORUM DCE tools. In response to the OSF request for technology (RFT), two camps proposed enhancements of their existing distributed computing frameworks. On one side was Open Network Computing with AT&T, Sun, Novell, and Netwise supporting new developments on top of the existing ONC RPC system. On the other side was an enhanced NCS, the

Network Computing System, from HP/Apollo with backers IBM, DEC, Apollo, and Microsoft.

Many people figured that the OSF would go with the ONC proposal because it already had established itself in the market. ONC RPC source code also had been made freely available to the public.

When it made its decision, OSF selected pieces from both submissions for inclusion in the DCE. However, it selected NCS as the primary RPC mechanism over ONC RPC.

Much of what ONC and NCS/OSF propose in their initial announcements is aimed for future release. You can't get either of the *complete* NCS/OSF or ONC distributed computing environments today.

OSF has made the *DCE developer's kits* available for licensing from OSF to members and non-members. The kit contains an integrated set of tools and services for developing and running distributed applications. It includes remote procedure calling, local directory (naming) services, time services, and lightweight threads for concurrent programming. Applications developed under this early version of the kit will run with the formal Release 1.0 of the DCE.

NCS and ONC do have a couple of things in common. As they exist today, both are integral parts of existing operating systems. Development tools and the API are shipped with the systems (either standard or as an option). ONC development tools are even available from Internet archives.

Even though both contemporary ONC and NCS are out to accomplish the same goals, they are by no means compatible. There are some major technical differences and we will look at these differences in upcoming sections. I also present the Netwise RPCTOOL, based on the ONC distributed computing environment. RPCTOOL has characteristics of both, but it is not a stand-alone environment; it is a distributed application development toolkit that assumes an ONC RPC system is in place.

Before we look at both of these standards, let's define the elements of a distributed computing environment.

Features of a Distributed Computing Environment

We can list a number of defining features of a distributed computing environment:

- Machine independent data representation tools to allow different machines to exchange data.
- A protocol to specify the low-level client and server responsibilities during a remote procedure call.

- A protocol compiler that takes a remote procedure definition, including argument and return types, and generates RPC interface stubs. A protocol compiler further isolates the application from the underlying protocol and other low-level network programming by generating code to handle data encoding, decoding, service registration, and look-up.

- Authentication services to augment standard operating system security systems, and required as part of any remote accesses.

- Network naming services that allow applications to locate conventional network objects (like users, hosts, or mailboxes) and bind to services which have registered themselves on the network.

- A network time service for host synchronization to establish a single absolute network time.

- A distributed file system to eliminate file redundancy. It must provide fast, secure, fault-tolerant file-sharing. For networked, heterogeneous machines to efficiently share large amounts of data, a distributed file system with a file-locking mechanism is required.

Though the emphasis here will be on remote procedure calling, the other utilities are essential. These utilities are typically built on top of the platform's machine-independent data representation and its RPC library.

Now, let's elaborate on the two leading RPC solutions and understand what their parent distributed computing environments actually include. Note that the functionality described here will be significantly enhanced as time goes on.

NCS

The Network Computing Architecture (NCA), developed by Apollo/HP, is a collection of concepts and guidelines for distributed computing. The Network Computing System (NCS) is a particular implementation of NCA. NCS is the software available for a distributed application developer to use. NCS itself is a combination of two Apollo/HP products: NCS/NCK and NCS/NIDL.

NCK is the Network Computing Kernel (NCK). It is a run-time library that includes RPC support and network resource-manager service with access routines called the Location Broker (NCS). Low-level RPC network communication is carried out through use of a proprietary Network Data Representation (NDR) format.[†] The Location Broker is the naming or mapping service that keeps track of network resource objects (e.g., servers).

The second NCS component, NIDL, is a distributed application development toolkit, including a protocol compiler. NIDL stands for the Network Interface Description Language (NIDL) (more on this later). It translates interface and

---

† This proprietary format may be augmented with standards in the future.

protocol descriptions into C code to implement NCA-style RPCs and provide NCK routines for use by cooperating clients and servers. Table 2-1 summarizes the Apollo/HP acronyms.

Table 2-1. Apollo/HP Distributed Computing Acronyms

Acronym	Description
NCA	Network Computing Architecture
NCS	Network Computing System
NCK	Network Computing Kernel
LB	Location Broker
NDR	Network Data Representation
NIDL	Network Interface Description Language

The NCS broker service is worth more discussion. The Location Broker is divided into two interfaces. The Local Location Broker service gives information about local resources relevant to the host. The Global Location Broker conveys information about the network at large. These brokers inherit their behavior from the underlying NCS RPC transports. This stateful behavior means that clients have a sense of history about server interactions and it is possible to embed error and server crash detection. Stateful behavior can be both an asset and a liability. Often the limited additional overhead is warranted. The protocol behind the Local and Global Broker services is extensible, illustrated by Hewlett-Packard's HP license broker product which monitors licensed software utilization on a network. With no authentication routines built directly into NCS RPC, a separate authentication broker is required to round out the network services.

The NCS/NCK and NCS/NIDL products (we'll call them NCS or the NCS system from now on) are supported under Domain/OS, HP-UX, SunOS, VAX/VMS, and VAX/ULTRIX operating systems. Figure 2-1 outlines the inter-relationships of the pieces of the NCA environment.

ONC

Sun's Open Network Computing refers to a suite of products. The suite includes the ExternalData Representation for low-level RPC communication, which is publicly available. It also includes the Network Information Service (NIS), which is similar to the NCS Location Broker, for managing and tracking network resources. It also includes the RPCGEN protocol compiler that reads an interface description written in RPCL and generates the C code implementing ONC-style RPCs for client and server. Versions of RPCGEN and other ONC RPC support tools are freely available from Sun, with free licensing. ONC also includes a stateless Network File System

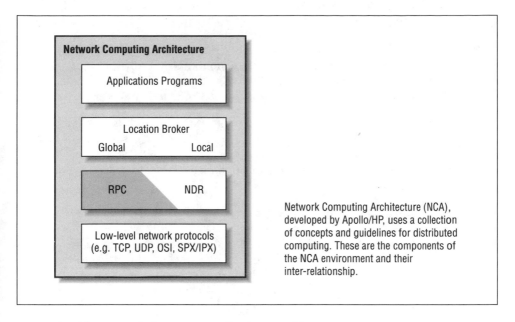

Figure 2-1. The Network Computing Architecture and System

(NFS) with automatic remote volume mounting, file-locking, and status monitoring mechanisms built on top of ONC RPC.

Table 2-2. Sun/AT&T Distributed Computing Acronyms

Acronym	Description
ONC	Open Network Computing
XDR	External Data Representation
NIS	Network Information Service, was Yellow Pages
RPCGEN	RPC protocol compiler, uses RPCL language
REX	Remote EXecution service
NFS	Network File System
NLM	Network Lock Manager

ONC NIS merits more elaboration. We will access it repeatedly throughout the examples in the book.

Each NIS master server manages a set of mappings between network resources (keys) and values for a domain of machine. Each map corresponds to and is built from the standard system ASCII data files: */etc/passwd, /etc/group, /etc/hosts, /etc/net-*

works, */etc/protocols*, */etc/ethers*, and */etc/netgroup*. Each machine in a domain runs a slave server, replicating and keeping the maps loosely consistent across the domain. In this way the standard */etc* information is augmented or in some cases replaced by on-line NIS map queries. The standard get... (3N)[†] and set... (3N) system call interface for retrieving this information is preserved. Other routines are provided within the ONC RPC library to get information in and out of the databases directly, although these routines are rarely needed.

NFS was one of the first services built on top of ONC RPC and uses NIS (then the Yellow Pages). It inherits a stateless protocol from ONC RPC using UDP.[‡] That is, servers don't have any sense of previous client interactions. The concept of state required for file-locking is accomplished through an additional service, the Network Lock Manager (NLM).

ONC makes use of yet another service, the Network Status Monitor, to watch for things like client crash recovery; something a stateless RPC protocol must do. A remote command execution service, rex (3R) (RPC remote execution protocol) is also defined. It copies the current environment (e.g., working directory and environment variables) to the remote machine before execution occurs there. on (1C) makes use of the rexd (8C) daemon using the rex protocol. rexed () is different from the low-level socket-based server, rexecd (8C). A license server also exists, the SunNet License. All are ONC RPC-based.

Figure 2-2 outlines the inter-relationships of the ONC distributed computing pieces.

Examining ONC and NCS

Let's take a look the main features of ONC and NCS as we compare and contrast the approaches.

Machine-independent Data Representation

Current NCS and ONC use their own (different) data representation schemes. NCS uses a *receiver-makes-it-right*, multi-canonical approach while ONC uses a single-canonical format.

The receiver-makes-it-right approach means that data translation, if necessary, is performed by the receiver. The exchange of data between like-machines is expedited because no translations are required. If the receiving machine requires a

---

† "..." is used to denote a group of functions or filenames that share a common prefix or suffix. In this example, get... (3N) and set... (3N) refer to the following functions: getnetent (3N), getnetbyaddr (3N), getnetbyname (3N), setnetent (3N), gethostent (3N), gethostbyaddr (3N), gethostbyname (3N), and sethostent (3N). You can find these functions using a command like: man -k get | egrep '(3N)'.

‡ ONC RPC inherits or borrows a sense of state from the transport being used. The TCP transport retains its state.

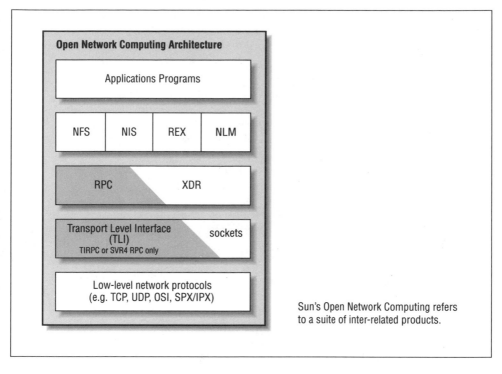

Figure 2-2. The Open Network Computing architecture

different data representation, it must invoke the appropriate conversion routine. Thus, with NCS, the sending machine can send data in one of 16 different formats, and the protocol tells the receiving machine which filter to use to read the data. Should a new machine type be added to an existing distributed application, the new requirements for translation are placed on client/server code that can cause major library rewrites or at least the recompilation of the application.

Single-canonical forms, though potentially requiring more overhead, present a more consistent application interface. The ONC XDR uses a single, neutral, intermediary data format, encoding and decoding data irrespective of the machines involved. Encode and decode steps are necessary even when compatible machines are communicating. That puts an extra burden on the send and receive processing, but with a single-canonical standard, all the applications know what format the data is in.

I have found that when big-endian (MSB first) machines are communicating, the impact of the big-endian byte-ordering used by XDR is minimal. The worst case is when two small-endian machines communicate. Bytes will have to be re-ordered at both send and receive ends to accommodate the XDR single-canonical order.

Like the NCS NDR, ONC XDR supports a finite number of data types and structures. To allow sharing of data with any kind of machine at run-time, the stubs surrounding your application must reduce your data structures to elements manageable by the NDR or XDR routines. If you happen to be writing for machines that are the same or compatible, no translation is necessary. The NCS RPC handles this special case at run-time. Neither RPC data representation can handle completely arbitrary data structures. Caution and planning is required when passing convoluted structures across the network. The encoding and decoding routines and macros understand only the built-in C types and some vector, array, and string types. XDR supports pointer-chasing, the ability to walk-down pointer-linked structures such as a linked list or tree. So, while there are a few constraints for application design, you will find that XDR does a pretty good job of allowing you to transfer elaborate data structures between clients and servers.

In the future, the ISO/OSI[†] standards should play an important role in bringing these two standards together. At the very least, there should be a basis for compatibility. Both NCS and ONC are moving to accommodate the ISO/OSI ASN.1 Basic Encoding Rules (BER) single-canonical standard, while maintaining backwards compatibility.

Both NCS and ONC are moving to allow migration to ISO/OSI network libraries via compile-time switches in the protocol compilers. Today, RPC libraries bundled with operating systems reference low-level TCP/IP and proprietary network protocol libraries. Both NCS and ONC will maintain the ability to use these standard low-level network communication libraries while including transport-independent communications in the future.

Of course, ONC TIRPC makes transport independence a reality for ONC as of AT&T UNIX System V, Release 4.0. The TIRPC release is available for SunOS 4.X machines.

RPC Mechanism

The RPC systems within NCS and ONC are built upon transports of different types.

Transport Protocols

ONC RPC 4.0 supports TCP and UDP Internet Protocols.[‡] TCP is a connection-oriented transport protocol. UDP is a connectionless transport protocol used for logically loose communications. We will cover these protocols in more detail in "A Network Protocol Primer" in Chapter 5. The current NCS suite supports UDP transport and the proprietary Apollo/HP Domain DDS transport.

---

† ISO—International Organization for Standardization, OSI—Open Systems Interconnection.

‡ IP—the Internet Protocols, of which TCP, the Internet Transmission Control Protocol and UDP, the Internet User Datagram Protocol, are members.

Under UNIX, connectionless Internet clients and servers use the UDP protocol. Even with additional user-level code, the UDP connectionless client/server communication is not completely reliable. If a datagram is lost, neither server nor client are aware of it. You can use a timer to gauge retransmission criteria and include some embedded data to sequence packets that allow re-assembly. The problem is that you don't know whether a request was successfully honored by the server or the reply was simply lost. I'll cover a cheap way to take care of these problems with the sockets examples in Chapter 5.

TCP, on the other hand, is reliable and manages these issues internally. Only a small amount of (mostly initial) overhead is required. It should also be noted that if an Internet-based RPC channel connects two processes on the same machine, both UDP and TCP become more reliable as they share a common operating-system kernel. UDP buffer overrun can still occur. UNIX domain sockets, local by their nature, are not used by RPC. They support more reliable protocols.

Under TIRPC, it is not necessary to specify transport protocol when writing protocol definitions or client and server code. The structure of the code is identical, whether the connection-oriented or connectionless protocol is selected. TIRPC sits on top of the network transport protocol and provides run-time transport independence. It uses the Transport Layer Interface (TLI) in SVR4, isolating the RPC mechanism from underlying transports. The name-to-address translation and network-selection libraries are separate entities that select the protocol and perform the necessary associations or look-ups to find server processes.

The current NCS RPC system specifies the transport layer. It is dependent upon which protocol is in use (e.g., UDP datagrams or the Apollo domain DDS datagrams). Plans have been announced for accommodating ISO/OSI TP4 and DECnet transports, but transport independence has not yet been announced. Even with old releases of ONC and NCS, specifying and developing code specific to a transport protocol is not that difficult, and to some degree can provide higher performance.

One disadvantage to working above the protocol (with TIRPC) is the need to perform more error detection and correction, especially if you're using an unreliable transport. If your application needs reliable behavior, your ONC RPC client and server code should watch host status on their own, if that function is not performed by the selected transport. For example, when using the unreliable UDP transport, things like number and duration of retries may need to be managed by your application. This is code you don't want to write and potentially represents a performance problem. The TCP transport handles many of these things itself.

The NCS RPC, given its depth of specification down communication layers, guarantees an application will perform in a robust, somewhat fault-tolerant fashion, independent of underlying protocols and transports problems. Nevertheless, I have not had any ONC RPC problems that I attribute to using UDP or TCP/IP. That's probably because I work late at night when even a wimpy network seems fast and robust. It is simple enough to write the extra code. Besides, by using ONC RPC, I can get at most of our lab's 300+ machines, many supporting only bare-bones ONC RPC systems.

The examples presented in this book will not use the transport-independent features of ONC TIRPC. I will use either TCP or UDP because it is common among networked UNIX machines today and is supported in the ONC RPC Release 4.0. I'll show the error detection and correction that I do on top of TCP or UDP protocols. The stateless nature of ONC RPC with UDP is not a problem to handle, but if server connections fade, things do get messy. If you use TCP instead of UDP, packet order and retry management are transparent by virtue of the transport.

Concurrency at the Server and Client

To process multiple requests at the same time at a server, you need some form of concurrent processing or multi-tasking. While less common, you may also have a need to post multiple requests from one client. Given the synchronous nature of any procedure call, this requires concurrent processing or multi-tasking at the client.

There are two ways to accommodate this: heavyweight and lightweight processing. Heavyweight processing copies the complete process context, address space and all, forking-off another copy of the current program. Lightweight processing starts another thread of execution in the same process address space. Lightweight processing is much leaner but requires that any shared code segments be re-entrant. That is, multiple threads must be able to execute the same code segment without unintended side-effects.

Neither NCS nor ONC RPC inherently support any form of multi-tasking at the client. Several of the examples in this book touch upon adding either heavyweight or lightweight processing to clients.

Heavyweight Server Processing. ONC RPC, through use of its protocol compiler, supports the brand of `fork()`-based servicing compliant with the Internet super-server `inetd`. Neither NCS nor ONC support generic heavyweight processing within the server. You can add your own heavyweight processing to your service procedures or perform surgery on the compiler-generated service dispatch procedure. Several examples in this book touch upon this subject, especially at the low level of windowing systems and socket interfacing.

Lightweight Server Processing. Heavyweight multi-tasking is often slow, inefficient, or too resource-intensive. It is virtually impossible to write a network information server that performs reasonably well under load without lightweight processing. The X server, for example, has its own lightweight process package internally.

There are a number of mature lightweight processing packages. Sun has their LWP package. HP/Apollo has the Concurrent Programming Support (CPS) library. DEC has CMA, the foundation for OSF DCE's non-OSF/1 threading support. OSF/1 uses Mach kernel threads. The POSIX draft includes *pthreads*. Most lightweight processing libraries are converging on a pthreads solution.

If you're the macho type, you can do your own lightweight processing in your portions of the client and server code. It's pretty straightforward at the client, but be wary of the lack of re-entrancy at the server.

The ONC RPCSRC 4.0 and TIRPC libraries are in no way re-entrant. You must get below the socket watching and I/O performed in the ONC library to avoid threads stepping on each other. It's like performing brain surgery in the dark (see Chapter 9 for some examples). ONC has promised re-entrant libraries and LWP support before 1992.

NCS through the NIDL compiler can be directed to generate re-entrant server code to interface with CPS where it's available. Not all operating systems can support CPS.

Protocol Compilers: The Most Important Feature

The protocol compiler is *the* most important tool for writing distributed applications. You use it to generate the code to do the job that you describe in a specification. More often than not, the protocol compiler is the only part of the distributed computing environment you need to be concerned about.

Both NCS and ONC suites include protocol compilers. NCS provides the NIDL compiler and ONC provides the RPCGEN compiler. Both protocol compilers use extensions of C, with preprocessor directives and block structures to define the protocol to be used between client and server programs. NCS also supports a Pascal-like syntax. Programs, procedures, and versions are identified numerically. The NIDL compiler makes use of preprocessing to leverage off standard external and canned interfaces and protocols, allowing you to use templates and borrow from other protocols. RPCGEN has similar capabilities, although protocols are typically defined from scratch each time. Protocol definitions for the standard Sun ONC RPC services can be found in the include files in */usr/include/rpcsvc*, the system service protocol directory.

RPCGEN has undergone major enhancements in its new TIRPC release and is now dubbed RPCGEN.NEW. These enhancements include multiple and pass-by-value argument support, sample client and server application generation, and C++ support. See Chapter 11 for more details.

RPCTOOL is a second ONC protocol compiler from Netwise. It provides a number of features that RPCGEN doesn't. RPCTOOL, like NIDL, is a vended product. RPCGEN is free. It has been announced that RPCTOOL will become the commercially-supported ONC protocol compiler. So for obvious reasons, RPCTOOL should be discussed. Because the bulk of the ONC RPC applications developed to date have used RPCGEN, I have covered it in more detail while NIDL and RPCTOOL receive less coverage.

Sun's RPCGEN was first; it was readily available and supported most of the data type exchanging or marshaling that you need using XDR routines. Before RPCGEN.NEW, it had not changed much since its first release several years ago.

RPCTOOL is now the ONC party-line, with full support for all of the new ONC RPC features including transport independence, and the ability to throw a switch and get either ISO/OSI ASN.1 canonical data exchange format or the old XDR standard. The ASN.1 format will use the Net Lib interface library rather than the UNIX TLI package.

The NIDL protocol compiler was developed to comply with the NCS receiver-makes-it-right translation paradigm, supporting a number of canonical formats underneath, and large, potentially machine-specific network interface libraries. The new NIDL will eliminate these problems, also including an ASN.1 switch.

It's difficult to generalize and compare the options in protocol compilers at a high level. RPCGEN as found in ONC RPCSRC 4.0 is used for many of the examples in this book and is admittedly simple. It represents the '77 Chevette class of protocol compiler.[†] You don't need lots of horsepower; you need staying power to get the job done. RPCGEN.NEW as found in the newer ONC TIRPC release falls into a racing class. RPCTOOL and NIDL, with many of the same additional features, also fall into the racing class. If RPCGEN.NEW is a Porsche, then the price tag of RPCTOOL or NIDL makes them resemble Ferraris. All three compete in the same class.

Authentication Services

The NCS by itself specifies no authentication services. The ONC distributed computing environment has three levels of security built-in: none, UNIX-style user-name and password, and a Data Encryption Standard (DES) mode. User security and authentication schemes could be implemented in either RPC mechanism. Both environments will move to support the MIT Kerberos authentication system.

Network Resource Naming Services

NCS has a Location Broker, whose job is similar to NIS, performing maintenance and look-up services for network objects. Some reports claim the Location Broker is somewhat more sophisticated and robust. This is possibly due to the inheritance of state from the NCS RPC. The stateless ONC NIS needs separate servers to detect server crashing (actually recoveries) and enforce file-locking. Both NCS and ONC plan to support the ISO/OSI X.500 directory-naming protocol.

RPCGEN command-line switches can generate services that the inetd(8C) Internet super-server can start.

Network Time Service

Both ONC and NCS support the Network Time Protocol (NTP) for synchronizing time-critical tasks across a network.

[†] Some say the vehicle is an extension of the man. I agree and drive a '77 Chevette with well over 150,000 miles.

Distributed File System

There sure are enough distributed file systems around: RFS, AFS, UFS, and NFS. NFS will continue to be the cornerstone of the ONC distributed computing environment; it has the largest number of installed units by far (well over 1 million). NCS does not explicitly include a file system, though both Apollo and HP machines ship with distributed file systems. The Andrew File System (AFS) was selected by OSF and will be included in the NCS DCE. OSF selected PC-NFS as the best solution for a PC file system.

There May be a Common Application Environment in Your Future

The computer-aided software engineering community has been developing integration framework standards since 1980. For example, the early ANSI/NIST[†] Information Resource Dictionary System is now part of the government's FIPS specifications. The more recent CAD Framework Initiative (CFI) and Object Management Group (OMG) are first concentrating on tool integration issues and with time will attend to data management. The Portable Common Tool Environment attempts to specify a complete environment for tool operation. Each group includes different commercial vendors, each with their own agenda. See the article, "CASE Integration Frameworks," by G.R. Lewis in the July 1991 issue of *SunWorld* for more details on evolving framework standards.

The OMG was formed in 1989 and has more than 100 international members including vendors of hardware platforms, object-oriented databases, applications, and tools as well as end users. Members represent different network, operating system, and hardware cultures. Sun, HP, NCR, DEC, HyperDesk, IBM, and Architecture Projects Management Limited are members. The goal of OMG is to make application development easier across major heterogeneous hardware and software systems. OMG is not a standards group; rather it will endorse or establish specifications that make up an Object Management Architecture (OMA). The OMG seeks to establish a distributed object programming paradigm based on technology that enables transparent access to objects across a network.

The OMA is comprised of four pieces: the Object Request Broker (ORB), object services, common facilities, and application objects. All pieces interact through the ORB. The ORB is a general-purpose distributed object management facility. By adhering to the ORB interfaces, the application developer is isolated from the details of the underlying network, operating, and RPC systems. It promises to provide a higher-level notion of distributed computing than OSF/DCE or ONC. Different ORBs can be gatewayed together to allow applications on heterogeneous environments to interoperate. Source compatibility of applications across different

---

† American National Standards Institute and the National Institute of Standards and Technology.

ORB implementations (which may be built on different operating and communications systems) is a goal.

In 1991 Hewlett-Packard and Sun announced intentions to work towards bringing their respective RPC systems closer together, targeting interoperability. The first step was a joint proposal to the Object Management Group's ORB RFP. A task force was set up to issue the RFP, evaluate the submissions, and select a specification. A common specification submitted by Sun, HP, DEC, HyperDesk, NCR, and ODI was endorsed. It includes both static type checking done at compile time and the ability for an application to dynamically create object requests using information from an interface repository. Full corporate OMG membership approval is expected. OSF, UI and a number of commercial vendors may elect to support the OMG-endorsed ORB specification. The X/Open Common Applications Environment plans to include OMG-approved specifications.

Netwise: A Second ONC Alternative

While Sun/AT&T and HP/Apollo struggle to grab market-share, Netwise, Inc. (Boulder CO), a network software vendor, seems to have taken the best features of both, as well as consideration of the evolving ISO/OSI and OSF standards, and come up with a number of versions of RPC-based network programming. Their RPC environment contains only some of the pieces that the ONC and NCS environments include, while layering upon existing or soon-to-be standards.

Like the NCS environment, Netwise began its development after ONC was established. Netwise specified or developed everything required for distributed application development from external data representation to the application protocol compiler. Netwise has a long established, strong presence in remote procedure calling and job entry for mainframes, including communications with UNIX machines. They are quickly building a commercial UNIX base and have a presence in the PC community as well.

The Netwise distributed computing environment consists of:

1. Network libraries that are different for each machine type.

2. Server control procedures for a number of different server binding and concurrency selections.

3. A protocol compiler, RPCTOOL.

4. RPC extensions that perform such tasks as server registration and look-up with ONC naming services.

The Netwise RPC suite is more flexible than either NCS or ONC RPC, at least in terms of API, server control, and concurrency. Yet the Netwise product does not have the same breadth and depth that the NCS and ONC environments have.

Earlier in this chapter, we stated that a distributed computing environment must perform a number of functions. Let's see how Netwise attempts to fulfill each.

Machine-independent Data Representation

The RPCTOOL Version 3 API has a command-line switch on the protocol compiler to specify whether the ISO application, presentation, and session layers (including ASN.1 BER) or ONC RPC's socket transport should be used. In effect, client and server stubs are generated with either ASN.1 BER or XDR single-canonical formatting. If OSI encoding and decoding is used, run-time selection of OSI-based network libraries is supported. Netwise neither specifies nor provides the actual source for the low-level networking, but rather layers on top of publicly- or commercially-available libraries. One major drawback to this approach is that on heterogeneous machines, there is a risk of needing a copy of Netwise RPCTOOL, or at least support libraries, on each machine to generate the necessary client and server interface code.

RPC Mechanism

Protocol compilers can be visualized as generating a software machine that steps the client and server from state to state to fulfill the defined communication scheme. With RPCTOOL the user has an almost unlimited ability to intervene in the state machine generation: inserting directives before, during, and after states in client, server, and dispatch processing.

A number of different server and client styles are supported automatically: synchronous, asynchronous, single- and multi-threaded servers, and multiple binding styles.

Concurrency is supported through RPCTOOL as well as provisions for idempotent procedure handling.

Concurrency at the Server and Client

With RPCTOOL, multiprocessing is heavyweight in the sense that it uses UNIX process creation via `fork()` and `exit()`.

The ability to multi-task within the server allows you to put together a concurrent service, which is able to handle multiple requests at the same time. On the client side, multi-tasking can allow a client process (or thread when available) to stay blocked while waiting for the normal request/reply cycle of an RPC to complete. Other processes could be executing asynchronous to the I/O operations. Once the processes receive a reply from the server and become unblocked, execution within that process can be terminated or branch somewhere else. This allows a client to make multiple requests at the same time.

Both ONC and NCS RPC libraries plan to support fully the use of multiple lightweight threads of execution within the same process space. This approach completely avoids the copying process context. Netwise is likely to implement some form of multi-threading.

Handling Idempotent Procedures

Like NCS, RPCTOOL allows special user extensions to handle *idempotent* procedures. A procedure is idempotent if it can be called more than once without changing the server state or the reply to the client. A client can repeat a request any number of times when a reply is not received before timeout. The server might thus receive and execute multiple redundant requests. If a procedure is designed and declared as non-idempotent, this type of treatment is avoided.

For example, a procedure that increments a value in a server-controlled database cannot be an idempotent RPC. Multiple tries are not acceptable and timeouts indicate an error condition.[†] In addition, just because no server responded, this does not indicate whether or not the procedure was executed. NCS and RPCTOOL provide mechanisms to handle non-idempotent procedures differently while ONC requires the use of a reliable transport.

Protocol Compiler

The RPCTOOL protocol compiler is more flexible than the ONC and NCS tools. It allows intervention into almost any phase of the client and server communication state machines and dispatch routine. Users can include their own code or choose from a variety of canned control procedures.

Authentication Services

RPCTOOL, like NCS, specifies no authentication services. User code must be developed to use the standard UNIX security equivalents. The current ONC release includes not only standard UNIX username and password verification, but also a DES encrypted security scheme. Low-level XDR calls can be used under RPCTOOL to facilitate ONC-style authentication.

Network Resource Naming Services

RPCTOOL under DOS depends on Novell's Netware product. Under UNIX, for either OSI or ONC sockets-based communications, the standard /etc files are consulted with the standard get...(3N) and set...(3N) routines. Services at well-known ports can be accessed through the inetd Internet super-server or through NIS if running. Use of inetd and the /etc files requires root privileges every time a server at a well-known port is installed or de-installed. If you do have the ONC NIS server running, you probably have the ONC XDR and RPC libraries. If this is the case, you can use the ONC RPCGEN protocol compiler, too.

---

† As an aside, ONC RPC today is reliable, without added user application coding, if the TCP transport is used. Use of UDP requires lower-level calls to set retry limits and time-outs.

Network Time Service

The Netwise suite does not specify network time services.

Distributed File System

Netwise does not specify a distributed file system.

Summary of Distributed Computing Environments

Table 2-3 lists the features of a distributed computing environment, with emphasis on the enabling RPC technology. There is no clear winner. Note that the OSF submission is not yet completely available. The NCS and ONC features are based on versions available in 1991.

Table 2-3. Distributed Computing Environment Features

Function	ONC (as in SVR4)	NCS (rev 1.5.1)	RPCTOOL (rev 3.0)	OSF/1 DCE
Product Description	Free source or included with AT&T & Sun OS.	Binary only, proprietary, optional with OS.	Commercial product, LAN Magazine product of the year.	Member organizations now, resale later.
• Operating systems supported	UNIX - SVR4, SunOS, HP-UX, Domain/OS, ULTRIX, AIX, Mac,etc.), DOS, OS/2, MVS, VM, TLI version included in SVR4	UNIX - Domain/OS, HP-UX, VMS, ULTRIX	UNIX (C and ADA), ULTRIX, VMS, DOS, OS/2, MS-Windows, VS (all don't interoperate).	OSF/1
• Supported transports	TLI, TCP, UDP, PC LAN support thru Netwise, Novell, 3Com, Banyan, PC-NFS	TCP, DDS (proprietary) future PC LAN support thru Microsoft.	TCP, Netware, NetBIOS, OSI, TLI (OSI, TCP, UDP, SPX/IPX) DECnet, LAN mng., VINES	Same as NCS plus OSI/ISO.
Data Representation	XDR	NDR	Either XDR or ASN.1 BER	OSI/ISO 8825, ASN.1 BER, NDR
• Canonical levels	1	16	1	1,16

Table 2-3. Distributed Computing Environment Features (Continued)

Function	ONC (as in SVR4)	NCS (rev 1.5.1)	RPCTOOL (rev 3.0)	OSF/1 DCE
• Pointer support	Full pointer chasing.	Pass-by-reference context only.	Full pointer chasing.	Greater than or equal to NCS.
• Supported types	C built-ins, arbitrary user structures, and opaque data.	C built-ins, primitive user structures.	Same as ONC.	Greater than or equal to NCS.
RPC User Base				
• Installed base	Approx. 1.2 M	Approx. 200,000	ONC support announced only.	Just underway.
• Licensees	Approx. 290	Approx. 200	0	Same as NCS.
• Implementations	Approx. 90	Approx. 10	Limited	Same as NCS.
• ISVs include	Lotus, Oracle, Ashton Tate, Informix, Interactive, Sybase	IBM, DEC, Microsoft	N/A	N/A
RPC Mechanism				Note: Enhanced NCS
• Protocol	State of transport, connection, or connectionless; time-out and retry control.	Stateful, connection, or connectionless; no time-out or retry control.	Same as ONC.	Same as NCS.
• Available client-server binding states	Persistent (TCP, UDP), non-persistent (UDP).	Fully-bound, unbound handles.	Persistent, non-persistent.	Same as NCS.
• Client and server error encapsulation	Yes	Yes, plus potential resource re-binding for fault tolerance.	Same as ONC.	Same as NCS.
• Broadcast	Yes	Yes	Yes	Yes
• Server multi-request (socket) processing	Use of select() on queued requests, manual heavyweight multi-processing.	Same as ONC plus use of lightweight threads where available.	Select() plus heavyweight processing hidden by protocol compiler.	Same as NCS.

Table 2-3. Distributed Computing Environment Features (Continued)

Function	ONC (as in SVR4)	NCS (rev 1.5.1)	RPCTOOL (rev 3.0)	OSF/1 DCE
• Client multi-request posting	Low-level user code or async, if no reply required.	Low-level user code.	Low-level user code.	Low-level user code.
• Authentication	None, UNIX, or DES.	N/A	N/A	Kerberos authentication.
• Callback (client can be a server)	Yes, but not by protocol compiler.	(See Chapter 9.)	Yes, supported by protocol compiler.	Yes, supported by protocol compiler.
Protocol Compiler	RPCGEN = C + XDR, arg typing and data definitions, no control constructs.	NIDL = C | Pascal + NDR, arg typing and data definitions, no control constructs.	RPCL—arg typing and data definitions, server control constructs, network protocol definitions.	Same as NCS RPC (NIDL).
• Service dispatching	Fixed: single-binding, multi-bindings, and multi-tasking performed by user.	Options: single or multi-binding, multi-tasking performed by user.	Options: single or multi-binding (heavy multi-tasking option with multiple bindings).	Options: single or multi-binding (light multi-tasking option with multiple bindings).
• Client processing	Synchronous (async possible but user responsibility).	Same as ONC.	Same as ONC.	No information (multi-thread capability possible).
• Concurrency at client and server	1:1 (iterative), concurrency at client or server done by user with lightweight processing or heavy multi-tasking.	1:1 or many:1 (multi-threaded servers require Concurrent Programming Support, CPS).	1:1 or many:1 (multi-tasking servers use heavy process creation).	1:1 or many:1
• Marshaling (data encoding-decoding)	Automatic	Automatic	Automatic with user extensions.	No information.

Table 2-3. Distributed Computing Environment Features (Continued)

Function	ONC (as in SVR4)	NCS (rev 1.5.1)	RPCTOOL (rev 3.0)	OSF/1 DCE
Network Resource Naming (Brokers)	/etc routines or NIS, extension of standard UNIX network system calls.	Local and Global Location Brokers, extensible object management approach.	N/A—but access to /etc/get... routines and ONC NIS.	NCS Location Broker, DEC naming and file services, extensible object management.
Network Time Service	N/A	N/A	N/A	NTP
Distributed File System	NFS—with locking, automount, status, PC-NFS.	N/A	N/A	Andrew file system (AFS) plus foreign systems, PC-NFS

Rapid Evolution

We can summarize the future enhancements that HP/Apollo and Sun have announced. Note that the word is *announced,* not delivered. You can anticipate that the Netwise RPCTOOL enhancements will track or even lead the ONC road map.

The ONC Future

Table 2-4 shows a development road map for the ONC distributed computing environment and its RPC.

Table 2-4. The ONC Development Road Map[a]

Feature	1990	1991	Beyond
RPC	• Run-time transport independence. • Asynchronous call support.	• Multi-thread support.	N/A
RPC Compiler	• Netwise RPC Tool.	N/A	• rpcgen remains available.
Naming	N/A	• Greater consistency. • Improved security. • Location/binding interface.	• Standards interoperability • Object orientation.
Filesystem	N/A	• Local disk caching. • Enhanced performance.	N/A

Table 2-4. The ONC Development Road Map[a] (Continued)

Feature	1990	1991	Beyond
Security	N/A	• Kerberos authentication.	N/A
Synchronization	• Network Time Protocol (NTP).	N/A	N/A

a. Extracted from Sun Microsystems, Inc. *Distributed Computing Roadmap*, May 1990.

Transport independence is one of the most important additions to ONC. The System V Transport Level Interface is used in ONC's new release, the same application programming interface as X/Open Transport Interface (XTI). There are already 800,000+ TLI seats installed. The new ONC distributed computing environment is also now available for SunOS as TIRPC. The examples and discussions in this book are based on the earlier TCP + UDP release 4.0, RPCSRC 4.0. They are compatible with TIRPC.

The NCS Future

NCS development will not sit still either. Fueled by OSF support, HP/Apollo plans to add many of the same features ONC has promised. By adding additional, non-proprietary transport protocol support, they can address a broader UNIX network market. They will improve integration of lightweight multiple threads of execution into the standard product. They have also promised extensions to speed bulk data transfers that cross packet boundaries. They will also move to support a single-canonical external data representation.

Table 2-5 shows a list of features that HP/Apollo plan to add to Release 2 of the NCA NCS DCE.

Table 2-5. DCE Development for NCS Release 2.0

Feature	Description
RPC	• Improved lightweight multi-threading for asynchronous RPCs. • Support TCP transport (have UDP and DDS now). • Add bulk data transfer.
Data Representation	• Add ASN.1 BER to NDR, for single- and multi-canonical support. • Add more intelligent marshaling. • Support non-Roman character set.
File System	Andrew File System.
Security	Kerberos authentication.

Which One Should You Choose?

The toughest part of deciding on which distributed computing environment or RPC suite to use is sorting fact from future. My personal decision in the 1989/1990 time frame was based on availability; I *had* to use the ONC RPC solution. The examples here are based on developments in that time frame. Much has happened since then. ONC has released the TI version and a number of development tools have become available.

NCS has won a small victory in the OSF/DECORUM contest, but all the pieces will not exist or be integrated for some time.

The benefits of distributed computing are too great to be sitting on the sidelines waiting for the market to shake out. The final dominance of one standard or the other will not be clear, especially as both NCS and ONC grow in the same direction. For this reason, NCS and ONC programming differences will close. Agreeing on one common canonical data representation, a set of common transports with optional transport independence, and the standardization of network services will make NCS and ONC programming at least logically similar. The concerns about the connection-oriented nature of the underlying protocol, as well as non-idempotent procedure handling will be hidden.

Each of the standards has enough marketing mass to survive, so go ahead and write your code using either distributed computing environment without fear. One strategy might be to develop your distributed application under ONC today, and migrate your application to comply with evolving standards. If you organize your application with this type of maintenance in mind, it should increase its lifetime.

Put the ONC Suite on Your Machine for Free

The ONC RPC system is a *de facto* standard for network communication. Library calls look and behave identically regardless of the host machine. ONC RPC as well as XDR libraries can be found on machines ranging from DOS PCs to Crays. Many public domain and officially supported ports of the ONC/NFS services have been made, including DOS, Macintosh OS, AIX, VM, MVS, VMS, Mach, RTU, PRIMOS, and others.

If you use an operating system other than SunOS or System V Release 4, and the suite is not bundled with the OS, check with your distributor to see if there is a vendor-supported ONC interface. Development software is available from Sun Microsystems, Netwise, and Novell.[†] To date, some 290+ organizations, including 150+ computer and software developers, are licensed to use ONC/NFS with their operating systems. An estimated 1.2 million NFS nodes have been installed.

---

† Novell's Netware C Interface-DOS package provides the foundation for PCs. See the Aug-90 issue of *Dr. Dobb's Journal.*

Having your own copy of the ONC source code has its advantages. I've had success installing the protocol compiler and the other RPC utility programs on a number of different machines. We have everything from just the subordinate XDR libraries to the protocol compiler and the Portmapper compiled and running on DECs, Convex, Solbournes, and Suns. It should compile without intervention on any BSD4.2 or 4.3 compatible machine. A big challenge when porting any RPC system occurs if the target machine does not support multi-tasking, like a Macintosh or PC. This makes the port mapping function difficult to implement.

It should be noted that Sun's ONC RPC (RPCSRC 4.0, TIRPC or bundled with UNIX SVR4) does not require the added purchase of libraries and protocol compilers for each unique machine type, as is the case with RPCTOOL and NCS NIDL. Once packaged into OSF/1, the DECORUM DCE may also be portable but will have some as-yet-undetermined price tag. The Sun ONC source is publicly available today.

In this chapter:
- *Development Overview*
- *Define the Protocol*
- *High-level ONC RPC Library Calls*
- *Shared XDR Routines*
- *Writing the Client and Server Programs*
- *Why High-level Calls and Not Protocol Compiling?*

3

Developing High-level RPC Applications

In Chapter 1, we showed how to create a client/server application using a protocol compiler. In this chapter, we generate the client and server stubs by hand. The application is simple enough—producing a remote directory listing—so that we can build it without a protocol compiler. There are a lot of good reasons to use a protocol compiler, as we'll demonstrate in the next chapter. Nonetheless, this manually-generated application gives you a better sense of how the client and server communicate.

☞ In Chapter 4, the emphasis is on hiding as many details as possible with a protocol compiler. Read Chapter 4 first if you are a *top-down* learner; otherwise forge ahead.

Development Overview

The beauty of RPC clients and servers is that the underlying IPC is hidden. When programmed at a high level, you never have to deal with host or network service databases, nor concern yourself with the sockets being used. You just need host and procedure names. This does not preclude using the lower-level RPC calls to tweak things, however.

Figure 3-1 shows the pieces of a typical RPC application development. To build up both sides of the application, you'll need to call a few RPC routines at the client and server. While there are a number of RPC calls available, as documented in the *The ONC RPC Programming Reference*, only a few of them are required to get a high-level application off the ground. Indeed, you don't even need a protocol compiler.

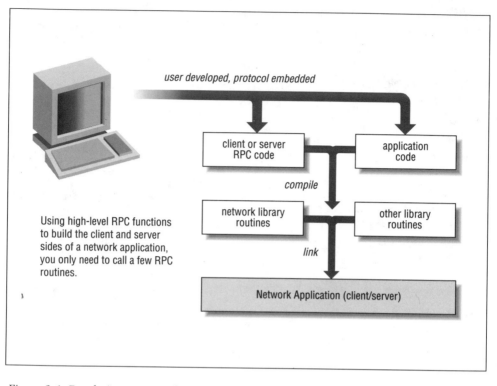

Figure 3-1. Developing a network application with high-level RPC

From Local to Remote Directory Reading

In this section, we look at a remote directory listing application, which we will also use in other chapters in this book. You will find the same kind of application in Sun's *Network Programmer's Guide.* If you compare the two, my version is more straightforward and better written. I will use it to expose in more detail the inner workings of the program, and later augment the client and server sides.

Let's say we currently have a local procedure that reads directory files the way ls might do. We want to place a server on a remote machine to look at its directories (assume that it is not running NFS or exporting all its volumes!). The local procedure is shown in Example 3-1.

Example 3-1. Directory listing with local procedure calling: lls.c

```
/*
 * ls.c: local directory listing main - before RPC
 */
#include <stdio.h>
#include <strings.h>
#include "rls.h"          /* we'll specify this in a moment */

main (argc, argv)
```

Example 3-1. Directory listing with local procedure calling: lls.c

```
int argc; char *argv[];
{
char    dir[DIR_SIZE];

  /* call the local procedure */
  strcpy(dir, argv[1]); /* char dir[DIR_SIZE] is coming and going... */
  read_dir(dir);

                        /* Spew out the results and bail out of here! */
  printf("%s\n", dir);
}
```

At this point the header file *rls.h* need only include the line:

```
    #define DIR_SIZE 8192
```

The read_dir() procedure in Example 3-2 performs all the work. We'll use it
repeatedly, so it is broken-out here. Note that it modifies the directory name string
passed to it to reflect the directory contents. The pointer passed-in has 8K bytes allocated, which should be large enough for most directory listings.

Example 3-2. Directory listing procedure: read_dir.c

```
/*
 * read_dir.c: directory lister
 */
#include <sys/types.h>
#include <sys/dir.h>        /* use <xpg2include/sys/dirent.h> (SunOS4.1) or
           <sys/dirent.h> for X/Open Portability Guide, issue 2 conformance */
#include "rls.h"

read_dir(dir)
char    *dir;               /* char dir[DIR_SIZE] */
{
  DIR * dirp;
  struct direct *d;

  /* open directory */
  dirp = opendir(dir);
  if (dirp == NULL) return(NULL);

  /* stuff filenames into dir buffer */
  dir[0] = NULL;
  while (d = readdir(dirp)) sprintf(dir, "%s%s\n", dir, d->d_name);

  /* return the result */
  closedir(dirp);
  return((int)dir);
}
```

Compile the program with the command:

```
    rodson> cc lls.c read_dir.c -o lls
```

Run the local program to produce output like this:

```
    rodson> lls .
    .
    ..
    read_dir.c
    lls.c
    lls
```

Now we want to get this function to work over the network, allowing us to inspect the directories of a remote server from across the network. Let's walk through the steps required to prepare the network application.

Figure 3-2 illustrates the steps behind a remote procedure call. The server must first register itself with the portmapper, making itself available over the network. The RPC system is checking for requests within the dispatcher, prepared to invoke your procedure if a client requests it. The client calls a high-level function, `callrpc()`, to perform two steps: locate the server procedure and execute the remote procedure call.

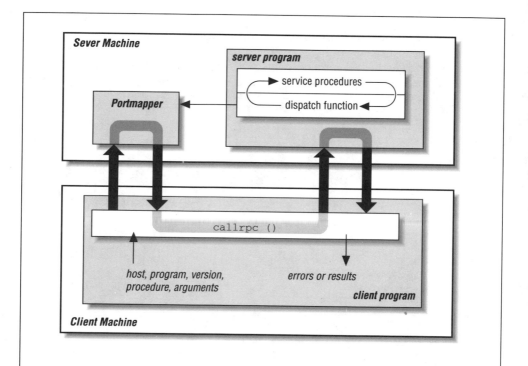

It is assumed that the server registers itself with the portmapper making it available to the network. The RPC server system is checking for requests, prepared to dispatch a procedure if a client requests it.

A client uses the high-level interface to perform two steps: locate the server procedure and execute the remote procedure call.

Figure 3-2. High-level RPC

Note that when programming at the high level *or* when using a protocol compiler, you will never concern yourself with the inner workings of the dispatcher. In the case of high-level RPC programming, the dispatching functions of validating and calling the requested service procedure are handled internal to the RPC system. The ONC RPC protocol compiler generates the dispatcher code for you, placing it in the server stub. The dispatcher is started after registration and runs forever.

Define the Protocol

To define the protocol for our appliaction, we must specify the data types passed between procedures and identify the remote procedure or service.

Data Types

NULL-terminated strings will suffice for both the directory name (request argument) and the directory contents (reply parameter). The data typing of request and reply arguments can be embedded directly in our client and server code.Without the protocol compiler to marshal our parameters, it is our responsibility to adhere to this data typing. We'll discuss the data typing issues more completely in the section "Shared XDR Routines."

Program, Procedure, and Version Numbers

A server needs to know the logical address where it should register itself. A client needs to know where to look for the server. Whether your protocol is defined manually or generated with a protocol compiler, client and server must agree ahead of time on what logical addresses they will use. Whether they use high- or low-level RPC calls, their physical addresses don't matter to the service procedure. The portmapper hides this information.

Service dispatching and network I/O details are hidden from both sides of your application. All your server code must do is register *program*, *procedure*, and *version* numbers with registerrpc(). The portmapper advertises the program and version availability of the RPC address, sending interested clients the necessary address information to open a channel with the server.[†] The availability of specific procedures is determined at run-time by a dispatch function, hidden deeply within the high-level calls. You will be exposed to the server dispatch function once we get into lower-level RPC calls and protocol compiling.

Only the service program *number* is registered in the portmap. You can't tell what service *procedures* are available by looking at a host's portmap. The portmap contains the program name and number, version, protocol, and the associated address. Many procedures may be associated with one program, and none of the procedures are explicitly advertised in the portmap.

---

† The new TIRPC binding service is called rpcbind. It deals with universal addresses instead of IP-specific port numbers. Chapter 11 covers these new features in more detail.

You register services with the RPC system and the portmapper using long integers for program, version, and procedure numbers. Be sure both client and server are using the same numbers (a common include file is a good idea) and be sure no other service, now or in the future, plans to live at that RPC address. Program and version numbers can be useful to enforce gross version changes or to allow different generations of clients and servers to co-exist. If the request or reply data types have changed with the version number, the request should be refused.

Program number ranges, as shown in Table 3-1, are mandated by Sun.

Table 3-1. ONC RPC Program Numbers

Range	Description
0x00000000 to 0x1FFFFFFF	Defined by Sun.
0x20000000 to 0x3FFFFFFF	User-defined.
0x40000000 to 0x5FFFFFFF	Transient.
0x60000000 to 0xFFFFFFFF	Reserved.

If you are running ONC RPC, take a look at the */etc/rpc* list of system program numbers, and the associated protocol files with suffix *.x* that reside in */usr/include/rpcsvc*. If you would like to register a protocol specification for a commercial product, mail a request to rpc@sun.com or write to: RPC Administrator, Sun Microsystems Inc., 2550 Garcia Ave., Mountain View, CA 94043.

In our example, we use symbolic constants: the program number is DIRPROG; the version number is DIRVERS; and there is only one procedure, READDIR. The definitions of the numeric associations are shared by the client and server programs in a single include file, *rls.h*, shown in Example 3-3. DIR_SIZE is used by the client and server to establish the size of the directory name (the request argument) and returned listing (the reply argument) to be 8K bytes.

Example 3-3. Common include definitions for the RPC directory lister: rls.h

```
#define DIR_SIZE 8192
#define DIRPROG ((u_long) 0x20000000)   /* server program # */
#define DIRVERS ((u_long) 1)            /* program version number */
#define READDIR ((u_long) 1)            /* procedure num for look-up */
```

High-level ONC RPC Library Calls

In the case of remote directory reading, client and server communication can be accomplished with just a few high-level RPC calls. Note that high-level functions apply only to the UDP transport protocol.

At the Server

Let's take a look at the ONC RPC library calls that we will use on the server side.

registerrpc()

registerrpc(3N) tells the server machine's portmapper that a procedure is ready to provide a service and should be registered. It also alerts the RPC system to make ready a dispatch routine to watch for incoming requests. The format of registerrpc() is shown below:

```
#include <rpc/rpc.h>
int registerrpc(prognum, versnum, procnum, procname, inproc, outproc)
u_long prognum, versnum, procnum;
char *(*procname) () ;
xdrproc_t inproc, outproc;
```

Once the service procedure is registered in the portmap, a client, given the server's hostname, can complete the association required for remote connection and execution. The client gets remote connection information from the server's portmapper. prognum, versnum, and procnum are the long integers used to register the service's program, version, and procedure numbers. Note that one server executable may install multiple programs, with different or even multiple versions of each program. Separate portmap entries and dispatchers are generated for each program.

When the high-level RPC server gets a request for prognum, versnum, and procnum, it attempts to execute procname. In this way, the RPC system performs dispatching for one program.

registerrpc() sets up UDP/IP communications only, compatible with using the UDP/IP callrpc(3N) call on the client side. To create communications with other than the default UDP/IP characteristics, or to register with TCP/IP, you must use lower-level RPC calls.

inproc() and outproc() are the XDR filters that data passes through when going on and off the network. We'll talk about the filters needed for this simple application in the section, *"Shared XDR Routines."* We defer detailed discussion until Chapter 4, where we cover the built-in XDR filters, as well as ways to put them together to encode and decode data at the client and server using the protocol compiler.

svc_run()

Once the server starts, it registers itself via a call to registerrpc(). It then goes to sleep, listening to the other end of a socket with a svc_run(3N) call. It waits to branch to the procedure mentioned in the registerrpc() call if the right client request comes along. The format for svc_run() is:

```
void svc_run();
```

svc_run() actually starts the process of waiting on the end of a socket, listening for a valid connection. Once accepted, the process branches to the named procedure with the input (request) argument, and returns the result (reply). svc_run() can be used independent of whether you use the UDP/IP or TCP/IP transport. You'll probably have to read Chapter 5 before the guts of svc_run() make sense to you. In Chapter 9, we discuss why you might want to augment what svc_run() does, and detail how to do it.

At the Client

On the client side, one RPC call is all you need, callrpc(3N).

callrpc()

The callrpc() function is called by the client to find and execute a UDP service on a host, given that the service is registered and responsive. The format of this call is:

```
int callrpc(host, prognum, versnum, procnum, inproc, in, outproc, out)
char *host;
u_long prognum, versnum, procnum;
char *in;
xdrproc_t inproc;
char *out;
xdrproc_t outproc;
```

callrpc() checks with the specified host's portmap and sets up the appropriate I/O channel to run a remotely-registered procedure. in and out are pointers to the remote procedure argument and the return value. inproc() and outproc() are XDR routines that encode the data at in to provide the server with request arguments and decode data into out from the server reply.

Both registerrpc() at the server and callrpc() at the client are designed only to use the UDP/IP transport. To use TCP/IP transport you must use lower-level RPC calls.

The callrpc() and default server dispatch pair do not attempt any form of authentication. They use the default form of credentials—namely none. More authentication and security measures can be added as described in Chapter 12 but lower-level RPC programming is required.

Shared XDR Routines

So far we've established how a client and server set up communications, but we haven't talked about the substance—that is, what is the data and in what form will it be exchanged. Let's assume we want to send the server a directory name. The server should send back the contents of that directory. Both request and reply arguments will be NULL-terminated strings of characters less than 8K (DIR_SIZE) bytes.

We define the data communication by first looking at the *problem requirements*. First, specify the data as if only a local procedure call were involved. In the example, we want to send and receive NULL-terminated strings.

Next consider the *RPC and XDR programming constraints*. RPC (Version 4.0) does XDR encoding and decoding of one argument only, and cannot handle arbitrary data structures easily. A multi-dimensional array, for example, must be cast into something else. Request and reply arguments must be packaged into single data structures using only structures understood by XDR. A protocol compiler does this packaging for you and should be used if anything but simple, built-in C data types are used.

We need an XDR routine to do encoding and decoding at the server and client ends, respectively. Since the request and reply parameters are the same type we only need one filter. The xdr_dir() routine will be used by both client and server in this example to put input and output into a known data representation.

xdr_string()

xdr_dir() calls the XDR primitive filter, xdr_string(). The format of this function is:

```
xdr_string(xdrs, &objp, DIR_SIZE) );
```

The xdrs handle indicates the direction, whether we are encoding or decoding. The data is pointed to by objp. The complete xdr_dir() procedure is not much longer, as shown in Example 3-4.

Example 3-4. XDR conversion routine shared by the RPC remote directory read client and server: rls_xdr.c

```
#include <rpc/rpc.h>
#include "rls.h"
bool_t xdr_dir(xdrs, objp)
XDR *xdrs;
char *objp;
{ return ( xdr_string(xdrs, &objp, DIR_SIZE) ); }
```

The xdr_string() filter must be used because strings may be stored differently at the client and server. Remember that XDR is a neutral intermediary form, requiring translations to and from a network format, even if it is not necessary—that is, even if the machines are compatible.

Using the XDR Library

The ONC XDR library routines or filters provide a conventional way of translating built-in C data types and pointer-based structures into an external bit-string representation. Extra fields are often required to provide the filters with the additional information required when translating data from one process' address space to another. To pass data more elaborate than that intrinsically supported by XDR, you can build encode/decode filters using the filters available with XDR.

Each of the XDR filters is bi-directional. Each routine operates on the data you pass it according to the state of information in the XDR data structure passed to it. For each built-in type, there's a single procedure which takes two arguments:

```
bool_t
xdrproc(xdrs, argresp)
    XDR *xdrs;
    <type> *argresp;
```

xdrs is an instance of an XDR handle. It's the address where the network-ready external form resides. If you are encoding to the external form, the filter looks through the argresp pointer for the data or structure to be converted. If decoding, data from xdrs is translated with the results placed in memory at the location xdrs. Each filter can perform one of three functions on the stream: encoding, decoding, or memory deallocation. The operation is specified in a field of the XDR handle containing either XDR_ENCODE, XDR_DECODE, or XDR_FREE.

XDR_DECODE will allocate space only if *argresp is NULL. This data may be freed later with an XDR_FREE operation. XDR_ENCODE causes the type at *argresp to be encoded into the *xdrs stream. XDR_DECODE causes the type to be extracted from the *xdrs stream and placed in *argresp. XDR_FREE can be used to release the memory allocated for xdrs space by an XDR_DECODE request. Be careful to use the XDR_FREE operation whenever required; otherwise you can wind up with a server that slowly runs out of memory.

As illustrated by our example, you should rarely have to mess with the elements of an XDR structure. Data goes into the filter on one end, and comes out the other with fields changed automatically.

The XDR library procedures are defined for each data type to keep them consistent, even though they actually share much of the same code across types. When you combine these routines to handle a user-defined type, it is a good idea to abide by the convention of having one filter for each data type that handles both encode (send) and decode (receive). That's what the protocol compiler does; it looks at your data type specifications and breaks them down into data types that the XDR library can handle. A bidirectional composite filter results. Any filters you assemble must be bi-directional to be usable by the RPC system.

ONC XDR filters fall into two classes: primitive and complex. The primitive filters in the ONC XDR library handle built-in C data types, as shown in Table 3-2.

Table 3-2. Primitive ONC XDR Filters for C Built-in Data Types

C Type	Filter	XDR Type
bool_t (actually C int)	xdr_bool(3N)	int
char	xdr_char(3N)	int
short int	xdr_short(3N)	int

Table 3-2. Primitive ONC XDR Filters for C Built-in Data Types (Continued)

C Type	Filter	XDR Type
unsigned short int	xdr_u_short(3N)	unsigned int
int	xdr_int(3N)	int
unsigned int	xdr_u_int(3N)	unsigned int
long	xdr_long(3N)	int
unsigned long	xdr_u_long(3N)	unsigned int
float	xdr_float(3N)	float
double	xdr_double(3N)	double
void	xdr_void(3N)	void
enum	xdr_enum(3N)	int

The ONC XDR library also handles more complex C data types, as shown in Table 3-3.

Table 3-3. ONC XDR Filters for Handling Complex C Data Types

Composite Data Type	Filter
Variable-length array with arbitrary element size.	xdr_array(3N)
Variable-length array of bytes.	xdr_bytes(3N)
Fixed-length data (uninterpreted).	xdr_opaque(3N)
Object references, including NULL pointers (for tree or linked-lists).	xdr_pointer(3N)
Object references.	xdr_reference(3N)
NULL-terminated character arrays.	xdr_string(3N)
Discriminated union (union with an enumeration acting as the discriminant).	xdr_union(3N)
Fixed-length array with arbitrary element size.	xdr_vector(3N)
Variable-length NULL-terminated character arrays.	xdr_wrapstring(3N)

The ONC RPC Programming Reference contains complete information on each filter.

Writing the Client and Server Programs

We have already discussed how to:

- Register a UDP service and make it wait for requests with registerrpc() and svc_run().

- Contact the server from the client with callrpc().

We have decided to pass a directory name to the server as a NULL-terminated string and expect to get back a NULL-terminated string listing all the files in that directory. Both strings will be DIR_SIZE or less in length. We have developed the routine xdr_dir() that can encode and decode the request and reply argument using the simple filter xdr_string(). We now need to write the actual client and server applications.

At the Server

The actual service procedure must return the filenames in a directory. Let's re-use the local read_dir() routine to open and read a directory file. Both the directory name argument and the returned listing are strings. Let's re-use the char * input parameter, placing the directory listing there when we're done. I'll do it this way for a few reasons:

- xdr_string() actually allocates a DIR_SIZE array of characters when invoked.[†] Since the 8K bytes is allocated by the decode of the directory name, we might as well use it again for the reply.

- Re-using the memory obviates the need for using xdr_free(3N) or a similar routine to deallocate unused memory.

- Space for the 8K bytes will be allocated and deallocated in the server's main(). In this way the memory need not be declared in the service procedure as static to assure its integrity when the main() is encoding the reply.

- I'm lazy.

RPC-compliant procedure calls take one input parameter and return the output. Both are passed by address. Return values should point to variables that are malloc()'ed, static, or that reside in the same procedure as that which sends the reply; the XDR filters must be able to access them.

---

† This undocumented feature of xdr_string() causes it to consume more space than it has to. Strings are NULL-terminated, but lots of space can be wasted.

Now we have everything we need to jump right into writing the server procedure. Example 3-5 shows a bare-bones server routine with minimal error checking, etc. We will perform the same function with servers developed in Chapters 4 and 5.

Example 3-5. RPC server for reading directory files: rls_svc.c

```
#include <rpc/rpc.h>
#include "rls.h"

main()
{
  extern bool_t xdr_dir();
  extern char * read_dir();

  registerrpc(DIRPROG, DIRVERS, READDIR,
              read_dir, xdr_dir, xdr_dir);
  svc_run();
}
```

It doesn't get much simpler than this! You'll notice there is no messing around with transport protocol, ports, services, or the network databases. This all happens within the RPC system. This server is *iterative* in the sense that it handles only one request at a time. Multiple independent servers could be started using different RPC program numbers or versions, but the right way to make it a *concurrent* server is to start a process or thread to service each request. In the meantime, the parent returns to listen for more requests. This server has the same limitations on queuing multiple requests as those discussed in Chapter 5. There you'll find background material on socket-based iterative servers.

Take a moment to look ahead and compare this sample server with Example 5-4, *UDP_AF_INETserver.c*. It is an equivalent socket-based IPC server that accomplishes the same thing, but requires more than four times the amount of code! The high-level RPC client routine that we look at in the next section is also simpler than its low-level socket IPC counterpart.

At the Client

The client routine, shown in Example 3-6, must first collect the hostname and directory name from the command line. The client program calls a local version of read_dir() which in turn uses callrpc() to place the RPC. When xdr_string() is called to encode a NULL-terminated string, it allocates only enough space for the string, with no extra padding in the request parameter. So the request packet that goes to the remote host does not contain any extra space. This keeps the network burden down.[†]

---

† In the current XDR, it is not until decoding at the server that space is wasted with xdr_string().

Example 3-6. RPC client for reading remote directory files: rls.c

```
/*
 * rls.c: remote directory listing client  manually prepared
 * protocol.
 */
#include <stdio.h>
#include <strings.h>
#include <rpc/rpc.h>
#include "rls.h"

main (argc, argv)
int argc; char *argv[];
{
char    dir[DIR_SIZE];

        /* call the remote procedure if registered */
        strcpy(dir, argv[2]);
        read_dir(argv[1], dir); /* read_dir(host, directory) */

        /* Spew out the results and bail out of here! */
        printf("%s\n", dir);

        exit(0);
}

read_dir(host, dir)
char    *dir, *host;
{
        extern bool_t xdr_dir();
        enum clnt_stat clnt_stat;

        clnt_stat = callrpc ( host, DIRPROG, DIRVERS, READDIR,
                        xdr_dir, dir, xdr_dir, dir);
        if (clnt_stat != 0) clnt_perrno (clnt_stat);
}
```

The `read_dir()` procedure goes by the same name in both client and server not
to confuse you, but to point out the ease with which you can make a remote call
look just like a local one. For that matter, with some editing it's possible to link
them together.

Compile, Link, and Run

To compile and link the client and server applications, follow these steps:

1. Compile your client application:

    rodson> **cc -c rls.c**

2. Compile your server application:

    rodson> **cc -c rls_svc.c**

3. Compile the common XDR routine:

    rodson> **cc -c   rls_xdr.c**

4. Make the client executable:

```
rodson> cc -o rls rls.o rls_xdr.o
```

5. Make the server executable:

```
rodson> cc -o rls_svc rls_svc.o read_dir.c rls_xdr.o
```

Then start a server on a remote machine. It's probably easiest to use rsh(1C) to start a process on the remote machine that executes the server directly. For example, to start a server on the machine cortex from your machine rodson, use the command:

```
rodson> rsh cortex $cwd/rls_svc &
```

$cwd is the C shell variable denoting your current working directory. Use $PWD if you are using the Bourne shell. Note that both the machine I am sitting at (rodson) and the server cortex must share a file system as I use the same path name for the server executable on both machines. When you use the -n flag with rsh, it redirects the input of rsh to */dev/null*. This can allow you to place the remote shell in the background to go through the log-in process without giving you a message at your terminal telling you the job is stopped waiting for input:

```
rodson> rsh -n cortex $cwd/rls_svc &
```

which is equivalent to:

```
rodson> rsh cortex $cwd/rls_svc < /dev/null &
```

I discuss a number of more elegant ways to start servers on other machines in Chapter 8 in the section, "How to Start the Remote Server." You may want to use the C shell built-in command, exec. It overlays the remote shell process with the named program. This is useful for reducing the resources consumed at the server.

```
rodson> rsh cortex -n exec $cwd/rls_svc &
```

Now you are ready to run the client. Let's see if you have the same files I do in this development directory.

```
rodson> rls cortex $cwd
.
..
lls.c
read_dir.c
lls
rls_svc.c
rls.h
rls_xdr.c
rls.c
rls.o
rls_svc.o
rls_xdr.o
rls
rls_svc
grocery_list
```

Why High-level Calls and Not Protocol Compiling?

You might be saying, "Hold on! Why didn't we use a protocol compiler to make things easier?" It's true that a protocol compiler like ONC RPCGEN generates virtually all the client/server interface code for you, but at the modest expense of forcing you to use lower-level ONC RPC library calls. If you can get a wimpy RPC application up and running quicker without a protocol compiler, all the better. Such is the case here.

We will discuss the use of a protocol compiler to ease the development of more complicated client/server interfaces throughout the balance of the book. But for many applications it is just as easy to implicitly define the protocol (data to be passed between the client and server, RPC program, procedure, and version numbers) within your own C code.

When you use high-level RPC calls, the dispatch function is called during the registration process vi a `registerrpc()`. For each program number, there is a dispatcher whose job it is to inspect the procedure numbers requested to see if that one is available. If so, it passes the request to the appropriate service procedure. In this way, even with high-level calls at the server side, multiple programs, and thus service procedures, may be registered and managed transparently by one application. Figure 3-2 shows the dispatch function embedded in the server.

As described in Figure 3-2, when a client calls a remote procedure using high-level RPC, it requires complete information about the host, program number, version number, and procedure number to make the client to server connection and affect the procedure call. The figure illustrates that as seen by the client, the RPC through `callrpc()` is a one-step, in and out procedure call. There are two steps taking place behind the scenes; the client finds the service and then calls it.

Some Limitations of the High-level Calls

The high-level calls have their limitations when compared to low-level calls. At the client side, each call to `callrpc()` first sends a remote procedure call to the server machine's portmapper and attempts to establish a new connection. If successful, the client establishes the link and sends its requests to the service. Repeating the process of creating and destroying network connections can consume significant OS resources, especially if TCP is used. If the application will make multiple RPCs, it is more efficient to work at the slightly lower level of a protocol compiler, re-using network connections.

The price you pay for not having to deal with network I/O details or dispatching at the server is reduced client performance for multiple RPCs.

At the server side, a server program can register more than one procedure for a given program/version number pair with `registerrpc()`. In this way you can use high-level calls to build up complex servers. `registerrpc()` registers the named server procedure and leaves dispatching up to the RPC system. It is the same as when you use the protocol compiler—all requests are funneled through one dispatch routine. It is the only program registered in the portmap. The dispatcher inspects the procedure number requested, and invokes it if available. This is more efficient than having a dispatch routine for each procedure.

You sacrifice some reliability when using the ONC RPC high-level calls. When using the high-level library calls documented in this chapter, you are constrained to using the UDP/IP transport. The low-level RPC calls are required to use TCP/IP.

TCP Transport Requires Lower-level Calls

In Example 3-6, the client program's `read_dir()` procedure could be changed slightly to accommodate TCP/IP, as shown below. The `callrpc()` call is replaced with two calls: `clnt_create()` specifies the TCP transport and creates a CLIENT handle and `clnt_call()` actually places the RPC using that handle. Both of these low-level ONC RPC functions work with UDP and TCP transports; they are presented in more detail later in the book.

```
read_dir(host, dir)
  char            *dir, *host;
{
  extern bool_t   xdr_dir();
  enum clnt_stat  clnt_stat;
  static struct timeval TIMEOUT = {25, 0};
  CLIENT          *clnt;

  clnt = clnt_create(host, DIRPROG, DIRVERS, "tcp");
  clnt_stat = clnt_call(clnt, READDIR,
                        xdr_dir, dir, xdr_dir, dir, TIMEOUT);
  if (clnt_stat != 0)
    clnt_perrno(clnt_stat);
  clnt_destroy(clnt);
}
```

A CLIENT is created with `clnt_create()` specifying TCP transport. Using `clnt_call()`, you specify the XDR routines to be used, just as with `callrpc()` with the addition of a TIMEOUT specification. The CLIENT handle is then used with `clnt_call()`, which works with either the TCP or UDP transport.

To call the service using TCP, the server in Example 3-5 can't use `registerrpc()`. Instead, the code must create a server transport handle with `svctcp_create(3N)` and register that handle with the portmapper and RPC system with `svc_register(3N)`. The server might look like this:

```
main() {
    static void dirprog_1(); /* a dispatcher that decodes arguments
                                with xdr_dir() and calls read_dir() */
    register SVCXPRT *transp;
    transp = svctcp_create(RPC_ANYSOCK, 0, 0);
```

```
        svc_register(transp, DIRPROG, DIRVERS, dispatcher, IPPROTO_TCP);
        svc_run();
}
```

If this additional server stub code is generated by the protocol compiler, as is typically the case, your service procedure need not concern itself with service
registration or transport handles. Your service procedure gets simplified to look
much like a local procedure.

We will discuss using lower-level calls, as well as using the TCP transport by using a
protocol compiler, in the next chapter.

In this chapter:

- *Development Overview*
- *Using RPCGEN*
- *The Protocol Definition Language*
- *Lower-level ONC RPC Library Calls*
- *An Example: One Client Talks to One Server*
- *Debugging*

4

Protocol Compiling and Lower-level RPC Programming

The ONC RPC protocol compiler RPCGEN produces client and server stubs that use lower-level RPC calls. RPCGEN supports multiple transports and it generates a dispatch routine that is capable of handling multiple procedures and versions. RPCGEN allows more flexibility in building the client and server with only a modest increase in programming complexity.

As Figure 4-1 suggests, developing an application that makes use of lower-level RPC function calls requires one additional step: the compilation of a protocol or RPC specification.

If you use a protocol compiler, you don't have to perform RPC communications in your client and server code. Instead, these functions are performed by the client and server stubs that the protocol compiler generates from your protocol specification. Encoding and decoding filters are also automatically generated to convey data between heterogeneous machines.

The single function call interface at the RPC client shown in the previous chapter is not used at the lower-level. Instead, a more efficient two-step process is used: finding the address of the service and then executing the RPC. The advantage is that it reduces the amount of time your application spends (synchronously) talking to portmappers and allows the re-use of service-addressing information.

The TIRPC version of ONC RPC has a new and improved protocol compiler named RPCGEN.NEW. It supports the generation of client and server templates for the application. These templates give you a framework in which to write your code. In this way I/O and function prototyping are correct by construction, as specified in your protocol definition. I strongly recommend the use of the RPCGEN.NEW

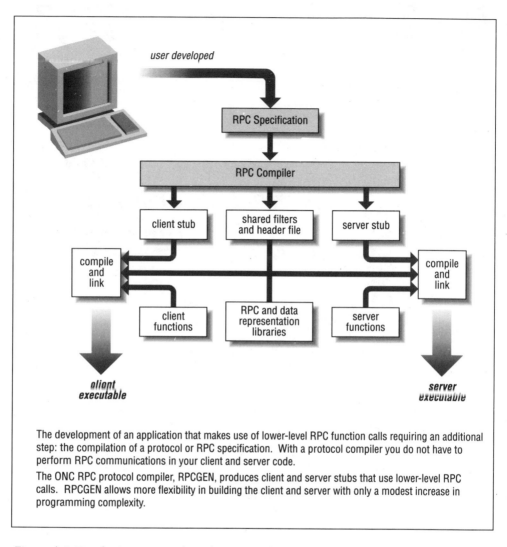

The development of an application that makes use of lower-level RPC function calls requiring an additional step: the compilation of a protocol or RPC specification. With a protocol compiler you do not have to perform RPC communications in your client and server code.

The ONC RPC protocol compiler, RPCGEN, produces client and server stubs that use lower-level RPC calls. RPCGEN allows more flexibility in building the client and server with only a modest increase in programming complexity.

Figure 4-1. Developing a network application with RPC Protocol Compiler

compiler, whether or not you intend to use the transport independence features of the new ONC libraries (backwardly-compatible code can be generated).

However, in this book, we will use the ONC RPC 4.0 protocol compiler RPCGEN. It must be on your search path as `rpcgen`.

Development Overview

In Chapter 1, you saw how we use a protocol compiler to generate the client and server stubs as well as the common XDR encode/decode filters. The stubs are pieces of code that interface with the XDR and RPC libraries and, in many cases, completely isolate the application from having to make even the high-level RPC calls covered in the previous chapter. The stubs put wrappers around the RPC calls, so that all you do is write what appears to be local server procedures and a client `main()` that appears to be making local procedure calls.

A protocol compiler doesn't create life. There are three programs you have to write. They include:

1. A definition of the protocol in the *application.x* file.

2. The service program in *application_svc_proc.c*. This contains the actual procedure(s) to be invoked by the server dispatch routine in the compiler-generated stub.

3. The client program *application.c*. This application must handle attaching to the appropriate services(s) as well as perform other `main()` functions.

Filename Conventions and Make

The examples in this book follow a set of filename conventions to make the discussion more coherent. These conventions also make it easier to use `make` to execute compile, link, and execute commands.

Figure 4-2 is a schematic of the filename and development process.

• The protocol definition file *application.x* is first processed by RPCGEN.

RPCGEN in turn generates:

• XDR wrapper routines in *application_xdr.c* (filters used by both the client and server).

• Associated common includes in *application.h*.

• Client stub in *application_clnt.c*.

• Server stub in *application_svc.c*.

These filenames are hard-wired into RPCGEN, though a smart *makefile* could take care of that. Rules to use RPCGEN might not be included in the default `make` rules (on a Sun, the default rules file is */usr/include/make/default.mk*). I use my own set of `make` rules to cover the process, as shown in Figure 4-2.

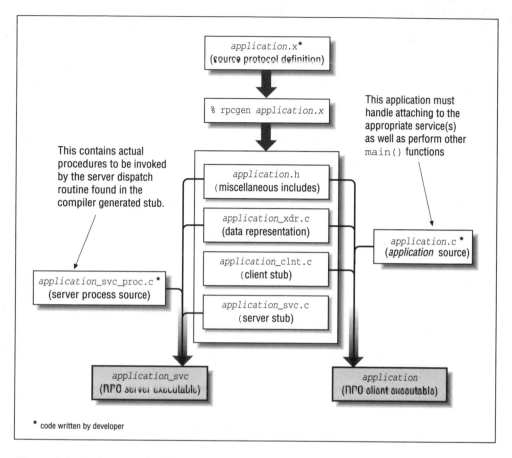

Figure 4-2. Application development with RPCGEN

Figure 4-2 can be expressed in terms of a *makefile* template suitable for inclusion in other makefiles. I will often make use of the rules in Example 4-1 to avoid lengthy cc commands.

Example 4-1. Rules for simple RPCGEN application development: makefile

```
# this makefile uses your sources:
# $(APPN).x - RPCGEN input, XDR protocol definition
# $(APPN)_svc_proc.c - define server process called by server stub
# $(APPN).c - tell the client what to do (talk to servers etc)
# $(APPN)_shared.h - shared include stuff (added since last month)
# to make the following:
# $(APPN)_xdr.c - client/server XDR library access
# $(APPN)_svc.c - server stub, a main() wrapper
# $(APPN)_clnt.c - client stub w/ function name defined in protocol
# $(APPN).h - miscellaneous includes generated from protocol def.
# $(APPN) - the executable for the client
# $(APPN)_svc - the executable for the server
```

Example 4-1. Rules for simple RPCGEN application development: makefile (Continued)

```
APPN=rls# put your favorite program name here,
        # or override/define it with -DAPPN= at make time

# change these for different machines and stages of development
CFLAGS=-g# says build the symbol table for the debugger
LFLAGS=# XDR & RPC are in libc.a

# compile the protocol
$(APPN)_xdr.c $(APPN)_svc.c $(APPN)_clnt.c $(APPN).h: $(APPN).x
        rpcgen $(APPN).x

# build the client application
$(APPN): $(APPN).h $(APPN).o $(APPN)_clnt.o $(APPN)_xdr.o
        $(CC)$(CFLAGS) -o $(APPN) $(APPN).o $(APPN)_clnt.o $(APPN)_xdr.o
$(LFLAGS)

# build the server application
$(APPN)_svc: $(APPN)_svc.c $(APPN).h $(APPN)_svc_proc.c $(APPN)_xdr.o
        $(CC) $(CFLAGS) -o $(APPN)_svc $(APPN)_xdr.o $(APPN)_svc.c \
        $(APPN)_svc_proc.c $(LFLAGS)
```

With the filename conventions selected, there may be an include file *$(APPN).h* conflict.

> ! *If your application uses an include file, **do not name it** application.h. RPCGEN already generates a file of that name from your protocol definition application.x file!*

Example 4-6 presents a more thorough makefile template that we'll use throughout the later parts of the book. It addresses techniques for debugging that are not yet relevant.

Using RPCGEN

RPCGEN as found in ONC RPC Release 4 can be invoked from the command line in a number of ways. We'll look at the simplest form first:

rpcgen *infile*

Typing rpcgen *application.x* will generate the header file, the XDR routines and the client and server stubs from the RPCL protocol definition in *application.x*. We'll describe the syntax of RPCL in a moment. The next form shows several options:

rpcgen [-D*name*[=*value*]] [-I [-K *seconds*]] [-L] [-T] *infile*

The -Dname[=value] option may be added at any time to define preprocessor symbols just as you do with the C compiler.

The -I and -K options are used to create services that run under inetd(8C), as explained fully in Chapter 5. RPCGEN can generate code in the server stub to allow inetd to watch its Internet address socket using the transport you choose. The -K

option tells the service how long it should wait between requests if it was started by
inetd. If the inetd-compatible server is started from the command-line, it forks a
child and exits, never returning. If more than seconds elapse, the server exits and
inetd must start it back up again at the next request. The -L option directs the
server stub code to use syslog when the server is started in foreground.

The -T option generates an RPC dispatch table in application_tbl. The entries
in the dispatch table contain:

- Pointers to the service routines used by the dispatcher.

- Pointers to the input and output arguments.

- The size of these routines.

Dispatch tables can be accessed by the client or server to perform bookkeeping.

The third form specifies either udp or tcp transport. It directs the server
side stubs to use a particular transport.

```
rpcgen -s transport [ -o outfile ] [ infile ]
```

Two -s options can be used to pick up both transports. This highlights the fact that
the code you are in charge of generating for the server side in no way mentions the
network connection. You define only the actual procedures to be executed. By
default, RPCGEN registers the service in the portmap twice; once with TCP transport and once with UDP transport.

Any of the options specified in the fourth form may be used to guide which files
RPCGEN produces.

```
rpcgen -c | -h | -l | -m | -t [ -o outfile ] [ infile ]
```

The command-line options for RPCGEN are described in Table 4-1.

Table 4-1. RPCGEN Command-line Options

Option	Description
-D*name*[=*value*]	Define a symbol (same as #define).
-I	Generate code for inetd support in server (for SunOS 4.1).
-K *seconds*	Server exits after *seconds* of inactivity.
-L	Server errors will be printed to syslog.
-T	Generate code to support RPC dispatch tables.
-s *transport*	Generate server code that supports *transport*.
-o *outfile*	Name of the output file.
-c	Generate XDR routines.

Table 4-1. RPCGEN Command-line Options (Continued)

Option	Description
-h	Generate header file.
-l	Generate client side stubs.
-m	Generate server side stubs.
-t	Generate RPC dispatch table.

RPCGEN.NEW as found within the TIRPC release (but not yet available in System V) has significantly enhanced functionality. Here is a summary of its forms:

```
rpcgen.new infile

rpcgen.new [-a][-b][-C][-Dname[=value]] -i size  [-I [-K seconds]] [-L][-N][-T] infile

rpcgen.new [-c I -h I -l I -m I -t I -Sc I -Ss] [-o outfile] [infile]

rpcgen.new [-s nettype]* [-o outfile] [infile]

rpcgen.new  [-n netid]* [-o outfile] [infile]
```

The new options are listed in Table 4-2.

Table 4-2. RPCGEN.NEW Command-line Options

Option	Description
-a	Generate all files, including sample client and server.
-b	Backward compatibility mode (generates code for SunOS 4.1).
-C	ANSI-C mode.
-i size	Size at which to start generating in-line code.
-N	Supports multiple arguments and call-by-value.
-s nettype	Generate server code that supports named nettype.
-Sc	Generate sample client code that uses remote procedures.
-Ss	Generate sample server code that defines remote procedures.
-Y path	Directory name to find C preprocessor (cpp).

Significant improvements include the ability to package-up multiple arguments, and pass them by value and support for C++. It also can generate client and server side templates. This is a real time-saver because misinterpreting the protocol and data types are common problems. RPCGEN.NEW will generate shells for both the

RPCGEN.NEW client and server as well as the stubs, header, and dispatch table files as before.

The Protocol Definition Language

RPCL, the protocol description language used by ONC's RPCGEN, is an extension of the XDR definition language. This is the language used in the *application.x* protocol definition file. The language is close enough to C that its syntax should be easy to pick up. If you're a seasoned programmer, you might skip this section for now, using it as a reference only when you get syntax errors.

We'll look at a structured syntax definition and give some simple examples. I also present the corresponding C code generated by the compiler to show you what goes into the header file. During the debugging process, the ability to navigate through the C or C++ header file becomes important.

Definitions

An RPCL protocol specification consists of a series of definitions:

    definition-list:
        definition ";"
        definition ";" definition-list

where there are six types of definitions:

    definition:
        const-definition
        enum-definition
        struct-definition
        union-definition
        typedef-definition
        program-definition

Each definition type (enum, struct, union, typedef, const, and program) has its own syntax. Though not always necessary in RPCGEN, types or variables should be defined before being used. Also, definitions may appear in any order in the *application.x* file.

There are four types of declarations allowed within definitions. These are described after the six definition types are discussed.

Symbolic Constants

Symbolic constants in the XDR or RPCL languages may be used wherever an integer constant might be used, for example in vector or array size definitions.

    const-definition:
        "const" const-ident "=" integer

Let's say you define a constant to dimension arrays or vectors of opaque data to 8K. The RPCL entry would look like this:

    const MAX_SIZE = 8192;

The result generated by RPCGEN and placed in the *application.h* header file would look like this:

    #define MAX_SIZE 8192

MAX_SIZE can be used subsequently within the RPCL definition or by the server and client routines (they must include the header file).

Enumerations

RPCL enumerations have the same form as in C:

    enum-definition:
        "enum" enum-ident "{"
            enum-value-list
        "}"

    enum-value-list:
        enum-value
        enum-value "," enum-value-list

    enum-value:
        enum-value-ident
        enum-value-ident "=" value

As an example, let's assume you set up a data structure in your shared protocol that defines some colors:

    enum color {
            RED = 0,
            GREEN = 1,
            BLUE = 2
        };

This enumeration gets compiled by RPCGEN into the *application.h* common header file to look like this:

```
enum color {
        RED = 0,
        GREEN = 1,
        BLUE = 2
    };
typedef enum color color;
bool_t xdr_color();
```

Notice that the enumeration gets typedef'ed to allow you to use the color type directly in the client and server procedures instead of enum color. RPCGEN has also generated the XDR encode/decode filter xdr_color() in *application_xdr.c* for use by client and server and prototyped it in the header file.

Structures

Structures are defined as in C:

struct-definition:

"struct" struct-ident "{"

declaration-list

"}"

declaration-list:

declaration ";"

declaration ";" declaration-list

For example, if you were interested in using an XDR structure to represent two-dimensional coordinates, it might look like this in the protocol definition:

```
struct point {
    int x;
    int y;
};
```

The following C form is placed in the header file:

```
struct point {
    int x;
    int y;
};
typedef struct point point;
bool_t xdr_point();
```

Notice the addition of the typedef. Subsequent RPCL entries, client, and server routines can use point types instead of struct point. The XDR filter xdr_point() has been prototyped here and resides in the *application_xdr.c* file.

Unions

XDR unions are discriminated unions. These are somewhat analogous to Pascal variant records, quite different from C unions.

> union-definition:
>
>   "union" union-ident "switch" "(" declaration ")" "{"
>
>   case-list
>
>   "}"

> case-list:
>
>   "case" value ":" declaration ";"
>
>   "default" ":" declaration ";"
>
>   "case" value ":" declaration ";" case-list

XDR unions make it easy to return results or errors on a conditional basis. Let's make up an example. If no error occurs at the server, it should return 8K bytes of data. If you have an error, it should return nothing. To accomplish this, the server could reply with the following union:

```
union result switch (int error) {
case 0:
     opaque data[MAX_SIZE];
default:
     void;
};
```

Here the integer `error` determines whether data will be sent or not. RPCGEN compiles this into the *application.h* header file as:

```
struct result {
    int error;
    union {
         char data[MAX_SIZE];
    } result_u;
};
typedef struct result result;
bool_t xdr_result();
```

Note again that we use `typedef result`. The union component of the resulting structure has the same `result` with a `_u` appended. The `xdr_result()` XDR filter is also generated by the compiler.

Typedefs

The RPCGEN compiler defines a type in the header file for every enumeration, structure, and union you define in the protocol. The associated XDR routines generated expect to encode and decode this type of variable.

In addition, you can make your own `typedef` statements in the protocol definition.

```
"typedef" declaration;
```

These get passed through RPCGEN unaltered. For example, the following might be used to represent a 4-sided polygon:

```
typedef point poly[4];
```

It appears exactly the same in the header file.

Programs

The program definition syntax is the only major difference between the XDR and RPCL languages. It allows you to specify the program name, program number, version and procedure information about the server. Once compiled into the header file, both the client and server stubs will make use of this information.

```
program-definition:
    "program" program-ident "{"
        version-list
    "}" "=" value


version-list:
    version ";"
    version ";" version-list



version:
    "version" version-ident "{"
        procedure-list
    "}" "=" value


procedure-list:
    procedure ";"
    procedure ";" procedure-list


procedure:
    type-ident procedure-ident "(" type-ident ")" "=" value
```

Your client application will make use of the program definition ...-ident information to find services. They show up as unsigned long integer preprocessor symbols. Here's a bogus program definition:

```
program BOGUS_PROGRAM {
    version BOGUS_VERSION {
        void BOGUS_PROCEDURE(void) = 1;
    } = 1;
} = 0x2000000;
```

And here's what gets inserted into the header file (shared by the client and server):

```
#define BOGUS_PROGRAM ((u_long)0x2000000)
#define BOGUS_VERSION ((u_long)1)
#define BOGUS_PROCEDURE ((u_long)1)
extern void *bogus_procedure_1();
```

Basically, for each RPC program you define in the protocol, the version(s) and procedure(s) it will provide are specified. You can define multiple RPC server programs within one RPCL protocol definition. A `program-definition` block is required for each. Multiple versions and procedures are of course accommodated.

As another example, let's tell RPCGEN we want to build a server whose symbolic name is TIMEPROG with RPC program number of 44 (that's in the reserved range, see Table 3-1). We want only one version (TIMEVERS=1). We'll have two procedures for the dispatcher to honor: TIMEGET and TIMESET, which will go by the procedure numbers of 1 and 2. Procedure number 0 is reserved for the default service provided in the server stub for client pinging of the server to see if it's alive.

```
/*
 * time.x: Get or set the time. Time is represented as number of seconds
 *             * since 0:00, January 1, 1970.  See /usr/include/rpcsvc,
 *             * system service protocol directory*.x for  other
 *             * interesting protocols.
 */
program TIMEPROG {
    version TIMEVERS {
        unsigned int TIMEGET(void) = 1;
        void TIMESET(unsigned) = 2;
    } = 1;
} = 44;
```

This gets compiled into the header file as:

```
#define TIMEPROG ((u_long)44)
#define TIMEVERS ((u_long)1)
#define TIMEGET ((u_long)1)    /* procedure #1 */
#define TIMESET ((u_long)2)    /* procedure #2 */
extern unsigned int *timeget_1();
extern void *timeset_1();
```

Notice that the service procedure names timeget_1() and timeset_1() are lowercase versions of the symbolic procedure names, TIMEGET() and TIMESET(), trailed by an underscore and the version number. For example, the TIMEGET procedure is declared as unsigned int *timeget_1().

RPCGEN adds indirection to the input and output variable types. The header file specifications make everything send and receive pointers. In the *time.x* protocol above, we specified TIMEGET as returning an unsigned int. The header file typed the service procedure as a pointer to an unsigned integer; extern unsigned int *timeget_1(). The same indirection holds true with the input argument sent with the request. It must be a pointer to a void.

The XDR filter routines work with pointers as they access memory starting at the address specified to perform either the encode or decode process. For this reason, RPC programming requires that you work with pointers. Be aware of this when you code your client's main() and the service procedures. The service procedures, timeget_1() and timeset_1(), must be designed to take and return pointers to the types specified in the protocol. The client calls must pass and receive pointers, too.

The simple fact is that pointers are required to encode and decode the data. If you ever get confused, design the protocol and pass it through RPCGEN, then inspect the dispatch routine generated in *application_svc.c* because that is the dispatcher that invokes the service routine. Type information is readily apparent there. In the above example, the RPCGEN-generated dispatch routine name will be time-prog_1(), a lowercase translation of TIMEPROG, followed by an underscore and the version number TIMEVERS.

If you use RPCGEN.NEW under the SVR4 or TIRPC release, it can generate both client and server application shells to guarantee consistent typing.

NULLPROC

The ONC RPC guidelines recommend that an extra service procedure be registered as procedure number 0, or the NULLPROC, for pinging purposes. When called, the NULLPROC returns no data but does reply to signify that the server at that address is healthy. When you use the RPCGEN protocol compiler, the NULLPROC procedure is hooked into the dispatcher along with your service procedures. Don't use procedure number 0 in your protocol specification.

Declarations

There are four types of declarations allowed in RPCL:

declaration:

    simple-declaration

    fixed-array-declaration

    variable-array-declaration

    pointer-declaration

There are simple declarations as in C:

```
simple-declaration:
    type-ident variable-ident
```

For example:

```
color c;
```

appears the same in the header file.

Fixed-length array declarations are like C fixed-length array declarations:

```
fixed-array-declaration:
    type-ident variable-ident "[" value "]"
```

For example:

```
color palette[8];
```

also appears the same in the header file.

There is currently no support of multi-dimensional arrays. As a workaround, you might think about serializing them yourself. You can pass offsets along with a fixed or variable length, one-dimensional vector. You could also redesign to use trees or linked lists.

Variable-length array declarations do not exist in C. XDR uses angle brackets.

```
variable-array-declaration:
    type-ident variable-ident "<" value ">"
    type-ident variable-ident "<" ">"
```

Specify the maximum vector size between the angle brackets. If the size is omitted, the vector may be of any size.

```
int x<MAX_SIZE>;    /* at most MAX_SIZE items */
int y<>;            /* any number of items */
```

With no explicit syntax in C, variable-length vector declarations are compiled into structures. For example, the x array declaration above gets compiled into the following:

```
struct {
    u_int x_len;   /* # of items in array */
    int *x_val;    /* pointer to array */
} x;
```

The number of items in the vector is stored in the _len component and the pointer to the vector is stored in the _val component. The first part of each of these components' names is the same as the name of the RPCL variable.

Pointer declarations are made in XDR the same way as they are in C. It makes no sense for XDR routines to send memory addresses (pointers) across the network. Addresses are only used to denote underlying structured data such as lists and trees.

pointor doolaration:

type-ident "*" variable-ident

For example, to reference one of the `point` data types we defined above:

```
pt *pNext;
```

You might want to take this a little farther to build up a structure to represent a linked-list of points to describe a polygon:

```
struct point {
        int x;
        int y;
};
struct poly {
        point *p;
        point *pNext;
};
```

An XDR filter is defined here for each variable type. The actual C code for the filters is compiled into *application_xdr.c*:

```
struct point {
        int x;
        int y;
};
typedef struct point point,
bool_t xdr_point();

bool_t xdr_pt();

struct poly {
        point *p;
        point *pNext;
};
typedef struct poly poly;
bool_t xdr_poly();
```

In this way a hierarchy of XDR filters can quickly be generated to handle almost any structure you can think of.

Special Cases

There are some exceptions to the rules described above.

Booleans

C has no built-in boolean type. However the XDR and RPC libraries use the boolean type `bool_t` that can take on a value of TRUE or FALSE. When you use the `bool` type in RPCL, it gets compiled into the output header file as a C `bool_t`.

For example:

```
bool busyFlag;
```

is compiled as:

```
bool_t busyFlag;
```

Strings

Similarly, C has no built-in string type. The convention of using NULL-terminated sequences of characters is also used in the RPCL language and the underlying XDR transfer routines. In RPCL a string is declared using the `string` keyword and gets compiled into the output header file as a `char *`. The maximum length of the string, in terms of characters, may be specified in angle brackets. This does not count the trailing NULL character. If the maximum size is left off, a string of arbitrary length is assumed. The string length merely affects how the associated XDR encode/decode filters are generated.

The following examples of string types:

```
string buffer<32>;
string longBuff<>;
```

are compiled as:

```
char *buffer;
char *longBuff;
```

Opaque Data

XDR and RPC use "opaque data" to describe sequences of arbitrary bytes with no explicit typing. Both fixed-length and variable-length vectors are supported.

The following examples:

```
opaque fixData[512];
opaque varData<1024>;
```

are compiled into:

```
char fixData[512];
struct {
        u_int varData_len;

        char *varData_val;
} varData;
```

The use of a structure to describe variable-length data vectors is described in the section on variable-length definitions.

Voids

Void declarations are only used in union and program definitions. When the keyword `void` is used, no variable is named. It effectively calls the `xdr_void(3N)` filter into action.

Preprocessor Symbols and Control

RPCGEN first passes the *application.x* file through the C preprocessor `cpp(1)`. You can specify symbols within the RPCL source (*application.x* file) directly with `#define` preprocessor directives or the `-Dname[=value]` command-line option to RPCGEN. RPCGEN itself generates `#define`'s for the `cpp` symbols listed in Table 4-3. These symbols can be used to add information to specific compilation units.

Table 4-3. Preprocessor Symbols Built-in to RPCGEN

Symbol	Description
RPC_HDR	Defined when in the header files.
RPC_XDR	Defined in the XDR routines.
RPC_SVC	Defined in the server side stub.
RPC_CLNT	Defined in the client side stub.
RPC_TBL	Defined in the RPC dispatch table

RPCGEN also does some built-in preprocessing itself. If you start a line with a percent sign (%), RPCGEN will pass that line directly through to the output. Here's one example of how this might be useful:

```
#ifdef RPC_SVC
%#define INIT_TIME 0
%int *
%timeget_1()
%{
%       static int theTime = INIT_TIME;
%
%       theTime = time(0);
%       return (&theTime);
%}
#endif
```

In this way the server stub could include the server procedure without the need for a separate *application_svc_proc.c* file. This feature should be used with care as you do not have control over exactly where RPCGEN will put the code in the server stub.

Lower-level ONC RPC Library Calls

While use of a protocol compiler increases flexibility, it slightly complicates the writing of the client application *application.c*. The client network access functions provided by the client stub *application_clnt.c* in many cases can be reduced to a few lines of code and imported into the client application. While I don't recommend this, as RPCGEN does a fine job, the resultant client application would still be much simpler than a client programmed at the socket IPC level.

Let's look in detail at the RPC calls you will have to make in the client. After that, we'll look at the server.

At the Client

A client is required to maintain a unique structure (pointed to by a CLIENT handle) for each client/server connection. Many of the RPC client routines take a CLIENT handle as an argument to specify the server. We will have occasions later in authentication and transport discussions to look into these handles. For now, we leave the creation and manipulation of these structures up to the lower-level ONC RPC library routines.

clnt_create()

To create a CLIENT handle, use low-level client clnt_create(3N):

```
CLIENT *

clnt_create(host, prognum, versnum, protocol)
    char *host;
    u_long prognum, versnum;
    char *protocol;
```

clnt_create() creates the CLIENT structure for the specified server host, program, and version numbers. Transport protocol is selectable as tcp or udp under ONC RPC 4.0. UDP RPC messages can be no larger than 8K bytes, so procedures requiring or returning more than 8K bytes of encoded data should use TCP. If it succeeds, that is, if the host portmapper has a copy of prognum registered, the CLIENT handle is returned. If it fails, NULL is returned, signifying that the query of the server's portmapper did not reveal a match in program number. A version number mismatch doesn't qualify as an error, but it will be revealed when placing the RPC with a clnt_call(3N).

clnt_destroy()

The clnt_destroy(3N) call deallocates memory associated with private data structures for the named CLIENT handle. If the RPC routines were used to open the associated socket, it is neatly closed.

```
clnt_destroy(clnt)
    CLIENT *clnt;
```

clnt_control()

Once a connection has been established with `clnt_create()`, you should use `clnt_control(3N)` to alter any of the characteristics of any anticipated RPC.

```
clnt_control(clnt, request, info)
    CLIENT *clnt;
    int request;
    char *info;
```

`clnt_control()` changes or retrieves `CLIENT` characteristics including the timeout value and socket descriptors (both ends), as well as their status. It works for both UDP and TCP transports. The supported values of request and their info argument types are discussed in *The ONC RPC Programming Reference*.

clnt_call()

`clnt_call(3N)` is what you use to actually place the RPC. It uses the `inproc()` XDR filters to encode the request argument from `in` and remains blocked until the reply comes. The `outproc()` XDR filter is used to decode the reply into `out`.

```
enum clnt_stat
clnt_call(clnt, procnum, inproc, in, outproc, out, timeout)
    CLIENT *clnt;
    u_long procnum;
    xdrproc_t inproc, outproc;
    char *in, *out;
    struct timeval timeout;
```

`clnt call()` uses the `CLIENT` handle to call the remote procedure, `procnum`. It encodes request arguments and reply results by the specified XDR procedures. A timeout interval is also controllable with `timeout`. Any value set by `clnt_control()` changes the default time-out and causes timeout values specified by `clnt_call()` to be ignored. See `<sys/time.h>` for discussion of the `struct timeval` field definitions.

```
struct timeval {
        long    tv_sec;          /* seconds */
        long    tv_usec;         /* and microseconds */
};
```

At the Server

The server procedures that you write in *application_svc_proc.c* typically won't need to call the RPC library. They are isolated by code in the server stub. All you need to do is code up the services to be performed while adhering to I/O types specified in the protocol definition file.

As a client has a `CLIENT` handle for each server, a server receives a server transport handle with each RPC request. A `SVCXPRT` handle, like CLIENT, is a typedef that points to a structure defined in the RPC header file. The server transport handle is created and maintained in the RPCGEN-generated server stub, *application_svc.c.* In some examples later in the book, we show servers that need to manage their own transport handles, but in most cases server procedures will not be concerned with these structures. When all the required RPC library calls are hidden in the server stub, the low-level RPC server application is simpler than its high-level equivalent (as shown in the previous chapter).

By default, RPCGEN generates server stubs that create both UDP and TCP transport handles with the low-level svcudp_create(3N) and svctcp_create(3N) ONC RPC library calls. You don't have to create them.

svctcp_create()

svctcp_create() creates and returns a TCP RPC service transport at a particular socket or creates a socket along with it.

```
SVCXPRT *
svctcp_create(sock, sendsz, recvsz)
    int sock;
    u_int sendsz, recvsz;
```

TCP-based RPC uses buffered I/O. If the sizes of the send and receive buffers, sendsz and recvsz, are zero, default buffer sizes are used. It returns NULL if it fails.

svcudp_create()

svcudp_create() creates and returns a pointer to a UDP/IP-based server transport.

```
SVCXPRT *
svcudp_create(sock)
    int sock;
```

The value of sock may be either that of an open socket descriptor or RPC_ANY-SOCK, in which case a socket is created. The socket is bound to an arbitrary local UDP port. It returns NULL if it fails.

The stub will use svc_register(3N) to register the dispatch routine. I'll leave further explanation of the low-level server stub calls until we use them in later chapters. The server procedures that we will write in this chapter do not require *any* RPC library calls.

An Example: One Client Talks to One Server

The best way to illustrate how to define a protocol and tie it into a server and client is by example. I recommend that you follow along, typing the code in as we go.

We shall build a client/server pair similar to the previous chapter's high-level RPC example. The client calls a remote service to get directory listings from the remote machine. We'll call the client application rls, also.

Let's start by building a protocol definition in *rls.x* as shown in Example 4-2.

Example 4-2. Remote directory listing protocol: rls.x

```
/*
 * rls.x: remote directory listing protocol
 */
const MAXNAMELEN = 512;
typedef string nametype<MAXNAMELEN>;     /* a directory entry */
typedef struct namenode *namelist;       /*a link in the listing */
/*
 * a node in the directory
 */
struct namenode {
    nametype name;      /* name of directory entry */
    namelist pNext;    /* next entry, struct namenode */
};
/*
 * the result of a READDIR operation
 */
union readdir_res switch (int errno) {
case 0:
    namelist list;    /* no error: return directory listing */
default:
    void;             /* error occurred: nothing else to return */
};
/*
 * the directory program definition
 */
program DIRPROG {
    version DIRVERS {
        readdir_res
        READDIR(nametype) = 1;
    } = 1,
} = 0x20000001;
```

We'll use a variable-length string `nametype` to hold the directory-name argument sent to the server. We'll use a linked-list handling of `namenode` structures to represent the filenames passed back to the client from the server in the reply. There will be one `namenode` structure for each node or entry in the directory file. Each `namenode` will contain a `nametype` to record the filename of the node as well as a next-pointer `pNext`. For sake of clarity, we shall generate a new type called `namelist` that is a pointer to a `namenode` structure.

The server is defined in the `program` definition section as having a request argument of type `nametype` and returning a reply argument of type `readdir_res`. Each `readdir_res` is a structure containing a union with contents discriminated by an integer error variable `errno`. Should all go well at the server and no error occur, a `namelist` containing the directory contents is passed back. If an error occurs, no data is returned in the `readdir_res` union.

As with C, I like to get data typing out of the way first. I used the `const` definition to define `MAXNAMELEN` for subsequent use within the protocol and in the stubs. The input and output data structures use variable-length strings. The request argument contains the directory in question. The reply argument includes a discriminated union which returns no data if there is a server error, or a linked list of variable-length string filenames, if successful.

In the `program` definition section, the server procedure is defined. The values (i.e., 1, 1, and 0x20000001) are bookkeeping numbers. If you use them wisely, choosing values with some method, they can be useful during development and at run-time.

We can run RPCGEN on the *rls.x* protocol definition file:

rodson> rpcgen rls.x

It produces the header file *rls.h*, shown in Example 4-3. It also produces the XDR filters in *rls_xdr.c*, along with client and server stubs *rls_clnt.c* and *rls_svc.c*.

The header file explains much of what goes on. It is included by the client and server stubs and should be included by your client and server code.

Example 4-3. Header file generated by RPCGEN: rls.h

```
#define MAXNAMELEN 255

typedef char *nametype;
bool_t xdr_nametype();

typedef struct namenode *namelist;
bool_t xdr_namelist();

struct namenode {
        nametype name;
        namelist pNext;
}; typedef struct namenode namenode;
bool_t xdr_namenode();

struct readdir_res {
        int errno;
        union {
                namelist list;
        } readdir_res_u;
}; typedef struct readdir_res readdir_res;
bool_t xdr_readdir_res();

#define DIRPROG ((u_long)0x20000001)
#define DIRVERS ((u_long)1)
#define READDIR ((u_long)1)
extern readdir_res *readdir_1();
```

`struct` and `union` definitions are followed by `typedef` statements, a programming style lots of people use anyway. Note the boolean data type `bool_t` unique to XDR. Union names use the suffix `_u`. Lastly, some `unsigned longs` act as the bookkeeping tokens in the calling process.

The server stub *rls_svc.c* will register program number 0x20000001, version number 1 with the portmapper service. Notice that I designated the previous chapter's high-level RPC program as 0x20000000. It is incompatible and should be indicated as such by a different program number.

The server stub includes a dispatch routine. If it receives a request for procedure number 1 (READDIR), it invokes `readdir_1()`. The name `readdir_1` was selected by using the lowercase version of the RPCL symbol used to define the procedure number READDIR, with an underscore (_), and the version number appended to the end.

The next thing to do is to develop the service procedures; the code the server will actually execute when requested should be put in *rls_svc_proc.c* as shown in Example 4-4. As we mentioned, the server dispatch expects the lone procedure to be named `readdir_1()`. The protocol specified that this procedure is expecting a pointer to a `nametype` as an input argument and returns a `readdir_res*`. The return variable must be declared as static and not an automatic variable. The reply variable isn't created in the server dispatch routine, so we must allocate it here, statically. With automatically allocated variables you run the risk of the values becoming undefined when you leave the scope of the service routine and return to the dispatcher function. Subsequent XDR filters and RPC library functions need access to the address to get the reply back.

Example 4-4. Remote read directory service: rls_svc_proc.c

```
/*
 * rls_svc_proc.c: remote readdir_1() implementation
 */
#include <rpc/rpc.h>
#include <sys/dir.h>
#include "rls.h"

extern int errno;
extern char *malloc();
extern char *strdup();

readdir_res *
readdir_1(dirname)
        nametype *dirname;
{
        namelist nl;
        namelist *nlp;
        static readdir_res res;/* Must be static! */
        static DIR *dirp = NULL;/* static to see if we've been called before */
        struct direct *d;

        /*
         * Open the directory.
         */
        dirp = opendir(*dirname);
        if (dirp == NULL) {
                res.errno = errno;
                return(&res);
        }

        /*
         * Free previous result if there was one.  It might be a long list
         * that eats up memory.
         */
        if (dirp) xdr_free(xdr_readdir_res, &res);


        /*
         * Collect directory entries.  Memory allocated here will
         * be xdr_free'd next time around.
```

Example 4-4. Remote read directory service: rls_svc_proc.c (Continued)

```
        */
        nlp = &res.readdir_res_u.list;
        while (d = readdir(dirp)) {
                nl = *nlp = (namenode *)malloc(sizeof(namenode));
                nl->name = strdup(d->d_name);
                nlp = &nl->pNext;
        }
        *nlp = NULL;



        /*
         * Return the result.
         */
        res.errno = 0;
        closedir(dirp);
        return(&res);
}
```

Keep in mind that RPC 4.0 procedures send and receive pointers. We'll use the errno(3) facility to get information back to the client (see intro(2)). This example demonstrates the need to dynamically allocate and free memory. After the server procedure finishes its task with return(&res), the malloc'ed memory is not freed; the XDR routines have it still. You should use the xdr_free(3N) routine the next time around or you will leave some memory tied-up. xdr_free() requires not just the XDR handle (&res), but also the filter or translation routine in order to free memory. Without the filter specification, it would not know what memory to free and how to free it. You should make sure that you don't attempt to free a readdir_res structure that is not initialized correctly, with NULL values where necessary, as it can give the XDR filters grief. We used a static dirp to be able to check that the procedure had been called and that the reply res had been initialized.

Next let's construct the main() client program used to oversee each RPC operation, *rls.c.* We create a CLIENT handle for a client/server association using clnt_create(). The CLIENT handle is formed if the specified server machine has a registered service with the appropriate program number and version running. We also specify the transport. Procedure number is not checked until the remote request is actually sent. We could get a good CLIENT handle that returns an error later when we attempt to execute the procedure number. The errors possible at the client are summarized at the end of *The ONC RPC Programming Reference.* A version number mismatch is reported at run-time but does not necessarily constitute an error.

The remote directory-listing client program appears in Example 4-5. It uses both system errno and RPC system error reporting to check the health of the remote call. At both the client and server side there are routines analogous to perror(3) to report error information. By just looking at their context and the error symbol names, I think you can quickly figure out how to use the important ones. RPC error reporting is summarized in *The ONC RPC Programming Reference* with further applications in Chapter 12.

Example 4-5. Remote directory listing client: rls.c

```
/*
 * rls.c - remote directory-listing client
 */
#include <stdio.h>
#include <rpc/rpc.h>
#include "rls.h"
extern int errno;
main (argc, argv)
    int argc;
    char *argv[];
{
    CLIENT *cl;
    char *server;
    char *dir;
    readdir_res *result;
    namelist nl;
    if (argc != 3) {
        fprintf(stderr, "usage: %s host directory\n", argv[0]);
        exit(1);
    }
    /*
     * Remember what our command-line arguments refer to.
     */
    server = argv[1];
    dir = argv[2];
    /*
     * Create client "handle" used for calling MESSAGEPROG on the
     * server designated on command line.  We tell RPC package
     * to use the "tcp" protocol when contacting the server.
     */
    cl = clnt_create(server, DIRPROG, DIRVERS, "tcp");
    if (cl == NULL) {
        /*
         * Couldn't establish connection with server.
         * print error message and die.
         */
        clnt_pcreateerror(server);
        exit(1);
    }
    /*
     * Call the remote procedure readdir on the server.
     */
    result = readdir_1(&dir, cl);
    if (result == NULL) {
        /*
         * An error occurred while calling the server,
         * print error message and die...
         */
        clnt_perror(cl, server);
        exit(1);
    }
    /*
     * Okay, we successfully called the remote procedure.
     */
    if (result->errno != 0) {
        /*
         * A remote system error occurred,
         * print error message and die.
         */
        errno = result->errno;
        perror(dir);
        exit(1);
    }
    /*
```

Example 4-5. Remote directory listing client: rls.c (Continued)

```
     * successfully got a directory listing, print it out
     */
    for (nl = result->readdir_res_u.list; nl != NULL; nl = nl->pNext) {
        printf("%s\n", nl->name);
    }
    exit(0);
}
```

The first thing this client does is parse the command line to pick up the names of the host and remote directory. The next step is to get hold of the named server, and then check the integrity of the connection. Since we will run RPCGEN with no command line options, it will generate a server stub that registers the dispatcher for the `readdir_1()` service with both UDP and TCP transports. Any reasonable directory listing length should be less than 8K bytes, so we could use either transport. I selected TCP for no real reason. To use UDP just replace the `tcp` in the `clnt_create()` call with `udp`.

If the server connection is okay, the remote procedure is invoked with the appropriate request argument and the client waits for a reply. When results arrive, execution continues and the results are analyzed.

If the attempt to create the `CLIENT` handle failed, `clnt_pcreateerror(3N)` is used to extract the error from the RPC system and print it at `stderr`. If the remote call failed, `clnt_perror(3N)` is used to decipher and print that error at `stderr`. We also passed-back the remote system's `errno` error code and print that at `stderr` with `perror(3)` if non-zero.

If you typed in the *makefile* in Example 4-1, you can use `make` to build the `rls` client executable and the `rls_svc` server executable. Let's review what you should have in the development directory:

```
rodson> ls
makefile        rls.c           rls.x           rls_svc_proc.c
```

In the directory, there is the *makefile*, the client `main()` application, the RPCL protocol definition, and the server procedure. Now run `make`. RPCGEN creates *rls.h*, the stubs *rls_svc.c* and *rls_clnt.c*, along with the XDR filters for encoding and decoding in *rls_xdr.c*.

```
rodson> make rls rls_svc
cc -g -c rls_xdr.c
cc -g -o rls rls_xdr.o rls_clnt.c rls.c
rls_clnt.c:
rls.c:
Linking:
cc -g -o rls_svc rls_xdr.o rls_svc.c rls_svc_proc.c
rls_svc.c:
rls_svc_proc.c:
Linking:
```

We ran the linker to make two executables: `rls_svc` is the remote server executable and `rls` is the client executable.

```
rodson> ls -F
makefile    rls.h     rls_clnt.c    rls_svc.c       rls_svc_proc.o
rls*        rls.o     rls_clnt.o    rls_svc.o       rls_xdr.c
rls.c       rls.x     rls_svc*      rls_svc_proc.c  rls_xdr.o
```

Note that, as required, you've got two executable programs. Now you are ready to try it! To make things easier to watch, launch the server on your own (client) machine. Run the client program with a command such as `rls yourMachine someDirectoryName`.

```
rodson> rls_svc &
[1] 29174
rodson> rls rodson $cwd
.
..
core
rls_xdr.c
rls.o
rls.x
rls_clnt.c
rls_svc.c
rls_clnt.o
rls.c
rls_xdr.o
makefile
rls.h
rls_svc_proc.c
rls_svc.o
rls
rls_svc_proc.o
rls_svc
rodson> rls rodson fred
fred: No such file or directory
```

Now that it works locally, let's try it out on the network. First, start a server on some remote machine. In this case, I'll use `cortex`.

```
rodson> rsh cortex -n exec $cwd/rls_svc &
```

Then launch the same RPC as before, but now directed at `cortex`.

```
rodson> rls cortex $cwd
.
..
core
rls_xdr.c
rls.o
rls.x
rls_clnt.c
rls_svc.c
rls_clnt.o
rls.c
rls_xdr.o
makefile
rls.h
```

```
rls_svc_proc.c
rls_svc.o
rls
rls_svc_proc.o
rls_svc
shoppingList
rodson> rls cortex fred
fred: No such file or directory
```

Debugging

The development of a client/server pair that operates in different process spaces is complicated by the fact that you cannot trace execution with a debugger. For this reason, both RPC and socket IPC-based network applications can be hard to debug.

When you start up the server process, the main() procedure in the compiler-generated *rls_svc.c* server stub registers the service with the local portmapper and goes into a suspended state with svc_run(3N). Consider what you'll see if you step through the client process using a debugger like dbx(1) or dbxtool(1).

After start-up overhead, you'll see your client program connect to the specified server and check connection status. Next your machine locally invokes the READDIR_version procedure or readdir_1() as defined in your protocol definition. This steps you into the client stub *rls_clnt.c*. There, return memory is first cleared and clnt_call() is used to contact the server stub's main() on the other side of the network. Your process now waits until the server returns its reply. dbx just hangs there until the results come back.

Once contacted, the server dispatch procedure in the server stub *rls_svc.c* inspects the request parameters to see which of the services under its control the client is requesting. If that service procedure exists, input parameters are translated as necessary with the XDR routines. The server dispatch then invokes the readdir_1() procedure. Results are returned through the server and client stubs back into the waiting client main().

You can't see what's going on at the server through a debugger at the client. If you trace execution with two debuggers, one at the client and one at the server, the XDR and RPC calls make it difficult to find potential errors in *your* code.

I like to go through three steps in debugging an RPC application:

1. Debug the code I wrote first without involving the network code.

2. Add the XDR and RPC network code to see what breaks next. This is still possible in one process using the Raw transport.

3. Use the target transport.

Step 1: Debug Without the Network

The purpose of the first step of debugging is to keep things simple. If you can come up with a way to run the client and server in the same process space, you can follow execution with a debugger. The general strategy is to debug service procedures incrementally in a local address space. Once these are verified, gradually add and debug the client/server functionality (steps 2 and 3).

The simplest thing to do is link the client main() and the server procedure code you wrote. This circumvents the XDR filters and RPC calls in the stubs generated by the protocol compiler, making it easier to debug the code *you* wrote. The common client and server procedure names generated by the RPCGEN protocol compiler make direct linking possible. Now you are debugging within a local procedure call model, which you are familiar with.

Let's look at this approach in the context of our example.

The client main()'s name for the remote procedure, in this case readdir_1(), is the same as the one we wrote for the server process in *rls_svc_proc.c*. That was by design. This allows you to do some local debugging and discover data or logic problems without going remote.

On the left of Figure 4-3 is a schematic of the structure of an RPC application, as glued-together with RPCGEN. The left side of the figure illustrates how we'll break things down to debug only our code. If you compile and run dbx on the reduced client application, you'll be able to look inside your server processing.[†]

```
rodson> cc -g -o local rls.c rls_svc_proc.c rls_xdr.c
rodson> dbx local
```

We did not link *rls.c* with the client stub *rls_clnt.c*. Instead we linked the client main() directly with *rls_svc_proc.c*. In this way the client's call to the service procedure readdir_1() is no longer a remote call, but rather a local call to readdir_1() performed in local address space.[‡]

This approach to local debugging still requires you to have a server running somewhere or at least registered in some portmap. Since we haven't altered the client main() in *rls.c*, it is still expecting to open a CLIENT handle for a server running the readdir_1() service. If you can't get a server registered, comment or edit out the client_create() call.

Using Conditional-compile Preprocessor Directives

We still linked the local debug application with the XDR filters in *rls_xdr.c*. *rls_svc_proc.c* uses xdr_free() with the xdr_dir() filter as an argument to free

---

† See the next section as to why the XDR filters are still linked in.

‡ The readdir_1() service procedure only uses one argument. readdir_1() as called from the client has two arguments. We no longer have a need for the second CLIENT handle argument.

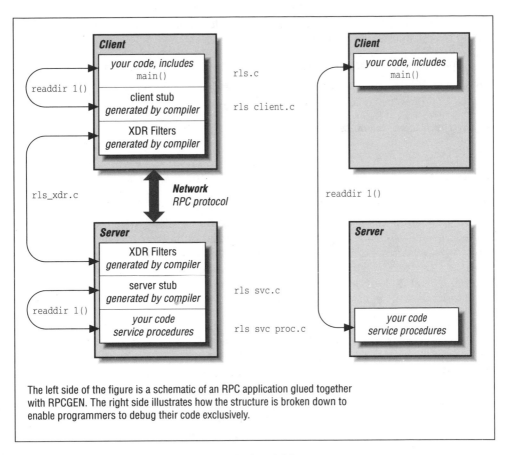

The left side of the figure is a schematic of an RPC application glued together with RPCGEN. The right side illustrates how the structure is broken down to enable programmers to debug their code exclusively.

Figure 4-3. Reducing an RPC application for local debugging

memory. If you comment-out or use `#ifdef` conditional compilation directives in *rls_svc_proc.c*, you can avoid the XDR calls and remove the need to link with *rls_xdr.c*. The XDR routines aren't actually used anyway as the RPC has been removed.

You could comment-out or use conditional compile directives to remove the RPC library used in *rls.c*. By removing calls like the `clnt_create()` and any dependent code, you'll avoid having to have a server process registered in a portmap. In Example 4-5, it is pretty simple—you augment the use of `clnt_ create()` with preprocessor directives.

```
#ifdef DEBUG
        cl = (CLIENT *)1; /* can be trouble if uninitialized */
#else
        cl = clnt_create(server, DIRPROG, DIRVERS, "tcp");
#endif DEBUG
```

The service program DIRPROG no longer needs to be registered in server's portmap. You must repeat this kind of conditional compilation logic around *all* instances of RPC library calls on the client side.[†] Compile and link the localD debug executable with a preprocessor directive.

```
rodson> cc -g -DDEBUG -o localD rls.c rls_svc_proc.c rls_xdr.c
```

No server needs to be started and the hostname on the command line can be bogus. The directory reading is executed locally.

```
rodson> local bogus /home
.
..
alydar .
cortex
unclejack
hp_9000
```

If you add more rules to your *makefile*, you can make a local test application local, useful for debugging with dbx or a similar debugger. Example 4-6 includes the previous makefile, then sets a few C compiler options and establishes new rules. "make clean" will remove all the files produced by the RPCGEN compiler, C compiler, and linker, leaving you with your three source files: *application.x*, *application.c*, and *application_svc_proc.c*.

"make local" will create a one-process space application as described above, suitable for stepping through with dbx. The *makefile* takes some dangerous liberties and just plain removes the references to XDR and RPC routines in the server procedure and client main(), respectively. In the client main() the CLIENT handle has some unknown value that can cause trouble. This is not a robust technique that will work with all applications. make removes the references with egrep -v, placing the results in filenames with extensions that reflect function and base names reflecting the current data. *Do not* change the temporary files. Make changes in the original sources.

Example 4-6. Two forms of local debugging: makefile

```
include ../makefile # bring-in Example 4-1

SRC=$(APPN).x $(APPN)_svc_proc.c $(APPN).c
CFLAGS= -g -DDEBUG      # turn on debugging,  cc builds tables, cond. compile
stmts.
TODAY=`date|awk '{print $$1$$2$$3}'`
# blast away
clean:
        $(RM) $(APPN) $(APPN)_svc $(APPN)_svc.c $(APPN)_xdr.c \
        $(APPN)_clnt.c $(APPN).h *.o *.*%

# Build a local-running, dbxtool-able version w/ no XDR use.  Note for
# link to succeed, keep your xdr_free()'s and the like in one compilation
# unit (file).  I keep them in $(APPN)_svc_proc.c
```

---

† For this reason, I often opt for the previous approach—that is, just starting a dummy server to minimize changes to code, even though the client won't send requests.

Example 4-6. Two forms of local debugging: makefile (Continued)

```
local: $(APPN).h $(APPN).c $(APPN)_svc_proc.c
        egrep -v xdr_ $(APPN)_svc_proc.c>`date|awk '{print
$$1$$2$$3}'`_svc_proc.c
        egrep -v clnt_create $(APPN).c>`date|awk '{print $$1$$2$$3}'`.c
        $(CC) -g -DDEBUG -o local `date|awk '{print $$1$$2$$3}'`*.c
        # $(RM) ${TODAY}.c and
        #       ${TODAY}_svc_proc.c after dbx-ing.
        # Do not edit them, change $(APPN)_svc_proc.c and $(APPN).c.

# OR if you have the #defines mentioned in $(APPN).c to remove
# clnt_create(), and that's your only use of RPC, try this.  Note use of
# -DDEBUG conditional compile flag, assumes
localD: $(APPN).h $(APPN).c $(APPN)_svc_proc.c
        egrep -v xdr_ $(APPN)_svc_proc.c>`date|awk '{print
$$1$$2$$3}'`_svc_proc.c
        $(CC) -g -DDEBUG -o localD  $(APPN).c \
                ${TODAY}_svc_proc.c $(LFLAGS)
        # $(RM) ${TODAY}_svc_proc.c after dbx-ing.
        # Do not edit it, change $(APPN)_svc_proc.c.

$(APPN).ar: $(SRC)
        bundle $(SRC) > $(APPN).a
```

"make localD" assumes your client main() program (in this case *rls.c*) is using the type of conditional compile directives mentioned earlier to remove calls to RPC CLIENT handle manipulation routines given the –DDEBUG C compiler option. This rule also assumes that if your service procedures make use of xdr_free(), each is on an isolated line (egrep -v again).

The last rule just gives you a way to package-up your sources using a bundle shell script such as the one shown in Example 4-7.

Example 4-7. A simple shell archiving script: bundle

```
: bundle:  group files into distribution package
echo ': To unbundle, sh this file'
for i
do
        echo "echo $i 1>&2"
        echo "cat >$i <<'End of $i'"
        cat $i
        echo "End of $i"
done
```

To unbundle the files, just type:

```
sh $(APPN).ar
```

! *Unless your* noclobber *environment variable is set, running this script will replace any of the files with the same name with the one in the archive.*

Several much more elaborate scripts can be found in use on Internet and in Usenet news groups. Check with your system administrator if you need a more robust archiving scheme.

If the server procedures you have defined in *application_svc_proc.c* have no XDR calls like xdr_free(), then you need not change your source code or include elaborate commands within make. If this is the case, you can replace the lines for the local rule above with a rule that just links the client application to the server procedure(s).

```
# If there are no xdr_...() calls in $(APPN)_svc_proc.c, 'make local'
# doesn't need to do anything but link the client main w/ the server
# procedure.
local: $(APPN)_svc_proc.c $(APPN).c
        $(CC) $(CFLAGS) -DDEBUG -o $(APPN) $(APPN)_svc_proc.c $(APPN).c
                $(LFLAGS)
```

Step 2: Use the Raw Transport

Once you are sure that your client and server agree on data types and that your code is bug-free, then you can use the ONC RPC's Raw transport[†] to test the client/-server protocol, including the XDR routines, within one address space.

The Raw transport is for intra-process rather than network communication. It is basically a memory-based transport used for testing and timing. The Raw functions replace the low-level RPC calls we've seen in the client and server stubs and applications with similarly-named calls. They perform the RPC on the local machine in the start-up process' address space.

At the client, you replace the use of clnt_create() to create the CLIENT handles with clntraw_create(3N). At the server, you generate Raw transport handles with svcraw_create(3N) rather than creating TCP or UDP transport handles with svctcp_create() and svcudp_create(). (See *The ONC RPC Programming Reference* for more details.)

While the clnt_create() calls are all in code you're responsible for, the svc..._create() calls were generated by RPCGEN in the server stub, so you'll have to edit that.[‡] Plus, you wind up executing code generated by RPCGEN, as in step 3. Personally, I like to attack the debugging of the network protocol using the target transport (e.g., UDP or TCP) as generated by the protocol compiler. Practically speaking, I often skip this approach to single-process debugging because it complicates testing. In step 3, you have the additional challenge of catching transport-oriented abuses which, in my experience, are rare and easy to catch.

Here's a quick overview of what you must do to debug the rls application with the Raw transport.

---

† The Raw transport does not work properly under Version 4.0 of ONC RPC or under SunOS 4.0. It has been fixed with SunOS 4.1 and Transport Independent RPC.

‡ RPCGEN currently only generates UDP and TCP transport connections.

First, run RPCGEN over the protocol as before:

```
rodson> rpcgen -s rls.x
```

The *rls_svc.c* server stub now must be edited:

- Rename `main()` to something like `svc_main()`. You will be invoking it to set up the Raw server from the client `main()`.

- Delete any `svc..._create()` calls. Replace them with one call to `transp = svcraw_create()`.

- Tell the RPC system about the dispatch routine `dirprog_1()` and specify a zero protocol so that RPC does not register it with the portmapper.

The server stub, *rls_svc.c*, should now look like Example 4-8. Major changes to the auto-generated file are in bold.

Example 4-8. Server stub edited to use Raw transport for local debugging: rls_svc.c

```
#include <stdio.h>
#include <rpc/rpc.h>
#include "rls.h"

static void dirprog_1();
svc_main()
{
    SVCXPRT *transp;

    (void) pmap_unset(DIRPROG, DIRVERS); /* might as well leave this */

    transp = svcraw_create();
    if (transp == NULL) {
            fprintf(stderr, "cannot create raw service.");
            exit(1);
    }
    if (!svc_register(transp, DIRPROG, DIRVERS, dirprog_1, 0 )) {
            fprintf(stderr, "unable to register (DIRPROG, DIRVERS, zero
proto).");
            exit(1);
    }

}

static void
dirprog_1(rqstp, transp)
{
        /* untouched by human hands - RPCGEN generated */
}
```

The default TCP and UDP transport creations were replaced with one Raw transport. Your client `main()` now establishes the service within its process, as shown in Example 4-9, performing dispatching only when required. The changes to *rls.c* are minimal, including the creation of a Raw transport CLIENT handle.

Example 4-9. Client application using Raw transport for local debugging: rls.c

```
#include <stdio.h>
#include <rpc/rpc.h>
#include <sys/errno.h>
#include "rls.h"

extern int        errno;

main(argc, argv)
   int            argc;
   char           *argv[];
{
   CLIENT         *cl;
   char           *dir;
   readdir_res    *result;
   namelist       nl;

   if (argc != 2) {
     fprintf(stderr, "usage: %s directory\n", argv[0]);
     exit(1);
   }
   dir = argv[1];

   /*
    * Create and register the local raw server transport.
    */
   svc_main();

   /*
    * Create local raw client handle.
    */
   cl = clntraw_create(DIRPROG, DIRVERS);

   /*
    * As before, call the procedure readdir on the server.
    */
   result = rd_1(&dir, cl);   /* note the procedure name change */
   if (result == NULL) {
     clnt_perror(cl, "raw deal");
     exit(1);
   }
   if (result->errno != 0) {
     errno = result->errno;
     perror(dir);
     exit(1);
   }
   for (nl = result->readdir_res_u.list; nl != NULL; nl = nl->next) {
     printf("%s\n", nl->name);
   }
   exit(0);
}
```

The only other change we must make before linking all the code into one executable is to change the name of the service procedure called in the client from readdir_1() to something like rd_1(). Otherwise the client and server are both making calls to readdir_1(). As seen above, I renamed the call in the client main() *rls.c* and as defined in the client stub *rls_clnt.c*.

```
rodson> sed 's/readdir_1/rd_1/g' < rls_clnt.c | into rls_clnt.c
```

Now we link everything together:

```
rodson> cc -g -o rls *.c # (I hope this is the only C code in this
                    directory:-)
rls.c:
rls_clnt.c:
rls_svc.c:
rls_svc_proc.c:
rls_xdr.c:
Linking:
```

To prove that your service is really getting called you will have to set a break-point within the dispatch or remote procedure. This is because it is called indirectly when the `clnt_call()` puts something into its socket.

```
rodson> dbx rls
Reading symbolic information...
Read 497 symbols
(dbx) stop in dirprog_1
(2) stop in dirprog_1
(dbx) run ./
Running: rls ./
stopped in dirprog_1 at line 42 in file ".../rls_svc.c"
   42            switch (rqstp->rq_proc) {
(dbx) c
.
..
rls.x
rls_svc_proc.c
rls.c
rls_xdr.c
rls.h
rls_clnt.c
rls_svc.c
rls_xdr.o
rls_clnt.o
rls.o
rls_svc.o
rls
rls_svc_proc.o

execution completed, exit code is 0
program exited with 0
```

This allows you to see the RPC and XDR calls at work, potentially debugging them from one process before you decouple client and server with the UDP or TCP transports.

Step 3: Debug Over the Network

Let's assume you've completed steps 1 and 2 such that your client and server code is debugged and you have a good feeling about adherence to the protocol specified in the *application.x* file. The next step is to pull the code apart again and see if it still works. If it doesn't, more often than not it is a case of not exactly adhering to the protocol or some transport abuse. You are probably passing bad data into XDR filters or possibly too much data to a UDP transport. In my experience, protocol compilers don't make mistakes; faulty protocol interpretations or adherence by the programmer will usually be the source of the problem.

Note that if you skipped step 2, this is the first time you'll see many protocol problems.

The client and server don't need to be on the same machine for step 3. You can start dbx(1) sessions on both machines, putting one in each of two windows on your workstation. You can then step through the client and place the RPC request. In the server, if you set the appropriate breakpoint(s), you can catch the arrival of the request in the dispatch routine. That is usually where any protocol errors first show up as the XDR filters fail to decode or encode request and reply parameters. The difficulty is that you didn't write this code; the protocol compiler did, and so debugging it can be tough. However, once you've stepped through one auto-generated server dispatch routine, you've seen them all. Watch for the XDR decode routine to bomb.

If you make it all the way into one of the service procedures that you wrote, you're half of the way there. The next most likely place for a problem is where your procedure returns its results to the dispatcher and the XDR filter is called to encode the reply argument at the server.

While you step through your service procedure and dispatcher to watch for these problems, the client will not wait for you and it will time-out. You can get around this by changing your code. Before the RPC is placed at the client, use clnt_control(3N) to set the TIMEOUT to some interval that is long enough to allow you to step through the server and still get a reply back to the client without timing-out. See *The ONC RPC Programming Reference* for a discussion of controlling client parameters.

```
struct timeval DebugTime;
CLIENT *cl;
.

.
open CLIENT handle cl
.

.
#ifdef DEBUG                      /* set RPC time-out */
        DebugTime.tv_sec = 10000;
        DebugTime.tv_usec = 0; /* Slow things down */
        clnt_control(cl, CLSET_TIMEOUT, (char *)&DebugTime);
#endif
```

If you are using UDP, your client by default will continue to retry its request every 4 seconds. Your server may buffer these up, giving you numerous requests to service. Usually I step through only once and restart, dump the buffer, and naturally avoid a problem. You can explicitly avoid request buffering by making another clnt_control() call at the client to stretch out the retry time.

```
#ifdef DEBUG /* set UDP retry timeout */
        DebugTime.tv_sec = 10000;
        DebugTime.tv_usec = 0;
```

```
                clnt_control(cl, CLSET_RETRY_TIMEOUT, (char *)&DebugTime);
    #endif
```

Or you could choose to turn on the server caching mechanism with a call to the undocumented `svcudp_enablecache()` routine.

```
svcudp_enablecache(transp, size)
    SVCXPRT *transp;
    u_long size;
```

This turns on the building and maintenance of a reply. Pointers to previous reply buffers are copied into a FIFO cache with buffers retransmitted if a retransmission is detected. More on this in Chapter 12.

Remake the `rls` client and server applications, being sure none of the step 2 edits are still in effect. Next I like to start two `dbxtool` windows, one for the client and one for the server. Then I set a breakpoint in the server to stop in the dispatch function. If your server stub was generated by RPCGEN, the name of the dispatch routine is the lowercase version of the symbolic RPCL program variable with a `_version` suffix. For our example, the dispatch routine is `dirprog_1()`.

Start the server and set yourself up to inspect the incoming request with the following:

```
rodson> dbx rls_svc # this is the server
Reading symbolic information...
Read 382 symbols
(dbx) stop in dirprog_1
(2) stop in dirprog_1
(dbx) run
Running: rls_svc
```

In another local shell, debug the client. I started the server on the same machine, `rodson`, on which I'll do the client debugging. There is no real reason for that other than laziness. I didn't want to bother running a remote login shell to debug the server on a remote machine. It will work the same whether the server is run locally or remotely.

```
rodson> dbx rls # this is the client
Reading symbolic information...
Read 340 symbols
(dbx) run rodson ./
```

Watch the server dbx process to see if the request even gets there. If so, continue stepping through the dispatching procedure and into the requested service procedure. Be watching for bad encode or decode steps. You can use all the standard debugging tricks from there on in.

If the XDR filters in *rls_xdr.c* fail, the first step is to determine whether the server is having trouble decoding the request or encoding the reply. Do this by using the up command in dbx to find out who is calling the failing filter. If the dispatch routine is having trouble decoding parameters, you probably sent data of the wrong length or not terminated from the client. The name of the failing low-level XDR filter call will suggest what piece of the request data structure is not being decoded correctly.

If the call to `svc_sendreply(3N)` is causing an XDR filter error, the reply data you assembled does not adhere to the protocol definition. Again, you should use the name of the failing low-level XDR filter as an indication of where the trouble lies in the reply data structure.

The following are five common protocol mistakes:

1. Strings without NULL termination.

2. NULL string pointers (C allows this, but XDR barfs).

3. Vectors or arrays that are longer than the specified maximum.

4. Linked-lists or trees without NULL next pointers.

5. Arguments that don't fit into the 8K byte limitation of the UDP transport.

Many protocol and RPC system errors are easy to resolve if you use the client and server error checking and reporting ONC library functions. We discuss these in more detail in later chapters, especially in Chapter 12 and in *The ONC RPC Programming Reference.*

Deploying Servers During Development

During the development of a client/server pair, you might want to launch server processes in a window or by a script where you can easily `kill(1)` them. To launch a server on my own machine, I can enter:

```
rodson> rls_svc &
```

If there's a need to run remote servers, start a remote shell:

```
rodson> rsh remoteHost -n exec $cwd/rls_svc &
```

`$cwd` expands to the current directory (the directory with the server code) and should expand to the same directory at the remoteHost. Different versions of SunOS and NFS mounting nuances sometimes cause problems. See Chapter 8 for a discussion of these problems. If the `rexd(8C)` daemon is alive at `serverhost`, an easier way to get the server started (handling all the environment issues) is:

```
rodson> on remoteHost rls_svc &
```

given that your current directory is that of the server code, and NFS can mount it, etc. Sticking these remote execution jobs in the background (using &) may plug things up a bit, using unnecessary process space, but it gives you a handle to kill them without directly accessing the remote machine. If you've lost track of the servers that are running, I have a script named `slay` that gets a lot of exercise when I'm running RPC jobs (see Example 4-10).

Example 4-10. A shell script to kill processes by name: slay

```
#!/bin/csh -f
set pgm=`echo $1 | cut -c1-24`
set DeathTo=`ps g | egrep $pgm | egrep -v egrep | egrep -v $0 | awk '{print $1}'`
#sed could do all that I'll bet, but I never read that Nutshell
echo $DeathTo; kill $DeathTo
```

Commands like `slay rls` or `rsh host slay rls` are quick ways to clean the slate and get the system management people off your back. This script handles one small peculiarity of `ps(1)`. `ps` only gives you 24 characters worth of program name. The name of your server might get chopped off with only the leading 24 characters visible. I used `cut(1)` to truncate the server name. If it is not unique and is the same as some other unrelated program you have running, it will terminate that one, too! A cleaner execution would save the `rsh` PIDs and terminate them as required. For a formal product or delivery, something a little more elegant is required, like starting the servers at boot time along with the myriad of system daemons.

Also notice that the signal sent with `kill` is the default SIGTERM or terminate (15) signal. We didn't use `kill -9 PID` or `kill -KILL PID`, as signal 9 is the SIGKILL signal that cannot be caught by a process. If you do this to an `rsh` process, `rsh` won't have a chance to clean up by terminating the process on the remote host first.

In Chapter 8, I'll cover a number of useful ways to start and control servers plus I'll introduce the ONC RPC utility `rpcinfo(8C)` to get server information.

Real RPC Power Means Using IPC

With a basic understanding of RPC programming behind us, the balance of the book focuses in on the real power of RPC: getting one or more clients talking to one or more servers, potentially at the same time. To get through the supporting examples, especially those dealing with concurrency or windowing systems, you need a working understanding of UNIX interprocess communication mechanisms. You need to know some of the low-level protocol and transport trade-offs that you must make during design. You need to understand some parallel programming paradigms as well. These topics are addressed in Chapter 5.

In this chapter:

• *A Network Proto-col Primer*

• *Adding a Server to the System*

• *An Overview of UNIX Interprocess Communication*

• *Berkeley Sockets*

• *Advanced Socket Programming Issues*

5

UNIX Networking and Interprocess Communication

This chapter covers some basic information about UNIX networking, leading up to the development of an interprocess communication application based on Berkeley sockets. If you are already familiar with UNIX networking, you can skip this chapter after looking over the IPC application in the last section. If you don't know much about TCP/IP networks and the interprocess communication (IPC) tools in UNIX, you might wonder why you need to know this information, given that an RPC API helps to isolate the programmer from the underlying networking mechanisms. Here's why:

• RPC makes *extensive* use of IPC mechanisms. Understanding IPC makes it easier to develop and debug RPC code. If nothing else, understanding IPC aids in your understanding and appreciation for RPC and increases your ability to use it.

• You'll have to use IPC to implement asynchrony, concurrency, and scheduling algorithms within RPC servers and clients. Most of the advanced RPC issues can only be resolved with low-level IPC programming.

• IPC mechanisms alone are enough to implement network applications. In some cases it makes more sense to develop a simple socket-based client/server pair than a full-blown RPC application, especially when services are available locally. We'll develop socket-based applications in this chapter.

As a tool for accessing remote computers, IPC allows access to resources similar to RPC. You can get at another host's processor or its attached peripherals; for example, tape drives, array processors, data acquisition units, etc. Most of the network applications written before RPC were developed with low-level IPC functions. Any application can make use of many powerful features of UNIX and the network using IPC.

As a tool for programming one computer, IPC allows a problem to be broken into processes, which can prove to be a valuable programming abstraction. When you work with processes, as opposed to procedures, you can use UNIX tools for scheduling, multi-tasking, and monitoring execution in a flexible fashion using run-time parameters. The IPC tools found in System V, BSD UNIX, and their derivatives are powerful. BSD provides sockets and daemons with which processes and utilities can interact, either locally or across a network. System V's message structure, shared memory, and semaphores provide other paradigms for coordinating processes and communication.

In this chapter, we begin by talking about the network transports and protocols that are required for two machines to communicate across a network. This is helpful in understanding the design of network servers. Then we cover how to install servers at boot-time that run under the control of the inetd daemon. Finally, we give an overview of the different facilities available in UNIX for interprocess communication and then concentrate on building a simple socket-based IPC application.

A Network Protocol Primer

A TCP/IP network is based on a model that assumes a large number of interconnected networks (the "catenet model"). Gateways and routing are necessary to get on and off the local networks and to facilitate inter-machine communication. A gateway is physically connected to two different networks and serves to assist in routing information between the two networks. A message may have to travel through several other machines, each acting as gateways, to get to its destination.

To convey a message across a network, the program and supporting network services have to:

1. Determine the addresses of the sending and receiving computers.

2. Break the data stream into datagrams.

3. Send the datagrams to the receiving computer.

4. Reassemble the datagrams into a data stream.

In the sections that follow, we will look at how addresses are specified, how datagrams are created, and how the connection is made between two machines.

Internet Addressing

Each destination on a network has a unique Internet address. It is a 32-bit number represented as four separate numbers, each covering 0-255 and expressed in 8-bits. For example, 3.1.4.93 is the Internet address of the gateway where I work. Most people prefer to use the name of a system to identify it. For instance, 3.1.4.93 goes by the name of crdgw1. Names are mapped to Internet numbers in */etc/hosts* or a shared network database equivalent.

My Sun's name is rodson, and it lives at 3.1.5.226. The first two numbers in rodson's and crdgw1's addresses, 3 and 1, denote the *domain*. Both machines reside in the *crd.ge.com* domain. The com represents a primary commercial domain, and ge denotes the General Electric Company. The remaining domain level is left to GE to configure as required. I work at the Corporate R&D center or crd.

There is a (logical) name server at each domain level to allow domains below to change. In other words, instead of fixed lists, there's a hierarchy of machines to check with on the global network to get the latest routing and connectivity information.

You might wonder how an Internet address is used to locate an Ethernet address. The address resolution protocol (ARP), which is actually outside of the Internet protocols, is used for translating Internet addresses into Ethernet addresses. ARP tables typically contain Internet/Ethernet address mappings for machines on your network. If the mapping is not there, the ARP protocol is used to send a request out on the network. It packages them in its own datagrams,which are different from the IP datagrams we'll discuss later. The request is passed from machine to machine, where each is required to see if the information they have can satisfy the request.

Connectionless at the Lowest Level

At the lowest level, network communication is made up of datagrams traveling back and forth. The term *datagram* describes the unit of data sent or received, one at a time, over the network. A datagram comprises a single message. The term *packet* is often used as a synonym, although it implies a physical thing flying around an Ethernet or wire. A datagram can be thought of as data encapsulated in, or surrounded by, headers and trailers.

Because datagrams are sent, and not a data stream, TCP/IP is considered *connectionless* technology. Even though it is called connectionless, an application can remain virtually *connected* to another machine, for example, listening on a pipe. It is possible that datagrams will arrive out of order, or never arrive at all. You have to handle this through higher-level protocols or within your application.

The size of a datagram can greatly affect network performance, yet the size is typically fixed when a transfer is initiated. Actual hardware or software packet size is often a constraint, so packets can range in size from the 1500 or 576 octet (byte) typical of Ethernet to say 128-byte packets when TCP/IP is layered on top of X.25.

Internet Protocols

TCP/IP is a layered set of protocols. From an application's point of view, there are four layers, as shown in Figure 5-1. It pre-dates the OSI model, but they can be correlated. The Internet protocols span the data-link, network, transport, and process layers of the reference model.

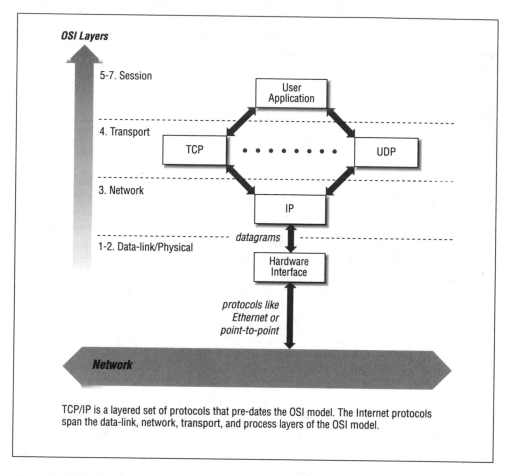

OSI Layers

5-7. Session

User
Application

4. Transport

TCP • • • • • • • • UDP

3. Network

IP

datagrams

1-2. Data-link/Physical

Hardware
Interface

protocols like
Ethernet or
point-to-point

Network

TCP/IP is a layered set of protocols that pre-dates the OSI model. The Internet protocols
span the data-link, network, transport, and process layers of the OSI model.

Figure 5-1. The TCP/IP Internet Protocol suite layers

Since the creation of a standardized network protocol in the 1980s, application
code no longer needs to directly address reliable network communications with
another computer. An application makes calls to transport libraries. Even an RPC
application must do this. When the TCP transport is used, TCP takes responsibility
for making sure commands get through to the other end. If a message is too large
for a single datagram, including headers and trailers, TCP will split (or fragment) it
into multiple datagrams. TCP keeps track of what is sent, and the order it is sent in.
This allows TCP to re-assemble the message upon receipt and retry different pieces
of the message if errors occur. TCP uses datagram checksums to watch for errors.
TCP is called a reliable transport.

Within the Internet protocol suite, one can choose UDP (user datagram protocol) as an alternative to TCP.[†] UDP sends single datagrams. Although it does include checksums, UDP makes no attempt to fragment your messages and resynchronize or reassemble them correctly at the other end. If an error occurs, UDP doesn't save your message, so your application will have to retransmit. No acknowledgment of receipt is built-in as is the case with TCP. UDP is called an unreliable transport.

Moving down the OSI layers at run-time, TCP and UDP call upon the services of IP. Figure 5-1 doesn't show the application talking directly to the IP layer, but it can. Indeed some down-and-dirty applications don't need the TCP or UDP layers. However, since we will be dealing well above the IP layer here, I will generalize.

Like TCP and UDP, IP was put together to alleviate problems common to all network applications. At this lowest software level, the IP routines handle the routing and actual transmission of the datagrams. Typically there is not much to do in most computing environments. There are probably only a couple of gateways to get through. But if your application ventures out onto a wide-area network or possibly Internet, routing and transmission tasks will compound fast. More header information is added to packets, for example, to tell the other computer that it is going to be reconstructed by TCP or UDP; the datagram is then sent and a response anticipated.

Applications Protocols

So far we have described how a stream of data is broken up into datagrams if necessary, sent to another computer, and put back together. What's missing is a way to put this to use. How do you open a connection and log-on to a specified computer, tell it what I/O you want, and then control the communication process? These steps are handled by application protocols that run on top of TCP/IP. TCP/IP routines are called to handle reliable message sending and receipt, with TCP and IP taking care of all the low-level networking details. Application protocols typically treat network connections as a stream of bytes flowing in one direction or the other (or both) like a phone line or terminal.

Connections and Well-known Ports

The first step in any network communication is finding the process you want to communicate with. This is true regardless of whether you are programming with TCP/IP sockets or RPC.

[†] There is also another protocol in the suite, ICMP, but it's not that prevalent and won't be addressed here.

IP assigns a port number to individual conversations. Many are *well-known* in the sense that they are standard port numbers used throughout the network. They might be used to contact daemons that control file transfers, handle remote terminal logins, mail, etc.[†] For example, a machine's file transfer protocol server can be found at port number 21. For an `ftp` session, there's an `ftp` application started on your end, using some random port number (who cares where you live!), and `ftp` attempts to contact port 21 on the specified machine. If successful, port 21 is alive and well with the `ftp` server now listening. *User ports* are allocated at run-time, randomly placed in a number range separate from well-known ports.

A connection is specified by four numbers: the Internet addresses and port numbers at each end. Each datagram assembled has these numbers in it. The IP header contains the Internet addresses, and the TCP header contains the port numbers. To maintain uniqueness, no two connections can have the same four numbers. A problem could only result if two machines were using the same ports for two different instances of an application. With well-known port numbers only available for one end of an application (e.g., like `ftp` servers), the other end is always allocated at run-time. Thus, two connections will get different port numbers.

Once we have established a connection, both ends use some predefined protocol to exchange data and commands. This involves some kind of finite-state machine that starts in a known state on each system. For example, let's look at a mail application that connects to a machine's mail server. First, the mailer sends your machine's name and address. Then it sends a command to denote the beginning of a message, followed by the message itself. When the message has been sent, it sends a " . " in the first column. Both programs understand that the mailer is now going to send more commands.

A file transfer protocol might include two connections: one dedicated to the data transfer, the other left available to monitor long transfers or issue commands, like abort. A remote terminal application typically uses just one connection. When a special character is found in the data stream, the application knows the following character is a command. If you are interested in the details of the protocols, get the relevant Request for Comments (RFC) as described in Appendix A. There are many caveats and special cases both in the specifications and in actual implementations.

Types of Servers

There are two different types of server protocols: connection-oriented and connectionless. When TCP/IP is used over a network, reliable communication can only be guaranteed with the former. There are two different servicing strategies: iterative and concurrent.

[†] See the section, "inetd and Other Lurking Network Daemons," for examples of well-known ports in the */etc/services* file.

Network Transport Selection: UDP or TCP?

The UDP and TCP transports are quite different. The connection-oriented nature of TCP and connectionless nature of UDP, as well as the associated overhead differentiates them. Also, you can look ahead to Figure 5-3 to compare the socket library calls for connected and connectionless communications.

The number of times that a remote procedure gets executed is determined by the protocol. If you execute a remote procedure on top of an unreliable protocol like UDP, you can't be sure whether or not it was executed. The ONC RPC calls that place a UDP-based RPC, perform a number of time-out/retry cycles. If, after several retries, you still fail to receive a reply message, your application can only be sure the remote procedure was executed *zero or more times*. If the remote procedure returned a reply message, the application knows the remote procedure was executed *one or more times*.

The reliability of TCP, on the other hand, means that if a reply message is received, the procedure was executed *exactly once*. If no reply is heard, like UDP, you cannot assume the remote procedure *was not executed*. So if reliability is an issue, as with non-idempotent procedures that affect server state, the connection-oriented nature of TCP can help. If speed is the main goal, the reduced packet and initial protocol overhead of UDP is a better choice.

UDP is a better alternative for most short-winded network applications, like querying a name server or NIS database. It can also be used in a network application that does not cross a router or a gateway where datagram order is due to be mixed-up. The initial UDP overhead is less and headers are smaller, so overall transfer rate is incrementally better. When used beneath RPC, only the first UDP RPC call is significantly faster. After that, the performance advantage of UDP over TCP for RPCs is only incremental.[†] It requires significantly fewer resources at the client to create and maintain UDP connections as compared with TCP. In summary, it makes sense to use UDP when performance is more important than reliability.

The following guidelines can help you choose between the two transports. Use connection-less UDP if:

- Remote procedures are idempotent, meaning they can be executed more than once with no problems.

- Server request messages and client reply messages can each fit completely within one UDP packet (8 KBytes on most machines).

- The server handles multiple clients. UDP is stateless, saving no information about clients. A TCP server is required to keep connections open, with the number of connections limited by operating system resources. The same holds true for a client communicating with multiple servers simultaneously.

---

† ±5% differences according to Sun's RPC development group.

Use the connection-oriented TCP transport if:

- Reliability is paramount.

- Procedures are not idempotent, with accidental execution of remote procedure more than once causing a problem.

- The size of the reply or request exceeds that of one UDP packet.

Iterative and Concurrent Servers

A server that takes a short period of time to render the service, like a time-of-day service, can be performed in the server process. It is called an *iterative* server. A server that might take longer to service the request usually replicates itself (fork(2V)), allowing the parent server to go back to sleep, listening for more client requests. It is called a *concurrent* server. The child server then renders the service and terminates.

In practice, there are also two categories of concurrent servers; those for which more than one instance can be activated at once in multiple processes, and those for which only one server may be run at one time (single process). It is often desired for the sake of performance or data integrity to have only one instance of a certain concurrent service running at the same time.

inetd(8C), the Internet super-server, provides several standard Internet services within itself as iterative services. One of the services gives the time-of-day in machine and human-readable form. Most of the services provided through inetd are concurrent services, driven by the /etc configuration files.

So in all, you could construct one of six types of servers based on protocol (connection-oriented or connectionless) and servicing strategy (iterative or concurrent). This matrix is shown in Figure 5-2.

Note that when performing server/client communication confined to the machine or address, as a rule, local protocols appear reliable regardless of connection type.

Adding a Server to the System

Anyone can manually add an RPC or Internet service to the system. Let's take a look at how to start frequently-used services automatically. Much like adding Internet daemons, the process involves editing some */etc* files, then kicking some supervisory daemons (inetd(8C) and Network Information Service).

The best way to run any network server is through inetd. Most default Internet (and RPC) servers are usually executed through inetd already. We'll look at its configuration file */etc/inetd.conf* in the next section.

RPCGEN as well as RPCGEN.NEW support code generation for inetd compatibility. They also allow you to specify how long the RPC server should stay in

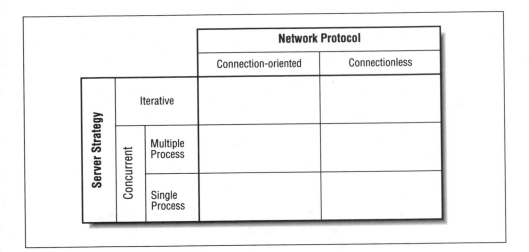

Figure 5-2. Network servers can be one of six different types

memory, listening to its own socket. When told to expire, an RPCGEN service will unregister itself from the portmap and explicitly exit.

If you are interested in a better understanding of how this works or how to add Internet and RPC services to your system, read on. Otherwise, skip to the section, "An Overview of UNIX Interprocess Communication."

inetd and Other Lurking Network Daemons

This section is devoted to understanding the well-established boot-up and Internet service mechanisms. The best way I know of to describe what UNIX is doing in the background is to take a look at the servers or daemons.

Quite often applications are clients calling standard UNIX or Internet servers. For example, to examine some of the root-owned servers ready and waiting for action, enter the following command:

```
ps aux | egrep root
```

You might find servers for mail (sendmail) or printing (lpd):

```
root         1  0.0  0.0   56    0 ?  IW   Jan 21  0:00 /sbin/init -
root         0  0.0  0.0    0    0 ?  D    Jan 21  0:28 swapper
root         2  0.0  0.0    0    0 ?  D    Jan 21  0:00 pagedaemon
root        99  0.0  0.0   40    0 ?  S    Jan 21  1:31 (nfsd)
root        55  0.0  0.0   80    0 ?  IW   Jan 21  0:17 portmap
root        60  0.0  0.0   56    0 ?  IW   Jan 21  0:00 keyserv
root        68  0.0  0.5   48  144 ?  S    Jan 21  4:50 in.routed
root        72  0.0  0.0   24    0 ?  I    Jan 21  0:13 (biod)
root        84  0.0  0.0   64    0 ?  IW   Jan 21  0:00 syslogd
root        92  0.0  0.0  112    0 ?  IW   Jan 21  0:00 /usr/lib/sendmail -bd -q
```

```
root        111  0.0  0.0   96     0  ?   IW   Jan 21   0:00  rpc.lockd
root        106  0.0  0.0   72     0  ?   IW   Jan 21   0:05  rpc.mountd -n
root        116  0.0  0.8  304   240  ?   S    Jan 21   4:36  automount
root        110  0.0  0.0   56     0  ?   IW   Jan 21   0:00  rpc.statd
root        127  0.0  0.0   64     0  ?   IW   Jan 21   0:00  cron
root        132  0.0  0.0   66     0  ?   IW   Jan 21   0:03  inetd
root        135  0.0  0.0   72     0  ?   IW   Jan 21   0:00  /usr/lib/lpd
root        124  0.0  0.1   24    16  ?   S    Jan 21   5:01  update
root       1269  0.0  0.0   56     0  ?   IW   Jan 22   0:00  rpc.rquotad
root      11323  0.0  0.2   48    64  ?   S    21:44    0:00  in.telnetd
bloomer   11396  0.0  0.9  120   288  q2 S    22:07    0:00  egrep root
```

Most root daemons are initiated when you boot-up the machine. The `IW` status indicates that they have been idle for more than 20 seconds and swapped-out.

inetd Started at Boot-time

Near the tail end of the boot procedure, the UNIX operating system invokes `init(8)`. By default, `init` runs the */etc/rc.boot* shell script to check and repair the file system and then it proceeds to run the */etc/rc* and */etc/rc.local* to begin multi-user operation.[†]

The Internet super-server daemon, `inetd(8C)`, is started from */etc/rc*. `inetd` is in charge of managing all the requests made of your machine for Internet services such as `rexec(3N)`, `rex(3R)`, `ping(8C)`, etc. `inetd` was developed for BSD 4.3 to avoid having lots of socket and I/O set-up code duplicated within each network service. Prior to BSD 4.3, each server sat waiting on its own socket. Now `inetd` opens and binds a socket to a port on behalf of each interested server and listens to all of them for requests with one big `select(2)`. If a request arrives, `inetd` forks a child process which takes over communications to perform the associated service. The child process executes the server program, sends the results and exits (as necessary). During this time, `inetd` has been monitoring the service sockets for connection requests.

`inetd(8C)` is a common front-end for servers, handling the `select()` and connection-request processing. It awakes or restarts a service, passing it `stdin` and `stdout` file descriptors for network I/O through the socket. While it does reduce server resource consumption, it often requires a forked process to make an `execl(3V)` call that brings an expired server executable back into memory from the file system. In the old days, the program was always loaded and ready to go.

`rusers` is a classic example of how `inetd`-managed RPC servers have replaced older services. `rwhod(8C)`, the service daemon for `rwho(1C)`, is started by itself (if at all) in one of the */etc/rc* family of scripts. Its functionality has been superseded by `rusers(1C)`, an RPC-based utility that can see through gateways. The related `rusersd(8C)` daemon is now started under `inetd`. It doesn't consume as much

---

† `init(8)` can be directed to begin single-user operation instead, giving the superuser a shell on the console.

memory as the old `rwhod`, nor is it prone to causing broadcast storms. `rwhod` could cripple large networks by starting numerous, simultaneous broadcast queries.

Using inetd Requires No Code Changes

Recall that RPCGEN will generate the necessary server stub code to permit the service to be handled by `inetd()`. If you use RPCGEN, you don't need to make any changes to your portion of the server (or client) application. What RPCGEN does is alter the server transport-creation calls to reflect the fact that `inetd` will pass the socket as file descriptor 0.

```
transp = svcudp_create(0);       /* for UDP */
transp = svctcp_create(0,0,0);   /* for TCP */
transp = svcfd_create(0,0,0);    /* for connected TCP sockets */
```

Services are already registered with the portmapper by `inetd`, so the registration calls now end with a 0 argument:

```
svc_register(transp, PROGNUM, VERSNUM, service, 0);
```

This same stub as generated by RPCGEN with the `-I` flag can be started as any other server from the command line. The stub is smart enough to see who or how it was started, using `syslog()` if it is an `inetd` server, or else acting like a standard I/O server.

Installing a Server Yourself

The above approach of altering */etc* files is handy for system services and promotes clean process management. Only the `root` login is authorized to configure `inetd` and make changes to global services database (*/etc* files or NIS). Every time something changes, access to `root` is needed, and that's not always practical.

As a development alternative, any user can register and provide non-`inetd` services to the network (socket- or RPC-based). If your final application must register and unregister services dynamically, this is the only alternative. Socket-based servers added by users (not at well-known ports) aren't readily advertised to the network. RPC-based servers added by users are listed in the server host's portmap. Interested clients search these databases for the presence of the servers. This method makes RPC server development easier because `root` isn't required (no */etc* files to change) and services are advertised as opposed to being well-known.

Keep in mind that RPCGEN generates all the `inetd` interface code. When your application is stable, install it under `inetd` to conserve resources and avoid any manual starting and stopping of services.

A Digression on Remote Execution Daemons

At the highest command-line level, Berkeley UNIX gives you two socket-based servers to execute commands remotely: `rshd(8C)` and `rexecd(8C)`. You can access these through the command-line client rsh(1C) or the C code client rexec(3N), respectively.

rexec() returns a stream to a remote command, using the rexecd remote execution server. This server does authentication based on user names and encrypted passwords, then provides remote execution facilities. It is usually invoked as needed by inetd. The rsh utility behaves similarly from the command line, providing remote execution facilities with authentication based on privileged ports through the rshd server. An alternative to rshd and rexecd is the BSD 4.3 user-contributed software shell that can distribute tasks among machines, depending upon load.

rex(3R), the RPC-based remote execution protocol, is accessed with on(1C) at the command line or may be accessed from C by following the protocol specified in */usr/include/rpcsvc/rex.[xh]*. Requests are serviced by the rexd(8C) daemon. The actual */usr/etc/rpc.rexd* daemon is typically started by inetd at boot-time. Only recently has this daemon performed any authentication.

Configuring inetd

/etc/inetd.conf is the default configuration file read by the inetd daemon. It lists a number of network services, some of which are still socket-based as specified in */etc/services* and some are RPC-based as specified in */etc/rpc*. Each entry in */etc/inetd.conf* has the following format:

```
{ service-name    socket-type    protocol    wait-status    user
server pathname    server arguments }
```

The service-name for an Internet TCP/IP service is described in */etc/services*. This file has the following format:

```
service-name    port/protocol    aliases
```

For each named service, you specify port/protocol, the port number and transport through which the service is provided, and aliases, a list of alternative names the service may go by. A sample */etc/services* entry might be:

```
hostnames 101/tcp  hostname # usually to sri-nic
sunrpc    111/udp
```

At the end of this section is an annotated excerpt from */etc/services* which is included to help TCP/IP service implementors.

RPC service-names are denoted in the */etc/rpc* file with entries of the form as follows:

```
rpc-program-server    rpc-program-number    aliases
```

Sample */etc/rpc* entries might look like:

```
portmapper    100000    portmap sunrpc
pcnfsd        150001    # the PC-NFS daemon
```

The remaining fields for */etc/inetd.conf* are as follows:

socket-types   Supported by inetd are sockets using stream or dgram transports.

protocol   Either tcp or udp. When the socket is being listened to by an RPC server, prefix the transport specification with an rpc/.

wait-status   Specifies whether or not inetd should wait for any active requests to that service to be fulfilled before it starts another child process.

server-program Specifies where inetd can find the executable to be used by the child process, passing it the server-arguments.

Sample */etc/inetd.conf* entries are:

```
shell    stream    tcp       nowait   root   /usr/etc/in.rshdin.rshd
exec     stream    tcp       nowait   root   /usr/etc/in.rexecdin.rexecd
talk     dgram     udp       wait     root   /usr/etc/in.talkdin.talkd
rstatd/2-4dgram   rpc/udp   wait     root   /usr/etc/rpc.rstatdrpc.rstatd
ypupdated/1 stream rpc/tcp  wait     root   /usr/etc/rpc.ypupdated\
                                            rpc.ypupdated
```

Sample /etc/inetd.conf, /etc/services, and /etc/rpc

Let's examine the relevant entries of an */etc/inetd.conf* configuration file from a Sun SPARCstation 1+ running SunOS 4.1. in.ftpd(8C) and in.telnetd(8C) are the ftp(1C) and telnet(1C) daemons managed by inetd. These are standard Internet services, available under most UNIX implementations.

```
ftp      stream    tcp    nowait    root    /usr/etc/in.ftpd     in.ftpd
telnet   stream    tcp    nowait    root    /usr/etc/in.telnetd  in.telnetd
```

in.tnamed(8C) handles an outdated name server protocol, kept here for compatibility.

```
name     dgram     udp    wait      root    /usr/etc/in.tnamed   in.tnamed
```

Next are the BSD protocols for remote shells, logins, execution, biff(1) mail notification, and terminal conversation, respectively.

```
shell    stream    tcp    nowait    root    /usr/etc/in.rshd     in.rshd
login    stream    tcp    nowait    root    /usr/etc/in.rlogind  in.rlogind
exec     stream    tcp    nowait    root    /usr/etc/in.rexecd   in.rexecd
comsat   dgram     udp    wait      root    /usr/etc/in.comsat   in.comsat
talk     dgram     udp    wait      root    /usr/etc/in.talkd    in.talkd
```

The uucp(1C) daemon manages UNIX-to-UNIX copy protocol.

```
uucp     stream    tcp    nowait    root    /usr/etc/in.uucpd    in.uucpd
```

tftp(1C) is the trivial (low-level, minimal-function) baseline version of ftp() , found on just about any machine that claims to communicate over a network. Its primary use here is for booting.

```
tftp     dgram    udp    wait    root    /usr/etc/in.tftpd \
         in.tftpd -s /tftpboot
```

finger(1) supports the server side of the RFC-742 remote information protocol. If enabled, systat(8C) and netstat(8C) give potentially dangerous information to outsiders with regards to system and network status, so be careful.

```
finger    stream  tcp    nowait  nobody  /usr/etc/in.fingerd in.fingerd
#systat   stream  tcp    nowait  root    /usr/bin/ps         ps -auwwx
#netstat  stream  tcp    nowait  root    /usr/ucb/netstat    netstat -f inet
```

Next are the time services, one on each TCP and UDP, used for synchronization.

```
time      stream  tcp    nowait  root    internal
time      dgram   udp    wait    root    internal
```

Next are a number of RPC-based servers. Notice that database updating with rpc.ypupdated and mountd automounting are commented-out and independently started from the */etc/rc.local* boot-script along with portmap. The status and user information daemons below are not using secure RPC.

```
#mountd/1   dgram rpc/udp wait    root /usr/etc/rpc.mountd    rpc.mountd
#ypupdated/1      stream    rpc/tcp    wait root \
            /usr/etc/rpc.ypupdated rpc.ypupdated
rquotad/1   dgram  rpc/udp wait    root /usr/etc/rpc.rquotad  rpc.rquotad
rstatd/2-4  dgram  rpc/udp wait    root /usr/etc/rpc.rstatd   rpc.rstatd
rusersd/1-2 dgram  rpc/udp wait    root /usr/etc/rpc.rusersd  rpc.rusersd
walld/1     dgram  rpc/udp wait    root /usr/etc/rpc.rwalld   rpc.rwalld
```

The RPC one-way packet spraying tool, spray(8C), is useful for testing the quality of a remote link.

```
sprayd/1    dgram    rpc/udp    wait    root    /usr/etc/rpc.sprayd rpc.sprayd
```

In this file, there's an interesting RPC service, rpc.cmsd(1), which is run for the Open Look calendar management tool, cm(1).

```
100068/2  dgram  rpc/udp wait  root/usr/openwin/bin/xview/rpc.cmsd \
          rpc.cmsd
```

Many people disable the rexd(8C) remote execution server as old versions do no authentication. The difference between rexd and rexecd(8C) is that the former honors one request at a time (wait) while the latter honors multiple simultaneous requests (nowait).

```
#rexd/1     stream    rpc/tcp    wait root /usr/etc/rpc.rexd    rpc.rexd
```

Transport Layer Interface (TLI) services will be added as they become available. I left out some superfluous server entries used for network testing.

Now let's look at an */etc/services* file that goes with the preceding */etc/inetd.conf* file.

```
# Network services, Internet style
# This file is never consulted when the NIS is running.
# NIS databases are created from this and other /etc ASCII files.
tcpmux          1/tcp                           # rfc-1078
systat          11/tcp          users
netstat         15/tcp
ftp-data        20/tcp
ftp             21/tcp
telnet          23/tcp
smtp            25/tcp          mail
time            37/tcp          timserver
time            37/udp          timserver
name            42/udp          nameserver
whois           43/tcp          nicname         # usually to sri-nic
domain          53/udp
domain          53/tcp
hostnames       101/tcp         hostname        # usually to sri-nic
sunrpc          111/udp
sunrpc          111/tcp
#
# Host specific functions
#
tftp            69/udp
rje             77/tcp
finger          79/tcp
link            87/tcp          ttylink
supdup          95/tcp
iso-tsap        102/tcp
x400            103/tcp                         # ISO Mail
x400-snd        104/tcp
csnet-ns        105/tcp
pop-2           109/tcp                         # Post Office
uucp-path       117/tcp
nntp            119/tcp         usenet          # Network News Transfer
ntp             123/tcp                         # Network Time Protocol
NeWS            144/tcp         news            # Window System
#
# UNIX specific services, these are NOT officially assigned
#
exec            512/tcp
login           513/tcp
shell           514/tcp         cmd             # no passwords used
printer         515/tcp         spooler         # line printer spooler
courier         530/tcp         rpc             # experimental
uucp            540/tcp         uucpd           # uucp daemon
biff            512/udp         comsat
who             513/udp         whod
syslog          514/udp
talk            517/udp
route           520/udp         router routed
new-rwho        550/udp         new-who         # experimental
rmonitor        560/udp         rmonitord       # experimental
monitor         561/udp                         # experimental
pcserver        600/tcp                         # ECD Integrated PC board srvr
cadlock         845/udp                         # cadence license server
cadlock         1017/udp                        # cadence license server
```

```
ingreslock    1524/tcp
ims_server    2113/tcp              # IMS logic master
guru          2050/tcp              # Alida, Inc (guru daemons)
gds_db        3050/tcp              # interbase (Ray&Bruce)
license       1700/tcp              # Matlab license server
```

The last eight entries are site-specific, added manually by `root`. Take, for example, the Matlab floating license monitor that appears as the last entry. When someone attempts to start a Matlab executable, it first checks in with the floating license administrator using TCP at port number 1700. If the server says too many copies are already running, the user is asked to try again later.[†]

If you declared a new RPC service in */etc/inetd.conf*, you must mention it in the */etc/rpc* file. Here's a compatible sample:

```
portmapper       100000    portmap sunrpc
rstatd           100001    rstat rup perfmeter
rusersd          100002    rusers
nfs              100003    nfsprog
ypserv           100004    ypprog
mountd           100005    mount showmount
ypbind           100007
walld            100008    rwall shutdown
yppasswdd        100009    yppasswd
etherstatd       100010    etherstat
rquotad          100011    rquotaprog quota rquota
sprayd           100012    spray
3270_mapper      100013    # it's scary, but we must talk to IBMs
rje_mapper       100014
selection_svc    100015    selnsvc
database_svc     100016
rexd             100017    rex
alis             100018
sched            100019
llockmgr         100020
nlockmgr         100021
x25.inr          100022
statmon          100023
status           100024
bootparam        100026
ypupdated        100028    ypupdate
keyserv          100029    keyserver
sunlink_mapper   100033
tfsd             100037
nsed             100038
nsemntd          100039
showfhd          100043    showfh
ypxfrd           100069    ypxfr
pcnfsd           150001
```

Remember if you aim to make the service available throughout a domain, you must rebuild the `dbm(3X)` files in */var/yp* with `ypmake(3N)`. NIS is told to update its internal databases by manual (`yppush(8)`) or automatic execution of

---

[†] I wish the license server would tell me who the hog is that has 10 copies checked out at once, so I could screw up his server's portmap.

`yp_update(3N)`. If you need to alert any `inetd` servers, send them a `SIGHUP` signal to re-read the configuration file.

If you modify a configuration file, you can force a currently running inetd daemon to re-read it by sending it a SIGHUP signal with something like `kill -1 PID` or `kill -HUP PID`, where PID is the process ID of the running inetd daemon.

An Overview of UNIX Interprocess Communication

There are several ways to communicate between processes, either locally or on different networked machines. The options available to UNIX programmers include the following application program interfaces (API):

- Pipes and FIFOs.

- System V Release 3.0 IPCs—message queues, semaphores, and shared memory.

- Berkeley BSD sockets.

- System V Release 4.0 Transport Layer Interface (TLI).

In general, a model for communication between two different processes located on a network requires five things to facilitate any IPC:

- Protocol.

- Local address.

- Local process.

- Remote address.

- Remote process.

First, the protocol must be agreed upon before a communication channel can be established at either end. The local process then needs to attach itself to a local memory address. The remote process needs to do the same in its memory space. In the end, the bytes from one process are being exchanged or shared with another. Communication can be carried out when the two addresses are known, usually as coordinated through the UNIX kernel or other external register and look-up process.

Each IPC API accomplishes the same tasks in a little different fashion. Berkeley sockets are the dominant IPC API today. However, before we concentrate on sockets, let's consider the broad class of IPC APIs you'll find under UNIX.

Pipes and FIFOs

Pipes are uni-directional interprocess channels, accessed by integer socket descriptors. They are analogous to file descriptors. One call to `pipe(2V)` establishes a one-way channel; a descriptor is open for reading with `read(2V)` at one end, and one is open for writing with write(2V) at the other. The real utility of a pipe is when the ends of it are connected to different processes. At the command line, you tie together commands with pipe (|).

FIFOs (first in, first out) are similar to the one-way pipe, but have names associated with them, hence the term *named-pipes*. Don't be confused by the term FIFO; pipes are really FIFOs, also. It is better to stick with named-pipes. The naming scheme allows an external process to find and access both ends of a pipe. In System V, named-pipes are actually file descriptors with read and write ends. Named-pipes are used within the print spooler; but you won't find them in unadorned BSD 4.3.

Named-pipes are created with a mknode(8) call and externally accessed with open(2V). Like pipes, named-pipes can also be created from the command line:

    /etc/mknod name

A trailing p argument causes the creation of a pipe. c and b are used by the super-user to create special character- and block-type device files.

The limitation of named-pipes, implied by the fact that ends are really file descriptors pointing at the same file, is that they can only act as an IPC tool if processes (e.g., client and server) share a common file system. Sharing a file system is pretty straightforward if they share the same kernel, but it might depend on a remote procedure calling mechanism to implement a distributed or networked file system. A similar argument holds for pipes. A (pipe) descriptor means nothing unless the processes share the same kernel. Both pipes and named-pipes are one-way, as bi-directional communication requires two different logical channels.

On the up side, both pipes and named-pipes are simple to use. They are accessed on either end with standard I/O library calls. A pipe() system call opens a pipe and returns an integer descriptor; fdopen(3V) and close(2) manipulate the descriptor. Since a named-pipe includes a filename, it can be opened with a high-level fopen(3V) and closed with fclose(3V). I suggest that when you have some local IPCs to do, you use these calls.

Message Queues, Semaphores, and Shared Memory

Pipes and FIFOs both work on a stream communication model; that is, raw bytes flow back and forth with no concept of packaging. The next higher level of intelligence is a message queue.

Messages are passed through (file) descriptors, for example, as with pipes or FIFOs. Messages are defined by a type identifier, length, and the actual message data. The msgget(2) system call is used at both client and server ends to create a usable channel. Data is received with msgrcv(2) and sent with msgsnd(2). msgctl(2) provides a number of control mechanisms for message queues. A number of send and receive messages may also be queued-up, transparent to the user, to allow for buffered, asynchronous message exchanges. Message queues provide a means to define an elegant communication scheme between processes, which is useful when more than just raw data is exchanged.

Semaphores are a synchronization agent. They aren't useful for the exchange of large amounts of data as is the case with pipes, FIFOs, and message queues. As found in System V, semaphores are an atomic test-and-set routine that allows a process to access status flags in memory, usually to signal another process. Semaphores are commonly used to signify the busy status of a resource like a file or a piece of hardware.

Pipes, FIFOs, and message queues all require the UNIX kernel to make potentially multiple copies of the data sent and received at either end. Shared memory provides a way to reduce temporary storage overhead. By letting processes share memory segments, copying is eliminated. Semaphores are used to coordinate data sharing across multiple processes. Lightweight process thread libraries, discussed later in the book, typically use shared memory and semaphores for communications, scheduling, and resource sharing between multiple (concurrent) threads of local execution.

Berkeley Sockets and System V TLI

Berkeley sockets and System V TLI are becoming the two most prevalent network IPC APIs. Berkeley sockets (as found in BSD 4.3) will be treated in detail in a separate section. The Transport Layer Interface first appeared in Release 3.0 of System V in 1986. Before this, the only real network programming option was Berkeley sockets. TLI provides an interface to the ISO transport layer, modeled after the ISO Transport Service Definition. It uses the Network Services Library, or the `-lnsl_s` link flag.

Sockets and TLI are not that different from a programmer's perspective, so most of what will be said about sockets applies to TLI. Most RPC schemes are built on one or the other API, with the only major difference being that with TLI RPC, transport decisions can be made at run-time.

Data Representation or Byte Ordering

When you build an RPC application, XDR isolates your network application from the differences in data representations across machines. It is handled consistently and elegantly below the application. If you write a network IPC application, you must isolate both sides of the network application from byte order issues. Both incoming and outgoing data must be explicitly converted to *network order*—or most significant byte first. Different processors store numbers in different order and formats. The following functions provide a variety of conversions:

`ntohs(3N)`   Convert network to host short-integer.

`ntohl(3N)`   Convert network to host long-integer.

htons(3N)   Convert host to network short-integer.

htonl(3N)   Convert host to network long-integer.

For example, before you send a short integer out through a network IPC, you should first pass it through the htons() filter function:

```
u_short is;
is = htons(is);
your_network_write_routine(ipc_w_descriptor, &is, sizeof(is));
```

Any incoming short integers should be sanitized as follows:

```
your_network_read_routine(ipc_r_descriptor, &is, sizeof(is));
is = ntohs(is);
```

You should get in the habit of using the conversion filters, even if you know the networked machines are compatible. Take a look in the <netinet/in.h> include file and you'll probably find the macros that actually do the work. On Motorola or SPARC processors, the macros are empty as network order is the same as host order. On Intel (e.g., 80386) processors, the macros swap byte order. In other words, if you call them and they are not needed, the compiler will remove them. It pays to be safe, making it possible for future heterogeneous clients and servers to work without revision.

Also worth thinking about is using byte-oriented, memory-access functions instead of operations that depend on processor-specific addressing, like that used for string manipulation. Below are the BSD 4.3 routines:

bcopy(3)   Copy a string of specified length (no NULL-termination assumed).

bcmp(3)   Compare byte by byte, again no NULL-termination assumed.

bzero(3)   Write a specified number of NULLs in memory.

System V has equivalent memory(3) functions: memcpy(3), memcmp(3), and memset(3).

You should also be aware of the chance that your machines may use different dialects at other levels like ASCII characters versus EBCDIC, or a wide choice of floating-point formats. For example, floating-point numbers cannot be shared between DEC and Sun processors unless you coerce or convert them.

Retrieving Host, Network, and Address Information

A server needs to establish its address, making its location and address available to the client once it is started. Getting this information is made easier by several system procedures. The gethost...(3N) family of network functions let a client call NIS or slurp-up its /etc/hosts file and format entries into the ever popular struct hostent (see <netinet/netdb.h>).

gethostent(3N)   Get this host's entry.

gethostbyaddr(3N)   Get a host's entry by address.

gethostbyname(3N)   Get a host's entry by name.

gethostname(2)   Can also come in handy to get your name.

The hostent structure is:

```
struct     hostent {
   char *h_name;                /* official name of host */
   char **h_aliases;            /* alias names this host uses */
   int  h_addrtype;             /* address type - Internet */
   int  h_length;               /* length of address */
   char **h_addr_list;          /* list of addresses from name server */
};
```

The h_aliases element is a zero-terminated array of alternate names for the host. An Internet address is currently returned in the h_addr_list. It is a pointer to a list of network addresses for the named host, each in network byte order.

On the server end, the getserv... (3N) routines are available to sift through the network services data base, */etc/services*, or to call NIS.

getservent(3N)   Get this service entry.

getservbyport(3N)   Get a service attached to a certain port.

getservbyname(3N)   Get a service by its name.

Each of these returns a pointer to a servent structure (again see <netinet/netdb.h>) with the following elements, as found in database entries:

```
struct servent {
    char *s_name;                /* official name of service */
    char **s_aliases;            /* alias list */
    int  s_port;                 /* port service resides at */
    char *s_proto;               /* protocol to use */
};
```

The alias list is like that in struct hostent. The s_port element is also in network short byte order. s_proto specifies the name of the protocol that must be used when communicating with the service.

There are also a number of routines to access the */etc/protocols* file (or the NIS server). getprotoent(3N) retrieves entries from this file.

By using these routines within both the client and server applications, all the information we need for the five-piece association will soon be available. All we have to do is get the client and server (local and remote) communication points or addresses nailed down. We will do that by opening sockets.

Command-line NIS Utilities

If you are running ONC NIS on your network, the above calls are actually consulting an NIS server database. In addition, there are a few command-line utilities worth mentioning. ypwhich(1) is a utility to ask your local NIS server to report the host on which it is running or dump the map master. The map master is a cross-reference of all the network information controlled by NIS. In this example, the NIS server for my machine rodson is running on alydar. The map master details eight maps. Each map contains information compiled from the appropriately-named /etc files using ypmake(1).

```
rodson> ypwhich
alydar
rodson> ypwhich -x
Use "passwd" for map "passwd.byname"
Use "group" for map "group.byname"
Use "networks" for map "networks.byaddr"
Use "hosts" for map "hosts.byaddr"
Use "protocols" for map "protocols.bynumber"
Use "services" for map "services.byname"
Use "aliases" for map "mail.aliases"
Use "ethers" for map "ethers.byname"
```

If you wanted to take a look at one or more keys stored in a particular NIS map, use ypmatch(1). Let's take a look at the addresses of two machines I make frequent reference to, both of which reside in the same NIS domain.

```
rodson> ypmatch rodson cortex hosts
3.1.5.226        rodson
J.1.0.5J         cortex
```

Getting ONC RPC Information

There are a few utilities to read the ASCII file /etc/rpc. As shown earlier, this file contains entries detailing service name, number, and any aliases the server might go by. The functions provided to access this file are summarized in this section. Information about starting and registering ONC RPC servers is kept in other ASCII files in /etc. Zero or NULL pointers are returned if these functions fail. We won't use these functions much in this book because consulting the portmapper is a better way to determine what services are running and where.

getrpcent(3N) reads the next entry in /etc/rpc, opening the file if necessary. Its format is:

```
#include <netdb.h>
struct rpcent *getrpcent();
```

getrpcbyname(3N) and getrpcbynumber(3N) search from the beginning of /etc/rpc until a matching RPC program name or number is found. NULL is returned if end-of-file is encountered during the search.

```
struct rpcent *getrpcbyname(name);
char *name;
```

```
struct rpcent *getrpcbynumber(number);
int number;
```

The structure returned contains the matching information found in _/etc/rpc_.

```
struct rpcent {
      char *r_name;                 /* name of this RPC program */
      char **r_aliases;             /* name alias list, NULL-terminated */
      long r_number;                /* service RPC program number */
};
```

Any number of RPC service procedures may share an RPC program name and its aliases. RPC programs are not typically accessed by their names but rather by their numbers (there is usually a unique, one-to-one mapping between names and numbers).

setrpcent(3N) opens _/etc/rpc_ with the pointer at the top of the file.

```
int setrpcent (stayopen);
int stayopen;
```

If the stayopen flag is non-zero, the _/etc/rpc_ database will be left open after calls to any of the getrpc...(3N) functions mentioned in this section.

Finally, endrpcent(3N) closes the file.

```
int endrpcent ();
```

Berkeley Sockets

Now that we know where the client and server process ports are, we must open a communication channel. The workhorse of network IPC tools today is Berkeley sockets. A socket is an IPC channel with its endpoints described by descriptors. Once connected, processes can read and write through these communication channels.

Before we delve into how to establish and use a socket between processes, let's not forget the real reason for investigating any of this. Most RPC systems are based on such IPCs. One of the goals of a good RPC API is to isolate you from all the networking issues we are about to talk about. In reality, an API can only speed up code generation. My experience has been that understanding the underlying technology leads to writing better code, faster, with fewer hidden or hard to find errors. And when you do get the strange hidden errors (like host: connection refused) you know where to start looking. So, stick with me. Programmers interested in integrating socket applications or windowing systems with RPC should pay special attention to socket maintenance and I/O functions.

The process of opening sockets and communicating between processes is basically:

1. **server**—establish a socket and listen at it for requests.

2. **client**—if undefined, determine the server host and port address.

3. **client**—establish a socket and use it to reach the server to issue a request.

4. **server**—honor the client's request then return to listening.

The process is pretty much the same regardless of protocol used (e.g., TCP or UDP) or whether the socket is addressed in terms of a file system or across the network. There is a finite number of socket-level system calls needed to maintain processes communication.

In Figure 5-3, the left-hand side illustrates the socket system calls used during a connection-oriented client/server communication, for example when using the TCP transport. The right-hand side shows a connectionless transaction, for example, when using the UDP transport.

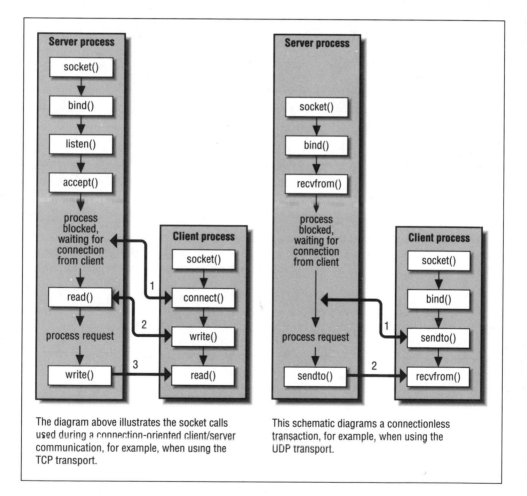

The diagram above illustrates the socket calls used during a connection-oriented client/server communication, for example, when using the TCP transport.

This schematic diagrams a connectionless transaction, for example, when using the UDP transport.

Figure 5-3. Connection-oriented (left) and connectionless (right) IPC protocols

A connection-oriented server gets a socket descriptor from the kernel with `socket(2)`, binding it to a local address (with `bind(2)`), then listens to it with `listen(2)`, accepting or denying client requests. Once accepted, a request is read in, evaluated, then results are written back to the client. The client had created a socket on its end, connected to the server, and then exchanged data accordingly.

A connectionless communication scheme posts requests and listens for responses, without the formality of defining a connection with `listen(2)` at the server side or `connect(2)` at the client side. It uses `read(2V)` and `write(2V)` calls similar to the connected scenario.

Yeah, But How Do I Use Sockets?

There are several UNIX system calls available to establish and configure sockets:

`accept(2)`	Accept a connection on a socket.
`bind(2)`	Bind a name to a socket.
`close(2)`	Close an end point descriptor.
`connect(2)`	Initiate a connection on a socket.
`getsockname(2)`	Get socket name.
`getsockopt(2)`	Get options on sockets.
`setsockopt(2)`	Set options on sockets.
`listen(2)`	Listen for connections on a socket.
`socket(2)`	Create an end point for communication.
`socketpair(2)`	Create a pair of connected sockets—good for local process communication.

To get the data in and out of the ends of a socket, use the following if connection-oriented:

`read(2V)` or `send(2)` Send a message out a connected socket.

`write(2V)` or `recv(2)` Retrieve a message from a connected socket.

There is a potential problem with these calls. The OS will try to send/receive the amount of data you specify, and if it's not there, or if the OS can't send the data all at once, `read()` and `write()` will return with only a portion of the job done. There are a couple of ways to fix this problem. One is to repeat the command until all the specified bytes have been sent or received; the other is to set up the socket to block if the complete package can't be handled. We'll detail the workarounds in the section, "Advanced Socket Programming Issues."

To get the data in and out of the ends of a connectionless socket, use the following functions:

sendto(2) or sendmsg(2)   Send a message through a connectionless socket.

recvfrom(2) or recvmsg(2)   Receive a message through a connection-less socket.

In actuality, the above four routines can be used for sockets in any state, connection-oriented or connectionless. Because a socket is really an I/O point with a descriptor, read() and write() are the most straightforward, reliable way to handle connected communications.

In addition, fcntl(2V) allows you to manipulate socket descriptors as you do files; see <sys/filio.h> and fcntl(5) for the available options. setsockopt(2) also gives you access to a number of specialized I/O controls, as listed in <sys/sockio.h>. I didn't mention bindresvport(2), a superuser call that allows you to bind a socket to a privileged IP port in the range 0-1023. Typically, any of the ports you find in the */etc/services* file are ports that users cannot bind to from their own applications. Users cannot bind to the ports associated with servers in */etc/inetd.conf* as this mixture of RPC and Internet daemons gets started first, and no one else can bind to an active port.

To establish your own well-known service, you can as superuser advertise it to the rest of the world by defining it in every client's */etc/inetd.conf.* A socket-based server is further defined in */etc/services* and RPC-based servers in */etc/rpc* files. This information is distributed via NIS if running. As a lowly user, you can register your service with a local portmap but cannot make it well-known, leaving it to clients to know or find the service (via broadcast or repeated connection tries).

Socket Examples

In this section we will look at three client/server pairs that demonstrate:

1. UNIX domain addressing.

2. Internet domain addressing using TCP.

3. Internet domain addressing and UDP.

The first two are examples of using a connection-oriented protocol and the last one uses a connectionless protocol.

The actual service returns the contents of the directory specified on the command line. Given that one of these servers is started on a machine described in your */etc* network database files, the associated client will ask for directory contents, then both server and client will gracefully exit. The server port address will be compiled into the client/server pair. Thus, we will not modify */etc* files to make the server known to all. The ONC RPC daemons do not need to be running for these examples.

We'll re-use the `read_dir()` function shown in Example 3-2. It takes the name of a directory, and returns the names of the files contained. It is used by all three of the socket servers developed in this chapter. Like the high- and low-level RPC version, we will drop the listing in the same 8K byte array `dir` that we got the request parameter in.

Connection-oriented, UNIX Domain Addressing

Let's develop a server to communicate with clients on the same machine; *AF_UNIXserver.c* uses UNIX domain addressing. To do UNIX domain addressing, you must include `<sys/un.h>`. The declarations for *AF_UNIXserver.c* are shown in Example 5-1 and we'll present the rest of the code as a succession of fragments.

Example 5-1. AF_UNIXserver.c – UNIX domain socket server

```
#include <stdio.h>
#include <string.h>
#include <sys/types.h>
#include <sys/socket.h>
#include <sys/un.h>
#define DIRSIZE 8192

main()
{
        char    dir[DIRSIZE];    /* used for incoming dir name,
                                  * and outgoing data */
        int     sd, sd_current;  /* socket descriptors */
        struct sockaddr_un sin;  /* socket address stuff */
```

First we use a `socket()` call to create a file descriptor that refers to the server end of an IPC channel:

```
/* get a UNIX domain AF_UNIX reliable socket */
        strcpy(sin.sun_path, "./socket"); /* name the actual file used */
        if ((sd = socket(AF_UNIX, SOCK_STREAM, 0)) == -1) {
                perror("socket");
                exit(1);
        }
```

Note that we are using the `sockaddr_un` structure as defined in the UNIX-domain specific `<sys/un.h>` include file. AF_UNIX tells `socket()` that we want a UNIX domain-addressed socket, with SOCK_STREAM or stream-type protocol. We'll take a look at AF_INET Internet addressing and SOCK_DGRAM protocol later.

Next the `bind(2)` command is used to bind the local address to the socket. The server must have a point at which to listen for requests.

```
/* bind the socket to the socket filename ./socket */
        if (bind(sd, &sin, sizeof(sin)) == -1) {
                perror("bind");
                exit(1);
        }
```

listen(2) is then used to let the OS know that there is some process at this socket prepared to receive data from a client request.

```
/* make available the fact that we are listening */
        if (listen(sd, 5) == -1) {
                perror("listen");
                exit(1);
        }
```

The second listen() parameter defines the size of the queue for incoming requests. Here the backlog parameter is set to 5, which is currently the maximum. This allows as many as 5 outstanding requests at that socket to remain unanswered before client connect(2) requests will return with the error ECONNREFUSED.

accept(2) is used by the server to manage requests. It can deal with a queue of client requests. accept() pops the first one off, and creates a new file descriptor, sd_current, that also points at the socket. Duplication of descriptors becomes useful if the service was compute-intensive, and the server needs to handle multiple concurrent client requests. You could fork-off here, thereby creating a copy of the descriptor in a child process. We don't have much to do in this iterative server (directory reading), so we don't use fork.

```
/* wait for a client to talk to us */
        if ((sd_current = accept(sd, 0, 0)) == -1) {
                perror("accept");
                exit(1);
        }
```

Notice that we didn't retrieve the address of the client, available in the second two fields of accept(). It can be useful. The server must now retrieve the actual request message: the directory name. I re-used the dir[] vector just for brevity. The size of the message transfer is set at both ends and will cause an error if the associated addresses and counts are not compliant. As the application is connection-oriented, I could have used read(), but I might have to do some retries to wait for sizeof(dir) bytes, so I use recv().

```
/* get a message from the client */
if (recv(sd_current, dir, sizeof(dir), 0) == -1) {
        perror("recv");
        exit(1);
}
```

The server then needs to respond, as the client is waiting. Note again that with a connection-oriented protocol we could use just about any output routine, but I choose send(2) here. The size of the transfer is by design 8K bytes. Things will blow up if there is a huge directory.

```
/* get the directory contents */
read_dir(dir);

/* acknowledge the message, reply w/ the filenames */
if (send(sd_current, dir, strlen(dir), 0) == -1) {
        perror("send");
```

```
                   exit(1);
        }
```

It is essential that you not only deallocate descriptors, but also unlink(2V) or otherwise remove them from the file system. Sockets cannot replace existing links. If in a child process, don't unlink the file if other processes, such as the parent, are still using it. Using a call to exit(3) in the child process will flush and close any descriptors. If you don't close the unused sockets, you may exceed the number of open files allowed by the operating system.

```
        /* close up both sockets */
        close(sd_current); close(sd);

        /* don't forget to clean-up */
        unlink("./socket");
}
```

That completes *AF_UNIXserver.c*. Compile the server and link it with read_dir.o as follows:

```
    rodson> cc -g -o AF_UNIXserver AF_UNIXserver.c read_dir.c
```

Or use this little *makefile* to make AF_UNIXserver.

```
CFLAGS = -g
.c :
        $(CC) -o $@ $(CFLAGS) $< $(LFLAGS) read_dir.c
```

It should suffice for all the samples in this chapter. It is brain-damaged in the sense that it links *everything* with read_dir.c, but the suffix rules keep things brief. It just takes a little longer.

With the server executable prepared, we are now ready to generate a client to call the server. Remember, we are dealing with UNIX domain addressing, which is only good within the same kernel. We don't need any network host information to open the client socket as it is actually the local *./socket* file.

The client is designed to take a directory from the command line, and pass it to the server, who will return the contents of the directory. The client then sends it to stdout. The client and server are on the same machine, so we use no byte-swapping calls. Directories are returned as characters or bytes anyway, so all we assume is that the client and server use the same character code set.

Now let's look at the client, *AF_UNIXclient.c*. The declarations are shown in Example 5-2.

Example 5-2. AF_UNIXclient.c – connection-oriented UNIX domain socket client

```
#include <stdio.h>
#include <string.h>
#include <sys/types.h>
#include <sys/socket.h>
#include <sys/un.h>
#define DIRSIZE 8192
```

Example 5-2. AF_UNIXclient.c – connection-oriented UNIX domain socket client (Continued)

```
main(argc, argv)
int argc; char **argv;
{
        char    dir[DIRSIZE];
        int     sd;
        struct sockaddr_un sin;
```

The socket instantiation looks identical to that in the server.

```
        /* set up a unix domain socket */
        strcpy(sin.sun_path, "./socket");
        if ((sd = socket(AF_UNIX, SOCK_STREAM, 0)) == -1) {
                perror("socket");
                exit(1);
        }
```

connect(2) attempts to tie the sd socket in our client to the *./socket* socket descriptor common to the client and server.

```
        /* connect to the UNIX socket ./socket */
        if (connect(sd, &sin, sizeof(sin)) == -1) {
                perror("connect");
                exit(1);
        }
```

Now both addresses are bound to the socket and data can flow. We'll first send over a message with the directory name requested. Notice that the size argument on the client's send() need only be smaller than the size specified in the server's recv(). recv() returns the actual length of the message sent. If the message sent is too long to fit into the recv() buffer, trouble can occur.

```
        /* send a message to the server */
        if (send(sd, argv[1], strlen(argv[1]), 0) == -1) {
                perror("send");
                exit(1);
        }
```

Once the message is sent, oftentimes there's a significant wait for a response. You could fork() and get something else done, but we'll remain blocked. We retrieve results with a recv() for up to DIRSIZE bytes.

```
        /* wait for a message to come back from the server */
        if (recv(sd, dir, DIRSIZE, 0) == -1) {
                perror("recv");
                exit(1);
        }
```

The result is by construction a NULL-terminated string, so we'll just print it out, then proceed to close our end of the socket.

```
        /* print out the results */
        printf("%s\n", dir);

        /* close the socket connection */
        close(sd);
}
```

Compile and link the client application the same as the server:

```
rodson> cc -g -o AF_UNIXclient AF_UNIXclient.c
```

Or use make:

```
rodson> make AF_UNIXclient
```

Now let's launch `AF_UNIXserver` in this directory, and then call it with `AF_UNIXclient` to get a directory listing.

```
rodson> AF_UNIXserver &
[1] 2606
rodson> AF_UNIXclient ./
.
..
AF_UNIXserver.c
read_dir.c
makefile
socket
AF_UNIXserver
AF_UNIXclient.c
AF_INETserver.c
TCP_AF_UNIXclient
[1]    Exit 1               AF_UNIXserver
rodson> ls -1
.
..
AF_UNIXserver.c
read_dir.c
makefile
AF_UNIXserver
AF_UNIXclient.c
AF_INETserver.c
AF_UNIXclient
```

Notice two things: the file `socket` appears only for the lifetime of the server, and by design, the server exits when complete.

Next let's tackle going out onto the network. The server will be making use of the same `read_dir()` utility, but there will be some additional socket overhead to make use of Internet addressing. The first example will be connection-oriented, using TCP.

Connection-oriented, Internet Addressing Using TCP

Using Internet addressing provides access to processes outside the reaches of the local kernel. Example 5-3 shows the declarations for our server, *AF_INETserver.c*, which uses the reliable TCP transport with Internet addressing. It accomplishes the same function as Example 5-1.

The includes are pretty much the same as for the UNIX domain client/server pair, but now we must include the Internet addressing definitions from `<netinet/in.h>` and `<netdb.h>`.

Example 5-3. TCP_AF_INETserver.c – TCP Internet socket server

```
#include <stdio.h>
#include <string.h>
#include <sys/types.h>
#include <sys/socket.h>
#include <netinet/in.h>
#include <netdb.h>

#define PORT            0x1234        /* some arbitrary user IP port */
#define DIRSIZE         8192

main()
{
        char    dir[DIRSIZE];        /* used for incoming dir name,
                                      * and outgoing data */
        int     sd, sd_current, cc, fromlen, tolen;
        int     addrlen;
        struct  sockaddr_in sin;
        struct  sockaddr_in pin;
```

We must use socket(2) to define an Internet domain socket with AF_INET. Again we are using the SOCK_STREAM transport.

```
        /* get an Internet domain socket */
        if ((sd = socket(AF_INET, SOCK_STREAM, 0)) == -1) {
                perror("socket");
                exit(1);
        }
```

To bind an address to the socket, we've got a little more work now. We must fill the sockaddr_in structure, including protocol family, port, and socket selection. The use of the INADDR_ANY socket address tells the OS to use any user address it likes. Notice that we used htons(3N) here. The port we chose out of the air (an unreserved port) must be advertised in a network-normal form.

```
        /* complete the socket structure */
        bzero(&sin, sizeof(sin));
        sin.sin_family = AF_INET;
        sin.sin_addr.s_addr = INADDR_ANY;
        sin.sin_port = htons(PORT); /* put in net order */

        /* bind the socket to the port number */
        if (bind(sd, &sin, sizeof(sin)) == -1) {
                perror("bind");
                exit(1);
        }
```

Just like the UNIX domain example, we tell the OS that there is a server here, read-blocked, ready to service client requests. The listen(), accept(), recv(), processing, and send() steps are also identical.

```
        /* show that we are willing to listen */
        if (listen(sd, 5) == -1) {
                perror("listen");
                exit(1);
        }
```

The same points about forking to affect concurrent servicing as mentioned in the UNIX domain server example hold true here. After all, the request queue is only 5 deep. After that, clients will get refused.

```
/* wait for a client to talk to us */
if ((sd_current = accept(sd, &pin, &addrlen)) == -1) {
        perror("accept");
        exit(1);
}

/* get a message from the client */
if (recv(sd_current, dir, sizeof(dir), 0) == -1) {
        perror("recv");
        exit(1);
}

/* get the directory contents */
read_dir(dir);




/* acknowledge the message, reply w/ the filenames */
if (send(sd_current, dir, strlen(dir), 0) == -1) {
        perror("send");
        exit(1);
}
```

When an `AF_INET` Internet domain addressing server exits, we don't need to worry about leaving a UNIX file around.

```
        /* close up both sockets */
        close(sd_current); close(sd);
}
```

The client routine to access this server is again more complex than the UNIX domain client. If nothing else, there are more data structure values to fill in, which are necesary to specify network endpoints to the socket. The client functions as before, taking a directory name from the command line, attempting to access the HOST compiled into the client code, and receiving from the server the contents of the directory. The declarations for the client, *TCP_AF_INETclient.c*, are shown in Example 5-4.

Example 5-4. TCP_AF_INETclient.c – TCP Internet socket client

```
#include <stdio.h>
#include <sys/types.h>
#include <sys/socket.h>
#include <netinet/in.h>
#include <netdb.h>

#define PORT        0x1234
#define HOST        "cortex" /*Start server on "cortex"*/
#define DIRSIZE     8192

main(argc, argv)
int argc; char **argv;
{
```

Example 5-4. TCP_AF_INETclient.c – TCP Internet socket client (Continued)

```
char    dir[DIRSIZE];
int     sd;
struct sockaddr_in sin;
struct sockaddr_in pin;
struct hostent *hp;
```

First look in the */etc/hosts* file for the HOST we're after.

```
/* go find out about the desired host machine */
if ((hp = gethostbyname(HOST)) == 0) {
        perror("gethostbyname");
        exit(1);
}
```

Next use this information to set-up the sockaddr_in data structure (see <netinet/in.h>). It is important to clear things out before using the structure; use something like bzero(3).

```
/* fill in socket structure with host information */
bzero(&pin, sizeof(pin));
pin.sin_family = AF_INET;
pin.sin_addr.s_addr
        ((struct in_addr *)(hp->h_addr))->s_addr;
pin.sin_port = htons(PORT);
```

You are now ready to ask for an Internet domain socket, TCP type.

```
/* grab an Internet domain socket */
if ((sd = socket(AF_INET, SOCK_STREAM, 0)) == -1) {
        perror("socket");
        exit(1);
}
```

Attach yourself to the business end of the server, and push, just like with AF_UNIX domain sockets. The send(2) and recv(2) are identical, so see the comments on their subtleties above.

```
/* connect to PORT on HOST */
if (connect(sd, &pin, sizeof(pin)) == -1) {
        perror("connect");
        exit(1);
}

/* send a message to the server PORT on machine HOST */
if (send(sd, argv[1], strlen(argv[1]), 0) == -1) {
        perror("send");
        exit(1);
}

/* wait for a message to come back from the server */
if (recv(sd, dir, DIRSIZE, 0) == -1) {
        perror("recv");
        exit(1);
}
```

Using the same utility routine, the server again returned NULL-terminated text characters to be printed out.

```
/* Spew out the results and bail out of here! */
printf("%s\n", dir);
```

It is wise to use either `close(2)` or `exit(3)` to shut down this end of the socket. `shutdown(8)` may be used to handle unilateral shutdowns in a little neater fashion.

```
        close(sd);
    }
```

Now compile and link the server to the utility routine (`read_dir.c`) mentioned above.

```
rodson> make TCP_AF_INETserver TCP_AF_INETclient
```

You are now ready to start the server on the machine named HOST. The simplest way is to use the `rsh` command, which makes use of the remote shell daemon `rshd` that `inetd` started at boot-time. Start `TCP_AF_INETserver` on the machine specified in HOST:

```
rodson> rsh -n cortex cd $cwd/TCP_AF_INETserver &
```

`cortex` better be listed in the local machine's */etc/hosts* file or we won't be able to get to it. Note we used the −n flag on `rsh` to tell it to take `stdin` from */dev/null* at the `cortex` machine. Now run the client once to get a listing of the development directory.

```
rodson> AF_INETclient $cwd
.
..
AF_UNIXserver.c
read_dir.c
makefile
TCP_AF_INETclient
AF_UNIXserver
AF_UNIXclient.c
AF_INETserver.c
AF_INETclient.c
AF_INETserver
AF_UNIXclient
[1]  Done  rsh -n cortex cd /home/cortex/bloomer/src/ipc/AF_UNIXserver
```

Connectionless Protocol, Internet Domain Addressing, and UDP

We now proceed to an example of connectionless client/server communication using the UDP protocol. We'll also use Internet domain addressing to put things out on the network. It is quite similar to the last example, excepting the use of `connect()` by the client and `accept()` at the server side. The socket I/O routines have to be changed to accommodate the lack of a negotiated connection, as well as the lack of reliable transmission. The unreliable nature of UDP is hidden by a built-in `wait(2V)` routine, that uses signaling and `alarm(3C)` to enforce a time-out. I'll talk more about signals in Chapter 6, where we'll use it for job scheduling.

We need to define the name for the service. This name must be registered in the */etc/services* file. This, again, is the job of the superuser. The getserv...(3N) routines expedite accessing network services, but require superuser, root-level conformity across the network. All the network database information must be in sync across the network.[†] In the connection-oriented Internet addressing application (see Examples 5-3 and 5-4), we avoided the use of network databases by "hard-wiring" the hostname and port number right in the client and server routines. There was no question about which machine and port the server end of the socket was at.

One way to avoid embedding port information is to connect to the rexec() server of the remote machine. As it lives at a well-known port, you could use it to execute the local service program. But with the rexec() server you are restricted to command-line argument passing. You could use rexec() to run a main() wrapped around the remote read_dir() procedure. We shall cover one example of remote execution at the end of the chapter. RPC, as we will see later, gets around most of these complications, building a framework to perform the information retrieval.

The declarations for the server, *UDP_AF_INETserver.c*, are shown in Example 5-5. We use the same include files as in the connection-oriented example (still using Internet addressing).

Example 5-5. UDP_AF_INETserver.c – UDP Internet socket server

```
#include <stdio.h>
#include <sys/types.h>
#include <sys/socket.h>
#include <netinet/in.h>
#include <netdb.h>
#include <errno.h>
/* note - must add this service as su to /etc/services */
#define UDP_SERVICE    "my_udp_read_dir_server"
#define DIRSIZE            8192

main()
{
        char    dir[DIRSIZE];               /* used for incoming dir name,
                                             * and outgoing data */
        int     sd, cc, addrlen;
        struct sockaddr_in structure myaddr;  /* my Internet location */
        struct sockaddr_in claddr;            /* the client's Internet
                        location */
        struct servent *sp;                 /* the port map for my service */
```

As with the other Internet socket instances, we must build up the elements of a sockaddr_in structure, clearing them first.

---

† The local and global network resources databases are automatically kept fairly consistent across a network. In this way information held by servers like the NCS Location Broker or ONC Network Information System is used rather than the ASCII /etc files.

```
/* clear and initialize the socket descriptors */
bzero((char *) &myaddr, sizeof(struct sockaddr_in));
bzero((char *) &claddr, sizeof(struct sockaddr_in));
myaddr.sin_family = AF_INET;
myaddr.sin_addr.s_addr = INADDR_ANY;
```

We search the */etc/services* file for the service. If it is there, we need its port number. In my case, `getservbyname()` is really calling NIS, so the database better be updated, too.

```
sp = getservbyname(UDP_SERVICE, "udp");
if (sp == NULL) {
        printf("Cannot find %s in /etc/services\n",
                UDP_SERVICE);
        exit(1);
}
myaddr.sin_port = sp->s_port;
```

For UDP, a socket using Internet domain addressing (AF_INET) and datagram socket protocol (SOCK_DGRAM) is called for. We `bind()` the socket to the port address.

```
/* qrab an Internet socket descriptor */
if ((sd = socket(AF_INET, SOCK_DGRAM, 0)) == -1) {
        perror("socket");
        exit(1);
}

/* bind the socket to our port description as specified above */
if (bind(sd, &myaddr, sizeof(struct sockaddr_in ))
== -1) {
        perror("bind");
        exit(1);
}
```

`recvmsg(2)` and `recvfrom(2)` may be used for connectionless receipts. Here the `recvfrom()` waits for a message with interesting things left in `errno`.

```
/* wait for a message to arrive */
errno = 0;  /* no errors at this point */
addrlen = sizeof(struct sockaddr_in );

/* get the message which is being sent */
cc =
    recvfrom(sd, dir, sizeof(dir), 0, &claddr, &addrlen);
if (cc == -1) {
        perror("recv");
        exit(1);
}
```

Do the real work, then return the data with a `sendto(2)` in a fashion complimentary to the above `recvfrom()` as the client sits waiting at a `recv()`.

```
/* get the directory contents */
read_dir(dir);

/* acknowledge the message, reply w/ the filenames */
if (sendto(s, dir, strlen(dir), 0, &claddr, addrlen)
```

```
                        == -1) {
                        perror("sendto");
                        exit(1);
              }
```

Then close down this end of the socket. Notice that since we are connectionless, accept() was not used, so the extra socket descriptor was not generated. If we wanted to change the iterative nature of the above processing into iterative serving, we'd have to dup(2) the descriptor.

```
                 /* connectionless - no accept() extra socket descriptor to close */
                 close(sd);
         }
```

We must compile and link the connectionless UDP server with the above *read_dir.c* utility routine, then launch it on the server named below in the client's HOST #define. Remember, if you stick with using the getservbyname() routine, you'll have to put the server into the */etc/services* file. If you are running NIS, you must re-make the dbm files in */var/yp* and force an update, also.

Now the final socket example—the client half of a connectionless communication. Here we take some lengths to detect, but not necessarily correct, for missed datagrams. Considering it is less than 100 lines of code, and by far the most complicated piece of our socket IPC exercise, sockets really aren't that hard to use.

Example 5-6 shows the declarations for the client, *UDP_AF_INETclient.c*.

Example 5-6. UDP_AF_INETclient.c – UDP Internet socket client

```
#include <stdio.h>
#include <sys/types.h>
#include <sys/socket.h>
#include <sys/errno.h>
#include <signal.h>
#include <netinet/in.h>
#include <netdb.h>

#define UDP_SERVICE        "my_udp_read_dir_server"
#define HOST               "rodson"
#define DIRSIZE            8192
```

We need a way to monitor transport time-outs, checking for lost requests. We will be using a signal handler to catch SIGALRM indicating that the receive attempt failed.

```
        void t_nop()
        {
                fprintf(stderr, "waiting for a reply...");
        }
```

The process of establishing a socket is the same as for the server. Notice that in both SOCK_DGRAM client and server the addresses must be calculated for use by sendto() and recvfrom().

```
        main(argc, argv)
        int argc; char **argv;
        {
```

```
        char    dir[DIRSIZE];
        int     sd, retry, addrlen;
        extern int      errno;     /* error type */
        struct hostent *hp;        /* our port descriptor */
        struct servent *sp;        /* server's port descriptor */
        struct sockaddr_in myaddr; /* our Internet descriptor */
        struct sockaddr_in svaddr; /* server descriptor */
        struct sockaddr_in claddr; /* recvfrom - client's internet location
                */

        /* clear and initialize the socket descriptors */
        memset((char *) &myaddr, 0, sizeof(struct sockaddr_in));
        memset((char *) &svaddr, 0, sizeof(struct sockaddr_in));
        svaddr.sin_family = AF_INET;
        hp = gethostbyname(HOST);
        if (hp == NULL) {
                fprintf(stderr, "%s not found in /etc/hosts\n", HOST);
                exit(1);
        }
        svaddr.sin_addr.s_addr =
        ((struct in_addr *)(hp->h_addr))->s_addr;

#ifndef PORT
        sp = getservbyname(UDP_SERVICE, "udp");
        if (sp == NULL) {
                fprintf(stderr, "%s not found in /etc/services\n",
            UDP_SERVICE);
                exit(1);
        }
        svaddr.sin_port = sp->s_port;
#else
         svaddr.sin_port = htons(PORT);

#endif

        /* create the socket */
        sd = socket(AF_INET, SOCK_DGRAM, 0);
        if (sd == -1) {
                perror("socket");
                exit(1);
        }

        /* add some home truths about ourselves */
        myaddr.sin_family = AF_INET;
        myaddr.sin_port = 0;
        myaddr.sin_addr.s_addr = INADDR_ANY;

        /* bind the socket to our port */
        if (bind(sd, &myaddr, sizeof(struct sockaddr_in ))
        == -1) {
                perror("bind");
                exit(1);
        }
```

Next, we install a signal handler to catch the SIGALRM signal that we generate with alarm(3C) after 5 seconds. We'll catch the alarm, resetting it each time, for up to five times. Each time through we'll attempt anew to send a message to the server, and get some acknowledgment through a subsequent reply. If the reply (recv())

doesn't find the message buffered-up on our client side by the server within five seconds, we try again up to five times.

```
/* attempt to send a message to the server */
signal(SIGALRM, t nop);
retry = 5;
addrlen = sizeof(struct sockaddr_in );

again:
if (sendto(sd, argv[1], strlen(argv[1]), 0, &svaddr, addrlen)
        == -1) {
        perror("sendto");
        exit(1);
}
alarm(5); /* a SIGALRM signal is repeated every 5 seconds */
if (recvfrom(sd, dir, DIRSIZE, 0, &claddr, &addrlen) == -1) {
        if (errno == EINTR) {
                if (--retry) {
                        goto again;
                } else {
                        perror("recvfrom");
                        exit(1);
                }
        } else {
                perror("recvfrom");
                exit(1);
        }
}
alarm(0); /* reset the alarm */
```

Finally, we show the world the results of the server, and put this end of the socket out of its misery.

```
/* success - spew out results and close up shop */
printf("%s\n", dir);
close(sd);
}
```

Advanced Socket Programming Issues

We used send() and recv() and their relatives above to avoid an issue with read() and write() when dealing with descriptors that are sockets, instead of just files. read() and write() are not aware of the message or buffer size associated with the socket in the kernel. read() and write() need to be used in a fashion so as to check the amount of data successfully transferred. It should also be noted that some non-BSD TCP/IP implementations don't allow read() and write() to be used with connectionless sockets. Example 5-7 presents two sample routines that check for bytes read and written from/to a socket, trying repeatedly, until failure, to satisfy the request.

Example 5-7. Reading and writing a socket requires special care: myReadWrite.c

```
my_read(sd, buf, n)
int     sd, n;
char    *buf;
{
        int     bcount,                 /* counts total bytes read */
        bread;                          /* bytes read this pass */

        bcount =  bread = 0;
        while (bcount < n) {            /* loop until full buffer */
                if ((bread =  read(sd, buf, n - bcount)) > 0) {
                        bcount  += bread; /* inc. byte count */
                                          /* move buffer ptr for next read */
                        buf += bread;
                }
                if (bread < 0)          /* signal an error */
                        return(-1);
        }
        return(bcount);
}

my_write(sd, buf, n)
int     sd, n;
char    *buf;
{
        int     bcount,                 /* counts total bytes written */
        bwrit;                          /* bytes written this pass */

        bcount =  bwrit = 0;
        while (bcount < n) {            /* loop until full buffer */
                if ((bwrit =  read(sd, buf, n - bcount)) > 0) {
                        bcount  += bwrit; /* inc. byte count */
                                          /* move buffer ptr for next written */
                        buf += bwrit;
                }
                if (bwrit < 0)          /* signal an error */
                        return(-1);
        }
        return(bcount);
}
```

If `send()` finds inadequate buffer space available at the socket to hold the message to be transmitted, it normally blocks the process, waiting for space. A socket may be placed in the non-blocking I/O mode through use of an `ioctl(2)` or `fcntl(2V)` call. If non-blocking, `errno` records a premature return status. This can be useful in time-critical applications where blocking is unacceptable. `select(2)` may be used to determine when in the future it is possible to send more data. Similarly, `recv()` will block, unless the socket has been placed in non-blocking I/O mode, if there is no complete message to receive yet.

I tend to use `send()` and `recv()` more than the `my_read()` and `my_write()` routines, unblocking with `fcntl()` and using `select()` when performance is critical. In speed-critical applications, or where you need to get down to the behavior of the IPC channel, it is worth looking at `ioctl()` and `fcntl()`. Here's an example of how to use `fcntl()` to avoid blocking a process while it reads or writes a socket:

```
if( fcntl( my_socket, F_SETFL, FNDELAY ) == -1)
    fprintf( stderr, "trouble unblocking socket\n" );
```

This kind of low-level mode switching is not for the lily-livered. Use `fcntl()` and `ioctl()` only when absolutely necessary. It is easy to get a socket into an unusable state. `getsockopt(2)` and `setsockopt(2)` can get at a number of the socket options and status indicators, which are useful during debugging.

Other socket-related calls worth looking at are `readv(2V)` and `writev(2V)`. These allow you to read and write into `iovcnt` buffers to organize or encapsulate before actually pulling the chain and sending it.

`sendmsg(2)` and `recvmsg(2)`, like `sendto()` and `recvfrom()`, are usable for either connection-oriented or connectionless protocols. They let you ship message entities as mentioned above in the section, "Message Queues, Semaphores, and Shared Memory."

`shutdown()`, as mentioned above, provides a mechanism to close down one or both paths of a (full-duplex) socket. `select()` for synchronous I/O multiplexing is useful when you have multiple sockets to work with. It allows you to non-destructively inspect the status of descriptors (e.g., ready for writing, ready for reading). You pass it a structure specifying the descriptor to be inspected for reading, writing, and exceptional activity separately. These sets are maintained with a number of `select()` add and delete macros. `select()` returns bit masks that highlight one or the three types of activities at the specified sockets, if there is anything pending. It can be the key to an asynchronous server scheduler or load balancer. `socketpair(2)` is a useful way of generating both sides of the socket (client and server) within one process, then typically splitting it up using forks for multi-processing under the same kernel.

Most all of these system calls are usable on *any* descriptor, not just sockets.

Remote Execution, Security, and Authentication

None of the above examples even go so far as to check username and password against the server */etc/passwd* database. If a machine is running any of these servers, a client can access it. The clients could be augmented to pass username and password as part of the `accept()` or `sendto()` protocol phase, which can then be checked by the server machine.

Even one of the simplest service daemons, `rexecd()` described above, at least does a form of password checking. In Example 5-8, a call is used to run a command (`argv[2]`) on the host you specify (`argv[1]`). If username and password are not specified in the `rexec()` call, first the environment and then your *~/.netrc* file is searched. Though the level of authentication is minimal, it is better than nothing. The authentication differs from `rsh`, where UNIX authentication credentials are checked in NIS or in the user's *~/.rhosts* file if NIS is not running or the authentication isn't available.

Example 5-8. Using rexec() for remote execution: remote.c

```
#include <stdio.h>
#include <netdb.h>

main(argc, argv)
int     argc; char    **argv;
{
        struct servent *out;
        int     sock;
        char    buf[1024];

        out = getservbyname("exec", "tcp");
        sock = rexec(&argv[1], out->s_port, NULL, NULL,
            argv[2], 0);

        while (read(sock, buf, 1024) > 0)
            printf("%s\n", buf);
}
```

This example behaves poorly due to some of the buffering issues mentioned in the previous section. I'll leave the task of fixing it as an exercise.

The rexec() call contacts the local inetd rexecd daemon. It runs TCP protocol. rexec() returns a socket descriptor at which the results of the execution will arrive. All the socket I/O stuff is nicely hidden. All you need to do is build the remote program and then run it,

```
    rodson> cc -o remote remote.c
    rodson> remote server MyService &
```

where server is the name of the remote server and MyService is the name of the program to run remotely. Note that unlike rsh, *remote.c* does not provide a mechanism to send a signal to the remote process. In other words, if you terminate the background job with something like kill -INT PID or slay remote, you leave a dangling server on the server.

In this chapter:

• *Developing Paral-
  lel Algorithms for a
  Multi-server
  Network*

• *System Require-
  ments and Network
  Constraints*

• *Brute-force
  Scheduling Using
  Process Control*

• *Remote Image
  Processing (RIP)*

• *Testing and Run-
  ning the Program*

6

*Application
Development:
Networked Parallel
Image Processing*

The last few chapters have explained some of the basics of RPC and IPC programming. The examples have been pretty simple: a small, single-server application. In
this chapter we look at the development of a complex distributed application, one
that makes use of multiple servers working in parallel to speed up the work of
image processing. This chapter covers:

• A strategy for designing parallel RPC applications.

• Network and system requirements and constraints on application design.

• Use of UNIX scheduling facilities to coordinate multiple RPC servers working in
  parallel.

• Steps in the development of a real distributed processing application.

My initial reason for using RPC was to build parallel, distributed image processing
applications on a network. I wanted my old Sun 3/60 to grab all the available
computations it could from under-exploited resources on our network. The Remote
Image Processing (RIP) application that I present in this chapter is an abstraction of
the stuff I use every day. It's put together for the sake of illustration. It works *okay*
but was never intended to be industrial-strength. I'm not trying to show you how to
do image processing efficiently. I am using it as a tool to demonstrate techniques
that can be applied to many different kinds of distributed applications. Type it in
and you'll notice a few shortcuts and kludges necessary to shoe-horn it into one

chapter. Also, you'll notice that the local RIP client calls *SunView* procedures.[†]
Every effort has been made to allow you to run the server on virtually any machine
because it does not rely on Sun-specific data structures or procedure calls. You
could use almost any machine as a server that supports built-in C data types and
ONC RPC. But enough caveats; besides, I'm a hardware guy anyway.

Developing Parallel Algorithms for a Multi-server Network

Designing an application that runs across a network can be an easy task if only one
client and server communicate synchronously at any one time. But your network
can do much more.

Is it possible that your problem can be solved much faster by partitioning it and
giving different pieces to different networked computers? Or do you have a
resource (a database, some hardware, etc.) that you want shared across the
network? This section examines general strategies for parallel processing, especially
as it applies to a bunch of networked computers running RPC.

With RPC at your disposal, you have the tools to implement multiple-process or
multiple-processor algorithms. But before you can do this, you need a good representation of available computational resources plus parallelism techniques to
partition your algorithm. The best I can do in a brief treatment of this huge research
area is to give you a simple, abstract (but hopefully usable) model, and suggest
some partitioning approaches.

If you are new to the science (art?) of multi-processing, consult Appendix D,
Parallel Processing in a Nutshell, to pick up all the appropriate buzz words.

Parallel algorithms can be devised using any of the following strategies:[‡]

Divide-and-conquer	Decompose into smaller problems, solve each, then combine.
Greedy method	Heuristically search for possible solutions, without considering potential penalties.
Dynamic programming	Useful when in search of a sequence of decisions.
Search and traversal	Break the problem into graphs or trees.

---

† It would help if you have some SunView programming experience, or have the `pixwin` *SunView Programmer's Manual* around. The first major application developed here uses *old* Sun-specific windowing. We move to more contemporary (but slower) windowing systems in later chapters.

‡ For a better, in-depth discussion, see *Parallel processing: principles and practice,* by E.V. Krishnamurthy (Addison-Wesley, 1989, ISBN 0-201-17532).

Backtracking	Move forward until failure, then backtrack to last good alternative.
Branch and bound	Avoid exhaustive searching by using earlier search results.
Algebraic transform	Transform, solve, then inverse transform.
Random trials	Probabilistic search.
Approximation	Save time; compromise accuracy/resolution for time.

I've had luck applying "divide-and-conquer" and "algebraic transform" in image processing and synthesis applications. These approaches seem to appeal to the simpler, more obvious properties of a problem, for example, carving up an image and transforming it to the Fourier domain before filtering. Each of us unknowingly uses these techniques in algorithm development already, as well as in mental processing.

When you look at your own machine, you have a form of multi-processing available in multi-tasking. The `fork(2V)` mechanism developed later in this chapter is a cheap and dirty way to get your machine running two threads of code in a time-sliced fashion. Controlling execution priority, data sharing, information exchange, synchronization, and process joining are also pretty straightforward. Multi-tasking is a commonly overlooked but valuable programming tool. You can partition your algorithm into processes that are easily decoupled from the main thread of operation.

One example is when you access external hardware that is slow or a database that is large and you don't want to hold up the `main()` process until the response arrives. Processes on the same machine can also be used to debug distributed processing applications. With some clever conditional execution and compiling statements, one can still use a debugger like `dbx` to look at multi-tasked debug versions of full-blown distributed applications.

Another advantage of single-machine multi-processing is the flexibility of the communication model. You can implement both loosely or tightly coupled models, using semaphores, shared memory, data flow—the works. It's a good environment in which to emulate multi-processing and understand the benefits as well as the design challenges. Personally, I usually just `fork()` child processes with their environment inherited from the parent, placing child results back in the parent process memory space somehow. The default process scheduling in UNIX is usually sufficient if one is not constrained by time. I'll cover some `fork()`, `signal()`, and `wait()` examples later, and base a simple distributed process scheduler on these concepts.

A Simple Model For Parallel Processing on a Network

Beyond your machine is a mass of processors eligible for true, simultaneous parallel processing. The simplest way to view this model is as a number of loosely-coupled processors that share memory and communicate through pretty poor, slow linkages, which are usually Ethernet cables.

The advent of shared file systems like NFS lets you extend this model to include some shared global memory in the form of disk space. An example of this model is shown in Figure 6-1. This is not very efficient or fast, but it can be good for initialization procedures as a (slow) global communication technique. After all, it's the same Ethernet cable, accessing one disk drive serially.

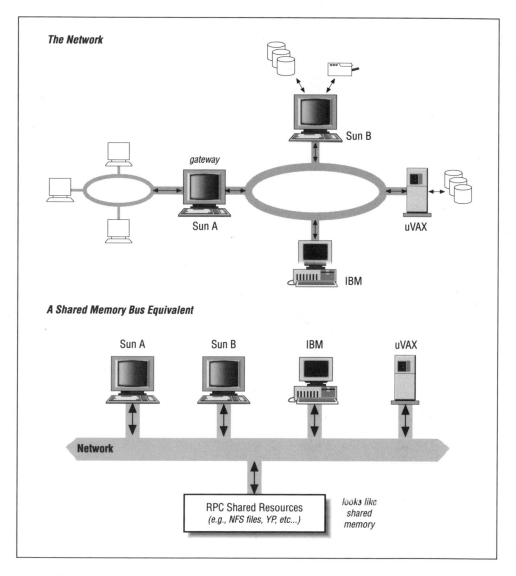

Figure 6-1. Modeling the distributed computing environment for parallelizing algorithms

System Requirements and Network Constraints

To develop a high-performance RPC application, you must look at the network and evaluate the machines that are available to you. Of course, you also have to look at your application; it might not be a good candidate for RPC parallel, distributed processing. You might only get the performance you need by adding some dedicated hardware or keeping the application local.

Server Access

The server machines on the network must be accessible to your local machine. As a general rule, if you can rsh(1C) to a host, you can use that machine as a server with UNIX authentication. Server processes started by other users work fine too, just set up the ~/.rhosts file on both machines. While ONC RPC/XDR supports three flavors of authentication (see Chapter 12), we shall apply none in this chapter.

So far we've seen some crude ways to start servers using standard Internet or ONC RPC remote execution daemons. While using rsh is a handy way to start a remote daemon from the command-line, a real programmer might want to implement a dynamic, run-time management technique from C. We'll import some of this functionality into the RIP client. Keep Chapter 4's slay script at your disposal, too—it's useful for disposing of lurking processes.

Server and Network Performance

The parallel processing model, shown earlier in Figure 6-1, described a typical UNIX Ethernet network as a loosely-coupled multi-processor with terrible interprocessor bandwidth. Shared memory, in the form of shared NFS files, comes at a high price—increased network traffic. Unless you have a caching drive or controller, network traffic is slowed to the drive's read/write rate with more overhead added for each seek. I've clocked my local Ethernet at effective data rates of 40-200KBytes/sec, depending on the time of day (and whether or not somebody is dumping core at the time!). That's pretty slow when you consider that newer Sun, IBM, HP/Apollo, and DEC workstations can crank through 20+ MIPS.

So what do you do? If your application now runs for minutes, and produces little output or interim data, you're a candidate for distributing your computations with RPC, given that you can partition or parallelize your algorithms. If you are I/O bound, you probably want to stay off the network until FDDI or another fiber optic network is installed.

You also have to look at the number and class of machines available. If you don't have a few big-MIPers in the pool, or don't schedule wisely, you may be sorry. There is some non-negligible overhead associated with your use of the RPC/XDR routines and the network data transfers involved. In some cases, you lose more than you gain.

There is no simple formula for this computation/bandwidth trade-off as each network and problem is different. In general, I've found that compute intensive applications alone warrant the overhead.

One trick I use for time-critical demonstrations is preprocessing or distribution. I get all the possible shared data and overhead functions out of the way before the clock starts. For example, for image processing, I put copies of the images in each server's RAM ahead of time, and perform client-server communications in terms of pixel addresses and ranges instead of pixel values.

If you have a changing mixture of computational and I/O loading, you can do what I do—keep the network loaded, keeping as many machines as busy as possible. That's what scheduling is all about.

Brute-force Scheduling Using Process Control

I call it BFS but I've heard our system management people call it worse things. Brute-force scheduling is a cheap and dirty approach to controlling multiple servers from a single client. It uses child processes to request jobs on remote servers and waits patiently for their reply. Accessing the server runs in the background, and we wait for output on the other end of a pipe, remaining idle until the server has the result ready. The child process then wakes up and dumps the data back into the environment it shares with the parent; that's where the client process is running.

BFS is *heavyweight processing* with the parent process reproducing itself in whole all over the place, whereas *lightweight processing* might be a better solution. In Chapter 2 we discussed the merit of lightweight threads and presented vendor development plans in this area. In Chapter 9, there is a section devoted to lightweight processing with Sun's LWP. I've used lightweight threads enough to know the sharing of variables in non-trivial applications can be complicated and a source of bottleneck.

Both threads and process creation can be avoided during scheduling of asynchronous remote calls. With memory and local MIPS increasing every day, I choose to use heavyweight processing. It's the easiest way to make multiple concurrent requests at the client for asynchronous processing.

Programming Asynchronous and Concurrent Processing at the Client

☞ If you understand signals, timers, and process creation under UNIX, you may want to skip the following section.

We can isolate the pieces of BFS and present them before we look at the RIP application. To get a feel for BFS, we will show a couple of simple examples which you can type in and run. Chapter 5 introduced fork(2V), signal(3), wait(2V), and other IPC routines and these BFS examples make use of fork() and wait() frequently. You can learn enough about IPC from these examples to design an even better scheduler.

Example 6-1 installs the sigchild() signal handler to be called whenever a child process' state changes via the SIGCHILD signal. It fork()'s a child process, then signals it using kill(2V) with the value you give it at stdin. If you send it a SIGCHILD signal, the number 20 as specified in my <signal.h> file, the signal handler is called, preventing the default action of process termination. Some signals actually abort the child process; others don't bother it. Nevertheless, sigchild() handler gets invoked when the child dies.

Example 6-1. Catching SIGCHLD from child deaths using fork(), kill(), and signal(): stest.c

```
#include <signal.h>
#include <stdio.h>

void        sigchild();
static int        visits - 0;

main()
{
  int              ppid, i;

  ppid = getpid(2V);
  printf("parent process id: \"%d\"\n", ppid);
  signal(SIGCHLD, sigchild);      /* do sigchild() when child is killed */
  while (scanf("%d", &i) == 1) {
    ppid = fork();
    if (!ppid) {
      printf("in child, sleeping...\n");
      sleep(2);
      printf("...but child died on its own...\n");
      exit();
    } else {
      sleep(1);
      printf("parent signalling child with %d...\n", i);
      kill(ppid, i);
    }
  }

}

intsig;
void
sigchild(sig) /* lots of other interesting args passed to sigchild() */
{
  visits++;
  printf("on the %dth signal\n", visits);
  printf("found signal \"%d\"\n", sig);
  return;
}
```

There are no special cc options needed, just use make's default rules. make stest should work even without a *makefile* if your default rules file is up to snuff. This holds true for all the examples in this section of the chapter.

```
rodson> make stest
cc -o stest stest.c
rodson> stest
parent process id: "20010"
0
in child, sleeping...
parent signalling child with 0...
...but child died on its own...
on the 1th signal
found signal "20"
1
in child, sleeping...
parent signalling child with 1...
on the 2th signal
found signal "20"
9
in child, sleeping...
parent signalling child with 9...

on the 3th signal
found signal "20"
```

Notice kill(ppid,0) did not kill the process while kill(ppid,1) caused an abrupt death. sigchild() reported the demise of every child process regardless of its cause of death.

In Example 6-2, *wtest.c* uses process control functions to launch child processes, which run their course, then die, to be recorded (reaped) later with a wait(2V) in the parent process. I'll use some of these ideas in BFS.

In Example 6-2 a child process is first started. If fork() returns -1, it failed. More than likely you have exceeded the number of processes allowed per user on your system (check the extern int errno to see). Once a child process is started, execution continues in both parent and child along the same path until the process ID is used to branch off. The child exits and the parent reaps its death with a wait() call.

Example 6-2. wait() watches for child processes that die: wtest.c

```
#include <stdio.h>
#include <sys/wait.h>

int             ServerStatus[10];

main()
{
  int           pid, ppid, DeadPid;
  int           i, j;

  ppid = getpid();
  for (i = 0; i < 10; i++) {
    while ((ServerStatus[i] = fork()) == -1) {
      sleep(1);
    }

    if ((pid = getpid()) != ppid) {       /* child */
      printf("child %d exits...\n", pid);
      exit(0);
    } else {                              /* parent */
```

Example 6-2. wait() watches for child processes that die: wtest.c (Continued)

```
      DeadPid = wait(0);
      for (j = 0; j < 10; j++) {
        if (ServerStatus[j] == DeadPid) {
          printf("parent caught child %d\n", DeadPid);
          break;
        }
      }
    }
  }
}
```

Make and run the program as follows:

```
rodson> make -f /dev/null wtest
cc -o wtest wtest.c
rodson> wtest
child 20031 exits...
parent caught child 20031
child 20032 exits...
parent caught child 20032
child 20033 exits...
parent caught child 20033
child 20034 exits...
parent caught child 20034
child 20035 exits...
parent caught child 20035
child 20036 exits...
parent caught child 20036
child 20037 exits...
parent caught child 20037
child 20038 exits...
parent caught child 20038
child 20039 exits...
parent caught child 20039
child 20040 exits...
parent caught child 20040
```

The fork/die sequence repeats ten times with the parent reporting each death.

If you don't want to waste time waiting for processes to return, design an alternative that can be used to make better use of your CPU. Use a SIGCHLD signal handler that is activated every time a child process changes status. You can also inspect the history of the returned child by way of checking its return status. In Example 6-3, *status.c* creates a child process and catches its death with a signal() handler like *stest.c* in Example 6-1. The difference is that the status information about the child process, including the process exit or return code, is inspected.

Example 6-3. Asynchronous concurrent processing using fork() and signal (): status.c

```
#include <signal.h>
#include <sys/wait.h>
#include <stdio.h>

void sigchild();
static int      visits = 0;

main()
{
```

Example 6-3. Asynchronous concurrent processing using fork() and signal (): status.c

```
int             ppid, i;

ppid = getpid();
printf("parent process id: \"%d\"\n", ppid);
signal(SIGCHLD, sigchild);      /* do sigchild() when child is killed */
while (scanf("%d", &i) == 1) {
  ppid = fork();
  if (!ppid) {
    printf("in child, sleeping...\n");
    exit(i);
  }
}

}

static int
void /* lots of other interesting args passed to sigchild() */
{
  union wait      status;
  int             DeadPid;

  while ((DeadPid = wait(&status)) == -1);
  printf("found status \"%d\"\n", status.w_retcode);
  return;
}
```

Make the program as follows. Start it and pass it values to be used as `exit(3)` status codes of the child process.

```
rodson> make status
cc -o status status.c
rodson> status
parent process id: "20060"
0
in child, sleeping...
found status "0"
1
in child, sleeping...
found status "1"
9
in child, sleeping...
found status "9"
-1
in child, sleeping...
found status "255"
```

I'll make use of this last approach to get many server connections opened and RPCs going, leaving them in the background for my client process to get pertinent post-mortem information from their obituaries.

Making Use of Timers to Watch Child Processes

In a multiple-process, scheduled application, it becomes important to know not only when and how a child returns, but how long it takes. One solution is to use the same signaling technique as discussed, augmented with a timer. In Example 6-4, the time that each child process is spawned will be recorded. On notification of a child death, the SIGCHLD signal catcher in the parent looks at the current time compared with the start time recorded for the child, and uses this to determine what the elapsed (clock) time was. This can be quite useful for monitoring and subsequently adjusting compute-loads on RPCs that might be placed within the children.

Example 6-4. Interval timer and signals monitor how long the kids are out: childTimer.c

```
#include <signal.h>
#include <stdio.h>
#include <sys/time.h>
#include <sys/wait.h>
#include <errno.h>

#define MAXCHLD 1000    /* Will surely get stopped first by process limit */

int             ChildStart[MAXCHLD];    /* When the child got started */
int             ChildTime[MAXCHLD];     /* Duration of the child process */
int             ChildPid[MAXCHLD];      /* Child process ID */
struct itimerval tval;

extern int      errno;
static int      sigchild();

main()
{
    int             i, child;

    /* Set the real-time timer */
    timerclear(&tval.it_interval);
    timerclear(&tval.it_value);
    tval.it_value.tv_sec =              /* Don't leave it zero! */
        tval.it_interval.tv_sec = 100;  /* seconds */
    setitimer(ITIMER_REAL, &tval, NULL);

    /* install SIGCHLD catcher */
    signal(SIGCHLD, sigchild);

    /* fork up to MAXCHLD children, and let them report back */
    while (scanf("%d", &i) == 1)
        for (child = 0; child < MAXCHLD; child++) {
            getitimer(ITIMER_REAL, &tval);
            ChildStart[child] = tval.it_value.tv_sec;
            if (ChildPid[child] = fork()) {
                /* in parent */
                if (ChildPid[child] == -1)
                    perror("can't fork another child");
                if (EAGAIN == errno) {
                    printf("ran out of processes after %d th child\n", child);
                    errno = 0;
                    break;
                }
            } else {
                /* in child */
                sleep(i);
                _exit(child);
            }
        }
}

void
sigchild()
{
    union wait      status;
    int             DeadPid;
    int             i;
```

Example 6-4. Interval timer and signals monitor how long the kids are out: childTimer.c

```
  getitimer(ITIMER_REAL, &tval);
  DeadPid = wait(&status);
  for (i = 0; i < MAXCHLD; i++) {
    if (DeadPid == ChildPid[i]) {
      ChildTime[i] = ChildStart[i] - tval.it_value.tv_sec;
      printf("found status \"%d\", took %d seconds\n",
             status.w_retcode, ChildTime[i]);
      return;
    }
  }
  printf("pid %d: bastard child\n", DeadPid);
}
```

Make and run the application:

```
rodson> make childTimer
cc -o childTimer childTimer.c
```

When you run the program, specify at stdin the length of time in seconds that each child process should last. If you supply it with a small value, like 1, child-Timer will have a chance to launch all 1000 of the child processes as they die as fast as it can fork() them.

```
rodson> childTimer
1
found status "0", took 1 seconds
found status "3", took 1 seconds
found status "4", took 1 seconds
.
.
.
found status "127", took 1 seconds
found status "126", took 1 seconds
found status "129", took 1 seconds
.
.
.
Alarm clock
```

Notice how the children get backed up and don't necessarily finish in order. The alarm clock goes off when a SIGALRM signal is not caught as the timer expires.

At my site I have a system named bach where the number of user processes is severely limited. Supply a larger child sleep() value on a machine, like bach, and you'll see something like this:

```
bach> childTimer
100
can't fork another child: No more processes
ran out of processes after 221st child
.
.
.
```

A different way of dealing with time is to use the time-of-day clock, as shown in Example 6-5. This might be preferred when running in a windowing system, which tends to have its own uses of some of the interval timers.

Example 6-5. Using time-of-day to watch child processing tim: day.c

```
#include <signal.h>
#include <stdio.h>
#include <sys/time.h>
#include <sys/wait.h>
#include <errno.h>

#define MAXCHLD 100

int         ChildStart[MAXCHLD];   /* When the child got started */
int         ChildTime[MAXCHLD];    /* Duration of the child process */
int         ChildPid[MAXCHLD];     /* Child process ID */
struct timeval tval;

extern int  errno;
void sigchild();

main()
{
  int         i, child;


  /* install SIGCHLD catcher */
  signal(SIGCHLD, sigchild);

  /* fork up to MAXCHLD children, and let them report back */
  while (scanf("%d", &i) == 1)
    for (child = 0; child < MAXCHLD; child++) {
      gettimeofday(&tval, NULL);
      ChildStart[child] = tval.tv_sec;
      if (ChildPid[child] = fork()) {
        /* in parent */
        if (ChildPid[child] == -1)
          perror("can't fork another child");
        if (EAGAIN == errno) {
          printf("ran out of processes after %d th child\n", child);
          errno = 0;
          break;
        }
      } else {
        /* in child */
        sleep(i);
        _exit(child);
      }
    }
}

void
sigchild()
{
  union wait    status;
  int           DeadPid;
  int           i;

  gettimeofday(&tval, NULL);
  DeadPid = wait(&status);
  for (i = 0; i < MAXCHLD; i++) {
    if (DeadPid == ChildPid[i]) {
      ChildTime[i] = tval.tv_sec - ChildStart[i];
      printf("found status \"%d\", took %d seconds\n",
```

Example 6-5. Using time-of-day to watch child processing tim: day.c (Continued)

```
              status.w_retcode, ChildTime[i]);
       return;
     }
  }
  printf("pid %d, bastard child\n", DeadPid);
}
```

Make and run the application. Again notice that the order in which children expire, and the length of time each took is irregular.

```
rodson> make day
cc -o day day.c
rodson> day
1
found status "0", took 1 seconds
found status "1", took 1 seconds
found status "4", took 1 seconds
.
.
.
found status "59", took 2 seconds
found status "62", took 1 seconds
found status "61", took 2 seconds
found status "63", took 1 seconds
.
.
.
found status "99", took 1 seconds
```

If MAXCHLD is increased and a machine that allows fewer processes is used, *day.c* is also bound to run into the limitations seen above.

Development Steps

Now we can begin to look at the development of the RIP application. We are out to build a client application (the calling procedure) that transparently calls our computational procedure on a remote server. This transparency is made possible by the client and server stubs. We plan to use Sun's RPCGEN protocol compiler to generate these stubs, along with shared XDR interface routines.

Figure 6-2 details the filenames and definitions we use for the example at hand. The application name is rip (Remote Image Processing). Notice that there is one additional file over that presented in Figure 4-2, *rip_shared.h*, which contains common definitions and variables. RPCGEN does allow you to start a line with a % to pass the line directly into the header file that it generates, but I find that a little too awkward to use for everything.

For the RIP application, there are three programs to write: (1) the protocol *rip.x*, where you define the service procedure for exchanging data between the client and server; (2) the server stub *rip_svc_proc.c*, where you define what the server is actually supposed to do; and (3) the client program, *rip.c*, where a locally-run main()

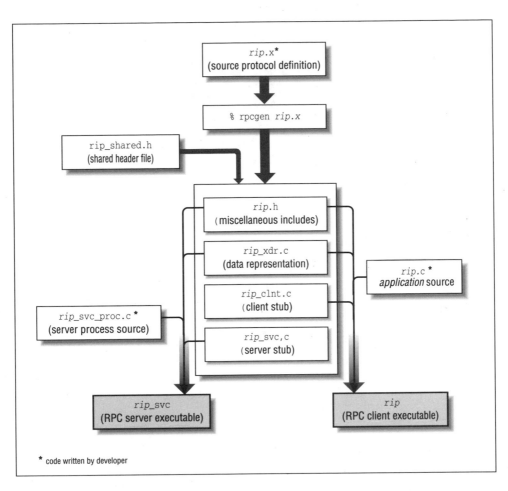

Figure 6-2. RIP application development layout

procedure runs the whole show, performing high-level communications with servers and any local processing.

To express Figure 6-2 in terms of a *makefile*, use Example 6-6. It will serve as a template to be included by other *makefiles*, providing a set of generic rules for most RPCGEN-based development. It's more thorough than the *makefiles* presented in Chapter 4.

Example 6-6. A template for RPCGEN RPC development: makefile

```
# NOTE - you MUST define APPN before including these rules...
#  CFLAGS and LFLAGS can be defined later as they aren't rules

# this makefile uses your sources:
# $(APPN).x            -   RPCGEN input, XDR protocol definition
# $(APPN)_svc_proc.c   -   define server process called by server stub
```

Example 6-6. A template for RPCGEN RPC development: makefile (Continued)

```
# $(APPN).c          -   tell the client what to do (talk to servers etc)
# $(APPN)_shared.h   -   shared include stuff (added since last month)
# to make the following:
# $(APPN)_xdr.c      -   client/server XDR library access
# $(APPN)_svc.c      -   server stub, a main() wrapper
# $(APPN)_clnt.c     -   client stub w/ function name defined in protocol
# $(APPN).h          -   miscellaneous includes generated from protocol def.
# $(APPN)            -   the executable for the client
# $(APPN)_svc        -   the executable for the server
RSRC=$(APPN).x $(APPN)_svc_proc.c $(APPN).c $(APPN)_shared.h

# change these for different machines and stages of development
#APPN=
CFLAGS= -g -DDEBUG
LFLAGS=

# compile the protocol
$(APPN)_xdr.c $(APPN)_svc.c $(APPN)_clnt.c $(APPN).h: $(APPN).x
        rpcgen $(APPN).x

# build the client application
$(APPN): $(APPN).h $(APPN)_shared.h $(APPN).o $(APPN)_clnt.o $(APPN)_xdr.o
        cc $(CFLAGS) -o $(APPN) $(APPN).o $(APPN)_clnt.o $(APPN)_xdr.o \
        $(LFLAGS)

# explicitly watch for .h files changes
$(APPN).o: $(APPN).c $(APPN).h $(APPN)_shared.h
        $(CC) -c -o $@ $(CFLAGS) $(APPN).c
$(APPN)_svc_proc.o: $(APPN)_svc_proc.c $(APPN).h $(APPN)_shared.h
        $(CC) -c -o $@ $(CFLAGS) $(APPN)_svc_proc.c

# build the server application
$(APPN)_svc: $(APPN).h $(APPN)_shared.h $(APPN)_svc_proc.o $(APPN)_svc.o \
$(APPN)_xdr.o
        cc $(CFLAGS) -o $(APPN)_svc $(APPN)_svc_proc.o $(APPN)_svc.o \
        $(APPN)_xdr.o $(LFLAGS)

# Build a local-running, dbxtool-able version w/ no XDR or RPC use. Note for
# link to succeed, keep your xdr_free()'s and the like in one compilation
# unit (file).  I keep them in $(APPN)_svc_proc.c.

local: $(APPN).h $(APPN).c $(APPN)_svc_proc.c
        egrep -v xdr_ $(APPN)_svc_proc.c>`date|awk '{print
$$1$$2$$3}'`_svc_proc.c
        egrep -v clnt_ $(APPN).c>`date|awk '{print $$1$$2$$3}'`.c
        $(CC) -g -DDEBUG -o local `date|awk '{print $$1$$2$$3}'`.c \
        `date|awk '{print $$1$$2$$3}'`_svc_proc.c $(LFLAGS)
#       $(RM) `date|awk '{print $$1$$2$$3}'`.c and
#             `date|awk '{print $$1$$2$$3}'`_svc_proc.c after dbx-ing.
#       Do not edit them, change $(APPN)_svc_proc.c and $(APPN).c.

# OR if you have the #defines mentioned in $(APPN).c to remove
# clnt_create(), and that's your only use of RPC, try this.  Note use of
# -DDEBUG conditional compile flag, assumes you used #ifdef DEBUG.

localD: $(APPN).h $(APPN).c $(APPN)_svc_proc.c
        egrep -v xdr_ $(APPN)_svc_proc.c>`date|awk '{print
$$1$$2$$3}'`_svc_proc.c
        $(CC) -g -DDEBUG -o localD  $(APPN).c \
        `date|awk '{print $$1$$2$$3}'`_svc_proc.c $(LFLAGS)
#       $(RM) `date|awk '{print $$1$$2$$3}'`_svc_proc.c after dbx-ing.
#       Do not edit it, change $(APPN)_svc_proc.c.

# There are no xdr_free() calls in $(APPN)_svc_proc.c, so 'make localS'
# doesn't need to do anything but link the client main w/ the server
```

Example 6-6. A template for RPCGEN RPC development: makefile (Continued)

```
# procedure.  A dummy server must be started as the client still
# builds handles.

localS: $(APPN).h $(APPN)_svc_proc.c $(APPN).c
        $(CC) $(CFLAGS) -DDEBUG -o $(APPN) $(APPN)_svc_proc.c $(APPN).c $(LFLAGS)

# blast away
clean:
        rm -f $(APPN) $(APPN)_svc $(APPN)_svc.c $(APPN)_xdr.c $(APPN)_clnt.c
$(APPN)
.h *.o *.*%

$(APPN).ar: $(RSRC)
        bundle $(RSRC) > $(APPN).a
```

The only major change made in the top half of the *makefile* is the addition of the shared header file `application_shared.h`. I used `$(APPN)_shared.h` instead of `$(APPN).h` because the latter is the header file produced by RPCGEN. The bottom half addresses the testing of server procedures and the `rip` application. I'll elaborate on this shortly.

Put this *makefile* somewhere to be used by other projects. It contains nothing particular to this application, just a set of rules to maintain the filenames in Figure 6-2. You could put a *makefile* in the development directory that looks something like this:

```
APPN    = rip
include ../Makefile

CFLAGS  = -O2  # note - don't try to use -O4 with signals...
LFLAGS  = -lm -lpixrect -lsuntool -lsunwindow

#got a FPU?: CFLAGS  = -f68881, LFLAGS  = /usr/lib/f68881/libm.i

# start the servers
ItGo:
        rsh c2a src/$(APPN)/$(APPN)_svc < /dev/null &
        rsh badlands $$PWD/$(APPN)_svc_4 < /dev/null &
        rsh calvin $$PWD/$(APPN)_svc_4 < /dev/null &
        rsh unclejack $$PWD/$(APPN)_svc_4 < /dev/null &
        rsh hobbes $$PWD/$(APPN)_svc_4 < /dev/null &
        rsh zeus $$PWD/$(APPN)_svc_3 < /dev/null &
        rsh glacier $$PWD/$(APPN)_svc_3 < /dev/null &
        rsh bach $$PWD/$(APPN)_svc_3 < /dev/null &
        $(APPN) script 512 512
        slay $$PWD/$(APPN)_svc
```

You could fix the compile and link flags in the previous *makefile* and just specify the application name by using the `-D` flag with `make`:

```
rodson> make APPN=application target
```

I also added on a rule to make `ItGo`. This starts a bunch of server processes and runs the `rip` client application. When that finishes, `make` runs the `slay` script (from Chapter 4) to terminate the server processes by killing the `rs` commands running in the background. This is handy while in the development stage but eventually I would embed the code for starting the remote server within the application. (See Chapter 8 for cleaner, neater ways to maintain servers.)

Remote Image Processing (RIP)

Figure 6-3 outlines the approach taken to distribute the pieces of an image processing application across the network. The local (client) process runs behind a SunView window. The images and filter coefficients are read into the client and passed to each server machine before any processing takes place. This is done explicitly by passing data values after the server connection is made.

I have had good results passing NFS filenames and having each server repeat the image reading process.[†] The alternative is to pass the image data the same number of times. That kind of implementation is left to the student as an exercise.

Once stuffed with data, the servers are ready to service requests from the client in the form of image processing commands like `Convolve`. These commands are read from a script. These operations are realized by passing image and kernel name input arguments to each server. Each server is also sent the coordinates of a *subimage*; that is, some rectangular subset of the whole image to be processed by that server. Once the subimage has been processed, its pixel values are then returned to the client. We're using a spatial divide-and-conquer strategy for parallelization.

Specifying Filter Coefficients

There are long-winded explanations of the mathematics behind the convolution of an image with a kernel. Suffice it to say that the object of the game is to treat small rectangular areas of the image. We will generate each pixel of a new image by weighting the pixels of a corresponding rectangular region in the old image. We multiply these old pixel values by the filter coefficients we define in a file. These weights are called filter coefficients. The complete collection of rectangularly-grouped coefficients is a convolution kernel.

What we will see here are some simple, fast operations being performed by servers. In this case, my Ethernet bandwidth limitation often becomes a performance-limiter. In the final application, things must be designed carefully to avoid making the target network's bandwidth a limitation.

With Figure 6-3 as a mental image, let's define what the user interface might be.We want to see the results of image processing operations on images, so we should open a window to put them in. We must specify the filter and image inputs for each operation. Each filter will be represented by a text file of coefficients. Images shall

---

† I'll talk more about ways to improve large data transfer rates between clients and servers in Chapters 8 and 10. Simple data compression schemes, like run-length limiting, often pay off.

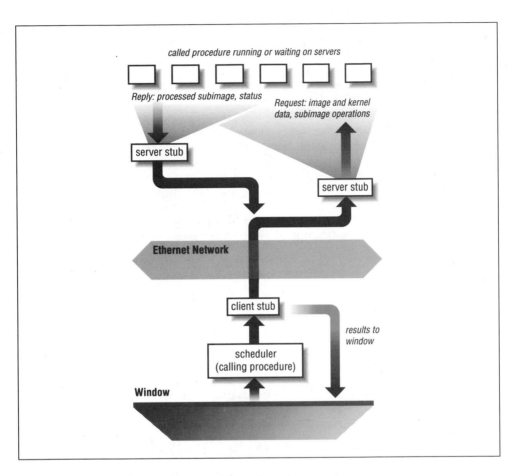

Figure 6-3. A model for Remote Image Processing

be stored in Sun `rasterfile(5)`, raster-scan pixel format. I don't want to get sidetracked with a protracted window, tool, and menu development, so we'll drive the client application with textual input at `stdin`. A session might consist of the commands shown in Example 6-7.

Example 6-7. Sample input script for rip

```
Help
AddServer c2a; a multi-processor Convex compute-server
        ; with RPCGEN software
        ; requires sed 's/rint(/((/' rip_svc_proc.c
AddServer badlands; a SPARC server w/ lots of RAM
AddServer calvin; a SPARC server w/ lots of RAM
AddServer unclejack; a SPARC server w/ lots of RAM
AddServer hobbes; a SPARC server w/ lots of RAM
AddServer zeus; sun 3/260
AddServer glacier; sun 3/260
AddServer bach; this sorry-little 3/160 went for coffee,
AddServer dspuv2; a u-vax - running my own
```

Example 6-7. Sample input script for rip (Continued)

```
              ; xdr_pointer() and strdup()
ReadKernel SobelX; read filter coefficients or kernels
ReadKernel SobelY
ReadKernel BoxCar
ReadImage /home/cortex/Images/Left.ras
Convolve /home/cortex/Images/Left.ras SobelX 4
Convolve /home/cortex/Images/Left.ras SobelY 4
Convolve /home/cortex/Images/Left.ras BoxCar 4
```

A series of `AddServer` commands puts servers on an availability list. The `ReadKernel` command reads the filter coefficients (convolution kernels) from a file and the `ReadImage` command reads image data. Copies of the kernels and the image data are then sent to each available server. We're then ready to try some distributed filtering operations (convolutions) and view the results.

Below is a sample of one of the kernel data files read in. This is a BoxCar average kernel. It has 9 elements, and is applied as a 3×3 kernel centered on each pixel.[†]

```
.111
.111
.111
.111
.111
.111
.111
.111
.111
```

This kernel has the effect of averaging surrounding detail, thereby smoothing or blurring the picture somewhat. This can be useful when attempting to remove high frequency artifacts or separating images into frequency bands.

rip Development: It's as Easy as 1 2 3

Let's follow the three development steps as outlined above, and look at the `rip` example.

Step 1: Define the Protocol

Defining the protocol is the best place to start. It forces you to define the inputs and outputs of the problem. I am referring to the data sent to servers (client requests) and that returned to the client (server replies). The form of the data exchanged frames the problem at both client and server ends.

Example 6-8 shows the protocol definition in *rip.x*. We use integers and floats in the `Image` and `Kernel` data structures that the client and server will exchange. For pixel values, we use the `opaque` data type with the number of pixels or byte-count

---

† A note to the signal/image processing readers: `rip_svc` makes no attempt to save the computations by exploiting the separability of filters like this.

determined at run-time. This is required as the data size will vary from time to time and from server to server.

Example 6-8. Protocol for client/server remote image processing exchanges: rip.x

```
/*
 * rip.x: remote image processing protocol between servers and client.
 * First, define the tokens referencing image processing functions, used in
 * the op fields.
 */
const       READIMAGE      = 0;
const       READKERNEL     = 1;
const       CONVOLVE       = 2;
const       OPENWINDOW     = 3;
const       ADDSERVER      = 4;
const       HELP           = 5;

const       SUCCESS        = 0xfd;        /* request processed */
const       ERROR          = 0xfe;        /* can't honor request */
const       EMPTY          = 0xff;
const       MAXKER         = 64;          /* maximum kernel size */
const       MAXSTR         = 256;         /* maximum string length */
const       MAXPIX         = 1036800;     /* handle 1152x900 pixel
                                           * regions */

/*
 * Define structures shared by client and server.
 */
struct Image {                        /* (sub)image, byte-deep pixels */
    string          sName < MAXSTR >; /* miscellaneous NULL-term'd strings */
    int             x;
    int             y;                /* tl corner of the pixel region */
    int             dx;
    int             dy;               /* region width and height */
    opaque          Data < MAXPIX >;  /* the raw data */
    struct Image    *pNext;           /* requires system w/ xdr_pointer()
                                       * support */
};

struct Kernel {
    string          sName < MAXSTR >;
    int             xsize;
    int             ysize;
    float           Value < MAXKER >;
    struct Kernel   *pNext;
};

/*
 * Define the client and server data exchanged.  Be consistent here. It's
 * important to fully define union structure elements at run-time. Pointers
 * left uninitialized to some random non-NULL value will cause erratic
 * errors as filters like xdr_pointer() try to look through them.
 */
union Packet switch (int op) {
    case ADDSERVER:      string sOp < MAXSTR >;
    case READIMAGE:      Image * pImage;
    case READKERNEL:     Kernel * pKernel;
    case CONVOLVE:       Image * pImage;
    case SUCCESS:        void;
    case ERROR:          string sOp < MAXSTR >;
    default:             string sOp < MAXSTR >;
};

/*
 * The rip server program and procedure definition.
 */
```

Example 6-8. Protocol for client/server remote image processing exchanges: rip.x (Continued)

```
program RIPPROG {
  version RIPVERS {
    Packet RIP(Packet) = 1; /* procedure # 1 will input and output
                             * Packets */
  } = 1;                    /* version # */
} =  0x20000001;            /* RPC program #, see Chapter 4 for
                            * explanation */
```

```
RPCGEN will transform the Packet union to the following:
struct Packet {
        int op;
        union {
                char *sOp;
                Image *pImage;
                Kernel *pKernel;
                Image *pImage;
                char *sOp;
                char *sOp;
        } Packet_u;
}
```

Notice we use only one data structure, `Packet`, for both request and reply argument.

This helps simplify things. Being a discriminate union, it allows run-time structure modification, but must be cast with care. Depending on the operation `op` specified (the constants from 0 to 5 in the protocol), the `Packet` can contain a string, an image, or a filter kernel.

The program definition block only defines the one procedure `rip_1()`. The server stub will contain a response mechanism in case someone calls the NULL procedure, but other than that, the server only has one registered procedure to dispatch. We will have a need to perform a number of different image processing procedures at each server. Instead of defining a large number of procedures in the protocol, I opted to do my own dispatching to call the different processing procedures. Our server procedure `rip_1()` will look at the `op` operation specifier instead of the request parameter to determine what procedure to call.

The only reason for doing your own operation (procedure) dispatching at the server is to simplify the program block of the protocol file. Examples in later chapters use multiple service procedures, relying on the RPCGEN-generated dispatcher to do the request decoding and procedure selection.

Step 2: Building the Client Procedure

Next let's define the `main()` client procedure. It needs to make the connections to remote servers, schedule the remote calls, and gather results—all in adherence to the protocol. To keep things simple, we have limited error logging and error checking at client and server. Error handling is essential for robust behavior and we will look at it in Chapter 12. For example, if a server fails, you should drop that handle and reissue any lost requests. The `main()` in *rip.c* establishes a SunView window to view the results in, then proceeds to parse input commands and handle them with a combination of local and remote processing (using BFS with RPC).

Before looking at *rip.c*, let's look at *rip_shared.h*, the file that contains the shared definitions, in Example 6-9.

Example 6-9. Definitions and macros shared between user client and server RIP code: rip_shared.h

```
/*
 * rip_shared.h - remote image processing common header file (different
 * from rip.h generated by RPCGEN).
 */
#define MAXSERVERS    8
#define MAXARGS       6
#define MIN(a,b)      (a<b)?a:b
#define MAX(a,b)      (a>b)?a:b
#define TRAVERSE(p,a) for(p=a; (p->pNext!=NULL); p=p->pNext)
#define FAILED(line_num, args, line) \
  { fprintf(stderr, "%s failed on line %d: \"%s\"\n", args[0], line_num, line); }

typedef char   *string;

/* Procedure definition stubs */
        /* Parsing in commands: */
ReadRIP();                  /* Read a rip command line from a file */
Parse();                    /* Parse a command line */
RemoveComments();           /* Helps out in above */

        /* Scheduling server jobs */
SubBFS();                   /* Launches and partitions server jobs */
ForkNextServer();           /* Used in SubBFS() to launch children */
FreeServer();               /* Used in SubBFS() to mark children as free */
RequestAll();               /* Send one request to every server */

        /* Client-side rip operations */
AddServer();                /* Try to add a server to the active list */
ReadImage();                /* Read a rasterfile, cc: to servers */
ReadKernel();               /* Reads in a filter kernel, cc: to servers */
Convolve();                 /* Tells servers what image and kernel to
                             * convolve */

        /* Server-side rip operations */
SAddServer();               /* Free local memory, reset */
SReadImage();               /* Copy this raster image */
SReadKernel();              /* "       "    kernel */
SConvolve();                /* Use the named image and kernel for convolution */

        /* Client window overhead */
OpenWindow();               /* Starts things off - all action thru the window */
MouseCaught();              /* Mouse notifier routine to fire-off rip
                             * operations */
Help();                     /* Lists know command usage */
```

The server procedures and the client's own procedures are now prototyped. The client and server both include the *rip_shared.h*, so to avoid any contention, procedure names are unique for each side. I did attempt to keep function names similar; for example, the client calls ReadKernel() when it encounters the ReadKernel in the command stream. The client reads the file and passes the filter coefficients to the server, requesting it to call SReadKernel() to record the new kernel.

Now let's look at the client code, *rip.c*, in Example 6-10. The RPC-related calls and definitions are in bold. You might notice the extensive use of conditional-compilation preprocessor directives. I use DEBUG here to defeat the `fork()`-based BFS scheme when I want to step through execution from the parent process.

Example 6-10. Client procedures for RIP: rip.c

```
/*
 * rip.c: remote image processing client main.
 */
#include <stdio.h>
#include <math.h>
#include <string.h>
#include <suntool/sunview.h>
#include <suntool/canvas.h>
#include <rpc/rpc.h>
#include "rip.h"
#include "rip_shared.h"

/*
 * Global server/client relationship stuff - max servers <= 8.
 */
char            ServersFree = 0x0;      /* bits are 1 if free, 0 if busy */
int             NumServers;             /* total # of servers connected */
int             ServerPid[MAXSERVERS];  /* used to record fork()'ed pids */
char            ServerName[MAXSERVERS][32];   /* record server names */
CLIENT          *cl[MAXSERVERS];        /* client handles */

/*
 * Client <--> server data structures, defined in protocol.
 */
Packet          *pRequest;
Packet          *pReply;
struct timeval  DebugTime;      /* fool w/ time out during REMOTE_debug */

/*
 * Global graphic, display and I/O stuff.
 */
Kernel          *pKernel = NULL; /* list of active kernels */
Image           *pImage = NULL;  /* list of active images */
Pixwin          *pPw;            /* the window canvas for the data */
Pixrect         *pPr;            /* the pixrect behind the window */
colormap_t      Colormap;        /* source colormap */
Pixrect         *pPrTmp;         /* a temporary subimage-sized pixrect */
FILE            *fp;             /* opened script */

/* rip.h token */
char            *pUsage[] = {
  "ReadImage", "ImageFileName",                          /* 0 */
  "ReadKernel", "KernelFileName",                        /* 1 */
  "Convolve", "ImageFileName KernelFileName BlockFactor", /* 2 */
  "OpenWindow", "WindowLabel Xsize Ysize",               /* 3 */
  "AddServer", "ServerName",                             /* 4 */
  "Help", "",                                            /* 5 */
NULL, NULL};

main(argc, argv)
  int           argc;
  char          *argv[];
{
  char          args[MAXARGS][MAXSTR];

  if ((argc != 4) || !(fp = fopen(argv[1], "r"))) {
    fprintf(stderr, "Usage: %s filename xsize ysize\n", argv[0]);
    exit(-1);
```

Example 6-10. Client procedures for RIP: rip.c (Continued)

```
    }
    pRequest = (Packet *) malloc(sizeof(Packet));
    pReply = (Packet *) malloc(sizeof(Packet));

    /*
     * Open a window, click to advance thru commands. SunView is the front-end
     * for all the processing, managing mouse events in the window.
     * OpenWindow() remains as an rip operation, but this version doesn't
     * support more than the one main() window.
     */
    strcpy(args[0], "OpenWindow");
    strcpy(args[1], argv[0]);
    strcpy(args[2], argv[2]);
    strcpy(args[3], argv[3]);
    OpenWindow(3, args);
}

/*
 * ReadRIP() - read a command line, clean-up & parse it in, then attempt to
 * fill a Request packet.  Note I avoided stdin, as SunView signals
 * complicate its use!
 */
ReadRIP()
{
    int             i, op = 0;
    char            line[MAXSTR];
    char            args[MAXARGS][MAXSTR];
    static int      line_num = 0;
    int             arg_count = 0;

    if (!fgets(line, MAXSTR, fp))
        exit(0);
    printf("%s", line);
    line_num++;
    RemoveComments(line);
    if (line[0] && ((arg_count = Parse(line, args)) >= 0)) {
        pRequest->op = EMPTY;
        /*
         * Establish tokens for the operation.
         */
        for (i = 0; pUsage[i] && strcmp(pUsage[i], args[0]); op++, i += 2);
        if (!pUsage[i])
            fprintf(stderr,
                    "don't know how to \"%s\" at line %d: \"%s\"\n",
                    args[0], line_num, line);
        switch (op) {
        case READIMAGE:                 /* send total image to each server */
            if (!ReadImage(arg_count, args))
                FAILED(line_num, args, line);
            RequestAll();
            break;
        case READKERNEL:                /* send kernel to each server */
            if (!ReadKernel(arg_count, args))
                FAILED(line_num, args, line);
            RequestAll();
            break;
        case CONVOLVE:                  /* split & schedule up job across servers */
            if (!Convolve(arg_count, args))
                FAILED(line_num, args, line);
            SubBFS();
            break;
        case OPENWINDOW:                /* locally open a window - careful ! */
            if (!OpenWindow(arg_count, args))
                FAILED(line_num, args, line);
            break;
```

Example 6-10. Client procedures for RIP: rip.c (Continued)

```
        case ADDSERVER:                 /* locally add a server */
          if (!AddServer(arg_count, args))
            FAILED(line_num, args, line);
          break;
        case HELP:                      /* locally do Help */
          if (!Help(arg_count, args))
            FAILED(line_num, args, line);
          break;
        default:
          break;
        }
    }    /* end of if non-null line, Request done (if there was one) */
    return (TRUE);
}


/*
 * SubBFS() - an operation is to be performed on an image. Break image into
 * subimages, and send subimage definition, along with the operation, to
 * each registered server.  Pixel-value results are then dumped to the open
 * window.
 */

SubBFS()
{
  Image           *pSubIm = pRequest->Packet_u.pImage;
  int             CPid;

  /*
   * Schedule-out one block of the image to be processed.
   */
  for (pSubIm->x = 0; pSubIm->x < pPr->pr_size.x; pSubIm->x += pSubIm->dx)
    for (pSubIm->y = 0; pSubIm->y < pPr->pr_size.y; pSubIm->y += pSubIm->dy) {
      /*
       * Keep all the servers busy.  Fork a process to manage I/O and
       * scheduling to the next available server, reflect allocation in
       * ServersFree and ServerPid[].  Note that process maint. must be
       * performed by the parent - children can't easily communicate their
       * own status and do all the logging.  Other approaches include shared
       * memory, signals, or the like - again, complicated by SunView.
       */
#ifndef DEBUG                 /* Using child processes if not debugging */
      while (ServersFree == 0x0) {
        /*
         * No servers free, loop until one becomes available.
         */
        while ((CPid = wait((union wait *) NULL)) == -1) {
          printf("everybody's busy i guess...");
          usleep(100000);
        }
        FreeServer(CPid);
      }
#endif
      ForkNextServer();
#ifdef DEBUG
      ServersFree = 0xff;   /* Debugging: free without concept of a child */
#endif
    }
  /*
   * Wait here to clean things up - till all children return.
   */
#ifndef DEBUG
  while ((CPid = wait((union wait *) NULL)) != -1)
    FreeServer(CPid);
#endif
```

Example 6-10. Client procedures for RIP: rip.c (Continued)

```
}

/*
 * ForkNextServer() - Fork and start remote procedure on the server (let UNIX
 * manage resource contention and detailed scheduling!). Record allocation
 * and pid in ServersFree and ServerPid[], resp.
 */
ForkNextServer()
{
  int            Server;        /* Number of who gets allocated */
  char           SMask;
  int            Parent = TRUE;

  /*
   * Direct computations to a free server.  The servers could get all
   * allocated so might have to wait for the next available server.
   */
  if (Parent) {
    for (Server = 0; Server < NumServers; Server++) {
      SMask = 0x1 << Server;
      if (SMask & ServersFree) {
        /*
         * Allocate the free server, record !free status. Parent returns.
         */
        ServersFree ^= SMask;
#ifdef DEBUG                           /* No fork()'s if debugging. */
        DebugTime.tv_sec = 1000;
        DebugTime.tv_usec = 0;  /* Slow things down - man rpc for help. */
        clnt_control(cl[Server], CLSET_TIMEOUT, (char *) &DebugTime);
        goto LAUNCH;
#endif
        if (ServerPid[Server] = fork())
            return (TRUE);
        Parent = FALSE;
        break;
      }
    }
  }
  /* Children only! - unless DEBUGging */
LAUNCH:
  pReply = rip_1(pRequest, cl[Server]);
  if ((pReply == NULL) || (pReply->op == ERROR)) {
    /*
     * An error occurred while calling the server, print error message and
     * move on.
     */
    clnt_perror(cl[Server], ServerName[Server]);
    if (ServerPid[Server])
      _exit(-1);                        /* Don't kill parent if debugging. */
  }
  /*
   * Okay, we successfully called the remote procedure, successfully got
   * back raster data, send it to the frame buffer.  Note the data is
   * assumed organized in raster order across a given subimage, reducing
   * client and server address calculation overhead.
   */

  (char *) ((struct mpr_data *) pPrTmp->pr_data)->md_image =
    pReply->Packet_u.pImage->Data.Data_val;
  pw_write(pPw, pReply->Packet_u.pImage->x, pReply->Packet_u.pImage->y,
           pReply->Packet_u.pImage->dx, pReply->Packet_u.pImage->dy,
           PIX_SRC, pPrTmp, 0, 0);

  if (!Parent)
    _exit(0);                           /* Kill child, don't kill debugging parent. */
```

Example 6-10. Client procedures for RIP: rip.c (Continued)

```
}

/*
 * RequestAll() - send the assembled request to each registered server.
 */
RequestAll()
{
  int            Server;
  for (Server = 0; Server < NumServers; Server++) {
    pReply = rip_1(pRequest, cl[Server]);
    if ((pReply == NULL) || (pReply->op == ERROR)) {

      clnt_perror(cl[Server], ServerName[Server]);
      _exit(-1);
    }
  }
}

/*
 * Marking servers as free from the child (in the parent's space) is
 * difficult and can cause collisions, so I do it in the parent process.
 */
FreeServer(CPid)
  int          CPid;
{
  int          i;
  char         mask = 0x1;

  for (i = 0; i < NumServers; i++)
    if (CPid == ServerPid[i])
      break;

  if (i == NumServers) {
    fprintf(stderr, "FreeServer: bad mask didn't");
    return (FALSE);
  }
  mask <<= i;
  ServersFree |= mask;
  return (TRUE);
}

Parse(line, args)
  char         line[];
  char         args[MAXARGS][MAXSTR];
{
  int          FoundArg = 0;
  int          line_index = 0;
  int          arg_index = 0;
  int          char_index = 0;

  args[0][0] = NULL;                 /* In case there are no args - should have
                                      * avoided this. */

  while (line[line_index] != NULL) {
    /* No leading or trailing spaces exist, RemoveComments(), start new arg. */
    if (line[line_index] == ' ') {
      args[arg_index][char_index] = NULL;   /* terminate the previous arg */
      arg_index++;
      char_index = 0;
    } else {
      FoundArg++;
      args[arg_index][char_index++] = line[line_index];
    }
    line_index++;
```

Example 6-10. Client procedures for RIP: rip.c (Continued)

```
    }
    args[arg_index][char_index] = NULL;
    if (FoundArg)
      return (arg_index);
    return (-1);
}

/* Included for completeness, not necessary if you constrain input text. */
RemoveComments(line)      /* Comment char ';', whitespace ' ', ',', '\t' */
  char            line[];
{
  char            *p_c;, new_line[MAXSTR];
  int             i = j = 0;

  /* swap tabs and ',' for spaces if there are any */
  while (p_c = strchr(line, '\t')) *p_c = ' ';
  while (p_c = strchr(line, ',')) *p_c = ' ';

  /* Stop at a ';', as well as remove multiple spaces. */
  for (i = 0; line[i] != NULL; i++) {
    if (line[i] == ';') { new_line[j] = NULL; break; }
    if (!((i > 0) && (line[i] == ' ') && (line[i - 1] == ' ')))
      new_line[j++] = line[i];
  } new_line[j] = NULL;

  /* Remove leading and trailing space if they exist. */
  while (new_line[0] == ' ') strcpy(new_line, &new_line[1]);
  j = strlen(new_line);
  for (i = 1; i < j; i++) {
    if (new_line[j - i] == ' ') new_line[j - i] = NULL;
    if (new_line[j - i] == '\n') new_line[j - i] = NULL;
    else break;
  } strcpy(line, new_line);

  return (TRUE);
}

/*
 * Operations from here on - client primitives for image processing. See
 * pUsage[][] as defined in main() for some use guidance.
 */
ReadImage(argc, args)                /* Reads rasterfile image file. */
  int             argc;
  char            args[MAXARGS][MAXSTR];
{
  Image           *pI;
  FILE            *fpIn;

  if (argc != 1)
    return (FALSE);

  if (!(fpIn = fopen(args[1], "r")) || !(pPr = pr_load(fpIn, &Colormap))) {
    fprintf(stderr, "cannot load image \"%s\"\n", args[1]);
    return (FALSE);
  }
  fclose(fpIn);

  /* Stuff it in the window */
  pw_rop(pPw, 0, 0, pPr->pr_size.x, pPr->pr_size.y,
         PIX_SRC, pPr, 0, 0);

  /* Go to end of list and add an image. */
  if (!pImage) {
    pI = pImage = (Image *) malloc(sizeof(Image));
  } else {
```

Example 6-10. Client procedures for RIP: rip.c (Continued)

```
      TRAVERSE(pI, pImage);
      pI->pNext = (Image *) malloc(sizeof(Image));
      pI = pI->pNext;
    }
    pI->pNext = NULL;

    /* Put the data into the Image structure for a local copy. */
    pI->sName = strdup(args[1]);
    pI->x = pI->y = 0;
    pI->dx = pPr->pr_size.x;
    pI->dy = pPr->pr_size.y;
    pI->Data.Data_len = pPr->pr_size.x * pPr->pr_size.y * pPr->pr_depth / 8;
    /* volatile - SHOULD REALLY COPY IMAGE */
    pI->Data.Data_val =
      (char *) ((struct mpr_data *) pPr->pr_data)->md_image;

    /* Build up Request packet - XDR handles struct ptrs... */
    pRequest->op = READIMAGE;
    pRequest->Packet_u.pImage = pI;
    return (TRUE);
}

/* Reads a kernel file - square, asymmetric, nonseparable filters assumed */
ReadKernel(argc, args)
    int              argc;
    char             args[MAXARGS][MAXSTR];
{
    FILE             *fpIn;
    Kernel           *pK;
    int              i, j, k;

    if (argc != 1)
      return (FALSE);

    if ((fpIn = fopen(args[1], "r"))) {
      fprintf(stderr, "cannot load kernel \"%s\"\n", args[1]);
      return (FALSE);
    }
    /* Go to end of list and add a kernel */
    if (!pKernel) {
      pK = pKernel = (Kernel *) malloc(sizeof(Kernel));
    } else {
      TRAVERSE(pK, pKernel);
      pK->pNext = (Kernel *) malloc(sizeof(Kernel));
      pK = pK->pNext;
    }
    pK->pNext = NULL;

    /* Read data file in. */
    pK->Value.Value_val = (float *) malloc(sizeof(float) * MAXKER);
    for (k = 0; (fscanf(fpIn, "%f", &pK->Value.Value_val[k]) == 1); k++) {
      if (k >= MAXKER) {
        fprintf(stderr, "%s: kernel too big\n", args[1]);
        return (FALSE);
      }
    }
    fclose(fpIn);

    /* Update the local kernel list. */
    pK->sName = strdup(args[1]);
    pK->xsize = pK->ysize = rint(sqrt((double) k));
    pK->Value.Value_len = k;          /* XDR only send this much, not MAXKER */

    /* Build up Request packet */
    pRequest->op = READKERNEL;
```

Example 6-10. Client procedures for RIP: rip.c (Continued)

```
    pRequest->Packet_u.pKernel = pK;
    return (TRUE);
}

AddServer(argc, args)/* Attempt to reset & add another server to the list. */
    int             argc;
    char            args[MAXARGS][MAXSTR];
{
    int             i;

    if (argc != 1)
      return (FALSE);

    /*
     * Create another client "handle" used for calling MESSAGEPROG on servers
     * designated on command line.  We tell RPC package to use the "tcp"
     * protocol when contacting the server.
     */
    if (NumServers >= MAXSERVERS) {
      fprintf(stderr, "%s: too many servers, max is %d\n",
              args[0], MAXSERVERS);
      return (NULL);

    }
    /*
     * Build-up Serverxxx information, attempt to reset the server, qualify
     * candidates.
     */
    cl[NumServers] = clnt_create(args[1], RIPPROG, RIPVERS, "tcp");
    if (!cl[NumServers]) {
       /*
        * Couldn't establish connection with server, print error message.
        */
       clnt_pcreateerror(args[1]);
       return (NULL);
    }
    /*
     * Attempt to initialize the server, to check its health.  I throw away
     * the returned server hostname.
     */
    pRequest->op = ADDSERVER;
    pRequest->Packet_u.sOp = strdup(args[1]);
    pReply = rip_1(pRequest, cl[NumServers]);
    if (!pReply || (pReply->op != ADDSERVER)) {
       fprintf(stderr, "%s: could not reset %s\n", args[0],
               ServerName[NumServers]);
       return (FALSE);
    }
    /*
     * This server is okay, register it.
     */
    strcpy(ServerName[NumServers], args[1]);
    ServersFree <<= 1;
    ServersFree |= 0x1;
    NumServers++;
    return (TRUE);
}

Convolve(argc, args)                    /* Convolve an image w/ a kernel. */
    int             argc;
    char            args[MAXARGS][MAXSTR];
{
    char            *sBuf[MAXSTR];
    Image           *pSubIm;
```

Example 6-10. Client procedures for RIP: rip.c (Continued)

```
  if (argc != 3)
    return (FALSE);

  /* Build up Request packet - passing image and kernel names is poorly
   * done. */
  pRequest->op = CONVOLVE;
  sprintf(sBuf, "%s %s", args[1], args[2]);

  /*
   * Define the subimage size.  Always zero the opaque data lengths and
   * unused struct pointers - XDR looks at them!
   */
  pSubIm = pRequest->Packet_u.pImage = (Image *) malloc(sizeof(Image));
  pRequest->Packet_u.pImage->Data.Data_len = 0;
  pSubIm->sName = strdup(sBuf);
  pSubIm->pNext = NULL;
  pSubIm->dx = pSubIm->dy = pPr->pr_size.x / atoi(args[3]);    /* square! */

  /* Update the local working subimage pixrect. */
  if (pPrTmp)
    mem_destroy(pPrTmp);
  pPrTmp = mem_create(pSubIm->dx, pSubIm->dy, 8);


  return (TRUE);
}

OpenWindow(argc, args)              /* Open a SunView window and loop on it. */
  int            argc;
  char           args[MAXARGS][MAXSTR];
{
  int            i;
  u_char         gray[256];
  Frame          frame;
  Canvas         canvas;

  if (argc != 3)
    return (FALSE);

  /* Create tool and get a hold of its pixwin, install mouse catcher. */
  frame = window_create((Frame) NULL, FRAME, FRAME_LABEL, args[1], 0);
  canvas = window_create(frame, CANVAS, WIN_WIDTH, atoi(args[2]),
                   WIN_HEIGHT, atoi(args[3]), WIN_EVENT_PROC, MouseCaught, 0);
  window_fit(frame);
  pPw = canvas_pixwin(canvas);


  /* Build and install a ramp color table if the image doesn't have one. */
  if ((Colormap.type == RMT_NONE) || !Colormap.length) {
    for (i = 0; i < 256; i++)
      gray[i] = i;
    pw_setcmsname(pPw, "ramp");
    Colormap.type = RMT_EQUAL_RGB;
    Colormap.length = 256;
    Colormap.map[0] = Colormap.map[1] = Colormap.map[2] = gray;
  } else {
    pw_setcmsname(pPw, "original");
  }
  pw_putcolormap(pPw, 0, Colormap.length, Colormap.map[0],
                   Colormap.map[1], Colormap.map[2]);

  /*
   * Watch out - indiscriminate mixing of signals with the dispatcher is
   * fatal!  Read the SunView Programmer's Guide.
   */
```

Example 6-10. Client procedures for RIP: rip.c (Continued)

```
    window_main_loop(frame);        /* never returns... */
}

/*
 * MouseCaught() - event procedure called by SunView Notifier. Click the
 * left button to consume an rip command.
 */
MouseCaught(canvas, event, arg)
    Canvas          canvas;
    Event           *event;
    caddr_t         arg;
{
    int             i, j;
    if ((event_action(event) == MS_LEFT) && event_is_up(event)) {
        ReadRIP();                  /* Process one command from script. */
    }
}

Help(argc, args)
    int             argc;
    char            args[MAXARGS][MAXSTR];

{
    int             zz;
    fprintf(stderr, "commands include:\n");
    for (zz = 0; pUsage[zz] != NULL; zz += 2)
        fprintf(stderr, "%s %s\n", pUsage[zz], pUsage[zz + 1]);
    return (TRUE);
}
```

We define some global data structures and on-line help information. The `main()` procedure then opens a SunView window and begins parsing lines from the file specified on the command line. If a valid command is found, the appropriate local action is taken. The local and remote actions to be taken are specified within each client procedure: `AddServer()`, `ReadImage()`, `ReadKernel()`, `Convolve()`, `OpenWindow()`, and `Help()`. There is a one-to-one mapping between a procedure and command in the input script.

Step 3: Developing the Server Procedure

Next we need to tell the server how to respond to requests. In the protocol definition and the client's `main()` procedure, we specified what operations we will support at the server. These were initially defined in *rip_shared.h*.

The server procedures are shown in Example 6-11. Excepting the #include statements, the server procedures need not concern themselves with the RPC system at
all.

Example 6-11. Server procedures for RIP: rip_svc_proc.c

```
#include <stdio.h>
#include <string.h>
#include <math.h>
#include <rpc/rpc.h>
#include "rip.h"
#include "rip_shared.h"
/*
 * Copies of image processing data (lists).
 */
static Kernel   *pKernel = NULL; /* list of active kernels */
static Image    *pImage = NULL;  /* list of active images */
/*
 * rip_1() - server procedure to execute one of many rip operations. As the
 * protocol suggests, Request Packets are returned with some error logging.
 */
Packet          *
rip_1(pRequest)
   Packet       *pRequest;
{
   /*
    * Allocate static space for the return data.
    */
   static Packet   Reply;
   char            sBuf[MAXSTR];
   /*
    * Reset last result & check to see what operation is requested.  I
    * precede the functions w/ and 'S' to avoid function name collision when
    * client and server routines are locally linked for debugging. This is a
    * good way to start testing as there's no XDR formatting. Once you have
    * things working, THEN include the XDR stuff, and tackle those problems
    */
   Reply.op = ERROR;
   switch (pRequest->op) {
   case READIMAGE:                    /* send total image to each server */
      SReadImage(pRequest, &Reply);
      break;
   case READKERNEL:                   /* send kernel to each server */
      SReadKernel(pRequest, &Reply);
      break;
   case CONVOLVE:                     /* split & schedule up job across servers */
      SConvolve(pRequest, &Reply);
      break;
   case ADDSERVER:                    /* locally add a server */
      SAddServer(pRequest, &Reply);
      break;
   default:                           /* below is the kind of thing you should do
                                       * in each function */
      gethostname(sBuf, MAXSTR);
      strcat(sBuf, ": don't understand operation");
      Reply.Packet_u.sOp = strdup(sBuf);
      Reply.op = SUCCESS;
   }
   return (&Reply);
}
/*
 * Server operations for image processing from here on out. Start with
 * SReadImage() - store a copy of this image in the linked list.
 */
SReadImage(pRequest, pReply)
   Packet       *pRequest, *pReply;
```

Example 6-11. Server procedures for RIP: rip_svc_proc.c (Continued)

```
{
  Image          *pI;

  /* Go to end of list and add an image. */
  if (!pImage) {
    pI = pImage = (Image *) malloc(sizeof(Image));
  } else {
    TRAVERSE(pI, pImage);
    pI->pNext = (Image *) malloc(sizeof(Image));
    pI = pI->pNext;
  }
  pI->pNext = NULL;

  /* Put the data into the Image structure for a local copy as it's
   * volatile. */
  bcopy(pRequest->Packet_u.pImage, pI, sizeof(Image));
  pI->sName = strdup(pRequest->Packet_u.pImage->sName);
  pI->Data.Data_val = (char *) malloc((int) pI->Data.Data_len);
  bcopy(pRequest->Packet_u.pImage->Data.Data_val, pI->Data.Data_val,
        pI->Data.Data_len);

  /* Build up Reply packet. */
  pReply->op = SUCCESS;
}

/*
 * SReadKernel() - store a copy of this kernel in the linked list.
 */
SReadKernel(pRequest, pReply)
  Packet          *pRequest, *pReply;
{
  Kernel          *pK;

  /* Go to end of list and add a kernel. */
  if (!pKernel) {
    pK = pKernel = (Kernel *) malloc(sizeof(Kernel));
  } else {
    TRAVERSE(pK, pKernel);
    pK->pNext = (Kernel *) malloc(sizeof(Kernel));
    pK = pK->pNext;
  }
  pK->pNext = NULL;

  /* Put the data into the Kernel structure for a local copy. */
  pK->sName = strdup(pRequest->Packet_u.pKernel->sName);
  pK->xsize = pRequest->Packet_u.pKernel->xsize;
  pK->ysize = pRequest->Packet_u.pKernel->ysize;
  pK->Value.Value_len = pRequest->Packet_u.pKernel->Value.Value_len;
  pK->Value.Value_val = (float *) malloc((int) pK->Value.Value_len *
sizeof(float));
  bcopy(pRequest->Packet_u.pKernel->Value.Value_val,
        pK->Value.Value_val, pK->Value.Value_len * sizeof(float));

  pReply->op = SUCCESS;
}

/*
 * SConvolve() - perform convolution between a subimage of the last
 * mentioned image and kernel.
 */
SConvolve(pRequest, pReply)
  Packet          *pRequest, *pReply;
{
  char            sk[MAXSTR], si[MAXSTR];
  Kernel          *pK;
```

Example 6-11. Server procedures for RIP: rip_svc_proc.c (Continued)

```
Image          *pI;
char           *pSubImage, *pMAC;
float          f;
int            x, xx, y, yy, dx, dxx, dy, dyy;
int            i, dxImage, SubImagePixelOffset;

/*
 * Try to find the kernel and the image mentioned, otherwise, use the last
 * one there...
 */
sscanf(pRequest->Packet_u.pImage->sName, "%s%s", si, sk);
TRAVERSE(pK, pKernel) if (!strcmp(pK->sName, sk))
    break;
TRAVERSE(pI, pImage) if (!strcmp(pI->sName, si))
    break;

/* Put the reply skeleton together. */
pReply->op = CONVOLVE;
bcopy(pRequest, pReply, sizeof(Packet));
dx = pRequest->Packet_u.pImage->dx;
dy = pRequest->Packet_u.pImage->dy;
pReply->Packet_u.pImage->Data.Data_len = dx * dy;
pMAC = pReply->Packet_u.pImage->Data.Data_val =
    (char *) calloc(dx * dy, sizeof(unsigned char));
pReply->Packet_u.pImage->sName =
    strdup(pRequest->Packet_u.pImage->sName);
pReply->Packet_u.pImage->pNext = NULL;

/*
 * Make the subimage copy larger - to control edge effects of the
 * convolution. Should really preserve derivative information instead of
 * zeroing...
 */
dxx = dx + pK->xsize;
dyy = dy + pK->ysize;
dxImage = pI->dx;
pSubImage = (char *) calloc(dxx * dyy, sizeof(unsigned char));
/* copy image a line at a time */
for (y = pRequest->Packet_u.pImage->y, yy = (pK->ysize >> 1);
     y < pRequest->Packet_u.pImage->y + dy; y++, yy++)

  bcopy(pI->Data.Data_val + y * dxImage + pRequest->Packet_u.pImage->x,
        pSubImage + yy * dxx + (pK->xsize >> 1), dx);

/*
 * Step thru the defined subimage and do a convolution.  Personally, I
 * find it conceptually easier to move thru each convolution window of the
 * subimage in raster-scan order, organized like the kernel, doing the
 * multiplication and accumulation in that order.
 */

/* Foreach non-edge pixel in SubImage(x,y)... */
for (y = (pK->ysize >> 1); y < dy + (pK->ysize >> 1); y++) {
  for (x = (pK->xsize >> 1); x < dx + (pK->xsize >> 1); x++) {
    /* Make a scan-line version of the conv. window (like pK). */
    i = 0;
    f = 0;
    for (yy = y - (pK->ysize >> 1); yy < y + (pK->ysize >> 1); yy++) {
      for (xx = x - (pK->xsize >> 1); xx < x + (pK->xsize >> 1); xx++) {
        SubImagePixelOffset = yy * dxx + xx;
        f += pK->Value.Value_val[i++] *
            (float) ((unsigned char) *(pSubImage + SubImagePixelOffset));
#ifdef VERBOSEDEBUG
        printf("pixel:%f kernel:%f product:%d ", fConvWin[i],
               pK->Value.Value_val[i], (unsigned) pMAC);
```

Example 6-11. Server procedures for RIP: rip_svc_proc.c (Continued)

```
#endif
        }
      }
      *pMAC = (unsigned char) rint(f);
      pMAC++;
    }
  }
  return (TRUE);
}

/*
 * SAddServer() - return hostname (free some rip memory too).
 */
SAddServer(pRequest, pReply)
  Packet          *pRequest, *pReply;
{
  char            sBuf[MAXSTR];
  Image           *pI, *pI1;
  Kernel          *pK, *pK1;

  /* Blast the images and kernels. */
  for (pI = pImage; pI; pI = pI->pNext, free(pI1)) {
    pI1 = pI;
  }
  for (pK = pKernel; pK; pK = pK->pNext, free(pK1)) {
    pK1 = pK;
  }

  /* Tell the client who you really are... */
  gethostname(sBuf, MAXSTR);
  pReply->Packet_u.sOp = strdup(sBuf);
  pReply->op = ADDSERVER;
}
```

Testing and Running the Program

As the *makefile* shown earlier suggests, it's easy to use dbx(1) or similar symbolic debuggers in a few different ways to debug the programs. I like to do this in a few steps. If not by design, I usually come back through these steps anyway when trouble develops!

Debug Steps 1 & 2: Start by removing any XDR calls. You can look at the simpler interface issue at this level. Just compile the protocol, client, and server procedures, but forget the XDR stubs. Link the client code, *rip.c*, with the server procedure, *rip_svc_proc.c* (debug step 1). You have to remove references to any XDR routines, for example, the xdr_free() call in *rip_svc_proc.c* must be removed. This is embedded in the *makefile* (e.g., make local). If you remove (manually or via #ifdef statements) the client's references to the RPC CLIENT handle, you won't have to start up dummy servers to make portmap entries. The application is now completely RPC-free. You may now use dbx to check out your algorithm and implementation with one local process.

Debug Step 3: Once the single-process works correctly, use the *makefile* to make two separate executables, rip and rip_svc, to run on the client and server, respectively. If you use both of the -DDEBUG definitions, you'll get around the RPC time-out and avoid the child-process forking done by the SubBFS() scheduler.

Child processes cannot be easily tracked with dbx, so -DDEBUG keeps all processing visible in the parent process.

Remove the -DDEBUG from CFLAGS and use only the -g flag to use dbx. To keep things simple, you probably want to start both the client and server on your own machine. Start up two dbx processes, one debugging the server (dbx rip_svc) and the other debugging the client (dbx rip). Start the server first to give it a chance to register itself with your portmap. The client process can now call the server process. Set break points appropriately to see if your data structures now make it through XDR unscathed. Mine usually don't the first time. Typically, some dangling pointers in opaque data types or bad, unassigned pointer values need to be NULL-ed out. To step through the code on the server side, you will have to set the RPC time-out value to an arbitrarily long number of seconds to allow you time to step through and get the reply back.

If your client and server make it through this inspection, and can run unattended under local dbx processes, it will run distributed over the network. So feel free to launch the server on a remote machine now. Personally, I like to structure the server to provide a little output (fprintf()'s to stderr or stdout as appropriate) to give me a warm feeling. It's easy, as we've seen, to redirect server output when launching, to discard this output. The shell command we've used previously takes input from the NULL device and places both stderr and stdout output in the same special bit bucket:

```
rodson> rsh server -n exec $cwd/rls_svc ">& /dev/null" &
```

RIP now accelerates the convolution or filtering of images by assigning portions of the computations to available servers. The speed-up is proportional to the number of servers applied to the task.

Extending RIP

RIP is missing several things which industrial-strength RPC applications should include:

• Server failure recovery and retry.

• Subimage dynamic sizing and load balancing/scheduling—right now these numbers are user-specified at run-time and have no bearing on network activity or number of servers.

• Extend the server image processing operations to lists and thus support operation pipelining on the servers for a better computation/communication ratio.

To make RIP into a full-blown image processing application, I'd also include:

- Run-length limiting (RLL) or other simple encoding to remove redundancy from communicated pixel values (compression). This puts a significant amount of additional burden on the client to decode the reply data. I have had success doing RLL decoding at the rate data returns over Ethernet. See the Sun `Pixrect` manuals for a discussion of Sun's style of run-length limiting in */usr/lib/rasfilters*.

- A better parser that could handle more data types and operators from standard input. Using `lex` and `yacc` might be a good idea.

- Multiple canvases to draw on.

- Use ttys and I/O descriptors to get commands and data in and out. I used `stdin` to avoid lengthy discussions about notifiers and event handlers. Add panels, buttons, and pop-ups to increase user interaction. What is here is merely a demo vehicle, with the windowing stuff stripped-out for legibility.

- Generalize the divide-and-conquer technique to work in other transform spaces— e.g., the spectral domain.

- Better convolution. It is abbreviated here, and only handles odd-sized, square kernels. It truncates the results into bytes and doesn't support DC offsets or scaling.

Fast SunView Frame Buffer Access Needed

When writing or reading pixel values to or from a frame buffer, there can be some significant performance considerations. These problems are universal to any raster-scan, bit-mapped, graphics device, independent of the windowing system you are using.

In the SunView `Pixwin` and `Pixrect` data structures, for example, Sun supports pixel accesses in memory and at the frame buffer. The single-pixel access functions, `pw_get()` and `pw_put()`, make `Pixwin` pixel reads and writes painfully slow. Frame buffer access is complicated by all sorts of things including hitting the video retrace window in time. The subimage functions, including `pw_rop()` and `pw_write()` (rectangular region functions), effectively access pixels faster by handling blocks. Use them whenever possible; even if pixels arrive serially, moving them in blocks is more productive.

For the sake of portability, there are no `Pixrect` or `Pixwin` structures or functions on the server side or in `rip_svc`. This allows you to run it on almost any machine that supports XDR. I exploit our center's multiprocessor Convex, Solbournes, Suns, and even our DEC machines.

Once I got used to low-level `char` * pixel access with XDR routines, things started to move more quickly. For example, dumping the contents of a long `char` * buffer of pixels, in raster-scan order, to a window might require:

```
Pixrect *pr;
unsigned char *p ;
p = (unsigned char *)((struct mpr_data *)pr->pr_data)->md_image ;
```

Now p is a pointer to the actual array of bytes forming the pixrect image data. Stuff your bytes into that array, then do a `pw_write()` into the window:

```
Pixwin *pw;
pw_write (pw, 0, 0, pr->pr_width, pr->pr_height, PIX_SRC, pr, 0, 0) ;
```

and magically the bytes appear in your window—*much* faster than the `pw_put()` equivalent.

There is an analogous issue with X11.[†] X `Pixmap` and `Windows` are both drawable, representing pixel image objects that live in memory, with the latter serving to update video RAM. Here the actual address of the `Window` pixel data is not readily available as above. `XImage` objects, beefy non-visible structures designed as vehicles to exchange image data between heterogeneous clients and servers, do have bare `char` * pointers to their pixel data. One strategy is to form an `XImage`, then dump the image into the `Window` or `Pixmap` in large rectangular pieces, as above with `pw_write()`. Use `XPutImage(3X11)` from the Xlib. If you are moving `Pixmaps` back and forth, use Xlib calls like `XCopyArea(3X11)` or `XCopyPlane(3X11)`.

Chapter 10 compares X and SunView frame buffer and memory efficiency. Appendix B includes an XView-based ray-tracing RPC application.

---

† X, along with its image handling in relation to RPC programming, is thoroughly covered in Chapter 10.

In this chapter:
- *A Local Image Manager*
- *Moving a Local Application to the Network*

7

Distributing Existing Applications

In this chapter, we examine the differences in the design of a local application and a distributed application. This discussion by example should help you in developing your own client/server applications and it should help modify an existing local application so that it can run out over the network.

Our example in this chapter is a new application, a distributed image manager named dim. We follow dim through a top-down design, first building a local image manager. Then we extend dim's lifetime by turning it into a distributed client/server application. We talk about ways to make the process of moving from a local to a remote execution model less painful.

A Local Image Manager

Here's the problem we have to solve: our image processing or synthesis group is running out of disk space. The cause of the problem is not just lots of pixels, but poor data management. There are redundant copies of images and rarely-used images that clog up our servers' disks. Images are also being lost or accidentally deleted by group members. All the user workstations are networked and have common NFS volumes but we can't seem to enforce a storage policy.

We need a centralized archive. We want users to be able to add, delete, list, and extract images from this archive. So we conceive of an image manager named im.

Using im, any user can add, delete, extract, or list images from a predefined archive on NFS. The command-line usage for im is:

im -a   imageName   "comments"   width height depth compressType

                                        add an image from file 'imageName'

    -d   imageName   *delete an image*

    -x   imageName   *extract an image to file 'imageName'*

    -l   *list contents of archive*

We could use a standard archive utility like cpio(1) or ar(1V). This would suffice if the only indexing information we need is a filename. We need to know more about an archived image, including its size and what compression algorithm it uses. If the image needs to be compressed, that is done prior to passing it to im. We can define a struct image to store the images; it consists of a header followed by the data.

```
struct image {
        int b;      /* total # of bytes, less opaque than data.data_len */
        int x;      /* width, height in pixels, depth in bytes */
        int y;
        int d;
        int c;      /* 0 if no compression, *_COMP type otherwise */
        pStr sN;    /* name of the image file */
        pStr sO;    /* owner, derived from uid */
        pStr sC;    /* comments, imaging conditions, etc. */
        pStr sU;    /* data, not at comment */
        struct {
                u_int data_len;/* bytes */
                char *data_val;/* pointer to pixel values */
        } data;
};
```

Note that data may (or may not) be in a compressed format.

The Header File

The data structures and function prototypes serve as the protocol connecting the main() and the subordinate archive access routines. The header file, *im.h*, shown in Example 7-1, defines the data structures to be passed (image, imageList, imageStat, and pStr), prototypes the functions, and defines constants and macros.

Example 7-1. Header file for the local image manager: im.h

```
struct image {
        int b;      /* total # of bytes, less opaque than data.data_len */
        int x;      /* width, height in pixels, depth in bytes */
        int y;
        int d;
        int c;      /* 0 if no compression, *_COMP type otherwise */
        pStr sN;    /* name of the image file */
```

Example 7-1. Header file for the local image manager: im.h (Continued)

```
        pStr sO;  /* owner, derived from uid */
        pStr sC;  /* comments, imaging conditions, etc. */
        pStr sD;  /* date, set at server */
        struct {
                u_int data_len;/* bytes */
                char *data_val;/* pointer to pixel values */
        } data;
};
typedef struct image image;

struct imageStat {/* package-up a comment along with an image */
        pStr status;
        image *pImage;
};
typedef struct imageStat imageStat;

struct imageList {/* a linked-list of images */
        image *pImage;
        struct imageList *pNext;
};
typedef struct imageList imageList;
typedef char *pStr;     /* unambiguous NULL-terminated string */

pStr add(/*image **/);       /* add an image, return status string */
pStr delete(/*pStr*/);       /* delete the named image, return status string */
pStr extract(/*pStr, image ***/); /* extract an image, return image and status */
imageList *list();           /* list archive - image list with no data in each */

/* miscellaneous macros and constants */
#define MAX(a,b)             (a>b)?a:b
#define MIN(a,b)             (a<b)?a:b
#define UIDTONAME(uid) \
(char *)strdup((char *)((struct passwd *)getpwuid((int)uid))->pw_name)
/* the following must be a writeable NFS volume */
#define SERVERDB    "/home/cortex/projects/vision/archive.dim"
#define LZW_COMP     1    /* Lempel-Ziv-Welch coded data */
#define HUFF_COMP    2    /* Huffman-coded data */
#define AHUFF_COMP   3    /* Adaptive Huffman-coded data */
#define ARITH_COMP   4    /* Arithmetic-coded data, 3-rd order model */
#define DPCM_COMP    5    /* Differential PCM-coded data, h1=1 1st order */
#define VQ_COMP      6    /* Vector quantized data */
#define DCT_COMP     7    /* Discrete Cosine Transformed data, JPEG */
#define MAXBUF 8192
#define MAXSTR 256
#define MAXPIX 0x100000
#define MAXIMG 256
```

The UIDTONAME() macro allows us to get the user's name to include in the sO owner name field of the image.

Modularity

We parse the command line within the main() procedure, then use a switch statement to call the local functions to get in and out of the archive. *im.c* in Example 7-2 contains main() while the subordinate functions are in *im_proc.c* in Example 7-3.

The main()

In addition to calling the appropriate function, the `main()` has a couple of extra functions to read and write raw-data images from local files, as required of the -a and -x options. The `PRINTHEAD()` macro is used to write the archive listing to `stdout` as requested by the -l option. *im.c* is shown in Example /-2.

Example 7-2. Main procedure for the local image manager: im.c

```
#include <stdio.h>
#include <string.h>
#include <pwd.h>
#include "im.h"
#define USAGE() { fprintf(stderr, "Usage: %s ", argv[0]); \
  fprintf(stderr, "\t-a imageName \"comments\" width height depth
compressType"); \
  fprintf(stderr, "\n\t\t\t\tadd an image from file 'imageName'\n"); \
  fprintf(stderr, "\t\t-d imageName\t\tdelete an image\n"); \

  fprintf(stderr, "\t\t-x imageName\t\textract image to file 'imageName'\n"); \
  fprintf(stderr, "\t\t-l\t\t\tlist contents of archive\n"); \
  exit(1); }
#define PRINTHEAD(pI) { \
  printf("name:\t%s\n\towner: %s\n\tcomments: %s\n\tdate: %s\n", \
         pI->sN, pI->sO, pI->sC, pI->sD); \
  printf("\tbytes: %d\twidth: %d\theight: %d\tdepth: %d\tcompress: %d\n",\
         pI->b, pI->x, pI->y, pI->d, pI->c); }

image            *readImage();
FILE             *fp;

main(argc, argv)
  int              argc;
   char           *argv[];
{
  pStr             expectEmpty;/* a single NULL if success, else an error string*/
  imageList        *pIL;
  image            *pI;
  pStr             sImageName;
  int              arg;

  /*
   * Parse the command line, doing local procedure calls as requested.
   */
  for (arg = 1; arg < argc; arg++) {
    if (argv[arg][0] != '-')
            USAGE();
    switch (argv[arg][1]) {
    case 't':
      arg++;
      break;
    case 'a':
      if ((argc - (++arg) < 6) || !(pI = readImage(argv, &arg)))
        USAGE();
      expectEmpty = add(pI);
      if (expectEmpty[0] != NULL)
                fprintf(stderr, "local call failed: %s", expectEmpty);
      break;
    case 'd':
      if (argc - (++arg) < 1)
        USAGE();
      sImageName = (pStr) strdup(argv[arg]);
      expectEmpty = delete(sImageName);
      if (expectEmpty[0] != NULL)
```

Example 7-2. Main procedure for the local image manager: im.c (Continued)

```
          fprintf(stderr, "local call failed: %s", expectEmpty);
        break;
    case 'x':
      if (argc - (++arg) < 1)
        USAGE();
      sImageName = (pStr) strdup(argv[arg]);
      expectEmpty = extract(sImageName, &pI);
      if (expectEmpty[0] != NULL)
        fprintf(stderr, "local call failed: %s", expectEmpty);
      else
      (void) writeImage(pI, sImageName);
      break;
    case 'l':{
        if (!(pIL = list((void *) NULL)))
          fprintf(stderr, "local call failed:");
        else
          for (pI = pIL->pImage; pIL->pNext; pIL = pIL->pNext, pI = pIL->pImage)
            PRINTHEAD(pI);
        break;
      }
    default:
      USAGE();
    }
  }
}

image          *
readImage(argv, pArg)
  char           **argv;
  int            *pArg;
{
  static image   im;
  char           buffer[MAXBUF];
  char           null = NULL;
  u_int          reallyRead;
  u_int          imageSize = 0;

  /*
   * Build the header information then look at stdin for data.
   */
  im.sN = (pStr) strdup(argv[*pArg]);
  im.sO = UIDTONAME(getuid());
  im.sC = (pStr) strdup(argv[++*pArg]);
  im.x = atoi(argv[++*pArg]);
  im.y = atoi(argv[++*pArg]);
  im.d = atoi(argv[++*pArg]);
  im.c = atoi(argv[++*pArg]);
  im.sD = &null;          /* Don't forget to terminate those empty strings! */
  im.data.data_val = (char *)malloc(0);

  if (!(fp = fopen(im.sN, "r"))) {
    fprintf(stderr, "error opening imageName \"%s\" for reading\n", im.sN);
    return (0);
  }
  while (reallyRead = fread(buffer, 1, MAXBUF, fp)) {
    im.data.data_val = (char *)realloc(im.data.data_val,imageSize+reallyRead);
    (void) bcopy(buffer, im.data.data_val + imageSize, reallyRead);
    imageSize += reallyRead;
  }
  im.b = im.data.data_len = imageSize;
  fclose(fp);
  return (&im);
}

writeImage(pImage, sImageName)
```

Example 7-2. Main procedure for the local image manager: im.c (Continued)

```
    image           *pImage;
    pStr            sImageName;
{
    if (!(fp = fopen(sImageName, "w"))) {
        fprintf(stderr, "error opening imageName \"%s\" for writing\n", sImageName);
        return (1);
    }
    PRINTHEAD(pImage);
    if (fwrite(pImage->data.data_val, 1, pImage->data.data_len, fp)
        != pImage->data.data_len) {
        fprintf(stderr, "error writing imageName \"%s\" data\n", sImageName);
        fclose(fp);
        return (1);
    }
    fclose(fp);
    return (0);
}
```

To add an image, the user must supply on the command line the image's filename, any quoted comments, as well as image width, height, and depth (bytes per pixel). We also record the compression type used as integer values from 0 through 7, as specified in *im.h.*

When adding or deleting a string, a status string is sent back: if the first character is NULL, we assume all went well; otherwise the included error message is printed at stderr. Similarly, if extracting an image produces an error, the status string's first character is non-NULL. Archive listing errors returns a NULL list.[†] We could have accomplished the same thing by designing an errno, perrno()-like approach, defining all the possible error situations symbolically and instead return those integers.

Functions

im_proc.c in Example 7-3 contains the guts of the application. This code does the reading and writing of the archive, sending either images, status, or both back to the main(). The functions were prototyped in *im.h.* We also require some memory management to allocate images. Deallocation is not necessary as the application exits after performing its work, automatically freeing memory.

There is a lot of code here, which you can skim for the comments. Then, as soon as you're tired of looking at somebody else's code, proceed directly to the section,

---

† Intelligible error reporting is at least as important with RPC. While RPC provides a mechanism for reporting RPC protocol-level problems, YOU the programmer must build up an application-level error reporting mechanism.

"Moving a Local Application to the Network." There, the emphasis is on the changes we need to make to create a distributed application.

Example 7-3. Archive access functions for the local image manager: im_proc.c

```
#include <stdio.h>
#include <sys/types.h>
#include <sys/time.h>
#include <time.h>
#include <pwd.h>
#include "im.h"

#define FGETS(ptr, max, fp) { fgets(ptr, max, fp); ptr[strlen(ptr)-1] = NULL; }
#define READHEADER(n, o, c, d) \
        { FGETS(n,MAXSTR,fp); FGETS(o,MAXSTR,fp); \
        FGETS(c,MAXSTR,fp); FGETS(d,MAXSTR,fp); }

FILE            *fp;
imageList       *iLAllocOne();
image           *iAllocOne();

pStr
add(argp)
  image         *argp;
{
  static pStr      result;
  static char      msg[MAXSTR];
  static char      N[MAXSTR], O[MAXSTR], C[MAXSTR], D[MAXSTR];
  char             head[MAXSTR];
  int              fstat, b, x, y, d, c;
  time_t           tloc;
  result = msg;
  msg[0] = NULL;

  if (!(fp = fopen(SERVERDB, "r"))) {
    sprintf(msg, "cannot open SERVERDB %s for reading\n", SERVERDB);
    return ((pStr) result);
  }
  /*
   * First make sure such an image isn't already archived.
   */
  while ((fstat = fscanf(fp, "%d%d%d%d%d\n", &b, &x, &y, &d, &c)) == 5) {
    READHEADER(N, O, C, D);
    if (!strcmp(N, argp->sN))
      brcak;
    fseek(fp, (long) b, 1);
  }
  switch (fstat) {
  case EOF:              /* not found - that's good */
    fclose(fp);
    if (!(fp = fopen(SERVERDB, "a"))) {
      sprintf(msg, "cannot open SERVERDB %s to append\n", SERVERDB);
      fclose(fp);
      return ((pStr) result);
    }
    break;
  case 5:                /* There already is one! */
    sprintf(msg, "%s archive already has a \"%s\"\n", SERVERDB, argp->sN);
    fclose(fp);
    return ((pStr) result);
  default:               /* not a clean tail... tell user and try to recover */
    repairDB(msg);
    fclose(fp);
    return ((pStr) result);
  }
  /*
```

Example 7-3. Archive access functions for the local image manager: im_proc.c (Continued)

```
   * Get the date, add the image header and data, then return.
   */
  time(&tloc);
  sprintf(head, "%d %d %d %d %d\n%s\n%s\n%s\n%s",
          argp->data.data_len, argp->x, argp->y, argp->d, argp->c,
          argp->sN, argp->sO, argp->sC, (char *) ctime(&tloc));
  if ((fwrite(head, 1, strlen(head), fp) != strlen(head))
      || (fwrite(argp->data.data_val, 1, argp->data.data_len, fp)
          != argp->data.data_len)) {
    sprintf(msg, "failed write to SERVERDB %s\n", SERVERDB);
  }
  fclose(fp);
  return ((pStr) result);
}


/*
 * This is included for the sake of completeness but is brute-force.
 */
pStr
delete(argp)
  pStr               argp;
{
  FILE               *fpp;
  int                fstat;
  static pStr        result;
  static char        msg[MAXSTR];
  char               N[MAXSTR], O[MAXSTR], C[MAXSTR], D[MAXSTR];
  char               *buffer;
  int                bufSize, bytesRead, b, x, y, d, c;
  int                seekPt = 0;

  msg[0] = NULL;
  result = msg;

  if ((fp = fopen(SERVERDB, "r"))) {
    sprintf(msg, "cannot open SERVERDB %s for reading\n", SERVERDB);
    return ((pStr) result);
  }


  /*
   * Look thru the DB for the named image.
   */
  while ((fstat = fscanf(fp, "%d%d%d%d%d\n", &b, &x, &y, &d, &c)) == 5) {
    READHEADER(N, O, C, D);
    fseek(fp, (long) b, 1);      /* fp stops at next entry */
    if (!strcmp(N, argp))
      break;
    seekPt = ftell(fp);
  }
  switch (fstat) {
  case EOF:                       /* not found */
    sprintf(msg, "%s not found in archive\n", argp);
    break;
  case 5:         /* This is the one! Remove it by copying the bottom up. */
    bufSize = MIN(MAX(1, b), MAXBUF);
    buffer = (char *) malloc(bufSize);
    fpp = fopen(SERVERDB, "r+");
    fseek(fpp, seekPt, 0);        /* fpp is at selected image */
    while (!feof(fp)) {
      bytesRead = fread(buffer, 1, bufSize, fp);
      fwrite(buffer, 1, bytesRead, fpp);
    }
    seekPt = ftell(fpp);
    fclose(fpp);
```

Example 7-3. Archive access functions for the local image manager: im_proc.c (Continued)

```
      truncate(SERVERDB, (off_t) seekPt);
      break;
   default:                              /* not a clean tail... */
      repairDB(msg);
   }
   fclose(fp);
   return ((pStr) result);
}


pStr
extract(argp, ppIm)
   pStr            argp;
   image         **ppIm;
{
   int             fstat;
   static pStr     result;
   static char     msg[MAXSTR];
   image          *pIm;

   result = msg;
   msg[0] = NULL;

   if (!(fp = fopen(SERVERDB, "r"))) {
      sprintf(msg, "cannot open SERVERDB %s for reading\n", SERVERDB);
      return ((pStr) result);
   }
   /*
    * Look thru the DB for the named image.
    */
   pIm = *ppIm = iAllocOne();

   while ((fstat = fscanf(fp, "%d%d%d%d%d\n", &(pIm->b), &(pIm->x), &(pIm->y),
                          &(pIm->d), &(pIm->c))) == 5) {
      READHEADER(pIm->sN, pIm->sO, pIm->sC, pIm->sD);

      if (!strcmp(pIm->sN, argp))
         break;
      fseek(fp, (long) pIm->b, 1);
   }
   switch (fstat) {
   case EOF:                             /* not found */
      sprintf(msg, "%s not found in archive\n", argp);
      break;
   case 5:                               /* This is the one! */
      pIm->data.data_len = pIm->b;
      pIm->data.data_val = (char *) malloc(pIm->b);
      if (fread(pIm->data.data_val, 1, pIm->data.data_len, fp)
            != pIm->data.data_len) {
         sprintf(msg, "couldn't read all of %s\n", argp);
         repairDB(msg);
      }
      break;
   default:                              /* not a clean tail... */
      repairDB(msg);
   }
   fclose(fp);
   return ((pStr) result);
}

static imageList *pIList = NULL;

imageList       *
list()
{
```

Example 7-3. Archive access functions for the local image manager: im_proc.c (Continued)

```
    imageList      *pIL;
    int             fstat;

    /*
     * Build a list.
     */
    pIL = pIList = iLAllocOne();

    if (!(fp = fopen(SERVERDB, "r"))) {
      sprintf(pIL->pImage->sN, "cannot open SERVERDB %s for reading\n", SERVERDB);
      return (pIList);
    }
    while ((fstat = fscanf(fp, "%d%d%d%d%d\n", &(pIL->pImage->b),
                           &(pIL->pImage->x), &(pIL->pImage->y),
                           &(pIL->pImage->d), &(pIL->pImage->c))) == 5) {
      READHEADER(pIL->pImage->sN, pIL->pImage->sO,
                 pIL->pImage->sC, pIL->pImage->sD);

      fseek(fp, (long) pIL->pImage->b, 1);

      pIL->pNext = iLAllocOne();   /* hang an empty one on the end */
      pIL = pIL->pNext;
    }
    if (fstat != EOF) {              /* not a clean tail... */
      repairDB(pIL->pImage->sN);
    }
    fclose(fp);
    return (pIList);
}

/*
 * the next two routines are just image linked-list maint. stuff
 */
imageList        *
iLAllocOne()
{                                  /* allocate one imageList structure */
    imageList      *pIL = (imageList *) malloc(sizeof(imageList));
    pIL->pImage = iAllocOne();
    pIL->pNext = NULL;
    return (pIL);
}
image            *
iAllocOne()
{                                  /* allocate one image structure */
    image          *pI = (image *) malloc(sizeof(image));
    pI->sN = (pStr) malloc(MAXSTR);
    pI->sN[0] = NULL;
    pI->sO = (pStr) malloc(MAXSTR);
    pI->sO[0] = NULL;
    pI->sC = (pStr) malloc(MAXSTR);
    pI->sC[0] = NULL;
    pI->sD = (pStr) malloc(MAXSTR);
    pI->sD[0] = NULL;
    pI->data.data_len = 0;
    pI->data.data_val = NULL;
    return (pI);
}

repairDB(s)                        /* doesn't do much, yet... */
    pStr           s;
{
    sprintf(s, "SERVERDB %s data hosed, don't know how to repair!\n", SERVERDB);
}
```

`repairDB()` is included as a stub to admit that the archive can get corrupted. If the application dies in the middle of writing the archive, we should have a way to recover. We'll address this in more detail once we have it on the network.

Compile, Link, and Run

Test it out by putting it all together:

```
rodson> cc -o im im.c im_proc.c
im.c:
im_proc.c:
Linking:
rodson> im -a MultispectralMalibu.4.Z \
"long- med- and short-wave IR image of Malibu CA coast" 512 480 3 1
local call failed: cannot open SERVERDB
  /home/cortex/projects/vision/archive.dim for reading
```

Oops, we must start things off by creating the archive:

```
rodson> echo > /home/cortex/projects/vision/archive.dim
rodson> im -a MultispectralMalibu.4.Z \
"long- med- and short-wave IR image of Malibu CA coast" 512 480 3 1
rodson> im -l
name:   MultispectralMalibu.4.Z
        owner: bloomer
        comments: long- med- and short-wave IR image of Malibu CA coast
        date: Sun Jun  2 05:50:26 1991
        bytes: 789241  width: 512    height: 480   depth: 3   compress: 1
```

Extraction and deletion work similarly. You can use this utility for archiving arbitrary file types, using bogus width, height, and depth parameters on the command-line.

Moving a Local Application to the Network

There is no cookbook for porting to RPC. If you ask yourself some questions, you can generate a porting strategy tailored to your application.

Answer Fourteen Questions First

Before you start rewriting an application to use RPC, devise a plan by asking the following questions:

Define the Client/Server Partitioning Strategy

After answering or reworking the local procedure calling code in response to questions 1-4, you should have code with an apparent client/server partitioning.

1. *Is there a functional client/server partition?* It's probably not as easy as putting `main()` at the client and major function calls at the server. Modular code is the easiest to port. If it's not modular, bite the bullet now.

2. *Is there a data-driven client/server partition?* Just because some module boundaries are functional does not mean that's a good client/server partition. If large amounts of data, as compared to computation, are passed on the stack or globally, that partitioning will drive the network bananas. You may need to rework module partitions to reduce request-and-reply passing overhead.

3. *Is there extensive use of global variables?* With RPC, all variables must get to the server via request messages. Two strategies for programming around global variables exist: (a) encapsulate them as another outgoing request argument for each procedure or (b) identify an additional remote procedure whose whole purpose in life is to convey global parameters to the server. This is especially useful if these parameters are infrequently updated. You may need RPCs in both directions (client-server and server-client).

4. *Does the current application use communication schemes other than procedure calling?* Network analogies to semaphores, signaling, or shared memory don't readily exist. The RPC equivalent requires that a request be constructed and sent across the network. Semaphores, signaling, and memory sharing can still be performed if isolated within the client or server.

RPC System Issues

5. *What security measures are needed?* All the examples we've developed so far don't even check standard UNIX credentials to see if the caller is who they say they are. You may require authentication credentials that are more difficult to falsify. Later, in Chapter 12, we address adding UNIX and DES authentication schemes and making the required client/server changes.

6. *What access control policy is required?* An authentication scheme only validates or invalidates credentials at the client and/or server. With the service made available to everyone on the network, you must decide what type of access protocol you will use. Before you start coding, decide what you will do if insufficient authentication occurs. Oftentimes some functions, like listing an archive, can be made available to all. Some functions might be restricted to certain users, whose identity must be validated.

7. *Got any non-idempotent procedures?* A lack of idempotence in a service procedure requires either the use of request/reply queuing on an unreliable transport or use of a reliable transport. Recall that UDP requests are unreliable and may never get to the server *or* they may get there multiple times. TCP requests are reliable but have more overhead.

8. *What about low-level networking issues?* Given that we are using ONC RPC and the XDR layer, client/server heterogeneity should not be an issue. The ONC RPC NIS daemon must be running on all machines. In many cases you must make a

protocol decision early, not just as a function of performance and fault tolerance, but out of reply/request packet size limitations. The UDP transport limits you to about 8K transactions while TCP does not limit size.

Fault Tolerance

When porting an application to RPC, we can insert code to achieve more robust behavior in the face of network problems. We address this by example in Chapter 12. If developing an RPC application from scratch, plan it in up front!

9. *What about error reporting and recovery?* As in the local procedure call application, you need some well-defined error reporting scheme. The RPC library provides error reporting at the RPC protocol level. But there are new areas you must now address: retaining state and recovering from crashes or dropped connections.

10. *Should your client or server retain state?* This determines what transport you should use.

11. *Should your client or server be able to recover from a crash?* Oftentimes you need more than a stateful or reliable transport to recover from a crash. Without some nonvolatile record of where the application was when the machine died (as available from a disk file or another client/server), the application might come back up in a bad state.

12. *What should you do about dropped connections?* If the client or server connection is severed during an RPC, should you attempt to reconnect, just stop, or look for another connection?

Synchronous or Asynchronous?

The purpose of 13 and 14 is to define what type, if any, of multi-tasking is required and whether any remote asynchronous calls will be required. Even if you require multiple clients or multiple servers, I suggest implementing the one-to-one version first, keeping an eye on how you will extend it. Once you have that debugged, move to the more complicated case.

13. *Why are you distributing the processing?* If you want to accelerate or parallelize an application across *multiple servers*, then be prepared to implement some form of multi-tasking at the client. If your goal is to share a server resource across multiple clients, ask yourself the next question.

14. *Should service processing be synchronous or asynchronous?* Multi-tasking at the server can only be rationalized by *multiple client* requests that take widely different times to process; where client fairness or processing priority is a concern. While stuck in the middle of a long request processing task, the server should be pre-empted by brief or high-priority requests. A multi-tasking server is actually slower overall than a single-threaded server.

If your current application already employs asynchrony or multi-tasking, consider splitting the client and server at those points.

The Strategy

Distributing an existing application can be involved. By following a set procedure, you can keep the process organized:

1. Partition the client and server.

2. Redefine the protocol (build the *.x* file).

3. Make changes to the client main().

4. Split out and augment the server procedures.

While porting im we won't see all the caveats suggested by the above questions, but it will illustrate many important points.

Partition the Client and Server

You must first clearly define the roles of the servers and clients. The ideal partitioning may be obvious, but you will have to weigh this against the constraints implied by the established procedure calling structure; otherwise you will have to redesign the whole protocol from scratch.

Start by putting the header file with all the procedure calls in front of you. If you have a calls utility, or something similar, use that to isolate the procedure calls at the first couple levels of the hierarchy:

```
rodson> calls -h
usage: calls [-aehitv] [-f function] [-F function[/file.c]] [-w width]
        [-D define] [-U undefine] [-I include-dir] [filename]"
        a       print all calls in every function body
        e       index external functions too
        f,F     start calling trace at given function
        h       print this message
        i       print an index of defined functions
        v       list only called functions in index output
        t       terse, list only trees that are requested
        w       set output width
        D,U,I   as in cpp
```

When applied to the im example I get:

```
rodson> calls im.c im_proc.c

    1    main [im.c]
    2            fprintf
    3            exit
    4            readImage [im.c]
    5                    strdup
    ...
    15                   fclose
    16           add [im_proc.c]
    17                   fopen
    ...
    29                   fwrite
    30           strdup
```

```
     31              delete [im_proc.c]
     32                  fopen
    . . .
     45                      repairDB [see line 25]
     46          extract [im_proc.c]
     47                  fopen
    . . .
     59                  fclose
     60          writeImage [im.c]
     61                  fopen
    . . .
     65                  fclose
     66          list [im_proc.c]
     67                      iLAllocOne [im_proc.c]
    . . .
     77                  fclose
     78          printf
```

We start by looking at the first level of hierarchy. fprintf(), exit(), strdup(), and printf() are system calls to be left alone. readImage() and writeImage() must be left at the client to provide local file I/O. With the server in charge of all archive I/O, it only makes sense to move add(), delete(), extract(), and list() over to the server.

Redefining the protocol in RPCL (from .h to .x)

Typically, the header files or preliminary declarations define the procedure input and output in terms of data types and structures. That is all we need to construct the RPCGEN input file. Define the necessary constants and data types first, followed by the remote procedure definitions. You can use cpp(1) definitions and controls within the *.x* file. You can test for the preprocessor symbols used by RPCGEN (Table 4-3) to achieve a variety of effects. You can use the following line:

```
#if RPC_HDR
```

and comment subsequent cpp lines with an initial percent sign (%) to direct lines into a new common header file.

We assume that you use Version 4.0 RPCGEN and so the user must (a) pass all variables by pointer, and (b) encapsulate all variables.[†] The only major difference between a well-designed local *.h* file and the *.x* file occurs in the procedure I/O data typing.

Arbitrary data structures can be translated from the form found in the original *.h* file into RPCL or XDR and placed in the protocol definition. In Chapter 4, see the section, "The Protocol Definition Language," for more information. Multidimensional arrays are not readily handled by RPCGEN today. The solution most often used here is to serialize the elements, building a vector of sub-vectors, each sub-vector being of an explicitly-defined length. This gets a little difficult to compre-

---

† In recently released versions of RPCGEN.NEW, passing multiple parameters and passing by value or address is supported.

hend and calculate offsets into for high-dimensional data. Although it takes some
extra time and memory, it can be productive to pass the data as opaque, then cast
or copy the data back into a multi-dimensional structure at the receive-end.

Now consider the RPCL program definition. The prototypes for the four local procedures in *im.h* were:

```
pStr add(/* image * */);
pStr delete(/* pStr */);
pStr extract(/* pStr, image ** */);
imageList *list();
```

In the RPCL program definition, we detail the data type that we are interested in.
While we detail values here, pointers are actually used. We must merge the status
string and image parameters of extract() into one structure so we use struct
imageStat.

By convention, we put procedure names in uppercase here. The automatically-
generated server dispatch, in turn, calls the lowercase equivalent with a trailing _1,
where the 1 is the specified DIMVERS version number:

```
program         DIMSERVER {
   version         DIMVERS {
     pStr            ADD(image) = 3;        /* -a */
     pStr            DELETE(pStr) = 4;      /* -d */
     imageStat       EXTRACT(pStr) = 5;     /* -x */
     imageList       LIST(void) = 6;        /* -t */
   } = 1;
} = 0x20000009;
```

I arbitrarily selected a DIMSERVER program number in the user range specified in
Table 3-1. The actual number assigned to each procedure can be any unique
number but 0.

Let's look at the complete protocol definition file, *dim.x*, in Example 7-4. Lines that
represent a significant departure from what was in *im.h* are indicated by change
bars in the margin. I introduce a couple of new functions, DIE() and RESTART(),
to do server maintenance such as that described in earlier chapters. The application
will now use a remote server, server executable and archive site, SERVERHOST,
SERVERPATH, and SERVERDB, respectively.

Example 7-4. RPCL protocol definition for the distributed image manager: dim.x

```
/*
 * Some glop we need in all the other C code via dim.h, not here.
 */
#if RPC_HDR     /* only generate the following in the header file */
%#define MAX(a,b)                (a>b)?a:b
%#define MIN(a,b)                (a<b)?a:b
%#define UIDTONAME(uid) \
% (char *)strdup((char *)((struct passwd *)getpwuid((int)uid))->pw_name)
%#define SERVERHOST   "c2a"      /* the server is now a convex */
%#define SERVERPATH   "/u/bloomer/dim/dim_svc"
%#define SERVERDB     "/u/bloomer/dim/archive.dim"
%
%#define DEFAULT_TRANSPORT "tcp"
```

Example 7-4. RPCL protocol definition for the distributed image manager: dim.x (Continued)

```
%#define LZW_COMP       1       /* Lempel-Ziv-Welch coded data */
%#define HUFF_COMP      2       /* Huffman-coded data */
%#define AHUFF_COMP     3       /* Adaptive Huffman-coded data */
%#define ARITH_COMP     4       /* Arithmetic-coded data, 3-rd order model */
%#define DPCM_COMP      5       /* Differential PCM-coded data, h1=1 1st order */
%#define VQ_COMP        6       /* Vector quantized data */
%#define DCT_COMP       7       /* Discrete Cosine Transformed data, JPEG */
#endif

/*
 * These integer constants we need now AND elsewhere, so we use const,
 * not #define.
 */
const   MAXBUF = 8192;      /* temporary buffer size maximum */
const   MAXSTR = 256;       /* maximum string length */
const   MAXPIX = 0x100000;  /* up to 1M pixels */
const   MAXIMG = 256;       /* maximum Images in the archive */

/*
 * Define structures used by client and server.
 */
typedef string  pStr < MAXSTR >;
struct image {
        int         b;      /* total # of bytes, augments data.data_len */
        int         x;      /* width, height in pixels, depth in bytes */
        int         y;
        int         d;
        int         c;      /* 0 if no compression, *_COMP type otherwise */
        pStr        sN;     /* name of the image file */
        pStr        sO;     /* owner, derived from uid */
        pStr        sC;     /* comments, imaging conditions, etc. */
        pStr        sD;     /* date, set at server */
        opaque          data < MAXPIX >;
};
struct imageStat {      /* status string and an image */
        pStr    status;
        image *pImage;
};
struct imageList {      /* a linked-list of images */
        image *pImage;
        imageList *pNext;
};

/*
 * The dim server procedure definition.
 */
program         DIMSERVER {
  version         DIMVERS {
     void         DIE(void) = 1;         /* for maint. */
     void         RESTART(void) = 2;     /* for maint. */
     pStr         ADD(image) = 3;        /* -a */
     pStr         DELETE(pStr) = 4;      /* -d */
     imageStat    EXTRACT(pStr) = 5;     /* -x */
     imageList    LIST(void) = 6;        /* -t */
  } = 1;
} = 0x20000009;
```

As an exercise, run a diff program comparing the old header file and the RPCL protocol:

```
rodson> sdiff -s ../local/im.h ../remote/dim.x.
```

You'll be surprised at the similarities. You could write a `sed` or `awk` script to auto-mate the conversion.

We now have a partitioning between client and server, as well as a detailed protocol definition. We've inherited the NULL-string error reporting mechanism. If the associated `pStr`'s first character is NULL, we can assume all went well; otherwise the NULL-terminated string details the error. All the low-level routines remain unchanged.

With the client/server partitioning clear and the protocol detailed, the hard work of aligning the client and server sides of the application is next.

Changes in the main()

The local `main()` now becomes the start of the client `main()`. The major changes are the use of pointers as parameters and return values, and parameter encapsula-tion. You are now calling local procedure stubs as generated by RPCGEN. Thus _VERSION is added to their names. To use RPCGEN stubs, you must also open any CLIENT handles and pass them as the second (last) parameter to each call. Don't forget to include `<rpc/rpc.h>` and *dim.h*.

In our example, *dim.c* has minimal changes. Here's an example of how the call to `extract()` changed:

```
<        expectEmpty = extract(sImageName, &pI);
<        if (expectEmpty[0] != NULL)
<          fprintf(stderr, "local call failed: %s", expectEmpty);
<        else
<        (void) writeImage(pI, sImageName);
---
>        pIS = extract_1(&sImageName, clnt);
>        if (pIS == NULL) {
>          clnt_perror(clnt, "remote call failed:");
>          exit(1);
>        }
>        if (pIS->status[0] != NULL) {
>          fprintf(stderr, "%s\n", pIS->status);
>          exit(1);
>        }
>        (void) writeImage(pIS->pImage, sImageName);
```

The address of the image name string is passed out along with the CLIENT handle with return parameters now encapsulated. The status string is printed if non-NULL.

The complete listing is shown in Example 7-5 for completeness. Changes and addi-tions from *im.c* are indicated by change bars in the margin. A command-line option to select between UDP or TCP (default) transports is also added. If you are familiar

with creating and using CLIENT handles, proceed to the next section on extracting
the service procedures.

Example 7-5. Client main for the distributed image manager: dim.c

```
#include <stdio.h>
#include <string.h>
#include <pwd.h>
#include <rpc/rpc.h>
#include "dim.h"
#define USAGE() { fprintf(stderr, "Usage: %s ", argv[0]); \
        fprintf(stderr, "\t-t [udp|tcp]\t\toverride transport default\n"); \
        fprintf(stderr, "\t\t-a imageName \"comments\" width height depth
compressType"); \
        fprintf(stderr, "\n\t\t\t\t\tadd an image from file 'imageName'\n"); \
        fprintf(stderr, "\t\t-d imageName\t\tdelete an image\n"); \
        fprintf(stderr, "\t\t-x imageName\t\textract an image to file
'imageName'\n"); \
        fprintf(stderr, "\t\t-l\t\t\tlist contents of archive\n"); \
        exit(1); }
#define PRINTHEAD(pI) { \
        printf("name:\t%s\n\towner: %s\n\tcomments: %s\n\tdate: %s\n", \
                pI->sN, pI->sO, pI->sC, pI->sD); \
        printf("\tbytes: %d\twidth: %d\theight: %d\tdepth: %d\tcompress: %d\n", \
                pI->b, pI->x, pI->y, pI->d, pI->c); }

image           *readImage();
FILE            *fp;

main(argc, argv)
  int               argc;
  char              *argv[];
{
  imageList       *pIL;
  image           *pI;
  imageStat       *pIS;
  pStr            sImageName;
  int             arg;
  CLIENT          *clnt;
  pStr            *expectEmpty;   /* a single NULL if RPC succeeded */
  char            *transport = DEFAULT_TRANSPORT;

    /*
     * Look thru the command line to see if a transport is specified.
     */
    if (argc < 2)
      USAGE();
    for (arg = 1; arg < argc; arg++) {
      if (!strcmp(argv[arg], "-t")) {
        if ((argc < 4) || (strcmp("udp", argv[++arg]) && strcmp("tcp", argv[arg])))
          USAGE();
        (void) strcpy(transport, argv[arg]);
      }
    }
    /*
     * Attempt to open a client handle to the SERVERHOST. We could use a
     * broadcast scheme to look for the closest server.
     */
    clnt = clnt_create(SERVERHOST, DIMSERVER, DIMVERS, transport);
    if (clnt == NULL) {
      clnt_pcreateerror(SERVERHOST);
      exit(1);
    }
    /*
     * Parse the command line, doing RPCs as requested.  I don't bother
     * xdr_free()'ing anything as it's a one-shot deal.
```

Example 7-5. Client main for the distributed image manager: dim.c (Continued)

```
    */
    for (arg = 1; arg < argc; arg++) {
      if (argv[arg][0] != '-')
                  USAGE();
      switch (argv[arg][1]) {
      case 't':
        arg++;
        break;
      case 'a':
        if ((argc - (++arg) < 6) || !(pI = readImage(argv, &arg)))
          USAGE();
        expectEmpty = add_1(pI, clnt);        /* assume RPCSRC 4.0, 1 arg */
        if (expectEmpty == NULL)
                    clnt_perror(clnt, "remote call failed:");
        else
                    fprintf(stderr, "%s", *expectEmpty);
        break;
      case 'd':
        if (argc - (++arg) < 1)
          USAGE();
        sImageName = (pStr) strdup(argv[arg]);
        expectEmpty = delete_1(&sImageName, clnt);
        if (expectEmpty == NULL)
          clnt_perror(clnt, "remote call failed:");
        else
          fprintf(stderr, "%s", *expectEmpty);
        break;
      case 'x':
        if (argc - (++arg) < 1)
          USAGE();
        sImageName = (pStr) strdup(argv[arg]);
        pIS = extract_1(&sImageName, clnt);
        if (pIS == NULL) {
          clnt_perror(clnt, "remote call failed:");
          exit(1);
        }
        if (pIS->status[0] != NULL) {
          fprintf(stderr, "%s\n", pIS->status);
          exit(1);
        }
        (void) writeImage(pIS->pImage, sImageName);
        break;
      case 'l':{
          if (!(pIL = list_1((void *) NULL, clnt)))
            clnt_perror(clnt, "remote call failed:");
          else
            for (pI = pIL->pImage; pIL->pNext; pIL = pIL->pNext, pI = pIL->pImage)
              PRINTHEAD(pI);
          break;
        }
      default:
        USAGE();
      }
    }
  clnt_destroy(clnt);
}

/*
 * If I used the rpcgen.new released with ONC's TIRPC, I would not need this
 * packaging function; the call to add_1() could take multiple parameters,
 * by value and/or reference.
 */
image          *
readImage(argv, pArg)
  char          **argv;
```

Example 7-5. Client main for the distributed image manager: dim.c (Continued)

```
    int             *pArg;
{
.
.
.
Identical to im.c.
.
.
.
.
}

writeImage(pImage, sImageName)
    image           *pImage;
    pStr            sImageName;
{
.
.
.
Identical to im.c.
.
.
.
.
}
```

The differences as shown by sdiff or diff are few.

Extracting the Service Procedures

If the service routines are not isolated in their own compilation unit(s) (files), you must do that first. Once in one file or group of files you should:

- Run RPCGEN to create the header file, client, and server stubs.[†]

- Add the proper #include statements (<rpc/rpc.h> and *application.h* at least.

- Change procedure names to reflect the lowercase, trailing version-number that is called out in the protocol definition.

- Alter the arguments associated with each procedure to reflect pass-by-pointer and encapsulation. An additional final parameter is passed into each service procedure. This struct svc_req * describes the service request:

```
        struct svc_req {
            u_long  rq_prog;            /* service program number */
            u_long  rq_vers;            /* service protocol versnum */
            u_long  rq_proc;            /* desired procedure number */
            struct opaque_auth rq_cred; /* raw credentials from wire */
            caddr_t rq_clntcred;        /* credentials (read only) */
        };
```

- Reflect the fact that the server dispatch procedure needs to work on your return parameter, making them static or using malloc().

---

† The new RPCGEN found in the SVR4, Transport Independent ONC RPC release can also generate client main and server procedure skeletons. These are a useful starting point. More in Chapter 11.

- Free any unused variables. While the server dispatch will take care of freeing the request-and-reply messages, you are responsible for monitoring the `static` or allocated memory use. Your server now runs forever, potentially running out of memory if things like strings or linked-lists aren't deallocated or reused. If the client were to make repeated remote calls, management of local and XDR/RPC memory would become important there, too. (See `clnt_freeres(3N)` in *ONC RPC Programming Reference*.)

We already have `add()`, `delete()`, `extract()`, and `list()` in the one file. *dim_svc_proc.c*, in keeping with our *makefile* convention, will contain the server routines. First, include the `<rpc/rpc.h>` and *dim.h* header files. Next, make the procedure naming and input/output parameter changes. All four get a trailing `_1`. They all must now accept and return pointers to variables. `extract_1()` also requires the encapsulation of the status and image variables.

All returned pointers point to `static` or allocated memory now. I elected to use `xdr_free(3N)` to do memory deallocation within the service procedures. I originally used `free()`, but then realized it was just extra code. Handle strings with care. See the comments in `iAllocOne()` below.

Recall that we added the two maintenance procedures, `die_1()` and `restart_1()`. Given that the server will now reside on some massive server, we've also moved the compression function into the application. In response to user complaints, `add_1()` and `extract_1()` now do compression and decompression at the server, as specified on the command line.

The differences between the new *dim_svc_proc.c* in Example 7-6 and the old support routines in *im_proc.c* in Example 7-3 are indicated with change bars in the margin.

Example 7-6. The server procedures for the distributed image manager: dim_svc_proc.c

```
#include <stdio.h>
#include <sys/types.h>
#include <sys/time.h>
#include <time.h>
#include <pwd.h>
#include <rpc/rpc.h>
#include "dim.h"

#define FGETS(ptr, max, fp) { fgets(ptr, max, fp); ptr[strlen(ptr)-1] = NULL; }
#define READHEADER(n, o, c, d) \
        { FGETS(n,MAXSTR,fp); FGETS(o,MAXSTR,fp); \
        FGETS(c,MAXSTR,fp); FGETS(d,MAXSTR,fp); }

FILE            *fp;
imagelist       *iLAllocOne();
image           *iAllocOne();

void            *
die_1()
{
  svc_unregister(DIMSERVER, DIMVERS);
  exit(0);
}
```

Example 7-6. The server procedures for the distributed image manager: dim_svc_proc.c (Continued)

```c
void            *
restart_1()
{
  svc_unregister(DIMSERVER, DIMVERS);
  (void) execl(SERVERPATH, (char *) 0);
}

pStr            *
add_1(argp, rqstp)
  image           *argp;
  struct svc_req *rqstp;
{
  static pStr     result;
  static char     msg[MAXSTR];
  static char     N[MAXSTR], O[MAXSTR], C[MAXSTR], D[MAXSTR];
  char            head[MAXSTR];
  int             fstat, b, x, y, d, c;
  time_t          tloc;
  result = msg;
  msg[0] = NULL;

  if (!(fp = fopen(SERVERDB, "r"))) {
    sprintf(msg, "cannot open SERVERDB %s for reading\n", SERVERDB);
    fprintf(stderr, msg);
    return ((pStr *) & result);
  }
  /*
   * First make sure such an image isn't already archived.
   */
  while ((fstat = fscanf(fp, "%d%d%d%d%d\n", &b, &x, &y, &d, &c)) == 5) {
    READHEADER(N, O, C, D);
    if (!strcmp(N, argp->sN))
      break;
    fseek(fp, (long) b, 1);
  }
  switch (fstat) {
  case EOF:                /* not found - that's good */
    fclose(fp);
    if (!(fp = fopen(SERVERDB, "a"))) {
      sprintf(msg, "cannot open SERVERDB %s to append\n", SERVERDB);
      fprintf(stderr, msg);
      fclose(fp);
      return ((pStr *) & result);
    }
    break;
  case 5:                  /* There already is one! */
    sprintf(msg, "%s archive already has a \"%s\"\n", SERVERDB, argp->sN);
    fprintf(stderr, msg);
    fclose(fp);
    return ((pStr *) & result);
  default:                 /* not a clean tail... tell user and try to recover */
    repairDB(msg);
    fclose(fp);
    return ((pStr *) & result);
  }

  CompressImage(1, argp); /* compress as specified */
  /*
   * Get the date, add the image header and data, then return.
   */
  time(&tloc);
  sprintf(head, "%d %d %d %d %d\n%s\n%s\n%s\n%s",
          argp->data.data_len, argp->x, argp->y, argp->d, argp->c,
```

*Example 7-6. The server procedures for the distributed image manager: dim_svc_proc.c
(Continued)*

```
                    argp->sN, argp->sO, argp->sC, (char *) ctime(&tloc));
    if ((fwrite(head, 1, strlen(head), fp) != strlen(head))
        || (fwrite(argp->data.data_val, 1, argp->data.data_len, fp)
            != argp->data.data_len)) {
      sprintf(msg, "failed write to SERVERDB %s\n", SERVERDB);
      fprintf(stderr, "failed write to SERVERDB %s\n", SERVERDB);
    }
    fclose(fp);
    return ((pStr *) & result);
}

/*
 * This is included for the sake of completeness but is brute-force.
 */
pStr            *
delete_1(argp, rqstp)
    pStr            *argp;
    struct svc_req *rqstp;
{
    FILE            *fpp;
    int             fstat;
    static pStr     result;
    static char     msg[MAXSTR];
    char            N[MAXSTR], O[MAXSTR], C[MAXSTR], D[MAXSTR];
    char            *buffer;
    int             bufSize, bytesRead, b, x, y, d, c;
    int             seekPt = 0;

    msg[0] = NULL;
    result = msg;

    if (!(fp = fopen(SERVERDB, "r"))) {
      sprintf(msg, "cannot open SERVERDB %s for reading\n", SERVERDB);
      fprintf(stderr, msg);
      return ((pStr *) & result);
    }
    /*
     * Look thru the DB for the named image.
     */
    while ((fstat = fscanf(fp, "%d%d%d%d%d\n", &b, &x, &y, &d, &c)) == 5) {
        READHEADER(N, O, C, D);
        fseek(fp, (long) b, 1);       /* fp stops at next entry */
        if (!strcmp(N, *argp))
          break;
        seekPt = ftell(fp);
    }
    switch (fstat) {
    case EOF:                         /* not found */
      sprintf(msg, "%s not found in archive\n", *argp);
      fprintf(stderr, msg);
      break;
    case 5:            /* This is the one! Remove it by copying the bottom up. */
      bufSize = MIN(MAX(1, b), MAXBUF);
      buffer = (char *) malloc(bufSize);
      fpp = fopen(SERVERDB, "r+");
      fseek(fpp, seekPt, 0),          /* fpp is at selected image */
      while (!feof(fp)) {
        bytesRead = fread(buffer, 1, bufSize, fp);
        fwrite(buffer, 1, bytesRead, fpp);
      }
      seekPt = ftell(fpp);
      fclose(fpp);
      truncate(SERVERDB, (off_t) seekPt);
      break;
```

Example 7-6. The server procedures for the distributed image manager: dim_svc_proc.c (Continued)

```
    default:                            /* not a clean tail... */
      repairDB(msg);
    }
    fclose(fp);
    return ((pStr *) & result);
}

static image    *pIm = NULL;

imageStat       *
extract_1(argp, rqstp)
  pStr          *argp;
  struct svc_req *rqstp;
{
    int               fstat;
    static imageStat iS;
    static char      msg[MAXSTR];

    iS.status = msg;
    iS.pImage = NULL;

    if (!(fp = fopen(SERVERDB, "r"))) {
      sprintf(msg, "cannot open SERVERDB %s for reading\n", SERVERDB);
      fprintf(stderr, msg);
      return (&iS);
    }
    /*
     * Re-use any previously allocated memory, look thru the DB for the named
     * image.
     */
    if (pIm!=NULL) xdr_free(xdr_imageStat, pIm); pIm = iAllocOne();
    iS.pImage = pIm;

    while ((fstat = fscanf(fp, "%d%d%d%d%d\n", &(pIm->b), &(pIm->x), &(pIm->y),
                          &(pIm->d), &(pIm->c))) == 5) {
            READHEADER(pIm->sN, pIm->sO, pIm->sC, pIm->sD);

        if (!strcmp(pIm->sN, *argp)) break;
        fseek(fp, (long) pIm->b, 1);
    }
    switch (fstat) {
    case EOF:                           /* not found */
      sprintf(msg, "%s not found in archive\n", *argp);
      fprintf(stderr, msg);
      break;
    case 5:                             /* This is the one! */
      pIm->data.data_len = pIm->b;
      pIm->data.data_val = (char *) malloc(pIm->b);
      if (fread(pIm->data.data_val, 1, pIm->data.data_len, fp)
          != pIm->data.data_len) {
        sprintf(msg, "couldn't read all of %s\n", *argp);
        fprintf(stderr, msg);
        repairDB(msg);
      }
      CompressImage(-1, pIm);    /* decompress */
      break;
    default:                            /* not a clean tail... */
      repairDB(msg);
    }
    fclose(fp);
    return (&iS);
}

static imageList *pIList = NULL;
```

*Example 7-6. The server procedures for the distributed image manager: dim_svc_proc.c
(Continued)*

```
imageList       *
list_1(argp, rqstp)
  void          *argp;
  struct svc_req *rqstp;
{
  imageList     *pIL;
  int           fstat;

  /*
   * Free any previously allocated memory, then build a list.
   */
  if (pIList) xdr_free(xdr_imageList, pIList);

  pIL = pIList = iLAllocOne();

  if (!(fp = fopen(SERVERDB, "r"))) {
    sprintf(pIL->pImage->sN, "cannot open SERVERDB %s for reading\n", SERVERDB);
    fprintf(stderr, pIL->pImage->sN);
    return (pIList);
  }
  while ((fstat = fscanf(fp, "%d%d%d%d%d\n", &(pIL->pImage->b),
                         &(pIL->pImage->x), &(pIL->pImage->y),
                         &(pIL->pImage->d), &(pIL->pImage->c))) == 5) {
          READHEADER(pIL->pImage->sN, pIL->pImage->sO,
                  pIL->pImage->sC, pIL->pImage->sD);

    fseek(fp, (long) pIL->pImage->b, 1);

    pIL->pNext = iLAllocOne();  /* hang an empty one on the end */
    pIL = pIL->pNext;
  }
  if (fstat != EOF) {          /* not a clean tail... */
    repairDB(pIL->pImage->sN);
  }
  fclose(fp);
  return (pIList);
}

/*
 * the next four routines are just image linked-list maint. stuff
 */
imageList       *
iLAllocOne()                          /* allocate one imageList structure */
{
  imageList      *pIL = (imageList *) malloc(sizeof(imageList));
  pIL->pImage = iAllocOne();
  pIL->pNext = NULL;
  return (pIL);
}
image           *
iAllocOne()                          /* allocate one image structure */
{
  /* Don't abuse the fact that in XDR, xdr_string(XDR_FREE) really
   * deallocates using "#define mem_free(ptr, bsize) free(ptr)", not
   * really looking for NULLs with strlen().  You should bzero() or
   * calloc() for MAXSTR length strings.
   */
  image      *pI = (image *) malloc(sizeof(image));
  pI->sN = (pStr) calloc(MAXSTR);
  pI->sO = (pStr) calloc(MAXSTR);
  pI->sC = (pStr) calloc(MAXSTR);
  pI->sD = (pStr) calloc(MAXSTR);
  pI->data.data_len = 0;
```

Example 7-6. The server procedures for the distributed image manager: dim_svc_proc.c (Continued)

```
  pI->data.data_val = NULL;
  return (pI);
}

repairDB(s)                        /* doesn't do much, yet... */
  pStr          s;
{
  sprintf(s, "SERVERDB %s data hosed, repaired\n", SERVERDB);
  fprintf(stderr, s);
}

CompressImage(d, pIm)              /* compression and decompression */
int         d;
image       *pIm;
{
  /* omitted */
}
```

Again, the differences between this version and the original *im_proc.c* are actually quite small. The overall structure and logic of the code is unchanged.

In this chapter:

• *How to Start the Remote Server*

• *Terminating Your Services*

• *Report Server Information with rpcinfo*

• *Data Sharing: NFS versus Sending it Yourself*

8

Managing RPC Servers

A distributed application can access servers throughout a network, but there is more involved than simply locating the server. For instance, you might need to inquire about the server's status or control execution of the server. You might encounter some of these problems:

• The server(s) you need isn't (aren't) alive. How can you start the remote server from the local machine?

• You're done and the service can now be removed. How can you remove it?

• The active service occupies too much in the way of resources. What can you do?

• The service needs to be reset; it's acting up or is out of sync. How do you reset it?

• You need to get the status of the server and perform various server maintenance functions. Can you do it from the command line? Or from within the client application?

• Clients and servers have different views of a common file system (file pathnames aren't the same). How do you share files between multiple clients and servers?

• Should you send the (distributed) filename or the actual file contents instead?

There are lots of ways to manage server status remotely, many of which make use of UNIX utilities and system calls outside the standard RPC utilities.

How to Start the Remote Server

The servers developed so far have been launched from the command line as a remote shell process or remote login. In Chapter 5, we discussed the UNIX system approach of starting things with the `inetd` daemon at boot-time.

If the necessary server processes are started by using remote execution on the local machine, there is a local process slot used up. On most machines, the number of processes available to you are limited; for example:

```
rodson> rsh    server MyService &
rodson> rsh -n server MyService &
rodson> on  -n server MyService &
```

These three approaches leave you a channel to transmit signals to the server process. For example, you can bring it to the foreground with `fg`, then use CONTROL-C to terminate both the local and remote processes. Don't send a SIGTERM signal (`kill  -KILL  PID`) or anything drastic like that because it will leave a dangling process on the server machine.[†] `rsh` is slow because it actually performs the complete log-in sequence on the remote `server`. The `-n` flag on `rsh` is the same as telling the process to read from */dev/null*. Without this flag, even if your server does not read from `stdin`, it will block, which is an unfortunate inter-action between the shell and `rsh`.

The `on` utility is incrementally faster to get started than `rsh`, and uses the same flag. `on` is a remote execution utility layered on top of ONC RPC. Both `on` and `rsh` utili-ties pre-suppose that `server` has the necessary daemons running, `rshd` and `rexd`, respectively. Only recently has `rexd` performed any authentication. System administrators should comment-out the */etc/inetd.conf* entry for `rexd` versions without authentication.

The *remote.c* code shown earlier in Example 5-8 is used in the fourth approach:

```
rodson> remote server MyService &
```

It's a simple, fast way to get a server started. It uses the `rexecd` daemon, which is enabled on most of the systems through `inetd`. Unlike the other alternatives, `remote`'s use of `rexec()` allows you to specify authentication credentials in a private *~/.netrc* file. `rexec()` does *not* handle signals across the network, however. Terminating this process will leave both a login shell and the server process running on the remote server.

---

† Example 4-10 addresses these issues with the `slay` script.

The four approaches suggested so far are useful when you want local termination-control over the server. This requires an extra process slot locally. The alternative is to have the remote shell `exec` the server executable:

```
rodson> rsh -n server exec MyService ">& /dev/null &"
rodson> on  -n server exec MyService ">& /dev/null &"
rodson> remote server "exec MyService </dev/null >&/dev/null &"
```

These approaches are a little more efficient (and faster) because each one forces the remote log-in shell started on the `server` machine to be overlaid with `MyService`. Note that it not only reads from */dev/null* as before, but also sends `stdout` and `stderr` to */dev/null*. There is no real reason to wait in the foreground for these remote shell processes to get started, so add an "`&`" on the end to hide them in the background. They return when the servers are established.

An even leaner approach would minimize the number of useless processes generated at *both* the server and client. Overlay both the local and remote processes with just what matters: the `rsh` on this end and the execution of the server on that end. To convince yourself, try something like this at the command line:

```
rodson> rsh server date &
```

Take a look at the processes used locally with a `ps -g`, then look at the processes generated on the server with `ps -g`. There are at least two processes on each end. The following command eliminates one extra process on the server side:

```
rodson> sh -c "rsh vision exec date &"
```

and by adding an `exec` at this end, you can eliminate one here, too:

```
rodson> sh -c "exec rsh vision exec date &"
```

Again, what you have lost is the ability to send signals to the server process directly. The alternative is to send them via other `rsh` commands, e.g., `rsh server kill -INT PID` or `rsh server slay program`.

When terminating any RPC service in this way, the server, unless specially designed to catch signals, will remain registered in the portmap.

Shell Scripts For Starting Servers

In this section, we look at a couple of shell scripts that start remote servers more effectively. The script `sstart.csh`, shown in Example 8-1, is a simple C shell script that starts the named service on the specified machines. It has no error detection and does not use any username information in a *~/.rhosts* file. The name of the server executable is specified as a complete local pathname because the `rsh` entry-point on the remote machine (the `~username` log-in directory) probably won't contain the server executable. Notice that the `rsh` commands placed in the background are reading from */dev/null*. This prevents the process from blocking on the local machine in anticipation of input.

Example 8-1. C shell script to start remote servers: sstart.csh

```
#!/bin/csh  f
#
# sstart.csh - establish the server processes
#
# Usage: sstart.csh service [host host host...]
#        without hosts, kills all services it can find, with
#        hosts, it starts the named service on the host

# Where is the server executable?  All sorts of NFS differences may
# exist...
set Server="$1"

#If no args, blast existing daemons
if ($#argv == 1) then
  foreach i \
  (`ps g|egrep "$Server"|awk '\\!/egrep/&&\\!/awk/&&\\!/sstart.csh/{print $1}'`)
    kill $i
  end
endif

#Launch the processes, up to 9 of them
foreach i ($2 $3 $4 $5 $6 $7 $8 $9 $10)
  rsh $i $Server < /dev/null &
end
exit
```

For example, try starting a bunch of network processes that just "sleep around," then proceed to remove them:

```
rodson> sstart.csh 'sleep 1000' cortex rodson zeus
[1] 23048
[2] 23049
[3] 23050
rodson> ps g | egrep 'sleep 1000'
23048 q0 I     0:00 rsh cortex sleep 1000
23049 q0 I     0:00 rsh rodson sleep 1000
23050 q0 I     0:00 rsh zeus sleep 1000
23064 q0 S     0:00 egrep sleep 1000
rodson> !ss
sstart.csh 'sleep 1000'
rodson> !ps
ps g | egrep 'sleep 1000'
23074 q0 S     0:00 egrep sleep 1000
```

The second script `sstart.sh` is more elaborate and more involved:

```
Usage: sstart.sh [-n] [-v] [-s] server [hosts...]
```

It accommodates the alternate remote usernames you often specify in your *~/.rhosts* file. `sstart.sh` also allows you to specify server machines and executable paths in a separate file. The `server` argument specifies which file to look in. If present, this *~/.server* file is used to select the hosts on which the named `server` should be started. Server hostnames may also be specified on the command line. This will start servers on just the named machines instead of *all* the machines detailed in the *~/.server* file.

sstart.sh, shown in Example 8-2, is somewhat more efficient than Example 8-1. It starts a shell on the remote machine which immediately overlays a call to the named service on top of the shell. This leaves only the one process on the remote machine, consuming minimal process space there as the original login shell process goes <defunct>. But we can no longer terminate these processes directly from the local command line.

Example 8-2. A Bourne shell script to start remote server process (better): sstart.sh

```
#! /bin/sh
#
# sstart - manual start-up of computation servers, RPC or otherwise
#
# Usage: sstart.sh [-n] [-v] [-s] server [hosts...]
#
#   -v means print the rsh commands before executing
#   -n means print the rsh commands but don't execute them
#   -s silence - means throw-away rsh command results
#

SILENCE=0
while true
do
  case $1 in
    -v) SHOPTS="${SHOPTS}v"; shift ;;
    -n) SHOPTS="${SHOPTS}nv"; shift ;;
    -s) SILENCE=1; shift ;;
     *) break ;;
  esac
done

SERVER=$1; shift ;
if test -s $HOME/.$SERVER; then
  echo reading hosts from $HOME/.$SERVER
  else
  echo $0: $HOME/.$SERVER not found
  exit
fi

tmp=/tmp/sstart_s$$
tmp3=/tmp/sstart_u$$

sort -b $HOME/.$SERVER | egrep -v '^#' >$tmp

# if arguments supplied, extract the named hosts
if test -n "$*"; then
  tmp2=/tmp/sstart_t$$
  for host in $*
  do
    echo $host
  done | sort -b >$tmp2
  cat $tmp | awk '{print $1}' | comm -13 - $tmp2 |
  awk \
'{printf "'$0': host %s not in $HOME/.$SERVER, ignored\n", $1}' 1>&2
  join $tmp $tmp2
  rm -f $tmp2
else
  cat $tmp
fi >$tmp3

cat $tmp3 |
  awk '
  { opts=""
     for(i=3; i<=NF; i++) opts=opts" "$i
     if (SILENCE == 1) {
```

Example 8-2. A Bourne shell script to start remote server process (better): sstart.sh (Continued)

```
        printf "%s \"%s%s%s >/dev/null </dev/null &\"\n", \
            $1, $2, SERVER, opts
    } else {
        printf "%s \"%s%s%s </dev/null &\"\n", \
            $1, $2, SERVER, opts
    }
}' SERVER=$SERVER SILENCE=$SILENCE >$tmp

# Check for a different login name in the ~/.rhosts file

sort -b $HOME/.rhosts |
    # if multiple user names for the same host, chooses one arbitrarily
    awk '{print $2, $1}' | uniq -1 |
    awk '{print $2, "-l", $1}' | join -a2 - $tmp |

# There is now a complete rsh command in the pipe for each
# host found.  We'll attempt to start all the servers in
# parallel, delaying some between each process creation to
# allow a process to get out onto the network before we load
# things down further. We send each command into the
# background to attempt to start them all in parallel.
# Because most servers and system error messages will
# come back without identification of the server (host),
# we'll pre-pend that with sed.

(
while read host rest
do
    # The quoted newline is necessary to get newlines in the output
    # when the -v and -n options are used. The redirect from </dev/null
    # is not just nice but essential here, as it would use the
    # standard input stream intended for the above read.
    sh -c$SHOPTS "exec rsh $host $rest 2>&1 | \
        sed -e 's/^/$host: /' 1>&2"'
' </dev/null &
    sleep 2
done

wait  # wait(1) for all messages to come back before exiting
)

rm -f $tmp $tmp3
```

sstart.sh uses the tertiary file *~/.server*, where server is the first argument, to specify the location and any host-specific command-line flags/arguments for the server. A sample file appears in Example 8-3. The specification of the directory and flags is optional. sstart.sh makes use of Bourne shell programming and awk.

Execute the script by typing:

```
rodson> sstart.sh -v ls
```

Use the −n flag and the rsh commands don't get executed, just echoed. Use the −s flag and server outputs go into their */dev/null* bit buckets. This is handy for compute servers who really have nothing valuable to say or who waste a lot of time writing needless things to stdout. Here's a sample *~/.server* file to use. It's intended to start a bunch of ls processes on a few machines, which just die after sending the results. I used a short-lived command like ls just to highlight the fact that this script and sstart.sh can be used to run just about any application or server on a UNIX network. The different ls executables listed could be replaced with different versions of server executables.

Example 8-3. Direct ls servers using sstart.sh: ~/.ls

```
#
#  Sample sstart.sh .server file
#
# Note that you should not include here machines already
# running the server either manually or thru inetd (creates
# multiple copies of the service).
#
# The format of this file is "host server_directory arguments".
# Don't specify the server name, that's tacked-on later.  Just
# for kicks, this $HOME/.ls file will run a couple different
# versions of ls on three machines with different args.
vision                  /usr/bin/ -F
pyramid                 /usr/5bin/ -g
rodson                  /usr/5bin/ -l
```

Alternatively, to augment the above *~/.ls* file, you could start one server with the following:

```
rodson> sstart.sh ls vision
```

Starting a Remote Server From within Your Client Application

The shell command-line use of rsh doesn't help you write a self-contained C application. The start-up of the server can easily be done by the client RPC application.

We can write a C application to read entries from a *~/.rhosts* file and start a server on the remote machine. This assumes that you have remote log-in permission as denoted by the NIS servers or if NIS is not running, then in the remote machine's *~/.rhosts* file. Often the local and remote machines reside in the same domain and/or share *~/.rhosts* via a distributed file system. We adhere to the application_svc naming convention adopted in Chapter 4 and assume that application is equivalent to argv[0] of the client application.

As servers come alive, we record their client handles along with hostnames and status bits. This will facilitate scheduling and tracking multiple server requests simultaneously. We pipeline any remote process creation by forking-off remote shells, and then checking for the server to make its portmap entry. If this doesn't occur in a timely fashion (RSHWAIT seconds), the server is dropped.

In Example 8-4, we execute `rsh` from inside `system()` calls. More efficient `exec` overlays could be added.

Example 8-4. A skeleton for starting servers from the client

```
#define ERRMSG(str) {fprintf (stderr, "%s\n", str); exit (-1);}
#define RSHWAIT 10
#define MAXSERVERS 32   /* allow up to sizeof(int) servers */
int NumServers;
int MaxServers;
int ServersFree;
char ServerName[32];
CLIENT cl[MAXSERVERS];
FILE *pf = NULL;

.... somewhere in main() ....
  /* Read ~/.rhosts and attempt to start/contact servers. */
  MaxServers = 14;
  StartServers(argv, 0);
....

StartServers(argv, online) /* calls itself until exhausted */
char *argv[];
int online;
{
  char sBuf[128];
  int  i, j;
  long ts;

  if (!pf) { /* Is it open already? */
    sprintf(sBuf, "%s%s", getenv("HOME"), "/.rhosts");
    if (!(pf = fopen(sBuf, "r")))
      ERRMSG ("can't open ~/.rhosts to get server names");
  }

  for (i=online; (i < MaxServers) &&
      (fscanf(pf, "%s%s", ServerName[i], sBuf)==2); i++) {

    cl[i] = clnt_create(ServerName[i],PGM,VERS,"tcp");

    /* If attempt to contact fails, try to (re)start the server. */

    if (!cl[i]) {
      sprintf(sBuf, "rsh %s -n '%s/%s_svc >& /tmp/%s &'",
        ServerName[i], NFSgetcwd(), argv[0], argv[0]);
      if (!fork())
        { system(sBuf); _exit(0); } /* pipeline the rsh pigs */
    }
  }
  NumServers = i;

  /* Keep checking to see if they're all alive. If it doesn't
   * happen within RSHWAIT seconds, move on... */
  for (i=j=online; i<NumServers; i++) {
    gettimeofday(&tval, NULL);
    ts = tval.tv_sec;
    while (tval.tv_sec - ts <= RSHWAIT) {/* wait for awhile */
      cl[j] = clnt_create(ServerName[i],PGM,VERS,"tcp");
      if (cl[j]) break;
      /* It failed, try again. */
      sleep(RSHWAIT);
      gettimeofday(&tval, NULL);
```

Example 8-4. A skeleton for starting servers from the client (Continued)

```
  }

  if (cl[j]) {   /* Designate an available server. */
    printf("server started on %s\n", ServerName[j]);
    ServersFree |= (0x1 << j);
    strcpy(ServerName[j++], ServerName[i]);
  } else {       /* It failed even after RSHWAIT seconds! */
    clnt_pcreateerror(ServerName[i]);
  }
}
NumServers = j;

/* Repeat until EOF or MaxServers really available. */
if ((!feof(pf)) && (NumServers < MaxServers))
  StartServers(argv, NumServers);

if (pf) fclose(pf);
}
```

In the above routine, we make a small effort to remove the often nonportable nature of local NFS directory paths by using the following function:

```
char *NFSgetcwd() {
  char path_name[MAXPATHLEN], *getcwd();

  getcwd(path_name, MAXPATHLEN);
  /* remove any local /tmp_mnt/home NFS mount differences */
  while (path_name[1] != 'h') strcpy(&(path_name[1]),
&(path_name[2]));
  return(path_name);
}
```

If a machine is not running an auto-mounting utility, then remote file systems are typically mounted via scripts at boot-time or manually by the superuser. In the SunOS 4.1 auto-mount environment that we run, automatically-mounted volumes appear with a */prefix* before the */home/hostname* part of the path (in our configuration it's */tmp_mnt*). Script or manually-mounted volumes do not have this prefix. Your mileage may vary. This is a site-specific, quick and dirty solution to accommodate differences in NFS paths. The information returned by fstab(5) is a good place to start to fashion a more robust approach. See the last section in this chapter.

There is an additional, potentially more elegant approach to starting servers from your client C code and that is to use the rex(3R), the RPC remote execution protocol as defined in */usr/include/rpcsvc/rex.[xb]*. It is a pretty generic terminal interface to remote machines. I did not explore it here because we won't run rexd() until all the security issues are cleared up.

Terminating Your Services

To remove the servers once you are done with them, you could either build in a lack-of-use timer or provide an external RPC procedure. Example 8-5 provides a template for a server that watches its own activity level with an alarm. alarm(3C) is a useful interface to set a timer which, when it expires, generates a signal SIGALRM that you can catch.

It is not a good policy to allow servers to terminate and leave registrations. To unregister a service from the portmap, you should delete portmap entries for every server procedure registered by the server.

```
svc_unregister(prognum, versnum)
    u_long prognum, versnum;
```

svc_unregister(3N) erases portmap entries for the named program and version number. If you use RPCGEN, you specified program and version number in the *application.x* file.

Example 8-5. A skeleton for server self-termination after lack of use

```
#define SLAVE_TIMEOUT(900);      /* time-out in secs. */

main()
{
  /*
   * Set-up an alarm signal function to be invoked if idle
   * for awhile.
   */
  signal(SIGALRM, die);

  /*
   * Register service if necessary and go dormant watching a
   * socket or using svc_run().
   */
  svc_register(...PGM, VERS...);

}

dispatch (..) {
  /*
   * Reset the alarm and do the servicing...
   ' '
    alarm(SLAVE_TIMEOUT);
  /*
   * Do the real work servicing here....
   */
  }
}

/*
 * This function is called when we get a SIGALRM so that we die
 * gracefully with exit status 0.  If started by inetd, it
 * takes interest in non-zero exit status and alarms.
 */
int die()
{
  /* Do this if you are registered in the portmap!! */
  svc_unregister(PGM, VERS);
  exit(0);
}
```

The above approach works equally well for any type of server, whether accessed with RPC or low-level socket calls. An alternative is to leave the server dormant and provide an RPC procedure to remove it completely with a client request. An example of such a procedure within a server program is shown in Example 8-6.

Example 8-6. Server termination through an RPC: die_1()

```
void *die_1()
{
  /*
   * Unregister the server and die gracefully, returning
   * nothing.  Could do a svc_sendreply() if so motivated...
   */
  svc_unregister(PGM, VERS);
  exit(0);
}
```

Recall that if RPCGEN is used with the -I flag to generate an inetd(8C)-compatible server, the -K flag can be used to set a desired waiting time. The -K argument is the number of seconds you want the server to hang around, watching for its own requests. After this time, the server explicitly exits, returning the responsibility of watching for requests to inetd. The server must stay registered with the portmap in this case to tell clients that, while it might not be running, it is still available.

When run from the command line, inetd-compatible RPC servers fork a process, but do not automatically remove themselves.

☞ Putting server functions like termination, priority setting, or restarting out as remote procedure calls makes a server vulnerable. Use them only during development, or protect them with some type of authentication and access policy.

System Error: "%STF-E-OPENIN, Server Too Fat"

Well, I got the attention of the VMS programmers. Idle servers should be terminated because they occupy process space and memory which may be critical to other applications, especially interactive ones. If the server must stick around for a while, change its process priority so it runs only when there are spare cycles. This allows it to be swapped-out and lets others access the CPU. It really makes people mad when they realize you use their machine as your compute server, so covert operations like these are often necessary!

By using the nice(3V) system call, the server process can set its process priority down, yet still take advantage of all spare CPU cycles.[†] To be even more elegant, you can manage priority from the client by defining and registering a procedure within the RPC server program that does something similar to Example 8-7.

---

† renice(8) and nice(1) are handy command-line utilities for setting process priority.

Example 8-7. A skeleton for setting server process priority

```
#define SLAVE_NICE (10)                 /* use nice 10 by default */

main()
{
   nice(SLAVE_NICE);

   /*
    * Register service if necessary and go dormant watching a
    * socket or using svc_run().
    */
}
```

Insert nice() into the server's main() to establish a new priority as soon as the server is started. Drive it with an alarm (interval or time-of-day) to set priority as a function of time. You could even set priority from the client using a separate service procedure. In this way, a server can control its own resource consumption or rely upon a client to do it.

Hit Reset

Oftentimes, especially during the development phase, a server needs to be restarted. This may be because an updated version is available or some re-initialization is required, such as when a new database comes on-line and needs to be read. The simplest scheme is to reserve a procedure within your RPC program for this purpose.

Once the server's dispatch program receives a call to the RESTART procedure, you can overlay the current process with one of the execl(3V) family of calls, pointing to the executable server image. Even if you plan to restart the service, it is also probably safest to remove the portmap entry; if the restart fails and the server dies, then a false program might be registered. Here's an example from the rtrace application discussed in detail in Appendix B. In Example 8-8, the only procedure registered was the dispatch procedure, RTRACESERVER, with version number RTRACEVERS.

Example 8-8. Restarting the server with an RPC: restart_1()

```
void             *
restart_1()
{
  /*
   * Unregister the server and start up again, returning
   * nothing.  Could do a svc_sendreply() first if you like.
   */
  svc_unregister(RTRACESERVER, RTRACEVERS);
  execl(RTRAVESERVERPATH, (char *) 0);
}
```

An even more elegant approach would be to pass the server pathname as a request argument. This is complicated by the issues of incompatible remote filenames.

If the server was left in a state where it is blocked, the remote procedure call to RESTART won't be heard. This might happen, for example, when waiting to return reply parameters to a client process who died prematurely. Unless you custom-designed a server dispatch routine, the server process is single-threaded, and capable of providing only one service at a time. You have to resort to drastic actions. One of my favorites is to remotely execute (via `remote`) the `slay` script discussed in Chapter 4. Although this does leave hanging portmap entries, they are easy enough to remove, as we will see in the next section.

Report Server Information with rpcinfo

The standard version 4.0 and TIRPC releases of the ONC RPC suite include a utility known as `rpcinfo(8C)`.[†] It allows you to look at the portmaps of networked machines from the command line and determine what procedure numbers and versions are registered. `rpcinfo` allows you to make remote procedure calls to a registered server's procedure number 0. `rpcinfo` even allows you to broadcast in search of a procedure/version match out on the network.

`rpcinfo` has the following forms of use:

> rpcinfo -p [*host*]
>
> rpcinfo [-n *portnum*] -u *host program* [*version*]
>
> rpcinfo [-n *portnum*] -t *host program* [*version*]
>
> rpcinfo -b *program version*
>
> rpcinfo -d *program version*

It makes RPC calls to servers and reports back what it finds. The program argument may be a system daemon name from */etc/rpc* or an RPC program number. The options are listed in Table 8-1 and we'll look at each option in turn.

Table 8-1. Rpcinfo Options

Options	Effect
-p	Probe the portmap of the local or specified remote machine.
-m	Use UDP to attempt a call to the NULLPROC of a host's server.
-t	Use TCP to attempt a call to the NULLPROC of a host's server.
-n	Override what portmap says with -u and -t and call NULLPROC at a specific port.
-b	Broadcast to all reachable NULLPROC's.
-d	Delete local portmap entries.

---

† `rpcinfo` is also available with the optional networking software with SunOS 4.1.

The -p flag makes remote calls to the portmapper service. It probes the portmap of the named host (or if not named, this host), dumping a list of all the registered RPC programs, specifying program and version numbers, the transport protocol used, and the port number assigned. Here is a portion of the results of a probe of the portmap on the machine rodson:

```
rodson> rpcinfo -p
   program vers proto    port
    100000   2   tcp     111   portmapper          ·
    100000   2   udp     111   portmapper
    100007   2   tcp    1024   ypbind
    100007   2   udp    1027   ypbind
    100007   1   tcp    1024   ypbind
    100007   1   udp    1027   ypbind
      .
      .
      .
    100012   1   udp    1042   sprayd
    100008   1   udp    1043   walld
    100015   6   udp    1587   selection_svc
 536870913   1   udp    3270
 536870913   1   tcp    1421
```

Notice that one of the rls_svc servers developed earlier in the book remains registered in the portmap, available at two different ports using UDP and TCP transports. I can verify this by using bc(1) to show that the decimal number listed is the hex program number I used in the protocol definitions:

```
cortex> bc
obase=16
536870913
20000001
```

When I probe the portmap of a remote machine cortex, I notice that there is a copy of the server registered over there, too. Remember just because it's registered in the portmap does not mean it's alive and available for use. The process could have terminated before using the svc_unregister() call mentioned earlier.

```
rodson> rpcinfo -p cortex
   program vers proto    port
    100000   2   tcp     111   portmapper
    100000   2   udp     111   portmapper
    100007   2   tcp    1024   ypbind
    100007   2   udp    1027   ypbind
    100007   1   tcp    1024   ypbind
    100007   1   udp    1027   ypbind
      .
      .
      .
    100012   1   udp    1042   sprayd
    100008   1   udp    1043   walld
    100015   6   udp    1880   selection_svc
 536870913   1   udp    3368
 536870913   1   tcp    1710
```

`rpcinfo` may also be used to find out if servers are alive by placing remote calls.

The `-u` flag uses UDP to attempt remote execution of the NULL procedure (0 or NULLPROC) for the specified host and RPC program. Version number may also be specified. `rpcinfo` reports regarding the response received. This is one of the reasons why it is good to provide a procedure number 0 service. It should return a `void` type.

The `-t` flag is the same, except that it uses TCP transport protocol. As used with either `-u` or `-t`, the `-n` flag overrides what the portmap might say, and explicitly directs the call to the 0 procedure at the named port. For example, let's make a call to the `rls_svc` service registered on `rodson`:

```
rodson> rpcinfo -u rodson 536870913
program 536870913 version 1 ready and waiting
```

The server is healthy enough to reply. This means it is listening to its UDP port and is not waiting to get rid of a reply or otherwise blocked. Now let's look at a server `program` by name:

```
rodson> rpcinfo -u cortex walld
program 100008 version 1 ready and waiting
```

The network `rwall` server `rwalld(8C)` is healthy, too.

Should you use `rpcinfo` to call a procedure that is registered in the portmap, and the procedure doesn't respond to the portmapper's bind attempt, the portmapper removes it from the mapping table. It is deemed dysfunctional. For example, I know the `rls_svc` server registered in `cortex`'s portmap was actually dead. `rpcinfo` reports it as unavailable:

```
rodson> rpcinfo -u cortex 536870913
rpcinfo: RPC: Program not registered
program 536870913 is not available
```

A subsequent probe into `cortex`'s portmap shows it now removed:

```
rodson> rpcinfo -p cortex
   program vers proto   port
    100000   2   tcp    111   portmapper
    100000   2   udp    111   portmapper
    100007   2   tcp   1024   ypbind
    100007   2   udp   1027   ypbind
    100007   1   tcp   1024   ypbind
    100007   1   udp   1027   ypbind
       .
       .

       .
    100012   1   udp   1042   sprayd
    100008   1   udp   1043   walld
    100015   6   udp   1880   selection_svc
```

The `rpcinfo -b` flag broadcasts requests for RPC procedure 0 of the named program and version. Broadcasting only makes sense with the UDP transport. By its nature (i.e., a lack of state), the server and client have no built-in mechanism to assure one-time execution. `rpcinfo` waits a pre-set length of time for replies to come back. A machine running the program may respond zero or more times. To get a good fix on who is running that program (with procedure zero of that version), pipe the results through `sort -u`. Let's look around the network for version 2 of the NIS binding service `ypbind(8)`. Instead of showing you all the 294 responses, I piped the results through the `nl(1)` line-numbering filter and `tail(1)` to look at the last lines:

```
rodson> rpcinfo -b ypbind 2 | sort -u | nl | tail
  285   3.1.7.53 sugarbush
  286   3.1.7.54 camelback
  287   3.1.7.58 antigua
  288   3.1.7.74 easygoer
  289   3.1.7.75 alydar
  290   3.1.7.76 manowar
  291   3.1.7.77 chico
  292   3.1.7.84 smds51
  293   3.1.7.88 ranger
  294   3.1.7.97 bigbird
```

Now let's broadcast requests to procedure 0 of our `rls_svc` server:

```
rodson> rpcinfo -b  536870913 1 | sort -u
3.1.4.213 dspuv2
3.1.5.126 c2a
3.1.5.226 rodson
```

There are only three servers running on the whole network: `dspuv2` is a DEC MicroVax, `c2a` is a multi-processor Convex, and `rodson` is this machine.

Broadcasting is considered an antisocial act. It should be discouraged, used infrequently, and not as something your application depends on. All the network portmappers (this side of any gateways) are exercised with the older non-TI portmappers forking for each response. It puts undue burden on every system on the network.

Under RPCSRC 4.0, the `-d` flag *should only be used by the superuser* as it calls `pmap_unset()` to delete the local portmap registration for the specified program/version combination. It does this with no respect for servers installed and running! In this way you can tell the portmapper to unregister a server, leaving it no way to communicate with the outside world. You can really cause some havoc by removing something important like the `selection_svc(1)` SunView selection service.

```
cortex> rpcinfo -p | tail -4
  100002   2   udp   1041   rusersd
  100012   1   udp   1042   sprayd
  100008   1   udp   1043   walld
  100015   6   udp   1587   selection_svc
cortex> rpcinfo -d selection_svc 6
cortex> rpcinfo -p | tail -4
  100002   1   udp   1041   rusersd
  100002   2   udp   1041   rusersd
```

```
100012   1   udp   1042   sprayd
100008   1   udp   1043   walld
```

Not a very nice thing to do. The server is still running, but now is unreachable.

Changes Under TIRPC

The `rpcinfo -d` loophole has been fixed. It uses loop-back transports to be sure who the caller is. The `-u` and `-t` flags specifying transport only make sense if the old `portmap(8C)` is running, instead of the new TI `rpcbind(8C)` binding service. The `-p` flag is also `portmap`-specific so it, too, disappears. You now have:

rpcinfo [*host*]

rpcinfo -T *netid host prognum* [*versnum*]

rpcinfo -a *serv_address* -T *netid prognum* [*version*]

rpcinfo -b *prognum versnum*

rpcinfo -d [-T *netid*] *prognum versnum*

The concept of a `netid` is explained in Chapter 11. It represents the token name of the transport on which the service is required. Servers are now defined in terms of universal addresses.

Data Sharing: NFS versus Sending it Yourself

NFS or any other distributed file system is no nirvana. Sharing data clogs up the network. Yet some of the newer, low-level, optimized Ethernet implementations (e.g., dynamic transport packet-sizing) transfer at greater than 30% of the theoretical maximum of the network's capacity. So the question is, should you ask clients and servers to retrieve shared data for themselves via a distributed file system or share data at the application level as part of the protocol?

High-level RPC and XDR calls are ideal for exchanging *small* amounts of data across a network. When an RPC client and server need to exchange or share *large* amounts of information, you still have the two options: do it yourself with replies and requests, or dump it to a file and depend on a common file system between the two.

When multiple connects are involved, with multiple clients and/or multiple servers, the case for using filenames to share data gets stronger. Locking and access control can be managed within the file system.

My experience has been that when using a conventional Ethernet network, with effective transfer rates of less than 100 KBytes/second, data compression is necessary for volumes exceeding hundreds of KBytes. When the time to transfer data between client and server processes increases to seconds, user interaction is greatly impaired.

The data compression, applied at both client and server side, may be as simple as standard `compress(1)` (Lempel, Ziv, Welch algorithm) or `oldcompact(1)` (an adaptive Huffman coding scheme).

Most graphics and imaging packages have command-line or C-callable filters for run-length encoding and decoding.[†] That's what I typically use for images. Simple compression schemes on occasion blow-up and actually increase the data size, but that's rare, usually delivering 1.5-2.0X compression.

I don't resort to calling `compress` with a `system()` or `exec()` call unless it is really necessary. The threshold of pain is about 4 MBytes for most of my applications on our network. The distributed ray tracing example covered in Appendix B discusses the merits of compression schemes.

Host-qualified Filenames

When you have decided to use filenames across the network, there's an additional caveat. Machines do not necessarily share the same exact pathname and occasionally use totally different syntax to represent filenames. One very plausible situation is when all your RPC applications need to access a central file. ONC NIS handles this functionality by providing RPC access to an on-line database. One centralized server is in charge with others slaved to it. See `ypclnt(3N)` for information on the programmatic interface to NIS servers and databases.

A simpler, but less fault-tolerant solution might place the shared data in one spot in the network file system. If all the associated clients of the database are mounted the same way, that spot might look like */home/cortex/projects/rpc/SCCS*. The problem is that some of the machines are different. An Apollo or even a native ONC machine not running `automount(8)` might see a different path or need a different representation syntax. Other common distributed file systems like AFS, RFS, UFS, or TFS construct their names differently, too.

One option is to define and share filenames in a neutral form. In this way, each side can translate it as necessary. In general, there is no set way to sanitize a filename. Different file systems mount files in different ways and places, though standards are emerging out of places like Berkeley and OSF. One strategy for expressing pathnames independent of the file system is to qualify the filename at the sending end:

• Use `statfs(2)` to retrieve information about a file system mounted by the local machine, given the filename.

---

† If you are using SunOS, exec the filters in */lib/rasfilters*.

- Follow this with `setmntent(3)` and `getmntent(3)` (or `getfsent(3)`) to inspect all the possible mounts, as involved volumes could be mounted in several places.

The `getmntent(3)` family of system calls allows you to look into the */etc/mtab* (and */etc/fstab*) databases. In this way you can get information about file systems. */etc/mtab* contains entries describing *currently* mounted file systems. This information will be passed with the filename, including hostname and mount information, to aid in translation. At the receiver end, the sanitized filename, with mount information spelled out, can be used to look for the mounted volume, or attempt to mount it.

The depth of this subject prohibits us from discussing it in any real detail. I hope that a standard mechanism or file system will be adopted soon enough anyway.

In this chapter:

• *Remote Asynchronous Calls, Multi-server Processing*

• *Multi-tasking at the Server*

• *Lightweight Processing*

• *Remote Asynchronous Calls with LWP*

9

Multiple Clients and Servers

This chapter is about designing distributed applications that require multiple RPC clients and/or servers. We will discuss:

• Remote asynchronous calling (RAC) from clients to facilitate concurrent, multiple-server processing.

• Methods for multi-tasking at the server, allowing one server to honor multiple requests in a time-slice fashion. We'll use heavyweight processing here.

• Lightweight processing as it applies to multi-tasking at the client and server.

We will look at a number of useful examples.

Remote Asynchronous Calls, Multi-server Processing

RPC systems are constructed such that the request/reply cycle keeps the client process I/O blocked until the reply is received, as shown in Figure 9-1. This can be unacceptable in mission-critical or interactive applications. As illustrated in Figure 9-2, there are three possible ways to perform RPCs asynchronously:

1. Heavyweight processing, as illustrated in Figure 9-2(a). We discussed this alternative in Chapter 6.

2. ONC RPC library support as illustrated in Figure 9-2(b). We can review the relevant building blocks within the ONC RPC suite, especially batch (one-way) and broadcast RPC.

3. Follow-up RPC (FRPC) as illustrated in Figure 9-2(c). By adding a second request/reply step a server can deposit results into the client in an asynchronous fashion. It allows each server to compute and reply at its own pace. Like heavy-weight processing, this type of client concurrency also avoids IPC programming but isn't so resource-intensive. A schematic for this approach appears. FRPC processing is useful if there are limited computer resources, the client has many other tasks to perform, or (my favorite) the client wants to tie up lots of servers at once.

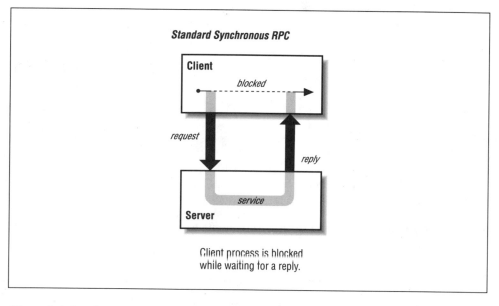

Figure 9-1. Synchronous RPC

We'll discuss the last two approaches in this chapter.

ONC RPC Support

So far we have seen that client requests placed in the ONC RPC system cause the calling process (the client) to block until the reply is returned. This model is inten-tionally the same as the local procedure-call model.

The ONC RPC system includes a few ways to avoid this blocking. Each technique makes use of the fact that you can place a request with a time-out value of zero. Control is returned to the calling process immediately after the request is sent to the remote service. The RPC system times-out before a reply can be received. To operate correctly in this scenario, servers must not send a reply because they will never be received. A reply with no client listening can leave the server blocked. If the server detects this type of *one-way* request, it should proceed to dispatch the appropriate service procedure but should not use `svc_sendreply()` when

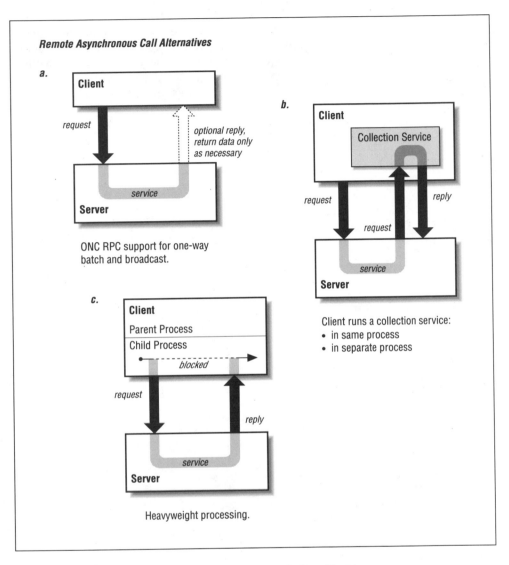

Remote Asynchronous Call Alternatives

a.

Client

request

optional reply,
return data only
as necessary

service

Server

ONC RPC support for one-way
batch and broadcast.

b.

Client

Collection Service

request   reply

request

service

Server

Client runs a collection service:
- in same process
- in separate process

c.

Client

Parent Process

Child Process

blocked

request

reply

service

Server

Heavyweight processing.

Figure 9-2. Three asynchronous alternatives to avoid client blocking

complete. You can think of a one-way RPC[†] as a simplex communication in which data travels in a single direction. Synchronous RPC is comparable to half-duplex communication, where data travels in either direction but not at the same time.

---

† Others use the term *non-blocking RPC*. I find this a little misleading because you greatly change the semantics of the RPC by removing the reply.

One-way RPC

We can create a one-way RPC by setting the RPC time-out interval at the client to zero. The RPC system returns control immediately instead of waiting for a reply. Thus, a client can send multiple requests, one at a time or in batches, without waiting around for a reply. In the ONC RPC suite, you can establish a time-out at the client on a per server basis by setting zero as the default time-out with `clnt_control()`. After the `CLIENT` handle is created, use a `struct timeval` as described in `<sys/time.h>`.

```
...
struct timeval timeOut;
...
    /* create CLIENT handle clntHandle */
if ((clntHandle = clnt_create(host, PROGNUM, VERSNUM, "tcp")) == NULL) {
    clnt_pcreateerror(host);
    return(1);
}
...
    /* set time-out to zero */
timeOut.tv_sec = timeOut.tv_usec = 0;
if (clnt_control(clntHandle, CLSET_TIMEOUT, &timeOut) == FALSE) {
    /* report an error */
  fputs("can't delay time-out\n", stderr);
  exit(1);
}
...
    /* place the remote call */
if (clnt_call(clntHandle, PROCNUM, xdr_prognum, &arom, NULL, NULL,
                    /*ignored*/timeOut) != RPC_SUCCESS) {
    clnt_perror(clntHandle, "PROCNUM failed");
    return(0);
}
...
    /*
     * Now send a normal RPC to signal the server to send a reply.
     * First you must set the time-out back to some realistic
     * non-zero value.
     */
timeOut.tv_sec = 25;
if (clnt_control(clntHandle, CLSET_TIMEOUT, &timeOut) == FALSE) {

    fputs("can't delay time-out\n", stderr);
      exit(1);
}
...
```

The default time-out value in ONC RPC Release 4.0 is 25 seconds. Once you have used `clnt_control()` to specify a new default timeout value, `struct timeval` specification in subsequent calls to `clnt_call()` are ignored, although they do need to be there.

As an alternative, you can specify a zero time-out when you place the remote call with `clnt_call()`. This approach is simply more visible:

```
    ...
    static struct timeval timeOut = {0, 0};
    ...
        /* create CLIENT handle clntHandle */
    if ((clntHandle = clnt_create(host, PROGNUM, VERSNUM, "tcp")) == NULL) {
        clnt_pcreateerror(host);
        return(1);
    }
    ...
        /* place the remote call */



    if (clnt_call(clntHandle, PROCNUM, xdr_procnum, &argp, NULL, NULL, timeOut)
                        != RPC_SUCCESS) {
        clnt_perror(clntHandle, "PROCNUM failed");
        return(0);
    }
    ...
```

Remember that if you want to receive a reply, such as on a subsequent RPC, you must make the remote call with a non-zero time-out.

My experience with ONC Release 4.0 is that the above use of `clnt_control()` to establish a new default RPC time-out works properly once, overriding that specified when `clnt_call()` is actually used. It does not work a second time, when you must set the time-out back to some non-zero value to receive a reply. The examples in this chapter instead modify the time-out structure specified with `clnt_call()`, avoiding the use of `clnt_control()` to set time-outs. I am told there is a bug report pending in this area.

The choice of transport is crucial here. If you use an unreliable transport like UDP, and you do not receive a reply for each request, you cannot be sure the request ever reached the server. By using a reliable transport like TCP, you can be sure the request gets there. The transport protocol may spend a significant amount of energy doing this.

Sometimes it makes sense to use an unreliable protocol; for example, if you wanted to update a number of distributed databases at a certain interval. Missing an update at one server might not be as important as delaying the update cycle. If one server is unable to acknowledge, it would bog down or potentially block the entire update process while the client's transport protocol either timed-out or continued to retry delivery.

A Client/Server That Uses One-way RPC

Let's build a client/server pair that makes use of a one-way RPC. The example here is an extension of the remote directory reading application. This time the protocol specifies two procedures, `dirname_1()` and `readdir_1()`. The latter works the same as `readdir_1()` in Chapters 3 and 4. It expects a directory name as the request argument and replies with a linked-list of directory contents. It is not the subject of a one-way RPC because it returns results.

The change to the protocol file, shown in Example 9-1, is the addition of `dirname_1()`, which tells the server to perform a directory listing and retain the contents locally. The listing gets added to the end of a linked-list kept in static server memory. The linked-list is dumped when a `readdir_1()` request is found and the complete list is sent back. `dirname_1()` returns nothing and will be the subject of a one-way RPC. Notice that within the new program declaration block `DIRNAME` is typed as returning `void`. Both `DIRNAME` and `READDIR` take as a request parameter a directory name within a NULL-terminated string. `READDIR` returns the listing in a `readdir_res` structure.

Example 9-1. Combined one-way and synchronous RPC protocol for remote directory listing: one-way.x

```
/*
 * one-way.x: no-reply remote multiple directory listing protocol
 */
const           MAXNAMELEN = 255;
typedef string  nametype < MAXNAMELEN >;  /* a directory entry */
typedef struct namenode *namelist;        /* a link in the listing */

/*
 * a node in the directory
 */
struct namenode {
  nametype      name;         /* name of directory entry */
  namelist      pNext;        /* next entry */
};

/*
 * the result of a READDIR operation
 */
union readdir_res switch (int errno) {
  case 0:
  namelist list;              /* no error: return directory listing */
default:
  void;                       /* error occurred: nothing else to return */
};

/*
 * The directory program definition, two procedures, one expects nothing,
 * the other retrieves any results.
 */
program         DIRPROG {
  version         DIRVERS {
    void
    DIRNAME(nametype) = 1;
    readdir_res
    READDIR(nametype) = 2;
  } =             1;
} =             0x20000001;
```

To make the stubs as well as to compile and link both sides of the application, use the simple *makefile* presented in Chapter 4. Or compile the protocol manually to generate the client and server stubs along with the shared XDR filters:

```
rodson> rpcgen one-way.x
rodson> rpcgen -s tcp -o one-way_svc.c one-way.x
```

The first use of RPCGEN generates the client and server stubs, plus the XDR filters and header file. The second use of RPCGEN with -s tcp generates a new *one-way_svc.c* server stub that accepts only clients using the TCP transport. Thus, we make sure that no client calls the service with the unreliable UDP transport.

There's just one problem with the code generated by RPCGEN. We need to alter the time-out value specified in each use of clnt_call() within the client stub. We alter this time-out value rather than adding calls to clnt_control(). In the client stub *one-way_clnt.c*, we replace the static global struct timeval with an external reference back to the client's main(), *one-way.c*, where we modify it as necessary. Type this command sometime after the protocol is compiled, or make the change indicated by hand. Below, we use sed in a shell script to make the change:

```
sed 's/static struct timeval TIMEOUT = { 25, 0 }/extern struct timeval TIMEOUT/'
< one-way_clnt.c > /tmp/$$
mv /tmp/$$ one-way_clnt.c
```

Now TIMEOUT is available in both the client's main() and the stub. It will be declared in *one-way.c* and its value changed there to reflect the type of RPC being placed.

Note that if you have an updated version of ONC RPC, the time-out control added to your client code via clnt_control() calls alleviates the need for modifying the RPCGEN-generated client stub.

If you are interested in modifying the Chapter 4 *makefile* stub, you must augment the rule defining actions required to make the client application pass *one-way_clnt.c* through sed first.

Now, let's move on to the service procedures. The two service procedures defined in the protocol, dirname_1() and readdir_1(), must be designed to accept the same directory-name request argument. dirname_1() will return nothing. By using return(void), you tell the server dispatch routine generated by RPCGEN to send *no* reply. svc_sendreply() is not called if a void return value is encountered. Look at the server stub *one-way_svc.c* to see how this is accomplished. Note that if you attempt to send a reply, no one is waiting for an answer so your server times out. This gets aggravating if the client is making request retries while the server ignores the requests, as it is busy repeating unwanted replies.

The server procedures are shown in Example 9-2. Note that there is a flaw in this server, detected by one of the reviewers. Read the next section before basing any real applications on this approach.

Example 9-2. Server procedures including a one-way, request-only RPC service:
one-way_svc_proc.c

```
/*
 * one-way_svc_proc.c: remote namedir_1() and readdir_1() implementations
 * for the multiple directory listing service
 */
#include <rpc/rpc.h>
#include <sys/dir.h>
#include "one-way.h"

extern int      errno;
extern char     *malloc();
extern char     *strdup();

static readdir_res res;            /* Must be static! */
static int      beginCycleFlag = TRUE;

void            *
dirname_1(dirname)
  nametype        *dirname;
{
  namelist        nl;
  namelist        *nlp;
  DIR             *dirp;
  struct direct   *d;

  /*
   * If this is the first time a no-reply request has been made in this
   * cycle, start a new res.readdir_res_u.list. Free previous result.  It
   * might be a long list that eats up memory.
   */
  if (beginCycleFlag == TRUE) {
    beginCycleFlag = FALSE;
    xdr_free(xdr_readdir_res, &res);
    res.readdir_res_u.list = NULL;
  }
  /*
   * Open the directory.
   */
  dirp = opendir(*dirname);
  if (dirp == NULL) {
    res.errno = errno;
    return (NULL);
  }
  /*
   * Add directory entries to the end of the list.
   */
  nlp = &res.readdir_res_u.list;
  while ((nl = *nlp) != NULL)
    nlp = &nl->pNext;

  while (d = readdir(dirp)) {
    nl = *nlp = (namenode *) malloc(sizeof(namenode));
    nl->name = strdup(d->d_name);
    nlp = &nl->pNext;
  }
  *nlp = NULL;

  /*
   * Return no result.
   */
```

Example 9-2. Server procedures including a one-way, request-only RPC service:
one-way_svc_proc.c (Continued)

```
    res.errno = 0;
    closedir(dirp);
    return (NULL);
}

readdir_res      *
readdir_1(dirname)
    nametype        *dirname;
{

    /*
     * Record this directory's contents.
     */
    dirname_1(dirname);

    /*
     * Start the cycle over and return the result.
     */
    beginCycleFlag = TRUE;
    return (&res);
}
```

Now let's look at the client side, shown in Example 9-3. As mentioned earlier, we will change the time-out structure used by the client stub's calls to `clnt_call()` to affect one-way RPCs. If you were to check the status fields within the CLIENT handle after the one-way RPCs to `dirname_1()` using the following,

```
    clnt_perror(clientHandle, server)
```

you would discover that the RPC_TIMEDOUT error was recorded. The RPC system was given no time to wait around for a reply, and wasn't sent one anyway. So, as far as it is concerned, the remote call failed. Ignore this error.

Example 9-3. Client places one-way RPC requests: one-way.c

```
/*
 * one-way.c: one-way remote multiple directory listing client
 */
#include <stdio.h>
#include <rpc/rpc.h>
#include "one-way.h"

extern int      errno;
struct timeval  TIMEOUT = {0, 0};      /* used by one-way_clnt.c */

main(argc, argv)
    int             argc;
    char            *argv[];
{
    CLIENT          *cl;
    char            *server;
    char            *dir;
    readdir_res     *result;
    namelist        nl;
    int             i;

    if (argc < 3) {
        fprintf(stderr, "Usage: %s host directory(s)\n", argv[0]);
        exit(1);
    }
    server = argv[1];
```

Example 9-3. Client places one-way RPC requests: one-way.c (Continued)

```
    /*
     * Create client "handle" used for calling the procedures of the program.
     * We use the "tcp" protocol to assure our one-way requests get there.
     */
    if ((cl = clnt_create(server, DIRPROG, DIRVERS, "tcp")) == NULL) {
        clnt_pcreateerror(server);
        exit(1);
    }
    /*
     * Call the remote procedure DIRNAME on the server each time for all but
     * the last directory specified on the command line.  Set the time-out for
     * this client handle to zero to tell RPC not to wait for a reply.
     */
    TIMEOUT.tv_sec = TIMEOUT.tv_usec = 0;
    for (i = 2; i < argc - 1; i++)   for (i = 2; i < argc - 1; i++) {
        dirname_1(&(argv[i]), cl);
        clnt_perror(cl, server);/* ignore the time-out errors */
    }

    /*
     * Now send a normal sync. RPC to signal the server to send the reply.
     * First you must set the time-out back to some realistic non-zero value.
     */
    TIMEOUT.tv_sec = 25;
    if ((result = readdir_1(&(argv[i]), cl)) == NULL) {
        clnt_perror(cl, server);
        exit(1);
    }
    /*
     * Successfully called the remote procedures.
     */

    if (result->errno != 0) {
        /*
         *A remote system error occurred, print error message and die.
         */
        errno = result->errno;
        perror(dir);
        exit(1);
    }
    /*
     * Got a directory listing, print it out.
     */
    for (nl = result->readdir_res_u.list; nl != NULL; nl = nl->pNext) {
        printf("%s\n", nl->name);
    }
    exit(0);
}
```

To compile and link everything takes a few extra steps now. You need to insert the
sed command in the *makefile*, or use the Chapter 4 template with some manual
post-processing.

```
rodson> make APPN=one-way one-way.h
rodson> sed 's/static struct timeval TIMEOUT = { 25, 0 }\
/extern struct timeval TIMEOUT/'one-way_clnt.c > tmp
rodson> mv tmp one-way_clnt.c
rodson> make APPN=one-way one-way one-way_svc
```

I didn't bother to use the $-s$ flag on RPCGEN and force use of only the TCP transport at the server. Run it by starting a remote server and executing the client `main()`.

```
rodson> rsh cortex $cwd/one-way_svc < /dev/null &
rodson> one-way cortex $cwd /home
cortex: RPC: Timed out # remember to ignore this 'error' as necessary
.
..
makefile
broadcast.c
one-way.c
one-way.x
one-way_svc_proc.c
one-way.h
one-way_clnt.c
one-way_svc.c
one-way_xdr.c
one-way_xdr.o
one-way_clnt.o
one-way_svc.o
one-way.o
one-way
one_way_svc_proc.o
one-way_svc
.
..
alydar
cortex
unclejack
bach
sparky
```

Retaining State

Example 9-3 illustrates two things:

1. One-way RPCs.

2. How *not* to retain state at the server.

We built the server to buffer-up replies, assuming that the client would get around to asking for the composite reply. If some other client intervened, or that client dies, then there's trouble. Every group of one or more `dirname_1()` calls from a server must be followed by a `readdir_1()` request from the same server, or else things get out of sync.

As a fix, let's add some logic to check the name of the client. First, get the address (in this case, the socket) of the caller, using `svc_getcaller(3N)`:

```
struct sockaddr_in * svc_getcaller(xprt)
    SVCXPRT *xprt;
```

If you wish to translate this address into the name of the client, you can use any one of a number of socket-to-name functions. The cleanest is probably getpeername(3N):

```
int getpeername(s, name, namelen)
int s;
struct sockaddr *name;
int *namelen;
```

The client address is unique to the instance of the client, so that's really what we want to base independent servicing on. We could simply refuse a request from a client until one client's request series has been satisfied. This is dangerous. What if the client dies before posting a readdir_1() request? Though that would possibly allow that client to recover its state, it denies the rest of the network access. Some form of multi-tasking at the server, with a process or thread associated with each client, would suffice.

One single-threaded solution is to build up a linked list of replies for each client address. Stale lists could be purged or left around to assist in restoring client state. Lists could also serve as a reply cache, a technique that we discuss in Chapter 12.

Batch RPC

Batch RPC keeps requests at the client side until the client lets them go over the network. This can be done if each RPC request from the client does not require a reply. One advantage of sending requests in batches is that it reduces network overhead. Batch RPC also compacts the number of replies to one. If several consecutive requests made to the same server are related, it may make sense to receive a reply when all the requests have been serviced.

Like one-way RPC requests, requests made in batch mode must not generate replies at the server. Send them with the time-out value set to zero. Batch-mode ONC RPC requests are queued at the client, then sent in one batch to the server when a request requiring a reply is encountered (a non-zero time-out is specified). For these reasons, reliable transmission of a request requires use of a reliable transport like TCP.

In addition, the address of the XDR routine that the client is supposed to use to decode the reply must be NULL as opposed to the void used with the one-way RPC. This means we must make not one but two sed changes to the client stub generated by RPCGEN. In addition to changing the TIMEOUT structure to be handled in your client's main(), you will also have to change the clnt_call() in the client stub. You need to change a call such as the following:

```
if (clnt_call(clnt, PROCNAME, xdr_filt, argp, xdr_filt, &res, TIMEOUT
) != RPC_SUCCESS) {
```

to something like this:

```
if (clnt_call(clnt, PROCNAME, xdr_filt, argp, NULL, &res, TIMEOUT
) != RPC_SUCCESS) {
```

There is no way to force RPCGEN to do this one either. You must change the client stub. So you'll need to run `sed` commands after the stub is created and before the client and server executables are compiled.

There are no changes required of the server. It knows nothing of the batch organization; it merely processes requests as they come in, providing a reply if that procedure requires one.

Let's build a version of the above `one-way` application that uses batched requests. This time we make a client executable called `batch`:

```
rodson> make APPN=one-way one-way.h
rodson> sed 's/static struct timeval TIMEOUT = { 25, 0}\
/extern struct timeval TIMEOUT/' one-way_clnt.c> tmp
rodson> mv tmp one-way_clnt.c
rodson> sed 's/xdr_void/NULL/' < one-way_clnt.c > batch_clnt.c
rodson> cc -g -o batch one-way_xdr.o batch_clnt.c one-way.c
```

When you run the `batch` client executable, it will appear exactly the same as the `one-way` example, except that the time-out error messages are now gone. (Don't accidentally execute */usr/bin/batch*.)

```
rodson> ./batch cortex $cwd /home
cortex: RPC: Success
.
..
makefile
one-way.c
one-way.x
batch
one-way_svc_proc.c
one-way.h
one-way_clnt.c
one-way_svc.c
one-way_xdr.c
one-way_xdr.o
one-way_clnt.o
one-way_svc.o
one-way.o
one-way
one-way_svc_proc.o
batch_clnt.c
one-way_svc
batch_clnt.o
.
..
alydar
cortex
unclejack
bach
sparky
```

Broadcast RPC

The ONC RPC system includes a high-level client-side call that allows you to probe the network for servers matching a certain description. It should be used with restraint because it tickles all the portmappers on this side of any gateways (packets are not broadcast through gateways). In fact, the older Release 4.0 ONC Portmappers fork children to service the broadcast request. Broadcasting in general is an antisocial act and should be kept to a minimum or you'll have the other net users at your door.

In Example 9-4, *broadcast.c* attempts to ask all the reachable portmappers if they have a record of the service designated on the command line. The client uses `clnt_broadcast(3C)` to ask the local network repeatedly for replies. Each time a server acknowledges by sending a reply, the reply procedure is called. Only UDP packets can be broadcast on the net, not TCP. Thus `clnt_broadcast()` only works for UDP transport services and will not find any TCP-based services. The format of this procedure is:

```
clnt_broadcast(prognum, versnum, procnum, inproc, in, outproc, out,
               eachresult)
    u_long prognum, versnum, procnum;
    char *in;
    xdrproc_t inproc;
    char *out;
    xdrproc_t outproc;
    bool_t eachresult;
```

`clnt_broadcast()` is a broadcast version of `callrpc()` that makes requests of all locally-connected network machines using AUTH UNIX style authentication (username, encrypted password). It adds one more argument, `eachresult()`, which is the procedure that is called to handle the results when it gets a reply.

Broadcast packets are limited in size by the underlying data-link transfer unit. For Ethernet, this limits the caller's argument portion of the request packet to 1400 bytes.

Example 9-4. Utility to ask the network if a service is available: broadcast.c

```
#include <rpc/rpc.h>
#include <stdio.h>
#include <sys/socket.h>          /* we'll need sockets here */
#include <netdb.h>

/*
 * replyProc collects replies from the broadcast. Pipe the output through
 * sort(1) -u to get a unique listing of responding servers.
 */

static          bool_t
replyProc(res, who)
    void           *res;         /* assume nothing comes back */
    struct sockaddr_in *who;     /* the address of who sent the reply */
{
    register struct hostent *hp;

    hp = gethostbyaddr((char *) &who->sin_addr, sizeof
                       who->sin_addr,
```

Example 9-4. Utility to ask the network if a service is available: broadcast.c (Continued)

```
                            AF_INET);
  printf("%s %s\n", inet_ntoa(who->sin_addr),
         (hp == NULL) ? "(unknown)" : hp->h_name);
  return (FALSE);
}

main(argc, argv)
  int            argc;
  char           **argv;
{
  enum clnt_stat  rpc_stat;
  u_long          prognum, versnum, procnum;

  if (argc != 4) {
    fprintf(stderr, "Usage: %s prognum versnum procnum\n",
            argv[0]);
    exit(1);
  }
  prognum = (u_long) atoi(argv[1]);
  versnum = (u_long) atoi(argv[2]);
  procnum = (u_long) atoi(argv[3]);

  /*
   * See if anybody is out there.  Note procnum should expect no request
   * arguments and send nothing back or we'll have some en/decode problems,
   * potentially hosing the server.  NULLPROC does this.
   */
  rpc_stat = clnt_broadcast(prognum, versnum, procnum, xdr_void,
                            (char *) NULL, xdr_void, (char *) NULL, replyProc);
  if ((rpc_stat != RPC_SUCCESS) && (rpc_stat != RPC_TIMEDOUT)) {
    fprintf(stderr, "%s: broadcast failed: %s\n",
            argv[0], clnt_sperrno(rpc_stat));
    exit(1);
  }
  exit(0);
}
```

This program doesn't need anything special, either make it with make
broadcast or manually compile and link it with cc -o broadcast
broadcast.c.

If you still have one of the one-way_svc server executables running on a
machine, try to locate it by calling on its procedure number 0, the NULLPROC.
You're looking for version number 1. I assume you created a one-way_svc that
registered both the TCP and UDP transports. clnt_broadcast() cannot see the
TCP servers.

```
rodson> broadcast 536870913 1 0
3.1.4.62 cortex
3.1.7.113 vision
3.1.4.62 cortex
3.1.7.113 vision
3.1.4.62 cortex
3.1.7.113 vision
3.1.4.62 cortex
3.1.7.113 vision
```

I left a server running on `vision`. `536870913` is the decimal equivalent of the `0x20000001` hex value specified as the RPC program number in *one-way.x* protocol definition in Example 9-1.

Alternatives to Broadcast and Batch Requests

We've discussed the ONC RPC broadcast mechanism for globally contacting servers and batching or queuing requests at the client to be used when replies aren't necessary. Both broadcasting and batching can be used to partition a problem space across servers. Neither approach uses full-duplex client/server communication. This makes scheduling and fault-tolerance more difficult at the application level. For these reasons, we will stick to RPCs that send replies, even if purely informational ones, when distributing problems across a network.

The Follow-up RPC

A server can return the results of a client's request in a few different ways. We've discussed making client-blocking (synchronous) replies with `svc_sendreply()`. Using a follow-up RPC (FRPC) mechanism can avoid the need to do process creation or multi-threading at the client to get multiple (asynchronous) servers working at the same time. Basically, the first RPC is placed to kick-off server processing. Before processing the request, the server sends a reply back to the client to acknowledge, allowing it to disconnect and move on. The result of the original request is sent back some time in the future, finding its way back into the requesting process.

For both the asynchronous and multi tasking services developed here, we need to become familiar with, and even write our own request loop; the `svc_run()` socket-watching routine. You must program at the lower RPC and IPC levels.

Designing the svc_run() Request Loop

`svc_run(3N)` is the heart of the server. It loops indefinitely, checking for requests at descriptors (socket descriptors in ONC Version 4.0), calling the requested service procedure. If you require a remote asynchronous-call interface at the client, multi-tasking at the server or must marry the server with other lower-level descriptors (e.g., a windowing system, user I/O), you must roll your own `svc_run()`.

Example 9-5 contains a sample server loop. The unadulterated ONC call implements something like this, with some refinements. Look back to Chapter 5 for more explanations of `select(2)` and the associated bit mask.

Example 9-5. Service request loop: svc_run()

```
#include <rpc/rpc.h>
#include <sys/errno.h>

void svc_run()
{
    fd_set      readfdset;
    extern int  errno;
```

Example 9-5. Service request loop: svc_run() (Continued)

```
static int      tsize = 0;

if (!tsize) tsize = getdtablesize(); /*how many descriptors can we have */

while (1) {
  readfdset = svc_fdset;
  switch (select(tsize, &readfdset, (fd_set*) NULL, (fd_set*) NULL,
                 (struct timeval *) NULL)) {
  case -1:
    if (errno == EBADF) continue;
    perror("select failed");
    return;
  case 0:
    /* perform other functions here if select() timed-out */
    continue;
  default:
    svc_getreqset(&readfdset);
  }
}
}
```

svc_run() puts the server into a loop, waiting for input at one of the descriptors denoted in svc_fdset, the RPC global file descriptor set. svc_fdset must be inspected anew each time through the loop because it changes with socket activity (requests). When input is detected, it uses svc_getreqset(3N) to call the associated service procedure, then returns to the loop.

errno takes a value of EBADF if a file descriptor refers to no open file or a read (write) request is made to a file that is open only for writing (reading). This is the only real reason why svc_run() should ever return.

If you are interested in writing your own svc_run() routine, one approach is to call select() with a non-zero time-out value. This way if select() returns with no activity, you proceed to case 0 above. At that point, insert procedure calls to perform any other tasks; for example, fielding window events or making FRPCs.

A Follow-up RPC From the Client Process

Sending a follow-up RPC to the client process uses more lower-level RPC functions because a server is run within the client process. The client must poll for socket activity, invoking a low-level response in its own procedure equivalent to svc_run() loop. Though incrementally more complex to program, it tends to have lower overhead than running a collection service in a separate process on the client machine. Figure 9-3 illustrates the steps involved.

The RPC service running in the client process is in charge of collecting results asynchronously from the server. The client process used to place the request, if signalled to jump somewhere by new data on a socket, can field the server's follow-up RPC request.

Let's go into detail on how you might construct the server side. We will send a quick reply to acknowledge the receipt of the initial client request, then move on to

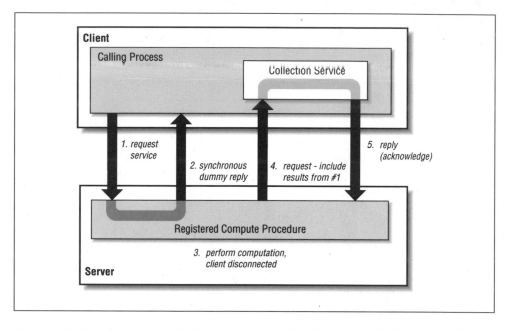

Figure 9-3. Asynchronously collecting results within the client avoids blocking at the client

do the processing. Next an RPC is made from the server, back to the client to deposit the results.

Let's assume you've constructed a protocol that facilitates `DOIT` requests and compiled the client and server applications. Once started, the server uses `svc_register()` followed by `svc_run()` to register itself and loop, looking for `DOIT` requests. A server procedure like Example 9-6 can be used to deliver results back to the client with a follow-up RPC.

Example 9-6. A service procedure makes an FRPC: doit_1()

```
doit_1(xprt)
SVCXPRT *xprt;
{
        static char ClientName[20];
        static int rv = 1;   /* some interesting status value */

        svc_getargs(xprt, xdr_ClientName, &ClientName[0]);
        /* Reply immediately to RPC client. */
        svc_sendreply(xprt, xdr_int, (char *)&rv);

        compute();      /* Do the computations, store results, */
        /* send results back to the server ClientName with an FRPC. */
        callrpc(ClientName, CL_PROG, CL_VERS, CL_CALLBCK,
                xdr_results, &results,
                xdr_int, &rv);
        return(0);
}
```

Notice that the only argument to the `doit_1()` request, decoded with `svc_getargs()`, is the client's name. We'll use the client's name to ask the port-mapper where to send the results back later using a second RPC (from server to client). It would have been more efficient to send the port number or address of the client's collection server as a request argument.[†] Here the only request argument specified is the NULL-terminated `ClientName` string. The XDR definition of the request parameter filter might be as follows:

```
#include <rpc/rpc.h>
bool_t xdr_ClientName(xdrs, objp)
XDR *xdrs;
char *objp;
{
        return ( xdr_string(xdrs, &objp, MAXNAMELEN) );
}
```

The `callrpc()` used for the follow-up call is a high-level RPC command.

```
int callrpc(host, prognum, versnum, procnum, inproc, in, outproc, out)
        char *host;
        u_long prognum, versnum, procnum;
        char *in;
        xdrproc_t inproc;
        char *out;
        xdrproc_t outproc;
```

CL_PROG represents the program number of a local RPC daemon registered and running back at the client. CL_VERS and CL_CALLBCK represent that service's version number and procedure number. Notice that by using the high-level RPC call, `callrpc()`, you've lost control over UDP time-outs and retries, but more often than not, that's acceptable.

A Client/Server Pair for Asynchronous Remote Directory Listing

In the following complete example, a client asks any number of servers to reply with the files in a named directory. Each request made to a server is given its own sweet time to return results; the client process does not wait. The server requests are sent out with a high-level `callrpc()`. The client needs to register an FRPC daemon, running a service itself to catch the replies returned by the servers.

---

† The port that we send the FRPC to is not the same as that used in the request. We could also get the client's name by looking at the request information. Other more elaborate ways of retrieving the caller information are illustrated later.

The header file included by the client and server is shown in Example 9-7. It must define not only the same old remote directory reading service, but also a new service, LOCALD, to be registered and controlled by the client.

Example 9-7. Header file included by asynchronous clients and servers: asyncRls.h

```
#define DIR_SIZE 8192
#define DIRPROG  ((u_long) 0x20000002)   /* server program (suite) number */
#define DIRVERS  ((u_long) 1)            /* program version number */
#define READDIR  ((u_long) 1)            /* procedure number for look-up */


#define DIRDPROG ((u_long) 0x20000003) /* local daemon to collect returns */
#define DIRDVERS ((u_long) 1)
#define LOCALD   ((u_long) 1)
```

In some cases, the client might register or unregister a unique FRPC daemon for each server to track results in a better way, allowing concurrent callbacks.

The Client

The code for the client is shown in Example 9-8. You can't just do a registerrpc() followed by a svc_run() because it would send us into a loop waiting on a request socket. Instead, you need to move to a lower level. You register the server the same way you would any service with a registerrpc().[†] With the FRPC service registered, to avoid the svc_run() loop, we'll devise our own logic to look at the activity on the socket descriptors associated with the service program, and provide the service only when necessary. In effect, we poll the descriptor status first by zeroing the time-out value specified with select(2), and then return immediately with the file-descriptor-set (fd_set) bit field modified to indicate which ports are being called upon. The global RPC variable svc_fdset provides you with the indication of candidate descriptors to be tested (see *The ONC RPC Programming Reference* for more details). Note that you should never pass the svc_fdset pointer to select(), as it will modify the bit mask. Make a copy of it and pass that in.

We also use a switch to look repeatedly at the result of the select() call, and service any outstanding requests with svc_getreqset(). You can fire off server requests from within this svc_run()-like loop whenever you are not busy checking select() or servicing requests.

There is no dispatcher layer mentioned in Example 9-8 because there is only one service offered. There is some extra code included to track the status (FRPCs pending) of a server to avoid multiple requests to the same server. Unless a server supports concurrent requests, a client can plug-up its request queue. Also, as this client is not designed for multi-processes or multi-threads, posting a request to a machine that is attempting to return results to our daemon will cause a deadlock. Read the comments in the example.

---

† Note this is for UDP only, see the associated server example for the low-level registration approach for both UDP and TCP with svc..._create().

Note that the XDR interface definition and filter is the same as it was in Chapter 4, containing a single call to xdr_string().

Example 9-8. Client side of an asynchronous server routine: asyncRls.c

```
/*
 * asyncRls.c: async remote directory listing client
 */
#include <stdio.h>
#include <sys/errno.h>
#include <sys/types.h>
#include <sys/socket.h>
#include <netdb.h>
#include <rpc/rpc.h>
#include "asyncRls.h"

#define SERVERFREE(argc, argv, h_name, k) for (k=1; k<argc; k+=2) \
        if (!strcmp(h_name, argv[k])) { k=(k-1)/2; break;} \
        if (k>=argc) { \
        fprintf(stderr, "%s: where did you come from!\n", h_name); \
        exit(-1); }

char        *locald();
extern bool_t  xdr_dir();
char        *host[DIR_SIZE];

main(argc, argv)                      /* Usage rls host dir host dir ... host dir */
    char       **argv;
    int         argc;
{
    extern int    errno;
    enum clnt_stat  clnt_stat;
    fd_set         readfds;
    struct timeval  timeout;
    int           i, j, k;
    int           ts = getdtablesize(); /* file descriptor table size */
    int           ServerBusy = 0;       /* outstanding requests bitmask */

    /*
     * Register a local UDP server daemon to collect results. We use
     * registerrpc() as we can afford to hide the server handle SVCXPRT *.
     * Data sent to this collection service includes the name of the
     * server asynchronously returning the results. There are more robust
     * ways to retrieve the name of the calling party developed elsewhere.
     * Note we really have no dispatcher here - just one single procedure -
     * locald().
     */

    registerrpc(DIRDPROG, DIRDVERS, LOCALD, locald, xdr_dir, xdr_void);

    /*
     * Clear the timeval to affect a poll when using select.
     */
    timeout.tv_sec = timeout.tv_usec = 0;

    /* repeatedly call an async request to a server if registered */
    for (j = 0, i = 1; 1; i = (i + 2) % (argc - 1), j = (i - 1) >> 1) {
        /*
         * Send repeated requests to the servers specified.  BE CAREFUL here as
         * attempting to send a request to a machine that is blocked trying to
         * return results to locald will in turn block us!  There is another way
         * to fix this (use clnt_create timeouts), but that requires checking
         * with the client to see if it can answer (time consuming). By creating
         * all the required client handles ahead of time, repeating the process
         * with callrpc() could be eliminated. Instead we keep track locally.
         * Another alternative could have been async. server child-processes.
         */
```

Example 9-8. Client side of an asynchronous server routine: asyncRls.c (Continued)

```
    */
    if (!(ServerBusy & (0x1 << j))) {    /* server is free */
      clnt_stat = callrpc(argv[i], DIRPROG, DIRVERS, READDIR,
                          xdr_dir, argv[i + 1], xdr_void, 0);
      if (clnt_stat != 0)
        clnt_perrno(clnt_stat);
      else
        ServerBusy |= (0x1 << j);
    }
    /*
     * Look for a response from the other socket.
     */
    readfds = svc_fdset;
    switch (select(ts, &readfds, (int *) 0, (int *) 0, &timeout)) {
    case -1:
      if (errno == EINTR) {
        printf("waiting...");
        continue;
        }
      perror("svc_run: - select failed");
      break;                        /* leave beat server marked as busy */
    case 0:
      break;
    default:
      svc_getreqset(&readfds);
      /*
       * You never know who came back and in what order, you'll need some
       * kind of monitoring mechanism like this.
       */
      SERVERFREE(argc, argv, host, k);
      printf("server %s, #%d returned!\n", host, k);
      ServerBusy ^= (0x1 << k);
    }
  }
}

char           *
locald(dir)        /*invoked if there is something at my socket... */
  char             *dir;           /* char dir[DIR_SIZE] */
{
  /*
   * As part of the protocol, we asked the server to send back its hostname
   * to expedite the monitoring process. It's easier to do here and now
   * than have the server determine it on its side.  Better yet we should
   * also send the server a private procedure number to reply to...
   */
  sscanf(dir, "%s", host);

  /* Spew out the results and bail out of here! */
  printf("%s\n", dir);

  /* must send something back, so here's a dummy reply */
  return;
}
```

The ServerBusy mask is used to monitor the activity of a server. You don't want to post a request to a server who is blocked and waiting for you to answer the return call. The only way around a deadlock situation is through the clever use of time-outs.[†] I chose to avoid the situation altogether and augment the directory server to tack its hostname on top of the list of files. This allows the client FRPC service to quickly determine which server has returned, without having to perform network/host information look-ups. Once successfully returned, that server is marked free and given another request the next time the client has a chance. There is a small performance compromise here because requests aren't buffered at the servers. You could make up for this loss by having the server fork-off processes for each procedure, handling request buffering in the server dispatch process.

Determining Where Requests and Replies Came From

You can autonomously determine which host a request or reply came from by looking at the struct sockaddr_in associated with the RPC system. We'll do this in the upcoming asynchronous server example, using svc_getcaller(3N) to get the caller socket information.

```
sock_in = (struct sockaddr_in *) svc_getcaller(transp);
```

If broadcasting requests with clnt_broadcast(),

```
clnt_broadcast(prognum, versnum, procnum, inproc, in, outproc, out,
               eachresult)
```

eachresult() gets invoked every time a reply arrives at a socket. If you wanted to know who sent the broadcast reply, do something like the following:

```
static bool_t eachresult(res, sock)
   void *res;
   struct sockaddr_in *sock;
{
   struct hostent *host =
   gethostbyaddr((char *) &sock->sin_addr,
      sizeof sock->sin_addr, AF_INET);
   printf("%s %s\n", inet_ntoa(sock->sin_addr), host->h_name);
}
```

See *The ONC RPC Programming Reference* for a more thorough definition of eachresult(). The inet(3N) family of system calls are quite useful, and could be applied at the server to determine which host made the RPC request.

The Server

The server routine, shown in Example 9-9, also has some major complications when compared to the simple synchronous server, *rls_svc.c*, in Chapter 4. Our asynchronous server can't be registered with registerrpc() because we must be able to get at the SVCXPRT server handles to tell where the request came from, and

---

† The SunOS 4.1 clnt_call() now uses exponential retry periods to help eliminate hitting a deadlock.

more importantly to determine where we should send the results. We'll have to use
svc_register() instead.

We will be completing the original RPC handshake as early as possible, closing and
losing the connection to the client. We can save the server handle from that transaction, and re-use pieces of it to build up a new connection to the client, making a
subsequent RPC on its locald() collection daemon.

Once the service dispatch procedure is registered, we go into a svc_run() loop,
where it does the monitoring of incoming requests. This is an efficient way to do
things, keeping down our use of resources. The dispatcher is called as appropriate;
it decides which remote procedure was requested by looking at the request arguments. If the NULL procedure is called, by convention, it sends an empty
xdr_void reply just to show the server is alive. If the READDIR procedure is
called, we first attempt to retrieve the required calling parameters from the request
packet. If this succeeds, we reply immediately with a svc_sendreply().

The client is now free to do what it pleases. The server reads the directory named in
the parameters, pre-pending its hostname for later identification at the client. The
server now makes a remote procedure call to the client machine, using the same
process that the request used. We make the call with a low-level equivalent of
callrpc(). We can't use callrpc() because what we have is the server handle,
not the client's hostname (as callrpc() wants). We can get the client's address
by using svc_getcaller(). By zeroing the sin_port field of the returned
sockaddr_in (see Chapter 4), we tell clntudp_create() that it must consult
the client machine's portmap to determine the address of the collection service
(DIRDIROG). clnt_create() then returns a client handle, completing the
connection back to the originating client. The actual call back is placed with a
clnt_call() using the client handle.

Status reporting is built into the RPC message returned to the client. You can call
svcerr_noproc(transp) to handle requests for nonexistent procedures; or
svcerr_decode(transp) to handle problems decoding request parameters; or
svcerr_systemerr(transp) for other non-RPC errors that are immediately
returned to the client. (transp is a SVCXPRT *.) At the client side, the family of
clnt_*err*() functions are used to interpret the remote status. Chapter 12 and
the *The ONC RPC Programming Reference* contain a more thorough discussion of
error reporting and recovery.

Example 9-9. Server responds asynchronously using FRPCs: asyncRls_svc.c

```
#include <stdio.h>
#include <string.h>
#include <sys/types.h>
#include <sys/socket.h>
#include <netdb.h>
#include <rpc/rpc.h>
#include "asyncRls.h"

static void      dispatch();    /* the server program - does dispatching */
extern bool_t    xdr_dir();
struct timeval   tval;
```

Example 9-9. Server responds asynchronously using FRPCs: asyncRls_svc.c   (Continued)

```c
/*
 * Register the service, then wait for requests without
 * consuming resources.
 */
main()
{
  SVCXPRT        *transp;

  (void) pmap_unset(DIRPROG, DIRVERS);

  transp = svcudp_create(RPC_ANYSOCK);
  if (transp == NULL) {
    (void) fprintf(stderr, "cannot create udp service.\n");
    exit(1);
  }
  if (!svc_register(transp, DIRPROG, DIRVERS, dispatch, IPPROTO_UDP)) {
    (void) fprintf(stderr,
                   "unable to register (DIRPROG, DIRVERS, udp).\n");
    exit(1);
  }
  /*
   * If we wished to simultaneously register the service w/ TCP
   * transport, we'd do the following, but since we use callrpc()
   * which uses UDP, we won't bother.
   */
  /*
  transp = svctcp_create(RPC_ANYSOCK, 0, 0); if (transp == NULL) {
    (void)fprintf(stderr, "cannot create tcp service.\n"); exit(1);
  } if (!svc_register(transp, DIRPROG, DIRVERS, dispatch, IPPROTO_TCP)) {
    (void)fprintf(stderr, "unable to register (DIRPROG, DIRVERS, tcp).\n");
    exit(1);
  }
   */
  /*
   * Set the time-out limit to 0 - makes the servers thrash a little
   * while attempting to return results, but after repeated retries,
   * they get there.  tval=0 also reduces the chance that the
   * callrpc() will get stuck when I ^C the client, reducing the need
   * to restart the servers.
   */
  tval.tv_sec = tval.tv_usec = 0;

  svc_run();
  (void) fprintf(stderr, "svc_run returned\n");
  exit(1);
}

/*
 * Decode the requested service and provide it.
 */
static void
dispatch(rqstp, transp)
  struct svc_req *rqstp;
  SVCXPRT        *transp;
{
  char           dir[DIR_SIZE];
  char           dhost[DIR_SIZE];
  struct hostent *host;
  struct sockaddr_in *sock_in;
  enum clnt_stat clnt_stat;
  CLIENT         *client;

  switch (rqstp->rq_proc) {
  case NULLPROC:/* it's a nice convention to provide a response */
```

Example 9-9. Server responds asynchronously using FRPCs: asyncRls_svc.c (Continued)

```
      (void) svc_sendreply(transp, xdr_void, 0);
      return;

  case READDIR:
      if (!svc_getargs(transp, xdr_dir, dir)) {
        svcerr_decode(transp);
        return;
      }
      if (!svc_sendreply(transp, xdr_void, 0)) {
        svcerr_systemerr(transp);
        return;
      }
      read_dir(dir);
      /*
       * Pre-pend the hostname to ease client-side tracking.
       */
      (void) gethostname(dhost, DIR_SIZE);
      strcat(dhost, "\n");
      strcat(dhost, dir);

      /*
       * Return the result with a call to the requestor's local daemon
       * - but where does it live? Translate this into caller host info
       * to call client back.
       */
      sock_in = svc_getcaller(transp);    /* get caller socket info */
      sock_in->sin_port = 0;            /* makes clntudp_create consult yp */
      client = clntudp_create(sock_in, DIRDPROG, DIRDVERS,
                              tval, &sock);
      clnt_stat = clnt_call(client, LOCALD, xdr_dir, dhost,
                            xdr_void, 0, tval);
      if (clnt_stat != 0)
        clnt_perrno(clnt_stat);

      /*
       * We'll re-use dhost, but should call this to free the XDR
       * struct, plus clean things up.
       */
      svc_freeargs(transp, xdr_dir, dhost);
      clnt_destroy(client);
      return;

      /*
       * put more procedures here...  case A: case Z:
       */

  default:
      svcerr_noproc(transp);
      return;
  }
}
```

There are a few important notes:

1. Destroy idle or stale client handles because you can run out of space to keep track of them sooner than you think.

2. Destroy unused XDR structures and associated arguments.

When communicating with the same clients and servers, it makes sense to maintain some history, keeping client (or server) handles around for potential future use. This reduces the number of synchronous `clnt_create()` or `callrpc()` calls.

You should exercise a little caution here since handles do occupy resources; plus, the most accurate, up-to-date associations are kept in system or network databases. Your associations may grow stale.

As discussed during client development, there are a number of ways the client's `locald()` collection service could be located by the server. We chose to have the client include its hostname and use the standard portmap access to send the FRPC. The client `hostname` instead could have been retrieved with a `gethostby-addr()` call. To do this requires that the server register itself with the lower-level `svc_register()` rather than `registerrpc()` to make it possible to inspect the addressing information associated with `SVCXPRT *transp`. We'll use `svc_get-caller()` in an upcoming asynchronous server example to get the caller socket.

The actual `read_dir()` routine is exactly the same as that generated in Chapter 4, so the compilation/linking process is as follows:

```
rodson> cc -g -o asyncRls asyncRls.c rls_xdr.o
rodson> cc -g -o asyncRls_svc asyncRls_svc.c read_dir.o rls_xdr.o
```

Start the server, `asyncRls_svc`, on a number of remote machines, then fire off the processing with something like:

```
rodson> asyncRls hosta dira ... hostz dirz
```

where the `hosts a-z` have registered servers running. The client is constructed to fire off requests as fast as it can, looping on the hostnames provided on the command line, until you cancel it (with CONTROL-C). Notice that some servers respond quite a bit faster (and therefore more often) than others. This is a function of the machine type and network distance from the file system named. That's the beauty of asynchronous server processing; you can get lots of things done in a short period of time.

A Follow-up RPC into a Different Client Process

A second alternative to getting results back to the client in an asynchronous fashion is for the server to send the results back to a different client process. These results could later be pulled from this process by the requestor with local IPC or RPC at some later date. In this way, a client machine is using something like the `callrpc()` interface we have seen in one process, plus registering and running a local server daemon in another process. Though this allows you to stay with high-level RPC calls, it requires that the client process make RPCs to a local process to retrieve results. In effect, the client polls the local daemon. Figure 9-4 outlines the dual-client-process approach. I won't illustrate this approach by example.

This approach gets the data back over the network as quickly as possible, with a low-latency local RPC (or IPC) required to actually get the results back into the original requestor process. By polling or placing a RPC to a local process, the original client process avoids blocking during the variable delays of a networked RPC. Another merit of this approach is the preservation of the high-level RPC interface.

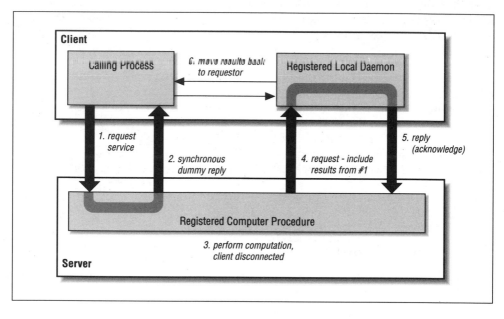

Figure 9-4. Using a second client process (a local collection daemon) FRPC to avoid blocking at the client

A Follow-up RPC Using Private Collection Services at the Client

To save even more time, the client can give the server the complete address information of the collection service as a parameter of the initial RPC. This saves the service from having to make a call to the portmapper to see where the collection service lives. If the client starts a collection service for each FRPC placed, servers can reply concurrently. These collection services might reside within the client process as in Figure 9-3 to avoid eating up process space as replicated local daemons would. The collection services need not be registered with the portmapper but their sockets are monitored by the RPC system. Remember to unregister the service from the RPC system when complete as you will run out of file descriptor space in the `select()` process within `svc_run()`.

Multi-tasking at the Server

You may have applications where a multitude of clients need to access a single server at the same time. The server may need to use some form of resource sharing through time-slicing, as shown in Figure 9-5.

For example, if the server manages a central database, and if a client's access might take a long time, other clients should not be deprived of service. Client time-outs and retries may result if a single-threaded server doesn't quickly acknowledge the request. Multi-tasking or multi-threading at the server is a logical solution. One way

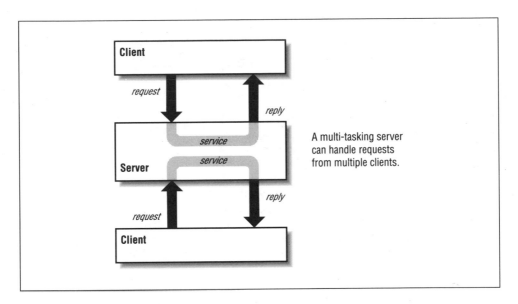

Figure 9-5. A multi-tasking server

to accomplish this is to apply some of the techniques developed in Chapter 6 to get multiple server child processes going, servicing each request concurrently.

Multi-tasking with Child Processes

Figure 9-6 illustrates one multiple-process approach to concurrent serving. Scheduling and I/O process blocking is managed by the UNIX kernel.

A naive approach to multi-processing is just to fork() as soon as the service has been requested. In Example 9-10 that doesn't work, but it serves to shed some light on why we must look deeper.

Nothing on the client side needs to change. The above server will run with the existing client, as long as you haven't changed any of the shared definitions. It is a rather crude way to *attempt* multi-tasking. Worse than that, it doesn't work. When the parent process returns, the nature of the svc_run() loop is that when it returns, the named XDR filter (xdr_dir()) processes the returned data and sends it back to the client. This tends to really confuse the client, or core-dump the server when you have NULLs where it wants data. Even if you replace the return with an _exit(), you are not looking at the svc_run() loop at the same time you are sending replies back out, so it's not really multi-tasking.

You need to reach a little lower into the RPC library, introduce a dispatcher where you can perform the necessary process creation and control. Process creation must be done during dispatching. Child processes should handle not only the service

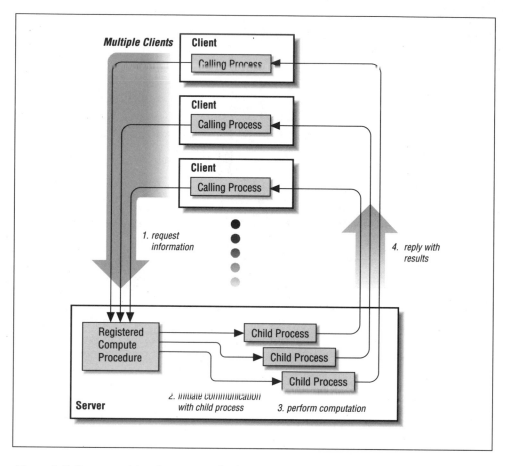

Figure 9-6. Server multi-tasking via multiple processes

procedure but encoding and sending the reply. It is then free to die without
adversely affecting the svc_run() loop.

Example 9-10. Server multi-tasking through process creation: HighLevelServer.c—DOES NOT
WORK!

```
#include <stdio.h>
#include <string.h>
#include <rpc/rpc.h>
#include "rls.h"

static int count = 0;

f_read_dir(dir)
char *dir;
{
        char ccount[32];

        /*
```

Example 9-10. Server multi-tasking through process creation: HighLevelServer.c—DOES NOT WORK! (Continued)

```
        * If you are the parent server process, return to the
        * svc_run() loop directly, otherwise, read the
        * directory and pass-back results - as the contents of
        * dir.
        */
        if (fork()) return; /* parent goes back to svc_run() */
        read_dir(dir);

        /*
        * Stuff the count on the end so you know what order
        * processing was performed in.
        */
        printf("%d\n", count++); fflush(stdout);
        sprintf(ccount, "%d", count);
        strcat(dir, ccount);
        return((int)dir);
}

main()
{
        extern bool_t xdr_dir();

        registerrpc(DIRPROG, DIRVERS, READDIR,
                        f_read_dir, xdr_dir, xdr_dir);

        svc_run();
        (void) fputs("svc_run died...\n");exit(1);
}
```

In Example 9-11, we can't use the high-level registerrpc() call so instead we use svcudp_create(3N) and svc_register(3N) to set up the dispatcher. We did the same earlier with the server that did asynchronous processing. Once registered, we start a svc_run() loop as usual, but when the dispatcher is called to look at a request, we provide the service in a child process. Replies are sent from the child and not the parent.

Example 9-11. Multi-tasking service that works: multi-Rls_svc.c

```
#include <stdio.h>
#include <rpc/rpc.h>
#include "rls.h"                    /* Early Chapter 3-1 example header will do. */

static void      dispatch();  /* the server program - does dispatching */
extern bool_t    xdr_dir();
struct timeval   tval;
static int       count = 0;

/*
 * Register the service, then wait for requests without consuming resources.
 */
main()
{
  SVCXPRT          *transp;

  (void) pmap_unset(DIRPROG, DIRVERS);

  transp = svcudp_create(RPC_ANYSOCK);
  if (transp == NULL) {
    (void) fprintf(stderr, "cannot create udp service.\n");
    exit(1);
  }
```

```
    if (!svc_register(transp, DIRPROG, DIRVERS, dispatch, IPPROTO_UDP)) {
      (void) fprintf(stderr,
                      "unable to register (DIRPROG, DIRVERS, udp).\n");
      exit(1);
    }
    tval.tv_sec = tval.tv_usec = 0;

    svc_run();
    (void) fprintf(stderr, "svc_run returned\n");
    exit(1);
}

/*
 * Decode the requested service and provide it.
 */
static void
dispatch(rqstp, transp)
  struct svc_req *rqstp;
  SVCXPRT        *transp;
{
  char           dir[DIR_SIZE];
  enum clnt_stat clnt_stat;
  CLIENT         *client;

  switch (rqstp->rq_proc) {
  case NULLPROC:
    (void) svc_sendreply(transp, xdr_void, 0);
    return;

  case READDIR:
    if (!svc_getargs(transp, xdr_dir, dir)) {
      svcerr_decode(transp);
      return;
    }
    count++;
      /
       * Parent sends no reply but goes back to listening for requests,
       * child does the work (doesn't that sound familiar!)
       */
       if (fork()) return;
       read_dir(dir);
       printf("%d\n", count);

    /*
     * Send the reply back.
     * Again, no need for clean-up - just die gracefully.
     */
    if (!svc_sendreply(transp, xdr_dir, dir)) {
      svcerr_systemerr(transp);
      _exit(-1);
    }

    _exit(0);

/*
 * put more procedures here...  case A: case Z:
 */

  default:
    svcerr_noproc(transp);
    return;
  }
}
```

The header file that is included needs an RPC program specification for the server. The one defined in Example 3-3 will do:

```
#define DIR_SIZE 8192
#define DIRPROG ((u_long) 0x20000001)   /* server program (suite) number */
#define DIRVERS ((u_long) 1)            /* program version number */
#define READDIR ((u_long) 1)            /* procedure number for look-up */
```

Now we can build the multi-tasking server as follows:

```
rodson> cc -o multiRls_svc multiRls_svc.c read_dir.o rls_xdr.o
```

Start it on a remote machine with, for example, the machine `cortex`:

```
rodson> rsh -n cortex exec $cwd/multiRls_svc "\
        </dev/null >& /dev/null" &
```

and try sending a few simultaneous `rls` requests to it from different terminal windows. Try the following command:

```
rodson> repeat 20 rls cortex ./
```

and at the same time from a remote login shell:

```
vision> repeat 20 rls cortex ./
```

You can use the Chapter 3 `rls` client or any of the `rls` clients we have developed that don't anticipate remote asynchronous calls. If you can manage to send enough requests from enough terminal windows at the same time, you'll find the replies do not always come back in the order submitted.

Alternatives to Avoid Run-time Process Creation

As an alternative, any number of child processes could be forked initially when the server is started, possibly several for each service procedure. The dispatcher could then use any one of the IPC techniques discussed in Chapter 5 to signal the child process to provide the service and tell it where to return the results by providing socket information for the requestors. This would avoid repeated forking which is consuming of time and resources.

A similar but somewhat simpler approach to code is to start a child process for each service procedure when the server is first started. The server parent process is in charge of running the dispatcher. When valid requests are encountered, the dispatcher in turn makes an RPC to the local server process, to be executed by what is really a child process. It may be important to realize UDP becomes reliable when performed within one kernel.

The originating client information, in the form of a server handle, is passed to the child along with the request arguments. The originating clients network address is required to get the reply back to the right place. This approach is simpler in that any IPC required takes the form of local RPC calls between parent and child processes. Note that authentication information as well as TCP connections cannot be forwarded

Combining Asynchronous and Multi-tasking at the Server

Concurrent request processing at one server can be designed using the same general structure as the asynchronous server (Example 9-11). The difference is that the server's dispatcher routine, dispatch(), forks-off processes to handle the requested service. In this way, Example 9-12 is both an asynchronous and multi-tasking service. It is tricky to verify to yourself that it really is servicing multiple clients, each asynchronously, but watch the server spit the count variable out, and see that in fact they are often out of sequence when you make requests from multiple clients.

Example 9-12. Asynchronous, multi-tasking service: multiAsyncRls_svc.c

```
#include <stdio.h>
#include <string.h>
#include <sys/types.h>
#include <sys/socket.h>
#include <netdb.h>
#include <rpc/rpc.h>
#include "../async/asyncRls.h" /* header file generated for the FRPC clients */

static void     dispatch();    /* the server program - does dispatching */
extern bool_t   xdr_dir();
struct timeval  tval;
static int      count = 0;

/*
 * Register the service, then wait for requests without consuming resources.
 */
main()
{
  SVCXPRT         *transp;

  (void) pmap_unset(DIRPROG, DIRVERS);

  transp = svcudp_create(RPC_ANYSOCK);
  if (transp == NULL) {
    (void) fprintf(stderr, "cannot create udp service.\n");
    exit(1);
  }
  if (!svc_register(transp, DIRPROG, DIRVERS, dispatch, IPPROTO_UDP)) {
    (void) fprintf(stderr,
               "unable to register (DIRPROG, DIRVERS, udp).\n");
    exit(1);
  }
  tval.tv_sec = tval.tv_usec = 0;

  svc_run();
  (void) fprintf(stderr, "svc_run returned\n");
  exit(1);
}

/*
 * Decode the requested service and provide it.
 */
static void
dispatch(rqstp, transp)
  struct svc_req *rqstp;
  SVCXPRT        *transp;
{
  char            dir[DIR_SIZE];
  char            dhost[DIR_SIZE];
  struct hostent *host;
```

Example 9-12. Asynchronous, multi-tasking service: multiAsyncRls_svc.c (Continued)

```
struct sockaddr_in *sock_in;
enum clnt_stat  clnt_stat;
CLIENT          *client;

switch (rqstp->rq_proc) {
case NULLPROC:
  (void) svc_sendreply(transp, xdr_void, 0);
  return;

case READDIR:
  if (!svc_getargs(transp, xdr_dir, dir)) {
    svcerr_decode(transp);
    return;
  }
  if (!svc_sendreply(transp, xdr_void, 0)) {
    svcerr_systemerr(transp);
    return;
  }
  count++;
  if (fork()) return;      /* parent goes back to listening for requests */
  read_dir(dir);
  /*
   * Pre-pend the hostname to case client-side tracking.
   */
  (void) gethostname(dhost, DIR_SIZE);
  strcat(dhost, "\n");
  strcat(dhost, dir);
  printf("%d\n", count);

  /*
   * Return the result with a call to the requestor's local daemon - but
   * where does it live? Translate this into caller host info to call
   * client back.
   */
  sock_in = svc_getcaller(transp);  /* get caller socket info */
  sock_in->sin_port = 0;            /* makes clntudp_create consult yp */
  client = clntudp_create(sock_in, DIRDPROG, DIRDVERS,
                          tval, &sock);
  clnt_stat = clnt_call(client, LOCALD, xdr_dir, dhost,
                        xdr_void, 0, tval);
  if (clnt_stat != 0)
    clnt_perrno(clnt_stat);

  /*
   * We're about to die, manual clean-up is unnecessary.
   */
  _exit(0);

  /*
   * put more procedures here...  case A: case Z:
   */

  default:
    svcerr_noproc(transp);
    return;
  }
}
```

Build this server with something like:

```
rodson> cc -o multiAsyncRls_svc multiAsyncRls_svc.c read_dir.o rls_xdr.o
```

We use the header file from the previous asynchronous client development
(Example 9-7) since we are making FRPCs from the server. Thus it needs the RPC

program, version, and procedure number definitions developed there. You must also call this server with clients that are using the FRPC scheme to make remote asynchronous calls (see Example 9-8).

Start this multi-tasking, asynchronous server on a (remote) machine and send lots of concurrent `asyncRls` requests to it and watch it feverishly field all the requests. Remember the `asyncRls` client sends repeated requests until you terminate (CONTROL-C) it. Running a few of these processes against one server generates a lot of output fast, with the service time-slicing performed by UNIX.

```
rodson> rsh -n cortex exec $cwd/multiAsyncRls_svc &
rodson> ../async/asyncRls cortex /usr/spool/
```

When I started the server, I left its `stdout` and `stderr` pointing back at us, so the results of the second line includes not only repeated asynchronous server replies, but also comments from the server about RPCs that timed-out.

Lightweight Processing

Lightweight processes share a single address space. Each thread shares all the resources of the originating process,[†] including descriptors and signal handlers. Each has its own stack segment for concurrent access to variables and procedures. The LWP library under SunOS includes functions for creating and destroying threads, sending messages between threads, pre-emptive and nonpre-emptive scheduling, sharing variables, event and exception handling (synchronous and asynchronous), as well as multiple time-outs.

Lightweight or multi-threaded processing can provide a way of avoiding blocking at the client when placing synchronous RPCs. Multiple threads of execution promise much higher performance as compared to full-blown forking. Synchronous RPCs may be placed by a client thread with other threads of execution continuing. The result is something equivalent to what was presented in Chapter 6, replacing the brute-force scheduling with process control using calls such as those found in Sun's lightweight process (LWP) library.

A good example can be found in the XView 2.0 contributed software *perfdemo*. It uses `fdset` information and `svc_getreqset()` calls similar to Example 9-8, while placing requests in independent threads. Multiple threads can also be used on the server side to perform the same sort of multi-tasking as in Examples 8-11 and 8-12. *perfdemo* required the alteration of the XView main notifier loop (source code) to reflect the coincident use of signals by XView and LWP.

In a future edition, I hope to show more examples of ways to exploit multiple threads of execution. Multiple threads of execution could be the subject of a complete chapter. Keep in mind that in the near future, RPC developers have promised to include multiple threads directly into the RPC libraries (see Chapter 2).

---

† In the case of SunOS, the address space is derived from a single forked process.

Remote Asynchronous Calls with LWP

The LWP library allows multiple threads of execution to be active, all in one process sharing the same address space. The collective group of threads is called a *pod*. When created, each thread is given a priority. All non-blocking threads are executed according to priority. Threads with the same priority execute in the order of creation (first-come, first-served).

Threads may block due to I/O requests (e.g., RPC requests and replies) or monitor locking. As there is currently no SunOS kernel support for Sun's LWP, non-blocking I/O library (*libnbio.a*) routines can be used to mitigate most of the blocking associated with thread I/O. *libnbio.a* basically provides you with reads and writes that don't block.

After introducing only the essential LWP library calls, we develop both an LWP client and LWP server.

A Minimal Set of LWP Routines

The first LWP call notifies the library to turn the current process into a thread itself. By default, the highest scheduling priority available (pod_getmaxpri(3L)) is assigned. All subsequent threads are created with lwp_create(3L).

```
#include <lwp/lwp.h>
#include <lwp/stackdep.h>
int lwp_create(tid, func, prio, flags, stack, nargs, arg1, ..., argn)
thread_t *tid;
void (*func)();
int prio, flags;
stkalign_t *stack;
int nargs, arg1, ..., argn;
```

This call creates a thread that starts at address func and has stack segment stack. If non-NULL, the identity of the new thread is filled in the reference parameter tid. prio is the scheduling priority with higher values favored by the scheduler. Using flags and the stack, threads can be started in a suspended state or directed how to act upon exit. nargs is the number of simple-type int arguments to be passed to the thread. Data can be explicitly placed on the stack by using lwp_datastk(3L).

The maximum priority of a pod and that of the current thread can be set by calling pod_setmaxpri(prio).

lwp_setstkcache(3L) allocates a cache of stacks. Whenever the cache is empty, it is filled with numstks new stacks, each containing at least minstksz bytes.

```
int lwp_setstkcache(minstksz, numstks)
int minstksz;
int numstks;
```

`lwp_newstk(3L)` returns a cached stack suitable for use with `lwp_create()`.

```
stkalign_t *lwp_newstk();
```

`lwp_setstkcache()` must be called prior to any use of `lwp_newstk()`. Stack space must be set up for every possible thread, making sure there is enough room, keeping stacks from overwriting one another. A number of stack maintenance calls exist. They need not be covered here. Stack variables may be completely inherited from the parent or have some degree of private information passed onto it.

When threads reach the end of their function, by default they gracefully exit and their stack is freed. The last (parent) thread of a pod should not exit and close descriptors without being sure all threads have finished I/O.

To change the schedule priority of a thread, use `lwp_setpri(3L)`.

```
int lwp_setpri(tid, prio)
    thread_t tid;
    int prio;
```

`tid` is a unique thread identifier. A `tid` of `SELF` identifies the current thread. Remember `tid` is returned at the time of creation.

Scheduling is pre-emptive with higher priorities pre-empting the execution of lower ones, but it is first-come, first-served within a priority. To explicitly yield execution to another process of the same schedule priority, use `lwp_yield(3L)`.

```
int lwp_yield(tid)
    thread_t tid;
```

If `tid` is `SELF`, the next thread of this schedule priority queue is brought forward and the current thread placed at the end of the queue. If `tid` specifies a valid thread of the same priority, that thread is scheduled and the current thread placed next in the queue. You cannot yield to threads of different schedule priorities.

You can use `lwp_resched(3L)` to shuffle the queue of a given schedule priority around, moving the thread currently at the head to the tail of the queue:

```
int lwp_resched(prio)
    int prio;
```

If this is attempted from a thread with only `prio` scheduling priority, it is equivalent to calling `lwp_yield()`.

You cannot use `sleep(3V)` or other process control system calls. To block the current thread for at least the amount of time specified in `*tv`, use `lwp_sleep(3L)`:

```
int lwp_sleep(tv)
    struct timeval *tv;
```

Client Multi-server Example

First let's develop a simplified version of the rdb client and server (Chapter 1) to make the LWP enhancements stand out. We'll cut back the application to provide only telephone numbers and addresses from a server database using last name as the search key. For example, if the database and rtele_svc server were on the remote machine cortex, running the rtele client on rodson would produce:

```
rodson> rtele cortex BLOOMER
name            location extension
JOHN J BLOOMER   KW C317  6964
```

The simplified protocol would look like this:

```
/*
 * rtele.x: remote telephone number listing protocol
 */
%#define DATABASE "/usr/local/lib/personnel.dat" /* put your database here */
%#define MAX_STR 256                    /* '%' passes it into "rtele.h" */
program RTELEPROG {
        version RTELEVERS {
                string RTELE(string) = 1;
        } - 1;
} = 0x20000001;
```

Compile the protocol.

```
rodson> rpcgen rtele.x
```

The client side of the application need only scan the argv for the server host and the last name you are interested in; then print the name, location, and extension as retreived from a remote procedure call.

```
/*
 * rtele.c: remote telephone number listing client
 */
#include <stdio.h>
#include <rpc/rpc.h>
#include "rtele.h"    /* generated from rtele.x by RPCGEN */
main(argc, argv)
   int          argc;
   char         *argv[];
{
   CLIENT       *cl; /* a client handle, discussed later */

   if (argc != 3) {
     fprintf(stderr, "Usage: %s server_host name\n", argv[0]);
     exit(1);
   }
   cl = clnt_create(argv[1], RTELEPROG, RTELEVERS, "udp");

   fputs("name location extension\n", stdout);
   fputs(*(rtele_1(&argv[2], cl)), stdout);
}
```

The client stub *rtele_clnt.c* generated by RPCGEN contains the rtele_1() interface code. The server stub *rtele_svc.c* is the server main(), containing the server

registration and dispatch monitoring loop. RPCGEN also put any necessary XDR
filters in *rtele_xdr.c*. The server reads the database looking for the argument string
name.

```
/*
 * rtele_svc_proc.c: remote telephone number listing server
 */
#include <stdio.h>
#include <string.h>
#include <rpc/rpc.h>
#include "rtele.h"

char          **
rtele_1(name)
   char          **name;
{
   char            sb[MAX_STR];
   static char     sa[MAX_STR];        /* pointer returned, must be static */
   static char     *s = sa;
   FILE            *fp = fopen(DATABASE, "r");

   sa[0] = NULL;
   while (fgets(sa, MAX_STR - 1, fp)) {
     sscanf(sa, "%s%s%s", sb,sb,sb); /* get the last name */
     if (!strcmp(sb, *name)) break;
   }
   if feof(fp) sa[0] = NULL; /* no match */
   fclose(fp);
   return ((char **)&s);
}
```

Compile, link, and run the server on a remote machine `cortex` as follows:

```
rodson> cc -o rtele_svc rtele_svc_proc.c rtele_svc.c rtele_xdr.c
rodson> rsh cortex -n $cwd/rtele_svc &
[1] 2924
```

Compile and run the client like this:

```
rodson> cc -o rtele rtele.c rtele_clnt.c rtele_xdr.c
rodson> rtele cortex BLOOMER
name            location extension
JOHN J BLOOMER   KW C317  6964
```

First let's introduce asynchrony at the client using LWP and leave the server
untouched.

In the new `rteleLWP` client, in Example 9-13, we parse the command line into
server/user name pairs. We loop, calling every server each time a "." is encountered at `stdin`, exiting only when some other character is encountered. Results of
the remote calls are sent to another tty, in this case */dev/console*. This is required
because `stdin/stdout` has been put in a raw-character processing state to allow
input of characters without a carriage return. For each client, we create a `CLIENT`
handle ahead of time to speed up the process.

The small number of LWP-related calls required to get a steady stream of requests asynchronously posted are shown in bold in Example 9-13. The first LWP call notifies the library to turn the main() into a thread itself. pod_setmaxpri(MAXPRIO) sets the current thread scheduling priority to this new peak value for the pod. lwp_setstkcache() is then used to allocate space for all the other threads. With potentially MAXCLNT servers and the main() thread, we could have MAXCLNT+1 threads active at once. Every time a "." is encountered at stdin, lwp_create() is called to start a new thread. The main() stack is made available with each thread, thus only the variable information outside of main() will be "shared memory." That's why we put server information there. request() is passed one argument and started in the new thread which in turn places the RPC. That thread then blocks, relinquishing control to another thread until it prints results in the */dev/console* window.

Note that while main() is reading from stdin, it is *not* blocked. main() is scheduled with a higher priority, but when the *libnbio.a*'s read() call sees no input, control is relinquished. If this were not the case, no RPCs would ever be performed.

*Example 9-13. Lightweight processing for asynchronous remote calls from a client:
rteleLWP.c*

```
#include <stdio.h>
#include <sgtty.h>
#include <lwp/lwp.h>
#include <rpc/rpc.h>
#include "rtele.h"
#define MAXPRIO 10
#define MAXCLNT 10
void lwp_perror() { };
#define RAW_ON(fd) { \
  struct sgttyb ttyb; \
  gtty(fd, &ttyb) ;  /* get current terminal characteristics */ \
  ttyb.sg_flags |= RAW ;  /* set RAW on */ \
  stty (fd, &ttyb) ;  /* set RAW on */ \
  }
#define RAW_OFF(fd) { \
  struct sgttyb ttyb; \
  gtty(fd, &ttyb) ;  /* get current terminal characteristics */ \
  ttyb.sg_flags ^= RAW ; \

  stty (fd, &ttyb) ;  /* set RAW off */ \
  }
/* need to keep these in all threads (inc. main) */
CLIENT          *cl[MAXCLNT];
char            *server[MAXCLNT];
char            *user[MAXCLNT];
int             numServers = 0;
FILE            *fp;

main(argc, argv)
    int             argc;
    char            **argv;
{
    char            c;
    thread_t        tid;
    int             request();
    int             i;

    /*
```

Example 9-13. Lightweight processing for asynchronous remote calls from a client:
rteleLWP.c (Continued)

```
 * Format of argv is "server username" pairs.  Open a client handle for
 * each server.
 */
if ((argc < 3) || ((argc-1)/2 > MAXCLNT)) {
   fprintf(stderr,
      "Usage: %s server username [server username [[[]]]]\n", argv[0]);
   fprintf(stderr, "\t\tup to %d pairs\n", MAXCLNT);
   exit(1);
}
if {
fp = fopen("/dev/console", "w");         /* give the threads somewhere to
                                          * write, stdout is RAW */
for (i = 1; i < argc; i += 2) {
   cl[i >> 1] = clnt_create(argv[i], RTELEPROG, RTELEVERS, "tcp");
   server[i >> 1] = (char *) strdup(argv[i]);
   user[i >> 1] = (char *) strdup(argv[i + 1]);
   numServers++;
}

/*
 * Establish an upper limit on priority for the whole pod, 1..10.  Main
 * becomes an LWP running at 10.
 */
pod_setmaxpri(MAXPRIO);
(puts("lwp main here");

/*
 * Initialize a cache of stacks (at least 1K bytes).  Let's assume we'll
 * never have more than MAXCLNT RPC requests out at once.
 */
lwp_setstkcache(1024, MAXCLNT + 1); /* probably too small */

/*
 * For each "server username" pair in argv, launch an LWP in a new thread.
 * Main will block when waiting for input, giving control to request().
 * Any char will terminate.
 */
RAW_ON(0);                           /* enables raw I/O at stdin/out */
while (read(0, &c, 1) && (c == '.')) {
   for (i = 0; i < numServers; i++) {
      /*
       * Start another lower-priority thread to follow-through w/ a blocking
       * RPC. Establish a stack for the thread that indicates which client
       * request we're interested in.  This must be private to keep others
       * from stepping on it.
       */
      fprintf(fp, "start: %dth request thread, server %s username %s\n",
                  i, server[i], user[i]);
      lwp_create((thread_t *) 0, request, MINPRIO, 0,
            lwp_newstk(), 1, i);
   }
}
RAW_OFF(0); /* Put tty back the way it was! */
exit(1);
}

request(serve)
  int             serve;
{
  /*
```

*Example 9-13. Lightweight processing for asynchronous remote calls from a client:
rteleLWP.c (Continued)*

```
* The RPC will block this thread for a while. Execution falls-thru and
* terminates this thread.  Could use lwp_destroy(lwp_self())).
*/
fprintf(fp, "return: %dth request thread, server %s username %s\n%s",
    serve, server[serve], user[serve], *rtele_1(&user[serve], cl[serve]));
}
```

To pick up the non-blocking I/O and the LWP functions, compile and link with the
liblwp.a and *libnbio.a* libraries. Don't bother turning the -g flag on as debugging is
a whole other can of worms.

```
rodson> cc -o rteleLWP rteleLWP.c rtele_clnt.o -llwp -lnbio
```

Now let's run the client, asking four different rtele_svc servers for telephone
information. We'll cycle through the argv server user name pairs twice.

```
rodson> rteleLWP vision SRINIVAS pyramid ABDEL-MALEK\
        cortex BLOOMER rodson SMITH
lwp main here
..
```

The following output appears at */dev/console*. Notice that the threads were started
in a 0-3 order but the replies returned in a different order. cortex is the fastest
machine. The balance are heavily-used Sun SPARCstation 1+ systems with rodson
the slowest (that's the same machine I'm running the client on). The order is
different from trial to trial.

```
start: 0th request thread, server vision username SRINIVAS
start: 1th request thread, server pyramid username ABDEL-MALEK
start: 2th request thread, server cortex username BLOOMER
start: 3th request thread, server rodson username SMITH
return: 2th request thread, server cortex username BLOOMER
JOHN J BLOOMER          KW C317  6964
return: 1th request thread, server pyramid username ABDEL-MALEK
AIMAN A ABDEL-MALEK       KW C614  7101
return: 0th request thread, server vision username SRINIVAS
CHUKKA SRINIVAS         KW C615  5461
return: 3th request thread, server rodson username SMITH
BRYAN L SMITH           K-1GARAGE  7836
      # start if second pass
start: 0th request thread, server vision username SRINIVAS
start: 1th request thread, server pyramid username ABDEL-MALEK
start: 2th request thread, server cortex username BLOOMER
start: 3th request thread, server rodson username SMITH
return: 1th request thread, server pyramid username ABDEL-MALEK
AIMAN A ABDEL-MALEK       KW C614  7101
return: 2th request thread, server cortex username BLOOMER
JOHN J BLOOMER          KW C317  6964
return: 0th request thread, server vision username SRINIVAS
CHUKKA SRINIVAS         KW C615  5461
return: 3th request thread, server rodson username SMITH
BRYAN L SMITH           K-1GARAGE  7836
```

Even if an EOF or non-"." character is encountered at stdin, servers still respond. The main() thread uses on_exit(3) through exit(3) to wait for I/O to finish before exiting.

Server Multi-tasking Example

Threads really find a home in database servers or other servers that must manage multiple concurrent accesses from the network. In the following example, we will make the rtele_svc telephone database server into a concurrent server.

Things get complicated fast when using ONC RPC along with Sun's LWP because the RPC library is not re-entrant. In other words, when a thread gets bumped by a higher-priority process or because it was I/O blocked, intervening threads can step all over variables. There was never any consideration for memory sharing between request threads. Sun is working on a re-entrant ONC RPC library, but in the mean-time you need to be *very* careful.

First, you need to develop your own svc_run() request watcher. I put mine in *svc_runLWP.c* shown in Example 9-14. Remember svc_run() is called by the server stub after everything is registered. This starts the dispatch loop, calling any valid requested procedures with svc_getreqset().

Before the service dispatch while(1) loop begins, the process will be transformed into a thread as the stack space is allocated (lwp_setstkcache()). The main thread then proceeds to check all the registered sockets for request activity as usual. The difference is that when the select() blocks the main thread, the non-blocking I/O library will yield control to the next eligible thread, if there is one.

If a new valid request does shows up (the default case in the switch()), we create a thread in which we call svc_getreqset() with the appropriate fd_set argument. Although the thread is of minimum priority, the main thread priority is immediately reduced to the same level. Control can then be yielded to the newly-created thread. The new thread retrieves the request message, deciphers the param-eters and starts the requested procedure. Once inside the procedure, your service procedure thread must then reduce its priority to allow the main thread to look for other requests. The service procedure thread can then provide the service and return the reply as schedule permits. Note that the main thread is not eligible to run until new requests show up during the synchronous select() call.

Example 9-14. Lightweight processing svc_run() server loop: svc_runLWP.c

```
#include <rpc/rpc.h>
#include <sys/errno.h>
#include <lwp/lwp.h>
#define MAXSVC 10
#define MAXPRIO 10
void lwp_perror() { };

void
svc_run()
{
    extern int        errno;
```

Example 9-14. Lightweight processing svc_run() server loop: svc_runLWP.c (Continued)

```
fd_set          readfds;
int             size = getdtablesize();
thread_t        tid;

lwp_setstkcache(1024, MAXSVC + 1);    /* go thread yourself */

while (1) {
  readfds = svc_fdset;

  /*
   * Block if there are no new requests, -lbnio yields the thread.  If
   * libnbio.a is not available, try select(timeval != 0) polling.
   */
  switch (select(size, &readfds, NULL, NULL, NULL)) {
  case -1:
    if (errno == EINTR) continue;
    perror("select failed");
    return;
  case 0:
    continue;
  default:  /* first discourage false activity */
    if (!bcmp(readfds, svc_fdset, sizeof(fd_set))) continue;
    puts("servicing...");
    lwp_create(&tid, svc_getreqset, MINPRIO, 0, lwp_newstk(),
      1, readfds);
    /*
     * Main thread - wait here until the new thread has removed the
     * pending input as found by select(), effectively starting the
     * request servicing.  If we had multiple requests at once, this logic
     * steps thru them one at a time, not letting the parent go on until
     * the last request packet is read...
     */
    lwp_setpri(SELF, MINPRIO); /* get behind the new thread */
    lwp_yield(tid);            /* returns when new thread is blocked
                                * or re-scheduled */
    lwp_setpri(SELF, MAXPRIO);
    puts("back to selecting...");
  }
 }
}
```

It is *your* responsibility to schedule the service procedures as required. You may need to:

• Prioritize across multiple procedures.

• Prioritize according to the request source, available within struct svc_req *rqstp, and give certain requestors preferred service.

• Schedule within one priority level. Options include round-robin scheduling with lwp_resched() or simply maintaining a FIFO (first in, first out) schedule with execution blocking only for higher priorities or I/O waits.

In this simple server example, shown in Example 9-15, we only address the last scenario. There are two services: NULLPROC automatically generated by RPCGEN and our rtele_1().

We will put some logic in the rtele_1() service procedure to schedule new requests at the tail of a queue. We don't want to schedule different requests at different priorities since it overly complicates things, plus we want to be fair to all

clients. All we need to do is re-order the MINPRIO queue as soon as we enter the
user code, that is immediately after the request decoding has been completed. After
that everything is pretty much the same as before, with two exceptions. I've added
a lwp_sleep() to make the remote call take longer, giving us an opportunity to
pass up to MAXSVC requests at the server before the first thread can reply.

The second critical addition is the boost in priority. The static reply variables
need to be shared by all the queued threads so you must use some mechanism to
grab control of them until the server thread sends the reply. LWP includes monitors
and other tools for marking critical sections of code, but boosting priority suffices
here. For the sake of brevity, well stretch the use of thread priority to solve our
problems. A robust, extensible application should make use of the myriad of other
undisclosed LWP functions to lock resources.

If the reason for using concurrency is to make multiple service procedures available
at one time with common variables that are read-only, the static variable contention
problem is avoided. Careful use of dynamic memory allocation routines can also
help.

*Example 9-15. Lightweight processing for asynchronous remote calls from a client:
rteleLWP_svc_proc.c*

```
#include <stdio.h>
#include <string.h>
#include <rpc/rpc.h>
#include <lwp/lwp.h>
#include "rtele.h"

char            **
rtele_1(name, rqstp)
   char            **name;
   struct svc_req *rqstp;
{
   char            sb[MAX_STR];
   static char     sa[MAX_STR];
   static char     *s = sa;
   FILE            *fp = fopen(DATABASE, "r");
   static struct timeval tv = {1, 0};

   /*
    * After announcing ourselves, give priority back to the dispatcher and
    * svc_run() to look for other requests.  Processing continues here only
    * when the main thread and older sibling threads of the same priority get
    * blocked (-lbnio) or yield, resp.
    */
   printf("thread %d started\t", SELF); fflush(stdout);
   lwp_resched(MINPRIO);         /* Be fair - move yourself to the back of
                                  * the queue if there is one. */
   lwp_sleep(&tv);               /* Pretend service takes a long time,
                                  * possible blocking.  This is where
                                  * main gets time to do selects. */
   lwp_setpri(SELF, MINPRIO+1);  /* IMPORTANT: lock all variables from
                                  * now on. */
   sa[0] = NULL;
   while (fgets(sa, MAX_STR - 1, fp)) {
     sscanf(sa, "%s%s%s", sb, sb, sb);  /* get the last name */
     if (!strcmp(sb, *name))
       break;
   }
```

Example 9-15. Lightweight processing for asynchronous remote calls from a client:
rteleLWP_svc_proc.c (Continued)

```
    if feof (fp) sa[0] = NULL;              /* no match */
    fclose(fp);

    printf("thread %d complete\t", SELF); fflush(stdout);
    return ((char **) &s);
}
```

Compile and link the server with the new svc_run() loop and the RPCGEN
server stub.

```
rodson> cc -o rteleLWP_svc rteleLWP_svc_proc.c \
    svc_runLWP.c rtele_svc.o -llwp -lnbio
```

To test the server out, start it on any machine and send it multiple requests concurrently with something like this:

```
rodson> rsh cortex exec $cwd/rteleLWP_svc
[3]  + Stopped (tty input) \
rsh cortex exec /home/cortex/bloomer/src/rpc/rtele/lwp/rteleLWP_svc
rodson> @ i=0
rodson> while ($i < 10)
? @ i++
? rtele cortex BLOOMER &
? end
```

The output comes back quickly. It's interesting to look at the server output. Bring it
to the foreground. It illustrates that the server threads were started and execution
was interleaved, allowing each to finish and send a reply in FIFO order.

```
rodson> fg
rsh cortex exec /home/cortex/u0/bloomer/src/rpc/rtele/lwp/rteleLWP_svc
servicing...back to selecting...servicing...back to selecting...
servicing...thread 383088 started   back to selecting...
servicing...back to selecting...
servicing...thread 407664 started   back to selecting...
servicing...back to selecting...
servicing...thread 432240 started   back to selecting...
servicing...back to selecting...
servicing...thread 456816 started   back to selecting...
servicing...back to selecting...
servicing...thread 481392 started   back to selecting...
servicing...thread 505968 started   back to selecting...
servicing...back to selecting...
servicing...thread 530544 started   back to selecting...
servicing...back to selecting...
servicing...thread 555120 started   back to selecting...
thread 383088 complete  thread 407664 complete
servicing...back to selecting...servicing...back to selecting...
servicing...back to selecting...servicing...
thread 407664 started   back to selecting...
servicing...back to selecting...
servicing...thread 383088 started   back to selecting...
thread 432240 complete  servicing...back to selecting...
thread 456816 complete  servicing...back to selecting...
thread 481392 complete  thread 505968 complete
servicing...back to selecting...
```

```
thread 530544 complete  servicing...back to selecting...
servicing...back to selecting...
thread 555120 complete  servicing...back to selecting...
thread 407664 complete  thread 383088 complete
```

Caveats

Watch your stack size and the number of threads. I did not use the return values from the LWP routines but using them will help you anticipate overflow and collision problems. Do not try to start more than MAXSVC+1 threads. Without enough stack space available, some strange errors are generated.

To really hammer on this example, recompile *svc_runLWP.c* with a MAXSVC of 100, then re-link the server. Start it on a remote machine. Increase the shell loop limit or use the LWP client rteleLWP to send this one server more than 10 requests at once. You'll notice that unless you significantly lengthen the lwp_sleep() in the service routine, the replies continue to come back in FIFO order. For longer, computationally-intense services, a more sophisticated scheduling heuristic may be called for.

In this chapter:
- *The X Window System*
- *Strategies for Using RPC Under X*
- *RPC and XView*
- *RPC and Xol/Xt*
- *Comparing Network Windowing Systems and RPC*

10

RPC Under
Windowing Systems

Some client and server RPC applications run under a windowing system such as X. There are special demands on such an application because it must maintain some level of interaction with the user, responding to mouse clicks, keystrokes, etc., even while an RPC is being placed or serviced. Long delays caused by I/O blocking of an RPC need to be avoided so asynchrony can be considered mandatory.

In this chapter, we discuss several aspects of integrating an RPC application with a windowing system, including:

- Placing synchronous and remote asynchronous calls.

- Waiting or polling for RPCs, in the context of asynchronous follow-up RPC (FRPC).

- Mixing low-level IPC and the X Window System.

We assume that you have some basic familiarity with the X Window System. For the programmer, the most significant aspect of a windowing system like X is that it requires event-driven programming. Your main routine loops to intercept and interpret events as generated by other processes or user input. Events of interest to the application are often used to instruct the window dispatch routine to execute a *callback* routine. For example, selecting the QUIT button causes the callback procedure cleanUpAndQuit() to be called in the client, and it closes windows and terminates the process.

The examples in this chapter use the XView toolkit, which inherits its API from SunView, and the Xol toolkit, also known as OLIT and Xt+. Either one can be used to create an OPEN LOOK compliant interface. The main difference between the two toolkits is that Xol is a widget set built on top of the Xt Intrinsics while XView provides its own event dispatch loop, derived from the SunView Notifier. Using Xt and in effect isolating the event handling from the widget set, makes it easier to design applications that must be written for Motif as well as OPEN LOOK.

Let me add, before we begin, that integrating RPC and a windowing system has its challenges. Some windowing systems use IPC techniques to watch for user events that are incompatible with the RPC system. The techniques developed in Chapters 6 and 9 for multiple client and server processing (asynchrony) won't work with all windowing systems. Integrating lightweight threads presents a similar challenge. So things can get complicated.

Client-side multi-tasking (Chapter 9) can often be applied to avoid parent-process blocking by blocking the child during a synchronous RPC. This technique is used in the networked ray tracing application developed in Appendix B. However, because the size of most windowing system processes is so large, forking child processes can be inefficient and slow. For example, it can be costly to duplicate the multi-megabyte process space of most X processes; they carry lots of extra baggage due to their high-level, networked, object-oriented interface.

The X Window System

The X Window System is the de facto standard network windowing system. In X and RPC systems, clients and servers mean different things. In X you have a display server operating on the machine that controls the terminal's screen display. Client processes which can run on any machine on the network, call the server to effect display activity. A separate process handles much of the common window management functions.

X uses socket-based IPCs to facilitate server/client communications. To compare the client and server relationships in X and RPC, we'd have to cover the complete details of the message-based X protocol, as well as pieces of layered widget sets or graphical user interface (GUI) toolkits like the Intrinsics or XView. Suffice it to say that although RPC libraries and associated utilities are more versatile for network IPC, they do not embrace many important windowing system abstractions. There is no concept of I/O devices, frame buffers, or interactive devices in RPC. On the other hand, both RPC and X have some kind of socket-level notification mechanism, and an RPC system does mandate something similar to the callback or event-driven program structuring of windowing systems.

X Toolkit Client Application Flow of Control

At a high level, most X toolkit client applications look the same. They instantiate objects (or widgets), then proceed to execute callback routines that you attach to widgets, as directed by an event dispatcher listening to inputs.

The client's `main()` routine must first initialize the appropriate toolkit, then proceed to make all possible widgets early-on. Managing and realizing a widget is necessary for it to show up as a usable user interface object. The last thing your `main()` procedure does is make a call to the windowing system's event dispatch loop that never returns. The dispatcher catches any interesting events and passes them to the appropriate widget, which in turn causes callback routines to be executed. Note that you the programmer determine which events are interesting and to what widget and callback function they apply.

Low-level RPC and X Protocol Similarities

Figure 10-1 puts three X client applications on a network. Each is running a different toolkit and widget set. All are accessing the same X display manager and server. In an abstract fashion, one could compare the functions of Xlib, and the X protocol with that of XDR and RPC, respectively. Both X and XDR/RPC provide a request mechanism (and reply when appropriate), with machine-independence. X does not (yet) include the network binding or association schemes that come with RPCs. An example is ONC's Network Information System. X, with its toolkits and widget sets, exists for the sole purpose of networked windowing, yet in order to do this the toolkits take on many of the same functions as XDR/RPC libraries.

Like RPCs, the network shown in Figure 10-1 is virtual in the sense that managers, servers, and clients may be run on any machine in any combination, even all on the local one. The only logistical constraint is that the X display server must be run on the machine whose windows and user I/O you are concerned with. The X window client application and manager are often run elsewhere, for example in the case of X terminals. Performance is often better when the display manager is run local to the display server.

Strategies for Using RPC Under X

The X protocol supports its own messaging system on top of sockets. It was designed with graphics and windowing in mind, and does not represent a general-purpose, high-level, remote execution environment like RPC. In order to mix RPC and X, you often have to reach down to low-level RPC and IPC programming. We will see several examples:

- Placing RPCs into the callback routines to be performed synchronously in response to some user action.

- Using a timer to do the same.

- Placing an RPC in a callback, returning immediately to look for the return FRPC with a timer.

- Performing asynchronous servicing of RPCs using event or socket-watching functions built into X toolkits.

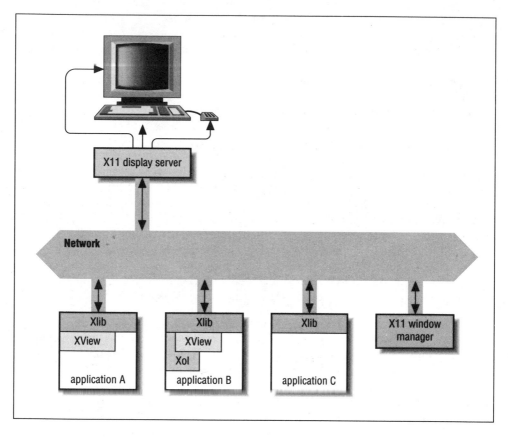

Figure 10-1. Distributed X Window applications using widget sets and toolkits

Functions are built into toolkits to watch or select socket activity, invoking a speci-fied callback function when data shows up (e.g., descriptors become ready to read or write). These toolkit functions are high-level IPC tools, layered on top of UNIX utilities like `listen()` and `connect()`.

In this chapter, we will borrow many of the techniques developed in Chapter 9 as well as the low-level IPC used in Chapter 5. We add another level of complexity as we make use of `select()` to monitor socket activity. Windowing systems perform similar processing because they need to monitor activity from a number of I/O sources simultaneously.

Placing and Servicing RPCs in an Event-driven Environment

RPC calls, like all application code in an X program, must be performed in callback procedures. These procedures can be activated by the event manager upon receiving a message about some event. These events might be user-generated or come from some external input, like a change in status of a socket or file descriptor. The simplest, and probably most common implementation is to connect an RPC to some user action.

Synchronous RPCs from a User-activated Callback

In this section, we show how to put a standard RPC into a procedure executed by a user action. A single synchronous RPC is made when the ACTION_SELECT event occurs—when the left mouse button is clicked in the window. The application waits until the reply containing a directory listing returns from the server. Both directory and server are named in the argument list. In this way, any of the synchronous rls RPC servers generated with RPCGEN in Chapters 4 or 9 are compatible. The *rls.h* include file therefore need only include:

```
#define DIR_SIZE 8192
#define DIRPROG ((u_long) 0x20000001) /* server program (suite) number */
#define DIRVERS ((u_long) 1)          /* program version number */
#define READDIR ((u_long) 1)          /* procedure number for look-up */
```

Notice the 0x20000001 RPC program number. This should tell you that the service is synchronous, and that the one-way RPC of Example 9-7 (DIRPROG 0x20000002) is not compatible.

The XView application in Example 10-1 defines an event procedure called event_proc(), that is executed by the XView Notifier when you click the left mouse button. This RPC client application requires a synchronous remote directory server. The directory you are interested in is argv[1] and the server names are all subsequent arguments. The client attempts to get a listing for a common directory on each server. The directory must be either a common distributed file system directory, or some relative pathname, since each server is asked for the same directory.

As an XView application, the example is trivial, displaying a text subwindow in a frame. The text subwindow is where the remote directory listing appears. An event procedure tells the application what to do when the action occurs. In this case it calls RPC.

Example 10-1. XView client with synchronous RPCs launched from callback function:
syncCallback.c

```
#include <XView/XView.h>
#include <XView/textsw.h>
#include <rpc/rpc.h>
#include "rls.h"

int             hosts;
char            **hostnames;
char            dir[DIR_SIZE];
static int      i = 0;
Textsw          textsw;
Frame           frame;

main(argc, argv)
    int             argc;
    char            *argv[];
```

Example 10-1. XView client with synchronous RPCs launched from callback function: syncCallback.c (Continued)

```
{
   Xv_window        window;
   void             event_proc();

   /*
    * Initialize XView and get hostnames and directory.
    */
   xv_init(XV_INIT_ARGS, argc, argv, 0);
   hosts = argc - 2;
   strcpy(dir, argv[1]);
   hostnames = &argv[2];

   /*
    * Create windows -- base frame and text subwindow.
    */
   frame = xv_create(XV_NULL, FRAME, FRAME_LABEL, argv[0], NULL);
   textsw = xv_create(frame, TEXTSW,
                      WIN_ROWS, 20,
                      WIN_COLUMNS, 80,
                      NULL);
   window_fit(frame);

   /*
    * ...and tell it what events to honor and how
    */
   window = (Xv_window) xv_get(textsw, OPENWIN_NTH_VIEW, 0);
   xv_set(window,
          WIN_EVENT_PROC, event_proc,
          WIN_CONSUME_EVENTS, WIN_UP_EVENTS, NULL,
          NULL);

   xv_main_loop(frame);
}

void
event_proc(window, event)
   Xv_Window        window;
   Event            *event;
{
   if (event_action(event) == ACTION_SELECT) {
      xv_set(frame, FRAME_BUSY, TRUE, NULL);
      i = (i + 1) % hosts;
      textsw_insert(textsw, hostnames[i], strlen(hostnames[i]));
      /*
       * This will block, so one could spawn children or threads as an
       * alternative. Extra signals, etc. REALLY complicate things...
       */
      read_dir(hostnames[i], dir);
      textsw_insert(textsw, dir, strlen(dir));
      xv_set(frame, FRAME_BUSY, FALSE, NULL);
   }
}

read_dir(host, dir)
   char             *dir, *host;
{
   extern bool_t    xdr_dir();
   enum clnt_stat   clnt_stat;

   clnt_stat = callrpc(host, DIRPROG, DIRVERS, READDIR,
                       xdr_dir, dir, xdr_dir, dir);
   if (clnt_stat != 0) clnt_perrno(clnt_stat);
}
```

Notice that we use xv_set(3XV) in main() to tell the window what events to honor and to establish a callback for WIN_EVENT_PROC events. WIN_EVENT_PROC represents not just one event, but a group of events. So the event_proc() callback must sift through the events to find any that interest it. XView callbacks are attached to objects by specifying the events you are interested in, followed by the function to execute. Here we modify the behavior of the text subwindow with xv_set(), attaching our own event procedure. event_proc() is called whenever any one of the NULL-terminated list of events (attributes) occurs. The list contains WIN_CONSUME_EVENTS and WIN_UP_EVENTS. Only upward mouse events are accepted.[†] If we were using Xt-based toolkit instead of XView, we would use XtAddCallback(3Xt) to attach callbacks to objects or widgets.

xv_set() was also used in the event_proc() to gray the frame bar and turn the cursor to an hourglass during the callback procedure. It is good programming style, plus it avoids the buffering of user events which can be fatal. If you are building CLIENT handles with clnt_create() before making the RPCs, you might mark the window as busy then, also. The busy frame attribute is actually part of the OPEN LOOK UI specification.

The callrpc() call in Example 10-1, as well as in Example 10-3, may be replaced with something like the high-level readdir_1() RPC call of Example 4-5. In this case the read_dir() remote interface is defined in the RPC language and a protocol compiler used.

Makefile for X Applications

When building the standalone XView and Xol/Xt examples in this chapter, use the makefile in Example 10-2. This assumes you have the XView libraries and include files, covering both XView and Xol. These reside in the directory pointed to by the OPENWINHOME environment variable. The X11 libraries and includes must also be installed in */usr/lib/X11*.

Example 10-2. makefile for Xt and Xv applications

```
INCLUDE         = -I${OPENWINHOME}/include
#
# if you want to compile for debugging, change "-O" to "-g"
#
CFLAGS          = ${INCLUDE} -O
# if you want special to pass special loader options to ld, set
# LDFLAGS= ...
#
LIB_PATH        = -L${OPENWINHOME}/lib
X11_LIBS        = -lX11
XVIEW_LIBS      = -lXView -lolgx
XT_LIBS         = -lXt -lXol

.c :
        $(CC) -o $* $(CFLAGS) $< rls_xdr.o $(LFLAGS) ${LIB_PATH} \
${X11_LIBS} ${XT_LIBS} ${XVIEW_LIBS}
```

---

† See the *XView Programming Manual*, by Dan Heller, O'Reilly and Associates, Inc.

There's one caveat. If you get the "`_XtInherit symbol undefined`" error at run-time with XView applications, remove the `-lXt` library. You are not initializing the Xt toolkit correctly. If this happens, you'll need different linker arguments for XView and Xt:

```
# for XView applications
.c :
        $(CC) -o $* $(CFLAGS) $< rls_xdr.o $(LFLAGS) ${LIB_PATH} \
${X11_LIBS} ${XVIEW_LIBS}
# for Xt/Xol applications
.c :
        $(CC) -o $* $(CFLAGS) $< rls_xdr.o $(LFLAGS) ${LIB_PATH} \
${X11_LIBS} ${XT_LIBS}
```

We will re-use the XDR filters in *rls_xdr.c*, as generated with the protocol in Example 4-2. The directory reading code in *read_dir.c* as well as the XDR routines from Chapter 4 may also be required for some of the RPC servers developed here.

RPC and XView

Another way to perform RPCs under XView is to use the interval timers XView makes available. There are complications if you are attempting to use the standard alarm, timer, or signal interfaces, as the XView Notifier uses these. More on that later. By calling `notify_enable_rpc_svc(3XV)`, you can enable or disable RPC event dispatching via the XView Notifier.

Synchronous RPCs with a Timer

Often it is necessary to make or check for RPCs on a regular basis. Interval timers are a logical choice to make RPCs in this case. XView provides an interval timer for events that is named `notify_set_itimer_func(3XV)` and allows the named function to be executed on a regular basis.

In Example 10-3, the same old synchronous remote directory listing server is called every two seconds. The directory and hosts you are interested in are the first and higher arguments, respectively. For example, compile and run the RPC client:

```
rodson> make itimer
rodson> itimer ./ hosta hostb hostc
```

This assumes, of course, that a Chapter 4 or 9 synchronous server is running on the named hosts. This example shares the same frame and text subwindow approach as Example 10-1. The callback procedure on the left mouse button is gone.

Example 10-3. Using an interval timer in XView to place synchronous RPCs: itimer.c

```
#include <XView/XView.h>
#include <XView/textsw.h>
#include <rpc/rpc.h>
#include "rls.h" /* as with the server used, synchronous from Ch 4/8 */

int             hosts;
char            **hostnames;
char            dir[DIR_SIZE];
static int      i = 0;
Textsw          textsw;
Frame           frame;

main(argc, argv)
  int             argc;
  char            *argv[];
{
  Xv_window       window;
  static struct   itimerval timeout = {{2, 0}, {2, 0}};
  Notity_value    rpcread();

  /*
   * Initialize XView and get host names and directory.
   */
  xv_init(XV_INIT_ARGS, argc, argv, 0);
  hosts = argc - 2;
  strcpy(dir, argv[1]);
  hostnames = &argv[2];

  /*
   * Create windows -- base frame and text subwindow.
   */
  frame = xv_create(XV_NULL, FRAME, FRAME_LABEL, argv[0], NULL);
  textsw = xv_create(frame, TEXTSW,
                     WIN_ROWS, 20,
                     WIN_COLUMNS, 80,
                     NULL);
  window_fit(frame);

  notify_set_itimer_func(frame, rpcread, ITIMER_REAL, &timeout, NULL);

  xv_main_loop(frame);
}

read_dir(host, dir)
  char *dir, *host;
{
  extern bool_t   xdr_dir();
  enum clnt_stat  clnt_stat;

  clnt_stat = callrpc(host, DIRPROG, DIRVERS, READDIR,
                      xdr_dir, dir, xdr_dir, dir);
  if (clnt_stat != 0) clnt_perrno(clnt_stat);
}

Notify_value rpcread(item, event)
  Panel_item      item;
  Event           *event;
{
```

Example 10-3. Using an interval timer in XView to place synchronous RPCs: itimer.c (Continued)

```
i = (i + 1) % hosts;
textsw_insert(textsw, hostnames[i], strlen(hostnames[i]));
read_dir(hostnames[i], dir);  /* read_dir(host, directory) */
textsw_insert(textsw, dir, strlen(dir));
return (NOTIFY_DONE);
}
```

rpcread() is activated by the XView Notifier on a regular basis, cycling through the provided hostnames, placing a remote directory listing RPC to each. The results are placed in the XView text subwindow. This again uses the synchronous RPC server, blocking the application while the timer-activated procedure does its RPCs.

Remote Asynchronous Calls, FRPC Polled with a Timer

If you are trying not to tie up the application while executing an RPC, mixing the follow-up RPC (FRPC introduced in Chapter 9) concept with interval timer notification can be useful. If you use a single synchronous RPC to perform a task that takes a while, the whole nature of the interface can be wrecked. Users quickly become despondent when events are not honored or buffered-up.

Example 10-3 illustrated how the XView Notifier can be told to do something on a regular basis with an interval timer. In Example 10-4, we place a synchronous RPC to ask the RPC client to start a task. Again, it is a directory listing. The server returns immediately, merely acknowledging the request, then proceeds to process the request. The RPC client watches for the subsequent FRPC that will return the real results. It uses an interval timer to place a select() call that looks at socket activity as described in Chapters 5 and 9, using the RPC svc_fdset file descriptor set. When an FRPC request is detected, the client retrieves the results and displays it in an XView text subwindow.

Figure 10-2 is a schematic of the example. After initializing the toolkit and creating the windows, an RPC collection server, locald(), is registered to listen for the return RPC. The XView Notifier is told to generate events every second that cause a callback routine to look for requests with getresults(). If present, the collection service puts the results into the window. The application then returns to the window event loop.

The application spends most of its time in the dispatch loop, idly monitoring activity. The process is not I/O blocked for very long due to the use of FRPC.

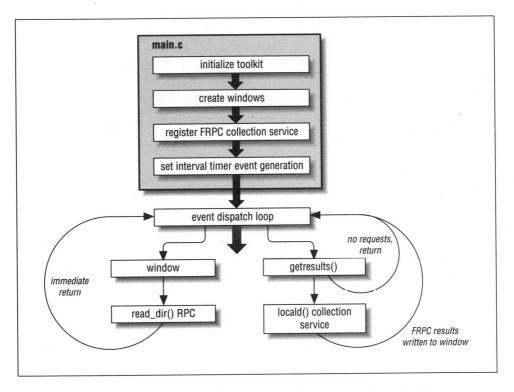

Figure 10-2. Remote asynchronous calls monitored with an interval timer in XView

Example 10-4. XView interval timer looks for asynchronous FRPC requests: asyncCallback.c

```
#include <XView/XView.h>
#include <XView/textsw.h>
#include <XView/panel.h>
#include <sys/errno.h>
#include <rpc/rpc.h>
#include "../async/asyncRls.h"/* must support client collection service */

int             hosts;
char            **hostnames;
char            dir[DIR_SIZE];
static int      i = 0;
Textsw          textsw;
Frame           frame;
int             ts;         /* file descriptor table size */
struct timeval  stimeout; /* select time-out values */
extern int      errno;

main(argc, argv)
   int          argc;
   char         *argv[];
{
   Xv_window    window;
   void         event_proc();
```

Example 10-4. XView interval timer looks for asynchronous FRPC requests: asyncCallback.c (Continued)

```
    static struct   itimerval timeout = {{1, 0}, {1, 0}};
    Notify_value    getresults();
    char            *locald();
    extern bool_t   xdr_dir();

    /*
     * Initialize XView and get hostnames and directory.
     */
    xv_init(XV_INIT_ARGS, argc, argv, 0);
    hosts = argc - 2;
    strcpy(dir, argv[1]);
    hostnames = &argv[2];

    /*
     * Establish some one-time use stuff for using select repeatedly.
     */
    ts = getdtablesize();
    stimeout.tv_sec = stimeout.tv_usec = 0;

    /*
     * Create windows -- base frame and text subwindow.
     */
    frame = xv_create(XV_NULL, FRAME, FRAME_LABEL, argv[0], NULL);
    textsw = xv_create(frame, TEXTSW,
                       WIN_ROWS, 20,
                       WIN_COLUMNS, 80,
                       NULL);
    window_fit(frame);

    /*
     * ...and tell it what events to honor and how
     */
    window = (Xv_window) xv_get(textsw, OPENWIN_NTH_VIEW, 0);
    xv_set(window,
           WIN_EVENT_PROC, event_proc,
           WIN_IGNORE_EVENTS, WIN_UP_EVENTS, NULL,
           NULL);

    /*
     * Register a collection daemon as a timer routine, then start looping.
     */
    registerrpc(DIRDPROG, DIRDVERS, LOCALD, locald, xdr_dir, xdr_void);
    notify_set_itimer_func(frame, getresults, ITIMER_REAL,
                           &timeout, NULL);
    xv_main_loop(frame);
}

void event_proc(window, event)
    Xv_Window       window;
    Event           *event;
{
    if (event_action(event) == ACTION_SELECT) {
        printf("sending request\n");
        i = (i + 1) % hosts;
        /*
         * Issue an async. rpc giving no real answer, proceeding
         * back to the Notifier loop. getresults() is called
         * by timer notices to check for returns.
         */
        read_dir(hostnames[i], dir);
    }
}

read_dir(host, dir)
```

Example 10-4. XView interval timer looks for asynchronous FRPC requests: asyncCallback.c (Continued)

```
  char              *dir, *host;
{
  extern bool_t    xdr_dir();
  enum clnt_stat   clnt_stat;

  /*
   * Place the call.  Notice the return value is not inspected.
   */
  clnt_stat = callrpc(host, DIRPROG, DIRVERS, READDIR,
                         xdr_dir, dir, xdr_void, 0);
  if (clnt_stat != 0) clnt_perrno(clnt_stat);
}

Notify_value getresults(item, event)
  Panel_item       item;
  Event            *event;
{
  fd_set           readfds;

  /*
   * Look for a response from the other socket, return otherwise.
   */
  readfds = svc_fdset;
  switch (select(ts, &readfds, (int *) 0, (int *) 0, &stimeout)) {
    case -1:
      if (errno == EINTR) break;
      perror("svc_run: - select failed");
      break;
    case 0:
      break;
    default:
      svc_getreqset(&readfds); /* calls locald() */
  }
  return (NOTIFY_DONE);
}

char *locald(dir) /* invoked if there is something at my socket... */
  char             *dir;         /* char dir[DIR_SIZE] */
{
  /*
   * As part of the protocol, we asked the server to send back its
   * hostname to expedite any required monitoring process.
   */
  textsw_insert(textsw, dir, strlen(dir));
  return;
}
```

If an ACTION_SELECT or left button click occurred in the text subwindow, the first client RPC of an FRPC pair is placed. When the Notifier timer value expires every second, the client application checks for an incoming request. The remote directory contents are retrieved and placed in an XView text window.

Make the RPC client and run it with one of the FRPC-based asynchronous servers developed in Chapter 9, such as Example 9-9.

```
    rodson> make asyncCallback
    rodson> rsh -n cortex $cwd/../async/asyncRls &
```

If you make the timer value a little longer, you will find that the interface is indeed honoring your input events. Try 5 or 10 seconds, and after you start an RPC with the left button, type some text into the window or do a redisplay. The Notifier has time to honor these events.

The Event Notifier and Associated Complications

We have introduced the XView Notifier by way of examples, but it warrants more discussion. Figure 10-3 shows how the XView Notifier monitors activity, turning it into events, and then activates any associated callback functions. XView doesn't actually listen to any hardware. That's the job of the X display server, which in turn communicates with the Notifier. XView Release 2.0 not only watches users, descriptors, and signals, but also higher-level RPC activity.

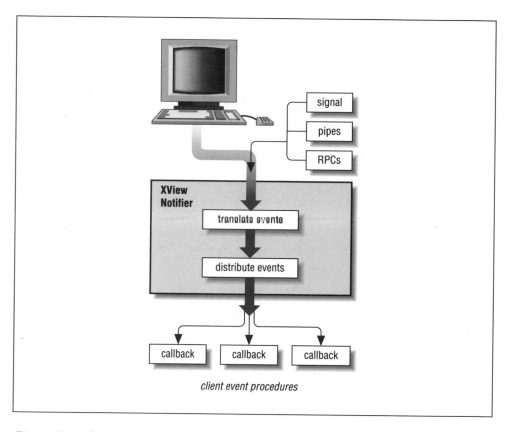

Figure 10-3. The Notifier as placed between the XView server and client application

The XView Notifier behavior is inherited from SunView. It is unlike the Xt event dispatcher in the way it uses signals and timers internally. Using them yourself can send the Notifier out to lunch or cause some events to be ignored. The API does provide a flexible way to augment or even replace the Notifier with your own type of event processing as necessary.

System calls you should avoid or replace when running the XView Notifier include:†

- `signal(3)` or `sigvec(2)`. The following signals are used by the Notifier, so substitute functions are provided. Instead of using `signal()`, use `notify_set_signal_func(3XV)` to install a signal handler through the Notifier. `signal()` can make the Notifier miss things. The `notify_set_..._func()` XView procedures below are invoked by the Notifier when the appropriate condition exists.

SIGALRM	Augment the Notifier with `notify_set_itimer_func()` instead.
SIGVTALRM	See above.
SIGTERM	Use `notify_set_destroy_client()` instead to signify that the Notifier client is disappearing.
SIGCHLD	The Notifier occasionally does its own child management. Use `notify_set_wait3_func()` to have the Notifier take action on a status change instead.
SIGIO	Use `notify_set_output_func()` or `notify_set_input_function()` if you want to watch your own file descriptors.
SIGURG	Use `notify_set_exception_func()` if you want to set up your own exception handling.

☞ You *may* use `signal()` to establish any signal handler you need *before* starting the XView Notifier main loop. XView augments the current signal handling, chaining them together, rather than blindly replacing the handlers you may have established.

- `setitimer(2)`, `getitimer(2)`, `alarm(3)` – The Notifier uses interval timers. Use `notify_set_itimer_func()` and `notify_itimer_value()` or the Notifier can miss an internal time-out.

- `wait3(2)` – The Notifier is watching for state change on its children. Use `notify_set_wait3_func()` to work within the constraints of the Notifier.

- `ioctl(2)` – Don't try to change blocking status (`FIONBIO`) or asynchronous I/O settings (`FIOASYNC`) through `ioctl(2)`. Use `fcntl(2)` instead as the Notifier need to know the status of these settings.

- `system(3)` – Under SunOS, `system(3)` uses `signal(3)` and `wait(2V)`. Avoid it.

---

† Dan Heller's *XView Programming Manual* does a better job of covering the nature of the Notifier with its caveats and workarounds. However, it doesn't address the Release 2.0 function we use: `notify_enable_rpc_svc()`.

Remote Asynchronous Call Servers Using notify_enable_rpc_svc()

XView 2.0 gives you a way to bring RPC event processing into the Notifier. Out of all the X/RPC merges presented, this is probably the cleanest, requiring the least amount of additional code. By calling notify_enable_rpc_svc(3XV), you can enable or disable RPC event dispatching via the XView Notifier. In this way an RPC server (or an RPC client who wants momentarily to become a server for FRPCs) can be notified of a pending request without locking things up with a svc_run() loop. It avoids the potentially wasteful use of an interval timer to poll for the same thing.

Example 10-5 contains an RPC server routine. Instead of using svc_run() to go into an endless loop looking for RPC socket activity, we use the XView Notifier. In this fashion, other window system tasks and callbacks can be performed. Here we just use the Notifier, and instantiate no interactive graphic objects. By replacing notify_start(3XV) with a window_main_loop(frame), you could perform notifications on objects subordinate to frame also, as in the previous examples.

Example 10-5. Using notify_enable_rpc_svc() in the XView Notifier: notifyServer.c

```
#include <stdio.h>
#include <xview/xview.h>
#include <xview/notify.h>
#include <rpc/rpc.h>
#include "rls.h"

main(argc, argv)
    int             argc;
    char            *argv[];
{
    SVCXPRT         *xprt;
    extern void dispatch();/* the server program - does dispatching */

    /*
     * Establish the UDP-transport server daemon.
     */
    (void) pmap_unset(DIRPROG, DIRVERS);
    xprt = svcudp_create(RPC_ANYSOCK);
    if (xprt == NULL) {
      (void) fprintf(stderr, "cannot create udp service.\n");
      exit(1);
    }
    if (!svc_register(xprt, DIRPROG, DIRVERS, dispatch, IPPROTO_UDP)) {
      (void) fprintf(stderr,
                   "unable to register (DIRPROG, DIRVERS, udp).\n");
      exit(1);
    }

    /*
     * Before starting the Notifier loop, tell it to look at the server socket
     * information in fd_set to notify us of RPC requests.
     */
    notify_enable_rpc_svc(TRUE);

    /* loops continuously */
    notify_start();
}
```

The Notifier event processing doesn't care whether it has an RPC event on a UDP or a TCP socket. Either transport works with `notify_enable_rpc_svc()`. I broke the dispatch routine out into its own compilation unit, *dispatch.c* in Example 10-6 because we use it again. It is a simple synchronous routine that checks for one of two request types, READDIR or NULLPROC, and provides the necessary service.

Example 10-6. Dispatcher registered for XView and Xt/Xol RPC server applications: dispatch.c

```
#include <stdio.h>
#include <rpc/rpc.h>
#include "rls.h"

/*
 * Decode the requested service and provide it. This is a synchronous
 * dispatcher, but there's no reason why you couldn't use the async.
 * asyncRls_svc.c dispatcher to avoid prolonged RPC client blocking.
 */
void
dispatch(rqstp, transp)
  struct svc_req *rqstp;
  SVCXPRT        *transp;
{
  extern bool_t   xdr_dir();
  extern char     *read_dir();
  char            dir[DIR_SIZE];
  char            dhost[DIR_SIZE];
  struct hostent *host;
  struct sockaddr_in *sock_in;
  enum clnt_stat  clnt_stat;
  CLIENT          *client;

  switch (rqstp->rq_proc) {
  case NULLPROC:
    (void) svc_sendreply(transp, xdr_void, 0);
    return;

  case READDIR:
    if (!svc_getargs(transp, xdr_dir, dir)) {
      svcerr_decode(transp);
      return;
    }
    read_dir(dir);
    /*
     * Pre-pend the hostname to ease client-side tracking.
     */
    (void) gethostname(dhost, DIR_SIZE);
    strcat(dhost, "\n");
    strcat(dhost, dir);

    /*
     * Return the result.
     */
    if (!svc_sendreply(transp, xdr_dir, dir)) {
      svcerr_systemerr(transp);
      return;
    }
    /*
     * We'll re-use dhost, but should call this to free the XDR struct, plus
     * clean things up.
     */
    svc_freeargs(transp, xdr_dir, dhost);
    return;

  /*
```

Example 10-6. Dispatcher registered for XView and Xt/Xol RPC server applications: dispatch.c (Continued)

```
 * put more procedures here...  case A: case Z:
 */
  default:
    svcerr_noproc(transp);
    return;
  }
}
```

Put everything together with:

```
rodson> cc -o notifyServer notifyServer.c dispatch.c rls_xdr.o \
       read_dir.o -I$OPENWINHOME/include \
       -L$OPENWINHOME/lib -lxview -lolgx -lX11
```

Start this server on your choice of host, then use the synchronous UDP remote directory listing RPC client (Example 4-5) to send it requests.

RPC and Xol/Xt

Before I get into the gory details of mixing RPC with Xt or Xol programming, let's start with a simple example that illustrates building widgets. In Example 10-7, we build two widgets. w_top is the top-level widget, under which everything else in the application is attached. w_text is a static text window, suitable for displaying the text "Hello, World."

Example 10-7. A simple Xt/Xol example: hello.c

```
#include <stdio.h>
#include <X11/Xlib.h>
#include <X11/Intrinsic.h>
#include <X11/StringDefs.h>
#include <Xol/OpenLook.h>
#include <Xol/StaticText.h>

#define STRING "Hello, World"

Arg             _tmpArgs[] = {
  {XtNstring, (XtArgVal) STRING},
};


main(argc, argv)
    int             argc;
    char            **argv;
{
  Widget          w_top, w_text;

  w_top = OlInitialize(argv[0],
                       "HelloWorld",
                       NULL,
                       0,
                       &argc,
                       argv
        );

  w_text = XtCreateManagedWidget("text",
                                 staticTextWidgetClass,
                                 w_top,
```

Example 10-7. A simple Xt/Xol example: hello.c (Continued)

```
                        _tmpArgs,
                        XtNumber(_tmpArgs)
        );

    XtRealizeWidget(w_top);
    XtMainLoop();
}
```

We use the Xt event dispatcher to watch the widgets for default events (e.g., redisplay, resize, etc.) when we invoke `XtMainLoop(3Xt)`.

Watching IPC with XtAppAddInput(3Xt)

Using the X11R4 Xt Intrinsics toolkit, you can call `XtAppAddInput(3Xt)` to establish a callback routine that gets activated by socket activity. `XtAppAddInput()` registers a new source of events with the Intrinsics' read routine, usually some file input or output. A file can be interpreted to mean any sink or source of data, like a socket descriptor. The conditions under which the source can generate events is specified. When this conditional input is pending at the source, the callback procedure is invoked. Its synopsis:

```
XtInputId XtAppAddInput(app_context, source, condition, proc, client_data)
        XtAppContext app_context;
        int source;
        caddr_t condition;
        XtInputCallbackProc proc;
        caddr_t client_data;
```

The arguments are:

id   A unique ID returned by the call.

app_context   The application context identifying the application.

source   The source file (socket) descriptor on a UNIX-based system—
                or some other operating-system dependent device specification.

condition   A mask specifying the read, write, or exception condition. It is
                operating-system dependent. On UNIX-based systems, you
                use some union of `XtInputReadMask`, `XtInputWrite-Mask`, and `XtInputExceptMask`.

proc   The procedure to be invoked when input is available.

client_data   Data to be passed to the specified procedure when the
                descriptor status condition is met.

The `XtRemoveInput(3Xt)` function tells the Intrinsics read routine to stop watching for inputs from a source. `XtRemoveInput()` is prototyped as follows:

```
void XtRemoveInput(id)
        XtInputId id;
```

Merely pass it the XtInputId input ID created with XtAppAddInput(). Also, XtAppAddTimeOut(3Xt) and XtRemoveTimeOut(3Xt) can be used to register and remove timer-invoked procedures, similar to that mentioned in the XView section.

Let's start by working at the level most X programmers are comfortable with. We'll use sockets in a fashion similar to what we did in Chapter 5. In Example 10-8, we build on the earlier simple Xol/Xt example, by adding a control area and a button, behind which we'll hang a callback routine. In ButtCallback() we use low-level socket calls to make a request to port PORT on each of the machines specified on the command line. This callback uses XtAppAddInput() to tell the Intrinsics to loop around in the dispatcher loop until it sees an FRPC request come in. ButtCallback() creates sockets and watches for readability. The routine installed by XtAppAddInput(), SocketInputCallback(), will be removed as a source of events and the socket closed. We could keep one socket open for each host specified on the command line, but I chose to show how sources are removed. Once triggered, SocketInputCallback() puts the server's reply into the static text widget.

Figure 10-4 outlines these steps. Note that the initial client RPC is designed to return quickly with no data. The FRPC made by the server to return results to the client will come sometime in the future. In the meantime, the RPC client, your window, will already have readied the label on the button, poised to place another RPC on the next host. In this way this RPC client might not get FRPC results back in the same order in which it asked for them.

This is a standalone, socket-based client application. Compile and link it with the necessary Xt/Xol libraries, or use the Example 10-2 *makefile*.

```
rodson> cc -o Xt_sockets_AF_INET_client -I$OPENWINHOME/include \
Xt_sockets_AF_INET_client.c  -lX11 -L$OPENWINHOME/lib -lXt -lXol
```

It anticipates a synchronous service using TCP transport and Internet addressing registered at PORT. Use the *TCP_AF_INETserver.c* from Chapter 5.

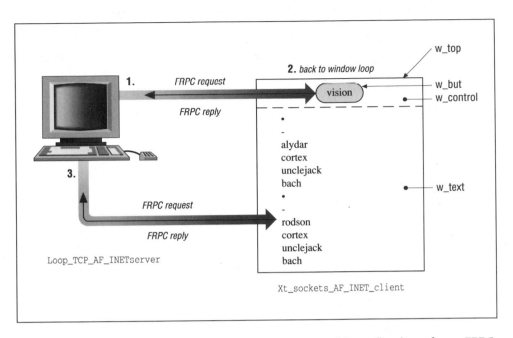

Figure 10-4. Asynchronous X client and server using XtAppAddInput() to listen for an FRPC

Example 10-8. Xt socket-based client, Internet addressing, and TCP transport:
Xt_sockets_AF_INET_client.c

```
#include <stdio.h>
#include <sys/types.h>
#include <sys/socket.h>
#include <sys/errno.h>
#include <netinet/in.h>
#include <netdb.h>
#include <X11/Xlib.h>
#include <X11/Intrinsic.h>
#include <X11/StringDefs.h>
#include <Xol/OpenLook.h>
#include <Xol/OblongButt.h>
#include <Xol/ControlAre.h>
#include <Xol/StaticText.h>

#define PORT        0x1234
#define DIRSIZE     8192

Arg             t_args[] = {
  {XtNstring, (XtArgVal) NULL},
  {XtNalignment, (XtArgVal) OL_LEFT},
};

Arg             b_args[] = {
  {XtNlabel, (XtArgVal) NULL},
};

extern int      errno;
Widget          w_top, w_text, w_control, w_but; /* need widgets outside */
```

Example 10-8. Xt socket-based client, Internet addressing, and TCP transport:
Xt_sockets_AF_INET_client.c (Continued)

```
XtAppContext      thisApp;
XtInputId         input_id;      /* keep one global extra input source around */
int               sockd;         /* it will be watching one socket */
int               hosts,
int               host_num = 0;

void
SocketInputCallback(clientData, source, id)
  caddr_t         clientData;    /* notice we just use to check socket # */
  int             *source;       /* tells us what socket it is */
  XtInputId       *id;           /* tells us which input source */
{
  char            dir[DIRSIZE];
  int             fromlen;
  char            **argv = (char **) clientData;

  if (*id != input_id || *source != sockd)
    XtAppError(thisApp, "unexpected input from who knows where");
  printf("request on input source %d callback\n", *id);

  /*
   * See comments in Chapter 5 regarding read() and recvfrom(), we'll use
   * the more general latter choice here.
   */
  if (recvfrom(*source, dir, DIRSIZE, 0, (struct sockaddr *) 0,
               &fromlen) == -1) {
    perror("recvfrom");
    XtAppError(thisApp, "slave input socket read");
  } else {
    XtSetArg(t_args[0], XtNstring, (XtArgVal) dir);
    XtSetValues(w_text, t_args, XtNumber(t_args));
  }

  /*
   * Remove the callback input or things go berserk - the descriptor
   * always appears to have input pending.  We're done with it, so
   * throw it away.
   */
  XtRemoveInput(input_id);
  (void) close(*source);

  /*
   * Set up for next server and return.
   */
  XtSetArg(b_args[0], XtNlabel, argv[(host_num++) % hosts + 2]);
  XtSetValues(w_but, b_args, XtNumber(b_args));
}

/*
 * Place an async remote request to a server.
 */
void
ButtCallback(widget, clientData, callData)
  Widget          widget;
  caddr_t         clientData, callData;
{
  char            **argv = (char **) clientData;
  struct sockaddr_in sin;
  struct sockaddr_in pin;
  struct hostent *hp;

  /*
   * Go find out about the desired host machine.
   */
```

Example 10-8. Xt socket-based client, Internet addressing, and TCP transport:
Xt_sockets_AF_INET_client.c (Continued)

```
  if ((hp = gethostbyname(argv[host_num % hosts + 2])) == 0) {
    perror("gethostbyname");
    XtAppError(thisApp, "gethostbyname");
  }
  /*
   * Fill in the socket structure with host information.
   */
  memset(&pin, 0, sizeof(pin));
  pin.sin_family = AF_INET;
  pin.sin_addr.s_addr = ((struct in_addr *) (hp->h_addr))->s_addr;
  pin.sin_port = htons(PORT);

  /*
   * Grab an Internet domain socket, TCP transport.
   */
  if ((sockd = socket(AF_INET, SOCK_STREAM, 0)) == -1) {
    perror("socket");
    XtAppError(thisApp, "socket");
  }
  /*
   * Connect to PORT on host.  We're not using /etc/services... or
   * any binding service here.
   */
  if (connect(sockd, &pin, sizeof(pin)) == -1) {
    perror("connect");
    XtAppError(thisApp, "connect");
  }
  /*
   * Send a message to the server PORT on machine HOST.
   */
  if (send(sockd, argv[1], strlen(argv[1]), 0) == -1) {
    perror("send");
    XtAppError(thisApp, "send");
  }
  /*
   * Unblock the socket - don't block when reading.
   */
  if (fcntl(sockd, F_SETFL, FNDELAY) == -1)
    XtAppError(thisApp, "unblocking socket");

  /*
   * Tell the widget to look at another source of events...
   */
  input_id = XtAppAddInput(thisApp,
                           sockd,
                           (caddr_t) XtInputReadMask,
                           SocketInputCallback,
                           (caddr_t) argv
      );
}

main(argc, argv)
  int            argc;
  char           **argv;
{

  w_top = OlInitialize(argv[0],
                       "HelloWorld",
                       NULL,
                       0,
                       &argc,
                       argv
      );
```

Example 10-8. Xt socket-based client, Internet addressing, and TCP transport:
Xt_sockets_AF_INET_client.c (Continued)

```
    /*
     * Create a control area and button to launch remote requests with.
     */
    w_control = XtCreateManagedWidget( "control",
                                       controlAreaWidgetClass,
                                       w_top,
                                       NULL,
                                       0
    );
    hosts = argc - 2;
    host_num = 0;
    XtSetArg(b_args[0], XtNlabel, argv[host_num + 2]);
    w_but = XtCreateManagedWidget("button",
                                  oblongButtonWidgetClass,
                                  w_control,
                                  b_args,
                                  XtNumber(b_args)
    );
    XtAddCallback(w_but, XtNselect, ButtCallback, argv);

    /*
     * Create a text window to spew results into.
     */
    XtSetArg(t_args[0], XtNstring, (XtArgVal) argv[0]);
    w_text = XtCreateManagedWidget("StaticText",
                                   staticTextWidgetClass,
                                   w_control,
                                   t_args,
                                   XtNumber(t_args)
    );

    XtRealizeWidget(w_top);
    thisApp = XtWidgetToApplicationContext(w_top);

    XtMainLoop();
}
```

In Example 10-9, we have modified the TCP_AF_INETserver. As originally
designed, it exits after replying once. We need to NULL-out the internal dir variable and loop-back up to the point where the socket is created by accept.

Example 10-9. TCP_AF_INETserver.c modified for repeated use:
Loop_TCP_AF_INET_server.c

```
#include <stdio.h>
#include <sys/types.h>
#include <sys/socket.h>
#include <netinet/in.h>
#include <netdb.h>

#define PORT            0x1234
#define DIRSIZE         8192

main()
{
        char    dir[DIRSIZE];   /* used for incoming dir name, and
                                 * outgoing data */
        int     sd, sd_current, cc, fromlen, tolen;
        int     addrlen;
        struct  sockaddr_in sin;
        struct  sockaddr_in pin;
```

Example 10-9. TCP_AF_INETserver.c modified for repeated use:
Loop_TCP_AF_INET_server.c (Continued)

```
          /* get an Internet domain socket */
          if ((sd = socket(AF_INET, SOCK_STREAM, 0)) == -1) {
                  perror("socket");
                  exit(1);
          }

          /* complete the socket structure */
          memset(&sin, 0, sizeof(sin));
          sin.sin_family = AF_INET;
          sin.sin_addr.s_addr = INADDR_ANY;
          sin.sin_port = htons(PORT);

          /* bind the socket to the port number */
          if (bind(sd, &sin, sizeof(sin)) == -1) {
                  perror("bind");
                  exit(1);
          }

          /* show that we are willing to listen */
          if (listen(sd, 5) == -1) {
                  perror("listen");
                  exit(1);
          }
again:
          /* wait for a client to talk to us */
          if ((sd_current = accept(sd, &pin, &addrlen)) == -1) {
                  perror("accept");
                  exit(1);
          }

          /* get a message from the client - note must now clear dir */
          bzero(dir, sizeof(dir));/* CHANGE */
          if (recv(sd_current, dir, sizeof(dir), 0) == -1) {
                  perror("recv");
                  exit(1);
          }

          /* get the directory contents */
          read_dir(dir);

          /* acknowledge the message, reply w/ the filenames */
          if (send(sd_current, dir, strlen(dir), 0) == -1) {
                  perror("send");
                  exit(1);
          }

          /* close up the one socket and continue */
          close(sd_current);
          goto again;   /* MINIMAL CHANGE: no prizes for neatness */
}
```

Start several servers, and then the client:

```
rodson> rsh -n hosta Loop_TCP_AF_INETserver &
...
rodson> rsh -n hostz Loop_TCP_AF_INETserver &
rodson> Xt_sockets_AF_INET_client directory hosta hostb ... hostz &
```

To send a request to a server, click the button. This steps through the hosts, sending a request to each of them. The `directory` listing results again show up in the window.

Remote Asynchronous Calls, Servers Using *XtAppAddInput()*

It's a lot easier to use low-level RPC calls to build a server than to use sockets directly. Not only that, but with RPC, you can use the portmap instead of /etc files or fixed PORT numbers.

Figure 10-5 illustrates the logic behind the server. You must use low-level RPC calls since the server handle and its socket information is required.

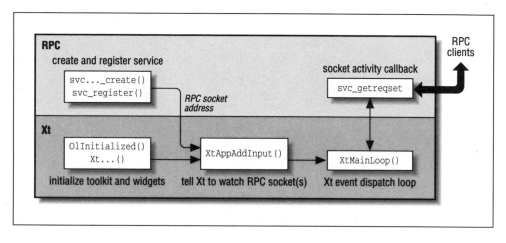

Figure 10-5. An RPC server using the Xt dispatch loop to replace svc_run()

After you use svcudp_create() and svc_register() to build a SVCXPRT and install a server, you can then register an Xt input callback function. It passes the socket associated with the SVCXPRT to XtAppAddInput(). In this way, the event dispatcher will look at the activity on this socket descriptor. Once the callback function gets invoked, you must then perform a svc_getreqset() and mimic the rest of the svc_run() steps. You look at the active file descriptor(s) and execute the registered RPC service routines.

In Example 10-10, we register only one dispatch routine. It's the same one we used in the previous XView application. We use the UDP transport here because the TCP transport complicates things. More on that in the next example.

Example 10-10. UDP transport RPC server activated by the Xt event dispatcher, using XtAppAddInput(): udpDispatchServer.c

```
#include <stdio.h>
#include <sys/types.h>
#include <X11/Xlib.h>
#include <X11/Intrinsic.h>
#include <Xol/OpenLook.h>
#include <Xol/ControlAre.h>
#include <rpc/rpc.h>
```

Example 10-10. UDP transport RPC server activated by the Xt event dispatcher, using
XtAppAddInput(): udpDispatchServer.c (Continued)

```c
#include "rls.h"

XtInputId       input_id;
SVCXPRT         *xprt;
XtAppContext    thisApp;

main(argc, argv)
  int           argc;
  char          *argv[];
{
  Widget        w_top, w_control;
  extern bool_t xdr_dir();
  extern char   *read_dir();
  extern void   dispatch();             /* the RPC server program -
                                         * does dispatching */
  static void   SocketInputCallback();  /* event dispatch routine */

  /*
   * Establish the server daemon.
   */
  (void) pmap_unset(DIRPROG, DIRVERS);
  xprt = svcudp_create(RPC_ANYSOCK);
  if (xprt == NULL) {
    (void) fprintf(stderr, "cannot create udp service.\n");
    exit(1);
  }
  if (!svc_register(xprt, DIRPROG, DIRVERS, dispatch, IPPROTO_UDP)) {
    (void) fprintf(stderr,
                "unable to register (DIRPROG, DIRVERS, udp).\n");
    exit(1);
  }
  /*
   * Build-up a minimal widget - though we won't be interacting w/ the
   * windows, we must manage some widgets.
   */
  w_top = OlInitialize(argv[0],
                    "rls server",
                    NULL,
                    0,
                    &argc,
                    argv
  );
  w_control = XtCreateManagedWidget("control",
                                controlAreaWidgetClass,
                                w_top,
                                NULL,
                                0
  );

  XtRealizeWidget(w_top);
  thisApp = XtWidgetToApplicationContext(w_top);

  /*
   * Before starting the dispatch loop, tell it to look at the server socket
   * information in fd_set to notify us of RPC requests.
   */
  input_id = XtAppAddInput(thisApp,
                        xprt->xp_sock,
                        (caddr_t) XtInputReadMask,
                        SocketInputCallback,
                        (caddr_t) NULL
  );

  /* loops continuously */
```

Example 10-10. UDP transport RPC server activated by the Xt event dispatcher, using
XtAppAddInput(): udpDispatchServer.c (Continued)

```
    XtMainLoop();
}

static void
SocketInputCallback(clientData, source, id)
    caddr_t         clientData;
    int             *source;
    XtInputId       *id;
{
    fd_set          readfds;

    if (*id != input_id || *source != xprt->xp_sock)
      XtAppError(thisApp, "unexpected input from who knows where");
    printf("request on input source %d callback\n", *id);

    readfds = svc_fdset;
    svc_getreqset(&readfds);        /* calls the dispatcher */
}
```

The `SocketInputCallback()` routine is greatly simplified over the socket-
based server approach. We only have the one descriptor for the single server kept
in `svc_fdset`. It must have changed status or we wouldn't have gotten into the
`SocketInputCallback()` callback routine. In this way we didn't call
`select()` first to sort-out the "ready-for-read" sockets from the rest. If you've got
multiple RPC registrants and sockets (or are using TCP), you'll need to add a
`select()` prior to `svc_getreqset()` (see Example 10-4). Put this UDP server
together with the dispatcher, `read_dir()`, and XDR objects, using the Xt and Xol
libraries:

```
    rodson> cc -o udpDispatchServer -I$OPENWINHOME/include -g \
    udpDispatchServer.c  -lX11 -L$OPENWINHOME/lib -lXt -lXol \
    rls_xdr.o read_dir.o dispatch.o
```

The difficulty when you choose to use the reliable TCP transport is that the socket
descriptor source that you register with the `XtAppAddInput()` routine does not
receive any traffic. That's the nature of the protocol. As in the Internet TCP socket-
level servers, they create a socket after the `accept()` succeeds. In this way, you
must register the primary socket with the Intrinsics' read routine, and once the
condition is met and the input callback invoked, you must look at all the file
descriptors RPC knows about. These are kept in `svc_fdset`.

Example 10-11 registers the primary TCP socket from a `svctcp_create()` with
`XtAppAddInput(3Xt)`. The same dispatch routine as above is registered with
RPC. Once the input event occurs and `SocketInputCallback()` is invoked, we
use `select()` and `svc_getreqset()` to service any and all requests made as
recorded in `svc_fdset`. Note that the `select()` time-out is greater than 0; that
gives `svc_fdset` time to change in response to newly created socket descriptors.
These are the sockets that actually get the traffic. When no more activity is found
within the time-out window, the application goes back into the event dispatch

loop. What saves us here is that `svc_getreqset()` when called on an inactive socket returns immediately, without invoking the registered dispatcher.

Example 10-11. TCP transport with XtAppAddInput is more complex: tcpDispatchServer.c

```
#include <stdio.h>
#include <sys/errno.h>
#include <sys/types.h>
#include <X11/Xlib.h>
#include <X11/Intrinsic.h>
#include <Xol/OpenLook.h>
#include <Xol/ControlAre.h>
#include <rpc/rpc.h>
#include "rls.h"

XtInputId       input_id;
SVCXPRT         *xprt;
XtAppContext    thisApp;
struct timeval  timeout;
int             ts;

main(argc, argv)
   int             argc;
   char            *argv[];
{
   Widget          w_top, w_control;
   extern bool_t   xdr_dir();
   extern char     *read_dir();
   extern void     dispatch();          /* the RPC server program -
                                         * does dispatching */
   static void     SocketInputCallback();  /* event dispatch routine */

   /*
    * Establish the server daemon.
    */
   (void) pmap_unset(DIRPROG, DIRVERS);
   xprt = svctcp_create(RPC_ANYSOCK, 0, 0);
   if (xprt == NULL) {
     (void) fprintf(stderr, "cannot create tcp service.\n");
     exit(1);
   }
   if (!svc_register(xprt, DIRPROG, DIRVERS, dispatch, IPPROTO_TCP)) {
     (void) fprintf(stderr,
                    "unable to register (DIRPROG, DIRVERS, tcp).\n");
     exit(1);
   }
   timeout.tv_sec = timeout.tv_usec = 1; /* give select time... */
   ts = getdtablesize();          /* file descriptor table size */

   /*
    * Build-up a minimal widget - though we won't be interacting w/ the
    * windows, we must manage some widgets.
    */
   w_top = OlInitialize(argv[0],
                        "rls server",
                        NULL,
                        0,
                        &argc,
                        argv
        );
   w_control = XtCreateManagedWidget("control",
                                     controlAreaWidgetClass,
                                     w_top,
                                     NULL,
                                     0
```

Example 10-11. TCP transport with XtAppAddInput is more complex: tcpDispatchServer.c (Continued)

```
     );

  YtRealizeWidget(w_top);
  thisApp = XtWidgetToApplicationContext(w_top);

  /*
   * Before starting the dispatch loop, tell it to look at the server socket
   * information in fd_set to notify us of RPC requests.
   */
  input_id = XtAppAddInput(thisApp,
                           xprt->xp_sock,
                           (caddr_t) XtInputReadMask,
                           SocketInputCallback,
                           (caddr_t) NULL
  );

  /* loops continuously */
  XtMainLoop();
}

static void
SocketInputCallback(clientData, source, id)
  caddr_t        clientData;
  int            *source;
  XtInputId      *id;
{
  fd_set         readfds;
  extern int     errno;

  if (*id != input_id || *source != xprt->xp_sock)
    XtAppError(thisApp, "unexpected input from who knows where");
  printf("request on input source %d callback\n", *id);

  readfds = svc_fdset;
  switch (select(ts, &readfds, (int *) 0, (int *) 0, &timeout)) {
  case -1:
    if (errno == EINTR)
      break;
    perror("my svc_run: - select failed");
    break;                            /* leave beat server marked as busy */
  case 0:
    break;
  default:
    /*
     * Calls the dispatcher - first time it's the inactive TCP descriptor.
     * Check for the active TCP descriptors that show-up in svc_fdset.
     */
    while (select(ts, &readfds, (int *) 0, (int *) 0, &timeout) != 0) {
      svc_getreqset(&readfds);  /* calls the dispatcher */
      readfds = svc_fdset;
    }
  }
}
```

Put this server together with:

```
rodson> cc -o tcpDispatchServer -I/$OPENWINHOME/include \
tcpDispatchServer.c  -lX11 -L$OPENWINHOME/lib -lXt -lXol \
rls_xdr.o read_dir.o dispatch.o
```

Of course, you need to run a compatible RPC client application that uses the TCP transport. Example 10-12 contains a version of the original synchronous

Example 4-5 `rls.c`, modified to use TCP. Note that ONC RPC does not include a TCP equivalent to `callrpc()` used for UDP. You must build up client handles first with `clnt_create()`, then use `clnt_call()` to place the RPC.

Example 10-12. Synchronous remote directory listing client using TCP transport: tcpRls.c

```
#include <stdio.h>
#include <strings.h>
#include <rpc/rpc.h>
#include "rls.h"

main(argc, argv)
    int             argc;
    char            *argv[];
{
    char            dir[DIR_SIZE];

    /* call the remote procedure if registered */
    strcpy(dir, argv[2]);
    read_dir(argv[1], dir);         /* read_dir(host, directory) */
    /* Spew out the results and bail out of here! */
    printf("%s\n", dir);
    exit(0);
}

read_dir(host, dir)
    char            *dir, *host;
{
    extern bool_t   xdr_dir();
    enum clnt_stat  clnt_stat;
    static struct timeval TIMEOUT = {25, 0};
    CLIENT          *clnt;

    clnt = clnt_create(host, DIRPROG, DIRVERS, "tcp");
    clnt_stat = clnt_call(clnt, READDIR,
                        xdr_dir, dir, xdr_dir, dir, TIMEOUT);
    if (clnt_stat != 0) clnt_perrno(clnt_stat);
    clnt_destroy(clnt);
}
```

We could just as easily have altered the high-level remote directory listing client compiled with RPCGEN in Chapter 4, first manually opening a TCP-transport client handle.

Comparing Network Windowing Systems and RPC

In the future, several major windowing system developers plan to migrate towards RPC-based implementations, thereby alleviating much of the redundancy between low-level network windowing and RPC processing. It's a simple fact that RPC is the backbone of many distributed, networked system applications, so why not build on it?

Oftentimes the memory- and compute-intensive nature of a network window system is not required. Many embedded applications won't need RPC-like function-ality to work across a network. For better performance, it's often worth sticking with your old typical windowing system, and adding RPCs underneath to perform necessary network functions. That was the approach taken in using SunView for the RIP networked image processing application developed in Chapter 6.

A Digression: Performance of Typical versus Network Windowing Systems

The typical window system (e.g., Microsoft Windows, Presentation Manager, and SunView) is physically or logically part of the operating system (O/S). The X Window System is independent of the O/S, and can be distributed. The display server must be run locally, but the peer-level client window manager, as well as any application, can run remotely. This is all by virtue of the underlying IPC-based network protocol.

A hardware-specific protocol like that of SunView is not necessarily bad, however. Most people think that since typical windowing systems are part of the O/S, graphic applications must run on the same machine—i.e., share the same kernel. It is true that a network protocol like X has several advantages, but you pay for it in performance. X11 has turned my 10 MIP machine into what looks like a 5 MIP machine when doing graphics or image-intensive functions. Whether it can be attributed to the extra baggage associated with network protocol, its object-oriented nature, or its outrageous consumption of memory when loaded (lots of shared libraries, too), the fact remains that it is slower then typical windowing systems.

I submit that to some first-order approximation, the equivalent to a typical windowing system must always be run locally. It is the only thing that has enough low-level knowledge to perform user I/O (including display, mouse, keyboard, and network driving). It's analogous to the X display server. The window manager functions (part of typical windowing systems, logically remote from the X display server) cut down overhead when closely coupled with window system functions. In addition, low-level hardware access is often required in the application. Frame buffer access is extremely painful with X.

Windowing System Evolution Can Hide a Frame Buffer

One example of abstraction being harmful stands out in my mind. X11 provides a number of Xlib routines for creating, destroying, and manipulating X drawables (Pixmaps, on and off screen, and XImages). Pixmaps (arrays of pixel values) exist at the display server. XImages are more elaborate structures, used to express images across the network between client and server in a machine-independent fashion. For this reason XImages must support all possible target representations. So to move pixel data across the network and a into frame buffer, it's a two-step process from XImage to Pixmap.

X11 Pixmaps, unlike their SunView equivalent Pixrects, do not specify an address that points to the raw pixel data. To write remotely-gathered data to a SunView window, it's as easy as computing the offsets and filling in the data yourself; then you refresh the window and it is visible. The fastest equivalent approach with X11 is to pass opaque data through an `XImage` to a `Pixmap` for display. Because you are unable to write images to the frame buffer `Pixmap` directly from the client application, the data has to be buffered an additional time, causing the performance to be slower than that of SunView.

The X11 approach is illustrated in gory detail in the code for the network-parallel ray tracer in Appendix B. See in particular the client routine. The last section of Chapter 6 discusses in more detail the issues of fast pixel access in SunView. The client presented in that chapter uses fast, low-level frame-buffer access to fill a SunView window.

X11 Pixmaps versus SunView Pixrects

Example 10-13 illustrates a number of important aspects of X when using images of pixel values. Hopefully, it is also moderately useful. `xwload` is a simple X11 application that makes use of both Xlib and XView libraries to load a Sun `rasterfile(5)` format image into a window. The Xlib routines were necessary to get fast low-level streams going. The utility routines for doing rasterfile format I/O are presented later. The `rasterfile` format image to be read is specified on the command line. An XView window is opened, the image is read in and the display server copies the data to the window.

Example 10-13. X client loads a Sun rasterfile(5) format image into a window: xwload.c

```
/*
 * A sample X11/XView program that stuffs Sun rasterfile format images into
 * an XView canvas window.  It uses X11 XImages and Pixmaps.
 */
#include <stdio.h>
#include <X11/X.h>
#include <X11/Xlib.h>
#include <XView/XView.h>
#include <XView/canvas.h>
#include <XView/cms.h>
#include "raster.h"
#define error(a) {fprintf(stderr, "Usage: %s rasterfile\n", a); exit(-1);}

/*
 * X11 and XView stuff
 */
Frame           frame;
Canvas          canvas;
Xv_cmsdata      cms_data;
Cms             cms;
int             scrn;
XImage          *ximage;
Pixmap          pixmap;
GC              gc;
XGCValues       gcvalues;
unsigned long   gcmask;
Display         *dpy;

/*
 * My own pixel I/O stuff, see "raster.h" and "raster.c" below.
```

*Example 10-13. X client loads a Sun rasterfile(5) format image into a window: xwload.c
(Continued)*

```
 */
u_char          *d;
colormap_t       cm;
rasterfile       rast;
FILE            *fp;

/*
 * We'll use some Xlib stuff to get the pixels (a Pixmap) out.  This
 * gets called first thing, so it will effectively fill the window.
 */
void
repaint_proc(canvas, paint_window, dpy, win)
  Canvas          canvas;
  Xv_Window       paint_window; /* not used */
  Display        *dpy;
  Window          win;
{
  XCopyArea(dpy, pixmap, win, gc, 0, 0, rast.ras_width, rast.ras_height, 0, 0);
}

main(argc, argv)
  int             argc;
  char           *argv[];
{
  int             x, y;
  /*
   * Take a look at and modify the command line if necessary, then read-in
   * input image to size things up.
   */
  xv_init(XV_INIT_ARGC_PTR_ARGV, &argc, argv, NULL);
  if (argc != 2)
    error(argv[0]);
  fp = fopen(argv[1], "r");
  if (!fp || !(d = (u_char *) ReadRasterfile(fp, cm, rast)))
    perror("can't read rasterfile\n");

  /*
   * Build and install a ramp color table if the image doesn't have one.
   */
  cms_data.type = XV_DYNAMIC_CMS;
  cms_data.index = 0;

  if (cm.type == RMT_NONE) {
    unsigned char   grey[256];
    cms_data.size = cms_data.rgb_count = 256;
    for (x = 0; x < 256; x++)
      grey[x] = (unsigned char) x;
    cms_data.red = cms_data.green = cms_data.blue = grey;
  } else {
    cms_data.size = cms_data.rgb_count = cm.length;
    cms_data.red = cm.map[0];
    cms_data.green = cm.map[1];
    cms_data.blue = cm.map[2];
  }

  /*
   * Establish a window w/ a repaint procedure.
   */
  frame = (Frame) xv_create(NULL, FRAME,
                            FRAME_LABEL, argv[1],
                            FRAME_SHOW_FOOTER, TRUE,
                            NULL);
  canvas = (Canvas) xv_create(frame, CANVAS,
                              WIN_WIDTH, rast.ras_width,
```

Example 10-13. X client loads a Sun rasterfile(5) format image into a window: xwload.c (Continued)

```
                              WIN_HEIGHT, rast.ras_height,
                              CANVAS_WIDTH, rast.ras_width,
                              CANVAS_HEIGHT, rast.ras_height,
   /* Don't retain window -- we'll repaint it all the time. */
                              CANVAS_RETAINED, FALSE,
   /* We're using Xlib graphics calls in repaint_proc(). */
                              CANVAS_X_PAINT_WINDOW, TRUE,
                              CANVAS_REPAINT_PROC, repaint_proc,
                              OPENWIN_AUTO_CLEAR, FALSE,
                              WIN_DYNAMIC_VISUAL, TRUE,
                              WIN_CMS_NAME, "XisBrainDead",
                              WIN_CMS_DATA, &cms_data,
                              NULL);
   window_fit(frame);

   /*
    * All I want to do is stream some client pixels into a server window.
    * This client application as well as the server and window manager are
    * all local in my case.  This kind of thing is easy w/ low-level
    * windowing systems.
    * First I must create an XImage out of the raw pixel data.
    * XImages have LOTS of extra baggage, as they are designed for
    * X11 client use - then passed to server w/ XPutImage().  Pixmaps live at
    * the display server, and have little penalty associated w/ them.  I
    * could use the pixmap data formatting routines in Xlib, but I'm
    * assuming the application wants to work with pixel addresses.
    */
   dpy = (Display *) xv_get(canvas, XV_DISPLAY);
   scrn = DefaultScreen(dpy);
   ximage = XCreateImage(dpy, DefaultVisual(dpy, scrn),
                         rast.ras_depth, ZPixmap, 0, d,
                         rast.ras_width, rast.ras_height, 8, rast.ras_width);

   /*
    * ... Next create a pixmap and the associated graphics context GC ...
    */
   pixmap = XCreatePixmap(dpy, DefaultRootWindow(dpy),
                          rast.ras_width, rast.ras_height, rast.ras_depth);

   gcvalues.function = GXcopy;
   gcmask |= GCFunction;
   gcvalues.plane_mask = AllPlanes;
   gcmask |= GCPlaneMask;
   gcvalues.foreground = 1;
   gcmask |= GCForeground;
   gcvalues.background = 0;
   gcmask |= GCBackground;
   gcvalues.graphics_exposures = False;
   gcvalues.background = WhitePixel(dpy, DefaultScreen(dpy));
   gcvalues.foreground = BlackPixel(dpy, DefaultScreen(dpy));
   gc = XCreateGC(dpy, DefaultRootWindow(dpy), gcmask, &gcvalues);

   /*
    * ... Now get the image over here!  This is slow - should keep it local!
    */
   XPutImage(dpy, pixmap, gc, ximage, 0, 0, 0, 0,
             rast.ras_width, rast.ras_height);
   XDestroyImage(ximage);

   /*
    * Good nite!
    */
   xv_main_loop(frame);
}
```

`XImages` are equivalent to building pixel arrays on an RPC server, then sending them across through XDR routines to take care of any format incompatibilities, e.g., byte swapping. If the network interface is not required, the use of X protocol IPCs or RPCs can be eliminated and speeds things up. To read the data in, more than likely you are using some form of distributed file system layered on top of RPC anyway, so why do it again? One way to resolve the problem is to make available the memory address to Pixmaps. X image processing toolkits are coming out that may help resolve these problems. Nevertheless, let's compare performance with SunView.

In SunView, pixrects are rectangular arrays of pixel values, along with other header or descriptive information. `Pixwins` are a layer on top of `Pixrects` that, in effect, put a `Pixrect` behind a visible window. In Example 10-14, I use plain `Pixrect` and `Pixwin` operations on the local machine to move pixels around, accomplishing the same thing as Example 10-13. Note that the memory address of a `Pixrect` is readily available. A visible (versus memory) `Pixrect` of a `Pixwin` is updated when `pw_write()` is called.

Example 10-14. Load a Sun rasterfile(5) format image into a SunView window: wload.c

```
#include <stdio.h>
#include <pixrect/pixrect_hs.h>
#include <suntool/sunview.h>
#include <suntool/canvas.h>
#define error(a) {fprintf(stderr, "Usage: %s rasterfile\n", a); exit(-1);}

void            MouseCaught();
Pixwin          *pw;
colormap_t      cm;
struct rasterfile rast;
FILE            *fp;
Pixrect         *pr_src;
u_char          *d;


main(argc, argv)
    int         argc;
    char        **argv;
{
    Frame           frame;
    Canvas          canvas;
    register int    i;

    /* read the source rasterfile */
    if (argc != 2)
        error(argv[0]);
    fp = fopen(argv[1], "r");
    if (!fp || !(d = (u_char *) ReadSunRaster(fp, &cm, &rast)))
        perror("can't read rasterfile\n");

    /* create frame and canvas */
    frame = window_create(NULL, FRAME,
                        FRAME_LABEL, argv[1],
                        0);
    canvas = window_create(frame, CANVAS,
                        WIN_HEIGHT, rast.ras_height,
                        WIN_WIDTH, rast.ras_width,
                        WIN_EVENT_PROC, MouseCaught,    /* kill window */
```

Example 10-14. Load a Sun rasterfile(5) format image into a SunView window: wload.c
(Continued)

```
                              0);
    window_fit(frame);

    /* get the canvas pixwin to draw into */
    pw = canvas_pixwin(canvas);


    /* build and install a ramp color table if the image doesn't have one */
    if (cm.type == RMT_NONE) {
      unsigned char    grey[256];
      for (i = 0; i < 256; i++)
        grey[i] = (unsigned char) i;
      pw_setcmsname(pw, "original");
      pw_putcolormap(pw, 0, 256, grey, grey, grey);
    } else {
      pw_setcmsname(pw, "original");
      pw_putcolormap(pw, 0, cm.length,
                     cm.map[0], cm.map[1], cm.map[2]);
    }

    /* load the image to the pw manually */
    pr_src = mem_point(rast.ras_width, rast.ras_height, rast.ras_depth,
                       (short *) d);
    pw_write(pw, 0, 0, rast.ras_width, rast.ras_height, PIX_SRC, pr_src, 0, 0);
    pr_destroy(pr_src);

    /* loop till dead */
    window_main_loop(frame);
}

void
MouseCaught(canvas, event, arg)
    Canvas          canvas;
    Event           *event;
    caddr_t         arg;
{
    if (event_action(event) == MS_RIGHT) {
      exit(0);
    }
}
```

Compile the two applications:

```
rodson> make raster.o
rodson> cc -o xwload -I$OPENWINHOME/include xwload.c raster.o \
-lX11 -L/home/cortex/software/openwin2.0/lib -lXView
```

and

```
rodson> cc -o wload wload.c raster.o -lpixrect -lsuntool -lsunwindow
```

The support routines in Example 10-15 are required to read and write the `raster-file(5)` file format. I used the same I/O routines in both examples to assure that

the performance comparison would document only the extra X network operations
that were required.

Example 10-15. Sun rasterfile format utilities: raster.c

```
#include <stdio.h>
#include "raster.h"

char            *
ReadSunRaster(fp, pColormap, pRast)
   FILE          *fp;
   colormap_t    *pColormap;
   rasterfile    *pRast;
{
   int            pixels;
   char          *pImage;

   if (fread(pRast, 1, sizeof(rasterfile), fp)
       != sizeof(rasterfile))
     fprintf(stderr, "ReadSunRaster: Error reading raster header\n");
   if (pRast->ras_type != RT_STANDARD)
     fprintf(stderr, "ReadSunRaster: not an RT_STANDARD rasterfile\n");
   pColormap = (colormap_t *) malloc(sizeof(colormap_t));
   if (fread(pColormap, 1, pRast->ras_maplength, fp)
       != pRast->ras_maplength)
     fprintf(stderr, "ReadSunRaster: Error reading colormap\n");

   /* allocate room for and read in the image */
   pixels = pRast->ras_width * pRast->ras_height;
   switch (pRast->ras_depth) {
   case 8:
     break;
   case 16:
     pixels <<= 1;
   default:
     fprintf(stderr, "ReadSunRaster: image must be 8.or 16 deep\n");
   }
   pImage = (char *) malloc(pixels);
   if (fread(pImage, 1, pixels, fp) != pixels)
     free(pImage);
   if (!pImage)
     fprintf(stderr, "ReadSunRaster: no memory or bad read\n");

   return (pImage);
}

WriteSunRaster(fp, pColormap, pRast, pData)
   FILE          *fp;
   colormap_t    *pColormap;
   rasterfile    *pRast;
   char          *pData;
{
   int            pixels;

   if (fwrite(pRast, 1, sizeof(rasterfile), fp)
       != sizeof(rasterfile))
     fprintf(stderr, "WriteSunRaster: Error writing raster header\n");
   if (pRast->ras_type != RT_STANDARD)
     fprintf(stderr, "WriteSunRaster: not an RT_STANDARD rasterfile\n");

   /*
    * If we have a valid colormap, write it out, should
    * catch errors here!
    */
   if ((pRast->ras_maptype == RMT_NONE) && (!pRast->ras_maplength) && !pColormap)
   {
```

Example 10-15. Sun rasterfile format utilities: raster.c (Continued)

```
      if (fwrite(pColormap, 1, pRast->ras_maplength, fp)
          != pRast->ras_maplength)
        fprintf(stderr, "WriteSunRaster: Error writing colormap\n");
  }
  /* write-out image data */
  pixels = pRast->ras_width * pRast->ras_height;
  switch (pRast->ras_depth) {
  case 8:
    break;
  case 16:
    pixels <<= 1;
  default:
    fprintf(stderr, "WriteSunRaster: image must be 8 or 16 deep\n");
  }
  /*
   * if pData is NULL, assume we repeat 0's... useful for
   * some things...
   */
  if (pData) {
    if (fwrite(pData, 1, pixels, fp) != pixels)
      fprintf(stderr, "WriteSunRaster: bad write\n");
  } else
    while (pixels--)
      fputc((char) 0, fp);

  fflush(fp);
}
```

The include file *raster.h* is shown in Example 10-16. It is an abstracted version of
the `<pixrect/pixrect_hs.h>` SunView file under SunOS. It defines the
colormap and header information of the rasterfile format.

Example 10-16. Sun rasterfile format support: raster.h

```
/* define some image file format stuff (vestigial Sunview stuff) */
typedef struct colormap_t {
        int             type;
        int             length;
        unsigned char   *map[3];
} colormap_t;

typedef struct rasterfile {
        int     ras_magic;          /* magic number */
        int     ras_width;          /* width (pixels) of image */
        int     ras_height;         /* height (pixels) of image */
        int     ras_depth;          /* depth (1, 8, or 24 bits) of pixel */
        int     ras_length;         /* length (bytes) of image */
        int     ras_type;           /* type of file; see RT_* below */
        int     ras_maptype;        /* type of colormap; see RMT_* below */
        int     ras_maplength;      /* length (bytes) of following map */
        /* color map follows for ras_maplength bytes, followed by image */
} rasterfile;
#define RAS_MAGIC       0x59a66a95

        /* Sun supported ras_type's */
#define RT_OLD          0     /* Raw pixrect image in 68000 byte order */
#define RT_STANDARD     1     /* Raw pixrect image in 68000 byte order */
#define RT_BYTE_ENCODED 2     /* Run-length compression of bytes */
#define RT_FORMAT_RGB   3     /* XRGB or RGB instead of XBGR or BGR */
#define RT_FORMAT_TIFF  4     /* tiff <-> standard rasterfile */
#define RT_FORMAT_IFF   5     /* iff (TAAC format) <-> standard rasterfile */
#define RT_EXPERIMENTAL 0xffff  /* Reserved for testing */

        /* Sun registered ras_maptype's */
```

Example 10-16. Sun rasterfile format support: raster.h (Continued)

```
#define RMT_RAW          2      /* Sun supported ras_maptype's */
#define RMT_NONE         0      /* ras_maplength is expected to be 0 */
#define RMT_EQUAL_RGB    1      /* red[ras_maplength/3],green[],blue[] */

#define INITRAST(r, w, h) { \
  r.ras_magic = RAS_MAGIC; \
  r.ras_width = w; \
  r.ras_height = h; \
  r.ras_depth = 8; \
  r.ras_length = w*h; \
  r.ras_type = RT_STANDARD; \
  r.ras_maptype = RMT_NONE; \
  r.ras_maplength = 0; }
```

I timed the execution of both SunView and XView applications, reading the same size, uncompressed 1Kx1K, 8-bit deep rasterfiles. Each had a 768-byte color table included. By choosing unique files, and not repeating the commands, I was careful not to allow local caching on my SPARCstation 1+ to affect read times. The following are representative numbers:

```
time ./xwload image3.ras
0.6u 1.2s 0:04 42% 0+1408k 1+0io 1pf+0w
time ./xwload image0.ras
0.5u 1.2s 0:04 40% 0+1364k 0+0io 0pf+0w

time ./wload /image2.ras
0.8u 0.9s 0:02 80% 0+1452k 0+1io 0pf+0w
time ./wload image1.ras
0.8u 0.9s 0:02 80% 0+1412k 0+1io 0pf+0w
```

The XView application took twice as long to load the equivalent rasterfile through an Xlib XImage into a local Pixmap as did the SunView application to access the frame buffer through a `Pixrect` address.

Augment Typical Windowing Systems with RPCs

With all this in mind, if performance, not portability is your main goal, it may be beneficial to augment a typical (low-level) windowing system with RPCs to execute remote graphics applications. RPC does not have any windowing support, but it does provide a robust IPC and remote execution scheme that X does not.

In this chapter:
- *Maintains the ONC RPC Protocol*
- *Run-time Transport Independence*
- *TIRPC API*
- *Availability*

11

ONC Transport-independent RPC

A transport-independent RPC system provides a single, consistent programming interface across machines and network transport protocols.

A new version of RPC that supports transport independence now ships with AT&T's System V, Release 4 (SVR4). This version has been separately ported to SunOS as TIRPC but it will not be an integral part of SunOS until Solaris 2.0. TIRPC is compatible with the existing socket-based UDP + TCP version, RPCSRC 4.0, as long as your code makes no socket calls. It is freely licensed and its source and specifications are in the public domain.

TIRPC was produced without affecting the existing ONC RPC protocol, which was always transport independent. Because of that, ONC RPC applications can be run as is, and even recompiled under TIRPC.

ONC enhanced RPC to true transport independence to get the programmer above transport and low-level networking issues. Programmers wanted:

- Run-time transport independence. Transport selection should be driven by user preferences and client/server constraints.

- Uniform addressing. Addresses must be independent of transport, name binding, and resolution mechanisms.

- A transport-independent API. The client and server application code should not demand mention of transport.

Figure 11-1 illustrates the new TIRPC software structure. Your application code sits at the top. The interface to the RPC library looks much as it did but with many new procedures. Three new elements are added (in bold). You will typically call the topmost layer of the RPC Interface Library. Very rarely will you need to use the Network Selection (NS) library and almost never call the Name to Address Translation (N2A) modules.

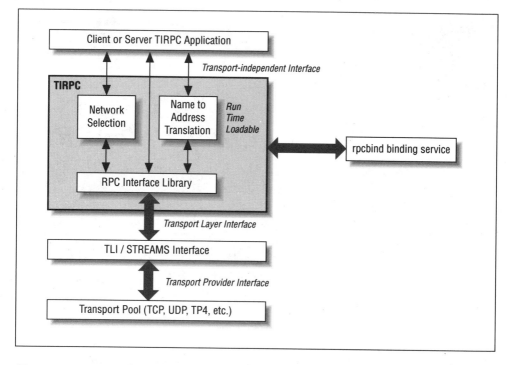

Figure 11-1. Layers of the TIRPC interface

Network selection facilitates run-time transport selection. Name-to-address translation provides universal addresses that are independent of the chosen transport. Thus, hostnames can be mapped to transport addresses. TLI/STREAMS provides the RPC library with a generic way to communicate with all transports.

The Portmapper portmap(8C) is replaced by rpcbind(8C) to provide a logical (versus IP and port number) interface. rpcbind makes a registry of RPC service addresses available to the network. RPC services do not need well-known transport addresses specific to a transport. As with portmap, clients consult the rpcbind server on remote hosts to find the addresses of specified servers.

Maintains the ONC RPC Protocol

The original ONC RPC protocol remains unchanged. The protocol was always independent of the underlying transport. With no call semantics built in, it adapts to any semantics implied by the transport. For example, if no reply is received when using an unreliable datagram transport like UDP, it's assumed a packet was lost, so after a time-out period, RPC retransmits the request for potential re-execution. No reply simply implies the remote procedure was executed zero or more times. If a reply is received from a reliable virtual-circuit transport (e.g., TCP) request, you know the remote procedure was executed once, while no reply means at most one execution.

Run-time Transport Independence

The original ONC RPC library supported only UDP and TCP transports (plus the single-process, memory-based Raw transport for testing). Transports may now be specified by the application, either by class or specific transport, potentially leaving the decision up to the user at run-time. A machine's available transports are now listed in */etc/netconfig*, and each user has the ability to reflect personal preferences via the NETPATH environment variable.

The */etc/netconfig* file specifies one transport per line, identifying each of the following:

```
netid
type
flags
family
protocol
device address
loadable module
```

A few sample entries in the file are:

```
udp    tpi_clts       v    inet    udp    /dev/udp    /usr/lib/tcpip.so
tcp    tpi_cots_or    d    vinet   tcp    /dev/tcp    /usr/lib/tcpip.so
tp4    tpi_cots       v    osi     -      /dev/tp4    /usr/lib/iso.so
```

Each transport is now known by netid. Type specifies whether the transport is connectionless, connection-oriented, or connection-oriented with orderly release. This is often a criterion for selecting a transport as it implies call semantics. flags specifies whether the transport is visible to applications. family and protocol allow additional transport selection mechanisms. device address specifies the name of the transport device. The loadable module specifies the name-to-address translation software the RPC library will use to perform name resolution. These must be dynamically loadable shared libraries. Multiple modules may be specified to allow multiple name-resolution attempts.

Network Selection

The ONC RPCSRC 4.0 `clnt_create()` interface has been enhanced. A `CLIENT` handle for the classes of choices listed in Table 11-1 may be requested through the assistance of the Network Selection module.

Table 11-1. Net Type Values and Transport Selection

Value	Description
VISIBLE	Use a transport from */etc/netconfig* regardless of the NETPATH environment variable.
CIRCUIT_V	Use a connection-oriented `VISIBLE` transport.
DATAGRAM_V	Use a connectionless `VISIBLE` transport.
NETPATH	If set, choose from among the transports specified by `NET-PATH` environment variable; otherwise `VISIBLE`.
CIRCUIT_N	Use a `NETPATH`, connection-oriented transport.
DATAGRAM_N	Use a `NETPATH`, connectionless transport.
udp	Use UDP, as it was in RPC 4.0.
tcp	Use TCP, as it was in RPC 4.0.

Uniform Addressing

The RPCSRC 4.0 release used the BSD sockets approach to networking. While sockets are predominantly transport-independent, they retain a degree of nonportability for transport addressing. To come up with a truly uniform addressing scheme, ONC could have added to the sockets interface or chosen the Transport Layer Interface (TLI) as found under AT&T's UNIX. They opted for the latter as uniform addressing is already built-in.

The concept of *well-known ports and IP addresses* should all but disappear. There are instead *universal addresses* that are string representations of a transport address. Transport-specific characteristics are hidden, as the mechanism for interpreting it is specific to the transport.

TIRPC API

The new library is a superset of the old. We shall discuss its compatibility with RPCSRC 4.0 and then abstract the library into a number of levels.

Backward Compatibility

Many routines have been added to the TI release but all the old interfaces remain for source compatibility reasons. The most significant changes you should make in programming involve the procedures listed in Table 11-2.

Table 11-2. The New Preferred Calls

Old RPC 4.0 Routines	TIRPC Routines
clnttcp_create(), clntudp_create()	clnt_tli_create()
svctcp_create(), svcudp_create()	svc_tli_create()
callrpc()	rpc_call()
registerrpc()	rpc_reg()
clnt_broadcast()	rpc_broadcast()

Caution: While the TIRPC release easily brings you up a level of abstraction, it disallows fiddling with sockets. Sockets are gone; replaced by TLI/STREAMS. While you may still use sockets on your transport, the addressing is different, making it difficult to find socket addresses and names. getsockname(3N) no longer works. In this fashion, many of the low-level windowing system or concurrency/asynchrony approaches developed in this book become unusable.

Levels of the Library

While the TIRPC API isn't that different, there are more levels of abstraction at which a programmer can work. We will present five levels, which we number from one to five, with one being the highest level. Obviously you should work at the highest level possible. Programming at a lower level is more verbose and error-prone but gives you the ability to control the network interface, often resulting in improved performance and functionality.

We will not mention the slightly altered functions in the areas of:

- Secure RPC, authentication.
- Direct XDR access through the xdr_...() functions.
- Enhanced interfaces to the default services including rstat(8C) and keyserv(8C).
- When using rpcbind(8C), direct calls are rarely required.

One: Simplified Interface

If you write code at this high level, you don't consider the characteristics of the transport, the operating system or other low-level implementation mechanisms.

Client and server communication handles are never even seen. The client specifies the server and procedure along with the type of transport and (hopefully) gets the results.

At the server:

- `rpc_reg(3N)` – Registers a procedure as an RPC service with a unique, system-wide procedure-identification number.

At the client:

- `rpc_call(3N)` – Uses the unique number (above) to make a remote call on a specified host.

- `rpc_broadcast(3N)` – Broadcasts a request across all networks of a specified type.

These replace `registerrpc()`, `callrpc()`, and `clnt_broadcast()` in RPCSRC 4.0, which impose a transport specification.

While this approach is lean, it is not advised for repeated calls because it hides the synchronous, resource-intensive client-and-server handle creation. It also requires the client (transparently) to call to the Network Selection. Without the ability to specify transport, a server could waste valuable resources listening on multiple transports.

Careful choice of the NETPATH variable, as shown in Table 11-1, can improve efficiency when using these calls.

Two: Middle Level

Moving to the next level down, the programmer still won't be concerned with transports, specifying only a general class of transports to use or `nettype` as with the simplified interface. We are back to generating client-and-server handles as with the lower-level RPCSRC 4.0 discussions of Chapter 4, but it is done specifying only transport type (`nettype`).

At the server:

- `svc_tp_create(3N)` – Creates a server handle for a specified transport, specifying the dispatch routine to be used for specific program/version number requests.

At the client:

- `clnt_tp_create(3N)` – Specify the server location and the transport type and get a generic client handle.

Client handle manipulation, remote procedure calling, and error reporting functions are similar if not identical to RPCSRC 4.0 at this level.

Three: Lower Level

At the next level down, the programmer deals with the specifics of transports. You need not go down to this level unless you need more control of clients and servers. At the server:

- `svc_tp_create(3N)` – Creates a server handle for a specified network, specifying the dispatch routine to be used for specific program/version number requests.

At the client:

- `clnt_tp_create(3N)` – Given the server hostname and the transport, creates a client handle.

The same client handle manipulation, remote procedure calling, and error reporting functions are used here as with the Middle Level.

Four: Lowest Level

This consists of a large number of procedures for specifying transport and controlling it more precisely.

At the server:

- `rpcb_set(3N)` – Calls `rpcbind` to establish a RPC service to network address mapping.

- `rpcb_unset(3N)` – Destroys a mapping.

- `svc_reg(3N)` – Associates a dispatch procedure with a given program and version number.

- `svc_unreg(3N)` – Destroys an association created by `svc_reg()`.

- `svc_tli_create(3N)` - Creates a server handle for a specified network, specifying the dispatch routine to be used for specific program/version number requests. It allows finer control of the client characteristics than `svc_tp_create()`.

At the client:

- `clnt_tli_create(3N)` – Given the server transport address and the transport, creates a client handle allowing fine control of the server characteristics. A `clnt_tp_create()` with more parameters.

- `rpcb_getaddr(3N)` – Given a transport, program, and version number, this instructs `rpcbind` to return the server address.

Five: Basement

Here's where you get full control of the interaction. The smallest details of the transport are controllable here.

At the server:

- `svc_dg_create(3N)` – For creation of server handles with a connectionless transport.

- `svc_vc_create(3N)` – Ditto for connection-oriented transports.

At the client:

- `clnt_dg_create(3N)` – For creation of connectionless transport client handles.

- `clnt_vc_create(3N)` – Ditto for connection-oriented transports.

An Example

In this section, we revise the `rtele` application developed in Chapter 1 for transport-independent RPC. I assume you have TIRPC installed under SunOS 4.1.x.

No changes need to be made to the existing protocol definition or service procedures to make them TIRPC-compatible. The new protocol compiler does most of the work. Minimal changes must be made to the client. I suggest you make a new directory and point links to the Chapter 9 *rtele.x* protocol and *rtele_svc_proc.c* service procedures. Copy over *rtele.c*. Pass the protocol definition through the *new* protocol compiler.

```
cortex> rpcgen.new rtele.x
```

This creates the enhanced client and server stubs. The service will by default register services with transports specified in the NETPATH environment variable. If NETPATH is undefined, the VISIBLE transports in */etc/netconfig* are used. In most cases this means udp and tcp.

Create the new server as before but with additional link libraries:

```
cortex> cc -DDEBUG -o rtele_svc rtele_svc_proc.c rtele_svc.c \
rtele_xdr.c -lrpc -ldl -lnsl
```

By using the `-DDEBUG` flag, the server runs in the foreground, otherwise TIRPC servers fork a child process and return.

You can augment the Chapter 1 `rtele.c` `clnt_create()` call to reflect use of run-time transport selection. Let's assume you want a connection-oriented tcp session. In *rtele.c* replace:

```
cl = clnt_create(argv[1], RTELEPROG, RTELEVERS, "tcp");
```

with:

```
cl = clnt_create(argv[1], RTELEPROG, RTELEVERS, "netpath");
```

or:

```
cl = clnt_create(argv[1], RTELEPROG, RTELEVERS, "circuit_n");
```

Make sure the NETPATH variable reflects the tcp preference (e.g., set NETPATH tcp:udp). NETPATH elements are each looked at, in order. To communicate, a client and server must have the same transport named in their NETPATH or have compatible defaults if the variable is undefined.

To force the use of tcp, leave the line:

```
cl = clnt_create(argv[1], RTELEPROG, RTELEVERS, "tcp");
```

as it is, or replace it with:

```
cl = clnt_create(argv[1], RTELEPROG, RTELEVERS, "visible");
```

or:

```
cl = clnt_create(argv[1], RTELEPROG, RTELEVERS, "circuit_v");
```

The latter form requires that the server use the tcp transport. The server should be started with NETPATH including tcp or undefined. You could force the use of udp in a similar fashion.

Compile the client as before, including the extra link libraries:

```
cortex> cc -o rtele rtele.c rtele_clnt.c rtele_xdr.o \
-lrpc -ldl -lnsl
```

The server and client will behave essentially as they did in Chapter 9, with sensitivity to the NETPATH variable. For example, if the client were compiled using netpath and you specify no environment variable, you get the following:

```
cortex> unsetenv NETPATH
cortex> rtele_svc &
[1] 2924
cortex> rtele cortex BLOOMER
name            location extension
JOHN J BLOOMER   KW C317  6964
```

Specify a particular transport use as follows:

```
cortex> kill %1
[1]    Terminated            rtele_svc
cortex> setenv NETPATH tcp
cortex> rtele_svc &
[1] 2930
cortex> rtele cortex BLOOMER
name            location extension
JOHN J BLOOMER   KW C317  6964
```

You'll get an error by constraining transport use to something not available:

```
cortex> setenv NETPATH udp
cortex> !rt
```

```
rtele cortex BLOOMER
cortex: RPC: Program unavailable
```

To automate the make procedure, you might use a *makefile* that looks like this:

```
# assumes "rpcgen" now accesses either the TI-RPC protocol compiler
# rpcgen or rpcgen.new (feature-filled successor).
LFLAGS = -lrpc -ldl -lnsl # comment out LFLAGS in ../../makefile
include ../../makefile    # the old chapter 4 makefile template
```

Availability

The availability and continued backward compatibility of ONC source makes it a good candidate for long-term distributed processing. Sun's freely licensed implementation of TIRPC is now available as source code via anonymous ftp from uunet.uu.net in the */networking* directory as a compressed tar file *tirpcsrc.tar.Z*. This implementation of TIRPC is compatible with SunOS 4.1 *only*, and requires root privileges and optional software for installation.

To use anonymous FTP, use the ftp program to connect to uunet.uu.net. When prompted for a username, enter anonymous. When prompted for a password, enter your user ID. Then change directory (cd) to networking where you will find *tirpcsrc.tar.Z*. In binary transfer mode, up-load the file with get. You may then place the file above some target file space and uncompress and extract the files with a command like zcat tirpcsrc.tar.Z | tar xf -.

Advanced Programming Issues

In this chapter:
- *Authentication
  and How to Use It*
- *Error Reporting
  Summarized*
- *Fault Tolerance,
  Connection Errors,
  and Crash Recov-
  ery*

This chapter covers several advanced programming topics: authentication, error reporting and fault tolerance. Authentication is important for a secure network. Proper error reporting is necessary to detect problems with an application. Fault tolerance includes recovering from lost connections and other client or server failures. These topics are presented along with error reporting.

Authentication and How to Use It

Authentication is essential when implementing any kind of security scheme. Authentication is comprised of two elements: credentials and verifiers. Credentials are a statement of your identity. An example is the text portion of your driver's license. The picture provides the verification that you are (or aren't) who you say you are. Most authentication schemes in RPC are relatively easy to break through. This chapter describes DES authentication, which is the most secure type currently available for RPC. We will not fully explore the power of the ONC RPC secure authentication system or API here.

In Chapter 7, our distributed image manager, dim, allowed any user to add, delete, extract, or list the archive. Any user can also restart or terminate the server. We need to check the identity of the users, rejecting certain actions by unauthorized users. The authentication mechanism within ONC RPC provide a means for you to build up such an access control strategy.

Before we delve into the details of how the client and server applications must be changed, there are some ONC RPC data structures and techniques you should become familiar with. If you are more interested in the high-level issues, skip over the sections within "ONC RPC Credentials and Verification at the Client" and "Authentication at the Server" that detail the changes made to the dim application. You can go back and read them later when you get stuck.

ONC RPC Credentials and Verification at the Client

Authentication data structures were designed to be opaque to client applications. Nevertheless, you will eventually need to know what they are.

The AUTH handle as found within each CLIENT handle as cl_auth completely describes the authenticator:

```
     typedef struct {
-->      AUTH     *cl_auth;                        /* authenticator */
         struct clnt_ops {
                 enum clnt_stat  (*cl_call)();  /* call remote procedure */
                 void            (*cl_abort)();    /* abort a call */
                 void            (*cl_geterr)();   /* get specific error code */
                 bool_t          (*cl_freeres)();  /* frees results */
                 void            (*cl_destroy)();  /* destroy this structure */
                 bool_t          (*cl_control)();  /* the ioctl() of rpc */
         } *cl_ops;
         caddr_t         cl_private;           /* private stuff */
         char            *cl_netid;            /* network token */
         char            *cl_tp;               /* device name */
     } CLIENT;
```

The AUTH structure can be opaque to the client, with values established solely through library routines:

```
     typedef struct {
             struct  opaque_auth     ah_cred; /* client credentials */
             struct  opaque_auth     ah_verf; /* associated verification */
             union   des_block       ah_key;
             struct auth_ops {/* not really important */
                     void    (*ah_nextverf)();
                     int     (*ah_marshal)(); /* nextverf & serialize */
                     int     (*ah_validate)();;/* validate varifier */
                     int     (*ah_refresh)(); /* refresh credentials */
                     void    (*ah_destroy)(); /* destroy this structure */
             } *ah_ops;
             caddr_t ah_private;
     } AUTH;

     struct opaque_auth {
             enum_t  oa_flavor; /* flavor of authentication */
             caddr_t oa_base;   /* address of more auth stuff */
             u_int   oa_length; /* not to exceed MAX_AUTH_BYTES */
     };
```

Once properly initialized, cl_auth->ah_cred contains the user's credentials while cl_auth->ah_verf contains the information required for verification. In case you forgot what type of authentication you are using with a certain server, check cl_auth->ah_cred.oa_flavor. There are currently three distinct varieties of authentication supported under ONC RPC; none (the default), UNIX-style credentials (UID, group IDs), and Data Encryption Standard (DES). The symbols used to describe authentication are listed in Table 12-1. You are free to develop your own, too.

Table 12-1. Flavors of Authentication, (CLIENT *clnt)->cl_auth->ah_cred.oa_flavor

Preprocessor Symbol	Description
AUTH_NONE or AUTH_NULL	No authentication.
AUTH_UNIX	UNIX-style (UID, GIDs), not verified.
AUTH_SHORT	Shorthand UNIX, encapsulated credentials, not verified.
AUTH_DES	DES style (encrypted timestamps), verified.

The ONC RPC functions and secure RPC functions include functions to *build* credentials at the client, *marshal* and pass them back and forth through XDR, *validate* them at either end, *refresh* or *destroy* them when unused. The ONC RPC library handles the marshaling and communication of the credentials within the request and reply messages. Your server code should never have to worry about credential refreshing during multiple request sessions. The automatic refreshing performed by clnt...call() routines should suffice. Credential validation is automatically performed on any provided credentials. You only need to concern yourself with building and destroying credentials.

Building credentials is flavor-specific. We'll discuss each of the three flavors next. Once you have finished with your credential data structures, they should be destroyed for security reasons with auth_destroy(3N):

```
(void) auth_destroy(auth);
AUTH *auth;
```

If you are done with the server connection, simply destroy that CLIENT handle with clnt_destroy(3N). This destroys any associated credentials.

AUTH_NONE—No Credentials to Check (Default)

AUTH_NONE provides no security at all. When a CLIENT handle is created with one of the clnt..._create() functions, the credential fields are NULL, signifying no credentials or verification to be performed at the server. Calling authnone_create(3N) to assign a value to the an initialized CLIENT structure would have the same effect:

```
CLIENT *clnt;
(AUTH *) (clnt->cl_auth) = authnone_create();
```

AUTH_UNIX—UNIX-style Credentials, No or Limited Verification

UNIX-style credentials offer a degree of casual security, which can be useful for preventing accidents:

```
CLIENT 'clnt,
(AUTH *) clnt->cl_auth = authunix_create_default();   †
```

The request through `clnt` will now carry with it the following authentication information:

```
/* UNIX-style credentials. */
struct authunix_parms {      /* becomes authsys_params in TIRPC */
    u_long  aup_time;        /* credentials creation time */
    char    *aup_machname;   /* hostname where client is */
    int     aup_uid;         /* client's UNIX effective uid */
    int     aup_gid;         /* client's current group id */
    u_int   aup_len;         /* element length of aup_gids */
    int     *aup_gids;       /* array of groups user is in */
};
```

`authunix_create_default(3N)` calls `authunix_create()` along with several system functions to fill-in the `authunix_parms` fields.

The `AUTH_UNIX` system is quite weak. The client uses no encryption for its credentials and sends no verifiers (`NULL`). The server sends back the `NULL` verifiers or optionally a verifier that suggests a new, leaner form for representing the credentials. In this way, if the response verifier in the `CLIENT` handle becomes flavor `AUTH_SHORT`, the body of the response verifier specifies a new credential of the form:

```
struct short_hand_verf {
        struct opaque_auth new_cred;
};
```

AUTH_DES—DES Credentials and Verification

Secure RPC provides answers to the limited security of UNIX credentials through Data Encryption Standard encoding of authentication information. The `AUTH_DES` system also implies verification. Note that to use Secure RPC, you will need the `keyserv(8C)` daemon running on *both* the client and server. Encryption keys are kept in the `publickey(5)` database.

Use `authdes_create(3N)` to build up the DES authentication information on the client-side.‡

```
AUTH * authdes_create(netname, window, syncaddr, deskeyp)
char *netname;
unsigned window;
```

---

† `authunix_create_default()` is superceded by `authsys_create_default()` in the SVR4 or TIRPC release.

‡ `authdes_create()` is made obsolete by `AUTHdes_seccreate()` in the SVR4 or TIRPC release.

```
struct sockaddr_in *syncaddr;
des_block *deskeyp;
```

The first argument is the network name of the owner of the server process. Often services are run as root processes and their netname can be derived using the following call:

```
char serverOwn[MAXNETNAMELEN+1];
host2netname(serverOwn, rhost, (char *)NULL);
```

Here `rhost` is a `char *` pointing to the NULL-terminated hostname of the server machine. `serverOwn` will contain the root process's netname. `user2net-name(3N)` can be used to get netnames for regular user processes. The second parameter is now a UID. To get a netname for a server process with the same UID as the client process:

```
user2netname(serverOwn, getuid(), (char *)NULL);
```

The last argument to both these calls is the NIS domain in which the server is located. Specifying NULL means to look in this domain.

`getnetname(serverOwn)` checks to see what your client process UID is. If root (UID==0), it uses `host2netname()`, otherwise `user2netname()`.

The second argument to `authdes_create()` is the lifetime of the credentials. When this time at the server is exceeded, the credentials expire and must be refreshed or replaced before a request is granted. If a mischievous user attempts to use expired credentials, requests are denied. Any subsequent of these credentials again within a lifetime starts another rejection timeout.

Time synchronization between client and server is important, especially for short-lived credentials. The third parameter to `authdes_create()` is the socket address of the host you want the client to synchronize with.

The final parameter to `authdes_create()` is the DES encryption key you want to use for encrypting timestamps and data. If NULL, this directs the client to generate one at random. The key resides in the `ah_key` field of the client's authentication handle.

Here's an example of creating a CLIENT handle with DES authentication for a server called SERVER, version VERS, on the machine `cortex`. The credentials last 60 seconds, no synchronization is performed, and the DES key is chosen at random.

```
char serverOwn[MAXNETNAMELEN+1];
CLIENT *clnt = clnt_create("cortex", SERVER, VERS, "tcp");
getnetname(serverOwn);
clnt->cl_auth = authdes_create(serverOwn, 60, NULL, NULL);
```

You are now ready to make a secure RPC to a remote machine.

Errors as Returned by the Server

Upon return of a `clnt_call()`, authentication status from the server can be found in the `CLIENT` structure, as shown in Tables 12-2 and 12-3.

The `rpc_err` structure can be decoded with a number of client error printing functions.

Table 12-2. Functions for Error Reporting at the Client after an RPC

Function	Description
void clnt_perrno(stat) enum clnt_stat stat;	Sends a message to stderr corresponding to the condition indicated in stat. Used with `callrpc()` and `clnt_broadcast()`.
char * clnt_sperrno(stat) enum clnt_stat stat;	Instead of printing the error string, return a pointer to it. The string is static (overwritten on subsequent calls). Handy for applications that want to log errors.
void clnt_perror(clnt, str) CLIENT *clnt; char *str;	Print an error message at stderr regarding why the RPC failed.
char * clnt_sperror(clnt, str) CLIENT *clnt; char *str;	Instead of printing the error string, return a pointer to it. The string is static.
struct rpc_err clnt_geterr(rh, errp); CLIENT *rh; struct rpc_err errp;	Extract values of an error structure from a CLIENT handle after a `clnt_call()`.

`clnt_perrno(3N)` and `clnt_perror(3N)` append newlines to the `stderr` message. `clnt_sperrno(3N)` and `clnt_sperror(3N)` do not append newlines to the string.

`clnt_sperror()` can be used to extract server errors, telling you if an authentication problem occurred (e.g., credentials that are deemed invalid or too weak by the server). You can extract the particular authentication error to take your own (evasive) actions using the `clnt_geterr(3N)` macro. As defined in ONC's `<rpc/clnt.h>`, given the `CLIENT` handle, `clnt_geterr()` fills in the fields of an `rpc_err` structure.

```
struct rpc_err {              /* client error information */
    enum clnt_stat re_status;
    union {
```

```
        int RE_errno;          /* related system error */
        enum auth_stat RE_why;/* why the auth error occurred */
        struct {
            u_long low;        /* lowest version supported */
            u_long high;       /* highest version supported */
        } RE_vers;
        struct {               /* may be meaningful if RPC_FAILED */
            long s1;
            long s2;
        } RE_lb;               /* life boot & debugging only */
    } ru;
#define  re_errno      ru.RE_errno
#define  re_why      ru.RE_why
#define  re_vers      ru.RE_vers
#define  re_lb      ru.RE_lb
};
```

The higher-level client error printing routines use this same structure.

Possible values of `rpc_err.re_why` generated by the server (and one generated at the client) are listed in Table 12-3.

Table 12-3. Possible Authentication Errors, rpc_err.re_why

Preprocessor Symbol	Description
AUTH_OK	Authentication OK.
AUTH_BADCRED	Invalid client credential (security seal broken).
AUTH_REJECTEDCRED	Server rejected credential, client must begin new session.
AUTH_BADVERF	Invalid client verifier (security seal broken).
AUTH_REJECTEDVERF	Server rejected verifier (verifier expired or was replayed).
AUTH_TOOWEAK	Server denies access, client credential too weak.
AUTH_FAILED	Failed (unspecified error).
AUTH_INVALIDRESP	Invalid server verifier (server response rejected by this client).

When the client succeeds in connecting to the server, the server's identity is obviously known. The client automatically attempts to verify a server's identity via authentication information provided in the reply message. Failure is denoted by a `rpc_err.re_why` value of AUTH_INVALIDRESP.

Adding Authentication to the dim Client

It's no trivial job to add authentication with error reporting to the client. But if you do it once, the code is *very* re-usable.

To add authentication to the dim client, include a command-line flag, -c
[unix|des] to control which type of credentials are added to the client handle.
The error reporting done by ONC clnt_...perr..() routines is minimal, and
only textual. So I decided to go a step lower and look at the actual status values.
This could, for example, allow the application to try different credentials. I chose
only to print some more error information.

Example 12-1 contains the revised source code for *dim.c,* shown earlier in
Example 7-5.

Example 12-1. Adding authentication to the client: dim.c

```
#include <stdio.h>
#include <string.h>
#include <pwd.h>
#include <rpc/rpc.h>
#include "dim.h"
#define USAGE() { fprintf(stderr, "Usage: %s ", argv[0]); \
 fprintf(stderr, "\t-c [unix|des]\t\toverride AUTH_NONE default
authentication\n"); \
.
. same as in Example 7-5
.

char          *my_clnt_sperror();
image          *readImage();
FILE           *fp;

main(argc, argv)
   int          argc;
   char          *argv[];
{
.
. same as in Example 7-5
.

   /*
    * Look thru the command line to see if a transport is specified.
    */
.
. same as in Example 7-5
.
   /*
    * Attempt to open a client handle to the SERVERHOST.  We could use a
    * broadcast scheme to look for the closest server.
    */
.
. same as in Example 7-5
.
   /*
    * Before we place an RPC, we set the authentication choice.
    */
   for (arg = 1; arg < argc; arg++) {
     if (!strcmp(argv[arg], "-c")) {
       if ((argc < 4) || (strcmp("unix", argv[++arg]) && strcmp("des",
argv[arg])))
         USAGE();
       if (!strcmp(argv[arg], "unix"))
         clnt->cl_auth = authunix_create_default();
       else {
         char servername[MAXNETNAMELEN+1];
         getnetname(servername); /* good for root or users */
         clnt->cl_auth = authdes_create(servername, 60, NULL, NULL);
```

Example 12-1. Adding authentication to the client: dim.c (Continued)

```
      }
    }
  }
  /*
   * Parse the command line, doing RPCs as requested.  I don't bother
   * xdr_free()'ing anything as it's a one-shot deal.
   */
  for (arg = 1; arg < argc; arg++) {
    if (argv[arg][0] != '-')
      USAGE();
    switch (argv[arg][1]) {
    case 'c':
    case 't':
      arg++;
      break;
    case 'a':
      if ((argc - (++arg) < 6) || !(pI = readImage(argv, &arg)))
        USAGE();
      expectEmpty = add_1(pI, clnt);/* assume RPCSRC 4.0, 1 arg */
      if (expectEmpty == NULL)
        fputs(my_clnt_sperror(clnt, "remote call failed"), stderr);
      else
        fprintf(stderr, "%s", *expectEmpty);
      break;
    case 'd':
      if (argc - (++arg) < 1)
        USAGE();
      sImageName = (pStr) strdup(argv[arg]);
      expectEmpty = delete_1(&sImageName, clnt);
      if (expectEmpty == NULL)
        fputs(my_clnt_sperror(clnt, "remote call failed"), stderr);
      else
        fprintf(stderr, "%s", *expectEmpty);
      break;
    case 'x':
      if (argc - (++arg) < 1)
        USAGE();
      sImageName = (pStr) strdup(argv[arg]);
      pIS = extract_1(&sImageName, clnt);
      if (pIS == NULL) {
        fputs(my_clnt_sperror(clnt, "remote call failed"), stderr);
        exit(1);
      }
      if (pIS->status[0] != NULL) {
        fprintf(stderr, "%s\n", pIS->status);
        exit(1);
      }
      (void) writeImage(pIS->pImage, sImageName);
      break;
    case 'l':{
        if (!(pIL = list_1((void *) NULL, clnt)))
          fputs(my_clnt_sperror(clnt, "remote call failed"), stderr);
        else
          for (pI = pIL->pImage; pIL->pNext; pIL = pIL->pNext, pI = pIL->pImage)
            PRINTHEAD(pI);
        break;
      }
    default:
      USAGE();
    }
  }
  auth_destroy(clnt->cl_auth); /* could just clnt_destroy() and exit...*/
  clnt_destroy(clnt);
}
```

Example 12-1. Adding authentication to the client: dim.c (Continued)

```
image           *
readImage(argv, pArg)
  char          **argv;
  int           *pArg;
{
.
. no changes
.
}

writeImage(pImage, sImageName)
  image         *pImage;
  pStr          sImageName;
{
.
. no changes
.
}

extern char *sys_errlist[]; /* pick up some error information */
static char *auth_errmsg();

/*
 * Print reply error info. Much of this is borrowed from the RPCSRC 4.0 source.
 */
char *
my_clnt_sperror(rpch, s)
CLIENT *rpch;
char *s;
{
    struct rpc_err e;
    void clnt_perrno();
    char *err;
    static char buffer[MAXSTR];
    char *pBuf = buffer;

    CLNT_GETERR(rpch, &e);

    /*
     * Build up a return message.
     */
    (void) sprintf(pBuf, "%s: ", s);
    pBuf += strlen(pBuf);

    (void) strcpy(pBuf, clnt_sperrno(e.re_status));
    pBuf += strlen(pBuf);

    switch (e.re_status) {
    case RPC_SUCCESS:
    case RPC_CANTENCODEARGS:
    case RPC_CANTDECODERES:
    case RPC_TIMEDOUT:
    case RPC_PROGUNAVAIL:
    case RPC_PROCUNAVAIL:
    case RPC_CANTDECODEARGS:
    case RPC_SYSTEMERROR:
    case RPC_UNKNOWNHOST:
    case RPC_UNKNOWNPROTO:
    case RPC_PMAPFAILURE:
    case RPC_PROGNOTREGISTERED:
    case RPC_FAILED:
        break;
    case RPC_CANTSEND:      /* we will make better use of these two later */
    case RPC_CANTRECV:
        (void) sprintf(pBuf, "; errno = %s", sys_errlist[e.re_errno]);
```

Example 12-1. Adding authentication to the client: dim.c (Continued)

```
                pBuf += strlen(pBuf);
                break;
        case RPC_VERSMISMATCH:
                (void) sprintf(pBuf,
                    "; low version = %lu, high version = %lu",
                    e.re_vers.low, e.re_vers.high);
                pBuf += strlen(pBuf);
                break;
        case RPC_AUTHERROR:
                err = auth_errmsg(e.re_why);
                (void) sprintf(pBuf,"; why = ");
                pBuf += strlen(pBuf);
                if (err != NULL) {
                    (void) sprintf(pBuf, "%s",err);
                } else {
                    (void) sprintf(pBuf,
                        "(unknown authentication error - %d)",
                        (int) e.re_why);
                }
                pBuf += strlen(pBuf);
                if  (e.re_why == AUTH_TOOWEAK) {
                 /*
                  * Tell user to add authentication info to the handle and try again.
                  */
                    switch (rpch->cl_auth->ah_cred.oa_flavor) {
                    case NULL: /* was AUTH_NON, try AUTH_UNIX */
                        (void) sprintf(pBuf, ", try -c unix");
                        break;
                    case AUTH_UNIX:
                        (void) sprintf(pBuf, ", try -c des");
                        break;
                    case AUTH_DES: /* already tried DES... */
                        (void) sprintf(pBuf, ", try -c unix");
                        break;
                    default: /* must have some foreign credential type... */
                        (void) sprintf(pBuf, "unknown, unsuccessful credentials");
                        break;
                    }
                    pBuf += strlen(pBuf);
                }
                break;
        case RPC_PROGVERSMISMATCH:
                (void) sprintf(pBuf,
                    "; low version = %lu, high version = %lu",
                    e.re_vers.low, e.re_vers.high);
                pBuf += strlen(pBuf);
                break;
        case BEER:
                /* drink */
        default:      /* unknown */
                (void) sprintf(pBuf,
                    "; s1 = %lu, s2 = %lu",
                    e.re_lb.s1, e.re_lb.s2);
                pBuf += strlen(pBuf);
                break;
        }
        (void) sprintf(pBuf, "\n");
        return(buffer) ;
}

struct auth_errtab {
    enum auth_stat status;
    char *message;
};
```

Example 12-1. Adding authentication to the client: dim.c (Continued)

```
static struct auth_errtab auth_errlist[] = {
   { AUTH_OK,
      "Authentication OK" },
   { AUTH_BADCRED,
      "Invalid client credential (security seal broken)" },
   { AUTH_REJECTEDCRED,
      "Server rejected credential, client must begin new session" },
   { AUTH_BADVERF,
      "Invalid client verifier (security seal broken)" },
   { AUTH_REJECTEDVERF,
      "Server rejected verifier (verifier expired or was replayed)" },
   { AUTH_TOOWEAK,
      "Server denies access, client credential too weak" },
   { AUTH_INVALIDRESP,
      "Invalid server verifier (server response rejected by this client)" },
   { AUTH_FAILED,
      "Failed (unspecified error)" },
};

static char *
auth_errmsg(stat)
   enum auth_stat stat;
{
   int i;

   for (i = 0; i < sizeof(auth_errlist)/sizeof(struct auth_errtab); i++) {
      if (auth_errlist[i].status == stat) {
         return(auth_errlist[i].message);
      }
   }
   return(NULL);
}
```

You may choose to compile and link the client application now, or wait, as we will make it all after the server is modified.

Authentication at the Server

The `struct opaque_auth.ah_cred` from the CLIENT handle is passed through XDR to the server. It shows up within the request message `struct svc_req`. This is the first parameter to your server dispatch routine, and is passed to each subordinate service procedure:

```
struct svc_req {
    u_long  rq_prog;              /* service program number */
    u_long  rq_vers;              /* service protocol versnum */
    u_long  rq_proc;              /* desired procedure number */
--> struct opaque_auth rq_cred;   /* raw credentials from wire */
    caddr_t rq_clntcred;          /* credentials (read only) */
};
```

Your server dispatch or procedures may inspect `rq_cred.oa_flavor` to decide what type of authentication was provided. It can then cast the `rq_clntcred` into either `authunix_parms` or `authdes_cred` authentication structures.

The first thing your server should do is look at the flavor of authentication issued by the client and decide whether it is secure enough, e.g., if you needed AUTH_DES encoded credentials and you only got AUTH_UNIX credentials, return an error message. The ONC RPC library server error-reporting functions listed in Table 12-4 are used to report errors, including authentication errors. They are the counterpart to the Table 12-2 routines.

Table 12-4. Functions for Error Reporting at the Server

Procedure	Description
void svcerr_auth(xprt, why) SVCXPRT *xprt; enum auth_stat why;	Called when a server dispatch routine refuses to provide a service due to an authentication error.
void svcerr_decode(xprt) SVCXPRT *xprt;	Called when a server dispatch routine cannot properly decode the request parameters.
void svcerr_noproc(xprt) SVCXPRT *xprt;	Called by a server dispatch routine that does not implement the procedure number requested.
void svcerr_systemerr(xprt) SVCXPRT *xprt;	Called by the server dispatch routine if a system error is detected outside the scope of RPC.
void svcerr_weakauth(x-prt) SVCXPRT *xprt;	Called when a server dispatch routine refuses to grant a request due to insufficient authentication. Calls svcerr_auth(xprt, AUTH_TOOWEAK).

See *The ONC RPC Programming Reference* for a more complete discussion of error reporting. svcerr_progvers(3N) and svcerr_noprog(3N) are not presented here as version and program number error reporting is handled by the RPC system itself. If RPCGEN generated your server dispatch stub, you'll have no need to call svcerr_noproc(3N) yourself either.

Security: Authentication Plus Access Control

A secure application must specify *both* an authentication flavor and an access control policy.

Although the request parameters, including the authentication structure, are available with the service procedures, it is best to do the authentication and verification as soon as possible in the server dispatch routine. This serves to:

- Turn the potentially mischievous user away before penetrating your application.

- Centralize and re-use the same authentication code.

- Address authentication issues in *one* place.

An access control policy specifies which users are or are not entitled to your application's services. It assumes the authentication process is complete, and valid user credentials exist to be compared with an access list. The access control policy will

grossly affect the structure of your server, so it is best to define it before you write
the application.

Adding Access Control to the dim Server

We proceed now to illustrate how to add the three authentication flavors, along
with a limited access control policy to the dim server. We allow only the owner of
an image to delete it from the archive.

First, adding security measures to the dispatcher might require that we manually
edit the RPCGEN-generated stub *dim_svc.c*. I don't like that option. All we really
need is to insert some code within the appropriate cases of the dispatch function.
Currently *dim_svc.c* looks something like this:

```
        .
        .
main() {
        .
        .
svc_run();
}

static void
dimserver_1(rqstp, transp)
        struct svc_req *rqstp;
        SVCXPRT *transp;
{

        switch (rqstp->rq_proc) {
        case NULLPROC:
        .
        .

        case DIE:
        .
        .

        case RESTART:
        .
        .
        case ADD:
        .
        .
        case DELETE:
        .
        .
        case EXTRACT:
        .
        .
        case LIST:
        .
        .
        default:
        .
        .
        }
```

```
     .
/* actually do the local call here and return */
     .
}
```

By convention, we don't check the credentials of a client just interested in pinging NULLPROC. If this were not the case, we could simply insert some code before the switch validating credentials, returning immediately with a call to either svcerr_ auth(transp, (enum auth_stat)why), or svcerr_weakauth(transp).

Thus we must check authentication on a service-specific basis. We probably should only allow the process owner to use DIE or RESTART, but we are really interested in checking credentials of requesters of the DELETE service. We need to add some code within the DELETE case to reformat the credentials, peeling them out into something usable for later access control. We will use cpp to expand a macro inserted by an awk script from our *makefile*:

```
case DELETE:
    AUTH[NONE|UNIX|DES](rqstp,transp,uid,gid,gidlen,gidlist)
```

Granted AUTH_NONE credentials cannot supply us with UID or group membership information, but if we are consistent, we only need to add a few lines to the *makefile* of Example 4-1 as shown in Example 12-2. Recall that this application is not using the *dim_shared.h* common header file used in other chapters. I will use statements in the protocol file only.

Example 12-2. Automating authentication changes to server dispatch stub: makefile

```
#AUTH=   tell what kind of authentication should be used, NONE, UNIX, or DES
AUTH=DES
#APPN=   provide your application basename at the make command line
#        with "make APPN=... AUTH=... target"
RSRC=$(APPN).x $(APPN)_svc_proc.c $(APPN).c
CFLAGS= -g -DDEBUG
LFLAGS=

# compile the protocol, add requested authentication and externs
 to the server
$(APPN)_xdr.c $(APPN)_svc.c $(APPN)_clnt.c $(APPN).h: $(APPN).x
        rpcgen $(APPN).x
awk 'BEGIN {print "extern int uid,gid,gidlen,gidlist[16];\n"} \
    {`print $$0; if(($$1=="case")&&($$2=="DELETE:")) \
    printf("AUTH $(AUTH)(rqstp,transp,uid,gid,gidlen,gidlist)\n") }' \
    $(APPN)_svc.c > tmp \
    mv tmp $(APPN)_svc.c

# build the client application
$(APPN): $(APPN).h $(APPN).o $(APPN)_clnt.o $(APPN)_xdr.o
        cc $(CFLAGS) -o $(APPN) $(APPN).o $(APPN)_clnt.o $(APPN)_xdr.o $(LFLAGS)

# build the server application
$(APPN)_svc: $(APPN).h $(APPN)_svc_proc.o $(APPN)_svc.o $(APPN)_xdr.o
        cc $(CFLAGS) -o $(APPN)_svc $(APPN)_svc_proc.o $(APPN)_svc.o \
        $(APPN)_xdr.o $(LFLAGS)
```

Example 12-2. Automating authentication changes to server dispatch stub: makefile (Continued)

```
clean:
        rm -f $(APPN) $(APPN)_svc $(APPN)_svc.c $(APPN)_xdr.c \
        $(APPN)_clnt.c $(APPN).h *.o *.*%

$(APPN).ar: $(RSRC)
        bundle $(RSRC) > $(APPN).ar
```

This causes awk to be run after RPCGEN, inserting a line at the top of *dim_svc.c* to declare the cooked pieces of the credentials we will need: UID and group information. It also tags a line after the DELETE case to perform client authentication. We use three different cpp macros as specified on the make AUTH= command line. Acceptable values for AUTH are NONE, DES, or UNIX. An additional header file, which we name *auth.h*, is required to tell cpp what to do. Make the following addition to the top of the *dim.x* file:

```
#if RPC_SVC          /* added some authentication-testing macros */
%#include "auth.h" /* could pass extern int uid into services */
#endif
```

auth.h will only be included with *dim_svc.c. auth.h*, shown in Example 12-3, contains three macros: AUTHNONE() can do nothing as there are no credentials or verifiers. AUTHDES() returns an error to the client if the user is unknown or if credentials are too weak. It also assigns values to the global UID and group information for later use. AUTHUNIX() basically does the same thing, but only requires UNIX credentials (no verification).

Example 12-3. Macros included into the server dispatch routine for authentication: auth.h

```
#define AUTHNONE(rqstp,transp,uid,gid,gidlen,gidlist) { \
                fprintf(stderr, "not checking credentials\n"); \
        }
#define AUTHDES(rqstp,transp,uid,,gid,gidlen,gidlist) { \
                switch (rqstp->rq_cred.oa_flavor) { \
                case AUTH_DES:  { \
                        struct authdes_cred *des_cred = \
                          (struct authdes_cred *) rqstp->rq_clntcred; \
                        if (! netname2user(des_cred->adc_fullname.name, \
                        &uid, &gid, &gidlen, gidlist)) { \
                                /* could use syslog(3) here */ \
                                fprintf(stderr, "unknown user: %s\n", \
                                  des_cred->adc_fullname.name); \
                                svcerr_systemerr(transp); \
                                return; \
                        } \
                        break; \
                } \
                case AUTH_NULL: \
                default: \
                        /* could use syslog(3) here */ \
                        svcerr_weakauth(transp); \
                        return; \
                } \
        }
#define AUTHUNIX(rqstp,transp,uid,gid,gidlen,gidlist) { \
                switch (rqstp->rq_cred.oa_flavor) {    \
```

*Example 12-3. Macros included into the server dispatch routine for authentication: auth.b
(Continued)*

```
            case AUTH_UNIX: {   /* AUTH_SYS will obsolete this */ \
                struct authunix_parms * unix_cred =   \
                        (struct authunix_parms *)rqstp->rq_clntcred; \
                uid = unix_cred->aup_uid;   \
                gid = unix_cred->aup_gid;   \
                gidlen = unix_cred->aup_len;   \
                gidlist = &(unix_cred->aup_gids);   \
                break;   \
                } \
            case AUTH_NULL:   \
            default:   \
                    /* could use syslog(3) here */ \
                    svcerr_weakauth(transp);   \
                    return;   \
            } \
        }
```

We now need to change the server procedures to allow only the owner to delete an image. The changes to *dim_svc_proc.c* are quite small, as shown in Example 12-4. Again we use cpp and the symbolic constant AUTH as passed from make to determine whether or not we are compiling this application to be secure. The type of authentication used is not important at this point; only user identity is.

We must add the global UID and group integers uid, gid, gidlen, and gidlist that *auth.b* and *dim_svc.c* need. Case 5 of the switch statement in delete_1() signifies that the image has been found in the archive, and deletion is about to begin. This is where we check user identity and reject the non-owner. A message is sent back to the client in the pStr error message.

Example 12-4. Access control added to server delete procedure: dim_svc_proc.c

```
int             uid, gid, gidlen, gidlist;

pStr            *
delete_1(argp, rqstp)
  pStr             *argp;
  struct svc_req *rqstp;
{
.
.
.
Same as in Example 7-6.
.
.
 case 5:            /* This is the one! Remove it by copying the bottom up. */
#if (AUTH)
     if (strcmp(UIDTONAME(uid), 0)) {        /* No delete rights for you! */
        sprintf(msg, "attempt to delete %s by %s denied!\n", N, UIDTONAME(uid));
        fprintf(stderr, msg);
        fclose(fp);
        return ((pStr *) & result);
     }
#endif
    bufSize = MIN(MAX(1, b), MAXBUF);
```

Example 12-4. Access control added to server delete procedure: dim_svc_proc.c (Continued)

```
buffer = (char *) malloc(bufSize);
fpp = fopen(SERVERDB, "r+");
.
.
.
}
```

Error Reporting Summarized

So far our examples have done limited error reporting. In Chapters 4, 7, and 9, we've used the `svcerr...()` family of functions to build and return an error from the server and interpret them at the client with `clnt...err...()`. You can get more guidance regarding non-RPC system errors by sending the remote system's `errno` back within your own status message. We saw that to implement any non-trivial access control policy also requires status reporting in excess of that native to RPC.

Figure 12-1 is a schematic of the error reporting we've seen to date. Refer to Tables 12-2 and 12-4 for a description of the error-reporting functions.

In Figure 12-1, it is assumed that the client has built a `CLIENT` handle for the server, having called the associated Portmapper and determined whether the program and version number required are resident. When an RPC is placed by the client (`foo = bar_1()`), the request message is sent to the server named in the `CLIENT` handle. Once received by the server, the message (`struct svc_req`) is decoded to determine which procedure is requested. The dispatcher will use `svcerr_noproc(3N)` to send back an error. If the dispatcher has trouble decoding the request parameters, it sends a message back with `svcerr_decode(3N)`. Subsequent authentication errors are sent back with either `svcerr_auth(3N)` or `svcerr_weakauth(3N)`. The server can return a record of an arbitrary system error with `svcerr_systemerr()`. To find out more information about the request, you may have to look inside the `struct svc_req` or even the associated authentication structures.

The enum `clnt_stat` returned by `clnt_call()` or `callrpc()`[†] should be passed through `clnt_perrno()` or `clnt_sperrno()` to decode any errors. `clnt_perror()` and `clnt_sperror()` are designed to look within the client's `rpc_err` structure and put the problem to words. If you need more information or want to take evasive maneuvers, you will have to look inside the `rpc_err` structure yourself.

[†] `callrpc()` returns 0 if it succeeds. Cast non-zero return values into enum `clnt_stat`'s.

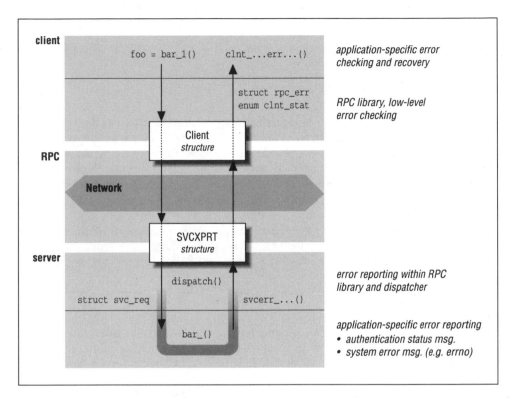

Figure 12-1. ONC RPC error reporting framework

Fault Tolerance, Connection Errors, and Crash Recovery

It's time we made both client and server more immune to errors and able to recover from them. If we assume your code is bug-free (a big assumption), the only errors we will see are related to the RPC protocol, transport, or client/server crashes. We've already covered the RPC protocol and transport error reporting built into the ONC library. Here we address what to do for abnormal connection termination or system crashes.

Connection Errors and Recovery

We covered detection and reporting of RPC and some transport errors earlier. The emphasis here is on the abnormal termination of the client/server connection. Later we will discuss crash recovery, especially as it affects the state of the clients and servers.

In this section, we add some structure to the application-specific, free-form art of error detection and recovery. Solid lines denote features that are important for elementary fault-tolerance. With RPC clients and servers, two of the most significant issues are caching replies at the server and catching connection problems. The choice of transport affects error and recovery strategy

Reply Caching for UDP

With the lack of execute-at-most-once semantics, a request may never arrive, may arrive multiple times, or may arrive out of order. This represents a problem for non-idempotent remote procedures. By building a finite-depth reply cache at the server, you can enforce execute-at-most-once semantics at the application level, making UDP somewhat reliable. Reply/request pairs must be given a unique identifier to prevent honoring a request more than once, or placing them out of order. If you incrementally save the server's reply cache to disk, you have a non-volatile record available for server crash recovery. Disk I/O intervals and logistic limitations on cache size are application-specific. This becomes difficult to orchestrate with concurrency and many clients and servers. Caching of UDP replies can also assist in state recovery.

Reply Caching for TCP

With the TCP transport, requests are received at most once, in order. Thus, reply caching isn't necessary to guarantee at-most-once execution of your non-idempotent procedures. Yet a non-volatile cache can be useful for retaining client state during a crash. If the server knows what requests it recently serviced, and retains replies, a client could query the cache to recover its state

Broken Pipe Handling with TCP

UDP (cached or not) as well as TCP do not *guarantee* that your request or reply ever gets through. Receiving parties may crash, time-out, or find a broken connection. Crash recovery may require some sense of state (e.g., a cache).

When a connection is dropped, the other party of the conversation has prematurely closed its end of the pipe (socket). Attempts to write to a connection-oriented pipe with a closed end causes a SIGPIPE signal to be generated. If not caught by your application, this can cause a process to hang or it can cause abnormal termination.

When using TCP, this is your only major worry. If calls are idempotent, the strategy from the client may be to just try again, or try a different server. Non-idempotent TCP requests may have been serviced and the reply never returned. A cache would be handy to check for this error and restart the client from there.

A TCP server detecting a SIGPIPE while acknowledging a request should not be alarmed. That's the client's problem. It should try again. A failure to write a reply should prompt the server to take some action, e.g., saving the client state into the reply cache.

Broken Pipe Handling with UDP

As you shouldn't be remotely executing non-idempotent procedures using UDP anyway, handling broken pipes within a UDP application is optional. SIGPIPEs are only caused with connected sockets. If your procedures are non-idempotent, you should use a reply cache or some other protective measure to guard against multiple executions. Detecting a broken connection should prompt a client to try the server again, or look for another server. Closed pipes detected at the server are the problem of the client, with optional server reply caching being of some merit.

Caching Replies at the Server

One approach to uniquely identifying request-reply pairs within the server cache is to place a time stamp on them. If the client is first synchronized with the server, this will completely identify the request (given no major clock drift). You might even think about inspecting the verifier time stamp provided with DES credentials (see <rpc/auth_des.h>) or use the simple RPCL time-protocol developed earlier in Chapter 4 in the section, "The Protocol Definition Language."

Deciding on the size of the cache (number or type discrimination of the replies saved) is a function of the transport used and the level of activity. UDP replies, by their nature, are at most 8K apiece. TCP replies can be huge.

A simpler approach for idempotent procedures is to save the last request from every client. Assuming each client will take subsequent action if a reply is lost, this guarantees a potent cache. On the downside, memory or disk consumption is now proportional to the number of clients, given no special exemptions are made for large or stale replies.

If procedures are non-idempotent, requests change server state and reply content. Only the most recent reply for each non-idempotent procedure should be saved. A complete sense of history of non-idempotent requests can only be reconstructed from a cache kept from the start of the server. In the case of dim, we are better off making periodic backup copies of the complete archive.

Broken Connections and Testing

To get a better feel for what happens, let's venture into a debugger with the dim application. There we will cause some SIGPIPE signals to be generated, indicating that a read or a write on a closed socket was attempted. If SIGPIPEs are not caught at the server, abnormal termination will occur. At the client, a clnt_call() will return a clnt_stat indicating whether the far-end of the connection was found closed during a request or reply.

One way to cause a SIGPIPE signal at the client or server is to close the other end of a socket prior to a write attempt. You can use this technique to test the fault tolerance of your application. Similarly, a read attempted from a pipe with a closed end will cause a `SIGPIPE`. It is difficult to manually close a socket during an RPC read as the reading is buffered below your code.

Note that when playing with signals in a debugger or using your own signal handlers, you may need to issue debugger commands to explicitly ignore or catch signal to guide execution.

At the Server

TCP: Change the `CFLAGS` in your *makefile* to add symbols for debugging. Use a debugger to set a break point within the dispatch stub at the point where valid requests are dispatched, e.g., within `svc_getreqset()`:

```
CLIENT dbx process              SERVER dbx process

                                cortex> dbx dim_svc
                                Reading symbolic information...
                                Read 745 symbols
                                (dbx) stop in svc_getreqset
```

Start the client from another process (it doesn't have to be in a debugger). Make a TCP request that will require a reply big enough to fill the write buffer at the server side (in my case with SunOS4.1 it's about 4KB). Kill it as soon as the debugger hits the break point, signifying that the server has a request buffered-up at its side of the socket. Continue ahead with server execution and you'll see that after servicing the request, the server generates a `SIGPIPE` when it attempts to send the reply:

```
rodson> dbx dim                 (dbx) stop in svc_getreqset
Reading symbolic information... (dbx) run
Read 568 symbols
(dbx) run -x imageName
^C                              stopped in svc_getreqset at 0xf76f1894
interrupt in select at          svc_getreqset:save %sp, -1376,.%sp
0xf77537e8                      Current function is svc_run
(dbx) print exit()              (dbx) cont
                                (dbx) cont
                                signal PIPE (broken pipe) in write at
                                0xf76e22d8
                                write+8: bgeu write+0x30
```

The `print exit()` dbx command at the client closed the pipe and now nobody's listening. If you are not using a debugger on the client, it isn't necessary to explicitly exit or close that end of the socket. This default action of the `SIGPIPE` is to terminate the server.

If we add a line like `signal(SIGPIPE, SIG_IGN);` to the server, we can avoid termination. In some applications, it may be necessary to add a SIGPIPE handler and take evasive action. You might log errors in decoding arguments (reading) or sending replies (writing). If the error occurred during a reply, you may want to buffer or save the data somewhere for the anticipated reconnect. In this way you are helping to save the client's state.

UDP: In our application, optional use of UDP as well as the need to tolerate client crashes prompts us to build a reply buffer. We could store on disk the latest request/reply pairs, saving the associated SVCXPRT, struct svc_req, and reply argument, along with the time, to uniquely identify the failed transaction.

To show yourself that TCP requires more overhead, repeat the procedure, but let the client finish. Try both UDP and TCP transports (small requests and replies). Notice that with UDP requests you hit the svc_getreqset() only once but with TCP it's twice, with a third time after the reply has already been sent. There is more overhead with TCP and its creation of new descriptors.

At the client

TCP: This time run the server in a debugger with a break point in svc_run(). This gets the server registered and tells the RPC system that it is ready to process requests. If you break just inside the svc_run() loop, then you stop the program before there is socket activity. Run the client with a small request (e.g., a packet size less than 8K):

```
                              cortex> dbx dim_svc
                              Reading symbolic information...
                              Read 686 symbols
                              (dbx) stop in svc_run
                              (1) stop in svc_run
                              (dbx) run
                              Running: dim_svc
                              stopped in svc_run at 0xf77023e8
                              svc_run: save   %sp, -128, %sp
rodson> dim -1                (dbx)
                              (dbx) print exit()
remote call failed:: RPC: Unable to receive;
errno = Connection reset by peer
```

The client was waiting for a request confirmation when the server end of the socket was closed. While this didn't cause a SIGPIPE at the client, it did set clnt_stat to reflect the closing, returning the call to the client immediately. If you send larger requests, your client will generate a SIGPIPE, with clnt_stat telling you when the pipe broke: RPC_CANTRECV or RPC_CANTSEND. Note that SIGPIPEs at the client are not catastrophic. The default action does not terminate the client, but allows you to fall-through, inspecting the returned client status, clnt_stat, to decide what to do. A signal handler at the client isn't necessary, though it may be a more convenient, centralized location to perform server crash recovery. Note that within a signal handler the client status may not yet be updated, so do not depend on it to make decisions at that point.

UDP: It is difficult to manually generate SIGPIPEs at the client when using UDP. Even when SIGPIPEs are generated, as detected by a handler, clnt_stat comes back indicating a time-out. All the client knows is that it didn't receive a reply. In this way it's not worth catching SIGPIPEs in UDP applications. A clnt_stat of RPC_TIMEOUT is the only information you will definitely get. This is because TCP includes request confirmations while UDP does not; in UDP applications the client must wait for the final reply.

Rebinding to a Server

If a connection is lost, and your client application wishes to press on, the first thing you might do is close the old CLIENT handle, destroying any credentials, then blindly attempt another clnt_create(). If it fails, you might have a secondary server already running if fault tolerance is a significant issue. You could also search for an equivalent service via broadcasting to the NULLPROC.

To avoid time-outs during reconnect, you can exec ping(8C) with a short time-out value to see if the machine is alive first. You could avoid an execl() or system() call by sending a ECHO_REQUEST packet to the host's icmp(4C) daemon yourself.

If you are interested in the availability of the server or its current loading, the rstatd(8C) daemon can be called directly without an exec(). The protocol in */usr/include/rpcsvc/rstat.x* gives you the ability to search for an attached disk (RSTATPROC_HAVEDISK procedure) or get general remote kernel information (RSTATPROC_STATS procedure).

If calls to these utilities come back with the network or the server as currently unavailable or not reachable, these can be seen as transient problems. In some applications it will be worth repeating the reconnect until it succeeds.

Crash Recovery

In general, crash recovery is application-specific. At best we can generalize according to transport. Most references address only server crash recovery. If your server is more than just a compute or information server and, for example, alters a database, things can get challenging and quite application-specific. But don't forget about the client. Often you don't want it to block while waiting for the server to come back. NIS is one example. Instead, it could look elsewhere on the network for the same service. Request queues and reply caches at the server and client can be useful.

Because writing to the archive is non-idempotent, our dim client/server pair needs a strategy to recover from server crashes. Adding to and deleting from the archive are server functions prompted by client requests, but they are de-coupled from the requests. If the server crashes while modifying the archive, the client may see a time-out or a closed pipe. It doesn't know for sure what happened.

If the server failed while writing the archive (during delete or add), we want to recover by discarding incomplete trailing archive entries, leaving the archive read-only to other servers until repaired. A function that demonstrates how to restore a database upon a crash is shown in Example 12-5.

Example 12-5. repairDB() now restores the database

```
#define FIX_RETURN(fp, seekPt, s) { \
        fclose(fp); \
        truncate(SERVERDB, (off_t) seekPt); \
        sprintf(s, "SERVERDB %s data hosed at %ld, repaired\n", \
          SERVERDB, seekPt); \
        fprintf(stderr, s); \
        return; \
    }

repairDB(s)         /* Does something now! */
  pStr              s;
{
  int               fstat, b, x, y, d, c;
  long              seekPt, fo;
  static char       N[MAXSTR], O[MAXSTR], C[MAXSTR], D[MAXSTR];
  static char       msg[MAXSTR];
  char              dummy;
  msg[0] = NULL;

  /*
   * Don't know exactly where the file pointer is at this time,
   * so rewind and stop at a point where the database gets funky.
   * If we cannot read a complete entry, we assume it's a corrupted add
   * or delete operation.  A BIG assumption just for purpose of
   * illustration.
   */
  fclose(fp);
  if (!(fp = fopen(SERVERDB, "r"))) {
    sprintf(s, "cannot open SERVERDB %s for reading\n", SERVERDB);
    fprintf(stderr, s);
    return;
  }
  for (seekPt = 0;
          (fstat = fscanf(fp, "%d%d%d%d%d\n", &b, &x, &y, &d, &c)) != EOF;
          seekPt = ftell(fp) ) {
    switch (fstat) {
      case 5:   /* everything is fine, try to get to next one */
        READHEADER(N, O, C, D);
        if (feof(fp)) FIX_RETURN(fp, seekPt, s);
        fo = ftell(fp);
        fseek(fp, (long) b-1, 1);
        dummy = fgetc(fp);
        if (feof(fp) || ((ftell(fp) - fo) != b)) FIX_RETURN(fp, seekPt, s);
        break; /* all went well */
      default  /* didn't get all 5 values, blast it */
        FIX_RETURN(fp, seekPt, s);
    }
  }
}
```

The ONC RPC
Programming Reference

Section One: ONC XDR Library Routines

Synopsis 368

Section Two: ONC Portmap Library
Routines

Synopsis 378

Section Three: ONC RPC Library Routines

Functional Summary 381
Synopsis 387
Error Codes 404

Section One:
ONC XDR Library Routines

Overview

The External Data Representation (XDR) library functions are used to represent data structures in a machine-independent form. The XDR protocol is documented in the ARPA Network Information Center's RFC1014. XDR provides the functions of the ISO presentation layer, and is similar to the X.409 ISO Abstract Syntax Notation. The only major difference is that X.409 uses explicit typing, where as XDR uses implicit typing.

Being a single-canonical data representation, XDR defines a single byte-order (big-endian or MSB first), a single floating-point representation (IEEE), etc. XDR was developed to allow any complying machines to share data regardless of compiler, operating system, or architecture differences. For example, strings can be NULL-terminated or PASCAL-style, data alignment can differ from compiler to compiler, or a 64-bit architecture might need to talk to an 8-bit architecture. Some data representations cannot be completely represented on foreign architectures (e.g., extended or non-standard floating-point numbers.)

Instead of describing the protocol or data representation here, we shall emphasize the programming interface provided through the ONC XDR library.[†] XDR supports the ONC RPC routines to directly communicate built-in C data types and strings between heterogeneous clients and servers. XDR function invocations can be grouped to encode and decode user-defined, arbitrary data structures. Both XDR and the ASN.1 data representations attempt to put the data in a neutral form. Data passed between client and server are encoded by the sender and decoded at the receiver using XDR routines. More often than not, it is more productive to define client/server data protocol at a higher level and allow a protocol compiler (e.g., RPCGEN or RPCTool) to do the hard work of stringing together XDR calls.

With the ONC RPC tool suite installed on a machine, the XDR and RPC libraries are included in the default /usr/lib libraries and thus do not require additional linker directives. With the TIRPC, SVR4 release you must link with /usr/lib/libnsl. Though documented as C routines, there is no reason why other programming languages could not (carefully) use the same library. With source readily available, they can be ported to most machines. There is also no reason why XDR routines couldn't be

---

† Routines used to describe messages for remote procedure calling in XDR language are not discussed: `xdr_accepted_reply()`, `xdr_authunix_parms()`, `xdr_callhdr()`, `xdr_callmsg()`, `xdr_opaque_auth()`, `xdr_rejected_reply()`, and `xdr_replymsg()`. These can be used by those who want to design their own RPC package.

used locally to maintain machine-independent databases, allowing applications across different platforms to share information.

Use of XDR routines require including the `<rpc/xdr.h>` header file. The underlying common XDR data structure itself is defined in Sun Microsystem's *RPC/XDR Library Definitions of the Network Programming*. CLIENT and SVCXPRT data structures (also described in the same document) include information about each client/server relationship. CLIENT handles are created by the client application with `clnt_create()`, and are unique to each client/server pair. The SVCXPRT server handles in the server routines describe the transport protocol being used.

The XDR routines fall into four categories: (1) creating and (2) managing XDR streams, (3) simple (built-in) conversions and (4) complex data type conversions. XDR streams are buffers into and out of filters, whose presence is managed by the filters. You should have little need to mess with XDR streams if you use a protocol compiler to string together conversion procedures.

The simple and complex conversion procedures act as filters to encode and decode data. Three actions may be performed with a filter: encoding, decoding, or memory freeing. All filter procedures have the same general synopsis:

```
bool_t xdrproc(xdrs, argresp)
       XDR *xdrs;
       <type> *argresp;
```

Each procedure takes two arguments, xdrs is an instance of a XDR handle. This is the incoming or outgoing data location, where the external XDR representation lives.

```
typedef struct {
          enum xdr_op     x_op;            /* operation to perform on stream */
          struct xdr_ops {
                    bool_t  (*x_getlong)(); /* get a long from under
                                             * stream */
                    bool_t  (*x_putlong)(); /* put a long to " */
                    bool_t  (*x_getbytes)();/* get some bytes from " */
                    bool_t  (*x_putbytes)();/* put some bytes to " */
                    u_int   (*x_getpostn)();/* returns bytes off from
                                             * beginning */
                    bool_t  (*x_setpostn)();/* lets you reposition the
                                             * stream */
                    long *  (*x_inline)();  /* buf quick ptr to buffered
                                             * data */
                    void    (*x_destroy)(); /* free privates of this
                                             * xdr_stream */
          } *x_ops;
          caddr_t         x_public;        /* users' data */
          caddr_t         x_private;       /* pointer to private data */
          caddr_t         x_base;          /* private used for position
                                            * info */
          int             x_handy;         /* extra private word */
} XDR;
```

The operation is specified in the enum xdr_op field of the XDR structure: XDR_ENCODE, XDR_DECODE, or XDR_FREE.

```
enum xdr_op {
        XDR_ENCODE=0,
        XDR_DECODE=1,
        XDR_FREE=2
};
```

argresp in the filter synopsis is a pointer to the local machine's structure of type <type>. Decoding will allocate space only if argresp is NULL. The freeing operation will deallocate the associated memory. Basically a procedure exists to decode/encode each data type. Most procedures return a bool_t TRUE if they succeed, FALSE if they fail. xdr_free() described below is used to free memory pointed to within composite XDR structures, making XDR_FREE requests with all the involved filters.

XDR Streams and Their Management

Three XDR library routines allow for the birth of XDR streams. XDR streams have to be created before using filters to provide memory for data encoding and decoding. If you are using XDR with RPC, the client and server-side RPC library calls take care of stream management. In other words, if you are using RPC, you'll never have to concern yourself with streams, just XDR filters. Thus there is little chance that you should have to work at this level. Nevertheless, there are three different types of XDR stream objects as shown in the following table.

Procedure	Description
xdrmem_create(3N)	Create an XDR stream in memory.
xdrrec_create(3N)	Create a record-oriented stream.
xdrstdio_create(3N)	Create an XDR stream connected to a file through standard I/O mechanisms.

Once an XDR stream object has been instantiated, it has associated with it routines to perform a number of functions as shown in the following table. Routines are provided to manage the XDR stream in a fashion similar to other stream management procedures under UNIX. If the ONC RPC man pages have been installed, look at xdr_admin(3N) for more details. The xdrrec_...() routines work only with record-oriented streams, created with xdrrec_create() above.

Procedure	Description
xdr_destroy(3N)	Destroy a stream, de-allocating resources.
xdr_getpos(3N)	Return position in the XDR byte stream.

Procedure	Description
`xdr_inline(3N)`	Return a pointer to a contiguous piece of the stream.
`xdrrec_endofrecord(3N)`	Mark a record as complete, optionally write out.
`xdrrec_eof(3N)`	Test for EOF after the next record.
`xdrrec_readbytes(3N)`	Read a number of bytes from a stream.
`xdrrec_skiprecord(3N)`	Skip to the beginning of the next record.
`xdr_setpos(3N)`	When possible, reposition yourself in a stream.

The stream creation and management routines are elaborated on at the end of this section.

Conversion Filters

The XDR library conversion filters fall into two categories: (1) simple filters or those converting between built-in C data types and their XDR external expression, and (2) complex filters or those designed for use in converting higher-level structures.

Simple Conversion Filters and Macros

A group of library routines is designed for translating built-in C data types into and out of their external data representation (see the following table). If you have the RPC manual pages installed, you may want to reference `xdr_simple(3N)`. XDR streams must first be created (see above), or created implicitly when using the filters. Note that each filter serves three purposes: it can either encode data into the XDR format, decode it back, or free the memory associated with the XDR structure.

C Type	Filter	XDR Type
`bool_t (C int)`	`xdr_bool(3N)`	`int`
`char`	`xdr_char(3N)`	`int`
`short int`	`xdr_short(3N)`	`int`
`unsigned short int`	`xdr_u_short(3N)`	`unsigned int`
`int`	`xdr_int(3N)`	`int`
`unsigned int`	`xdr_u_int(3N)`	`unsigned int`
`long`	`xdr_long(3N)`	`long`
`unsigned long`	`xdr_u_long(3N)`	`unsigned long`
`float`	`xdr_float(3N)`	`float`

C Type	Filter	XDR Type
double	xdr_double(3N)	double
void	xdr_void(3N)	void
enum	xdr_enum(3N)	int

Each simple filter returns a `bool_t` TRUE if it succeeds, FALSE otherwise. Failure can be brought on by bad data as the second argument or an XDR stream error, such as insufficient disk space when the XDR stream is pointing to a disk file. An instance of an XDR handle is passed-in, to which or from which, the data type is to be converted, along with a pointer to the structure to be converted. The one-of-three operations (XDR_ENCODE, XDR_DECODE, or XDR_FREE) is specified in the XDR handle xdr_op operation field. XDR_DECODE may allocate space if the data pointer is NULL. This data may be freed with an XDR_FREE operation.

As an example of using the simple filters with manually-created XDR steams, the following code opens a data file and writes four short integers to it in XDR form. They actually appear in the file occupying four bytes each with the current Sun implementation. Once written, the example then opens the stream back up and reads the data back from the beginning.

Example R-1. Reading and writing XDR data through simple filters: portable.c.

```
#include <rpc/xdr.h>
#include <stdio.h>

short           sarray[] = {1, 2, 3, 4};

main()
{
  FILE          *fp;
  XDR           xdrs;
  int           i;

  /*
   * Encode the 4 shorts.
   */
  fp = fopen("data", "w");
  xdrstdio_create(&xdrs, fp, XDR_ENCODE);
  for (i = 0; i < 4; i++)
    if (xdr_short(&xdrs, &(sarray[i])) == FALSE)
      fprintf(stderr, "error writing to stream\n");

  xdr_destroy(&xdrs);
  fclose(fp);

  /*
   * Decode the 4 shorts.
   */
  fp = fopen("data", "r");
  xdrstdio_create(&xdrs, fp, XDR_DECODE);
  for (i = 0; i < 4; i++)
    if (xdr_short(&xdrs, &(sarray[i])) == FALSE)
```

Example R-1. Reading and writing XDR data through simple filters: portable.c (Continued)

```
        fprintf(stderr, "error reading stream\n");
    else printf("%d\n", sarray[i]);

    xdr_destroy(&xdrs);
    fclose(fp).
}
```

At the end of this section, the simple filter routine synopses are listed, along with the other XDR routines, in alphabetical order. Note that there is one utility routine, `xdr_free()`, that you will need to use with these routines.

In-line Routines for Fast Conversion

The library and include file `<rpc/xdr.h>` also provide in-line routines for fast encode/decode of primitive data types. These use single memory cycles to get or put the data from/to the underlying buffer. They will fail to work correctly if the data is not aligned. One way to use these is to use the `XDR_INLINE()` macro to obtain the required contiguous length of XDR stream buffer, then invoke the macro to encode or decode:

```
    if ((buf = XDR_INLINE(xdrs, count)) == NULL)
        return (FALSE);
    <<< macro calls >>>
```

where `count` is the number of bytes of data occupied by the primitive data type, `xdrs` is the XDR * stream handle. The following macros from `<rpc/xdr.h>` decode and encode data from and to the `buf` XDR * stream and increment the pointer along. They return or expect as input the obvious data type.

```
#define IXDR_GET_LONG(buf)           ((long)ntohl((u_long)*(buf)++))
#define IXDR_PUT_LONG(buf, v)        (*(buf)++ = (long)htonl((u_long)v))

#define IXDR_GET_BOOL(buf)           ((bool_t)IXDR_GET_LONG(buf))
#define IXDR_PUT_BOOL(buf, v)        IXDR_PUT_LONG((buf), ((long)(v)))

#define IXDR_GET_ENUM(buf, t)        ((t)IXDR_GET_LONG(buf))
#define IXDR_PUT_ENUM(buf, v)        IXDR_PUT_LONG((buf), ((long)(v)))

#define IXDR_GET_U_LONG(buf)         ((u_long)IXDR_GET_LONG(buf))
#define IXDR_PUT_U_LONG(buf, v)      IXDR_PUT_LONG((buf), ((long)(v)))

#define IXDR_GET_SHORT(buf)          ((short)IXDR_GET_LONG(buf))
#define IXDR_PUT_SHORT(buf, v)       IXDR_PUT_LONG((buf), ((long)(v)))

#define IXDR_GET_U_SHORT(buf)        ((u_short)IXDR_GET_LONG(buf))
#define IXDR_PUT_U_SHORT(buf, v)     IXDR_PUT_LONG((buf), ((long)(v)))
```

These macros are not useful with `stdio` streams as buffer size isn't available. As an example of how to use these fast macros, below is a segment of code that assumes you've already opened the file and XDR stream for reading. We use `XDR_IN-LINE()` to retrieve a buffer with sufficient space to write the same four short integers we are interested in. Notice the use of `BYTES_PER_XDR_UNIT` to calibrate ourselves with the number of bytes (a constant) that XDR uses in this implementation to encode a unit of data. If the buffer allocation fails, go back to using the slower filter procedures, truly failing if these, too, don't work. Reading (XDR_DECODE) four long integers from a stream and printing them out might look like this.

Example R-2. Using fast XDR macros: macro.c

```
...
long * buf;
if (xdrs->x_op == XDR_DECODE) {
  buf = XDR_INLINE(&xdrs, BYTES_PER_XDR_UNIT * 4);
  if (buf == NULL) {
    fprintf(stderr, "XDR_INLINE: couldn't get a buffer\n");
    for (i = 0; i < 4; i++) {
      if (!xdr_int(xdrs, buf) || (printf("%d\n", buf) != 1))
        return (FALSE);
    }
  } else { /* got a buffer - do it the fast way */
    for (i = 0; i < 4; i++)
      printf("%d\n", IXDR_GET_LONG(buf));
  }
...
```

Complex Data Type Filters

A group of the library routines is designed for translating more complex C data types than mentioned above, into and out of their external data representation. These routines handle vectors, arrays, unions, strings and pointers, or references. If you have the RPC manual pages installed, try looking at xdr_complex(3N). XDR streams must first be created (see above) or implicitly created when using the filters through RPC calls. These routines adhere to the same bool_t return status value (TRUE or FALSE) and the three-use filter nature mentioned above. The XDR filter routines in the following table translate the associated composite C data types into and out of their portable, external XDR form. These routines are also alphabetically tabulated in the next section.

Composite Type	Filter
Variable-length array with arbitrary element size.	xdr_array(3N)
Variable-length array of bytes.	xdr_bytes(3N)
Fixed-length data (uninterpreted).	xdr_opaque(3N)
Object references, including NULL pointers (for tree or linked-lists).	xdr_pointer(3N)
Object references.	xdr_reference(3N)
NULL-terminated character arrays.	xdr_string(3N)
Discriminated union (union with an enumeration acting as the discriminant).	xdr_union(3N)

Composite Type	Filter
Fixed-length array with arbitrary element size.	xdr_vector(3N)
Variable-length NULL-terminated character arrays	xdr_wrapstring(3N)

Synopsis

In this section, the XDR library routines are described briefly.

xdr_array()

```
#include <rpc/xdr.h>
bool_t xdr_array(xdrs, arrp, sizep, maxsize, elsize, elproc)
    XDR *xdrs;
    char **arrp;
    u_int *sizep, maxsize, elsize;
    xdrproc_t elproc;
```

xdr_array() is the conversion routine for a variable-length array, pointed to by *arrp, containing *sizep elements each elsize bytes. sizep must be established for encoding and is set when decoding. If the array is longer than maxsize, it fails (returns FALSE). Memory must be allocated for the array before decoding into *arrp. The xdrproc_t elproc is the XDR filter procedure used to translate each element.

xdr bool()

```
bool_t xdr_bool(xdrs, bp)
    XDR *xdrs;
    bool_t *bp;
```

xdr_bool() converts between a boolean, actually a C integer, and its XDR external data representation with value either 0 or 1.

xdr_bytes()

```
bool_t xdr_bytes(xdrs, arrp, sizep, maxsize)
    XDR *xdrs;
    char **arrp;
    u_int *sizep, maxsize;
```

xdr_bytes() converts an array of bytes in and out of XDR format like this:

```
xdr_array(xdrs, arrp, sizep, maxsize, 1, xdr_opaque()).
```

It treats the array as opaque bytes starting at *arrp. If *arrp is NULL when decoding from the XDR *xdrs structure, memory is allocated. It, too, is freed with xdr_free(). Like xdr_array(), sizep is the number of bytes and must be set for encoding and is set by decoding. It fails if more than maxsize bytes are encountered, returning FALSE, otherwise TRUE.

xdr_char()

```
bool_t xdr_char(xdrs, cp)
    XDR *xdrs;
    char *cp;
```

xdr_char() converts between a C char and the associated XDR external form. Due to the fact that xdr_char() characters occupy four bytes, when working with arrays or strings of characters, you're better off using the xdr_bytes(), xdr_o-paque(), or xdr_string() described in the complex filter section.

xdr_destroy()

```
void xdr_destroy(xdrs)
    XDR *xdrs;
```

xdr_destroy() invokes the destroy routine associated with the named XDR structure. It frees the memory associated with an XDR stream and must be performed along with xdr_free() if streams are destroyed outside of RPC functions.

xdr_double()

```
bool_t xdr_double(xdrs, dp)
    XDR *xdrs;
    double *dp;
```

xdr_double() converts between C double and the associated XDR external form.

xdr_enum()

```
bool_t xdr_enum(xdrs, ep)
    XDR *xdrs;
    enum_t *ep;
```

xdr_enum() converts between the C enum types (effectively your machine's int) and the associated XDR external form.

xdr_float()

```
bool_t xdr_float(xdrs, fp)
    XDR *xdrs;
    float *fp;
```

xdr_float() converts between C float types and the associated XDR external form.

xdr_free()

```
void xdr_free(proc, objp)
    xdrproc_t proc;
    char *objp;
```

xdr_free() frees the memory associated with the XDR object (or composite object) pointed to by objp, with data conversion routine specified in proc. In this way it can be used to de-allocate linked-list memory, too. It does not free the actual pointer passed-in. It returns nothing.

xdr_getpos()

```
u_int xdr_getpos(xdrs)
    XDR *xdrs;
```

xdr_getpos() returns the position of the current byte stream read/write pointer. Note that XDRs are objects; the routines in this category are effectively invoking procedures (methods) attached to the instance of the XDR specified. Here the get-position routine is called.

xdr_inline()

```
long * xdr_inline(xdrs, len)
    XDR *xdrs;
    int len;
```

xdr_inline() returns a pointer to a len byte long buffer within the stream. If one does not exist, NULL is returned. It, along with XDR_INLINE(), is defined as the same macro in <rpc/xdr.h>.

xdr_int()

```
bool_t xdr_int(xdrs, ip)
    XDR *xdrs,
    int *ip;
```

xdr_int() converts between C integers and the associated XDR external form.

xdr_long()

```
bool_t xdr_long(xdrs, lp)
    XDR *xdrs;
    long *lp;
```

xdr_long() converts between C long integers and the associated XDR external form.

xdrmem_create()

```
void xdrmem_create(xdrs, addr, size, op)
    XDR *xdrs;
    char *addr;

    u_int size;
    enum xdr_op op;
```

xdrmem_create() initializes the XDR stream object in memory at *xdrs. Up to size bytes of stream data can be written to or read from memory starting at addr.

op defines the direction of future XDR operations—either XDR_ENCODE, XDR_DECODE, or XDR_FREE.

xdr_opaque()

```
bool_t xdr_opaque(xdrs, cp, cnt)
    XDR *xdrs;
    char *cp;
    u_int cnt;
```

xdr_opaque() converts fixed-size opaque data. Opacity in this context means that what the data is has no relevance, it's a number of bytes (cp of them in this case) to be encoded on one end, and restored into the same thing in the other end.

xdr_pointer()

```
bool_t xdr_pointer(xdrs, objpp, objsize, objproc)
    XDR *xdrs;
    char **objpp;
    u_int objsize;
    xdrproc_t objproc;
```

xdr_pointer() converts indirect data like xdr_reference() but it can handle NULL pointers. Thus it works with things like binary trees and linked lists. Be sure you NULL any unused or terminated pointers! It can cause some strange, irregular behavior. objsize is the size of (**objpp), the size of the structure pointed to by *objpp. objproc is the XDR filter for the data it will encounter.

xdrrec_create()

```
void xdrrec_create(xdrs, sendsz, recvsz, handle, readit, writeit)
    XDR *xdrs;
    u_int sendsz, recvsz;
    char *handle;
    int (*readit) (), (*writeit) ();
```

xdrrec_create() initializes a record-oriented XDR *xdrs stream object. sendsz and recvsz specify buffer size for writing and reading the stream. Zero directs xdrrec_create() to use a suitable default buffer size. The procedure named by writit() (readit()) is called when the stream's output (input) buffer is full (empty).

xdrrec_endofrecord()

```
bool_t xdrrec_endofrecord(xdrs, sendnow)
    XDR *xdrs;
    int sendnow;
```

xdrrec_endofrecord() forces the data in the output buffer to be marked as a complete record, and optionally written-out if sendnow is non-zero. Can only be used with record-oriented streams created with xdrrec_create(). Returns TRUE upon success, FALSE if it fails.

xdrrec_eof()

```
bool_t xdrrec_eof(xdrs)
    XDR *xdrs;
    int empty; ·
```

xdrrec_eof() is only for streams created by xdrrec_create(). It returns
TRUE if the stream has no more input, after finishing the current record.

xdrrec_readbytes()

```
int xdrrec_readbytes(xdrs, addr, nbytes)
    XDR *xdrs;
    caddr_t addr;
    u_int nbytes;
```

xdrrec_readbytes() reads nbytes bytes from an XDR created by
xdrrec_create() into the addr buffer. Number of successfully read bytes is
returned (or -1 if failure).

xdrrec_skiprecord()

```
bool_t xdrrec_skiprecord(xdrs)
    XDR *xdrs;
```

xdrrec_skiprecord() discards the rest of a record in the stream input buffer
associated with the named xdrrec_create() created XDR. Returns TRUE if
successful, FALSE otherwise.

xdr_reference()

```
bool_t xdr_reference(xdrs, pp, size, proc)
    XDR *xdrs;
    char **pp;
    u_int size;
    xdrproc_t proc;
```

xdr_reference() recursively chases down pointers, encoding/decoding the
data elements (of size size) pointed to. It starts at *pp, and will use the XDR filter
proc() on your data. It *does not* understand NULL pointers. It basically deserial-
izes pointers.

xdr_setpos()

```
bool_t xdr_setpos(xdrs, pos)
    XDR *xdrs;
    u_int pos;
```

xdr_setpos() sets the XDR stream's position. Returns TRUE upon success,
FALSE if it fails.

xdr_short()

```
bool_t xdr_short(xdrs, sp)
    XDR *xdrs;
    short *sp;
```

xdr_short() converts between C short integers and the associated XDR external form.

xdrstdio_create()

```
void xdrstdio_create(xdrs, filep, op)
    XDR *xdrs;
    FILE *filep;
    enum xdr_op op;
```

xdrstdio_create() is like xdrrec_create() except the standard I/O stream filep is used for writing or reading, determined by the mode of the operation op either XDR_ENCODE, XDR_DECODE, or XDR_FREE. This must correspond to the mode the file was opened with. Note the destroy routine (used by xdr_destroy()) calls fflush(), but does not close the file.

xdr_string()

```
bool_t xdr_string(xdrs, strp, maxsize)
    XDR *xdrs;
    char **strp;
    u_int maxsize;
```

xdr_string() is for converting between xdrs, XDR, and a C NULL-terminated string representation at *strp. If more than maxsize characters are encountered, it fails and returns FALSE. If *strp is NULL when decoding, xdr_string() allocates the appropriate space. xdr_free() will deallocate that memory. strp cannot be NULL itself; it must point to some valid memory location at the head of a string of zero or more characters.

xdr_u_char()

```
bool_t xdr_u_char(xdrs, ucp)
    XDR *xdrs;
    unsigned char *ucp;
```

xdr_u_char() converts between C unsigned characters and the associated XDR external form.

xdr_u_int()

```
bool_t xdr_u_int(xdrs, up)
    XDR *xdrs;
    unsigned *up;
```

xdr_u_int() converts between C unsigned integers and the associated XDR external form.

xdr_u_long()

```
bool_t xdr_u_long(xdrs, ulp)
    XDR *xdrs;
    unsigned long *ulp;
```

xdr_u_long() converts between C unsigned long integers and the associated XDR external form.

xdr_union()

```
bool_t xdr_union(xdrs, dscmp, unp, choices, defaultarm)
    XDR *xdrs;
    int *dscmp;
    char *unp;
    struct xdr_discrim *choices;
    bool_t (*defaultarm) ();   /* may be NULL */
```

xdr_union() converts a discriminated C union. After converting type enum_t discriminant at dscmp, the union located at unp is converted. choices is a pointer to a NULL-terminated array of structures containing a pair of [value,proc]. If the discriminant is the same as any of the values, the associated proc is used to translate the contents of union. If no discriminant/value matches are found, the defaultarm procedure is used for conversion if it is not NULL.

xdr_u_short()

```
bool_t xdr_u_short(xdrs, usp)
    XDR *xdrs;
    unsigned short *usp;
```

xdr_u_short() converts between C unsigned short integers and the associated XDR external form.

xdr_vector()

```
bool_t xdr_vector(xdrs, arrp, size, elsize, elproc)
    XDR *xdrs;
    char *arrp;
    u_int size, elsize;
    xdrproc_t elproc;
```

xdr_vector() converts a size-length array, starting at arrp, with each element elsize bytes, using the elementary filter elproc.

xdr_void()

```
bool_t xdr_void()
```

xdr_void() always returns TRUE. It's used in conjunction with routines that input or output nothing, as a parameter placeholder.

xdr_wrapstring()

```
bool_t xdr_wrapstring(xdrs, strp)
    XDR *xdrs;
    char **strp;
```

xdr_wrapstring() converts a NULL-terminated C string at *strp. This is equivalent to, yet more terse than, xdr_string(xdrs, strp, MAX); where MAX is the biggest possible unsigned integer. Like xdr_string(), if *strp is NULL on decode, memory will be allocated, to be freed later with xdr_free().

Section Two:
ONC Portmap
Library Routines

Overview

The `portmap(8C)` network service maintains the mappings between a machine's service programs and their universal addresses or TCP/IP ports. `portmap` converts TCP/IP protocol port numbers into RPC program numbers, thereby providing access to subordinate remote procedures. RPC servers first register their programs with the `portmap` server, including the port number they are listening at and version number of the program they are running (the binding process). Clients use these numbers to contact the server and look for specific procedures, with the `portmap` server returning the appropriate port to connect with. `portmap` is started before `inctd` at boot-time, as many RPC servers are started by `inetd()`.

More often than not, you will not be using these calls yourself when constructing RPC clients and servers. Their use is embedded in the higher-level calls described in the sections, "Creation and Manipulation of CLIENT Handles" and "Registering Servers." `rpcinfo(8C)` makes use of many of these procedures. The `portmap(3C)` routines summarized in the following table provide mechanisms for C clients to make procedure calls to this network RPC binder service.

Procedure	Description
`pmap_getmaps(3C)`	Get a remote host's program-to-address maps.
`pmap_getport(3C)`	Get the port number of a remote service.
`pmap_rmtcall(3C)`	Use a remote portmap service to call a service.
`pmap_set(3C)`	Register a service with a local portmap.
`pmap_unset(3C)`	Erase portmap service registration (association).
`xdr_pmap(3C)`	Create portmap call parameters yourself.
`xdr_pmaplist(3C)`	Get a portmap dump outside of `pmap_getmaps()`.

Synopsis

pmap_getmaps()

```
#include <rpc/rpc.h>
struct pmaplist * pmap_getmaps(addr)
    struct sockaddr_in *addr;
```

Returns a complete list of program-to-address mappings from the portmap of the machine with IP address *addr. It returns NULL if the portmap service cannot be contacted.

pmap_getport()

```
u_short pmap_getport(addr, prognum, versnum, protocol)
    struct sockaddr_in *addr;
    u_long prognum, versnum, protocol;
```

Returns the port number the specified service is waiting at. You specify RPC program number prognum, version versnum, and the transport protocol protocol, either IPPROTO_UDP or IPPROTO_TCP. The socket address is returned in addr, which should be pre-allocated. Zero is returned if the mapping does not exist or the remote portmap service couldn't be contacted. If the remote portmap couldn't be contacted, the RPC status is left in the global variable rpc_createerr (see rpc_clnt_create(3N)). The port number for a different version number is returned if no exact match is registered. The port number is host byte order. Convert it with htons(3N) if it is to be used as part of the sockad-

pmap_rmtcall()

```
enum clnt_stat pmap_rmtcall(addr, prognum, versnum, procnum, inproc, in, outproc,
                    out, timeout, portp)
    struct sockaddr_in *addr;
    u_long prognum, versnum, procnum;
    char *in, *out;
    xdrproc_t inproc, outproc;
    struct timeval timeout;
    u_long *portp;
```

Requests the portmap service at the IP address *addr to directly make an RPC to a procedure on that host. *portp reflects the program's port number if the procedure succeeds. The parameter definitions, including the return value, are discussed in callrpc() and clnt_call() (see Reference Section Three). No authentication is performed. If the requested remote procedure is not registered, no error response is returned and the call times-out.

pmap_set()

```
bool_t pmap_set(prognum, versnum, protocol, port)
    u_long prognum, versnum;
```

```
    int protocol;
    u_short port;
```

Registers with the local machine portmap service an association or mapping triple [prognum, versnum, protocol]. It ties an RPC program number prognum, version number versnum, and transport protocol protocol with a port number port. The value of protocol may be IPPROTO_UDP or IPPROTO_TCP. This routine returns TRUE if it succeeds, FALSE otherwise. Servers use this to register themselves with the local portmap when they call svc_register().

In the SunOS 4.1 version of the library, pmap_set() and pmap_unset() are disallowed from a remote host. These functions cannot be called to affect reserved ports when the caller is an unreserved port.

pmap_unset()

```
    bool_t pmap_unset(prognum, versnum)
        u_long prognum, versnum;
```

Tells the local portmap to remove registrations for triples that match [prognum, versnum, *]. Returns TRUE if it succeeds, FALSE otherwise.

xdr_pmap()

```
    bool_t xdr_pmap(xdrs, regp)
        XDR *xdrs;
        struct pmap *regp;
```

Used to create low-level XDR parameters for portmap calls outside of the above portmap interface. Returns TRUE if it succeeds, FALSE otherwise.

xdr_pmaplist()

```
    bool_t xdr_pmaplist(xdrs, rp)
        XDR *xdrs;
        struct pmaplist **rp;
```

Used to create a low-level port mapping list outside of the above interface. Returns TRUE if it succeeds, FALSE otherwise.

Section Three:
ONC RPC Library Routines

Overview

The ONC RPC library routines isolate the C programmer from the specialized data structures developed on top of UNIX IPCs for the purpose of remote procedure calling. The basic process consists of the client finding the appropriate service, checking authentication, and placing a request to run a service procedure. After a client request is made and validated, the server replies to the client with results generated by the selected procedure.

If you use a protocol compiler like RPCGEN or RPCTool, you need not read this entire section. The only call you'll need to make is `clnt_create(3N)` to create a `CLIENT` handle. The compiler will do the rest. If you do have a need to go below the protocol compiler and can use the unreliable UDP transport, the high-level client RPC library routine, `callrpc(3N)`, will perform RPCs in a single call. You can register and run a UDP service with just `registerrpc(3N)` and `svc_run(3N)`. The rest of the high-level as well as the low-level RPC library routines are covered here. In this sense the ONC RPC library can be split into two pieces: high-level and low-level calls, as illustrated in the following figure.

The ONC RPC library is presented in a summary of routines by function and then alphabetically listed to present a brief synopsis. Using any of these RPC routines requires #include <rpc/rpc.h>.

We cover the ONC RPC library as found in SunOS 4.1. This is a superset of the RPCSRC 4.0 release or the SunOS 4.0 version of the library. Additions are denoted in the "Synopsis" section.

Functional Summary

Building Client Authentication

In ONC RPC, a `CLIENT` handle is first created by the client to reach a server. Next, before a request can be made, some level of authentication must be made by the server of the client: AUTH_NONE, AUTH_UNIX, or AUTH_DES. AUTH_NONE requires no checking before requests are serviced; AUTH_UNIX requires standard username/password checks; AUTH_DES uses encryption and verification.

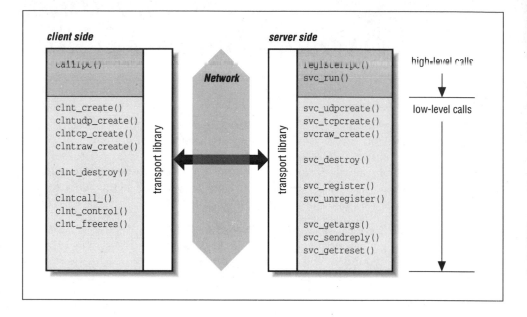

An AUTH authentication structure (described in Chapter 12) is passed to the server for each RPC.

auth_destroy()	Destroy authentication information
authnone_create()	Create default authentication information, no usable authentication information is passed with each RPC.
authunix_create(), authunix_create_default()	Build authentication information from UNIX credentials.

Making the Call from the Client

callrpc() is the simplest approach. callrpc(), clnt_broadcast(), and clnt_call() are the client-side functions used to actually send the RPC request, staying blocked until the reply is sent. The clnt_stat status structure is returned, and if non-zero, denotes a problem that can be explained by the error routines. clnt_call() is used after CLIENT handle and authentication have been assembled. The balance of the functions in this section of the library are dedicated to error handling.

clnt_call()	Make an RPC call using client handle.
callrpc()	Make a high-level UDP RPG.

clnt_broadcast( )	Broadcast an RPC request to all locally-connected broadcast nets.
clnt_freeres( ), clnt_geterr( ), clnt_perrno( ), clnt_perror( ), clnt_sperrno( ), clnt_sperror( )	Error handling and reporting at the client.

CLIENT Handle Management

A client is required to maintain a unique CLIENT structure for each open client/-server connection. Many of the RPC routines take a CLIENT handle as an argument to specify the client/server association. The handle is typically a twice indirect pointer to a CLIENT structure. The library routines isolate the programmer from the details of the structure.

A client object (referenced by its handle) contains information about the client-to-service connection.

clnt_control( )	Change and retrieve client object information.
clnt_create( )	Generic client handle creation.
clnt_create_vers( )	Generic client creation with version checking.
clnt_destroy( )	Release resources associated with a client handle.
clnt_pcreateerror( )	Report client creation errors to stderr.
clntraw_create( )	Create a client handle for intraprocess RPCs.
clnt_spcreateerror( )	Like `clnt_pcreateerror( )` but returns a string.
clnttcp_create( )	Create a TCP transport Internet client handle.
clntudp_create( ), clntudp_bufcreate( )	Create a UDP transport Internet client handle.
rpc_createerr	A global variable recording client creation errors.

Server Registration With The Portmap

After a server is started, it must register itself in the port mapping. A number of procedures are provided to expedite the communication with the portmap(8C) service. If you are writing a server stub by hand, you'll need to use these to tell portmap the program and version numbers associated with your dispatch function. A protocol compiler can alleviate using any of the calls in this section.

The simplest interface is registerrpc().

registerrpc()	Register a UDP service procedure with the local port-map.
svc_register()	Register a service with the local portmap.
svc_unregister()	Unregister a service from the local portmap.
xprt_register(), xprt_unregister()	Register service transports with RPC.

A Programming Tip on Avoiding Conflicts

Whether you use registerrpc() or svc_register() to register the service, you may accidentally displace the portmap registration of a service that is already running on that machine. This leaves a process running that is hard to contact. David Brownell suggests that when the server is first started, you attempt to bind to it, attempting to create a CLIENT handle. If this succeeds and a subsequent ping to the NULLPROC shows it to be healthy, your server should exit before registering itself with the portmap.

SVCXPRT Service Transport Handle Management

As the CLIENT requires structures to associate information with the client, servers need similar structures. The SVCXPRT data structure or service transport handle describes server communications.

svc_destroy()	Destroy the service transport structure and free associated resources.
svcfd_create()	Create a service transport on top of an already open, bound descriptor.
svcraw_create()	Creates a local process space transport for intra-process RPCs.
svctcp_create()	Creates a TCP service transport.
svcudp_bufcreate(), svcudp_create()	Creates a UDP service transport.

Server Side Error Handling And Reporting

A number of routines are provided to try to make server errors recognizable. This is one of the classic difficulties of remote programming—you can't see what's going on at the server. These routines are used by the server-side dispatch function (the code responsible for directing things) to declare client transaction problems like

XDR decoding, authentication, procedure, program, and version errors, as well as overall execution problems.

The server calls these routines to indicate error conditions and handle them.

svcerr_auth( )	Called by the server to indicate service cannot be provided due to authentication errors.
svcerr_decode( )	Arguments cannot be decoded from the request; see `svc_getargs()`.
svcerr_noproc( )	Dispatch indicates a procedure number isn't available.
svcerr_noprog( )	Indicates a program number isn't available (usually not a server issue).
svcerr_progvers( )	Indicates a program version number mismatch (usually not a server issue).
svcerr_systemerr( )	An error outside of the RPC transport/protocol has occurred.
svcerr_weakauth( )	Service routine indicates the service was not provided due to insufficient authentication.

Server I/O and Utility

A number of library routines exist to simplify the server/socket interface. If you can live within the constraints imposed by the protocol compiler, you never have to use these functions because they are hidden within the dispatcher and server stub. Should you require a socket interface, multi-tasking, or an access control policy, you need to become familiar with them.

The server typically is looping, checking for requests. Once found, it provides services using these functions.

svc_fds, svc_fdset	Global variables reflecting the RPC server's read file descriptor bit mask, used to `select()` activity.
svc_freeargs( )	Free any XDR/RPC data allocated by a `svc_getargs()`
svc_getargs( )	Decode the incoming request arguments.
svc_getcaller( )	Get the service network address from the SVCXPRT.
svc_getreq( ), svc_getreqset( )	For building your own service loop, provides services to sockets with activity (see `svc_fds, svc_fdset`).

| svc_run() | Called by a server dispatch function or the like to loop in wait of requests. |
| svc_sendreply() | Server sends a solicited reply to the requesting client. |

Direct XDR Access

These RPC XDR library routines can be used to implement low-level remote procedure calling actions. The routines describe RPC messages (authentication information, replies, requests, etc.) in the XDR neutral form. They can be used to implement your own ONC RPC-like transactions for remote procedure calling. Typically they return `bool_t` TRUE on success, FALSE on failure. If the ONC RPC manual pages are installed, see `rpc_xdr(3N)`. You've got to be a little twisted to use these.

xdr_accepted_reply()	Encode RPC reply.
xdr_authunix_parms()	Describe UNIX credentials.
xdr_callhdr()	Used to describe the RPC call header message.
xdr_callmsg()	Used to describe the RPC call message itself.
xdr_opaque_auth()	Builds RPC authentication information messages.
xdr_rejected_reply()	Records the rejection reply message in XDR format.
xdr_replymsg()	Builds an XDR format RPC reply message.

Making Secure RPCs

Because it can be easy to impersonate a user, additional remote procedure call security is provided through use of the secure RPC library routines. The circa 1990 versions of ONC RPC support three authentication schemes: AUTH_NONE, AUTH_UNIX, and AUTH_DES, with more sophisticated security schemes released soon after. The section, "Client Authentication," covers AUTH_NONE and AUTH_UNIX authentication types.

The routines described here are for using the AUTH_DES NBS Data Encryption Standard (DES) algorithm for authentication. Typically they return `bool_t` TRUE on success, FALSE on failure. `authdes_create()` and `authdes_getucred()` implement the actual DES authentication, the balance of the routines provide support. It encrypts and decrypts data in a secure fashion. The algorithm is driven by a user-supplied key, or in some uses a randomly generated one. See Data Encryption Standard (DES), `des(1)`, for a UNIX implementation of the DES algorithm. `crypt` and associated routines are used for UNIX DES password maintenance.

For the RPC DES authentication system to work, both client and server must have their encryption keys in the publickey(5) database and both have the keyserv(8C) daemon running. Many of the routines use or return AUTH * authentication handles. The keyserv(8C) service must be running on client and server, as keys for both sides are kept there.

authdes_create( )	Create DES authentication.
authdes_getucred( )	Server maps DES credentials into UNIX equivalent.
get_myaddress( )	Return the machine's IP address.
getnetname( )	Return the unique, operating system-independent net-name.
key_decryptsession( ), key_encryptsession( )	Keyserver daemon interface routines, users rarely need these. They use a public key from the keyserver and a secret key associated with the effective user ID of the calling process to decrypt or encrypt a DES key.
key_gendes( )	Ask the keyserver for a secure DES conversation key.
key_setsecret( )	Tell the keyserver to set the secret key for the effective user ID of the calling process.
netname2host( ), host2netname( )	Convert between operating system-independent net-name and domain.
netname2user( ), user2netname( )	Convert between operating system-independent net-name and domain.

Synopsis

In this section, RPC library routines are briefly described.

authdes_create()

```
AUTH *
authdes_create(netname, window, syncaddr, deskeyp)
    char *netname;
    unsigned window;
    struct sockaddr_in *syncaddr;
    des_block *deskeyp;
```

authdes_create() returns the client an authentication handle to use with the secure authentication system. It takes as input the server machine's netname, as returned by procedures below, and a time `window` in seconds for which the credentials are valid. These may be DES encoded by a random or user-specified key.

authdes_getucred()

```
int
authdes_getucred(adc, uidp, gidp, gidlenp, gidlistp)
    struct authdes_cred *adc;
    short *uidp;
    short *gidp;
    short *gidlenp;
    int *gidlistp;
```

`authdes_getucred()` is used on the server side to convert operating system-independent DES credentials into UNIX format credentials. Different from `netname2user()` described below, it gets information from a cache, avoiding repeated NIS name service look-ups. It returns TRUE on success, FALSE on failure.

auth_destroy()

```
void
auth_destroy(auth)
    AUTH *auth;
```

`auth_destroy()` destroys the authentication information in the given AUTH.

authnone_create()

```
AUTH *
authnone_create()
```

`authnone_create()` creates and returns a new authentication handle for AUTH_NONE authentication, the default authentication used by ONC RPC.

authunix_create()

```
AUTH *
authunix_create(host, uid, gid, grouplen, gidlistp)
    char *host;
    int uid, gid, grouplen, *gidlistp;
```

`authunix_create()` is the same as above, but for AUTH_UNIX type authentication, using standard UNIX credentials.

authunix_create_default()

```
AUTH *
authunix_create_default()
```

`authunix_create_default()` calls `authunix_create()` filling in the standard authentication parameters for that user.

callrpc()

```
int
callrpc(host, prognum, versnum, procnum, inproc, in, outproc, out)
    char *host;
    u_long prognum, versnum, procnum;
    char *in;
    xdrproc_t inproc;
    char *out;
    xdrproc_t outproc;
```

callrpc() makes a remote procedure call to a specified program, version, and procedure number on the specified host. Inputs and outputs are passed through the specified conversion routines for both XDR encoding and decoding. callrpc() will retry the request 5 times, every five seconds, returning with a time-out error if the 25 seconds has elapsed with no reply. Return value is 0 if successful, or a status integer if failure. clnt_perrno() (described below) can be used to translate the error into something meaningful. RPCs made this way use UDP/IP transport with no control of time-outs or authentication.

clnt_broadcast()

```
enum clnt_stat
clnt_broadcast(prognum, versnum, procnum, inproc, in, outproc, out, eachresult)
    u_long prognum, versnum, procnum;
    char *in;
    xdrproc_t inproc;
    char *out;
    xdrproc_t outproc;
    bool_t eachresult;
```

clnt_broadcast() is a broadcast version of callrpc(). It makes requests of all locally-connected network machines using AUTH_UNIX style authentication. Each time a reply is received, the eachresult() procedure is called to handle the results. Broadcast packets are limited in size by the underlying data link transfer unit. For Ethernet, this limits the caller's argument portion of the request packet to 1400 bytes.

clnt_call()

```
enum clnt_stat
clnt_call(clnt, procnum, inproc, in, outproc, out, timeout)
    CLIENT *clnt;
    u_long procnum;
    xdrproc_t inproc, outproc;
    char *in, *out;
    struct timeval timeout;
```

clnt_call() uses the CLIENT handle to call the remote procedure, procnum. It encodes request arguments and reply results by the specified XDR procedures. Time-out interval is also controllable. Under the SunOS 4.1 release, clnt_call() now uses an exponential back-off scheme when retrying requests.

clnt_control()

```
bool_t
clnt_control(clnt, request, info)
    CLIENT *clnt;
    int request;
    char *info;
```

clnt_control() changes or retrieves CLIENT characteristics, including: time-out, UDP retry time-out, socket descriptor (both ends), and their status. Works for both UDP and TCP transports. It returns TRUE if successful, FALSE otherwise. The supported values of request, their info argument types, and what they do are listed in the tables below. Note: send a pointer to the info.

Request Value	Info Argument	Description
CLSET_TIMEOUT	struct timeval	Set total time-out.
CLGET_TIMEOUT	struct timeval	Get total time-out.
CLGET_FD	int	Get associated socket.
CLSET_FD_CLOSE	void	Close socket on clnt_destroy().
CLSET_FD_NCLOSE	void	Leave socket open on clnt_destroy().
CLGET_SERVER_ADDR	struct sockaddr_in	Get server's address.

The following operations are valid for UDP only:

Request Value	Info Argument	Description
CLSET_RETRY_TIMEOUT	struct timeval	Set the retry time-out.
CLGET_RETRY_TIMEOUT	struct timeval	Get the retry time-out.

If you set the time-out using clnt_control(), the time-out parameter passed to clnt_call() will be ignored in all future calls. The retry time-out is the time that UDP RPC waits for the server to reply before retransmitting the request. Setting the time-out value to 0 for a clnt_call() affects an RPC request without waiting for a reply—a one-way RPC. In this case clnt_call() always indicates a time-out error on return. The service should be written so as not to issue a svc_sendreply() in one-way RPCs. This routine returns TRUE if it succeeds and FALSE otherwise.

clnt_create()

```
CLIENT *
clnt_create(host, prognum, versnum, protocol)
    char *host;
    u_long prognum, versnum;
    char *protocol;
```

clnt_create() creates the CLIENT structure for the specified server host, program, and version numbers. Transport protocol is selectable, but note that UDP RPC messages are at most 8K bytes, so procedures requiring or returning more than 8K bytes of encoded data should use TCP. If it succeeds, the CLIENT handle is returned. If it fails, that is if the query of the named server's portmap does not reveal a match in program number, NULL is returned. A version number mismatch doesn't qualify as an error, but will be revealed later by a clnt_call().

clnt_create_vers()

```
CLIENT *
clnt_create_vers(host, prognum, vers_outp, vers_low, vers_high, protocol)
    char *host;
    u_long prognum;
    u_long *vers_outp;
    u_long vers_low, vers_high;
    char *protocol;
```

clnt_create_vers() is like clnt_create() except that it allows specification of a candidate version number range. This heads off later errors that a subsequent clnt_call() would produce due to a version mismatch. It allows you to group versions according to generations of request and reply arguments.

clnt_destroy()

```
void
clnt_destroy(clnt)
    CLIENT *clnt;
```

clnt_destroy() deallocates memory associated with private data structures for the named CLIENT handle. If the RPC routines were used to open the socket, the socket is neatly closed.

clnt_freeres()

```
bool_t
clnt_freeres(clnt, outproc, out)
    CLIENT *clnt;
    xdrproc_t outproc;
    char *out;
```

Free any data allocated by the RPC/XDR system from the decoding of a reply at the client. out is the address of the results, outproc the XDR routine used with them. It's equivalent to calling xdr_free(outproc, out). It returns TRUE upon success, FALSE otherwise.

clnt_geterr()

```
void
clnt_geterr(clnt, errp)
    CLIENT *clnt;
    struct rpc_err *errp;
```

clnt_geterr() copies the error structure out of the client handle into pre-allocated memory.

clnt_pcreateerror()

```
void
clnt_pcreateerror(str)
    char *str;
```

clnt_pcreateerror() translates CLIENT handle creation errors into something useful at stderr. It is handy when used with clnt_create(), clntraw_create(), clnttcp_create(), or clntudp_create().

clnt_perrno()

```
void
clnt_perrno(stat)
    enum clnt_stat stat;
```

clnt_perrno() processes the client status returned by callrpc() and clnt_broadcast(). It sends the results to stderr.

clnt_perror()

```
void
clnt_perror(clnt, str)
    CLIENT *clnt;
    char *str;
```

clnt_perror() is like clnt_perrno(), though it is an error utility for use with clnt_call(). It puts an error message and your string to stderr.

clntraw_create()

```
#include <rpc/raw.h>
CLIENT *
clntraw_create(prognum, versnum)
    u_long prognum, versnum;
```

clntraw_create() is used to create a local CLIENT handle to communicate with a server in the same process address space, itself created with svcraw_create(). This approach is useful for debugging, with the communication carried out through a buffer, though independent of the kernel, to simulate RPC overhead. A CLIENT handle is returned upon success, otherwise NULL.

Under SunOS 4.1, the Raw transport now works. It does not work correctly under Release 4.0.

clnt_spcreateerror()

```
char *
clnt_spcreateerror(str)
    char *str;
```

clnt_spcreateerror() returns a pointer to a static string containing an error message like that in clnt_pcreateerror().

clnt_sperrno()

```
char *
clnt_sperrno(stat)
    enum clnt_stat stat;
```

clnt_sperrno() is like clnt_perrno() but returns a pointer to the message instead of placing at stderr.

clnt_sperror()

```
char *
clnt_sperror(clnt, str)
    CLIENT *clnt;
    char *str;
```

clnt_sperror() returns a pointer to a static message, otherwise like clnt_sperrno().

clnttcp_create()

```
CLIENT *
clnttcp_create(addr, prognum, versnum, sockp, sendsz, recvsz)
    struct sockaddr_in *addr;
    u_long prognum, versnum;
    int *sockp;
    u_int sendsz, recvsz;
```

clnttcp_create() creates a TCP transport CLIENT handle for the specified program and version number on Internet addressed server machine (if possible). If not specified, port and socket information is returned. The size of the TCP send and receive buffers may be specified, or zeroed to issue defaults. Success returns a CLIENT handle, otherwise NULL. The same potential for version mismatch exists as in clnt_create() above.

clntudp_bufcreate()

```
CLIENT *
clntudp_bufcreate(addr, prognum, versnum, wait, sockp, sendsz, recvsz)
    struct sockaddr_in *addr;
    u_long prognum, versnum;
```

```
        struct timeval wait;
        int *sockp;
        u_int sendsz;
        u_int recvsz;
```

clntudp_bufcreate() is similar to clnttcp_create() but creates UDP transport protocol CLIENT handles. The wait time for retries and time-outs is specified for the UDP transport. The total time allowed for RPC completion can be specified by clnt_call(). Buffer sizes may be specified or defaulted. The same potential for version number mismatch exists. Success returns the CLIENT handle, failure NULL.

clntudp_create()

```
        CLIENT *
        clntudp_create(addr, prognum, versnum, wait, sockp)
            struct sockaddr_in *addr;
            u_long prognum, versnum;
            struct timeval wait;
            int *sockp;
```

clntudp_create() is the same as clntudp_bufcreate() but lacks buffer size definitions, instead taking the defaults.

get_myaddress()

```
        void
        get_myaddress(addr)
            struct sockaddr_in *addr;
```

get_myaddress() returns a pointer to a struct sockaddr_in (see "Berkeley Sockets" in Chapter 5) containing the machine's IP address and portmap port number.

getnetname()

```
        int
        getnetname(netname)
            char netname[MAXNETNAMELEN];
```

getnetname() fills a character array with the machine's operating-system independent netname, NULL-terminated. It returns TRUE on success, FALSE on failure.

getrpcport()

```
        int getrpcport(host, prognum, versnum, proto)
            char *host;
            int prognum, versnum, proto;
```

The ONC RPC library includes a way to check for a specific portmap registration without using portmapper functions directly.

getrpcport(3R) returns the port number used by an RPC server on host. You specify the version number versnum, program number prognum, and the protocol `proto`. It returns NULL if it cannot contact the `hosts`'s portmapper, or if `prognum` using protocol `proto` is not registered. Notice the version number `versnum` need not match that specified in the portmap. Version mismatches are detected and subsequent client decisions made at the time the remote call is placed. This allows for compatibility across versions of servers.

Any number of RPC service procedures may share an RPC program number.

host2netname()

```
int
host2netname(netname, host, domain)
    char netname[MAXNETNAMELEN];
    char *host;
    char *domain;
```

`host2netname()` fills a character array with the machine's operating-system independent netname, NULL terminated, given a domain-specific hostname. Often used by servers, who then pass netname to `authdes_create()` to get an authentication handle. It's the inverse of `netname2host()`. It returns TRUE on success, FALSE on failure.

key_decryptsession()

```
int
key_decryptsession(netname, deskeyp)
    char *netname;
    des_block *deskeyp;
```

`key_decryptsession()` interfaces with the keyserver daemon used for RPC secure authentication. It takes the server's `netname` and the DES key, looks up the public key of the server and secret key associated with the calling process to decrypt the DES key. `key_encryptsession()` performs the inverse function. You will rarely need to interact with the keyserver daemon at this low level, minimizing the use of `key_decryptsession()`, `key_encryptsession()`, `key_gendes()`, and `key_setsecret()`. Login and other system commands, as well as the above- mentioned RPC library routines use these. It returns TRUE on success, FALSE on failure.

key_encryptsession()

```
int
key_encryptsession(netname, deskeyp)
    char *netname;
    des_block *deskeyp;
```

`key_encryptsession()` is similar to above, but encrypts the DES key using the public key of the server and the secret key from the calling process. It returns TRUE on success, FALSE on failure.

key_gendes()

```
int
key_gendes(deskeyp)
    des_block *deskeyp;
```

key_gendes() gets a secure conversation key from the keyserver. Better than attempting to choose one at random. It returns TRUE on success, FALSE on failure.

key_setsecret()

```
int
key_setsecret(keyp)
    char *keyp;
```

key_setsecret() sets the secret key at the keyserver for the effective user ID of the calling process. It returns TRUE on success, FALSE on failure.

netname2host()

```
int
netname2host(netname, host, hostlen)
    char *netname;
    char *host;
    int hostlen;
```

netname2host() is the inverse of host2netname(), converts netnames (operating-system independent) to a domain-specific hostname. It returns TRUE on success, FALSE on failure.

netname2user()

```
int
netname2user(netname, uidp, gidp, gidlenp, gidlistp)
    char *name;
    int *uidp;
    int *gidp;
    int *gidlenp;
    int *gidlistp;
```

netname2user() converts a netname to a domain-specific user ID. It returns TRUE on success, FALSE on failure.

registerrpc()

```
int
registerrpc(prognum, versnum, procnum, procname, inproc, outproc)
    u_long prognum, versnum, procnum;
    char *(*procname) () ;
    xdrproc_t inproc, outproc;
```

registerrpc() allows a UDP protocol RPC server to register its (string) name, program, version, and procedure numbers. When an appropriate request arrives, the named procedures decode the XDR input arguments and encode the output into XDR form. It returns a 0 if it succeeds; -1 if it fails to register.

rpc_createerr

```
struct rpc_createerr
rpc_createerr;
```

This is a global variable whose value is set by any RPC client-creation failure. It's used by `clnt_pcreateerror()`, etc.

svc_destroy()

```
void
svc_destroy(xprt)
    SVCXPRT *xprt;
```

`svc_destroy()` deallocated the memory associated with the named `SVCXPRT` service transport handle.

svcfd_create()

```
SVCXPRT *
svcfd_create(fd, sendsz, recvsz)
    int fd;
    u_int sendsz;
    u_int recvsz;
```

`svcfd_create()` creates and returns a `SVCXPRT` service transport handle using the named descriptor and send and receive buffer sizes (or defaults). It returns `NULL` if it fails.

svc_fds

```
int
svc_fds;
```

`svc_fds` is made obsolete by `svc_fdset` which is similar but limited to 32 descriptors because it is an `int`.

svc_fdset

```
fd_set
svc_fdset;
```

`svc_fdset` is a read-only global variable, the server read file descriptor bit mask of type `fd_set`, a file descriptor set. Useful to programmers interested in doing their own asynchronous request processing (instead of just `svc_run()`) as `svc_fdset` is a suitable parameter for working with multiple descriptors (e.g., with `select()`). See `xprt_register()` and `xprt_unregister()`.

svc_freeargs()

```
bool_t
svc_freeargs(xprt, inproc, in)
    SVCXPRT *xprt;
    xdrproc_t inproc;
    char *in;
```

svc_freeargs() frees memory allocated by decoding with svc_getargs().
Returns TRUE if successful, otherwise FALSE.

svc_getargs()

```
bool_t
svc_getargs(xprt, inproc, in)
    SVCXPRT *xprt;
    xdrproc_t inproc;
    char *in;
```

svc_getargs() decodes server arguments from XDR neutral form given data
pointer and decode routine. Returns TRUE if successful, otherwise FALSE.

svc_getcaller()

```
struct sockaddr_in *
svc_getcaller(xprt)
    SVCXPRT *xprt;
```

svc_getcaller() goes back and gets the network address of the client. It's
really just a macro that looks at the transport fields:

```
#define svc_getcaller(xprt) (&(xprt)->xp_raddr)
```

svc_getreq()

```
void
svc_getreq(rdfds)
    int rdfds;
```

svc_getreq() is an ancestor to svc_getreqset(), limited to 32 socket
descriptors.

svc_getreqset()

```
void
svc_getreqset(rdfdsp)
    fd_set *rdfdsp;
```

svc_getreqset() can be used instead of svc_run() to implement your own
asynchronous request processing. Use a select() system call to determine if
there are outstanding RPC request(s) at any of the socket(s) generated when registering. The read file bit mask returned by select() is used to call
svc_getreqset(), which returns only when the read bits (requests at sockets)
are cleared. This can provide a valuable way to monitor or control servicing on a

per client basis. See select(2) or the brief explanation of select() in the section, "Advanced Socket Programming Issues," in Chapter 5 as well as Chapters 9 and 10 for a discussion of fd_set and bit masks.

svcerr_auth()

```
void
svcerr_auth(xprt, why)
    SVCXPRT *xprt;
    enum auth_stat why;
```

svcerr_auth() is called by a server when refusing an RPC because of an authentication error.

svcerr_decode()

```
void
svcerr_decode(xprt)
    SVCXPRT *xprt;
```

svcerr_decode() is used if the service cannot decode the request parameters; e.g., svc_getargs() fails.

svcerr_noproc()

```
void svcerr_noproc(xprt)
    SVCXPRT *xprt;
```

svcerr_noproc() is used if the service does not have the procedure number requested.

svcerr_noprog()

```
void
svcerr_noprog(xprt)
    SVCXPRT *xprt;
```

svcerr_noprog() is used to report that the service is not registered. It is typically not required of RPC developers.

svcerr_progvers()

```
void
svcerr_progvers(xprt)
    SVCXPRT *xprt;
```

svcerr_progvers() reports a version number problem. This is rarely needed by RPC developers because problems stemming from version incompatibility can be avoided.

svcerr_systemerr()

```
void
svcerr_systemerr(xprt)
    SVCXPRT *xprt;
```

svcerr_systemerr() reports some undetermined system error, not covered by a particular protocol; e.g., insufficient memory.

svcerr_weakauth()

```
void
svcerr_weakauth(xprt)
    SVCXPRT *xprt;
```

svcerr_weakauth() reports insufficient authentication parameters, then itself calls svcerr_auth().

svcraw_create()

```
#include <rpc/raw.h>
SVCXPRT *
svcraw_create()
```

svcraw_create() creates and returns a dummy service transport, suitable for local process-space buffered client/server communication (outside of the kernel). See clntraw_create() on rpc_clnt_create(3N). It returns NULL if it fails.

svc_register()

```
bool_t
svc_register(xprt, prognum, versnum, dispatch, protocol)
    SVCXPRT *xprt;
    u_long prognum, versnum;
    void (*dispatch) ();
    u_long protocol;
```

svc_register() works directly with the portmap to register a dispatch routine of a specified protocol. It returns TRUE if it succeeds, otherwise FALSE.

svc_run()

```
void
svc_run()
```

svc_run() is used to indefinitely service requests as they arrive, returning only if there is an unrecoverable error. It basically puts the server in an indefinite loop. It effectively issues a select(), with an infinite time-out period, launching a svc_getreqset() when select() returns with an eligible read file descriptor(s). This denotes an incoming request.

See Chapter 5 for more details on how to write your own svc_run(). This can become necessary when you have other low-level descriptors involved, e.g., those of a windowing system, or want to implement asynchrony or concurrency at the client or server.

svc_sendreply()

```
bool_t
svc_sendreply(xprt, outproc, out)
    SVCXPRT *xprt;
    xdrproc_t outproc;
    char *out;
```

`svc_sendreply()` is used by service dispatch routines to reply to the client, passing the specified data through the specified XDR encoder. It returns TRUE if it succeeds, FALSE otherwise.

svctcp_create()

```
SVCXPRT *
svctcp_create(sock, sendsz, recvsz)
    int sock;
    u_int sendsz, recvsz;
```

`svctcp_create()` creates and returns a TCP RPC service transport at a particular socket, or creates a socket along it. Like the client-side equivalent `clnttcp_create()`, TCP-based RPC uses buffered I/O, with specified or default buffer sizes. It returns NULL if it fails.

svcudp_create()

```
SVCXPRT *
svcudp_create(sock)
    int sock;
```

`svcudp_create()` creates and returns a pointer to a UDP/IP-based RPC transport. The value of `sock` may be either that of an open socket descriptor or RPC_ANYSOCK, in which case a socket is created. The socket is bound to an arbitrary local UDP port. It returns NULL if it fails.

svcudp_bufcreate()

```
SVCXPRT *
svcudp_bufcreate(sock, sendsz, recvsz)
    int sock;
    u_int sendsz, recvsz;
```

`svcudp_bufcreate()` creates and returns a pointer to a UDP/IP RPC transport. If directed, it generates a socket. If necessary, the socket is bound to an arbitrary local UDP port. Similar to its client counterpart `clntudp_bufcreate()`, `svcudp_bufcreate()` allows specification of the maximum send and receive packet sizes for the UDP-based RPC messages. It returns NULL if it fails.

svc_unregister()

```
void
svc_unregister(prognum, versnum)
    u_long prognum, versnum;
```

svc_unregister() erases portmap entries for the named program and version number.

user2netname()

```
int
user2netname(netname, uid, domain)
    char name[MAXNETNAMELEN];
    int uid;
    char *domain;
```

user2netname() is the inverse of netname2user(), converts a domain-specific username (including user ID of owning process) to a netname. Servers use this to get netname used to call authdes_create() to get an authentication handle. It returns TRUE on success, FALSE on failure.

xdr_accepted_reply()

```
bool_t
xdr_accepted_reply(xdrs, arp)
    XDR *xdrs;
    struct accepted_reply *arp;
```

xdr_accepted_reply() encodes RPC replies in XDR form.

xdr_authunix_parms()

```
bool_t
xdr_authunix_parms(xdrs, aup)
    XDR *xdrs;
    struct authunix_parms *aup;
```

xdr_authunix_parms() puts UNIX authentication information into an XDR structure to facilitate future validation.

xdr_callhdr()

```
void
xdr_callhdr(xdrs, chdrp)
    XDR *xdrs;
    struct rpc_msg *chdrp;
```

xdr_callhdr() creates an XDR representation of an RPC header message.

xdr_callmsg()

```
bool_t
xdr_callmsg(xdrs, cmsgp)
```

```
        XDR *xdrs;
        struct rpc_msg *cmsgp;
```

xdr_callmsg() creates an XDR representation of an RPC call message.

xdr_opaque_auth()

```
    bool_t
    xdr_opaque_auth(xdrs, ap)
        XDR *xdrs;
        struct opaque_auth *ap;
```

xdr_opaque_auth() creates an XDR representation of an RPC authentication information message.

xdr_rejected_reply()

```
    bool_t
    xdr_rejected_reply(xdrs, rrp)
        XDR *xdrs;
        struct rejected_reply *rrp;
```

xdr_rejected_reply() encodes a rejection reply into XDR format (due to version number mismatch or authentication errors).

xdr_replymsg()

```
    bool_t
    xdr_replymsg(xdrs, rmsgp)
        XDR *xdrs;
        struct rpc_msg *rmsgp;
```

xdr_replymsg() encodes an accepted, rejected, or NULL reply into XDR format.

xprt_register()

```
    void
    xprt_register(xprt)
        SVCXPRT *xprt;
```

xprt_register() is a low-level call, typically not required to register service transport handles with the RPC system.

xprt_unregister()

```
    void
    xprt_unregister(xprt)
        SVCXPRT *xprt;
```

xprt_unregister() unregisters service transport handles with RPC.

Error Codes

The enum `clnt_stat` as returned by many of the client-side ONC RPC library calls can take on a number of values:

RPC_SUCCESS   The RPC was successful.

RPC_CANTENCODEARGS
          An attempt to encode a request failed. Either the XDR filters couldn't encode your request parameters or the RPC message header couldn't be built.

RPC_CANTSEND   A transport error occurred while sending the request to the service.

RPC_CANTDECODERES An attempt to decode reply results from the service failed. The XDR routines could not decode either the RPC header or the results.

RPC_CANTRECV   A transport error occurred while receiving the reply from the service.

RPC_TIMEDOUT   A time-out while waiting for the service to reply.

RPC_VERSMISMATCH   The service does not have the same version of the protocol that the client has specified. The RPC may continue.

RPC_AUTHERR   An authentication error occurred at the server.

RPC_PROGUNAVAIL   `svcerr_noprog()` on the server side says the specified program is unavailable. Usually you gained server access through the portmap, so this is not used.

RPC_PROGVERSMISMATCH
          The specified version and program are not matched. This error is sent back from a call to `svcerr_progvers()` at the server.

RPC_PROCUNAVAIL   The requested procedure is not available on the server machine. The server uses `svcerr_noproc()` to send this message back to the client.

RPC_CANTDECODEARGS
          The service reports back to the client with `svcerr_decode()` that it cannot decode the request arguments to the procedure.

RPC_SYSTEMERROR   The service encountered some system error outside of the RPC system. The server sends this one back to the client with `svcerr_systemerr()`.

RPC_UNKNOWNHOST   The specified host is not known.

`RPC_UNKNOWNPROTO`   The specified transport protocol is not known.

`RPC_PMAPFAILURE`   An error occurred when the RPC system was making a call to the portmapper function.

`RPC_PROGNOTREGISTERED`
                      The program specified is not registered in the specified hosts's portmap.

`RPC_FAILED`   None of the above. An error other than the above occurred.

A

Obtaining RFCs (Internet Standards, Request for Comment)

RFCs are Internet Standards Request for Comment. Each proposed standard has to pass through this documentation phase. RFCs and related documents define the foundations of networking today. The most important RFCs are in a three-volume set, the *DDN Protocol Handbook*, available from:

```
DDN Network Information Center, SRI International
333 Ravenswood Avenue
Menlo Park, California 94025
(telephone: 800-235-3155)
```

You can obtain RFCs via anonymous ftp from *ftp.nisc.sri.com, nis.nsf.net, nisc.jvnc.net, venera.isi.edu, wuarchive.wustl.edu, src.doc.ic.ac.uk, ftp.concert.net,* and *nic.ddn.mil* (in the */inet/rfc* directory). See the preface of this book for RPC software availability discussions on using anonymous ftp. You can get more information about obtaining RFCs via ftp or e-mail by sending an e-mail message to *rfc-info@isi.edu* with the message body "help: ways_to_get_rfcs":

```
To: rfc-info@ISI.EDU
Subject: getting rfcs

help: ways_to_get_rfcs
```

Requests for special distribution should be addressed to either the author of the RFC in question, or to *nic@nic.ddn.mil.* Unless specifically noted otherwise on the RFC itself, all RFCs are for unlimited distribution.

B

An RPC Case Study: Networked Ray Tracing

In this case study, we cover in detail the construction and performance of a distributed application that renders synthetic images using the ray tracing paradigm. Previous efforts to accelerate ray tracing are surveyed. Remote procedure calling, RPC, is applied in multiplicity to the computationally demanding task of ray tracing. A parallel, distributed network application is developed, including scheduling and dynamic load balancing. Network and computational bandwidths are traded off to dynamically optimize ray tracing. Data distribution to facilitate parallel, recursive ray tracing is discussed. Performance results show a nearly optimal speed-up as additional networked computers are added. This makes photo-realistic animation easier to attain, exploiting the spare cycles on a multitude of networked, heterogeneous computers.

Introduction to Ray Tracing

Image synthesis by ray tracing approximates diffuse and specular reflections as well as refraction using a geometric optics model [Whit80]. (References begin on Page 423.) The quality of the resultant image is a function of the appropriateness and typical complexity of the model and the precision of object representations. As shown in Figure B-1, ray tracing casts rays from a viewpoint, through the image plane to intersect a display pixel. Each of these primary rays is checked for intersection with an object, identifying the surface closest to the viewpoint. If an intersection is found, secondary rays are cast into object space to check for shadow—present if an object stands between the surface intersection and the light source(s). Secondary rays are also used to model translucence or opacity. Secondary ray castings can in turn produce more secondary rays. By recursively tracing the rays refracted and reflected by the surface, a more physically accurate rendition is generated. This does require that optical parameters be defined for each object surface.

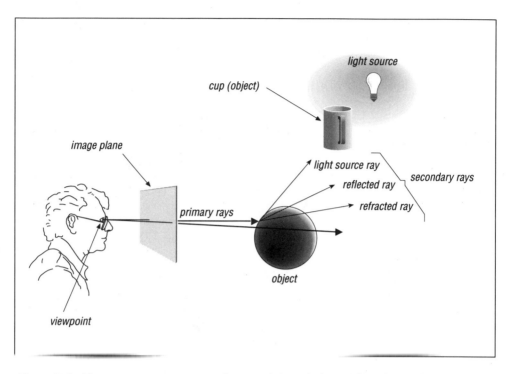

Figure B-1. The ray tracing, image synthesis paradigm (adapted from [Sam89])

Ray tracing, using even simple shading models, provides some of the most realistic scenes generated. With processor bandwidths and parallelism on the rise, 3D visualization is becoming practical, displacing faster surface-based 2D projection approaches [Mei89], [Udu90]. Note that projection approaches to image synthesis can be seen as degenerate ray tracing. They are equivalent to tracing primary rays and potentially select secondary rays, depending on the complexity of the shading model used [Weg84]. A scene equivalent to a parallel projection rendered via hidden-surface elimination using Z-buffering or a painter algorithm, can be generated by tracing parallel primary rays from the display. A perspective projection results when diverging primary rays are traced from a viewpoint.

Research efforts in ray tracing have attempted to:

1. *Increase realism of simulated natural phenomenon*—[Cia90] and [Kno89] summarize current realistic image synthesis and ray tracing models. Over-sampling (anti-aliasing), radiosity, and distributed ray tracing [Kaj86][Coo86] significantly improve image quality, but at additional computational cost [Lev88].

2. *Develop better geometric definitions*—the use of combinatorial solid geometry (CSG) models [Mor89] or 3D volume pixel (voxel) data (e.g., computed tomography [Udu90]) increases the range of geometric definitions available to a database designer.

3. *Speed up the process*—a very active area. We shall look at these efforts more closely, as our research addresses this topic using parallel network computations.

Accelerating Ray Tracing

The computational complexity of ray tracing warrants acceleration as the generation of even moderate-complexity scenes can take from minutes to hours on a serial mini-super computer. Research in this area can be further broken down:

    A.   Applying data structures to expedite ray/object intersection calculations.

    B.   Exploit object and image space coherence.

    C.   Exploit the parallelism inherent to ray tracing.

After surveying efforts in these areas, we present our efforts to exploit the parallelism inherent to ray tracing.

Checking rays for object intersections represents the majority of the ray tracing computations. Hierarchic data structures, including BSP trees and octrees, have been successfully applied to obtain significant computational savings [Sam89]. Enhancements to Whitted's original bounding volume help reduce the number of intersection checks. [Rub80] suggests objects be organized into a hierarchical tree of bounding volumes. [Kay86] bounds objects with convex hulls of parameterized tightness. [Gla88] extends an adaptive bounding volume subdivision algorithm to 4D for sequence rendering. Tessellation preprocessing [Sny87] may prove costly, but produces hierarchical lists and 3D grids efficient for casting. Rayshade, a public domain ray tracer (Craig Kolb, Yale), was developed along these lines. Rayshade also exploits parallelism, supporting multi-computers that have a parallel Linda language compiler.[†] The casting of each ray is essentially independent of all others.

Exploiting scene coherence and parallelism can be discussed in the context of object and image space [Gre89]. In ray tracing, *object space* defines the world to be rendered in a 3D coordinate system. Many different model representations are used, ranging from constructive solid geometry, CSG [Mor89], to octree or 3D

---

† To the best of my knowledge, the author(s) have not published their work.

volume pixel (voxel) organizations [Sam88]. Object space partitioning is complicated by the fact that it is inevitable that (secondary) rays cross boundaries at all scales, dependent upon object, lighting, and viewing parameters. *Image space* refers to the display pixels associated with each coincident ray to be cast into the object space. Exploiting coherence in this space seems straightforward, as each ray can be cast or checked for object intersections independently. The subset of the object database to which any ray casting process will require access, cannot be completely determined *a priori*. The generation of secondary rays—to trace-out reflections, shadowing, etc.—complicate the data distribution issue. It is difficult to effectively distribute the required object information within an image space-parallel partitioning as a preprocessing step. Non-uniform sampling, be it probabilistic or stochastic, can help reduce the number of rays generated. [Kaj86] discusses much of this work in a unified framework, presenting a variance-reduction technique that traces fewer rays.

Successful accelerations of ray tracing have been reported on specialized, parallel architectures—ranging from programmable hardware to massively-parallel VLSI systems. [Deg86] uses a hierarchical processor tree and star topology. [Mor89] uses a processor farm for a dataflow algorithm. [Kob87] divides object parallelism into multi-scale global and local computations with different global and local processors. [Cas89] uses an MIMD machine with a hypercube-like topology to exploit object parallelism with bounding volumes and intersections computed at each processor. Image space parallelism is exploited in both distributed and shared memory architectures in [Muu87]. [Ran90] uses Transputers with OCCAM and a 3D temporal/image space processor mapping, with each processor assigned a region over time to process. [Dew87] uses Transputers in a ring, with a hybrid image/object space distribution scheme. The [Pri89] MIMD hypercube 3D object region allocation is performed with an adjacency graph, which establishes both region connectivity and interprocess communication. [Gre89] looks at the efficiency of different multi-processor object space caching approaches, presenting a mixed dynamic/static partitioning that produces results nearly as good as having complete data at each node of their distributed-memory multi-processor.

The emphasis of our work is on parallelism. We seek to speed up ray tracing without the use of special-purpose hardware, exploiting the spare cycles on the multitude of conventional computers typically found on a local area network. The development of low level software is minimized to allow portability and heterogeneity.

Multiple Processor Ray Tracing and Data Distribution

The generation of secondary rays seriously complicates object space data distribution as a preprocessing step. [Gre89] assumes memory-limited multiple processors, making the object distribution and caching mandatory. [Muu87] eliminates the data distribution problem in his distributed network model by copying all data into large local memories.[†] We will proceed with this as an acceptable alternative, as network computers with 10's of megabytes of memory are becoming the norm—enough to handle databases of moderate complexity. Virtual memory and operating system caching techniques help extend this. We will address the details of how data is distributed from a client application, and how server processes can direct their own memory management.

Figure B-2 abstracts a network parallel ray tracing application into several modular pieces. To simplify discussion, any database preprocessing to orient or organize objects for a selected viewpoint occurs off-line. For moderately complex scenes, we will distribute a copy of the complete database to each processor. The lack of a deterministic network data broadcast mechanism or shared memory complicates things, though NFS provides a reasonably efficient approximation to shared memory. Without NFS, a network of processors can only be modeled as a loosely-coupled multi-processor.

Assuming a client/multiple server model, the client is in charge of assigning rays (portions of image space) to each server. Server performance, network speed, and other issues are dynamically considered for the fastest overall scene generation. We use a scan-line as the fundamental unit of distribution. For each pixel in the requested scan-line(s), a server traces a ray, generating secondary rays in a recursive fashion and applying a shading model. Once complete, pixel values for each scan-line(s) are returned to the client. Both the supported geometric models and shading models are simple. We have concentrated on the network interprocess communications, scheduling, loading, and data distribution aspects of the problem.

Step 4, the actual ray tracing performed at each server, is accomplished by a fixed-grid ray tracer with five levels of primary/secondary recursion applied in all simulations. A global, Whitted-style illumination model reflects rays at surface intersections, as well as making use of surface index of refraction to transmit refracted secondary rays through the surface. Intensity at a specified angle due to a single ray is given by the weighting of ambient, diffuse, and reflected light. The intensity as observed at a primary ray source (pixel) is the ensemble total of primary and secondary ray intensities. Additional rays are shot towards light sources to check for incident objects—indicating shadow. (Refer to Figure B-1.) The model and intersection processing used in our simulations supports sphere objects of the form: *x y z rad ior refract reflect diffuse ambient*, where x, ·y, and z instantiate a sphere of radius `rad`, with index of refraction `ior`. The four appended optical characteristics serve to weight the components of intensity used at the surface.

---

† [Muu87] also provides a good comparison of closely versus loosely coupled (network) parallelism.

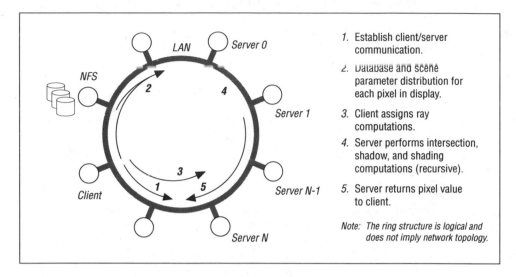

Figure B-2. Overview of the network parallel ray tracing application

During implementation, some interesting things became evident:

1. The use of redundant NFS file reading by each server during step 1, the initialization, required incrementally less time than the client reading the data once, and sending the data to each server. Ideally, if a request broadcast mechanism were available,[†] initialization time would be reduced by a factor of N. The speed up is due to the use of caching disk controllers at the `fread()` level. Note that communicating filenames requires isolating servers from the fact that NFS mount points can be different across a network.

2. When data size is small, initialization is best carried out via data, not qualified NFS filename, avoiding the `fread()` overhead at each server.

3. Data compression is *extremely* important. Regardless of which data distribution scheme is used (qualified NFS filename or direct data), a simple run-length limiting filter typically provides a 1.5 to 2X data reduction, with minimal client and server overhead.

Figure B-3 is the 840×640×8 grey-scale scene generated by most of the simulations. For a moderate complexity like this, the initialization overhead proves to be on the order of seconds per server, regardless of the number of servers involved. In this case it is a total of 15773 bytes for the background image and 422 bytes of sphere

---

† Most LAN protocols available today are point-to-point. The ONC RPC clnt_broadcast() function can broadcast and listen for responses. In this sense it does not broadcast, nor provide one-time server/client interaction. Its use of UDP on Ethernet also limits broadcast socket (transfer) size to 1500 bytes.

database. These numbers reflect the run-length encoding. The background image tends to be common across fixed-viewpoint animations

Networked Ray Tracing Using RPC

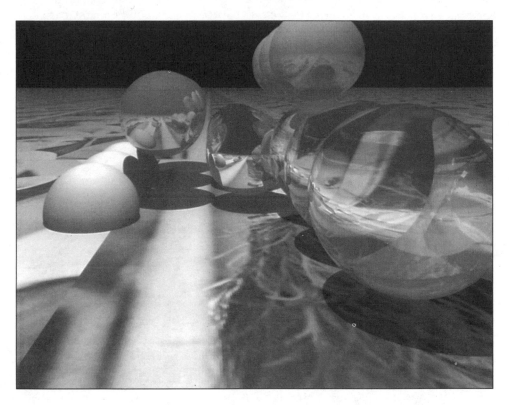

Figure B-3. Benchmark scene generated by the ray tracer

Blocking the client process is not acceptable if multiple servers are to be applied to a problem simultaneously. By programming below the level of RPCGEN, manually using the svc_sendreply() return function, the server can be made to reply immediately, then be polled and reply later when the final result is ready. We have opted for asynchronous server management using process control at the local machine—effectively forking child processes to be blocked until results return. Process exit() status can be inspected using signal() and wait() derivatives, making load balancing and scheduling possible. When waiting is done by child client processes, the default RPC time-out period may need to be increased. See Example 6-3, *status.c*, that outlines the use of fork(), sleep(), wait(), and signal() for asynchronous process monitoring.

We now take a detailed look at the communications used for partitioning ray tracing across multiple RPC servers. Figure B-4 (see Page 418) outlines the approach taken. It illustrates not only the network connections, but also the fact that process control and interprocess communication are at work. Each server process naturally gets blocked while waiting on the other end of a pipe for a client to make a request. At the client side, we have implemented something similar, adding signals to watch child process status, to make use of it in scheduling and load balancing heuristics. Shared address space between children and parent is required to capture server replies (pixel values) in one place. Hardware frame buffers or seeking on NFS file descriptors provide crude forms of shared memory. The former requires careful integration between the windowing system (if in use) signal handler, typically called an *event notifier*, and the client's use of signal().

The sequence of events used to render a given scene is as follows. REQUESTs and REPLYs represent RPCs and returns by the CLIENT, respectively:

```
------- parent process -------
foreach SERVER candidate (pipelined):
   ------- fork child process -------
      check for registered SERVER process, retrieve CLIENT handle
      if SERVER not registered, start SERVER with rsh and retry
      until TIMEOUT
      REQUEST: SERVER database initialization, background NFS
      path and SPHERE data
   ------- child process exits -------
    REPLY: error disallows use of CLIENT handle
end SERVER candidate
foreach SCAN-LINE in image
   wait while no idle SERVERs
   size REQUEST according to prior performance
   ------- fork child process -------
   REQUEST  SCAN-LINES loop count
      at SERVER:
         foreach PIXEL in SCAN-LINES
            generate PRIMARY RAY
            recursive ray casting - hit a SPHERE or the floor?
            generate SECONDARY RAYs
             shading: reflect, refract, diffuse, shadow, returning
            one pixel value
         end PIXEL in SCAN-LINES
         SERVER returns SCAN-LINE pixel values to CLIENT
      back at CLIENT:
      waiting for REPLY
      REPLY: error  - exit(ERROR)
             success - dump SCAN-LINES to window, exit(SUCCESS)
      ------- parent process -------
      signal(SIGCHLD): catches dying child
      if STATUS == ERROR disallows use of CLIENT handle,
      reschedule its SCAN-LINEs
      else /* perform load re-sizing */
          if SERVER faster than others (slower), increase
          (decrease) SCAN-LINE loading
         mark SERVER as available
   end REQUEST SCAN-LINEs
end SCAN-LINEs in image
```

First, to facilitate an arbitrary number of servers at run-time, the rhosts file is consulted in order. If the Portmapper has no record of the service, a remote execution utility is used to attempt to start the server. If the service still fails to be registered in a timely fashion, the next host is tried. Attempts to contact or (re)start servers are performed in parallel from child processes, to amortize the remote execution login and start-up latency. A server is further tested by an optional initialization phase—new object and background data (optional) and scene-specific rendering parameters (e.g., viewpoint, field-of-view, etc.) are defined. If server initialization succeeds, the ray tracing process begins.

The process is partitioned into groups of scan-lines, where the size of the group is determined by the run-time performance of each server. In this way the number of scan-lines requested of the server is proportional to its performance. A child process is started for each server request. While each child process wait for a reply, the server associated with that request is generating and tracing the required rays through the database, with up to 5 levels of recursion.[†] A server reply tagged as successful causes the client to transfer the incoming pixel values to the windowing system. This process is complicated by the use of signals by event handlers. Nevertheless, a frame buffer or canvas in a windowing system provides an effective shared memory that child processes can all write to. Signals are used to monitor the health of the reply back in the parent process, which is responsible for scheduling and loading. Child process exit status indicates either successful completion, failure, or time-out. Bad replies cause servers to be removed from candidacy and scan-lines to be reprocessed. Successful replies mark the server as available, typically being re-used immediately by a new child process.

Dynamic Scheduling and Load Balancing

An efficient parallelization of an application results only if each processing element is kept loaded to its limit with minimal interprocessor communication overhead. With these two goals in mind, several other researchers have proposed scheduling and load balancing techniques for ray tracing. Both static and run-time scheduling and loading are proposed, on both conventional networks and special-purpose hardware.

[Pri89] and [Cas89] develop MIMD load balancing techniques. [Pri89] uses static load balancing on a hypercube topology. [Cas89] develops a self-balancing, demand and data-driven loading. It uses a hierarchical (in space) data distribution, making use of some redundancy. [Mur88] also presents a static load balancing, but on a cellular array. [Mor89] gives a dynamic dataflow algorithm for balancing CSG object space parallelism on a processor farm. [Sto88] presents VERA—a networked ray tracing application for photorealistic animation using a coarse-grained, frame-by-frame partitioning. The [Muu87] network application uses scan-line partitioning. Like the latter network application, ours, too, uses a central dispatcher or client, and many servers.

---

† Experience shows that any more than five levels of recursion do not significantly affect picture quality.

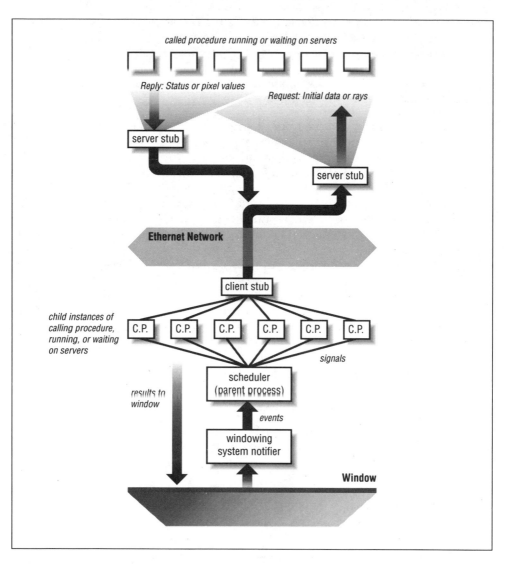

Figure B-4. Multiple ray tracing servers using process control

But Why Scan-line Parallelism and Not Frame Parallelism?

[Sto88] describes a mature environment, successfully used to ray trace a number of animated sequences. It divides the problem into frames, with a central client managing the division of labor, queuing-up frames at each server. They address the issues of fault tolerance and recovery—logically at the resolution of frames. Their goal was to produce long, animated sequences (minutes) using all spare network CPU cycles—idle time during the day and night.

Before designing our approach, we have to consider the level of processing granularity we desired. Some pros and cons of fine-grained, scan-line parallelism and coarser-grained partitioning across frames in an animation sequence follow in Table B-1.

Table B-1. Parallel Ray Tracing: Frames or Scan-lines?

	Frame Parallel	**Scan-line Parallel**
Interactive Visualization	no speed-up	accelerated
Animation	accelerated	accelerated
Network Control Overhead	low	higher
Network Database Overhead	low, server-specific databases maintained	higher, but common server database
Fault Tolerance	coarse-grained	fine-grained
Recovery	coarse-grained	fine-grained

Our application requires not only animation but interactive single-frame processing. Therefore, we needed an approach that could accelerate both. A logical choice was to pursue dynamic processing granularity—to inherit the ability of scan-line parallelism to process single views in parallel, and to reduce network overhead as with frame-parallelism. We accomplished this through dynamic sizing of the number of scan-lines requested of each server. The number of lines is increased until an acceptable middle-ground is reached. Note that parallelism at the scan-line level does require that each server be working from the same database (as we implemented), or the client must maintain work queues across frames. The efficiency reported later suggested that the extra complexity was not required.

When confronted with heterogeneous processors, and a non-deterministic communication environment like that found in a large commercial or academic engineering environment, these methods break down. The original goals for efficient parallelization remain: keep each processor busy, and keep communication latency low. Several attempts at attaining these goals showed that the process had to be asynchronous to prevent slow processors or communication links from delaying synchronization points. This would cause all processors to wait. The faster machines had to proceed unencumbered. Add the fact that extraneous processor and network loading is unpredictable and uncontrollable, attempts at modeling load balancing as a multi-variate minimization problem proved too difficult. Instead, we opted to implement a simple servo, or PD control algorithm. Handling the unpredictable processing times of servers could be done by having the client poll each server to check for completion,† but we found process control and IPCs a cleaner way to implement remote asynchronous calls.

We have devised a simple, but effective UNIX-based scheduling mechanism that allows as many server requests to be posted as there is process room on the client machine. To avoid blocking the parent task, or closing the socket opened for communication to allow completely asynchronous server processing, child processes are forked. These children make the requests and handle the replies, in a conventional fashion—becoming blocked as they wait for a reply. Reply data is deposited in memory shared by the child and parent processes. A number of shared memory or passing techniques exist, but for the case of image synthesis, writing values directly into a frame buffer or window canvas has proven effective. Another option is seeking on a descriptor—as they are common between parent and child processes. Once reply values have been deposited, a child exits with a status indicating what transpired. The parent client process catches the SIGCHLD signal and inspects the status. In the case of an error, the server is disabled, left marked as busy, and basically dropped from re-use. Any lost scan-lines must be rescheduled elsewhere. In the case of a successful return, the lifetime of the child is checked, and future loading, in terms of scan-lines, is adjusted.

A PD control mechanism is used to keep the response time of each server as close as possible, thereby eliminating dangling RPCs at synchronization points. When rendering an animation, the initialization phase required of each new scene or viewpoint requires that all involved servers be re-initialized. This requires synchronization at the end of a scene. A timer is kept to denote the length of time the child process took while making the RPC. The time elapsed during each RPC is compared with a low-passed average of response time for all healthy servers. Differences above or below a threshold cause the number of scan-lines to be sent next to that server to be reduced or increased, respectively, by a delta. This has the effect of reducing or increasing time for the next RPC. See Example 6-4 as an illustration of these methods.

Error recovery proved to be a large issue. As stated in [Sto88], recovery—rather than restarting—is essential. We have the ability to inspect a server's status through its response or time-out. Unhealthy servers may be restarted, or merely marked as unusable. Any lost scan-lines must be rescheduled.

It is also essential, when processing a long animated sequence, that processing not significantly affect interactive use of the servers. In our case, most of these machines are used during the day for text and graphics editing, mail, and limited interactive simulation. After registering, the server processes reduce their priority level, making daytime processing unnoticed, while consuming all available CPU time at night.

---

† rpcmand, an RPC-based network-parallel application for computing Mandelbrot sets uses this technique. It appears in the April '87 *Sun Users Group Tape*, written by Philip Heller (sun!terrapin!heller).

Performance Results

Figures B-5 and B-6 illustrate the time required to ray trace a scene, as a function of the number of servers invoked. These times represent averages of a large number of sample runs. Two different scene sizes were used, 840×640 and 420×320, one-quarter of its size. A includes server initialization—using the mixed data/qualified NFS filename approach mentioned previously. B shows performance without initialization. As more and more servers are involved, initialization becomes a more significant penalty. The ideal performance curve is generated by assuming linear speed-up, with no communication overhead. The communication overhead of the baseline, single-server simulation is reflected in the ideal performance. All simulations were done off-hours, with minimal Ethernet traffic. Each server is a Sun 4/65 with 16MB of memory. The client is a Sun 3/60.

The dynamic load sizing is of reduced value in these performance runs, as the machines were evenly matched, though utilization is a variable. But with heterogeneous servers, e.g., mixing super-mini compute servers with Sun 4's, it proves essential. We have experienced 1.5-3 fold speed-ups over these numbers when high-end Sun 4 server-class machines, Solbourne and a Convex, are applied simultaneously.

Conclusions

Cost-effective parallel ray tracing in a networked environment makes tasks like sequence animation practical. By exploiting idle CPU time on a local area network, ray tracing is accelerated in a near-optimal. By using multiple concurrent remote procedure calls, one machine is in charge—the client—distributing computations to a variable number of heterogeneous server machines. An image-space computational partitioning is used. By allocating scan-lines to servers, efficient parallelism results, at the cost of requiring that the complete object database be available to each server. This mechanism is provided by the client passing databases to servers or use of a network file system—itself layered on top of RPC. By carefully managing processes, and controlling client loading as a function of performance, a near linear speed-up is achieved as more clients are added. A degree of fault-tolerance is available at the application level with client health monitored, and work-load redirected as necessary. Though a coarser-grained, parallel partitioning across frames in an animation sequence reduces network communication overhead, individual frame visualization remains unaccelerated and multiple server databases must be on-line.

In [Muu87] the PKG protocol was applied to parallel network ray tracing. Here we attempt to use a more standard scheme, making a larger variety of servers available. We have run this application on the following platforms: Sun 3, Sun 4, Solbourne, DEC Ultrix MicroVAX, and Convex multiprocessor. With XDR, and even RPCGEN publicly available, there should be no limitation on platform support. We anticipate that overall performance could be improved by increasing the TCP receive window sizing [Muu87]. Another limitation of our approach is that for each server, room in process tables is required—limiting the total number reachable. No spatial or

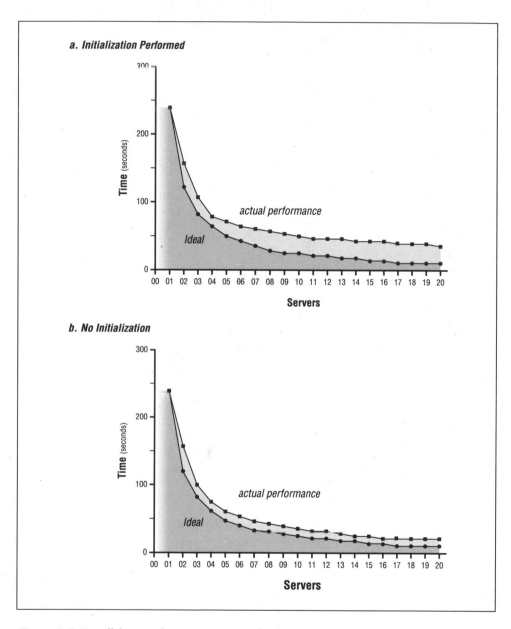

Figure D-5. Parallel network ray tracing time for 420x320 images as a function of number of servers

temporal coherence is exploited as in [Gla88]. This should significantly improve performance, also.

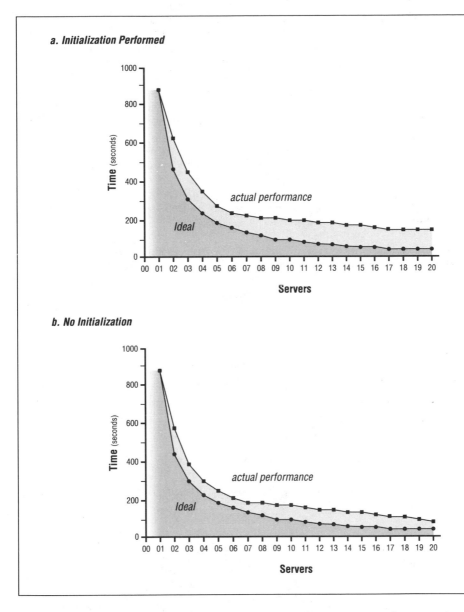

Figure B-6. Parallel network ray tracing time for 840x640 images, as a function of number of servers

References

[Cas89] Caspary, E.; and Scherson, I.D. "A self-balanced parallel ray-tracing algorithm," Parallel Processing for Computer Vision and Display, 1989, pp. 408-19.

[Cia90] Ciaria. C. "Image synthesis: a tutorial," *Circuit Cellar INK*, Issue 12, December '89/January '90, pp. 23-35.

[Coo86] Cook, R. "Stochastic sampling in computer graphics," *ACM Trans. on Graphics*, Vol. 5, No. 1, January 1986, pp. 51 72.

[Deg86] Deguchi, H.; Shirakawa, I.; Omura, K.; Nishida, M.; Nishimura, H.; and Kawata, T. "A tree-structured parallel processing system for image generation by ray tracing," *Syst. & Comput. Jpn.* (USA) 1986 Vol. 17, No. 12, pp. 51-62.

[Deg88] Deguchi, H.; Omura, K.; and Shirakawa, I. "A parallel processing scheme for tree-structured image generation system," *IEEE International Symposium on Circuits and Systems*, 1988, Vol. 1, pp. 569-72.

[Dew87] Dew, P.M.; de Pennington, A.; and Morris, D.T. "Programmable VLSI Architecture for solid modelling," *CG Tokyo 87*, April 1987.

[Dor87] Dorband, J.E. "3D graphic generation on the MPP," *Second International Conference on Supercomputing '87*, Vol. 2, pp. 305-9.

[Gla88] Glassner, A. "Spacetime ray tracing for animation," *CGA*, March 1988.

[Gre89] Green, S.A. and Paddon, D.J. "Exploiting coherence for multiprocessor ray tracing," *CGA* 9(6), 1989, pp. 12-26.

[Lev88] Levoy, M. "Display of surfaces from volume data," *CGA*, May 1988.

[Kaj06] Kajia, J.T. "The rendering equation," *Proceedings of SIGGRAPH '86*, 1986.

[Kno89] Knox, W.J., Jr. "Shading models for realistic image synthesis," *Proceedings of the IEEE 1989 National Aerospace and Electronics Conference*, 1989, Vol. 2, pp. 596-603.

[Kob87] Kobayashi, H.; Nakamura, T.; and Shigei, Y. "Parallel processing of an object space for image synthesis using ray tracing," *Visual Comput.* (Germany) 1987 Vol. 3, No. 1, pp. 13-22.

[Mei89] Meinzer, H.P.; Schaefer, R.; Heyers, V.; Saurbier, F.; and Scheppelmann, D. "Medical 3D-images," *SEAS. Proceedings Spring Meeting 1989, End User Computing*, Vol. 1, pp. 157-62.

[Mor89] Morris, D.T. and Dew, P.M. "Dynamic dataflow algorithms for ray tracing CSG objects," *Parallel Processing for Computer Vision and Display*, 1989, pp. 452-60

[Mur88] Murakami, K.; Hirota, K.; and Ishii, M. "Fast ray tracing," *Fujitsu Sci. Tech. J.* (Japan) June 1988, Vol. 24, No. 2, pp. 150-9.

[Muu87] Muuss, M.J. "RT & REMRT: shared memory parallel and network distributed ray-tracing programs," *USENIX Association Fourth Computer Graphics Workshop*, 1987, pp. 86-97.

[Pri88] Priol, T. and Bouatouch, K. "Experimenting with a parallel ray-tracing algorithm on a hypercube machine," *EUROGRAPHICS '88*, pp. 243-59.

[Pri89] Priol, T. and Bouatouch, K. "Static load balancing for a parallel ray tracing on a MIMD hypercube," *Visual Comput.* (Germany) 1989, Vol. 5, pp. 109-119.

[Que89] Quek, L.H. "Ray tracing with space subdivision on vector-multiprocessor system," Univ. Illinois at Urbana-Champaign, IL, USA; UIUCDCS-R-89-1491.

[Ran90] Ransen, O.F. "The art of ray tracing," *BYTE*, February 1990, pp. 238-242.

[Rub80] Rubin, S.M. and Whitted, T. "A 3-dimensionsal representation for fast rendering of complex scenes," *SIGGRAPH 1980 Conference Proceedings*, Vol. 14, No. 3, pp. 110-16.

[Sul89] Sullivan, M. and Anderson, D. "Marionette: a system for parallel distributed programming using a master/slave model," *9th International Conference on Distributed Computing Systems*, 1989.

[Sam88] Samet, H. and Webber, R.E. "Hierarchical data structures and algorithms for computer graphics II Applications," *IEEE CGA*, 1988, Vol. 8, No. 4, pp. 59-75.

[Sam89] Samet, H. Applications of Spatial Data Structures, Computer Graphics, Image Processing and GIS, Addison-Wesley, Chapter 7, 1989.

[Sto88] Stober, A.; Schmitt, A.; Neidecker, B., Muller, W.; Maus, T., and Leister, W. "Tools for efficient photo-realistic computer animation," *Eurographics '88* Elsevier Science Publishers B.V., pp. 31-41.

[Sun88] Network Programming, Sun Microsystems PN: 800-1779-10, Rev. A, May 1988.

[Weg84] Weghorst, H.; Hooper, G.; and Greenberg, D.P. "Improved computational methods for ray tracing," *ACM Transactions on Graphics 3*, Jan. 1984, pp. 547-554.

[Whi80] Whitted, T. "An improved illumination model for shaded display," *Communications of the ACM 23*, June 1980, pp. 343-349.

[Udu90] Udupa, J.K. "Visualization of biomedical data: principles and algorithms (short course notes)," *First Conference on Biomedical Computing*, Atlanta, Ga, May 1990.

Documentation and Source Code

Example B-1 represents a complete application that renders scenes via ray tracing. Neither client nor server require windowing system support. The client uses concurrent child process `fseek()` and `fwrite()` pairs to allow asynchronous-return RPCs to record their results in the right place. The XView preprocessor symbol integrates the RPCs with X11 through the XView toolkit. Results are then displayed in a window and not written to disk.

To start things off, here's a manual page that summarizes what we are about to develop. Credit for the base-line, single-thread ray tracing goes to an anonymous Usenet author.

Example B-1. Manual page for the network ray tracer rtrace

```
RTRACE(L)                       GRAPHICS                    RTRACE(L)


NAME
     rtrace - run a simple RPC ray tracing procedure

SYNOPSIS
     rtrace -o [filename] -i [filename] -b <filename> -B <number>
       -S <number> -d

DESCRIPTION
     Rtrace is a program developed originally to study how ray tracing
     works when distributed to multiple hosts using RPC.  Up to the
     first 10 successful RPC connections, as specified in the ~/.rhosts
     file, become servers.  NFS is used to share data among client and
     severs.  Options may be in any order, with any omitted to take
     defaults

     It is capable of depicting a number of balls (up to 1024) and a
     plane that is covered with a tiling of any bitmapped picture.

OPTIONS
     -o Chooses the output data file. If no argument is given, stdout
        is used. If the option is not used, the default is data.dis.

     -i Chooses the input (ball) data file. If no argument is given, stdin
        is used. If the option is not used, the default is bdata

     -b Chooses the file containing the tiling bitmap. It requires
        an argument. If the option is not used, the default is pat.def.

     -B Chooses contrast of the pattern. 0.0 is no contrast, 1.0 is maximum
        contrast. 1.0 is the default. (useful for fading during animation)

     -s Sets the number of servers to be used from the ~/.rhosts list.
        The default is 8.

     -d If option present (no arguments), servers are not initialized
        with ball and tiling bitmap data.  Handy for compute timing.


PROGRAM NOTES
     This program generates a file in Sun rasterfile(5) format,
     containing a header with x and y sizes, colormap, etc., followed
     by the data in 8-bit greyscale, one pixel to a character, in
     scanline order.  There are two necessary input files: ball data,
     and a pattern bitmap.  The tiling bitmap can be digitized data,
```

Example B-1. Manual page for the network ray tracer rtrace   (Continued)

```
it must be in the form of an 8-bit deep Sun rasterfile(5), no
bigger than 1Kx1K.  The ball data is of the following form:


x y z rad ior refract reflect diffuse ambient

On each line where x y & z are the coordinates of the center of
the ball, rad is the radius of the ball, ior is the index of
refraction for translucent materials (index of refraction for
glass is about 1.5) the last four numbers determine how much of
each attribute is used.  Thus a pure silver ball would have 0.0
1.0 0.0 0.0 as the last numbers, and a pure glass ball would have
1.0 0.0 0.0 0.0 .

Viewpoint and the viewing cone are fixed.


FILES
    ./bdata.i  default ball data
    ./pat.def  default floor pattern rasterfile(5)
    ./data.dis default output rasterfile(5)
    $HOME/.rhosts  specified list of servers started in order
```

First, let's define what we'll want to stuff into the ray trace. Here's one data file (see Example B-2) that contains 10 sphere primitives with its 10-tuple describing location and optical parameters. Spheres are all this ray tracer understands.

Example B-2. Input file for the network ray tracer rtrace: bdata.i

```
-30.0     10.0    400.0    50.0    0.0    0.0    0.0    0.9    0.1
210.0    175.0    400.0    50.0    0.0    0.0    0.3    0.6    0.1
 40.0    110.0    450.0    50.0    0.0    0.0    0.6    0.3    0.1
140.0     65.0    450.0    50.0    0.0    0.0    0.9    0.0    0.1
220.0     70.0    100.0    60.0    1.4    0.9    0.0    0.0    0.1
-30.0     10.0    300.0    50.0    0.0    0.0    0.0    0.9    0.1
210.0    175.0    300.0    50.0    0.0    0.0    0.3    0.6    0.1
 40.0    110.0    350.0    50.0    0.0    0.0    0.6    0.3    0.1
140.0     65.0    350.0    50.0    0.0    0.0    0.9    0.0    0.1
220.0     70.0    200.0    60.0    1.4    0.9    0.0    0.0    0.1
```

We can now start defining the protocol with which the one client will make repeated remote procedure calls on servers (see Example B-3). The bulk of these shared data definitions are used by either the client or the servers, and are never passed over the network, but this is as good a place as any to define them to be common. There are six remote procedures anticipated. The first procedure die_1() will unregister the service and cause it to exit cleanly. The second procedure restarts the service. This provides a mechanism for the type of maintenance mentioned in Chapter 8. The third procedure is for establishing global ray tracing parameters for subsequent remote procedure calls that load the background pixel pattern (procedure #4), load the spheres database (procedure #5), and start the actual ray tracing (procedure #6).

Example B-3. Protocol definition for the network ray tracer rtrace: rtrace.x

```
const           ERROR = 0x0,     /* status codes used for exiting children */
const           SUCCESS = 0x1;
const           MAXU = 1024;     /* maximum columns in the bkgnd. pat */
const           MAXV = 1024;     /* maximum lines in the bkgnd. pat */
const           MAXBALLS = 1024; /* guess */
const           MAXSTR = 256;    /* maximum string length */
const           MAXPIX = 40960;  /* handle one 1024x40 regions */
const           STIME = 1;       /* how long to sleep between forks */
const           RSHWAIT = 60;    /* how long to wait for rsh's to start */

/*
 * Define structures used by client and server.
 */
struct color {
    int         r;
    int         g;
    int         b;
};
struct vector {
    double      x;
    double      y;
    double      z;
    double      l;
    double      xzl;
};
struct ray {
    struct vector   org;
    struct vector   dir;
};
struct sphere {
    struct vector   cent;
    double          rad;
};
struct parameters {
    struct sphere   *ls;
    struct vector   *vp;
    double          *bkcon;
};
struct ball {
    struct sphere   s;
    double          ior;
    double          rfr;
    double          rfl;
    double          dif;
    double          amb;
};
struct mat {
    struct vector   x;          /* first !row! */
    struct vector   y;          /* second !row! */
    struct vector   z;
};                              /* third !row! */

/*
 * Attempts at sending raw pixel data to clients yields the
 * following times: 17, 42, 47, 180, 43, 25 seconds of init
 * times per server! Thus passing filename is opted for.
 * These init times are: 17, 27, 30, 37, 23, 13 seconds -
 * 2.4X faster!
 */
typedef string  filename < MAXSTR >;
typedef ball    balls < MAXBALLS >;
```

Example B-3. Protocol definition for the network ray tracer rtrace: rtrace.x   (Continued)

```
struct lines {                   /* start and stop
                    * assignments for servers */
  double          ymin;
  double          ymax;
};

/*
 * Define the client and server data exchanged.  Be
 * consistent here. It's important to fully define union
 * structure elements at run-time - leave a dangling field
 * or access a bogus one, and get very erratic behavior.
 * xdr_pointer() is handy but unforgiving.
 */
union reply switch (int op) {
  case SUCCESS:void;
case ERROR:
  string sOp < MAXSTR >;
default:
  string sOp < MAXSTR >;
};

typedef char    replypix < MAXPIX >;

/*
 * The rtrace server procedure definition.
 */
program         RTRACESERVER {
  version         RTRACEVERS {
    void            DIE(void) = 1;       /* dereg. and die */
    void            RESTART(void) = 2;   /* restart service */
    reply           SET_PARAMS(parameters) = 3;
    reply           LOAD_BKGND(filename) = 4;
    reply           LOAD_BALLS(balls) = 5;
    replypix        RAY_TRACE(lines) = 6;
  } =             1;
} =             0x20000001;
```

There are also a number of other things shared, which I placed in *rtrace_shared.h*.
There are a number of powerful vector and matrix math macros and Sun-style rasterfile image file format structures hidden in here.

Example B-4. Other shared definitions for the network ray tracer client and server procedures:
rtrace_shared.h

```
#include "raster.h" /* see Example 9-16 */
#define MAXSERV sizeof(int)*8
#define DEFLOAD 25      /* default starting server loading in scan-lines */
#define MINLOAD 15      /* minimum load */
#define MAXLOAD 35
#define HUGE 99999999999.0
#define XMIN 10.0       /* window size,  virtual units */
#define XMAX 220.0
#define YMIN 10.0
#define YMAX 170.0
#define SCALE 2.0       /* magnification factor  */
#define LEVEL 5         /* levels of recursion */
#define RLEV 3          /* don't want as many inside the ball,
                         * takes forever as it is */
#define ERRMSG(str)     { printf ("%s\n", str); exit (-1); }
#define WARNMSG(str)    { printf ("%s\n", str); }

/* some of the most important stuff in the program */
#define DOT(v1,v2) (v1.x*v2.x+v1.y*v2.y+v1.z*v2.z)
/* returns dot product of two vectors */
```

Example B-4. Other shared definitions for the network ray tracer client and server procedures:
rtrace_shared.h (Continued)

```
#define LN2(v)        (DOT(v,v))
/* returns the square of the length of a vector */
#define LEN(v)        sqrt(LN2(v))
/* guess */
#define XZL(v)        sqrt(v.x*v.x+v.z*v.z)
/* returns the component in the xz plane of a vector */
#define SCMLT(sc,vct) vct.x*= sc;vct.y*= sc;vct.z*= sc;vct.l*= sc;
/* multiplies a vector by a scalar */
#define MV(a,b,c,v)   v.x= a;v.y= b;v.z= c;
/* makes a vector. wouldn't need this with c++ */
#define SV(t,u,v)     t.x=u.x-v.x;t.y=u.y-v.y;t.z=u.z-v.z;
/* subtract vector t=u-v */
#define AV(t,u,v)     t.x=u.x+v.x;t.y=u.y+v.y;t.z=u.z+v.z;
/* add vector t=u+v */
#define MTV(v1,m,v2)  MV(DOT(m.x,v2),DOT(m.y,v2),DOT(m.z,v2),v1)
/* multiply transpose matrix by vector. v1=m*v2 */
```

Any image or pixel I/O to disk will be carried out using Sun rasterfile-format images. The client and server must be linked with the rasterfile utility routines in Example 9-15, *raster.c.* Note that run-length encoded images are not supported. For that I depend on standard filters. See the discussion in Chapter 8 regarding use of NFS.

After defining the protocol and other common items, the client local procedures are defined, as shown in Example B-5. The significant number of conditional compile statements (#ifdef XView and #ifndef XView) allow you to create two versions of the program. The former XView executable will run under X11 using XView toolkit calls. The latter writes pixels to a Sun rasterfile(5) format file. It has a lurking bug in that the seek and write actions are not atomic, and are performed in child processes. In this way multiple child processes could set seek points to place their RPC reply results at, and when writing begins, the file pointer may not be in the right place.

Example B-5. Client side of the network ray tracer: rtrace.c

```
#include <stdio.h>
#include <signal.h>
#include <sys/param.h>
#include <sys/wait.h>
#include <sys/time.h>
#include <errno.h>
#include <string.h>
#include <math.h>
#include <ctype.h>
#include <rpc/rpc.h>
#ifdef XView
#include <X11/X.h>
#include <X11/Xlib.h>
#include <xview/xview.h>
#include <xview/canvas.h>
#include <xview/notify.h>
#include <xview/cms.h>
#endif XView
#include "rtrace.h"
#include "rtrace_shared.h"

/*
 * Global server/client relationship stuff - max servers <= 32.
```

Example B-5. Client side of the network ray tracer: rtrace.c   (Continued)

```
    */
.int                NumServers;                 /* total # of servers connected */
int                 ServersFree = 0x0;          /* bits are 1 if free, 0 if busy */
int                 ServerPid[MAXSERV];         /* used to record fork()'ed pids */
char                ServerName[MAXSERV][32];    /* record server names */
int                 ServerLoad[MAXSERV];        /* server load capability */
int                 ServerTot[MAXSERV];         /* # times the server was used */
long                ServerTime[MAXSERV];
long                ServerStart[MAXSERV];
CLIENT              *cl[MAXSERV];               /* client handles */
struct timeval      DTime = {100, 0};
int                 MaxServ = 8;
int                 InitServ = TRUE;
int                 LoadSizing = FALSE;         /* don't do dynamic load balancing */
/*
 * Global graphic, display and I/O stuff.
 */
double              bkcon = 1.0;     /* background contrast */
char                *spat;           /* background file name */
balls               bl;              /* ball vector */
int                 height, width;
ray                 *pRays;
reply               *pReply;
FILE                *pFBal,          /* ball input data file */
                    *pFpat,          /* bkgnd. pattern input data file */
#ifndef XView
                    *pFOut,          /* output data file */
#endif XView
                    *pFRhosts = NULL;/* rhosts file */


#ifdef XView
/*
 * X11 and xview stuff - yuck blech rech.  I tend to keep them global as I
 * never know when I might need them.  I do occasionally step on them
 * (e.g., in the repaint procedure).
 */
Frame               frame;
Canvas              canvas;
Xv_cmsdata          cms_data;
Cms                 cms;
int                 scrn;
XImage              *ximage;
GC                  gc;
XGCValues           gcvalues;
unsigned long       gcmask;
Display             *dpy;


/*
 * My own vestigial rasterfile pixel I/O stuff - it's not
 * fair to require that you have SunView-era stuff around.
 */
colormap_t          cm;
rasterfile          rast;
#endif XView


/*
 * Signaling, timing, and error handling.
 */
extern int          errno;
struct timeval      tval;
#ifndef XView
void                CatchServer();
#endif XView
#ifdef XView
int                 CatchServer();
```

Example B-5.   Client side of the network ray tracer: rtrace.c   (Continued)

```
#endif XView

char             *
NFSgetcwd()
{
  char             path_name[MAXPATHLEN], *getcwd();

  getcwd(path_name, MAXPATHLEN);
  /* remove any local /tmp_mnt/home NFS mount problems */
  while (path_name[1] != 'h')
    strcpy(&(path_name[1]), &(path_name[2]));
  return (path_name);
}

main(argc, argv)
  int              argc;
  char             **argv;
{
  ray              rr;
  vector           vp;
  double           x, y, z;
  sphere           ls;
  parameters       params;
  int              i;
  char             *d;
#ifndef XView
  rasterfile       RasOut;
#endif XView

  /* Parse command-line options. */
  CommandLine(argc, argv);

  /* Read ~/.rhosts and attempt to start/contact servers. */
  StartServers(argv, 0);

#ifdef XView
  /* Open the window */
  width = (int) ((XMAX - XMIN) * SCALE + 0.9999999);
  height = (int) ((YMAX - YMIN) * SCALE + 0.9999999);
  INITRAST(rast, width, height);
  WindowInit(argc, argv);
#endif XView

  /* Make any new child deaths be recorded by CatchServer(). */
  while (wait((union status *) NULL) != -1) {
    sleep(STIME);
  }
  signal(SIGCHLD, CatchServer);

  /* Bring in ball data and ship it to the servers. */
  if (InitServ == TRUE) {
    GetBalls();
    EachServerOnce(load_balls_1, &bl);
    /*
     * Send NFS qualified filename for background to servers to read.
     * The easiest way to get at a RLL filter under SunOS is in
     * /usr/lib/rasfilters.  That really speeds things up.
     */
    EachServerOnce(load_bkgnd_1, &spat);
  }
  /*
   * Establish viewpoint & light source vector, background contrast.
   */
  MV(95.0, 140.0, -200.0, vp);
  MV(0.0, 900.0, 0.0, ls.cent);
```

Example B-5. Client side of the network ray tracer: rtrace.c   (Continued)

```
    ls.rad = 40;

    /*
     * Servers need to know light source & viewpoint vector,
     * background contrast.
     */
    params.ls = &ls;
    params.vp = &vp;
    params.bkcon = &bkcon;
    EachServerOnce(set_params_1, &params);

#ifndef XView
    /* Write a header and blank raster data to disk. */
    width = (int) ((XMAX - XMIN) * SCALE + 0.9999999);
    height = (int) ((YMAX - YMIN) * SCALE + 0.9999999);
    INITRAST(RasOut, width, height);
    WriteSunRaster(pFOut, NULL, &RasOut, NULL);

    /* Cast and trace all the rays at servers. */
    if (NumServers > 1)
      LoadSizing = TRUE;                 /* Turn on load sizing. */
    ReqRay();
    for (i = 0; i < NumServers; i++)
      printf("%s: %d\n", ServerName[i], ServerTot[i]);
#else XView
    /*
     * Good nite!  All the action starts when a CANVAS_REPAINT event occurs.
     */
    xv_main_loop(frame);
#endif XView
}

CommandLine(argc, argv)
    int            argc;
    char           **argv;
{
    int            i, c, in = 0, out = 0, tex = 0;
    char           resolved_name[MAXPATHLEN];

#ifdef XView
    /*
     * Take a look at and modify the command line if necessary, then read-in
     * read-in input image to size things-up - could use an XImage, but that's
     * not necessary if the data stays here...
     */
    xv_init(XV_INIT_ARGC_PTR_ARGV, &argc, argv, NULL);
#endif XView

    for (i = 1; i < argc; i++) {
      if (argv[i][0] != '-')
        ERRMSG("Start with a '-' ! ");
      c = argv[i][1];

      switch (c) {
      case ('i'):
        if (in)
          ERRMSG("You may only have one input file");
        in = 1;
        if ((i + 1) >= argc || argv[i + 1][0] == '-')      /* no arg */
          pFBal = stdin;
        else if ((pFBal = fopen(argv[++i], "r")) == NULL)
          ERRMSG("Input file not found");
        break;
#ifndef XView
      case ('o'):
```

Example B-5. Client side of the network ray tracer: rtrace.c   (Continued)

```
          if (out)
            ERRMSG("You may have only one output file");
          out = 1;
          if ((i + 1) >= argc || argv[i + 1][0] == '-')        /* no arg */
            pFOut    stdout;
          else
            pFOut = fopen(argv[++i], "w");
          break;
#endif XView
      case ('b'):
          if (tex)
            ERRMSG("You may have only one image file");
          if ((i + 1) >= argc || argv[i + 1][0] == '-')        /* no arg */
            ERRMSG("-b requires an argument");
          tex = 1;
          realpath(argv[++i], resolved_name);
          if ((pFpat = fopen(resolved_name, "r")) == NULL)
            ERRMSG("Background rasterfile not found");
          fclose(pFpat);
          spat = argv[i];
          break;

      case ('n'):
          if (argv[i][2] < '0' || argv[i][2] > '9') {
            printf("%c\n", argv[i][2]);
            ERRMSG("-n needs a numerical argument");
          }
          MaxServ = atoi(&(argv[i][2]));
          break;

      case ('B'):
          if (argv[i][2] < '0' || argv[i][2] > '9') {
            printf("%c\n", argv[i][2]);
            ERRMSG("-B needs a numerical argument");
          }
          Bkcon = atof(&(argv[i][2]));
          break;
      case ('s'):
          if ((i + 1) >= argc || (!isdigit(argv[i + 1][0])))
            /* no good arg */
            ERRMSG("-s requires a numeric argument");
          if (1 != sscanf(argv[++i], "%d", &MaxServ))
            ERRMSG("-s requires a numeric argument");
          if (MaxServ >= sizeof(int) * 8)
            ERRMSG("# servers must be < sizeof(int)*8");
          break;
      case ('d'):
          if ((i + 1) < argc && argv[i + 1][0] != '-')
            ERRMSG("-d doesn't take a parameter");
          InitServ = FALSE;
          ++i;
          break;
      default:
          ERRMSG("Unrecognized option. Better try again.");
      }
  }

  if (!in)
      if ((pFBal = fopen("bdata.i", "r")) == NULL)
          ERRMSG("bdata.i not found");
#ifndef XView
  if (!out)
      pFOut = fopen("data.dis", "w");
#endif XView
  if (!tex) {
```

Example B-5. Client side of the network ray tracer: rtrace.c (Continued)

```
      sprintf(resolved_name, "%s/pat.def", NFSgetcwd());
      if ((pFpat = fopen(resolved_name, "r")) == NULL) {
        WARNMSG(resolved_name);
        ERRMSG("not found");
      }
      fclose(pFpat);
      spat = strdup(resolved_name);
    }
}

StartServers(argv, online)       /* recursive */
  char              *argv[];
  int               online;
{
  char              sBuf[128];
  int               i, j;
  long              ts;

  if (!pFRhosts) {                  /* Is it open already? */
    sprintf(sBuf, "%s%s", getenv("HOME"), "/.rhosts");
    if (!(pFRhosts = fopen(sBuf, "r")))
      ERRMSC("Can't open ~/.rhosts to get server names");
  }
  for (i = online; (i < MaxServ) &&
        (fscanf(pFRhosts, "%s%s", ServerName[i], sBuf) == 2); i++) {

    cl[i] = clnt_create(ServerName[i], RTRACESERVER, RTRACEVERS, "tcp");

    /*
     * If attempt to contact fails, try to (re)start the server.
     */
    if (!cl[i]) {
      sprintf(sBuf, "rsh %s -n '%s/%s_svc >& /tmp/%s &'",
              ServerName[i], NFSgetcwd(), argv[0], argv[0]);
      if (!fork()) {
        system(sBuf);
        _exit(0);
      }                             /* Pipeline the rsh's! */
    }
  }
  NumServers = i;

  /*
   * Keep checking to see if they're all alive. If it doesn't
   * happen within RSHWAIT seconds, move on...
   */
  for (i = j = online; i < NumServers; i++) {
    gettimeofday(&tval, NULL);
    ts = tval.tv_sec;

    while (tval.tv_sec - ts <= RSHWAIT) {       /* wait for a while */
      cl[j] = clnt_create(ServerName[i], RTRACESERVER, RTRACEVERS, "tcp");
      if (cl[j])
        break;
      /* It failed, try again. */
      sleep(STIME);
      gettimeofday(&tval, NULL);
    }

    if (cl[j]) {
      /* Designate an available server. */
      printf("server started on %s\n", ServerName[j]);
      ServersFree |= (0x1 << j);
      strcpy(ServerName[j], ServerName[i]);
      ServerPid[i] = 0;
```

Example B-5. Client side of the network ray tracer: rtrace.c   (Continued)

```
        ServerLoad[j] = DEFLOAD;
        ServerTot[j] = 0;
        ServerTime[j] = 1000;

        /*
         * to avoid having to use svc_sendreply() in servers,
         * delay time-outs and use forks locally
         */
        clnt_control(cl[j], CLSET_TIMEOUT, (char *) &DTime);
        j++;
    } else {                        /* It failed even after RSHWAIT seconds! */
        clnt_pcreateerror(ServerName[i]);
    }
}
NumServers = j;

/* Repeat until EOF or MaxServers really available. */
if ((!feof(pFRhosts)) && (NumServers < MaxServ))
    StartServers(argv, NumServers);

if (pFRhosts)
    fclose(pFRhosts);
}

GetBalls()
{
    int             i;
    double          x, y, z, r, ior, rfr, rfl, dif, amb;
    ball            *bp;

    bl.balls_val = (ball *) malloc(sizeof(ball) * MAXBALLS);

    for (i = 0;
         fscanf(pFBal, "%lf %lf %lf %lf %lf %lf %lf %lf %lf",
         &x, &y, &z, &r, &ior, &rfr, &rfl, &dif, &amb) != EOF;
         i++) {
        if (i >= MAXBALLS)
            ERRMSG("Too many balls, MAXBALLS max.");
        bp = bl.balls_val + i;
        bp->s.cent.x = x;
        bp->s.cent.y = y;
        bp->s.cent.z = z;
        bp->s.rad = r;
        bp->ior = ior;
        bp->rfr = rfr;
        bp->rfl = rfl;
        bp->dif = dif;
        bp->amb = amb;
    }
    bl.balls_len = i * sizeof(ball);
}

#ifndef XView
void
#else XView
/*
 * Use a SIGCHLD handler to catch returning children.
 */
#endif XView
CatchServer()
{
    int             Server;
    int             DeadPid;
    union wait      status;
```

Example B-5.   Client side of the network ray tracer: rtrace.c   (Continued)

```
  DeadPid = wait(&status);
  if (DeadPid == -1)
    return;          /* doesn't happen if it's installed as a signal
                      * handler for SIGCHLD */

  /*
   * Catch them as they return, inspecting their exit() status.
   */
  for (Server = 0; Server < NumServers; Server++) {
    if (ServerPid[Server] == DeadPid) {
      /* if server failed, replace it */
#ifdef DBXTOOL
      if (status.w_status != 133) {      /* use this if window debug */
#else
      if (status.w_T.w_Retcode != SUCCESS) {
#endif
        printf("server %s had %d trouble and is being disabled\n",
               ServerName[Server], status.w_T.w_Retcode);
        ServerPid[Server] = 0;  /* Mark it as returned. */
      } else {
        if (LoadSizing) {
          gettimeofday(&tval, NULL);
          ServerTime[Server] = tval.tv_sec - ServerStart[Server];
          if (Total(ServerTime, NumServers) > (NumServers << 2)) {
            /* slow server down with more rays, low pass */
            if (ServerTime[Server] * NumServers <
                Total(ServerTime, NumServers)) {
              ServerLoad[Server] = MIN(ServerLoad[Server] + 1, MAXLOAD);
            } else {                  /* speed it up */
              ServerLoad[Server] = MAX(ServerLoad[Server] - 1, MINLOAD);
            }
          }
          printf("%s took %d secs., load now %d\n",
                 ServerName[Server], ServerTime[Server], ServerLoad[Server]);
        }
        ServerTot[Server]++;
        ServerPid[Server] = 0;  /* Mark it as returned. */
        ServersFree |= (0x1 << Server); /* Mark it as available. */
      }
      return;
    }
  }
  /* the returned child is not registered */
  printf("panic: a bastard child!");
}

#define myexit(val) _exit(val);
#ifdef DEBUG                         /* handy */
#define myexit(val) \
  {printf("child %d back from %s exit w/ %d\n",getpid(),\
  ServerName[Server],val);_exit(val);}
#endif

EachServerOnce(proc, arg)          /* pipeline requests to all servers */

  char           *(*proc) ();
  char           *arg;
{
  int            Server;
  int            pid;              /* Need this as CatchServer could step on
                                    * ServerPid[Server] */
  int            SMask;

  /*
   * Request a remote call of each server - only if healthy
```

Example B-5.   Client side of the network ray tracer: rtrace.c   (Continued)

```
     * (marked available).  If call fails, ServerPid is
     * cleared by CatchServer, ServersFree is left set.
     */
    for (Server = 0; Server < NumServers; Server++)
      CatchServer();
    if (ServersFree == 0x0)
      ERRMSG("No healthy servers left!");
    for (Server = 0; Server < NumServers; Server++) {
      SMask = 0x1 << Server;
      /* Check to see if it's sick. */
      if (!(SMask & ServersFree))
        continue;
      /*
       * Wait for it to come back if necessary - order could be important.
       */
      if (ServerPid[Server]) {
        printf("Waiting for initialization processes to return\n");
        sleep(STIME);
      }
      ServersFree ^= SMask;        /* Mark it as unavailable - and let's go. */
      while ((pid = ServerPid[Server] = fork()) == -1) {
        perror();
        sleep(STIME);                  /* fork failed, sleep awhile */
      }
      if (pid)
        continue;

      /* child */
      pReply = (reply *) (*proc) (arg, cl[Server]);
      if ((pReply == NULL) || (pReply->op == ERROR)) {
        clnt_perror(cl[Server], ServerName[Server]);
        fprintf(stderr, "%s", pReply->reply_u.sOp);
        myexit(ERROR);
      }
      myexit(SUCCESS);                /* success, child dies
                                       * without consequences */
  }
}                                    /* parent leaving with
                                      * living children... */

Total(vect, max)
  int               vect[MAXSERV], max;
{
  int               i, total = 0;
  for (i = 0; i < max; i++)
    total += vect[i];
  return (total);
}

#ifndef XView
ReqRay()
#else XView
/*
 * We'll use some Xlib stuff to get the pixels (an XImage) out in this repaint
 * callback procedure. It launches children to repaint the window, just to
 * show the use of children async. processing and reaping.
 */
ReqRay(canvas, paint_window, dpy, win)
  Canvas            canvas;
  Xv_Window         paint_window; /* not used */
  Display           *dpy;
  Window            win;
#endif XView
{
  int               i;
```

Example B-5. Client side of the network ray tracer: rtrace.c (Continued)

```
   double          yco;
#ifdef XView
  /* Cast and trace all the rays at servers. */
  if (NumServers > 1)
    LoadSizing = TRUE;              /* Turn on load sizing. */

  /*
   * Note a maximum-sized dummy XImage was already made in the WindowInit()
   * call - gives child processes dummies - saves LOTS of time.
   */
#endif XView

  /* Start casting rays... */
  for (yco = YMAX * SCALE; yco > YMIN * SCALE;) {
    if (InitServ)
      printf("Scan-line %d\n", (int) yco);

    /* launch the next free server, w/ load sizing */
#ifndef XView
    ForkNextServer(&yco);
#else XView
    ForkNextServer(&yco, win);
#endif XView
  }

  for (i = 0; i < NumServers; i++)
    printf("%s: %d\n", ServerName[i], ServerTot[i]);
}

/*
 * ForkNextServer() - Fork and start remote procedure on the server (let UNIX
 * manage resource contention and detailed scheduling!).  Record allocation
 * and pid in ServersFree and ServerPid[], resp.
 */
#ifndef XView
ForkNextServer(pyco)
#else XView
ForkNextServer(pyco, win)
  Window         win;
#endif XView
  double         *pyco;
{
  lines          lns;
  int            Server;          /* Number of who gets allocated. */
  int            SMask;
  replypix       *prp;
  int            Ppid;
  int            height;

  /*
   * Direct computations to a free server.  The servers could get all
   * allocated so might have to wait for the next available server.
   */
  Ppid = getpid();
  while (ServersFree == 0x0) {
    CatchServer();
    sleep(STIME);
  }
  for (Server = 0; Server < NumServers; Server++) {
    /* Allocate the next free server */
    SMask = 0x1 << Server;
    if (SMask & ServersFree) {
      ServersFree ^= SMask;
```

Example B-5. Client side of the network ray tracer: rtrace.c   (Continued)

```
        /*
         * Watch the timer, establish loading proportional to
         * last speed of response.
         */
        lns.ymax = *pyco;
        lns.ymin = (*pyco -= ServerLoad[Server]);
        gettimeofday(&tval, NULL);
        ServerStart[Server] = tval.tv_sec;

        while ((ServerPid[Server] = fork()) == -1) {
          perror("can't fork another server (sleeping)");
          if (EAGAIN == errno) {
            printf("ran out of processes (sleeping)");
            errno = 0;
          }
          CatchServer();
          sleep(STIME);                   /* fork failed, sleep to catch return child */
        }

        if (getpid() == Ppid)
          return (SUCCESS);
        break;
      }
  }

  /* Children only */
  prp = ray_trace_1(&lns, cl[Server]);
  height = (int) (lns.ymax - lns.ymin);
  if ((prp == NULL) ||
      (prp->replypix_len != height * width)) {
    clnt_perror(cl[Server], ServerName[Server]);
    _exit(ERROR);
  }
#ifndef XView
  /* Seek to the right position and write it out. */
  fflush(pFOut);
  fseek(pFOut, (long) (width * (YMIN * SCALE - lns.ymax)), 2);
  if (prp->replypix_len == fwrite(prp->replypix_val,
                  sizeof(char), prp->replypix_len, pFOut)) {
    fflush(pFOut);
#else XView
  /*
   * Stuff the pixels in the window and exit - must pass
   * both thru an XImage.
   */
  ximage->data = prp->replypix_val;
  XPutImage(dpy, win, gc, ximage, 0, 0, 0, (int) (YMAX * SCALE - lns.ymax),
            width, height);
  fflush(stdout);
  XFlush(dpy);
#endif XView
    _exit(SUCCESS);
  }
#ifndef XView
  _exit(ERROR);
}

#else XView

WindowInit(argc, argv)
  int         argc;
  char        *argv[];
{
  int         x;
```

Example B-5. Client side of the network ray tracer: rtrace.c   (Continued)

```
/*
 * build and install a ramp color table if the image doesn't have one
 */
cms_data.type = XV_DYNAMIC_CMS;
cms_data.index = 0;

if (cm.type == RMT_NONE) {
  unsigned char    grey[256];
  cms_data.size = cms_data.rgb_count = 256;
  for (x = 0; x < 256; x++)
    grey[x] = (unsigned char) x;
  cms_data.red = cms_data.green = cms_data.blue = grey;
} else {
  cms_data.size = cms_data.rgb_count = cm.length;
  cms_data.red = cm.map[0];
  cms_data.green = cm.map[1];
  cms_data.blue = cm.map[2];
}

/*
 * Establish a window w/ a repaint procedure.
 */
frame = (Frame) xv_create(NULL, FRAME,
                          FRAME_LABEL, argv[0],
                          FRAME_SHOW_FOOTER, TRUE,
                          NULL);
canvas = (Canvas) xv_create(frame, CANVAS,
                            WIN_WIDTH, rast.ras_width,
                            WIN_HEIGHT, rast.ras_height,
                            CANVAS_WIDTH, rast.ras_width,
                            CANVAS_HEIGHT, rast.ras_height,
/* don't retain window -- we'll repaint it all the time */
                            CANVAS_RETAINED, FALSE,
/* We're using Xlib graphics calls in repaint_proc(). */
                            CANVAS_X_PAINT_WINDOW, TRUE,
                            CANVAS_REPAINT_PROC, ReqRay,
                            OPENWIN_AUTO_CLEAR, FALSE,
                            WIN_DYNAMIC_VISUAL, TRUE,
                            WIN_CMS_NAME, "XisBrainDead",
                            WIN_CMS_DATA, &cms_data,
                            NULL);
window_fit(frame);

/*
 * The following section initializes some structures for repeated use in
 * child processes - saves the trouble of re-creating them each time.  It
 * has the side effects of initializing some global X11/Xview variables.
 * First create an XImage...
 */
dpy = (Display *) xv_get(canvas, XV_DISPLAY);
scrn = DefaultScreen(dpy);
ximage = XCreateImage(dpy, DefaultVisual(dpy, scrn),
      rast.ras_depth, ZPixmap, 0, (unsigned char *) NULL,
                        width, MAXLOAD, 8, width);


/*
 * ... then create a GC ...
 */
gcvalues.function = GXcopy;
gcmask |= GCFunction;
gcvalues.plane_mask = AllPlanes;
gcmask |= GCPlaneMask;
gcvalues.foreground = 1;
gcmask |= GCForeground;
```

Example B-5. Client side of the network ray tracer: rtrace.c   (Continued)

```
        gcvalues.background = 0;
        gcmask |= GCBackground;
        gcvalues.graphics_exposures = False;
        gcvalues.background = WhitePixel(dpy, DefaultScreen(dpy));
        gcvalues.foreground = BlackPixel(dpy, DefaultScreen(dpy));
        gc = XCreateGC(dpy, DefaultRootWindow(dpy), gcmask, &gcvalues);
}
#endif XView
```

Next the server side ray tracing and bookkeeping procedures are defined in
Example B-6. Notice the use of global memory, for a sense of history (state) across
RPCs.

Example B-6. Server procedures for the network ray tracer rtrace: rtrace_svc_proc.c

```
/*
 * rtrace_svc_proc.c: rtrace remote server procedures
 */
#include <stdio.h>
#include <string.h>
#include <math.h>
#include <sys/param.h>
#include <rpc/rpc.h>
#include "rtrace.h"
#include "rtrace_shared.h"

reply           Reply;

/*
 * Ray tracing stuff.
 */
double          bkgnd[MAXU][MAXV];
double          bkcon;
ball            *bl = NULL;
sphere          ls;
vector          vp;
int             level, nob;
int             xsue, ysue;
int             maxu, maxv;

void            *
die_1()
{
  /*
   * Unregister the server and die gracefully, returning nothing.
   */
  svc_unregister(RTRACESERVER, RTRACEVERS);
  exit(SUCCESS);
}

void            *
restart_1()
{
  /*
   * Unregister the server and start up again, returning
   * nothing.  Put the path to your server here.
   */
  svc_unregister(RTRACESERVER, RTRACEVERS);
  execl("/home/cortex/u0/bloomer/src/rpc/rtrace/rtrace_svc",
    (char *) 0);
}

reply           *
```

*Example B-6. Server procedures for the network ray tracer rtrace: rtrace_svc_proc.c
(Continued)*

```
set_params_1(pparams)
  parameters      *pparams;
{
  printf("set_params_1\n");
  bcopy(pparams->ls, &ls, sizeof(vector));
  bcopy(pparams->vp, &vp, sizeof(vector));
  bkcon = *(pparams->bkcon);
  Reply.op = SUCCESS;
  return (&Reply);
}

/*
 * load_bkgnd_1() - server procedure to load a database. As the protocol
 * suggests, Request Packets are returned with some error logging.
 */
reply            *
load_bkgnd_1(fname)
  filename        *fname;
{
  int             u, v;
  u_char          pval, big = 0, little = 255;
  colormap_t      cm;
  rasterfile      rast;
  u_char          *d;
  FILE            *fp;

  printf("load_bkgnd_1\n");
  Reply.op = ERROR;

  /* Read in a Sun rasterfile and make some room. */
  fp = fopen(*fname, "r");
  if (!fp || !(d = (u_char *) ReadSunRaster(fp, &cm, &rast))) {
    WARNMSG("can't load background raster file:");
    WARNMSG(*fname);
    Reply.reply_u.sOp = strdup("can't load background raster file");
    return (&Reply);
  }
  if (((maxu = rast.ras_width) > MAXU) ||
      ((maxv = rast.ras_height) > MAXV)) {
    WARNMSG("background pattern too big");
    Reply.reply_u.sOp = strdup("background pattern too big");
    return (&Reply);
  }
  /* Normalize and stuff into a double array. */
  for (v = 0; v < maxv; v++)
    for (u = 0; u < maxu; u++) {
      pval = (u_char) * (d + v * maxu + u);
      little = MIN(pval, little);
      big = MAX(pval, big);
    }
  big = big - little;
  for (v = 0; v < maxv; v++)
    for (u = 0; u < maxu; u++) {
      pval = (u_char) * (d + v * maxu + u);
      bkgnd[u][v] = (double) (pval - little) / (double) big;
    }

  /* Build up Reply packet. */
  Reply.op = SUCCESS;
  return (&Reply);
}

reply            *
load_balls_1(pBalls)
```

Example B-6. Server procedures for the network ray tracer rtrace: rtrace_svc_proc.c
(Continued)

```
  balls          *pBalls;
{
  printf("load_balls_1\n");
  Reply.op = ERROR;
  nob = pBalls->balls_len / sizeof(ball);
  if (bl)
    free(bl);
  bl = (ball *) malloc(pBalls->balls_len);
  bcopy(pBalls->balls_val, bl, pBalls->balls_len);

  Reply.op = SUCCESS;
  return (&Reply);
}

replypix        *
ray_trace_1(pLines)
  lines          *pLines;
{
  ray             rr;
  static replypix rp;
  static char    *data = NULL;
  char           *p;
  static double   xmin, xmax, ymin, ymax;
  double          xco, yco;

  /* Allocate some static return space. */
  if (!data) {
    xmin = XMIN * SCALE;
    xmax = XMAX * SCALE;
    ymin = YMIN * SCALE;
    ymax = YMAX * SCALE;
    data = malloc(nint((xmax - xmin) * (ymax - ymin)));
  }
  /* Cast rays for the assigned scan-lines  */
  p = data;
  ymin = pLines->ymin;
  ymax = pLines->ymax;
  for (yco = ymax; yco > ymin; yco--) {
    printf("Scan-line %d\n", (int) yco);
    for (xco = xmin; xco < xmax; xco++) {
      MV(xco / SCALE, yco / SCALE, 0.0, rr.org);
      SV(rr.dir, rr.org, vp);
      *(p++) = (char) shade(&rr);    /* trace them */
    }
  }
  rp.replypix_len = p - data;
  rp.replypix_val = data;
  return (&rp);
}

/*
 * This function does all the real work - calculating the
 * value (shade) each pixel should be. It uses recursion.
 */
int
shade(r)
  ray            *r;
{
  int             i, c, refract();
  ray             refr;
  double          lght, x, y, z, l, k, dot(), find(),
                  Shadow();
  int             sx, sy;
  double          stupid;
```

Example B-6. Server procedures for the network ray tracer rtrace: rtrace_svc_proc.c
(Continued)

```
vector          new, norm;
mat             trans;
sphere          ss;
ball            *b;

if (++level <= LEVEL) {
  c = -1;
  l = HUGE;
  /* get vector length and xz component for mt() */
  r->dir.l = LEN(r->dir);
  r->dir.xzl = XZL(r->dir);
  /*
   * Make a transform matrix that rotates something in space so that the
   * ray will be aligned with the x axis.
   */
  mt(&(r->dir), &trans);

  /* For starters we find out whether we hit anything. */
  for (i = 0; i < nob; i++) {
    b = bl + i;            /* ball pointer */
    ss.rad = b->s.rad;
    SV(ss.cent, b->s.cent, r->org);
    if ((k = find(&trans, &ss)) > 0.0 && k < l) {
c = i;
l = k;
    }
  }

  if (c >= 0 && (l * trans.x.y + r->org.y) > 0.0) {
    /* WE HIT SOMETHING */
    MV(l * trans.x.x, l * trans.x.y, l * trans.x.z, new);
    new.l = l;
    /* move the new origin of the ray to the intersection */
    AV(refr.org, new, r->org);
    AV(r->org, new, r->org);
    MV(r >dir.x, r->dir.y, r->dir.z, refr.dir);
    /* get a normal vector for the intersection point */
    b = bl + c;
    SV(norm, r->org, b->s.cent);
    norm.l = b->s.rad;

    /* ambient lighting */
    lght = 200.0 * b->amb;

    /*
     * shaded lighting (diffuse) subroutine Shadow is in find.c
     */
    if (b->dif != 0.0) {
SV(new, ls.cent, r->org);
new.l = LEN(new);
if ((k = DOT(new, norm)) > 0.0)
 lght += b->dif * Shadow(&(r->org)) * k / (new.l) / (norm.l);
    }
    /* reflection... easy */
    if (b->rfl != 0.0) {
/* make the normal unit length */
SCMLT((1.0 / norm.l), norm);
/*
 * get the length of the ray's component in the normal direction
 */
stupid = 2.0 * DOT(norm, r->dir);
SCMLT(stupid, norm);
/*
 * subtract double the normal component- !reflection!
```

Example B-6. Server procedures for the network ray tracer rtrace: rtrace_svc_proc.c
(Continued)

```
    */
    SV(r->dir, r->dir, norm);
    lght += b->rfl * (double) shade(r).
    }
    /*
     * refraction - this is ugly, which is why I choose to deal with it in
     * its own subroutine which comes after this one
     */
    if (b->rfr != 0.0) {
    lght += b->rfr * (double) refract(&refr, b);
    }
    } else {              /* hit no objects... */
      if ((r->dir.y) < 0.0) {    /* crosses floor */
    z = -(r->org.y) / (r->dir.y);
    (r->org.x) += z * (r->dir.x);
    (r->org.z) += z * (r->dir.z);
    (r->org.y) = 0.0;

    SV(new, ls.cent, r->org);
    new.l = LEN(new);
    sx = (int) (r->org.x / 1.5) % maxu;
    if (sx < 0)
      sx += maxu;
    sy = -(int) (r->org.z / 1.5) % maxv;
    if (sy < 0)
      sy += maxv;
    lght = (bkcon * bkgnd[sx][sy] + 1.0 - bkcon) * (0.8 *
        Shadow(&(r->org)) * (new.y) / (new.l) + 40.0);


      } else {            /* check to see if it hit lightsource */
    SV(ss.cent, ls.cent, r->org);
    ss.rad = ls.rad;
    if (find(&trans, &(ss.cent)) > 0.0)
      lght = 255;
    else
      lght = 0;
      }
    }
  }
  /* too many levels return 0 cause it shouldn't matter */
  else
    lght = 0;
  level--;
  if (lght < 0.0)
    lght = 0.0;
  if (lght > 255.0)
    lght = 255.0;
  return ((int) lght);
}

int             rlev;
int
refract(r, bll)
  ray           *r;
  bull          'bll,
{
  vector        new, norm;
  mat           trans;
  ray           ir;
  double        l, refk(), getcapt(), capt, inside();
  double        stupid;
  sphere        ss;
```

Example B-6. Server procedures for the network ray tracer rtrace: rtrace_svc_proc.c (Continued)

```
    SV(norm, r->org, bll->s.cent);
    norm.l = bll->s.rad;

    capt = getcapt(&norm, &(r->dir), bll->ior);


    /* get the addition factor for the normal for refraction */
    stupid = refk(&(norm), &(r->dir), bll->ior);
    SCMLT(stupid, norm);

    AV(ir.dir, r->dir, norm);
    MV(r->org.x, r->org.y, r->org.z, ir.org);

    /* now get it for reflection */
    SV(norm, r->org, bll->s.cent);
    norm.l = bll->s.rad;
    SCMLT(1.0 / norm.l, norm);
    stupid = 2.0 * DOT(norm, r->dir);
    SCMLT(stupid, norm);
    SV(r->dir, r->dir, norm);

    return ((int) ((1.0 - capt) * (double) shade(r) + ((capt) * inside(&ir,
bll)))));
}

double
inside(r, bll)
    ray             *r;
    ball            *bll;
{
    vector          new, norm;
    mat             trans;
    ray             er;
    double          findo(), lght, l, refk(), getcapt(),
                    capt;
    double          stupid;
    sphere          ss;

    if (++rlev < RLEV) {
        r->dir.l = LEN(r->dir);
        r->dir.xzl = XZL(r->dir);
        mt(&(r->dir), &trans);
        ss.rad = bll->s.rad;
        SV(ss.cent, bll->s.cent, r->org);

        l = findo(&trans, &ss);
        MV(l * trans.x.x, l * trans.x.y, l * trans.x.z, new);
        AV(er.org, r->org, new);
        AV(r->org, r->org, new);
        SV(norm, er.org, bll->s.cent);

        norm.l = bll->s.rad;
        capt = getcapt(&norm, &(r->dir), 1.0 / bll->ior);

        stupid = refk(&norm, &(r->dir), 1.0 / bll->ior);
        SCMLT(stupid, norm);
        AV(er.dir, norm, r->dir);

        SCMLT(1.0 / norm.l, norm);
        stupid = 2.0 * DOT(norm, r->dir);
        SCMLT(stupid, norm);
        SV(r->dir, r->dir, norm);
        lght = (1.0 - capt) * inside(r, bll) + (capt * (double) shade(&er));
    } else
```

Example B-6. Server procedures for the network ray tracer rtrace: rtrace_svc_proc.c (Continued)

```
    lght = 0.0;
   rlev--;
   if (lght < 0.0)
     lght = 0.0;
   if (lght > 255.0)
     lght = 255.0;
   return (lght);
}

double
refk(nrm, in, ior)
   vector        *nrm, *in;
   double        ior;
{
   double        dt, ln, li, ret;

   ior = ior * ior;
   dt = DOT((*nrm), (*in));
   ln = LN2((*nrm));
   li = LN2((*in));
   if (dt < 0)
     ret = (-dt - sqrt(dt * dt - ln * li * (1 - ior))) / ln;
   else
     ret = (-dt + sqrt(dt * dt - ln * li * (1 - ior))) / ln;
   return (ret);
}

double
getcapt(nrm, dr, ior)
   vector        *nrm, *dr;
   double        ior;
{
   double        dt, cs1, cs2, p, s;
   dt = DOT((*nrm), (*dr));
   dt = dt * dt / LN2((*nrm)) / LN2((*dr));
   cs1 = sqrt(dt);
   cs2 = sqrt(1.0 - (1.0 - dt) / ior);
   p = cs1 / (cs1 + ior * cs2);
   s = cs1 / (ior * cs1 + cs2);
   return (2.0 * (p * p + s * s));
}

double
findo(m, s)               /* Finds where a ray inside the ball exits. */
   mat           *m;
   sphere        *s;
{
   /* foops id the rotated position vector */
   vector        foops;
   double        t;
   MTV(foops, (*m), s->cent);
   /* see if it hits the ball (it better) */
   t = s->rad * s->rad - foops.y * foops.y - foops.z * foops.z;
   if (t > 0)
     t = foops.x + sqrt(t);
   else
     t = 0;
   /* Returns how far along the ray you were when you hit. */
   return (t);
}

double
find(m, s)                /* Finds whether a ray hits a ball. */
   mat           *m;
```

Example B-6. Server procedures for the network ray tracer rtrace: rtrace_svc_proc.c
(Continued)

```
  sphere          *s;
{
  vector          foops;
  double          t;
  MTV(foops, (*m), s->cent);
  t = s->rad * s->rad - foops.y * foops.y - foops.z * foops.z;
  if (t > 0)
    t = foops.x - sqrt(t);
  else
    t = 0;
  return (t);
}

double
finds(m, s)          /* Finds if a ball is between a point and a lightsource.
                      * Returns how obscuring the ball is. */
  mat             *m;
  sphere          *s;
{
  vector          foops;
  double          t;
  MTV(foops, (*m), s->cent);
  t = s->rad - sqrt(foops.y * foops.y + foops.z * foops.z);
  if (t > 0)
    t = t / foops.x;
  else
    t = 0;
  return (t);
}

double
Shadow(p)            /* Finds if a point is in a Shadow, or if it is on edge. */
  vector          *p;
{
  mat             trans;
  sphere          ss;
  vector          d;
  int             c, i;
  double          l, k, x, y, z, finds();
  ball            *b;

  l = 0.0;
  c = -1;
  SV(d, ls.cent, (*p));
  d.l = LEN(d);
  d.xzl = XZL(d);
  mt(&(d), &trans);

  for (i = 0; i < nob; i++) {
    b = bl + i;
    ss.rad = b->s.rad;
    SV(ss.cent, b->s.cent, (*p));
    if ((k = finds(&trans, &ss)) > l) {
      c = i;
      l = k;
    }
  }
  if (c == -1)
    k = 200.0;
  else {
    k = 1.0 - l / ((ls.rad) / (d.l));
    if (k < 0.0)
      k = 0.0;
    k *= 200.0;
```

*Example B-6. Server procedures for the network ray tracer rtrace: rtrace_svc_proc.c
(Continued)*

```
  }
  return (k);
}

/*
 * supportive subroutines...
 */
mt(vec, trans)
  vector          *vec;
  mat             *trans;
{
  if (vec->xzl == 0.0) {
    trans->x.x = 0.0;
    trans->x.y = 1.0;
    trans->x.z = 0.0;
    trans->y.x = -1.0;
    trans->y.y = 0.0;
    trans->y.z = 0.0;
    trans->z.x = 0.0;
    trans->z.y = 0.0;
    trans->z.z = 1.0;
  } else {
    trans->x.x = (vec->x) / (vec->l);
    trans->x.y = (vec->y) / (vec->l);
    trans->x.z = (vec->z) / (vec->l);
    trans->y.x = -(vec->x) * (vec->y) / ((vec->l) * (vec->xzl));
    trans->y.y = (vec->xzl) / (vec->l);
    trans->y.z = -(vec->z) * (vec->y) / ((vec->l) * (vec->xzl));
    trans->z.x = -(vec->z) / (vec->xzl);
    trans->z.y = 0;
    trans->z.z = (vec->x) / (vec->xzl);
  }
}
```

Example B-7. makefile for the rtrace network ray tracer

```
APPN      = rtrace
include ../makefile

# note - don't try to use -O4 with signals...
CFLAGS    = -O2 -I${OPENWINHOME}/include  -DXView=${XView}
LFLAGS    = -L${OPENWINHOME}/lib -lxview -lolgx -lX11 -lm $(APPN).a

$(APPN).a: raster.o
          ar rcv $(APPN).a raster.o
          ranlib $(APPN).a
```

To use the above *makefile* to put together the file-based approach, use:

```
rodson> make XView=0 raster.o rtrace rtrace_svc
```

Start the rtrace_svc servers on remote machines yourself or let the client do it.
The client reads your ~/.rhosts file in order, uses the standard UNIX rsh to attempt
to start the servers. The number of servers you are interested in is specified on the
command line. Make the XView version of the program with:

```
rodson> rm rtrace.o
rodson> make XView=1 rtrace
```

and run it in the same fashion.

Comments on Augmenting the Client to Run Under X11 with the XView Toolkit

If you've looked at the above client source code, there are some significant differences between the version that writes to an X11 window instead of disk. I'll document those differences here. The discussions in Chapters 6 and 10 about interacting with a windowing system should be consulted.

The servers did not change at all. I could have changed the RPC servers to use sockets and IPCs to communicate with the client, but chose rather to stay with RPC to simplify communications. The X11 XImage object is not used for communication, instead the servers return pixels values as raw XDR opaque character data. In this way the protocol didn't change either. None of the common or interface objects and data structures changed, so the input file *bdata.i*, shared definitions *rtrace_shared.h*, and *makefile* are also identical. The only changes required are to the client procedure, which instead of aligning descriptors and then writing, now sends pixel data through an X11 XImage to the window drawable.

Basically, the `RayReq()` procedure became an XView repaint callback. It still does RPC placing, keeping all the sound server connections open and active. Every time the canvas window is repainted, the rendering starts again. As server child processes return with pixel data, they place them into the window through an `XImage`, then they die. I made somewhat risky use of signals here. Instead of using the `wait3()` approach outlined in Dan Heller's book (*XView Programming Manual*), I chose to intercept all `SIGCHLD` signals, and check to see if the child is mine. This appears to work fine on a number of machines.

C

Generalized Server Initialization, Inquiry, and Removal

What we need is a generalized command-line tool to execute server initialization, inquiry, and removal mechanisms. If you extend the rpcinfo concept of accessing a remote portmap, you can think of finding, connecting to, and calling any remote procedure from the command line. This can be a powerful, dangerous technique if extra server functions are available to do things like shut the server down or reinitialize itself. We mentioned making server termination, restarting, and priority setting available as remote calls in Chapter 8.

> ☞ The changes made here to rpcinfo are done to illustrate how you might put together your own general-purpose RPC server maintenance tool. It does not suggest any deficiencies in rpcinfo, nor does the author take responsibility for this hack. I personally did it as a learning process, and thought you might benefit from it. That's why it's hidden here!

I augmented the original *rpcinfo.c* to reflect the ability to call arbitrary procedures directly or via broadcast. In this fashion, with one command line, you can restart or shut down all or one of the servers on your network. It's a lot faster than seeking out that process and attempting to kill it remotely. If the servers are implemented correctly, and unregister themselves, it tends to leave less of a mess in the portmap.

Due to the fact that the original utility is 672 lines, I decided to include just the results of a diff -e between the original and my new and improved version. Pass the following ed(1) script into patch, running it against the old version to produce the new with patch < patchfile. This assumes that *rpcinfo.c*, as found in the 4.0 ONC release, is in the current directory.

As an alternative it would be valuable for you to wander through *rpcinfo.c* to see how it works, making the changes manually on the noted line numbers.[†] The new `rpcinfo` has the following usage:

Usage: rpcinfo [-n portnum] -u host program [versnum [procnum]]

rpcinfo [-n portnum] -t host program [versnum [procnum]]

rpcinfo -p [host]

rpcinfo -b program versnum [procnum]

rpcinfo -d program versnum

Now we can call *any* valid procedure of a registered server, the NULLPROC, and more. If no procedure number is specified, NULLPROC is the default. A command like the following will de-install all the servers answering to a query for a certain UDP transport protocol `prognum` and `versnum`, with a `deinstall` procedure similar to that defined above:

```
rpcinfo -b prognum versnum deinstall
```

If you'd like to neatly terminate one in particular, use:

```
rpcinfo -u host prognum versnum deinstall .
```

I did not add a check for root privileges before honoring the `-d` flag. Under ONC RPC 4.0, it is not necessary to be the superuser to mess around with local portmap entries (i.e., with `pmap_unset()`). Unrestricted changes to the portmap can be lethal. There is no mechanism to protect entries. This loophole was closed with `rpcbind`, but portmap backward compatibility (calls to the old Version 2 of the portmap interface supported by `rpcbind`) is still available. The patch file for *rpcinfo.c* is shown in Example C-1.

Example C-1. Making RPCSRC 4.0 rpcinfo.c do other things: patchFile

```
644c
        vers = (int) atoi(argv[c]);
        if (argc > (c+1)) anyproc = (int) atoi(argv[c+1]);
.
639,640c
getvers(argv, c, argc)
        char **argv;
        int c, argc;
.
612,613c
        fprintf(stderr, "        rpcinfo -b program versnum [procnum]\n");
        fprintf(stderr, "        rpcinfo -d program versnum\n") ;
.
609,610c
        fprintf(stderr, "Usage: rpcinfo [ -n portnum ] -u host program [ versnum
[or
ocnum]]\n");
```

---

† If you cannot get this to work, watch UUNET for source availability. I'll attempt to make modified source available there.

Example C-1. Making RPCSRC 4.0 rpcinfo.c do other things: patchFile (Continued)

```
        fprintf(stderr, "        rpcinfo [ -n portnum ] -t host program [ versnum
[pr
ocnum]]\n");
.
598c
        version_num = getvers(argv, 1, argc);
.
596a
#endif
.
592a
#ifdef OLD
.
572,573c
        vers = getvers(argv, 1, argc);
        rpc_stat = clnt_broadcast(prognum, vers, anyproc, xdr_void,
.
567c
        if ((argc < 2) || (argc > 3)) {
.
435c
                rpc_stat = clnt_call(client, anyproc, xdr_void, (char *)NULL,
.
424c
                vers = getvers(argv, 2, argc);
.
414c
                rpc_stat = clnt_call(client, anyproc, xdr_void, (char *)NULL
,
.
377c
                rpc_stat = clnt_call(client, anyproc, xdr_void,
.
356c
                rpc_stat = clnt_call(client, anyproc, xdr_void, (char *)NULL,
.
334c
        if (argc < 2 || argc > 4) {
.
309c
                rpc_stat = clnt_call(client, anyproc, xdr_void, (char *)NULL,
.
296c
                vers = getvers(argv, 2, argc);
.
288c
                rpc_stat = clnt_call(client, anyproc, xdr_void,
.
251c
                rpc_stat = clnt_call(client, anyproc, xdr_void,
.
228c
                rpc_stat = clnt_call(client, anyproc, xdr_void, (char *)NULL,
.
198c
        if (argc < 2 || argc > 4) {
.
97c
        while ((c = getopt(argc, argv, "cptubdn:")) != EOF) {
.
81a
```

Example C-1. Making RPCSRC 4.0 rpcinfo.c do other things: patchFile (Continued)

```
/* stuff added to allow arbitrary procedure calling,
   modified getvers() and all its uses to pick up an optional
   proc. number */
u_long anyproc = NULLPROC;
```

Apply the patch file of ed(1) commands as follows:

```
rodson> cd /home/cortex/projects/RPCSRC4.0/etc
rodson> ls -lt rpcinfo*
-rw-r--r--  1 bloomer       16542 Dec  2  1988 rpcinfo.c
rodson> patch < patchFile
Hmm...  Looks like an ed script to me...
File to patch: rpcinfo.c
16542
16884
done
rodson> ls -lt rpcinfo*
-rw-r--r--  1 bloomer       16884 Feb 17 16:27 rpcinfo.c
-rw-r--r--  1 bloomer       16542 Dec  2  1988 rpcinfo.c.orig
```

We performed the patching in the directory that the file was in, though that's not necessary. You can use ed directly to produce the new file (see diff(1)). Patch is nice enough to keep the old file around.

D

Parallel Processing In A Nutshell

Like most other branches of evolving science, parallel computing is filled with many acronyms and buzz words. I'll try to clear some of them up.[†] The following are some of the more commonly used (or abused) terms:

- *Processor coupling* addresses how processors communicate. A *tightly-coupled* network typically shares global memory, is controlled by some centralized resource, and hard-wired together (e.g., a backplane bus). A *loosely-coupled* network typically has distributed memory and control, and may use a more abstract interprocessor communication scheme, like message-passing over a backplane or network bus. In recent years, loosely-coupled schemes have been employed when communication bandwidth is low compared to task computational requirements.

- *Task dependence* determines processing order. If a sequence of tasks is *mutually independent*, e.g., C=A+B and F=D*E, partitioning for parallel execution is readily apparent, with communication overhead occurring at start and end only. *Mutually dependent* tasks, e.g., C=A+B, B=X+Y, require temporal execution management and more communications overhead, for example, synchronization techniques. In many real-life cases, task dependencies are dynamic and time-varying.

- *Process granularity* determines the size of the parallel pieces. A *coarse-grained* partitioning of parallel processes typically implies a small number of processors, each with significant resources. The computations to intercommunication ratio is

---

† E.V. Krishnamurthy's *Parallel processing: principles and practice*, (Addison-Wesley, 1989, ISBN 0-201-17532) is a good, practical reference.

high. Vectorizing compilers on a multi-processor computer often manage coarse-grained partitioning. When the multiple processors are connected by a network instead of a local bus, the programmer typically does not have an automated solution to coarse-grained process partitioning and must do it through code design. We emphasize this aspect of parallel programming in this book.

- A *fine-grained* partitioning of parallel processes implies a massive number of processors, each capable of handling small processes. It is characterized by high I/O rates and minimal local resources. Oftentimes a compiler for a massively-parallel architecture performs fine-grained partitioning.

Parallelism

There are several different types of parallelism:

- *Concurrent processing* involves dependent processes operating at the same time. It implies that there are multiple processors communicating to maintain execution-time data requirements, etc.

- *Multi-processing parallelism* involves independent jobs running on multiple computers. Processor operation is generally autonomous, and no centralized memory switch or controller is employed. This processing architecture label is usually not extended to cover networked computers as emphasized here because the communication schemes employed by networks are comparatively slow, and memory (RAM) space is not shared across the network.

- *Pipelining* is a common form of chip-level parallelism. Data is operated on sequentially by different processors, each with its own instruction. Hardware designers may be familiar with this approach to parallelism. For example, many signal or image processing tasks require use of high-speed multiply-accumulate operations. Oftentimes you'll see a hardware multiplier followed by an adder. Each is a different processor with a very limited instruction set. Processing on a data stream can be overlapped, as the multiplier can multiply while the adder accumulates in memory the results of the previous multiply. That's pipelining.

- *Multi-pass, interleaving, and pipes* are ways of finding places to break an algorithm into subordinate pieces, each capable of sequentially operating on its predecessor's incremental result. I like this one best, as it allows you to structure the communication in a symmetrical, potentially data-independent fashion. If the interleaved subordinate processes (subalgorithms) have a clear data in-data out separation, it can become a pipe.[†] The UNIX OS itself makes heavy use of process interleaving as well as scheduling.

---

† See "An Overview of UNIX Interprocess Communication" in Chapter 5 for an explanation of pipes.

- *Vector or array processing* assigns a large number of closely-coupled processors to crunch away on different pieces of data with common operations. The Single Instruction, Multiple Data (SIMD) processor is an example. Typically these beasts need a centralized, microcoded controller as a front-end interface between your code and the vector/array.

- *Distributed computing* is a network of loosely-coupled processors. Different from a *distributed multi-processor*, the interconnect medium is a network, instead of a bus or backplane. Control is distributed across the network as each processor is an independent computer. This interconnect topology is capable of executing multiple instructions on multiple data streams (MIMD). On a grand scale, your local area network is an MIMD machine, as is ARPANET. The goal, of course, is to coordinate useful processing! SIMD machines are understandably easier to program in parallel.

Interprocess Control

Interprocess control is essential to keep processors dynamically and efficiently applied to the problem, with processors supplied with all the necessary data for pending computations. Some different techniques for interprocess control are described below:

- *Synchronization* – Processes or processors that operate with data interdependencies must use some technique to align their process execution to points in time when all the required input data is available. Shared variables and message passing are a couple of approaches to the problem.

- *Multi-thread control flow* – Modeling parallel processing as control-driven, where the execution of operations is explicitly managed through process control, such as `fork(2V)`, `wait(2V)`, etc.

- *Dataflow* – A data-driven, decentralized model of processing where execution occurs as data becomes ready. Data produced by one process is consumed by others without a need for shared memory.

- *Reduction* – Modeling the parallel processes as instructions which get executed only when their results are demanded by previously selected instructions.

Interprocess Communication

Processes may or may not be on separate machines (see Multi-programming). For this reason, processes may need to communicate using one of a couple of different approaches:

- *Message passing* – Communication through point-to-point, or broadcast passing of messages; that is, packets of information containing commands, status, data, etc.

- *Shared memory* – Communication via memory mapped into a space accessible to all processors. This memory may or may not be physically local to a processor; for example, it could be local RAM or a global memory card on the same bus.

Buzzwords: A Glossary

Here's a glossary of the important terms and acronyms you need to understand this book and the subject area:

asynchronous processing
> Execution proceeds in such a fashion that procedure calls do not suspend execution while waiting for results to be returned.

binding
> The act of associating a server with a socket. When ONC RPC server transport handles are created, they are *bound* to a certain network port (and a socket) address.

blocking
> Suspension of execution until some condition is satisfied. This term is used to describe synchronous RPC, where execution waits until the remote procedure returns.

broker or Portmapper
> An intermediary between clients and servers designated to assist in network resource communications.

client application
> A user-written application that requests remote procedure calls to be executed by a server application.

client process
> A process on the machine executing the client application. There may be more than one process associated with one instance of client application execution.

client stub Source code containing all the necessary functions to allow the client application to make remote procedure calls using a local procedure call model. A protocol compiler typically generates this file, which gets linked with any XDR filters and the client application.

DARPA Defense Advanced Research Projects Agency.

daemon A program designed to run continuously in the background, lying dormant until some condition is met. Most servers are daemons. Daemons have been around a lot longer than RPC, providing many local services within UNIX.

distributed computing environment
Generally a superset of other programming tools. These typically represent some coherent toolkit containing remote procedure calling and data representation libraries. They include network resource management tools and application development interfaces. OSF has trademarked the initials DCE.

DDS The default addressing scheme used on Apollo networks.

dispatch procedure or dispatcher
This routine receives the requests, attempts to validate and provide the service through a local procedure call on the client, then sends a reply to the client. Dispatchers are the most useful for multiple-service servers and are often generated by a protocol compiler.

distributed application
An application that executes code on two or more networked computers.

fork Start a child process that is an exact copy of the parent except for process ID and descriptors, which are useful for execution control and communication.

heterogeneous architectures
A diverse collection of computers with differences in processor or operating system requiring back-and-forth data translations to facilitate network communication.

homogeneous architectures
A collection of computers with the same or compatible processors and operating systems requiring no data translations for networking.

host A processor or "machine" connected to a network.

idempotent operation
An operation that, if performed, does not affect the outcome of any future operations. To read a value is an idempotent operation; incrementing a variable is not.

inetd(8C) The Internet services daemon (superserver) which listens for connections, invoking the named server daemon, no portmapping required. Normally, system standard RPC servers are started by `inetd`.

Internet A collection of networks including NSFnet, ARPAnet, and several commercial, military, academic, and regional/local networks. DDN (Defense Data Network) refers to the large portion of Internet managed by the Department of Defense.

Internet Protocols

Includes TCP, IP, and UDP. Often referred to as the TCP/IP protocol family, just to confuse people.

IP Internet protocol, an inter-network datagram delivery protocol. An IP address refers to a host. From the same Internet protocol suite as TCP.

IPC UNIX talk for interprocess communication, the sharing of data between processes, on the same machine or across a network.

ISO International Organization Standardization, developed the Open Systems Interconnection (OSI) standards.

LB or Location Broker

The NCS Location Broker is the naming or mapping service that tells where network resource objects (e.g., servers) are and how to access them. As part of the NCS DCE it consists of the Global and Local Locations brokers, responsible for expressing resource availability for the network at large, and as relevant to the local host, respectively. The Local Location Broker is comprised of a database of objects and servers on a single host. See NIS for the equivalent function in the ONC suite.

NCA The Network Computing Architecture (NCA), an Apollo/HP abstraction, is a collection of concepts and guidelines for distributed computing.

NCK The NCS Network Computing Kernel is a run-time library that includes RPC support and network resource manager service with access routines called the Location Broker. Low-level RPC network communication is currently carried out through use of NDR.

NCS The HP/Apollo's Network Computing System is a particular implementation of NCA. NCS is the software that a distributed application developer would use. NCS itself is a combination of two Apollo/HP products: NCS/NCK and NCS/NIDL.

NDR The NCS Network Data Representation, a proprietary multi-canonical form for expressing network data.

NFS Sun's Network File System, built on ONC RPC. It uses IP with UDP.

NIDL   The NCS Network Interface Description Language. This NCS component is a distributed application development toolkit, including a protocol compiler. It translates interface and protocol descriptions into C code to implement NCA-style RPCs and provide NCK routines for use by cooperating clients and servers.

NIS   The Sun Network Information Service, roughly equivalent to the Location Broker. Major pieces include the `ypserv()` and `ypbind()` daemons started at boot-time in the */etc rc.local* script, to handle NIS database communication at the server and client sides. An NIS server machine must also run a client daemon to talk to itself. NIS files are a distributed, replicated (with some level of consistency and time constraints) database of dbm files living in */var/yp./etc* files are no longer consulted directly. Content during change (prompted by intentional and unintentional network modifications) is weakly consistent, being updated gradually across the network.

NLM   The ONC Network Lock Manager.

ONC   Sun Microsystems' Open Network Computing. The ONC product suite includes RPC, XDR, NIS, NLM, rex, etc. AT&T and others support ONC tools.

OSF   Open Software Foundation (OSF) is a consortium of DEC, IBM, HP/Apollo, and other major UNIX hardware vendors.

OSI   Open Systems Interconnection. A set of ISO-developed standards that include the seven-layer reference model for data communication systems and the ASN.1 Basic Encoding Rules.

pipe   An interprocess communication channel, effectively a FIFO (first-in, first-out) buffer with separate read and write file descriptors.

port   A logical network communication channel. The Portmapper lives at port number 111. All other services are assigned statically or dynamically.

Portmapper
              The Sun utility service used by all other services to map ports to services on a machine (actually DARPA port to RPC program number mapping).

process   For the purpose of this book, a process is a unique entity, viewing the world through a table of descriptors.

process binding
              A logical association between client and server processes.

protocol A set of conventions used to exchange messages between entities over a medium. In this context it hosts communication over a network.

protocol compiler

A tool that generates structured C source code, including client and server stubs, common definitions (header file(s)), and data translation filters. Driven by a textural, usually C-like definition of the networked application, the protocol compiler allows the client and server applications to carry on remote procedure calls at the highest possible abstraction.

protocol definition

A formal grammar is used to define the nature of the client/server interface, including remote procedure declarations, input and output typing, and program, version, and procedure detailing.

register　To make something known as a network resource database(s), made accessible to hosts on that network. RPC servers register (and unregister) themselves with a broker or portmapping service.

remote procedure

A procedure so packaged as to be called within a server process indirectly by a client process.

remote procedure call system

A set of facilities including a programming library, and network resource mapping and binding services to provide a mechanism for a client process to execute a procedure on a remote server. A remote procedure call system is a subset of a distributed computing environment.

reply　Information assembled by the server RPC code and transmitted back to the client, according to RPC protocol, to return the results of the remote execution. The information in a reply connotes either a success procedure call or a failure at the server.

request　Information created by the client process RPC code and transmitted to the server, according to RPC protocol, to attempt to initiate the execution of a procedure within the server application. Necessary procedure arguments are included.

rex　The remote execution protocol, as defined in the ONC RPC protocol definition */usr/include/rpcsvc/rex.x*. This network service uses the TCP transport and a `rexd` server daemon. on uses `rex` to run commands on other systems with a copy of each one's current environment including NFS mounts. It uses standard username and password authentication.

rexec　An earlier, non-RPC remote execution protocol. `rexec` uses streams to communicate with a remote command, using your *~/.netrc* information when possible, to perform authentication with the `rexecd` daemon. `rexec()` and `rexd()` by themselves have some security shortcomings.

rlogin, rsh, rcp
> Non-RPC remote login, shell execution, and copy utilities, based on BSD networking facilities.

RPC   A remote procedure call (noun) or remote procedure calling (verb).

RPCGEN   The Sun ONC RPC protocol compiler, uses a C-like specification (RPCL language) of RPC applications and network data to generate code to handle low-level RPC mechanisms.

semaphores
> A facility for sharing data about the state of a process, developed in System V. Like messages and shared memory, these are useful for communicating and synchronizing multiple processes.

service or service procedure
> One isolated function performed by the server, fulfilled by one procedure within a server application.

server   Servers are daemons that make resources available to networked clients. Servers have port and program numbers associated with them for network access by clients.

server application
> A user-written application that handles and replies to requests made by client processes.

server process
> A process on the machine executing the server application. There may be multiple server processes necessary to fulfill services as detailed in the server application.

server stub Source code containing all the necessary functions to allow the server application to satisfy remote procedure requests using local procedure calls. A protocol compiler typically generates this file, which gets linked with any XDR filters and the server application.

signal   A BSD4.2 IPC tool, uses a predefined set of tokens to notify processes, typically prompting a result.

socket   An IPC channel. Once connected, processes can read and write to communicate.

state machine
> A virtual machine used to organize execution through a defined sequence of steps or states.

synchronous processing
> A mode of processing wherein execution is suspended until a procedure call returns.

TCP Internet Transmission Control Protocol, layered upon IP. As a *network transport*, it provides process-to-process message transfer across a network. A socket using TCP transport has a port and IP address bound to it.

UDP User Datagram Protocol, uses connectionless datagram sockets. It, too, is a network transport, layered on top of IP.

UI UNIX International. Sun, AT&T, and others teamed up to develop standards for the UNIX system software.

well-known ports
A port whose number is known as part of the definition of the network, making it known *a priori* to clients and servers. Assignments of well-known port numbers is coordinated by a centralized authority.

XDR External Data Representation, ONC's standardized specification for portable data transmission. Takes the form of a library of routines.

YP or Yellow Pages
Now known as NIS. YP is a trademark of British Telecom.

Index

A

accept() 130
access control policy 198, 345
access utilities (see setrpcent() &
        getrpcent())
address resolution protocol (ARP) 105
alarm() 137, 141
Andrew File System 39
anonymous FTP xxvii
ARP (see address resolution protocol)
asynchronous processing 199, 254
        defined 461
auth_destroy() 335, 388
authdes_create() 336, 387
authdes_getucred() 388
authentication 333–349
        AUTH structure 334
        authunix_params structure 336
        errors 338
        flavors 335
        high-level RPC 50
        opaque_auth structure 334
authnone_create() 335, 388
authunix_create() 388

authunix_create_default() 336, 388
awk 220

B

batch RPC 246
bcmp() 122
bcopy() 122
BER (see data representation)
BFS (see Brute-force Scheduling)
binding 127, 377
        bind() 127, 129
        defined 16, 461
        Internet domain 134, 139
        UNIX domain 129
bindresvport() 128
blocking 236, 461
        read/write 143
bool_t, status return 363
broadcast RPC
        as an antisocial act 248
        authentication 248
        transport and packet size limit 248
broker or binder service 16, 461
Brute-force Scheduling (BFS) 152
        lightweight alternative 270

BSD 4.3 112
bulk data transfers 39
bundle, shell script 93
byte order 24, 121
    macros in <netinet/in.h> 122
    network order 121
    support routines 121
byte-oriented memory access
        functions 122
bzero() 122, 136, 139, 141

C
CAD Framework Initiative (CFI) 31
callrpc() 50, 253, 381, 389
calls, UNIX utility 200
child process
    reaping 154
    return status 155
    timing 157
CLIENT
    handle 59, 79, 362, 381
    structure 334
client 1, 2
    application, defined 461
    asynchronous 254
    defined 16
    in X 1, 284
    multiple clients and servers 235
    one-way RPC 243
    process, defined 461
    starting servers 222
    state 246
        retaining 352, 354
    stub 61, 462
client/server partitioning strategy 197
clnt_broadcast() 248, 389
clnt_call() 59, 80, 389
clnt_control() 80, 98, 238, 390
clnt_create() 59, 79, 328, 381, 391
clnt_create_vers() 391
clnt_destroy() 79, 335, 391
clnt_dg_create() 330
clnt_freeres() 208, 391
clnt_geterr() 338, 392

clnt_pcreateerror() 87, 392
clnt_perrno() 338, 392
clnt_perror() 87, 338, 392
clnt_spcreateerror() 393
clnt_sperrno() 338, 393
clnt_sperror() 338, 393
clnt_stat status values 342, 404
clnt_tli_create() 329
clnt_tp_create() 329
clnt_vc_create() 330
clntraw_create() 94, 392
clnttcp_create() 393
clntudp_bufcreate() 393
clntudp_create() 258, 394
close() 127, 132
    for pipes 120
    for sockets 137
collection server or daemon,(see also
        follow-up RPC) 253
compression 185
    compress 232
    oldcompact 232
    run-length encoding 232
concurrent processing 458
Concurrent Programming Support
        (CPS) 28
concurrent server (see also server) 110
connect() 127, 130, 132, 136
connection
    error 130
    error detection 352
    Internet 108
    transport 105
connectionless versus connection-
        oriented programming 126
convolution
    in image processing 164
    kernel 164, 166
coupling 457
crash recovery 352, 356
credential
    building 335
    cooked 348
    defined 333
    destroying 335

lifetime or window 337
raw 207
cut() 101

D

daemon 16, 462
DARPA 462
Data Encryption Standard (DES) 30,
    335, 386
    crypt() 386
    des 386
    keyserv daemon 336
    publickey database 336, 387
data representation
    Basic Encoding Rules (BER) 26
    multi-canonical 24
    receiver-makes-it-right 24
    single-canonical 24
dataflow 459
datagram 27
    defined 105
    detection of loss 140
    IP 107
dbm 118, 140
dbx 89, 90, 94, 97, 183
    and Raw transport 97
    client/server breakpoints 99
    over the network 98
    up command 99
dbxtool 89
deadlock 254
debugging 89
    breakpoints for client/server 99
    client linked to server 90
    dbx 89
    dbxtool 89
    in one address space 90, 94
    over the network 97
    Raw transport 94, 97
        editing the client application 96
        editing the client stub 96
        editing the server stub 95
        linking 96
    via cpp directives 91

DECORUM DCE 19
deploying servers 100
DES (see Data Encryption Standard)
diff, UNIX utility 456
discriminated union 5
dispatch function 46, 47
    defined 462
    name 99
dispatch table, generated by
    RPCGEN 66
distributed applications
    defined 462
    design questions 197
distributed computing environment
    components of 20
    defined xxvi, 16, 462
    standards 19
Distributed Computing Environment
    (DCE) xxvi
distributed file systems 232
distributed filename normalization 232
divide and conquer, strategy for
    parallelization 148, 164
domain
    Internet 105
    UNIX 129
dup() (see also socket descriptor,
    duplication) 140

E

encapsulation 105
endrpcent() 125
errno 85, 139, 143, 157, 350
    during select 251
error codes 404
error reporting 338, 350
Ethernet 164
    address 105
    bandwidth 231
examples
    ~/.ls, directs ls servers using
        sstart.sh 221

examples (continued)

asyncCallback.c, XView interval tim-
    er looks for asynchronous
    FRPC requests 293

asyncRls.h, header file included by
    the asynchronous clients
    and servers 254

asyncRls_svc.c server, responds
    asynchronously using
    FRPCs 258

auth.h, macros included in server
    dispatch routine 348

bdata.i, input file for rtrace 427

bundle, shell archive script 93

childTimer.c, use of interval timer
    and signals 157

day.c, using time of day to watch
    child processing 159

die_1(), server termination through
    a RPC 225

dim.c, adding authentication to the
    client 340

dim.x, RPCL protocol definition for
    dim 202

dim_svc_proc.c, access control add-
    ed to server delete
    procedure 349

dispatch.c, dispatcher registration
    for X-based RPC server 299

doit_1(), a service procedure makes
    an FRPC 252

hello.c, a simple Xt/Xol
    example 300

HighLevelServer.c, server multi-
    tasking through process
    creation, DOES NOT
    WORK! 264

im_proc.c, archive access functions
    for local image
    manager 193

itimer.c, using an interval timer in
    XView 291

Loop_sockets_AF_INET_server.c,
    sockets_AF_INET_server.c

modified for repeated
    use 306

makefile
    automating authentication
        changes 347
    for the rtrace network ray
        tracer 450
    for two forms of local
        debugging 92
    for Xt and XView
        applications 289
    template for RPCGEN RPC
        development 161

manual page for rtrace 426

multiRls_svc.c, multi-tasking service
    that works 265

notifyServer.c, using notify_en-
    able_rpc_svc() in the
    XView notifier 298

one-way.c, client places one-way
    RPC requests 243

one-way.x, combined one-way and
    synchronous RPC protocol
    for remote directory
    listing 240

one-way_svc_proc.c, server proce-
    dures including a one-way,
    request-only RPC
    service 242

patchFile, making RPCSRC 4.0
    rpcinfo.c do other
    things 454

raster.c, Sun rasterfile format
    utilities 320

raster.h, Sun rasterfile format
    support 321

read_dir.c, directory listing
    procedure 45

remote.c, using rexec for remote
    execution 145

repairDB() now restores the
    database 357

restart_1(), restarting the server with
    a RPC 226

examples (continued)
rip_shared.h, include file for client
and server 169
rip_svc_proc.c, server procedures
for RIP 180
rls.c
remote directory listing
client 86
RPC client for reading remote
directory files 56
rls.h, common include definitions
for the RPC directory
lister 48
rls.h, header file generated by
RPCGEN 83
rls.x,remote directory listing
protocol) 82
rls_svc.c, server stub using Raw
transport for local
debugging 95
rls_svc_proc.c, remote read directory service 84
rteleLWP.c, lightweight processing
for asynchronous remote
calls from a client 275
rteleLWP_svc_proc.c, lightweight
processing for asynchro-
nous remote calls from a
client 280
rtrace.c, client side of the network
ray tracer 430
rtrace.x, protocol definition for
rtrace 428
rtrace_shared.h, shared definitions
for client/server
procedures 429
rtrace_svc_proc.c, server procedures for rtrace 442
sample input script for rip 165
skeleton for server self-termination
after lack of use 224
skeleton for setting server process
priority 226
skeleton for starting servers from the
client 222

sstart, C shell script to start remote
servers 218
sstart.sh, Bourne shell script to start
remote server process
(better) 219
stest.c, catching SIGCHLD using
fork(), kill() and
signal() 153
TCP_AF_INETclient.c, connection-
oriented client using Internet addressing 135
TCP_AF_INETserver.c, connection-
oriented server using Internet addressing 134
AF_UNIXserver.c, connection-oriented server using domain
addressing 129
tcpDispatchServer, TCP transport is
more complex 311
tcpRls.c, synchronous client using
TCP transport 313
UDP_AF_INETclient.c, connectionless client using Internet
domain addressing 140
UDP_AF_INETserver.c, connectionless server using Internet
domain addressing 138
udpDispatchServer.c, UDP transport RPC server activated
by the Xt event
dispatcher 308
wload.c, loads an image into a Sun-
View window 318
wtest.c, wait() watches for child
deaths 154
Xt_sockets_AF_INET_client.c, Xt
socket-based client 303
xwload.c, X client loads an image
into a window 315
exec, C shell built-in command 57, 217
execl() 112, 226
exit() 156, 278
for sockets 131, 137

External Data Representation (XDR) 10, 22, 25 (see also XDR)

F

fault tolerance in applications 199
fclose(), for named-pipes 120
fcntl() 128, 143
fdopen(), for pipes 120
FIFO 120, 279
filename conventions 63
filenames, host qualified 232
follow-up RPC (FRPC) 252
    collection daemon 253, 292
    polling for requests 254
fopen(), for named-pipes 120
fork() 110, 149, 153, 462
frame buffer 185
    SunView vs. X performance 314
fstab 223
ftp 108, 115

G

gateway
    defined 104
    IP 107
get_myaddress() 394
gethostbyaddr() 123, 248
gethostbyname() 123, 136, 141
gethostent() 123
gethostname() 123
getitimer() 157
getmntent() 233
getnctname() 337, 394
getpeername() 246
getpid() 153
getprotoent() 123
getpwuid() 189
getrpcbyname() 124
getrpcbynumber() 124
getrpcent() 124
getrpcport() 394
getservbyname() 123, 139, 141
getservbyport() 123
getservent() 123

getsockname() 127
getsockopt() 127, 144
global variables 198
gtty() 275

H

heavyweight processing 152
heterogeneous clients and servers 462
high-level ONC RPC library
            functions xxvi
homogeneous clients and servers 462
host, defined 462
host2netname() 337, 395
hostent structure 123, 136, 141
hosts file
    /etc/hosts, hostname to Internet ad-
            dress mapping 104, 122
HP license broker 22
htonl() 122
htons() 122, 134

I

idempotent procedure 33, 109
    defined 34, 462
    porting concerns 198
    TCP 352
inet() 257
inet_ntoa() 249
inetd
    adding services 110
    how it works 112
    re-init with SIGHUP 119
    rexecd 145
    RPCGEN support 28, 65, 111
    server timeout 225
    the Internet superserver 30, 34, 110,
            112, 377, 463
inetc.conf file
    /etc/inetd.conf, inetd configuration
            file 114
init 112

Internet
    addresses
        defined 104
        example 133, 138
        mapping to Ethernet
            addresses 105
        archive sites xxxi
    catenet model 104
    defined 463
    domain 105
    protocols 16, 26, 105, 463
    standards, obtaining RFCs 407
interprocess communication (IPC)
    application program interfaces
        (APIs) 119
    defined 463
    FIFOs 120
    file descriptors 120
    kernel sharing 120
    message queue 120
    model for communication 119
    named-pipes 120
    overview of methods 459
    pipes 120
    semaphores 121
    shared memory 121
interprocess control 459
interval timer 157
into, shell alias 244
ioctl() 143
iovcnt buffers 144
IP 14, 16, 463
ISO/OSI
    defined 17, 26, 463
    proposed guidelines 32
    TP4 27
    X.25 105
    X.409 ASN.1 Basic Encoding Rules
        (BER) 26, 30, 33, 361
    X.500 directory- naming
        protocol 30
iterative server (see also server) 110
itimerval structure 157

K

Kerberos authentication 30, 37, 39
key_decryptsession() 395
key_encryptsession() 395
key_gendes() 396
key_setsecret() 396
kill() 100, 216

L

libnbio.a 275
license broker 22
lightweight processing 152
    asynchronous RPC 275, 280
    DEC CMA 28
    defined 270
    HP/Apollo 28
    OSF/1 Mach kernel threads 28
    POSIX pthreads 28
    protocol compiler support for 34
    Sun LWP 28
        library 270
        lwp_create() 271
        lwp_datastk() 271
        lwp_newstk() 272
        lwp_resched() 272
        lwp_setpri() 272
        lwp_setstkcache() 271
        lwp_sleep() 272
        lwp_yield() 272
        need for re-entrant code 278
        non-blocking support 271, 275
        pod, defined 271
        pod_getmaxpri() 271
        pod_setmaxpri() 271
        scheduling queues 272
        SELF 272
        thread blocking 271
        thread scheduling priority 271
    threads of execution (see also
        threads)
    within X server 28
limitations of high-level functions 58

linking
    client to server 56, 90
    ONC RPC 4.0 362
    Raw transport, debug 97
    TLI 121
    XDR 362
listen() 127, 130
local and remote procedure call
        communication 3
Location Broker 21
    defined 463
    Global 22
    Local 22
lpd 111
LWP, see lightweight processing
lwp_create() 271
lwp_datastk() 271
lwp_newstk() 272
lwp_resched() 272
lwp_setpri() 272
lwp_setstkcache() 271
lwp_sleep() 272
lwp_yield() 272

M

macros, XDR in-line 366
mail, client/server protocol 108
make
    command-line symbol
            definition 163
    default rules 63, 153
    RPCGEN makefile template 161
memory(), byte oriented memory ac-
        cess functions 122
message
    defined 120
    passing 459
    queue (see also interprocess
            communication) 120
mknod file
    /etc/mknod, creating named-
            pipes 120
mknode 120

moving a local application to the
        network 187, 197
msgctl() 120
msgget() 120
msgrcv() 120
msgsnd(2) 120
multi-pass, interleaving and pipes 458
multiprocessing 458
    under UNIX 149
    with RPCTool 33
multi-tasking 149, 199, 262, 265

N

NCA (see Network Computing Architec-
        ture)
NCS (see Network Computing System)
Net Lib interface library 30
netid 231, 325
netname2host() 396
netname2user() 396
NETPATH, environment variable 325
~/.netrc, network user database 145,
        216
netstat 116
Netware 34
Netwise RPCTool 20
Network Computing Architecture
        (NCA) 16, 21, 463
Network Computing Kernel (NCK) 21,
        463
Network Computing System (NCS) 16,
        463
    acronyms 22
    compared to ONC 24
    overview 21
Network Data Representation
        (NDR) 21, 26, 463
Network File System (NFS) 22, 463
    data sharing 231
    defined 16
    filenames 164
Network Information Service (NIS) 22
    adding services 110
    command-line utilities 124

database updating 119
defined 464
domain 118, 124, 221
files 118
keys 124
maps 124
retrieving host, network and address
info 122
server 124
servers started by inetd 116
Network Interface Description Language
(NIDL) 21
defined 464
Network Lock Manager (NLM) 24, 464
Network Selection (NS) 326
Network Status Monitor 24
Network Time Protocol (NTP) 30
NFS (see Network File System)
nice() 225
NIS (see Network Information Service)
non-blocking RPC 238
non-idempotent procedure 198
Novell 34, 40
ntohl() 121
ntohs() 121
NULLPROC, RPC procedure 0 74

O

Object Management Group (OMG) 31
Object Request Broker (ORB) 31
OLIT (see Xol toolkit)
on 24, 100
to start servers 216
on_exit() 278
ONC RPC (see RPC)
ONC (see Open Network Computing)
one-way RPC 238
RPC_TIMEDOUT error 243
transport reliability 239
unreliable transport, when to
use 239
Open Network Computing (ONC) xxii
acronyms 23
defined 16, 464

future development 38
ONC RPC compared to NCS 24
overview 22
Transport-independent RPC 323
Open Software Foundation (OSF) xxiv,
19
DCE developer's kits 20
defined 16, 464
Open Systems Interconnection
(OSI) 464
reference model 13, 105, 361
open() 120
OSF (see Open Software Foundation)

P

packet size (see also datagram) 105
parallel processing 457–460
partitioning strategies 148
parallelism, types of 458
passwd file
/etc/passwd, system password
database 144
patchFile 454
perror() 85, 87, 130
ping 112
pipe() 119, 464
pipelining 458
pmap_getmaps() 378
pmap_getport() 378
pmap_rmtcall() 378
pmap_set() 379
pmap_unset() 379
pod 271
pod_getmaxpri() 271
pod_setmaxpri() 271
pointer chasing 26, 372
port 11
defined 17, 464
number, IP 108
privileged (reserved) 128, 379
TCP/IP and DARPA 377
user (unprivileged,
unreserved) 108, 134
well-known 108, 467

portmap 231, 383
    functions
        pmap_getmaps() 378
        pmap_getport() 370
        pmap_rmtcall() 378
        pmap_set() 379
        pmap_unset() 379
        xdr_pmap() 379
        xdr_pmaplist() 379
    portmap() 377
    portmapper, ONC 11, 464
    started by inetd 116
procedure number
    nonexistent procedure error 47
    RPC registration 47
process
    binding 464
    defined 464
    granularity 458
    ID 154
processor coupling, defined 457
program number
    mismatch 79
    ranges controlled by Sun 48
    register · protocol 48
    RPC registration 47
protocol
    client and server communication 47
    defined 464
    implicit, without a compiler 58
    one-way RPC 240
    specification 61
protocol compiler xxvi
    defined xxiv, 465
    NCS NIDL xxvi, 29
    Netwise RPCTool xxvi, 29
    ONC RPCGEN 29
    Sun's RPCGEN xxvi
    (see also RPCGEN)
protocol definition language (see RPCL)
protocols file
    /etc/protocols 123
ps 101, 111
pthreads (see lightweight processing)

Q

questions about distributed application
    design 197

R

rasterfile 165, 315
Raw transport 94
ray tracing 409
rcp 466
read()
    for pipes 119
    on sockets 127
readv() 144
reaping, of child process 154
recv() 127, 130, 132, 136, 142
recvfrom() 128, 139
recvmsg() 128, 139
reduction 459
re-entrant code 28
    problems with lightweight
        threads 278
references
    make xxxiii
    NCS RPC xxxiii
    ONC RPC xxxiii
    parallel processing 457
    RPCGEN 81
    SunView 148
    UNIX networking 104
    X xxxiii
    XView xxxiii, 289
register, defined 465
registerrpc() 47, 49, 381, 396
registration 47
remote asynchronous call (RAC) 235
remote procedure call 465
    defined xxv, ?
    system 17
reply 17
    caching 99, 246, 352
        as a protective measure 353
        cache sizing 353
    defined 465
    NULL for one-way RPC 246

static variables (see also static return variables) 280
void for no reply 241, 374
reporting server information 227
request 17
    defined 465
    queue size (socket) 130
Request for Comment (RFC) 108, 407
request/reply communication model 2
resetting server 226
rex, RPC remote execution protocol 24, 112, 114, 223, 465
rexd, on remote execution daemon 24, 100, 114, 116
    security 216
rexec, socket remote execution interface 112, 114, 138, 144, 465
rexecd, socket rexec remote execution daemon 24, 113, 116, 144, 216
~/.rhosts, remote permission database 145, 151, 218
rlogin 466
routing 107
    defined 104
RPC
    address 47
    administrator 48
    application development steps 4
    availibility of source 40
    batch 246
    blocking (synchronous) nature 236
    clnt_stat status codes 342, 404
    compared to X 285
    compatibility of 4.0 and TIRPC 327
    defined xxv, 466
    error codes 404
    error reporting functions 338
    fault tolerance 199
    follow-up RPC (FRPC) 252
    format of /etc/rpc 124
    lack of reentry (current ONC releases) 278
    names and numbers 125
    one-way protocol 240, 242, 243
    rpc_err status codes 342, 404

software availability
    Courier RPC xxxii
    examples in book xxxii
    NCS RPC xxxii
    Netwise RPCTool xxxii
    ONC source, TIRPC 323
    ONC Source,RPC 4.0 xxx
    OSF DCE xxxii
source availability
    RPCSRC 4.0 (Release 4.0) xxxii
strategies for use with X Window System 285
system issues 198
timeout 236, 238
Transport-independent RPC (TIRPC) 323
under windowing system 283
rpc file
    /etc/rpc, system RPC programs 48, 114, 124, 128
RPC functions
    authentication 381
        auth_destroy() 335
        authdes_create() 336
        authnone_create() 335
        authunix_create_default() 336
        getnetname() 337
        host2netname() 337
        user2netname() 337
    CLIENT handle management 381
    error reporting 350
        clnt_geterr() 338
        clnt_perrno() 338
        clnt_perror() 338
        clnt_sperrno() 338
        clnt_sperror() 338
        svcerr_auth() 345, 350
        svcerr_decode() 345, 350
        svcerr_noproc() 345, 350
        svcerr_systemerr() 345, 350
        svcerr_weakauth() 345
    high-level client
        callrpc() 50, 253, 381
    high-level server
        registerrpc() 47, 49, 381

RPC functions (continued)
    svc_run() 49, 250, 381
    limitations of high-level calls 58
    low-level client
        clnt_broadcast() 248
        clnt_call() 59, 80
        clnt_control() 80, 98
            parameters 390
            RPC timeout control 238
        clnt_create() 59, 381
        clnt_destroy() 79, 335
        clnt_freeres() 208
        clnt_pcreateerror() 87
        clnt_perror() 87
        clntraw_create() 94
        clntudp_create() 258
    low-level server
        svc_getargs() 253
        svc_getcaller() 245, 257
        svc_getreqset() 251, 254, 295
        svc_register() 59, 81, 265
        svc_sendreply() 100
        svcerr_decode() 258
        svcerr_noproc() 258
        svcerr_systemerr() 258
        svcraw_create() 94
        svctcp_create() 59, 81, 94
        svcudp_create() 81, 94, 265
        svcudp_enablecache() 99
    making the call from the client 381
    server registration with the
        portmap 381
    SVCXPRT service transport handle
        management 381
rpc.cmsd 116
rpc_broadcast() 328
rpc_call() 328
rpc_createer portmap global error
    variable 378
rpc_createcrr 397
rpc_err status values 342, 404
rpc_err structure 338
rpc_reg() 328
rpc_stat structure 249

rpcb_getaddr() 329
rpcb_set() 329
rpcb_unset() 329
rpcbind
    TIRPC binding service 231, 324
rpcbind() 11
rpcent structure 124
RPCGEN 61–100
    as found in ONC RPC Release 4 65
    common mistakes 100
    cpp preprocessing 78, 201
    defined 466
    inetd support 111
    overview of protocol compilers 29
    preprocessor symbols 65, 78
    RPCGEN.NEW 29
    RPCL (see RPCGEN)
    syntax of rpcgen command 65
RPCGEN.NEW 29
    client and server shells 68
    enhancements to RPCGEN 67
rpcinfo 101, 227–231
    source code modifications 453
    under TIRPC 231
RPCL 22, 68–78
    boolean type, bool_t 76
    built-in preprocessing 78
    discriminated union 71, 82, 168
    enumerations 69
    fixed-length array declarations 75
    linked-list handling 82
    multi-dimensional arrays 75
    opaque data types 77
    pointer declarations 76
    preprocessor symbols 73, 78, 201
    program definition 72, 73
    protocol definition 65
    service procedure names 73
    simple declarations 75
    string type, string 77
    structures 70
    symbolic constants 69
    typedef 72
    variable-length array
        declarations 75

variable-length string 82
void declarations 78
void replies 241
rpcsvc file
/usr/include/rpcsvc, system service
protocol directory 29, 48,
114, 356
RPCTool 20
rsh 57, 100, 114, 151
defined 466
signalling 145, 163
to start servers 57, 137, 216
rshd 113
rstat() protocol 356
rusers, RPC successor to rwho 112
rusersd, the service daemon for
rusers 112
rwhod, the service daemon for
rwho 112

S

security 198, 216
sed 220
select() 112, 143, 250, 292
polling with 254
semaphore 121, 466 (see also interprocess communication)
send() 127, 130, 132, 136
sendmail 111
sendmsg() 128
sendto() 128, 139, 142
servent structure 123, 138, 141
server 1, 2
application 466
classifications 111
concurrent 55, 110, 135
multiple processes 110
single process 110
connection-oriented 130, 133
crash recovery 352
defined 17, 466
deploying during development 100
handle, SVCXPRT 362
in X 1, 284

inetd registration with
svc_register() 113
initilization, inquiry and
removal 453
iterative 55, 110, 130, 140
multiple clients and servers 235
multi-tasking 262, 265
one-way RPC 242
portmap registration 379
process, defined 466
registration, avoiding conflicts 384
resetting 226
restarting 226
rpcinfo 227
server too fat system error 225
setting process priority 226
starting from client 222
starting remote servers 216
state 245
stateful 15
stateless 15
stub 61, 466
terminating via RPC 225
transport handle, SVCXPRT 59, 80,
461
with lack of use timer 224
server caching 99
service, defined 466
services file
/etc/services, Internet TCP/IP service names 108, 114, 117,
128
setmntent() 233
setrpcent() 125
setsockopt() 127, 128, 144
shared memory 121, 460
NFS as 150
shell archive 93
shutdown() 137, 144
SIGALRM signal 140, 141, 158
under XView 297
SIGCHLD signal 153, 155
under XView 297
SIGHUP signal 119
SIGIO signal 297

SIGKILL signal 101
signal 466
signal handler 141, 153
SIGTERM signal 101, 216
     under XView 297
SIGURG signal 297
SIGVTALRM signal 297
slay 101, 145
sockaddr_in structure, Internet domain
          socket 134, 136, 138, 141
sockaddr_un structure, UNIX-domain
          socket 129
socket
     blocking 143
     buffering issues 142
     client/server communication
               process 125
     connectionless server 127, 128
     connection-oriented server 127
     defined 17, 125, 466
     descriptor 130
          deallocation 131
          duplication 130
          manipulation and control 128,
               143
          status 144
     Internet addressing 133
     retrieving host, network and
               address 138
     shutting down 137, 140
     system functions 126
     UNIX domain addressing 129
     UNIX system calls 127
socket() 127, 132, 134
socketpair() 127, 144
spray 116
standards, distributed computing
          environments 19
state machine, defined 466
stateful server 22
statfs() 232
static return variables 54, 84
stream communication model 120
stty() 275
Sun User's Group xxvii

SunNet License server 24
Sun-Spots mailing list xxvii
SunView 164
     Pixrect structure 185, 314
     Pixwin structure 185, 318
     window 179
svc_create() 328
svc_destroy() 397
svc_dg_create() 330
svc_fds 397
svc_fdset 397
svc_fdset, global RPC file descriptor
          set 251, 254, 270, 292, 310
svc_freeargs() 398
svc_getargs() 253, 398
svc_getcaller() 245, 257, 398
svc_getreq() 398
svc_getreqset() 251, 254, 295, 398
svc_reg() 329
svc_register() 59, 81, 113, 265, 400
svc_req structure 207, 344, 355
svc_run() 49, 381, 400
     roll your own 250
svc_sendreply() 100, 401
svc_tli_create() 329
svc_tp_create() 328, 329
svc_unreg() 329
svc_unregister() 224, 402
svc_vc_create() 330
svcerr_auth() 345, 350, 399
svcerr_decode() 258, 345, 350, 399
svcerr_noproc() 258, 345, 350, 399
svcerr_noprog() 399
svcerr_progvers() 399
svcerr_systemerr() 258, 345, 350, 400
svcerr_weakauth() 345, 400
svcfd_create() 397
svcraw_create() 94, 400
svctcp_create() 59, 81, 94, 401
svcudp_bufcreate() 401
svcudp_create() 81, 94, 265, 401
svcudp_enablecache() 99
SVCXPRT, transport handle 59, 80
     associated socket 261
     structure 362

synchronization 459
synchronous processing 199
    defined 466
    I/O multiplexing (select()) 144
    remote procedure call 2
syslog(), RPCGEN support 66
systat 116

T

task dependencies 457
TCP
    as a reliable transport 27, 109
    defined 467
    handling connection errors 355
    protocol 26
    request sockets in windowing
        systems 310
    within OSI model 14
thread scheduling priority 281
threads (of execution) 459
timeout
    for client 98
    inetd 111
    RPC 80, 236
        controlling 238, 390
        default 238
    SIGPIPEs and UDP 355
    UDP retry 98, 109, 390
    using alarm() 138
timeval structure 80, 238, 272
TIRPC (see Transport-independent RPC)
TLI/STREAMS (see also Transport Layer
    Interface (TLI)) 324
transmission control protocol (see TCP)
transport
    connectionless 105, 108
    connection-oriented 105, 108
    DDS 26
    DECnet 27
    independence from
    ISO/OSI TP4 27
    libraries 106
    overhead 109, 355
    packet size 109

Raw 94
resource consumption 109
selection 66, 109
specific error and recovery
    strategies 352
TCP 106
UDP 107
Transport Layer Interface (TLI) 27, 116,
    119, 121, 326
Transport-independent RPC
    (TIRPC) 14, 26, 323–332
    application programming
        interface 327
    availability 332
    clnt_create() 328
    clnt_dg_create() 330
    clnt_tli_create() 329
    clnt_tp_create() 329
    clnt_vc_create() 330
    Name to Address Translation
        (N2A) 324
    netid 325
    NETPATH environment
        variable 325
    Network Selection (NS) 326
    ONC RPCSRC 4.0 compatibility 327
    protocol and semantics 324
    rpc_broadcast() 328
    rpc_call() 328
    rpc_reg() 328
    rpcb_getaddr() 329
    rpcb_set() 329
    rpcb_unset() 329
    rpcinfo changes 231
    socket incompatibility 327
    svc_create() 328
    svc_dg_create() 330
    svc_reg() 329
    svc_tli_create() 329
    svc_tp_create() 328, 329
    svc_unreg() 329
    svc_vc_create() 330
    transports in /etc/netconfig 325
    uniform addressing 326

U

UDP
    as an unreliable transport 27, 109
    defined 467
    handling connection errors 355
    maximum RPC data size 79
    statelessness 109
    within OSI model 14
union, in RPCL 5
universal address 231
UNIX International (UI) 17, 467
UNIX TLI 30
unlink() 131
user datagram protocol, see UDP
user2netname() 337, 402

V

vector or array processing 459
verifier, defined 333
version mismatch, avoiding 391
version number
    changes 48
    mismatch 79
    RPC registration 49

W

wait() 137, 153, 220
widgets, examples 300
write()
    for pipes 120
    on sockets 127
writev() 144

X

X Window System
    callback procedures 286
    client 284
    display server 284
    distributed applications 284
    Pixmap structure 186, 314
    protocol 285
    RPC comparison 284
    socket activity watching 286

standard 284
TCP RPC requests 310
Window structure 186
XImage structure 186, 314
X/Open Transport Interface (XTI) 39
XDR
    bool_t 363
    defined 467
    filter operation codes 363
    handle 52, 362
    in-line routines 366
    library overview 361
    macros 366
    multi-dimensional array 51, 202
    programming example 365
    protocol 361
    stream management 363
    streams 52, 362, 371
    wrapper routines as generated by
        RPCGEN 63
XDR filters 52, 74
    complex 53
        xdr_array() 53, 367, 368
        xdr_bytes() 53, 367, 368
        xdr_opaque() 53, 367, 371
        xdr_pointer() 53, 367, 371
        xdr_reference() 53, 367, 372
        xdr_string() 53, 367, 373
        xdr_union() 53, 367, 374
        xdr_vector() 53, 367, 374
        xdr_wrapstring() 53, 367, 375
    primitive 52
        xdr_bool() 52, 364, 368
        xdr_char() 52, 364, 369
        xdr_double() 53, 364, 369
        xdr_enum() 53, 364, 369
        xdr_float() 53, 364, 369
        xdr_int() 53, 364, 370
        xdr_long() 53, 364, 370
        xdr_short() 52, 364, 373
        xdr_u_char() 373
        xdr_u_int() 53, 364, 373
        xdr_u_long() 53, 364, 374
        xdr_u_short() 53, 364, 374
        xdr_void() 53, 364, 374

XDR functions
    xdr_destroy() 363, 369
    xdr_free() 85, 208, 370
    xdr_getpos() 363, 370
    xdr_inline() 363, 370
    xdr_setpos() 363, 372
    xdrmem_create() 363, 370
    xdrrec_create() 363, 371
    xdrrec_endofrecord() 363, 371
    xdrrec_eof() 363, 372
    xdrrec_readbytes() 363, 372
    xdrrec_skiprecord() 363, 372
    xdrstdio_create() 363, 373
xdr_accepted_reply() 402
xdr_array() 53, 367, 368
xdr_authunix_parms() 402
xdr_bool() 52, 364, 368
xdr_bytes() 53, 367, 368
xdr_callhdr() 402
xdr_callmsg() 402
xdr_char() 52, 364, 369
XDR_DECODE 52
xdr_destroy() 363, 369
xdr_double() 53, 364, 369
XDR_ENCODE 52
xdr_enum() 53, 364, 369
xdr_float() 53, 364, 369
XDR_FREE 52
xdr_free() 85, 370
xdr_getpos() 363, 370
xdr_inline() 363, 370
xdr_int() 53, 364, 370
xdr_long() 53, 364, 370
xdr_opaque() 53, 367, 371
xdr_opaque_auth() 403
xdr_pmap() 379
xdr_pmaplist() 379
xdr_pointer() 53, 367, 371
xdr_reference() 53, 367, 372
xdr_rejected_reply() 403
xdr_replymsg() 403
xdr_setpos() 363, 372
xdr_short() 364, 373
xdr_string() 53, 367, 373
xdr_u_char() 373

xdr_u_int() 53, 364, 373
xdr_u_long() 53, 364, 374
xdr_u_short() 53, 364, 374
xdr_union() 53, 367, 374
xdr_vector() 53, 367, 374
xdr_void() 53, 364, 374
xdr_wrapstring() 53, 367, 375
xdrmem_create() 363, 370
xdrrec_create() 363, 371
xdrrec_endofrecord() 363, 371
xdrrec_eof() 363, 372
xdrrec_readbytes() 363, 372
xdrrec_skiprecord() 363, 372
xdrstdio_create() 363, 373
Xlib
    XCopyArea() 186
    XCopyPlane() 186
    XPutImage() 186
Xol toolkit 283
Xol/Xt widgets 300
xprt_register() 403
xprt_unregister() 403
Xt
    dispatch loop 308
    event dispatcher 301
    watching descriptors 301
Xt functions
    XtAddCallback() 289
    XtAppAddInput() 301, 310
    XtAppAddTimeOut() 302
    XtMainLoop() 301, 302
    XtRemoveInput() 301
    XtRemoveTimeOut() 302
XView
    event dispatch loop 292
    event procedure 287
    events 289
    interval timers 290, 292
    Notifier 292
    RPC programming
        complications 296
        modifications required for
        threads 270
    notify_set_itimer_func() 290
    signal handling 297

    system calls to avoid 297
    toolkit 283
XView functions
    notify_enable_rpc_svc() 290, 298
    notify_set_itimer_func() 291, 292
    notify_set_signal_func() 297
    notify_start() 298
    window_main_loop() 298

Y

Yellow Pages (YP), defined 467
yp file
    /var/yp (see Network Information
        Service (NIS))
ypclnt() 232
ypmake 124
ypmatch 124
ypwhich 124

Books That Help People Get More Out of Computers

Please send me the following:

❑ A free catalog of titles.

❑ A list of Bookstores in my area that carry your books (U.S. and Canada only).

❑ A list of book distributors outside the U.S. and Canada.

❑ Information about consulting services for documentation or programming.

❑ Information about bundling books with my product.

❑ On-line descriptions of your books.

Name _____

Address _____

_____

City _____

State, ZIP _____

Country _____

Phone _____

Email Address_____
(Internet or Uunet)

Books That Help People Get More Out of Computers

Please send me the following:

❑ A free catalog of titles.

❑ A list of Bookstores in my area that carry your books (U.S. and Canada only).

❑ A list of book distributors outside the U.S. and Canada.

❑ Information about consulting services for documentation or programming.

❑ Information about bundling books with my product.

❑ On-line descriptions of your books.

Name _____

Address _____

_____

City _____

State, ZIP _____

Country _____

Phone _____

Email Address_____
(Internet or Uunet)

NAME _____

COMPANY _____

ADDRESS _____

CITY _____ STATE _____ ZIP _____

BUSINESS REPLY MAIL

FIRST CLASS MAIL PERMIT NO. 80 SEBASTOPOL, CA

POSTAGE WILL BE PAID BY ADDRESSEE

O'REILLY & ASSOCIATES, INC.

103 Morris Street Suite A
Sebastopol CA 95472-9902

NAME _____

COMPANY _____

ADDRESS _____

CITY _____ STATE _____ ZIP _____

BUSINESS REPLY MAIL

FIRST CLASS MAIL PERMIT NO. 80 SEBASTOPOL, CA

POSTAGE WILL BE PAID BY ADDRESSEE

O'REILLY & ASSOCIATES, INC.

103 Morris Street Suite A
Sebastopol CA 95472-9902

About the Author

John Bloomer has held microelectronic design positions with Texas Instruments and General Electric. He has been involved in the design and specification of memory, special-function graphics, and signal processing hardware at the chip and algorithmic level. John currently works within the Signal and Image Coding and Processing group at GE's Corporate R&D Center. His technical interests and areas of publication include distributed processing, multidimensional signal processing, and neural and parallel VLSI architectures.

John earned his BSEE at Clarkson University in 1983, and his MSCE at the University of Central Florida in 1986. He is pursuing a PhD at Rensselaer Polytechnic Institute. He currently lives in Schenectady, NY, with his wife, Cathy, and three children, Natalie, Megan, and Audrey.

Colophon

Our look is the result of reader comments, our own experimentation, and distribution channels.

Distinctive covers complement our distinctive approach to technical topics, breathing personality and life into potentially dry subjects. UNIX and its attendant programs can be unruly beasts. Nutshell Handbooks help you tame them.

The animal featured on the cover of *Power Programming with RPC* is a kangaroo. The kangaroo is a marsupial, an animal which raises its young in a pouch. When the young are born, they are only partially developed embryos, deaf, blind, and furless, and weighing about a gram. Once born, they make their way into their mother's pouch where they remain for up to six months before they are able to venture out into the world.

Kangaroos are native to Tasmania, Australia, New Guinea, and parts of the Bismark Archipelagos. They are herbivores who chew their cud like cows, and they are capable of existing on very coarse grasses, unlike cattle or sheep. They need very little water to survive and are capable of going for months without drinking at all. When they do need water, they dig "wells" for themselves, frequently going as deep as three or four feet. These "kangaroo pits" are a common source of water for other animals living in the kangaroo's environment.

Edie Freedman designed this cover and the entire UNIX bestiary that appears on other Nutshell Handbooks. The beasts themselves are adapted from 19th-century engravings from the Dover Pictorial Archive.

The text of this book is set in ITC Garamond Light; headings are ITC Garamond Book Italic; examples are Courier. Text was prepared using FrameMaker. Figures are produced with a Macintosh. Printing is done on a Varityper 5300.

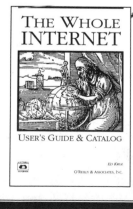

System Performance Tuning

By Mike Loukides

System Performance Tuning answers one of the most fundamental questions you can ask about your computer: "How can I get it to do more work without buying more hardware?" Anyone who has ever used a computer has wished that the system was faster, particularly at times when it was under heavy load.

If your system gets sluggish when you start a big job, if it feels as if you spend hours waiting for remote file access to complete, if your system stops dead when several users are active at the same time, you need to read this book. Some performance problems do require you to buy a bigger or faster computer, but many can be solved simply by making better use of the resources you already have.

336 pages, ISBN 0-937175-60-9

Essential System Administration

By Æleen Frisch

Like any other multi-user system, UNIX requires some care and feeding. *Essential System Administration* tells you how. This book strips away the myth and confusion surrounding this important topic and provides a compact, manageable introduction to the tasks faced by anyone responsible for a UNIX system.

If you use a stand-alone UNIX system, whether it's a PC or a workstation, you know how much you need this book: on these systems the fine line between a user and an administrator has vanished. Either you're both or you're in trouble. If you routinely provide administrative support for a larger shared system or a network of workstations, you will find this book indispensable. Even if you aren't directly responsible for system administration, you will find that understanding basic administrative functions greatly increases your ability to use UNIX effectively.

466 pages
ISBN 0-937175-80-3

Computer Security

**COMPUTER
SECURITY
BASICS**

Deborah Russell and G. T. Gangemi Sr.
O'Reilly & Associates, Inc.

Practical UNIX Security

By Simson Garfinkel & Gene Spafford

If you are a UNIX system administrator or user who needs to deal with security, you need this book.

Practical UNIX Security describes the issues, approaches, and methods for implementing security measures—spelling out what the varying approaches cost and require in the way of equipment. After presenting UNIX security basics and network security, this guide goes on to suggest how to keep intruders out, how to tell if they've gotten in, how to clean up after them, and even how to prosecute them. Filled with practical scripts, tricks and warnings, *Practical UNIX Security* tells you what you need to know to make your UNIX system as secure as it can be.

"Worried about who's in your Unix system? Losing sleep because someone might be messing with your computer? Having headaches from obscure computer manuals? Then *Practical Unix Security* is for you. This handy book tells you where the holes are and how to cork'em up.

"Moreover, you'll learn about how Unix security really works. Spafford and Garfinkel show you how to tighten up your Unix system without pain. No secrets here—just solid computing advice.

"Buy this book and save on aspirin."—Cliff Stoll

512 pages, ISBN 0-937175-72-2

Computer Security Basics

By Deborah Russell & G.T. Gangemi Sr.

There's a lot more consciousness of security today, but not a lot of understanding of what it means and how far it should go. This handbook describes complicated concepts like trusted systems, encryption and mandatory access control in simple terms.

For example, most U.S. government equipment acquisitions now require "Orange Book" (Trusted Computer System Evaluation Criteria) certification. A lot of people have a vague feeling that they ought to know about the Orange Book, but few make the effort to track it down and read it. *Computer Security Basics* contains a more readable introduction to the Orange Book—why it exists, what it contains, and what the different security levels are all about—than any other book or government publication.

464 pages, ISBN 0-937175-71-4

Managing UUCP and Usenet

10th Edition
By Tim O'Reilly & Grace Todino

For all its widespread use, UUCP is one of the most difficult UNIX utilities to master. Poor documentation, cryptic messages, and differences between various implementations make setting up UUCP links a nightmare for many a system administrator.

This handbook is meant for system administrators who want to install and manage the UUCP and Usenet software. It covers HoneyDanBer UUCP as well as standard Version 2 UUCP, with special notes on Xenix. As one reader noted over the Net, "Don't even TRY to install UUCP without it!"

368 pages, ISBN 0-937175-93-5

Using UUCP and Usenet

By Grace Todino & Dale Dougherty

Using UUCP shows how to communicate with both UNIX and non-UNIX systems using UUCP and *cu* or *tip*. It also shows how to read news and post your own articles and mail to other Usenet members. This handbook assumes that UUCP and Usenet links to other computer systems have already been established by your system administrator.

While clear enough for a novice, this book is packed with information that even experienced users will find indispensable. Take the mystery out of questions such as why files sent via UUCP don't always end up where you want them, how to find out the status of your file transfer requests, and how to execute programs remotely with *uux*.

210 pages, ISBN 0-937175-10-2

Understanding DCE

By Ward Rosenberry, David Kenney, and Gerry Fisher

Understanding DCE is a technical and conceptual overview of OSF's Distributed Computing Environment for programmers and technical managers, marketing and sales people. Unlike many O'Reilly & Associates books, *Understanding DCE* has no hands-on programming elements. Instead, the book focuses on how DCE can be used to accomplish typical programming tasks and provides explanations to help the reader understand all the parts of DCE.

266 pages (estimated), ISBN 1-56592-005-8

Guide to Writing DCE Applications

By John Shirley

A hands-on programming guide to OSF's Distributed Computing Environment (DCE) for first-time DCE application programmers. This book is designed to help new DCE users make the transition from conventional, nondistributed applications programming to distributed DCE programming. Covers the IDL and ACF files, essential RPC calls, binding methods and the name service, server initialization, memory management, and selected advanced topics. Includes practical programming examples.

282 pages, ISBN 1-56592-004-X

Learning GNU Emacs

By Deb Cameron & Bill Rosenblatt

GNU Emacs is the most popular and widespread of the Emacs family of editors. It is also the most powerful and flexible. (Unlike all other text editors, GNU Emacs is a complete working environment—you can stay within Emacs all day without leaving.) This book tells you how to get started with the GNU Emacs editor. It will also "grow" with you: as you become more proficient, this book will help you learn how to use Emacs more effectively. It will take you from basic Emacs usage (simple text editing) to moderately complicated customization and programming.

The book is aimed at new Emacs users, whether or not they are programmers. Also useful for readers switching from other Emacs implementations to GNU Emacs.

442 pages, ISBN 0-937175-84-6

Learning the vi Editor

5th Edition
By Linda Lamb

For many users, working in the UNIX environment means using *vi*, a full-screen text editor available on most UNIX systems. Even those who know *vi* often make use of only a small number of its features. This is the complete guide to text editing with *vi*. Early chapters cover the basics; later chapters explain more advanced editing tools, such as *ex* commands and global search and replacement.

192 pages, ISBN 0-937175-67-6

Learning the UNIX Operating System

2nd Edition
By Grace Todino & John Strang

If you are new to UNIX, this concise introduction will tell you just what you need to get started, and no more. Why wade through a 600-page book when you can begin working productively in a matter of minutes?

Topics covered include:

- Logging in and logging out
- Managing UNIX files and directories
- Sending and receiving mail
- Redirecting input/output
- Pipes and filters
- Background processing
- Customizing your account

"If you have someone on your site who has never worked on a UNIX system and who needs a quick how-to, Nutshell has the right booklet. *Learning the UNIX Operating System* can get a newcomer rolling in a single session."—;login

84 pages, ISBN 0-937175-16-1

MH & xmh:
E-mail for Users and Programmers

2nd Edition
By Jerry Peek

Customizing your e-mail environment can save you time and make communicating more enjoyable. *MH & xmh: E-mail for Users and Programmers* explains how to use, customize, and program with the MH electronic mail commands, available on virtually any UNIX system. The handbook also covers *xmh*, an X Window System client that runs MH programs.

The basics are easy. But MH lets you do much more than what most people expect an e-mail system to be able to do. This handbook is packed with explanations and useful examples of MH features, some of which the standard MH documentation only hints at.

728 pages, ISBN 1-56592-027-9

UNIX Text Processing

Learning
GNU Emacs

Debra Cameron and Bill Rosenblatt
O'Reilly & Associates, Inc.

Guide to OSF/1:
A Technical Synopsis

By O'Reilly & Associates Staff

OSF/1, Mach, POSIX, SVID, SVR4, X/Open, 4.4BSD, XPG, B-1 security, parallelization, threads, virtual file systems, shared libraries, streams, extensible loader, internationalization.... Need help sorting it all out? If so, then this technically competent introduction to the mysteries of the OSF/1 operating system is a book for you. In addition to its exposition of OSF/1, it offers a list of differences between OSF/1 and System V, Release 4 and a look ahead at what is coming in DCE.

This is not the usual O'Reilly how-to book. It will not lead you through detailed programming examples under OSF/1. Instead, it asks the prior question, What is the nature of the beast? It helps you figure out how to approach the programming task by giving you a comprehensive technical overview of the operating system's features and services, and by showing how they work together.
304 pages, ISBN 0-937175-78-1

POSIX Programmer's Guide

By Donald Lewine

Most UNIX systems today are POSIX-compliant because the Federal government requires it. Even OSF and UI agree on support for POSIX. However, given the manufacturer's documentation, it can be difficult to distinguish system-specific features from those features defined by POSIX.

The *POSIX Programmer's Guide*, intended as an explanation of the POSIX standard and as a reference for the POSIX.1 programming library, will help you write more portable programs. This guide is especially helpful if you are writing programs that must run on multiple UNIX platforms. This guide will also help you convert existing UNIX programs for POSIX-compliance.
640 pages
ISBN 0-937175-73-0

UNIX Network Programming

Power
Programming
with

RPC

John Bloomer
O'Reilly & Associates, Inc.

Managing NFS and NIS

By Hal Stern

A modern computer system that is not part of a network is an anomaly. But managing a network and getting it to perform well can be a problem. This book describes two tools that are absolutely essential to distributed computing environments: the Network Filesystem (NFS) and the Network Information System (formerly called the "yellow pages" or YP).

As popular as NFS is, it is a black box for most users and administrators. This book provides a comprehensive discussion of how to plan, set up, and debug an NFS network. It is the only book we're aware of that discusses NFS and network performance tuning. This book also covers the NFS automounter, network security issues, diskless workstations, and PC/NFS. It also tells you how to use NIS to manage your own database applications, ranging from a simple telephone list to controlling access to network services. If you are managing a network of UNIX systems, or are thinking of setting up a UNIX network, you can't afford to overlook this book.
436 pages, ISBN 0-937175-75-7

Power Programming with RPC

By John Bloomer

A distributed application is designed to access resources across a network. In a broad sense, these resources could be user input, a central database, configuration files, etc., that are distributed on various computers across the network rather than found on a single computer. RPC, or remote procedure calling, is the ability to distribute the execution of functions on remote computers outside of the application's current address space. This allows you to break large or complex programming problems into routines that can be executed independently of one another to take advantage of multiple computers. Thus, RPC makes it possible to attack a problem using a form of parallel or multiprocessing.

Written from a programmer's perspective, this book shows what you can do with RPC and presents a framework for learning it.
494 pages, ISBN 0-937175-77-3

Practical C Programming

By Steve Oualline

There are lots of introductory C books, but this is the first one that has the no-nonsense, practical approach that has made Nutshell Handbooks famous. C programming is more than just getting the syntax right. Style and debugging also play a tremendous part in creating well-running programs.

Practical C Programming teaches you how to create programs that are easy to read, maintain and debug. Practical rules are stressed. For example, there are 15 precedence rules in C (&& comes before || comes before ?:). The practical programmer simplifies these down to two: 1) Multiply and divide come before addition and subtraction and 2) Put parentheses around everything else. Electronic Archaeology, the art of going through someone else's code, is also described.

Topics covered include:

* Good programming style
* C syntax: what to use and what not to use
* The programming environment, including *make*
* The total programming process
* Floating point limitations
* Tricks and surprises

Covers Turbo C (DOS) as well as the UNIX C compiler.

420 pages, ISBN 0-937175-65-X

Using C on the UNIX System

By Dave Curry

Using C on the UNIX System provides a thorough introduction to the UNIX system call libraries. It is aimed at programmers who already know C but who want to take full advantage of the UNIX programming environment. If you want to learn how to work with the operating system and if you want to write programs that can interact with directories, terminals and networks at the lowest level, you will find this book essential. It is impossible to write UNIX utilities of any sophistication without understanding the material in this book.

250 pages, ISBN 0-937175-23-4

Managing Projects with make

2nd Edition
By Steve Talbott and Andrew Oram

Make is one of UNIX's greatest contributions to software development, and this book is the clearest description of *make* ever written. Even the smallest software project typically involves a number of files that depend upon each other in various ways. If you modify one or more source files, you must relink the program after recompiling some, but not necessarily all, of the sources.

Make greatly simplifies this process. By recording the relationships between sets of files, *make* can automatically perform all the necessary updating. The 2nd Edition of this book describes all the basic features of *make* and provides guidelines on meeting the needs of large, modern projects.

152 pages, ISBN 0-937175-90-0

Checking C Programs with lint

By Ian F. Darwin

The *lint* program checker has proven itself time and again to be one of the best tools for finding portability problems and certain types of coding errors in C programs. *lint* verifies a program or program segments against standard libraries, checks the code for common portability errors, and tests the programming against some tried and true guidelines. *lint*ing your code is a necessary (though not sufficient) step in writing clean, portable, effective programs. This book introduces you to *lint*, guides you through running it on your programs and helps you to interpret *lint*'s output.

"Short, useful, and to the point. I recommend it for self-study to all involved with C in a UNIX environment."—Computing Reviews

84 pages, ISBN 0-937175-30-7

Why Does 2+2=5986?

PracticalC
Programming

By Steve Oualline

O'Reilly & Associates, Inc.

DNS and BIND

By Cricket Liu and Paul Albitz

DNS and BIND is a complete guide to the Internet's Domain Name System (DNS) and the Berkeley Internet Name Domain (BIND) software, which is the UNIX implementation of DNS. DNS is the system that translates hostnames (like "rock.ora.com") into Internet addresses (like 192.54.67.23) Until BIND was developed, name translation was based on a "host table"; if you were on the Internet, you got a table that listed all the systems connected to the network, and their address. As the Internet grew from hundreds to thousands and hundreds of thousands of systems, host tables became unworkable. DNS is a distributed database that solves the same problem effectively, allowing the network to grow without constraints. Rather than having a central table that gets distributed to every system on the net, it allows local administrators to assign their own hostnames and addresses, and install these names in a local database.

418 pages, ISBN 1-56592-010-4

sed & awk

By Dale Dougherty

For people who create and modify text files, *sed* and *awk* are power tools for editing. Most of the things that you can do with these programs can be done interactively with a text editor. However, using *sed* and *awk* can save many hours of repetitive work in achieving the same result.

This book contains a comprehensive treatment of *sed* and *awk* syntax. Plus, it emphasizes the kinds of practical problems that *sed* and *awk* can help users to solve, with many useful example scripts and programs.

"*sed & awk* is a must for UNIX system programmers and administrators, and even general UNIX readers will benefit. I have over a hundred UNIX and C books in my personal library at home, but only a dozen are duplicated on the shelf where I work. This one just became number twelve."—Root Journal

414 pages, ISBN 0-937175-59-5

Programming Perl

By Larry Wall & Randal Schwartz

This is the authoritative guide to the hottest new UNIX utility in years, co-authored by the creator of that utility.

Perl is a language for easily manipulating text, files and processes. Perl provides a more concise and readable way to do many jobs that were formerly accomplished (with difficulty) by programming in the C language or one of the shells. Even though Perl is not yet a standard part of UNIX, it is likely to be available wherever you choose to work. And if it isn't, you can get it and install it easily and free of charge.

482 pages, ISBN 0-937175-64-1

UNIX for FORTRAN Programmers

By Mike Loukides

UNIX for FORTRAN Programmers provides the serious scientific programmer with an introduction to the UNIX operating system and its tools. The intent of the book is to minimize the UNIX entry barrier: to familiarize readers with the most important tools so they can be productive as quickly as possible. *UNIX for FORTRAN Programmers* shows readers how to do things that they're interested in: not just how to use a tool like *make* or *rcs*, but how it is used in program development and fits into the toolset as a whole.

"An excellent book describing the features of the UNIX FORTRAN compiler f77 and related software. This book is extremely well written."
—American Mathematical Monthly

264 pages, ISBN 0-937175-51-X